W9-CTW-554

Theories of Human Development

Key human development theories that continue to guide research and practice are examined in this engaging text. Ten key theories are grouped into three families—those that emphasize biological systems, environmental factors, and those that reflect an interaction between the two. This organization enhances students' ability to evaluate, compare, and contrast theories both within and across families. Each family is introduced with an overview of their unique perspectives and the rationale for grouping them together. Discussion of each theory includes the cultural/historical context during the theory's development, its key concepts and ideas, extensions of the theory in contemporary work, an example showing a modification of the theory, an application of how the theory is used to inform practice, and an analysis of how the theory answers six basic questions that a human development theory should address. Each chapter includes an overview of the strengths and weaknesses of the theories to facilitate comparisons. Theories that have a clear life-span focus along with cases and examples that address issues across the life span are included.

The second edition features:

- A new chapter on bioecological theory that highlights the increased use of this theory in the development of family, school, and community intervention programs.
- A new epilogue that examines the same case via each of the ten theories, illustrating their similarities and differences and how these ideas cast a unique light on a common situation.
- New *opening cases* that bring theory to life along with narrative that links the case to the chapter's concepts, *guiding questions* that help students compare theoretical perspectives, *critical thinking questions* that focus on using the theory to interpret the case and personal life experiences, and recommended resources that extend students' understanding.
- More examples from various disciplines that address topics students are likely to encounter as professionals.
- A new glossary that defines the boldfaced key terms.

- Enhanced website at www.psypress.com/9781848726673 that provides *instructors* with a test bank, PowerPoints, discussion questions and activities, additional cases with questions, teaching notes for using the book with various types of majors, and a conversion guide outlining changes to the new edition, and *students* with key terms with hot links to their definitions, chapter summaries and outlines, and additional resources for further study.
- Updated research and applications highlight the latest scientific developments.

Ideal for advanced undergraduate or beginning graduate courses in theories of development, life-span or child development taught in psychology, human development, family studies, education, and social work.

Barbara M. Newman is a professor emeritus at the University of Rhode Island in Human Development and Family Studies.

Philip R. Newman is a Fellow of the American Psychological Association, SPSSI, and the American Orthopsychiatric Association.

Theories of Human Development

Second Edition

Barbara M. Newman
Philip R. Newman

Psychology Press
Taylor & Francis Group

NEW YORK AND LONDON

Second edition published 2016
by Psychology Press
711 Third Avenue, New York, NY 10017

and by Psychology Press
27 Church Road, Hove, East Sussex BN3 2FA

Psychology Press is an imprint of the Taylor & Francis Group, an informa business

© 2016 Taylor & Francis

The right of Barbara M. Newman and Philip R. Newman to be identified as the authors of this work has been asserted by them in accordance with sections 77 and 78 of the Copyright, Designs and Patents Act 1988.

All rights reserved. No part of this book may be reprinted or reproduced or utilised in any form or by any electronic, mechanical, or other means, now known or hereafter invented, including photocopying and recording, or in any information storage or retrieval system, without permission in writing from the publishers.

Trademark notice: Product or corporate names may be trademarks or registered trademarks, and are used only for identification and explanation without intent to infringe.

First edition published by Psychology Press 2007

Library of Congress Cataloging in Publication Data
Newman, Barbara M.
   Theories of human development / by Barbara M. Newman and
   Philip R. Newman.—Second edition.
      pages cm
   Includes bibliographical references and index.
   1. Developmental psychology.   I. Newman, Philip R.   II. Title.
   BF713.N494 2016
   155—dc23   2014050034

ISBN: 978-1-84872-666-6 (hbk)
ISBN: 978-1-84872-667-3 (pbk)
ISBN: 978-1-315-87124-0 (ebk)

Typeset in Minion Pro
by Keystroke, Station Road, Codsall, Wolverhampton

Contents

Preface

Think about the power of ideas. Consider how concepts like freedom, justice, or equality have inspired action, or how ideas like loyalty, authority, and discipline have influenced family and military life. Scientific theories are logical, empirically grounded sets of ideas that can have a profound impact on the way one understands oneself and others. Theories draw you into a world of ideas, leading you to consider relationships, processes, time, culture, and self in new ways and suggesting methods for exploring human behavior. The goal of this book is to provide an engaging introduction to theoretical perspectives about human development. The ten theories that are presented have guided research, intervention, and practice in numerous fields including developmental psychology, life-span development, education, medicine and nursing, social work, human services, counseling, parenting, therapy, and mental health.

One weakness of several current books in this area is that they offer a "shotgun" approach to theory. Each chapter is typically devoted to a separate theory, but students have no idea why these theories were selected or how they relate to one another. In contrast, this book is designed to focus on three major families of theories: those that emphasize biological systems in guiding the direction of development; those that emphasize environmental factors in guiding the direction of development; and those that emphasize a dynamic interaction between biological, environmental, and self-directed forces in guiding the direction of development. Within each family, a small number of influential theories are presented. These theories were selected because they have had a major impact on developmental science and continue to evolve because of new insights from contemporary scholarly work. Our hope is that, in examining the concepts and perspectives of the ten theories, students will have new resources to think critically about theoretical ideas, begin to assess the strengths and weaknesses of the theories, and gain a deeper understanding of how the particular emphasis of a theory guides research, application, policy, and public opinion.

The book highlights the role of theories in building a knowledge base. Theories guide research, help to interpret behavior, and guide the design of interventions. Students will appreciate how theories are revised and extended as new issues are brought to light. They will observe, through examples, how the research process contributes to the evaluation and modification of theories. They will be able to appreciate how, over time, ideas that may have been introduced in one theory are revisited in another theoretical framework, and how an emerging societal issue or new research capability brings back the relevance of a theoretical concept from the past. Students will also be encouraged to consider the historical and cultural context within which each theory was developed. This perspective suggests that there are inevitable biases that accompany any individual's efforts to explain and predict human behavior, situated as they are in the prevailing scientific environment and influenced by the theorist's particular scholarly training, values, and beliefs.

The book was written for upper division undergraduates and beginning graduate students who have already taken one course in human development or developmental psychology. It is comprised of 12 chapters: an introduction, ten theory chapters divided into three families, and an epilogue. The introduction (Chapter 1) reviews the role that theories play in guiding the development of knowledge and the design of interventions. It also highlights some of the challenges of understanding human development across the life span. The introductory chapter introduces six guiding questions that a theory of human development is expected to address. These questions are addressed in each theory chapter, providing a vehicle for students to compare and contrast the contributions of each theory. Each family of theories is introduced with a brief interlude that provides some highlights of each theory and its unique perspectives, and an explanation for why the theories in that section have been grouped together.

The discussion of each theory includes the following sections:

A. Guiding questions: each chapter begins with a small set of guiding questions to help orient the reader to some big ideas and to introduce issues that will be central to the focus of the theory.
B. An opening case and brief narrative that links the case to themes from the theory.
C. The historical and cultural context in which the theory was developed.
D. An overview of the theory's key concepts and important ideas.
E. New directions that extend the theory in contemporary scientific work.
F. A research example that shows how the theory has been tested and modified.
G. An application that shows how the theory has guided the design of an intervention or program, or has been used to inform practice.
H. An analysis of how the theory answers six basic questions that a theory of human development is expected to address.
I. A critique of the theory, pointing out strengths and weaknesses, and a table which summarizes these points.
J. A set of critical thinking questions and exercises.
K. Key terms.
L. Recommended resources.

A major objective of this book is to foster critical thinking and an active approach to learning. The book is written in a clear, comprehensible style without sacrificing the integrity and complexity of ideas. Concepts are explained so that students can grasp the underlying logic of the theory and its basic contributions. Each theory chapter follows the same organization to allow students to do their own comparisons and to learn to anticipate the issues that are likely to be raised. By emphasizing three families of theories and selecting a few examples within each family, we hope to help students begin to grasp the essential features of the family of theories and appreciate how new theories they will encounter fit within one orientation or another. Within each chapter, the use of case material encourages application of concepts to real-life situations. By returning to the six questions that a theory of human development is expected to address, students begin to accumulate a broad and comparative view of the theories, and their relevance for understanding the complexities of human behavior. After reading the critique of each theory, highlighting strengths and weaknesses, students can begin to add their own ideas, possibly combining ideas from several theories to address limitations.

The Epilogue, Chapter 12, is new to this edition. The Epilogue describes a single case that is interpreted using each of the ten theories presented in the text. This approach is intended to foster complex thinking by illustrating how the variety of theoretical ideas and principles can cast a unique light on a common situation. The Epilogue also summarizes some of the similarities and differences among the theories, culminating in a table that compares the theories with regard to basic processes; conceptualizations about periods of life; the universal versus contextual emphasis of the theory; and the timescale that the theory features in its approach to development.

PEDAGOGICAL FEATURES

The pedagogical features of the text are intended to foster understanding and stimulate conceptual development. An initial outline provides a roadmap of ideas that will be covered in the chapter. The guiding questions help students to formulate a basis for their critical analysis of the theories. As they read several theories, these questions will become increasingly useful to guide efforts to compare and contrast the theories. The initial case vignette provides a real-life situation to help illustrate how the theory can be useful in dealing with individual, family, and/ or organizational situations. The narrative that follows the case vignette provides a link from the case to the concepts of the theory, even before the students have explored the theory in depth. Each chapter includes a discussion of strengths and weaknesses of the theory, in order to facilitate comparing theories and evaluating their usefulness for specific educational, counseling, human service, or policy goals.

The chapters close with a set of critical thinking questions and exercises which are intended to promote an analytical review of concepts, link the theory to personal life experiences, and encourage students to return to the opening case with enhanced appreciation for the insights provided by the theoretical lens. Key terms are boldfaced throughout each chapter, and the definition of these words and phrases can be found in the glossary as well as in the student e-resource. These glossary terms will support student assessment and outcomes. Recommended resources are suggested that extend the ideas of the theory through lectures, videos, websites, and additional readings. These resources suggest ways that students who are motivated can continue their exploration of the theory by examining its past as well as its current trends and application.

NEW TO THE SECOND EDITION

This edition preserves the basic organization and writing style of the first edition. It has been thoroughly updated with new references and contemporary examples of theoretical extensions, research, and applications. As noted above, many pedagogical elements were added to this edition. With respect to the content, a stronger emphasis on application can be seen in the use of opening cases for each theory chapter, a basic question about the practical implications of the theory, and critical thinking questions that focus on using the theory to interpret the case and personal life experiences. A new theory chapter, Chapter 10, Bioecological Theory, was added, based on its importance as a foundational framework in education, human services, and social work. The Epilogue, Chapter 12, was also added to provide a supplemental stimulus for analysis and comparison.

New topics are incorporated into the chapters. A few examples include: research on free-riders in Chapter 2; new research on the cognitive unconscious in Chapter 3; Robbie Case's theory of central conceptual structures in Chapter 4; a discussion of Albert Bandura's social cognitive theory in Chapter 5; an expanded discussion of gender role development in Chapter 6; a discussion of the effects of the accumulation of advantage and disadvantage over the life course in Chapter 7; a discussion of the practical implications of psychosocial theory in Chapter 8; an explanation of cultural historical activity theory (CHAT) in Chapter 9; and an explanation of Gilbert Gottlieb's concept of probabilistic epigenesis in Chapter 11.

This edition is accompanied by a website at www.psypress.com/9781848726673. The website provides *instructors* with a test bank, PowerPoints, cases, discussion questions and activities, tips for using the book with various types of majors, and a conversion guide outlining changes to the new edition. *Students* will find a summary, chapter outline, key terms with definitions, and additional readings and websites for further study.

We hope the text will serve instructors well in bringing the realm of theory to life. We hope the content will encourage students to see the field of human development as a living science that invites their critical thinking and creative contributions.

Acknowledgments

We would like to thank the reviewers who gave us their input on the revision: Davidio Dupree, University of Pennsylvania, Michele Gregoire Gill, University of Central Florida, Hillary Merk, University of Portland, Lydia B. Smith, University of North Carolina at Charlotte, and one anonymous reviewer.

About the Authors

Barbara M. Newman received her Ph.D. in developmental psychology from the University of Michigan. She is a professor emeritus at the University of Rhode Island in Human Development and Family Studies where she served for six years as department chair. She has been on the faculty at Russell Sage College and the Ohio State University, where she served as department chair in Human Development and Family Science, and as associate provost for faculty recruitment and development. As associate provost, she provided leadership for the recruitment of women and underrepresented minorities in the faculty, including innovative spousal advocacy initiatives. She was one of the founders of the Young Scholars Program as well as a program to provide access and coordinate resources for single mothers who wanted to complete an undergraduate degree. Dr. Newman received the outstanding teaching award from the College of Human Science and Services at the University of Rhode Island. Her teaching included courses in human development and family theories, life-span development, adolescence and young adulthood, and the research process. Dr. Newman's publications include articles on social and emotional development in adolescence, parent–adolescent relationships, and adjustment in the transition to high school and the transition to college. She is currently involved in two major research projects: a study of the sense of purpose and adaptation to the college environment for students with disabilities; and a multinational study of adolescent well-being.

Philip R. Newman received his Ph.D. in social psychology from the University of Michigan. He is a fellow of the American Psychological Association, the Society for the Psychological Study of Social Issues (SPSSI), and the American Orthopsychiatric Association. He has taught courses in introductory psychology, adolescence, social psychology, developmental psychology, counseling, and family, school and community contexts for development. He served as the director for research and evaluation for the Young Scholars Program at the Ohio State University, and as the director of the Human Behavior Curriculum Project for the American Psychological Association. His research focused on the transition to high school for low-income, minority students, and the relationship of group identity and alienation to adaptation in early adolescence. His current projects include a book about how high schools can meet the psychosocial needs of adolescents, and the development of a protocol for counselors to assess psychosocial maturity and problems in living based on the developmental framework presented in *Development through life: A psychosocial approach.*

Together, the Newmans have co-authored 13 books in the field of human development as well as numerous journal articles and book chapters on adolescent development, parenting, and psychosocial theory. Their life-span developmental text, *Development through life: A psychosocial approach*, is in its 12th edition.

1
Introduction

CHAPTER OUTLINE

GUIDING QUESTIONS

- What is the role of theory in the study of human development?
- What are some important features of a theory?
- How would you decide which theory is most appropriate for explaining behaviors that are of interest to you?

CASE VIGNETTE

Imagine the following situation. You are babysitting for Clark, who is 2½. You are getting ready to go to the park, which Clark loves, and you tell Clark that he needs to get his shoes on before you can leave the house. Clark sits down on the floor, pulls his shoes on, and starts to tie his laces. You see that he is having trouble, so you offer to help. "No!" says Clark, "I do it." You wait a while, and then you say, "Let me get that so we can go to the park." "No!" says Clark again, and pulls away. "Don't you want to go to the park?" you ask. Clark takes his shoes off and throws one at you. He falls on the floor, kicking and crying "no shoes, no help, no park!"

As a student of human development, you might begin to try to understand this situation by reflecting on what you observed. What did Clark say and do? What did you say and do? What was the context in which this interaction took place? Once you have taken careful account of the "what" of the situation, you will probably begin asking yourself some questions in order to understand the "why" of the situation and how to cope with it. You may wonder about the meaning of the situation for you and for Clark. You might consider that since you are an adult and Clark is a young child, the meaning of the situation might be different for each of you. Why won't Clark accept your help? Does Clark understand why he has to wear shoes to the park? Why is Clark so set on tying his own shoelaces? What role did you play in this situation? Did you say or do something that made Clark reject your help? How can you intervene so that Clark puts his shoes on and gets to go to the park?

In order to answer these questions, you need to link your observation of your behavior and Clark's behavior to ideas that explain them. These ideas are your theory of why things happened as they did for you, for Clark, and for you and Clark. The theory will lead you to a decision about what you might do next.

The world of **scientific inquiry** can be divided into two related components: **observation** and **theory**. Scientific observations describe what happens; scientific theories offer explanations about "how" and "why" these things happen.

In the study of human development, theories play a powerful role by shaping our ideas about the meaning of behavior, expanding our understanding of the scope and potential of complex human functioning, opening the way to new research, and guiding **interventions**. There is no single, agreed on theory that all scholars of human development endorse. Yet, many of the theories have given us a new lens for observing and interpreting behavior.

- Jean Piaget's theory of cognitive development led to a new appreciation for the way children create meaning out of their experiences. His theory has helped parents and teachers appreciate that as children develop they use different strategies for learning and thinking. This insight has had broad application in the design of age-appropriate curricula and learning environments.
- Sigmund Freud's theory of development provided insights into the unconscious, giving us a way of thinking about the tension between strong motives or desires and the constraints against expressing those desires. His emphasis on the early and continuing maturation of sexual drives has influenced parenting practices and approaches to psychotherapy. Current biopsychosocial theory draws on his work, linking internal sexual motives with patterns of reproductive behavior and their implications for human evolution.
- Albert Bandura's theory of social learning led to widespread use of the idea of modeling to characterize the social conditions under which children learn through observation and imitation of the behavior of others. His theory stimulated greater awareness of the social nature

of learning across many contexts. His ideas about self-efficacy have pointed to the importance of confidence as a person strives to meet new and challenging standards for performance. This concept has been applied in many fields including coaching, classroom instruction, and workplace performance.

- Erik Erikson's psychosocial theory highlighted the concept of identity, a creative synthesis of a sense of self in society, that emerges in later adolescence and guides the direction of development over the life span. His theory was one of the first to provide a model of development that extends over the entire life span. His theory has been applied broadly in the field of college student development with specific links to student achievement, career exploration, ethnic identity, and gender role development.

These are a few examples of how theorists have provided frameworks for identifying unobservable processes and mechanisms that account for behavior. In doing this, they have given us a new vocabulary for understanding and studying the dynamics of development.

This book is a selective introduction to ten theories that have inspired the study of human development and produced a rich heritage of research and intervention. Each theory not only has a distinguished history, but is also important in shaping the current focus of the field and guiding approaches to both research and practice.

This introductory chapter will address the following questions:

1. What is human development?
2. What is theory?
3. What do we expect from a theory of human development?
4. What are some of the challenges to understanding human development across the life span?
5. Why are there so many theories?

The chapter closes with an overview of the organization of the text.

WHAT IS HUMAN DEVELOPMENT?

The study of human development focuses on describing patterns of **constancy** and **change** across the **life span** and identifying the underlying processes that account for these patterns (Kagan, 1991). The term **development** implies change that occurs over time and has a direction. The direction is usually from simple to more complex, from less organized and coordinated to more organized and coordinated, or from less integrated to more integrated. In order to decide whether a particular change is developmental, one must ask if there is some pattern to the change that can be observed from one individual to the next, and if this change appears to have a direction that suggests a new level of complexity or integration. Consider the behavior of walking as an example. Walking is a new form of locomotion that can be observed from one child to the next. The change from crawling or scooting to standing and walking involves new levels of coordination in balance, and new integration of sensory and motor information.

The term *human development* suggests a focus on the human species, not all life forms. This focus brings with it special considerations. First, humans have ideas and experiences that influence their outlook. Scientists and theorists are similar to other humans in this regard. Scholars of human development are humans studying their own species. They have their own thoughts and experiences that may serve as a basis for expectations about the direction and meaning of behavior. Often, these personal thoughts and experiences serve to give focus and direction to the scholar's work. For example, Erik Erikson grew up in southern Germany with his mother and stepfather who was a Jewish pediatrician. It was not until he was older that he learned that his biological father was Danish. The experience of being an ethnically and religiously mixed child growing up in a tight knit, bourgeois community contributed to his heightened awareness of identity, self, and society which became key constructs in his theory. Each theory of human development must be understood as reflecting the education and training, historical context, and personal experiences, values, and beliefs of the human beings who invented it.

Second, humans enjoy a wonderful capacity for representational or symbolic thought. Thus, theories of human development must address more than a description of **behaviors** and explanations that account for these behaviors. They must also account for the nature of **mental activity** such as knowledge acquisition and use, imagination, aspirations and plans, emotions, problem solving, patterns of change and the direction of change in mental activity. Theories of development need to offer ideas about the mechanisms that link mental activity and behavior.

Third, humans have a comparatively long life span during which their capacities change dramatically. In contrast to many other species, humans are born in a dependent state, and their daily survival depends on the care and nurturance provided by others. This dependent state continues for quite some time. Humans may live to an advanced age of 100 years or more, achieving many new levels of complex thought and behavior, participating in a wide range of social relationships, and adapting to diverse physical and social settings. Theories of human development must address constancy and change of an organism over a long period of time.

WHAT IS A THEORY?

A theory is a logical system of concepts that helps explain **observations** and contributes to the development of a body of knowledge. We all have our informal, intuitive theories about why people behave as they do. For example, the adage "The acorn doesn't fall far from the tree," is an informal theory that predicts that children are going to grow up to behave a lot like their parents. However, a formal scientific theory is different from an informal set of beliefs. In order for a set of ideas to reach the level of a formal scientific theory, it has to be supported by extensive evidence, including systematic experimentation and observation (Zimmerman, 2009). A formal scientific theory is a set of interconnected statements, including assumptions, definitions, and hypotheses, which explain and interpret observations. The function of this set of interconnected statements is to describe unobservable structures, mechanisms, or processes and to relate them to one another in order to explain observable events. For example, in learning, the information or strategies that have been learned are not observable nor is the process of learning. The information becomes observable by asking questions, giving a test, or presenting a situation where the information must be used to solve a problem. However, the process of learning the information is not directly observable and our understanding of this process relies on theories that attempt to explain how new information is acquired, remembered, and produced when needed. Components of a theory and characteristics of a good theory are listed in Table 1.1.

In the field of human development, theory is differentiated from research and from facts. The research process may be guided by theory; however, the research process is a separate approach to building a knowledge base. For example, Piaget's cognitive developmental theory introduced the idea that through direct interaction with the physical world, infants gradually construct a scheme for the permanent object, and understanding that objects do not cease to exist when they are out

Table 1.1 What is a theory?

Components of a theory	Characteristics of a good theory
Assumptions	Logical
Domains	Internally consistent
Range of applicability	Parsimonious
Constructs	Testable
Hypotheses	Integrates previous research
	Deals with a relatively large area of science

of sight. A growing body of research, stimulated by this theory, has led to a more complex view of what infants know about objects depending on the nature of the task, the kind of response the baby is required to make, and the setting where the baby is studied.

Facts are distinct from the theories that might try to explain or account for them. For example, life expectancy at birth in the United States has increased considerably from 1900 to the present. This fact is indisputable. There may be several theories about factors that account for changes in longevity. Each theory might influence the direction of research about longevity. However, these theories do not change the facts.

Components of a Theory

Theories are like short stories with a situation, main characters, and a plot. The theory identifies a **domain** such as cognition, language, learning, motivation, or identity development that will be the focus of explanation. This is the situation or problem the theory is attempting to address. In order to understand a theory, one must be clear about which phenomena the theory is trying to explain. A theory of intellectual development may include hypotheses about the evolution of the brain, the growth of logical thinking, or the capacity to use symbolism. Such a theory is less likely to explain fears, motives, or friendship. Understanding the focus of the theory helps to identify its **range of applicability**. Although principles from one theory may have relevance to another area of knowledge, a theory is evaluated in terms of the domain it was originally intended to explain.

In reading about each theory, you will encounter certain **assumptions** about the scientific process, human behavior, or development. These assumptions may not be testable; they provide a platform upon which the theory is built. Assumptions are the guiding premises underlying the logic of a theory. In order to evaluate a theory, you must first understand what its assumptions are. Darwin assumed that lower life forms "progress" to higher forms in the process of evolution. Freud assumed that all behavior is motivated and that the unconscious is a "storehouse" of motives and wishes. The assumptions of any theory may or may not be correct. Assumptions may be influenced by the cultural context that dominates the theorist's period of history, by the sample of observations from which the theorist has drawn inferences, by the current knowledge base of the field, and by the intellectual capacities of the theorist.

Each theory is comprised of key **constructs** that refer to certain unobservable relationships or processes. You might think of these constructs as the principal characters in the story. We use constructs such as intelligence, motivation, and goals to explain human behavior, just as we use constructs such as electricity, gravity, and momentum to explain the physical world. In each case, the construct is not observable directly, although in the case of the physical world, scientists often have reached agreement on ways of measuring constructs. Developmental scholars work to measure explanatory constructs just as physical scientists do, but there is much less agreement about approaches to measurement.

Finally, theories offer *if–then* links or testable **hypotheses**. This is the plot. What does the theory predict? For example, Skinner's theory of operant conditioning offered the following testable hypothesis: "When a response is followed by a reward or reinforcement, the probability of its recurrence will increase." This means that successful actions (those that are rewarded) are more likely to be repeated than unsuccessful actions (those that are not rewarded). From this single hypothesis, one can interpret many observations about human behavior and predict others.

Requirements of a Good Theory

A formal theory should meet certain requirements. It should be logical and internally consistent, with no contradictory statements. The hypotheses can be explored through systematic research. As you read each theory, look for ways that the abstract concepts of the theory can be observed and measured. For example, a theory of learning might suggest that a behavior is more likely to occur when it is followed by a reinforcement. You can test this theory by monitoring a specific behavior, creating a specific reinforcement, and observing whether or not a person performs the behavior more often once the reinforcement has been presented.

The theory should be parsimonious, which means that the theory should be simple, relying on as few assumptions, constructs, and propositions as possible while still accurately accounting for the observations. Parsimony is relative. For example, Freud hypothesized that there were five stages of development. Erikson hypothesized that there were eight stages of development. Using the principle of parsimony, one might conclude that Freud's theory is a better one. However, Erikson's theory provides a more differentiated view of adulthood and aging, and, as a result, his theory offers more insight into the process of development over the life span. On the other hand, a theory that suggests 30 or 40 stages of life might be viewed as overly complex and less parsimonious than one that provides a smaller number of integrated periods. Finally, a theory should integrate previous research, and it should deal with a relatively large area of science (Miller, 2011).

Theories add new levels of understanding by suggesting causal relationships, by unifying diverse observations, and by identifying the importance of events that may have gone unnoticed. Once you agree to use the constructs of the theory as a way of talking about the domain, the theory takes you through a set of logical steps to predict the nature and direction of constancy and change.

Upon entering the world of a specific theory, it is easy to be caught up in its vocabulary and logic and to think of the theory as offering the truth about its domain. However, an important aspect of any scientific theory is that it is viewed as *tentative* and open to revision based on new observations. Scientific theories are different from beliefs. They are created with an understanding that new instrumentation, new observations, and new insights may result in new and better explanations. Thus, in your study of scientific theories you must realize that you are dealing with works in progress, and always treat them as providing descriptions and explanations that are useful until a more inclusive, accurate analysis is available (Bordens & Abbott, 2013).

WHAT DO WE EXPECT FROM A THEORY OF HUMAN DEVELOPMENT?

Theories of human development offer explanations regarding the origins and functions of human **behavior** and **mental activity**, and the changes that can be expected under certain conditions or from one period of life to the next. A theory of development should help to explain how people change and grow over time, as well as how they remain the same (Thomas, 1999). We expect a theory of human development to provide explanations for six questions:

1. What is the *direction* of change over the life span? We assume that there is a direction to development, that it is not random. Development is not the same as changing one's hair style or deciding one day to play tennis and the next to play soccer. Theories of development offer some big ideas about maturity, and shed light on important ways in which thought, self-understanding, the capacity for social relationships, and/or the capacity for adaptation become increasingly complex and integrated as life goes along. Theories of development provide a framework for thinking about **optimal development**, that is, age-related characteristics of social, physical, emotional and cognitive competence that can be expected when a person is highly motivated, physically healthy, and well-integrated into their social group.

2. What are the *mechanisms* that account for growth from conception through old age? Do these mechanisms vary across the life span? Theories of development suggest kinds of processes or experiences that bring about systematic change. In this book, we will present and explain the variety of mechanisms theorists offer for how growth and development occur. For example, Piaget's theory suggests that change occurs when a person encounters discrepancy between what is experienced in the world and the mental representations of that experience. He assumed that there is a natural tendency for people to resolve this discrepancy and seek equilibrium. Another theorist might offer a different kind of mechanism for explaining how change occurs. And in some instances, a theory suggests that different kinds of processes are at work at different periods of life.

3. How relevant are early experiences for later development? The theories presented in this book offer different ideas about the significance of early experiences for the psychological and behavioral organization of later periods of life. Some theories suggest that incidents from infancy and childhood play a powerful role in guiding the direction of development well into adulthood. Other theories emphasize the influence of contemporary events in guiding development by viewing the person as continuously adapting to new demands and opportunities.

   Two contrasting concepts inform this question: canalization and plasticity. **Canalization** means that responsiveness, whether at a neural or behavioral level, is shaped and narrowed as a result of repeated experiences (Gottlieb, 1991, 1997). For example, in infancy, babies are initially able to perceive sounds from a wide range of languages. However, some time between 6 and 10 months, infants are no longer able to differentiate the sounds of non-native languages, while their sensitivity to native language sounds and combinations becomes increasingly adept. Repeated exposure to early stressors, such as harsh parenting, has a similar canalizing impact at the neurological, hormonal, and cognitive levels (Blair & Raver, 2012). Children who have been repeatedly exposed to harsh, violent environments may develop neurological and hormonal responses that provide an advantage—a more rapid, sensitive awareness to threat, and the related ability to withdraw. However, this advantage comes at the cost of physical health, difficulties in concentrating, and impaired self-regulation.

   In contrast to the concept of canalization is the idea of **plasticity**, the capacity for adaptive reorganization at the neurological, psychological, and behavioral levels. The impressive ability of humans to learn from experience reflects this concept. Plasticity can be observed at the neurological level. For example, after a stroke, rehabilitation efforts allow a person to relearn many of the functions that were lost due to brain damage. Through repetition and practice, new neural networks and pathways are established. In some cases, new regions of the brain take over functions of regions that were damaged.

4. How do the *environmental* and *social contexts* affect individual development? Individuals develop in **contexts**, especially physical, cultural, family, school, work, and community contexts.

Theories of human development provide ways of conceptualizing contexts and of highlighting which aspects of context are especially important in shaping the directions of growth.

One of the most salient contexts impacting development is the culture in which a person grows up. **Culture** refers to the social, standardized ways of thinking, feeling, and acting that are shared by members of a society. Culture includes the concepts, habits, skills, arts, technologies, religions, and governments of a people. Cultures have implicit theories about the stages of life, the expectations for a person's behavior as one matures, and the nature of a person's obligations to the older and younger members of the cultural group.

Cultures exert influence directly through families as well as through networks of interacting individuals who may belong to common social organizations such as churches, clubs, schools, political and work organizations. In addition, cultures exert influence through media such as television, newspapers, magazines, online social media, music, books, and movies. Cultures provide a **worldview**, a way of making meaning of the relationships, situations, and objects people encounter in daily life. Culture is transmitted through a process of socialization whereby adults convey values and goals for themselves and their children, and structure the activities of daily life. We will analyze the salient aspects of each theory as it addresses the role of the environmental and cultural contexts in shaping development.

5. What factors are likely to place the person at risk at specific periods of the life span? Although humans have an enormous capacity for adaptation, some combination of conditions is likely to impede optimal growth. We look to theories of human development to help us understand **risk factors** that disrupt development. Each of the ten theories provides constructs that address vulnerabilities or risks and some predictions about the conditions that increase risk. Some of the theories also offer a differentiated view of risk over the life span.

   The idea of risk factors is often accompanied by a complementary concept of **protective factors** (Rutter, 1987). These are aspects of the person, the caregiving or intimate relationship, or the larger social environment that provide a positive influence on development. Protective factors may help to minimize or buffer the harm associated with threats, or contribute to the person's ability to rebound following a crisis (Ertem & Weitzman, 2011).

   Another related concept is resilience. People differ in their sensitivity to threat and their ability to recover following a crisis. **Resilience** refers to the ability to adapt successfully to events that threaten optimal functioning (Masten, 2014). Resilience may include the ability to anticipate threat, to adapt readily, and even become stronger or more competent under conditions that are otherwise known to disrupt or undermine functioning (Lerner et al., 2012). Differing environmental conditions at the cellular or behavioral levels can alter the expression of one or more genes, resulting in vulnerabilities or resilience (see Table 1.2). As illustrated, children with the same genetic profile become highly sensitive to environmental stressors if they are exposed to harsh parenting, but they can be especially resilient in the face of stress if they are exposed to warm, nurturing parenting (Caspi, Hariri, Holmes, Uher, & Moffitt, 2010). Theories differ in how they characterize risk and protective factors and how they account for individual differences in resilience.

6. What are the practical implications of the theory for prevention, intervention, or education? This is the big SO WHAT question. In what ways has the theory influenced practice? What big ideas from the theory contribute to the ways parents, caregivers, educators, counselors, social workers, health care providers, or other human service professionals engage in their work? Given the concepts and hypotheses of a theory, what guidance does the theory offer for action? What does the theory suggest that one should do to promote optimal development,

Table 1.2 Expression of the same gene in different environments

Genetic make-up	Parenting environment	Resilience
Child A: Gene A	Harsh parenting	Highly sensitive to stress
Child B: Gene A	Nurturing parenting	Resilient in the face of stress

prevent dysfunction, or promote recovery from disruptive experiences? What guidance does the theory offer about the timing of the intervention; the method of intervention; the duration of the intervention; or the intensity of the intervention? The practical implications of a theory are derived from its explanatory processes and mechanisms for change (Walton, 2014). In deciding to apply the theory in a particular context, one looks to empirical evidence of its effectiveness to determine if the guidance from that theory has been applied successfully to similar situations with similar individuals or groups.

WHAT ARE THE CHALLENGES TO UNDERSTANDING HUMAN DEVELOPMENT ACROSS THE LIFE SPAN?

Take a moment to reflect on your own development over the past ten years. Try to make an inventory of all the ways that you have changed. Include in this inventory your physical self, your interests, your plans and goals, the quality of your relationships, the settings in which you participate, the roles you play, the tasks you try to accomplish and your ability to succeed at those tasks, the way you use your time, the people with whom you spend time, and your level of self-insight.

Now, consider the ways you experience a sense of self-sameness, such as a constant sense of "I" who guides and directs your behaviors, certain continuous roles and relationships, your assessment of your underlying temperament and personality, your strengths and special talents, and a basket of early childhood memories that come along with you into each new phase of your life. Theories of human development face tremendous challenges in trying to offer scientifically based, empirically testable frameworks to account for the nature of stability and change over the life span. A few of these challenges are identified below; you may think of others.

1. Change in the person is taking place in the context of a changing environment. We do not have the luxury of placing a person in a "petri dish" and watching how he or she grows. A person develops over a long period of time, and as he or she grows, the environment changes. New siblings are born; parents get older; the society's norms for social behavior may change; opportunities for education and employment may change; new technologies and medical interventions may provide new resources; diseases, disasters, and war may place the person at risk. A challenge for each theory is to conceptualize the reality of a changing person in a changing environment (Magnusson & Cairns, 1996; Diehl et al., 2014).

2. Change is both quantitative and qualitative. Human beings grow by inches and pounds; these are **quantitative changes**. But they also grow through transitions from lying, to creeping, crawling, and walking; these are **qualitative changes**. Some changes, like a person's vocabulary, can be thought of as additive. At age 8 months, most infants typically have no real words; by 16 months most babies have about 24 words; and by 30 months most toddlers have about 570 words. In contrast to vocabulary, which grows incrementally, the creation of two-word sentences ("daddy bye-bye," "more juice") is a qualitative change in language use. At age 16 months,

few infants make these primitive sentences, but by 30 months almost all children create them (Fenson et al., 1994). Two-word expressions are an initial grammar through which children are able to convey their own complex meaning. The words "more" and "juice" each have meaning, but by putting them together, the child makes a primitive sentence that conveys an idea that is more complicated than the words alone. Two-word sentences are a qualitatively new language capacity that is a reorganization of vocabulary and meaning. Theories of human development face the challenge of accounting for both quantitative and qualitative changes and explaining how they operate together.

3. Human development is a product of the interaction of three dynamic systems: the biological, the psychological, and the societal. Each system is complex in its own right, and each has the potential for influencing the others (Erikson, 1963). The **biological system** includes all those processes necessary for the person's physical functioning, including genetic factors, physical maturation, vulnerability to disease, nutrition, exercise, sleep and rest cycles, reproductive and sexual functions. The **psychological system** includes all those mental processes needed to make meaning out of experiences, to learn, and to take action. Symbolic abilities, memory, language, the capacity for problem solving, emotion, coping strategies, and creativity are examples of components of the psychological system. The **societal system** includes all those processes through which a person becomes integrated into society. These include social roles, family, participation in social institutions such as school, work, and religion, cultural values and norms, exposure to discrimination or inter-group hostilities, and exposure to environmental toxins and hazards. Theories of human development may emphasize one or two of these systems more than the others, but without some recognition of the interaction of these systems, the analysis of human development is incomplete.

4. Human beings are conscious, reflective and goal-directed. The final challenge we want to raise in this introductory chapter is the need to recognize that humans are able to reflect upon and analyze their behavior, evaluating outcomes as successes or failures (Ellis, Carette, Anseel, & Lievens, 2014). The way people evaluate past experiences influences subsequent decisions. The capacity for conscious reflection and evaluation allows individuals to make choices that guide the direction of their own development.

   Often, the concepts of nature (a biological plan for development) and nurture (the environmental contexts of development) are presented as constructs that help account for the direction of growth. Current scholarly work emphasizes that these two factors interact with each other, so that we no longer seek a purely environmental or a purely biological explanation for human behavior. Rather, we look for evidence about how the expression of certain genetically guided patterns is mediated by environmental conditions. However, in these analyses, a third dimension, self-directed goal behavior, is often omitted.

   > The great variability and flexibility of human behavior and development are advantages in terms of enhanced adaptive potential. However, the organism needs to organize his or her resource investment by making choices and focusing resources accordingly. Thus, life-span development theory inherently raises questions of how individuals decide which domains or goals to select and how they remain focused on the domains or goals they have chosen. (Heckhausen & Schulz, 1999, p. 70)

The challenge to theories of human development is to offer an explanation for the choices individuals make that ultimately contribute to the direction of their development.

WHY SO MANY THEORIES? WHICH ONE SHOULD I CHOOSE?

Given the challenges to the study of human development noted above, it is probably not surprising that there is no one agreed upon theory that accounts for all aspects of human development. The ten theories you will review in this text address different domains of development, focusing to a greater or lesser extent on physical, cognitive, social, and emotional processes. The theories differ in their emphasis on particular periods of life, some more attuned to infancy and the childhood years; others more attuned to periods of adolescence, adulthood, and aging. The theories differ in their emphasis on universal patterns as compared to unique cultural and contextual factors that influence development. The theories also differ in their level of analysis. Some theories focus on very specific moments in daily life; others focus on broad, system changes that may occur gradually over long periods of time. As you study the ten theories, you will appreciate that each one offers a unique lens for the study of development.

The decision about which theory to use depends on your purpose. Think back to the case vignette of Clark. Your choice of a theory to guide intervention will be influenced by your goals. For example, do you want to understand the developmental significance of oppositional behavior for long-term species survival? Or do you want to help Clark learn new strategies for self-regulation? Or do you want to help Clark's parents develop a new approach to childrearing? Each purpose would implicate a different theory.

Once you understand the assumptions, scope, concepts, and hypotheses, and read about the research and application of each theory, you will have a clearer notion of whether that theory can be helpful in promoting optimal development. You will want to review how the theory addresses the following key issues:

- What is the direction of development?
- What are the mechanisms that account for development?
- How do early experiences influence later development?
- What are the key contexts and how do they influence development?
- What are the key risk and protective factors that influence development?

You will want to examine the evidence that addresses the effectiveness of interventions that have been guided by the theory. But, you may also think of some possible applications of the theory that have not been considered before. That is one of the most exciting aspects of the study of human development; it is a dynamic field with many new and emerging directions for intervention.

THE ORGANIZATION OF THE BOOK

The remainder of this book focuses on ten theories divided into three families of theories. Part I includes evolutionary theory, psychoanalytic theory, and cognitive developmental theory, which place a comparatively strong emphasis on *biological factors* that guide the direction of development. Part II includes learning theories, social role theory, and life course theory, which place a comparatively strong emphasis on *environmental factors* that guide the direction of development. Part III includes psychosocial theory, cognitive social-historical theory, bioecological theory, and dynamic systems theory, which emphasize the ongoing *interaction of the person and the environment*. As an initial orientation to the book, Table 1.3 provides an overview of the emphasis of each theory, its primary domain, and the methods it uses to gather information and evaluate its claims.

Of course, this division of the theories into three families is an overgeneralization. Each theory has something to say about biological factors, environmental factors, and person–environment interactions. However, we expect that this organization will help you recognize some of the common threads among the theories, compare and contrast them, and work out your own assessment of their strengths and weaknesses.

The presentation of each family of theories begins with a brief interlude or overview in which the issues that tie the theories together are introduced. The discussion of each theory includes the following sections:

A. The historical/cultural context within which the theory was developed.
B. An overview of key concepts.
C. New directions of the theory.
D. A research example that shows how some aspect of the theory has been tested.
E. An application that shows how the theory has been used to address a practical problem.
F. A review of how the theory answers the six questions discussed above that are expected to be addressed by a theory of human development.
G. A critique of the theory, pointing out its strengths and weaknesses.

As you read each theory, we encourage you to consider its broad impact as well as its scientific merit. You will be thinking about the contributions these theories have made to research and application, and their ability to shape the worldviews of people outside the narrow circle of human development researchers and scholars.

Table 1.3 Overview of ten theories

Theory	Emphasis	Primary domain	Unique methods
Evolutionary theory	Biological evolution	Fitness; sexual reproduction	Ethology; observation of behavior in natural settings
Psychoanalytic theory	The origins and development of mental life	Personality development, emotions, motivation, morality	Free association, dream interpretation, case analysis
Cognitive developmental theory	The origins and development of cognition	The development of reasoning and logical thought	Cognitive interview, problem-solving tasks, observation
Learning theories	The establishment of relatively permanent links between stimuli and responses	Learned behaviors, expectancies, vicarious learning; changes in behavior as a result of experience	Laboratory experimentation
Social role theory	Socially constructed roles and role relationships	The development of the self in social life	Survey, interview, and case material
Life course theory	Individual life in social and historical time	Transitions and trajectories over the life course	Archival data, demographic data, longitudinal studies, intergenerational studies
Psychosocial theory	The interaction of the individual and society	Stages of ego development, identity, worldview, and social relationships	Case material, play analysis, narratives and life stories, and psychohistory
Cognitive social-historical theory	The social and cultural basis of thinking	Cognition, the relationship of speech and thinking, the nature of consciousness, learning and development	Experimental demonstrations that promote or include learning and development, double stimulation method

Theory	Emphasis	Primary domain	Unique methods
Bioecological theory	The interaction of the person and the immediate and more remote environments	Development as a product of the interaction of characteristics of the person, specific processes, contexts and time	Observation, experimentation, and cross-setting comparisons of behavior
Dynamic systems theory	The function and change of complex systems	Emergence of novel patterns (e.g. motor behavior, skills, cognition, and social interactions)	Mathematical, multidimensional modeling; observation; experimentation

CRITICAL THINKING QUESTIONS AND EXERCISES

1. What should a theory of human development explain?
2. Why are there so many different theories of human development?
3. Think back to the case of Clark. What concepts that you have studied in the past are most useful to you in explaining Clark's behavior?
4. How might a babysitter, a parent, and a preschool teacher differ in their analysis of this situation? How might their theories of development differ? Make a table that summarizes the similarities and differences in the theoretical focus of each of these three roles.
5. Given what you have read about challenges to the study of human development, what more would you need to know about Clark and the context of this situation in order to account for his behavior?
6. Identify a theoretical concept that has proven useful to you in understanding a topic in development. What are the features of that concept that make it particularly useful? Identify a theoretical concept that you believe to be incorrect or disadvantageous in your efforts to understand a problem in development. What evidence do you have that the concept is incorrect? How has it disrupted your efforts to understand the topic?

KEY TERMS

assumptions
behavior
biological system
canalization
change
constancy
constructs
context
culture
development
domains
hypotheses
intervention
life span
mental activity

observation
optimal development
plasticity
protective factors
psychological system
qualitative change
quantitative change
range of applicability
resilience
risk factors
scientific inquiry
societal system
theory
worldview

RECOMMENDED RESOURCES

****Haig, B.D. (2009). Methods: Evaluating explanatory theories. Retrieved on April 2, 2014 from www.thepsychologist.org.uk/archive/archive_home.cfm?volumeID=22&editionID=181& ArticleID=1587
This article describes a qualitative approach, Inference to the Best Explanation (IBE), for evaluating theories.

****Popper, K.R. (1963). Science as falsification. Taken from *Conjectures and Refutations*. Retrieved on April 2, 2014 at www.stephenjaygould.org/ctrl/popper_falsification.html
The essay from a distinguished philosopher of science describes his early thinking about how to evaluate theories based on the principle of falsification.

**** Schermer, Michael (2006). "Why people believe weird things." Ted Talks. www.ted.com/talks/ michael_shermer_on_believing_strange_things
Schermer provides an amusing and insightful presentation about how beliefs can be based on questionable evidence.

****Sutton, R.I. & Staw, B.M. (1995). What theory is not. *Administrative Science Quarterly, 40,* 371–384. Stable URL: www.jstor.org/stable/2393788
Sutton and Staw offer a perspective that critically evaluates many social science papers by clarifying the elements that are not sufficient to be considered a theory.

****Wilson, T.D. (2011). *Redirect: The surprising new science of psychological change.* New York: Little Brown.
A review of interventions that target specific psychological processes, illustrating the power of theory in helping to guide change.

REFERENCES

Blair, C. & Raver, C.C. (2012). Child development in the context of adversity: Experiential canalization of brain and behavior. *American Psychologist, 67,* 309–318.

Bordens, K.S. & Abbott, B.B. (2013). *Research design and methods: A process approach.* 9th ed. New York: McGraw-Hill.

Caspi, A., Hariri, A.R., Holmes, A., Uher, R., & Moffitt, T.E. (2010). Genetic sensitivity to the environment: The case of the serotonin gene and its implications for studying complex diseases and traits. *American Journal of Psychiatry, 167,* 509–527.

Diehl, M., Chui, H., Hay, M.A. et al. (2014). Change in coping and defense mechanisms across adulthood: Longitudinal findings in a European American sample. *Developmental Psychology, 50,* 634–648.

Ellis, S., Carette, B., Anseel, F., & Lievens, F. (2014). Systematic reflection: Implications for learning from failures and successes. *Current Directions in Psychological Science, 23,* 67–72.

Erikson, E.H. (1963). *Childhood and society.* 2nd ed. New York: Norton. (Original work published 1950)

Ertem, I.O. & Weitzman, C.C. (2011). Child development: Monitoring and supporting early childhood development. In C. Rudolph, A. Rudolph, G. Lister, L. First, & A. Gershon (Eds.), *Rudolph's pediatrics.* 22nd ed. (pp. 34–42). New York: McGraw-Hill.

Fenson, L., Dale, P.S., Reznick, J.S., Bates, E., Thal, D.J., & Pethick, S.J. (1994). Variability in early communicative development. *Monographs of the Society for Research in Child Development, 59* (Serial No. 5).

Gottlieb, G. (1991). Experiential canalization of behavioral development: Theory. *Developmental Psychology, 27,* 4–13.

Gottlieb, G. (1997). *Synthesizing nature-nurture: Prenatal roots of instinctual behavior.* Mahwah, NJ: Erlbaum.

Heckhausen, J. & Schulz, R. (1999). Selectivity in life-span development. In J. Brandtstadter & R.M. Lerner (Eds.), *Action and self-development: Theory and research through the life span* (pp. 67–103). Thousand Oaks, CA: Sage.

Kagan, J. (1991). Continuity and discontinuity in development. In S.E. Brauth, W.S. Hall, & R.J. Dooling (Eds.), *Plasticity of development* (pp. 11–26). Cambridge, MA: MIT Press.

Lerner, R.M., Schmid, K.L., Weiner, M.B. et al. (2012). Resilience across the life span. In B. Hayslip, Jr. & G.C. Smith (Eds.), *Emerging perspectives on resilience in adulthood and later life* (pp. 275–299). New York: Springer.

Magnusson, D. & Cairns, R.B. (1996). Developmental science: Principles and illustrations. In R.B. Cairns, G.H. Elder, & E.J. Costello (Eds.), *Developmental science.* Cambridge, UK: Cambridge University Press.

Masten, A.S. (2014). Global perspectives on resilience in children and youth. *Child Development, 85,* 6–20.

Miller, P.H. (2011). *Theories of developmental psychology.* 5th ed. New York: Worth.

Rutter, M. (1987). Psychosocial resilience and protective mechanisms. *American Journal of Orthopsychiatry, 57,* 316–331.

Thomas, R.M. (1999). *Human development theories: Windows on culture.* Thousand Oaks, CA: Sage.

Walton, G.M. (2014). The new science of wise psychological interventions. *Current Directions in Psychological Science, 23,* 73–82.

Zimmerman, M. (2009, Spring). Why evolution is the organizing principle for biology. *Phi Kappa Phi Forum,* 4–7.

Part I
Theories That Emphasize Biological Factors

How do human beings emerge from a fertilized egg into their full-blown stature as an adult? In the sixteenth and seventeenth centuries, some scholars believed in the idea of an homonculus, a fully formed, miniature human believed to be contained in the spermatozoon. This theoretical construct helped to explain how the human body was guided toward its adult shape, structures, and functions. A more contemporary term that reflects this idea is epigenesis, the "approximately stepwise process by which genetic information, as modified by environmental influences, is translated into the substance and behavior of an organism" (Flexner, 1987, p. 653). You can think of this view as if humans were like plants. Seeds contain all the information necessary to grow into daisies, carrots, or marigolds. The role of the environment is to provide the basic, "just good enough," resources so that the potential embedded in the seed can reach its full expression. Just give seeds the correct amount of water, sun, soil, and the right temperature for their growing season, and the fate of the seeds is predetermined.

The three theories presented in this section are members of a family of theories that have a strong biological thread. In the literature about development, this is sometimes referred to as the *nature, innate*, or *nativist* camp. Of course, no theory of development claims that the story of growth is entirely about nature. No human, whatever his or her biological endowments, can live without environmental supports including air, food, water, and shelter. We are increasingly aware that humans also require social and cognitive stimulation. However, when we ask how development occurs, these theories give a strong role to biologically based capacities that guide the direction and nature of growth.

Evolutionary theory, psychosexual theory, and cognitive developmental theory address the process of adaptation. Evolutionary theory focuses on the long-term adaptation of the species over many generations. This theory highlights the importance of the reproductive process through which adaptive capacities emerge and are transmitted biologically from one generation to the next. The human beings alive today are a product of a long period of biological evolution, carrying with them the genes for specific physical structures, cognitive functions, and sensory capacities that allow them to find a mate, reproduce, and rear their young to reproductive age.

Psychoanalytic theory focuses on the psychological development that accompanies sexual maturation during a lifetime. The theory helps explain how sexual impulses and drives are experienced at the psychological level. The tension between individual survival and group survival is highlighted by constructing a model of the mind and its structures that allows some degree of impulse gratification within socially acceptable boundaries. The direction of development is predetermined and viewed as universal, from the oral-dependent status of the infant to the sexually mature, well-socialized status of the healthy adult.

Cognitive developmental theory focuses on the unfolding of cognitive capacities that accompany problem solving and adaptation to the challenges of coping with the physical and social worlds. The theory helps explain how the mind develops from the early reflexive capacities of the newborn to the abstract, hypothetical problem-solving capacities of the adult. Here, too, the direction of development is predetermined and viewed as universal, from reasoning that is based largely on direct interaction and manipulation of objects, to the capacity for mental representations of concepts, and finally the internal manipulation of variables guided by principles of logic.

The three theories are linked by their common emphasis on the biological bases of behavior as a guide to development, and their focus on development from an immature to a mature state. They all suggest that there are universal directions of development. These theories focus on different domains of development. Evolutionary theory addresses the adaptive capacities that contribute to reproductive success and species survival. Psychoanalytic theory focuses on personality development, emotions, motivation, and morality as a product of tensions between conscious and unconscious drives and constraints. Cognitive developmental theory emphasizes the emergence of reasoning and logical thought as primary adaptive capacities. The three theories differ in the mechanisms they suggest for change, and in the level of "conscious attention" they attribute to individuals in the process of change.

REFERENCE

Flexner, S.B. (1987). *Random House dictionary of the English language*. 2nd ed., unabridged. New York: Random House.

2
Evolutionary Theory

CHAPTER OUTLINE

GUIDING QUESTIONS

- What are the basic concepts of the theory of evolution? How can they be applied to individual development over the life span?
- How does the relatively long period of infant dependency shape human development and the nature of families?
- What might be the adaptive benefit of longevity? How might human survival into advanced later life contribute to species survival?
- What is the relationship between human cognitive capacities and complex social life? What are some bidirectional influences between cognitive complexity and the coordination of large social groups?

CASE VIGNETTE

Two strangers, Mark and Linda, get into the elevator in the Randolph Towers. They make eye contact and smile. Then Linda looks away. Mark continues to glance over at Linda; after a few moments she returns his gaze. Mark thinks that Linda is attractive. She has dark eyes, full lips, and smooth skin. She looks comfortable in her jacket and slacks, revealing an appealing, curvy figure. Linda thinks Mark looks very respectable in his suit and tie. His shoes are polished and he is carrying a smart leather briefcase. They ride to the 23rd floor where they both get off. Mark smiles again and asks Linda where she is going. She tells him she has an appointment with an attorney on that floor. She asks him what he is doing there; he says he is an accountant for a firm that is doing an audit of a company on that floor. Mark asks Linda if she would like to go for coffee when her meeting is over, and she grins and says, "Sure."

Evolutionary theory offers insights into how people established close, cooperative bonds long before language and symbolic systems were created. The case introduces basic ideas about attraction between strangers. Eye contact is an initial mode of nonverbal communication. Even very small babies are attuned to facial expressions and features as meaningful stimuli. The human brain has a specialized area that allows people to assess the mood, sex, age, direction of gaze, and trustworthiness of another person by scanning their face (Kanwisher, 2006). What might be the adaptive value of this sensitivity to eyes and faces?

A second theme is the nature of attractiveness. Describe the differences in the features that Mark and Linda notice in one another. What might be some explanations for these differences? From an evolutionary perspective, men and women have different lenses for assessing attractiveness because they have different reproductive motives. As you read further about evolutionary theory, you will be encouraged to think about the link between contemporary human behavior and its ancient antecedents derived from thousands of years of biosocial adaptation through the process of natural selection.

Humans are living beings, linked to all other forms of life through the process of evolution. The theory of evolution explains how diverse and increasingly complex life forms come to exist. Evolutionary theory assumes that the natural laws that apply to plant and animal life also apply to humans. This theory is important in the study of human development because it integrates human beings into the vast array of life forms and suggests explanations for a variety of characteristics that we regard as essentially human. Evolutionary theory emphasizes the importance of biological forces in directing growth, the gradual modification of species, and the emergence of new species as a result of adaptation to specific environments. The theory addresses change over many generations and thousands of years; it is not intended as a theory about how change and adaptation occur within short periods or even within one lifetime. This chapter focuses on the key concepts of evolutionary thought and their relationship to an understanding of human behavior through advances in the fields of ethology and evolutionary psychology.

HISTORICAL CONTEXT

Charles Darwin was born in Shrewsbury, England in 1809. He was from an educated family with a long-standing tradition of belief in the concepts generated by the theory of evolution. Darwin's grandfather Erasmus Darwin was a pioneer in the development of evolutionary theory. His ideas about the topic were published in a book entitled *Zoonomia* in 1794–96. In this book, Erasmus wrote about sexual selection: "The final cause of this contest among males seems to be that the strongest and most active animal should propagate the species which should thus become improved." However, the work was based largely upon theoretical hypotheses and generalizations rather than upon systematic evidence, and Charles Darwin denied that it had any significant impact on his own thinking.

As a schoolboy, Darwin rebelled against the classical pattern of learning by rote memorization. He preferred to spend long periods of time outdoors, exploring nature and puzzling over its mysteries. Darwin recalls that as a young boy of about 8 or 9, he already had a strong interest in collecting all sorts of things, including shells, coins, and rocks, and was interested in learning the names of the plants he found in his wanderings (Barlow, 1958). As a young man, Darwin explored careers in medicine and theology, but he found those studies uninteresting. He continued to spend much of his time outdoors, exploring nature.

In 1831, an opportunity arose that allowed Darwin to indulge his passion for the outdoors in a professionally acceptable way: he became the resident naturalist on *H.M.S. Beagle*. The crew's mission was to sail to South America, to survey the coast and the islands of the Pacific, to map this region, and to document its plant and animal life. The voyage lasted from 1831 to 1836. During those years, Darwin demonstrated unbounded energy in his exploration of the natural phenomena that he encountered.

Returning to England, Darwin settled down to work on the samples he had collected and to reflect on his observations. With painstaking attention to details, over a period of 20 years he developed his theory of how species can change and evolve into new plant or animal forms. However, he postponed writing about his views while he searched for examples that would support his argument. Not until 1859, when he learned that another naturalist, Alfred Russell Wallace, was about to introduce a very similar argument, was Darwin compelled to publish *The origin of species*.

KEY CONCEPTS

Natural Selection

Charles Darwin has been credited with the discovery of the basic mechanism that could account for the transformation of species over long periods and in many different environments. In line with Charles Lyell's (1830/1833) idea of uniformitarianism, Darwin believed that unchanging laws of nature apply uniformly throughout time. The challenge posed by this assumption was to discover the basic mechanism that could account for species change from the beginnings of life to the present. The mechanism that Darwin (1859/1979) discovered is natural selection.

The law of **natural selection** predicts that behavior is adapted to the environment in which it occurs. Natural selection operates, via organisms' reproductive success, from one generation to the next. Reproductive success, sometimes called **fitness,** varies among members of a species (Archer, 1991). Every species produces more offspring than can survive to reproduce because of limitations of the food supply and natural dangers. Darwin observed that there was quite a bit of variability among members of the same species in any given location. This variability may be a result of existing genetic diversity or a product of **mutations** that introduce new sources of variation in the species. Mutations are changes in the DNA that result in the substitution, deletion, insertion, or reordering of some segment of DNA which then modifies subsequent developmental processes. The term "genetics" was not even coined until 1905, more than 20 years after Darwin's death (Hayden, 2009). Thus, his theory about the variability and modification of species was based on his observations and collected samples.

According to the theory of natural selection, some individuals were better suited than others to their immediate environment and were more likely to survive, mate, and produce offspring. These offspring were also more likely to have characteristics appropriate for that location. Over long periods of time, those members of the species that had the selective advantage would be more likely to survive and reproduce, thus passing their characteristics on to future generations. If the environment changed (in climate, for example), only certain variations of organisms would survive, and again new species would evolve. Forms of life that failed to adapt would become extinct. Thus, in the context of changing environmental conditions, the variability within a species ensures the species' continuation or its development into new forms. Darwin viewed evolutionary change as taking place slowly and incrementally as individual organisms adapt and populations with similar adaptive characteristics dominate an environment or ecological niche.

The polar bears or white bears are an example of this evolutionary change. Roughly four or five million years ago, the white bears evolved from the brown bears. Some of the brown bears living in the harsh, cold, ice- and snow-capped regions near the Arctic began to show patches of white fur. Over generations, those bears with more white fur had better success at creeping up on their prey. Over time, the white bears became the dominant species in the Arctic, and brown bears were no longer found in these cold, snow-covered Arctic regions (Polar Bears International, 2014).

The concept of fitness has been expanded to consider the idea of **inclusive fitness** (Hamilton, 1964). This idea suggests that fitness is not only determined by an individual's reproductive success, but by promoting the survival and reproductive success of others who share one's genetic ancestry. In human groups, behaviors that support one's family members or that make it possible for one's kin to be more attractive in the mating process would be considered examples of inclusive fitness.

In the process of natural selection, new species may emerge, and existing species may become extinct. **Extinction,** just like the appearance of a new species, is a natural process. This may occur as the result of some catastrophe when many species that had been flourishing are destroyed. Some catastrophes, such as the collision of the Chicxulub asteroid with earth roughly 66 million years ago, resulted in enormous heat, tidal waves, and changes in the amount of oxygen in the atmosphere which led to the extinction of large numbers of existing species across the globe (Renne et al., 2013). Extinction can also occur when individuals in a specific species are reduced to a very small number so that inbreeding occurs. This weakens the genetic strain because anomalies are transmitted more rapidly from one generation to the next, threatening survival or reproductive capacity. Changes in environmental conditions such as new diseases, increases in predators, or changes in climate can result in extinction at the same time as they result in the formation of new species.

The law of natural selection has been referred to as the principle of *survival of the fittest*. Herbert Spencer (1864) first referred to it in this way. This phrase often calls up images of head-to-head combat between members of a species. This is not what Darwin's principle says. Darwin described the process in the following way:

> It may metaphorically be said that natural selection is daily and hourly scrutinizing, throughout the world, the slightest variation; rejecting those that are bad, preserving and adding up all that are good; silently and insensibly working, whenever and wherever opportunity offers, at the improvement of each organic being in relation to its conditions of life. We see nothing of these slow changes in progress, until the hand of time has marked the lapse of ages, and then so imperfect is our view into long-past geological ages, that we see only that the forms of life are now different from what they formerly were. (Darwin, 1859/1979, p. 77)

In fact, it is reproductive advantage, not survival per se, that results in the continuation of certain characteristics. For example, if a characteristic resulted in a relatively early death for mothers but the survival of her offspring, that characteristic might have an adaptive advantage.

Darwin described two aspects of evolution (Mayr, 1991). One is the gradual change within a species over time from earlier to later forms. For example, even though they are the same species, modern chimpanzees alive today are not identical to the chimpanzees that lived thousands of years ago. They have had to adapt to changing environmental conditions, including alterations in food sources, landscapes, and threats. The second aspect of evolution is the breaking away from an earlier evolutionary lineage and the establishment of a new branch in the phylogenetic tree. This is the process of speciation that contributes to biological diversity. For example, some combination of events led to the separation of the hominids from homo erectus to homo sapiens about 300,000 to 400,000 years ago.

Adaptation

Adaptation is the process that underlies evolutionary change—the process by which living things develop structures and problem-solving mechanisms that enable them to thrive in a particular environment. Adaptation is expressed in specific characteristics that are functional in the face of specific problems the organism must solve. For example, the need to distinguish edible from poisonous foods results in the adaptation of specific sensory capacities in taste, smell, and visual discrimination. The particular sensory abilities that evolve depend on the sources and variety of foods the organism encounters. Adaptation can operate at the biological level, as a change in some physical characteristic over generations. Adaptation can also operate at the behavioral level, as a change in some pattern of behavior.

Evolution and the Human Species

Imagine a cosmic calendar in which the history of the universe of 13.8 billion years is represented in one year, with the big bang occurring on January 1 and each month representing a little over

Figure 2.1 Adaptation Katydid
Source: H. Vannoy Davis © California Academy of Sciences

one billion years. The first mammals appeared on December 26, the first primates on December 29, and the first humans at 10:30 pm on December 31 (Sagan, 1977/2012; Cosmos: A Spacetime Odyssey, 2014). The evolution of the family of humans began only about 2 million years ago with the species homo habilis and homo erectus. Homo habilis lived between 1.9 and 1.8 million years ago, and fossil evidence of this species was found only in Africa. Homo erectus lived between 1.8 million and 300,000 years ago, with fossil remains discovered in Africa and throughout Europe and Asia. Modern humans are thought to have descended from this species. Modern humans, homo sapiens, most likely had their origins in Africa. Fossil evidence places them in Ethiopia roughly 200,000 years ago (O'Neil, 2013). This group of advanced humans then dispersed throughout the Old World and replaced other human species. With techniques from molecular biology it is possible to trace characteristics of mitochondrial DNA that show that the modern humans found in various areas of Europe, Asia, and America are quite similar to one another, suggesting common genetic ancestry. The DNA would not be so similar if they had evolved independently from local primitive ancestors (Lewin & Foley, 2004).

Thus the picture of human evolution that is taking shape is one of a common modern ancestor whose offspring migrated throughout the world and dominated other human species. Fossil evidence suggests that there were a variety of hominids alive at the same time. The question that continues to puzzle modern paleoanthropologists is how to account for the significant gap in capacity between these species of humans and those of modern homo sapiens (Tattersall, 2012). The domination of modern humans was probably subtle, not a case of open warfare or competition. Some superiority in hunting skills, tool making, and planning could have given the modern species an evolutionary advantage by enabling them to establish dependable sources of high-quality food (Simons, 1989). This domination was comparatively rapid, fueled by powerful mental evolution and the accompanying forms of cultural evolution that brought complex tool development, advanced techniques for hunting and gathering, the invention of agriculture, and the eventual growth of tribes, chiefdoms, and political states.

Wilson (1975) described the process through which humans achieved such a rapid and advanced level of functioning as the *autocatalysis model*. This term suggests that a capacity that emerged in the process of adaptation resulted in an acceleration of the change process itself.

When the earliest hominids became bipedal as part of their terrestrial adaptation, their hands were freed, the manufacture and handling of artifacts was made easier, and intelligence grew as part of the improvement of the tool-using habit. With mental capacity and the tendency to use artifacts increasing through mutual reinforcement, the entire materials-based culture expanded. Cooperation during hunting was perfected, providing a new impetus for the evolution of intelligence, which in turn permitted still more sophistication in tool using, and so on through cycles of causation . . . The autocatalysis model usually includes the proposition that the shift to big game accelerated the process of mental evolution. (pp. 567–568)

Humans Are Mammals. Humans have characteristics that link them to the larger group of mammals from which they descended. Humans produce live young. The mothers feed their young on milk produced by the mammary glands. Their bodies are covered with skin, which is protected by hair.

Humans Are Primates. Humans also have characteristics that link them to other primates, the class of mammals that includes humans, apes, monkeys, lemurs, and tarsiers. Primates share ten major characteristics:

1. Progressive movement of the eyes toward the midline of the head and consequent development of stereoscopic (three-dimensional) vision.
2. Retention of five-digit extremities and of the major bones of the arms and legs—clavicle, radius, and fibula.
3. Progressive development of the digits, particularly the thumb and big toe, which allows for increasing dexterity.
4. Development of flattened nails, instead of claws, and also of sensitive pads on the tips of the digits.
5. Progressive shortening of the snout, reduction in the size of the apparatus for smell, and consequent reduction in olfactory acuity.
6. Great increase in the size of the brain.
7. Prolongation of prenatal and postnatal development.
8. Decrease in the number of teeth and retention of a simple molar system.
9. Overall increase in body size, progressive development toward upright stature, and increased dependence on the hind limbs for locomotion.
10. Development of complex social organizations.

Humans Are a Unique Species. Humans also have some features which characterize **human nature**. All human beings, regardless of culture, share characteristics that tie them together as a species:

- They share a common body shape and specific organs such as eyes, nose, ears, hands, and feet, which can be recognized as human despite individual differences.
- They can mate and produce living children who in turn are capable of reproducing.
- Critical among the characteristics of humans is bipedalism as a primary means of locomotion, which leaves the hands free for tool use, holding, carrying, and gesturing.
- The structure of human hands permits the flexible manipulation of objects as tools.
- Reduced reliance on smell and relatively greater reliance on vision influence the human mode of exploring the environment.

- Because of the prolonged period of prenatal and postnatal development characteristic of human infants, humans are highly social; they are oriented toward social stimuli and have highly developed capacities for solving social problems.
- Perhaps the most critical aspect of human nature is the size, structure, and complexity of the brain. As a result of this brain, humans have extensive symbolic capacities and a remarkable ability to learn. They produce spoken symbolic language. They store information and pass it on from one generation to the next.
- Humans are self-conscious; they raise questions about their origin and anticipate their death.
- Humans are aware of what others are feeling and thinking. This social intelligence allows them to coordinate complex group activities and to form enduring social bonds.

NEW DIRECTIONS

Ethology

Have you ever been to a park where a number of dogs are playing together? Have you noticed how they chase each other, engage in a form of rough and tumble play, and bite at each other's legs and neck without actually harming each other? Playfulness is an example of a topic that is of interest to ethologists. What is the adaptive value of playfulness? Why do animals play? **Ethology** is the study of the functional significance of animal behavior in the natural environment from an evolutionary perspective (LaFreniere, 2000). Its roots lie in Darwin's ideas about behavioral adaptation. In addition to the evolution of physical organs and body structures, adaptation has produced patterns of motor activity, facial expressions, and emotional reactions. Darwin himself was very interested in the adaptive nature of emotions and wrote extensively about it in *The expression of the emotions in man and animals* (1872/2009).

Ethology examines how a particular behavior contributes not just to the future growth and development of the individual but to the adaptation and continuation of the species. The future of a species depends on the capacity of its individual members to survive, mate, reproduce, and rear their young. Some of the factors that contribute to the vigor and continuity of a species are the health of the individuals when they attain reproductive capacity, the characteristics of the environment that promote or inhibit procreation, and the capacity of sexually mature partners to rear their offspring.

From Darwin's interest in the evolution of species grew the ethologists' interest in those behaviors that are central to the species' survival, including feeding efficiency, competition among males for breeding females, and cooperation among males in warding off predators and competing primates. The field of ethology has emerged as the study of evolutionarily significant behaviors that appear to be innate and specific to a particular species. These behaviors are commonly associated with eating, mating, and protecting a species from harm.

Behaviors that are successful in coping with specific environmental conditions are supported by an integration of brain structures, physiological responses, and motivational underpinnings. Ultimately, those behaviors appear as spontaneous, unlearned actions that provide some type of adaptive advantage. An example is the infant's smile. Smiles occur early in the postnatal period. They function as a powerful signal that evokes a caregiving response. Over time, the infant's smile takes on more complex meanings within a social context. Yet, it begins as an unlearned behavior that has important adaptive value (Fogel, Hsu, Shapiro, Nelson-Goens, & Secrist, 2006).

Methods of Ethological Research. Ethology uses observation, experimentation, and the comparative method to investigate the proximal causes of behavioral acts, the relative contribution of inheritance and learning to these acts, and the adaptive significance and evolutionary history of various patterns of behavior within and across species. Ethologists emphasize the importance of studying behavior in natural settings. Laboratory experiments may be used to discover answers to questions derived from these observations (Eibl-Eibesfeldt, 2007).

Two early contributors to the field of ethology, Konrad Lorenz (1935/1981) and Niko Tinbergen (1951), focused on **innate behaviors** and how they are expressed under natural conditions. Innate behaviors are present in some standard or shared form in all members of a species. They are expressed without previous learning and remain relatively unchanged by experience. Innate behaviors include **reflexes**, which are simple responses to simple stimuli. A baby's grasp of a finger or other object that is placed in its palm is a reflex. Many infant reflexes disappear by the end of the first year. However, some reflexes including sucking, creeping, stepping, and grasping are replaced by very similar behaviors that come under voluntary control.

Some innate behaviors, called *fixed* or *modal action patterns,* are more complex than reflexes. Birds build nests, squirrels bury nuts, and goslings follow their mothers. These behaviors are genetically guided sequences that are prompted by a particular stimulus pattern that releases or signals the behavior. The *releasing stimulus* may be a certain odor, color, movement, sound, or shape. It may require a special relation between stimuli. Whereas fixed action patterns are more common in non-human animals, there are some human examples such as yawning. When you see a person yawn, you tend to yawn yourself. The behavior seems involuntary; you may not even feel tired yet you cannot resist the urge to yawn. Once a person starts to yawn, the behavior must be executed.

John Bowlby (1958, 1988) was influential in bringing the ethological perspective to the study of child development through his observations of infant–caregiver attachment. Bowlby described the **attachment behavior system** as a complex set of reflexes and signaling behaviors that bring about **caregiving** responses from adults. These responses in turn shape an infant's expectations and help to create an inner representation of the parent as a caring, comforting person.

The infant's innate capacities for smiling, cooing, grasping, and crying draw the adult's attention and provoke a sympathetic response. The adult's gentle cuddling, soothing, and smiling establish a sense of security in the child. Attachment, viewed in this light, is an innate behavior system that promotes the safety of offspring in infancy and provides the basis for the trusting social relationships that are necessary for mating and parenting in adulthood.

Bowlby argued that attachment behavior serves a basic survival function: protection.

> Whilst attachment behaviour is at its most obvious in early childhood, it can be observed throughout the life cycle, especially in emergencies. Since it is seen in virtually all human beings (though in varying patterns), it is regarded as an integral part of human nature and one we share (to a varying extent) with members of other species. The biological function attributed to it is that of protection. To remain within easy access of a familiar individual known to be ready and willing to come to our aid in an emergency is clearly a good insurance policy—whatever our age. (Bowlby, 1988, p. 27)

Subsequent research has demonstrated the importance of patterns of attachment in influencing adolescent and adult behaviors.

Ethology and Fitness. Focusing on a different behavioral system, William Charlesworth (1988) studied the importance of social interaction as a mechanism that allows humans to obtain resources from the environment at any point in the life span. He suggested that the resources required to resolve the crises of the psychosocial stages vary with the stage. The infant may require protection, food, or attention; the toddler may require a toy or someone to talk to; the child of middle school age may need tools and materials for education; and the early adult may need a mate. Strategies for obtaining resources change with development. Infants learn to signal their needs by crying or fussing. As they get older, children acquire an increasingly diverse set of strategies to use in their efforts to get the resources they need. Both aggressive and help-giving behaviors are strategies designed to elicit needed resources. Language strategies help people acquire needed resources of many kinds.

Many areas of human behavior which are functionally relevant to the fitness of individuals and groups are potential targets of study in the field of human ethology (Charlesworth, 1992). They include:

Reproductive strategies, such as having few or many sex partners

Infant immaturity requiring prolonged care

Infant–caregiver attachment

Parent–child conflicts

Sibling rivalry

Peer group formation and functions, especially cooperation, competition, dominance, and submission

Pair-bonding and mate selection

Helping behavior and altruism

Learning as adaptive behavior

Individual creation and modification of the environment

Elaboration of rites, rituals, and religions.

Evolutionary Psychology

Whereas ethology focuses on analyzing adaptive behavior patterns across species, the goal of **evolutionary psychology** is to draw upon principles of evolution to understand the human mind. "The mind is a set of information-processing machines that were designed by natural selection to solve adaptive problems faced by our hunter–gatherer ancestors" (Cosmides & Tooby, 1997). This focus takes us to a time when humans lived in small, nomadic groups traveling from place to place to find sources of food and trying to protect themselves from the dangers of predatory animals, weather, illness, and other humans. This way of life existed for over 2 million years, during which various human species (along with their human minds) emerged. From this perspective, the human mind is highly adapted to solve problems faced by these human ancestors, but it may not be well adapted to solve the new problems that have emerged in our recent industrial/post-industrial way of life.

According to evolutionary psychologists, the human brain is a physical system that is designed to generate responses that are effective in dealing with the information being received from specific environmental situations. It is comprised of a large number of complex mini-machines or subsystems that have evolved in response to the specific problems that humans faced in the thousands of years during which modern humans emerged from their hominid ancestors (Buss, 1995, 2012). Evolutionary psychologists view adaptation as resulting in the formation of functionally specific capacities as well as structures that can integrate information from a variety of sources. You might think of each structure as a tool designed to perform a specific task. The brain has an optic nerve that coordinates visual information; an olfactory center that receives and interprets smells; and an auditory system that receives, integrates, and interprets sound waves. The optic nerve is not designed to receive sound waves, and the auditory system is not sensitive to light. In this same sense, evolutionary psychologists seek to discover mental structures that contribute to performing other information-processing tasks such as recognizing faces, detecting threats, or recognizing and producing spoken language.

According to evolutionary psychologists, through the process of natural selection, certain mechanisms developed that are sensitive to specific environmental conditions. When activated by those conditions, these mechanisms function to produce an adaptive response or set of responses. The question of interest is "What are the psychological mechanisms that have emerged in this way?" In general, mechanisms of interest are linked to important adaptive functions (Buss, 1995, 2012).

Adaptive Problems. Evolutionary psychology focuses on how the mind may have become structured to resolve adaptive problems. **Adaptive problems** have two essential qualities: (a) they are likely to have occurred repeatedly in human evolutionary history; and (b) the solutions to these problems influenced reproductive success (Cosmides & Tooby, 1997). Adaptive problems include: how to tell if someone is a friend or a threat, how to select a mate, how to select a good dwelling, or how to collaborate in order to hunt large game.

Buss (1995, 2012) provided a concrete example of how evolutionary psychology might lead to the formulation of logically deduced hypotheses and testable predictions. He begins with Trivers's (1972) theory of parental investment and sexual selection. According to Trivers's theory, which is derived from Darwin's theory of sexual selection, the sex that has the greater investment in the offspring will be more selective in choosing a mate; the sex that has less investment will be more competitive with others of the same sex for sexual access. Beginning with this mid-level theory, the following hypothesis emerges: Where males contribute resources to the offspring, females select mates, in part, on the ability and willingness of males to contribute resources.

From this hypothesis, three specific testable predictions emerge:

1. Women have evolved preferences for men who are high in status.
2. Women have evolved preferences for men who show cues indicating a willingness to invest in them and their offspring.
3. Women will divorce men who fail to contribute expected resources, or who divert their resources to other women and their children.

These three predictions can all be evaluated through traditional social science methods. If they prove correct, the theoretical hypothesis from which they were derived is supported. If the evidence does not support these predictions, the underlying theoretical assumption is likely to be rejected. Thus, even though evolutionary psychologists seek explanations for the origins of mental mechanisms in the long-distant past, they can use evidence from contemporary behavior to assess whether their explanations have merit.

From an evolutionary perspective, any behavior can be assessed by asking a few basic questions (Neese, 2001):

1. What behavior is necessary to achieve a goal?
2. How much energy is needed to achieve the goal?
3. When should the person stop the activity?
4. What should the person do next?

These questions suggest that the person has to recognize the nature of a problem and bring to bear the best "tool" needed to solve the problem. There are start-up costs to beginning any new behavior, so the most adaptive responses will contribute to long-term fitness. Once a behavior has been started, the person has to assess how hard and long to persist at the task. There is risk in putting too much energy into one problem and ignoring other important tasks. There is also risk in giving up too soon before an important goal has been reached. Since environmental conditions fluctuate, the ability to make this assessment has to be flexible. Finally, once a goal has been achieved, the person has to redirect energy to a new task.

This analysis suggests that the person has a set of goals and has to direct energy to one or more of them in some priority. Fitness is enhanced when the person is able to meet goals for health and safety, reproductive success, social allegiances, and care and nurture of the offspring as conditions require. Thus, while respecting the complexity of the human mind, evolutionary theory offers a context for focusing on a select group of problems and their adaptive solutions.

A RESEARCH EXAMPLE: ATTACHMENT

With a focus on fitness, evolutionary theory highlights three phases of the life history: healthy growth and development leading up to the reproductive period, success in mating and the conception of offspring, and the ability to parent offspring so they can reach reproductive age and bear offspring of their own (Charlesworth, 1992). Primates, including humans, are most vulnerable during infancy and childhood; children require continuous care and protection if they are to survive to reproductive age.

John Bowlby proposed the concept of an attachment behavior system as an organized pattern of infant signals and adult responses that form the basis of a relationship during the very earliest stage of development and a corresponding behavioral system referred to as the **parenting or caregiving** system that is made up of the responses of the caregiver to the infant's signals (Bowlby, 1988; Ainsworth, 1985). From an ethological perspective, the coordinated attachment and caregiving systems form a pattern of mutual regulation through which the infant alerts the caregiver to distress, and the caregiver provides protection, comfort, and care. Given the prolonged dependent state of human infants, this attachment/caregiving system is the foundation of survival in infancy and early childhood. The nature of this relationship also shapes the child's ability to form close relationships in later life stages, which has implications for the two subsequent tasks: finding a mate and rearing one's young.

The Development of Attachment

Attachment theorists have described a sequence of stages in the formation of the attachment relationship (Ainsworth, 1973, 1985; Bowlby, 1969/1982, 1988; Marvin & Britner, 2008) (see Table 2.1). During the first 3 months of life, infants engage in a variety of behaviors, including

Table 2.1 Five stages in the development of attachment

Stage	Age	Characteristics
1	Birth to 3 months	Infant uses sucking, rooting, grasping, smiling, gazing, cuddling, crying, and visual tracking to maintain closeness with caregivers.
2	3 to 6 months	Infant is more responsive to familiar figures than to strangers.
3	6 to 9 months	Infant seeks physical proximity and contact with objects of attachment.
4	9 to 12 months	Infant forms internal mental representation of object of attachment, including expectations about the caregiver's typical responses to signals of distress.
5	12 months and older	Child uses a variety of behaviors to influence the behavior of the objects of attachment in ways that will satisfy needs for safety and closeness.

Source: From Newwman, B.M. & Newman, P.R. (2015). *Development through life: A psychosocial approach, 12th ed.* Stamford, CT: Cengage Learning, p. 154. © 2015 South-Western, a part of Cengage Learning, Inc. Reproduced by permission. www.cengage.com/permissions

sucking, rooting, grasping, smiling, gazing, cuddling, crying, and visual tracking or following, which serve to maintain closeness with a caregiver or bring the caregiver to the infant. Through these contacts, babies learn about the unique features of their caregivers. Caregivers, for their part, use a variety of strategies including eye contact, touching and holding, and vocalizing as means of establishing and maintaining social engagement with their infants (Akhtar & Gernsbacher, 2008). Caregivers and infants experience repeated interactions which result in the formation of predictable patterns. Rhythmic patterns of interaction lay the foundation for expectations about communication.

From about 3 to 6 months, an infant's attachment is expressed through preferential responsiveness to a few familiar figures. Infants smile more at the familiar person than at a stranger. They show more excitement at that person's arrival and appear to be upset when that person leaves. During this phase, babies initiate more interactions toward the familiar caregiver. They are able to control the interaction by linking a chain of behaviors into a more complex sequence. In Stage 1, for example, the baby may look intently at the primary caregiver. In Stage 2, the baby looks intently, reaches toward the caregiver's face, and pulls the caregiver's hair.

From about 6 to 9 months, babies want to be physically close to the object(s) of attachment. The ability to crawl and to coordinate reaching and grasping contribute to greater control over the outcomes of their actions. In this phase, babies experiment with finding an optimal distance from the caregiver. They may crawl away, look back, and then, depending on the caregiver's perceived availability, crawl back to the caregiver or smile and continue exploring. If the caregiver is preoccupied or out of sight, the baby may cry to bring the caregiver closer or to reestablish contact.

From about 9 to 12 months, babies form mental representations of their caregivers. This mental picture provides the first robust *working model* of an attachment relationship. Specific characteristics of a caregiver and expectations about how the caregiver will respond to the infant's actions are organized into a complex attachment scheme that includes expectations about how the caregiver will respond when the child is frightened, hurt, or distressed.

Formation of Attachments with Mother, Father, and Others

Most infants have more than one caring person with whom they form an attachment. Typically, the first object of attachment is the mother, but fathers, siblings, grandparents, and childcare professionals may also become objects of attachment. Several factors have been identified as important for predicting which people will form the infant's hierarchy or radius of significant attachment figures (Cassidy, 2008; Howes & Spieker, 2008):

1. The amount of time the infant spends in the care of the person.
2. The quality and responsiveness of the care provided by the person.
3. The person's emotional investment in the infant.
4. The presence of the person in the infant's life across time.

Patterns of Attachment

Consistent with an evolutionary perspective, the fact that the capacity to form an attachment is part of human nature does not mean that the expression of the attachment response will be the same in all humans. According to attachment theory, if an adult is present to interact with the infant, an attachment will be formed. However, research has discovered that individual differences emerge in the quality of attachment, depending on the accumulation of information the infant gathers over many instances when the infant is seeking reassurance, comfort, or protection from threat (Weinfield, Sroufe, Egeland, & Carlson, 2008). The adults' acceptance of the infants and their ability to respond to the infants' varying communications contribute to the formation of secure attachments. The caregivers' patterns of expressing affection and rejection influence how well babies can meet their needs for reassurance and comfort.

The Strange Situation. Differences in the quality of attachment have been highlighted by observations of babies and their caregivers in a standard laboratory procedure called the Strange Situation (Ainsworth, Blehar, Waters, & Wall, 1978; Bretherton, 1990). During an approximately 20-minute period, the child is exposed to a sequence of events that are likely to stimulate the attachment system. The situation introduces several potentially threatening situations including the presence of a stranger, the departure of the mother, being left alone with a stranger, and being left completely alone, all in the context of an unfamiliar laboratory setting. During this situation, researchers have the opportunity to make systematic observations of the child's behaviors, the caregiver's behaviors, and characteristics of their interactions, as well as to compare these behaviors across varying segments of the situation.

Four Patterns of Quality of Attachment. Using the Strange Situation methodology, four patterns of attachment behavior have been distinguished: (a) secure attachment, (b) anxious-avoidant, (c) anxious-resistant, and (d) disorganized attachment.

Infants who have a *secure attachment* actively explore their environment and interact with strangers while their mothers are present. In reunion after a brief separation, the babies actively greet their mothers or seek interaction. If the babies were distressed during separation, the mothers' return reduces their distress and the babies return to exploration of the environment.

Infants who show an *anxious-avoidant attachment* avoid contact with their mothers upon reunion after a brief separation or ignore their efforts to interact. They show less distress at being alone than other babies.

Infants who show an *anxious-resistant attachment* are very cautious in the presence of the stranger. Their exploratory behavior is noticeably disrupted by the caregivers' departure. When the caregiver returns, the infants appear to want to be close to the caregiver, but they are also angry, so they are very hard to soothe or comfort.

In the *disorganized attachment*, babies' responses are particularly notable in the reunion sequence. In the other three attachment patterns, infants appear to use a coherent strategy for managing the stress of the situation. The disorganized babies have no consistent strategy. They behave in contradictory, unpredictable ways that seem to convey feelings of extreme fear or utter confusion (Belsky, Campbell, Cohn, & Moore, 1996).

The attachment behavioral system and the caregiving system have also been studied in the home environment. When observed at home, babies who have a secure attachment are observed to cry less than other babies (Tracy & Ainsworth, 1981; Ainsworth, 1985). They greet their mothers more positively upon reunion after everyday separations, and appear to respond more cooperatively to their mothers' requests. Attachment theorists hypothesize that securely attached babies have a working model of attachment in which they expect their caregiver to be accessible and responsive.

Mothers of babies who are characterized as anxious-avoidant seem to reject their babies. It is almost as if they were angry at their babies. They spend less time holding and cuddling their babies than other mothers, and more of their interactions appear to be unpleasant or even hurtful. At home these babies cry a lot, they are not readily soothed by contact with the caregiver, and yet they appear to be quite distressed by separations.

Infants who are characterized as anxious-resistant have mothers who are inconsistent in their responsiveness. Sometimes these mothers ignore clear signals of distress. At other times they interfere with their infants in order to make contact. Although these mothers appear to be able to enjoy close physical contact with their babies, they do not necessarily do so in ways appropriate to the baby's needs. The result appears to be the formation of an internal representation of attachment that is highly unpredictable. These babies try to maintain proximity and to avoid unfamiliar situations that increase uncertainty about accessibility to their caregivers.

Research suggests links between the disorganized attachment and serious mental health problems among mothers, including abusive tendencies, depression, and other mental illnesses. Observations of mothers and infants who are described as having a disorganized attachment highlight two different patterns. Some mothers are negative, intrusive, and frighten their babies in bursts of intense hostility. Other mothers are passive, helpless, and rarely show positive or comforting behaviors. These mothers appear to be afraid of their babies, perhaps not trusting their own impulses to respond appropriately (Lyons-Ruth, Lyubchik, Wolfe, & Bronfman, 2002).

In U.S. samples, about two-thirds of the children tested have been characterized as securely attached. Of the remainder, more children fall into the anxious-avoidant category than into the anxious-resistant category (Ainsworth et al., 1978). Only a small percentage of infants show the disorganized pattern which is associated with very serious mental health problems in later childhood and beyond (Fonagy, 2003; George & Solomon, 2008).

The Relevance of Attachment to Later Development

The nature of one's attachment pattern has been found to influence expectations about the self, others, and the nature of relationships. The formation of a secure attachment relationship is expected to influence the child's ability to explore and engage the environment with confidence, knowing that the protective "other" is near at hand. Children who experience a secure attachment are less likely to be exposed to uncontrollable stress. They experience rhythmic, meaningful, and predictable interactions that contribute to their social competences. As a result, they are hopeful about their ability to form positive relationships with others (Weinfield et al., 2008).

The significance of attachment styles for the formation of emotional bonds has been the primary target of research. However, a growing body of research points to the role of attachment in the child's ability to manage stress. The synchronous, rhythmic relationship with the caregiver helps to reduce the infant's experiences of anxiety, and provides a model for recovery from distress. At the hormonal and neurological levels, the conditions that support a secure attachment also protect the child from the deregulating impact of environmental threats (Mikulincer & Shaver, 2012).

Long-term benefits of a secure attachment have been documented. Secure attachments in infancy have been associated with positive adaptive capacities when the child is 3 to 5 years old. Securely attached infants become preschoolers who show greater resilience, self-control, and curiosity (Schneider, Atkinson, & Tardif, 2001). In contrast, infants who have a disorganized attachment are very hostile, aggressive preschoolers (Hazan, Campa, & Gur-Yaish, 2006). Results of numerous studies indicate that, as they get older, children who have a disorganized attachment, especially boys, are at risk for externalizing problems (Fearon, Bakermans-Kranenburg, van IJzendoorn, Lapsley, & Roisman, 2010).

Despite the evidence that the secure attachment style is optimal, some researchers suggest that the diversity of attachment styles may have adaptive value. For example, those with insecure attachments are more vigilant, scanning the environment for evidence of threat. They are less likely to assume that they are safe, or to assume that someone is available to protect them and meet their needs. In the context of a dangerous environment, those with an insecure attachment may be quicker to detect a threat and take action to escape or avoid it (Ein-Dor, Mikulincer, Doron, & Shaver, 2010).

From a life-span perspective, the quality of the attachment formed in infancy influences the formation of later relationships (Ainsworth, 1989). Children who have formed secure attachments are likely to find more enjoyment in close peer friendships during their preschool years. In an analysis of the results of over 60 studies of the relationship of parent–child attachment and peer relations, the quality of attachment with mother was consistently predictive of the quality of close peer friendships, well into middle school and early adolescence (Schneider et al., 2001). Children who have secure attachments are more likely to attribute positive intentions to peers, whereas children with anxious attachments are more likely to view peers with wariness.

The attachment construct has been useful in helping to explain the nature of adult love relationships. Romantic relationships can be characterized along many of the same dimensions as infant attachments, including the desire to maintain physical contact with the loved one, increased disclosure and responsiveness to the loved one, the effectiveness of the loved one in providing comfort and reassurance that reduce distress, and an element of exclusiveness or preferential response to the loved one (Hazan & Shaver, 1987). Fears about loss and abandonment, born from anxious-avoidant attachments, are likely to result in anxiety about one's contemporary relationships. People who are consistently anxious about their relationships tend to be more coercive and mistrustful, thus pushing their partners away (Feeney, 2008; Tracy, Shaver, Albino, & Cooper, 2003).

I had a real problem trusting anyone at the start of any relationship. A couple of things happened to me when I was young, which I had some emotional difficulties getting over. At the start of our relationship, if P. had been separated from me, I would have been constantly thinking: 'What was he doing?'; 'Was he with another girl?'; 'Was he cheating on me?'; all that would have been running through my head. (Feeney, 2008, p. 465)

The parenting relationship can also be understood as an elaboration of one's childhood attachment. Adults who have experienced a secure attachment in their own infancy have been found to be more likely to be able to comfort and respond to their children. Adults whose childhood attachments were unpredictable or even hostile are more likely to have difficulty coping successfully with young infants' needs (George & Solomon, 2008). For example, in one study, parents were observed while their infants were having inoculations. Those parents who had an avoidant attachment style were less responsive to their infants' distress in this context (Edelstein et al., 2004). Parents draw on the model of attachment they formed as infants and young children which guides their perceptions of infant cues and their own responses.

It would be a mistake to assume that the quality of adult love relationships or parental behavior is determined solely by the quality of childhood attachments. Many experiences intervene to modify the attachment representation and to expand one's capacity to love another person after infancy. However, a growing body of research links the quality of early attachments with a person's orientation to and capacity for social relationships within the context of friendships, intimate relationships, and parent–child relations.

AN APPLICATION: THE FREE-RIDER PROBLEM

The evolution of human groups has required the coordination and cooperation of group members to achieve common goals, such as hunting for large game, building shelters, and clearing land for planting. These collective efforts continue to be essential to contemporary groups, from the training of military units for defense to the sharing of knowledge in websites like Wikipedia. Yet, we all know that there are some individuals who hold back from these shared efforts. In fact, a built-in conflict for group survival is the natural tension between individual self-interest and the collective good. If you have ever been assigned a group project for a class, you have probably experienced this conflict. While most members of the group take the assignment seriously and try to do their part, there is often one person in the group who does not contribute, or who does his or her own thing despite what the group has agreed upon. If everyone in the group gets the same grade, those who do not contribute benefit from the efforts of everyone else. This is the free-rider, the person who does not contribute his or her fair share to the production of a resource, but shares equally in the benefits of the resource (Hardin, 2013).

According to evolutionary psychology, the human mind is sensitive to cues that help to identify the free-rider. This is necessary in order for the group to survive. Consider a hypothetical situation where there are two kinds of people, those who cooperate to contribute resources for the betterment of the group, and those who benefit from the efforts of others, but hold on to their resources. Over time and across generations, this group of free-riders enjoys greater reproductive success because they have more resources, thereby populating the group with more of their kind. Eventually, the proportion of the free-riders dominates the group, undermining the group's capacity to act collectively for common goals (Delton, Cosmides, Guemo, Robertson, & Tooby, 2012).

What Strategies Allow the Cooperative Individuals to Flourish in the Face of Free-Riders?

First, there must be a mental structure that allows people to recognize and categorize individuals as free-riders. Second, when free-riders have been identified, the cooperators must exclude the free-riders from sharing in the collective benefits, punish the free-riders, or create some incentives that will encourage their cooperation. In other words, in order for groups to survive over time, they have to create conditions so that cooperators will benefit from repeated experiences of collaboration, resulting in a reproductive advantage in comparison to the free-riders. In the life of a group, cooperators must be protected from the ongoing exploitation of free-riders. At the same time, there must be a way to differentiate free-riders from people who are basically cooperators but who, for one reason or another such as illness or competing family demands, are unable to contribute in a particular effort or for a limited time. These people should not be unduly excluded or punished.

This evolutionary concern about distinguishing free-riders from those who under-contribute for other reasons has led to a long history of theory and research in economics, philosophy, social psychology, and evolutionary psychology (Hardin, 2013). The basic free-rider identification rule is as follows:

> If a member of a collective action intentionally fails to contribute even in the presence of other contributors, then categorize the member as a free rider. (Delton et al., 2012, p. 1255)

This rule requires the ability to make two important judgments about a person based on his or her behavior in the context of a collective effort: the person is benefiting from the resource by withholding from the group, or the person is benefiting by avoiding the costs of producing the resource. In a variety of experimental situations, participants are clearly able to distinguish free-riders from those who under-contribute for a variety of other reasons (e.g. lack of competence, poor health, or misfortune). In laboratory experiments, when participants perceive that a person is intentionally under-contributing to a collective effort, those free-riders are viewed as less trustworthy, deserving of more punishment, and being less desirable as potential work partners (Delton et al., 2012). This ability to detect free-riders is not specifically taught, but appears to be part of a person's social intelligence in the context of group efforts. Research has found that children as young as age 3 will share more with other children who participate equally in a group effort than they will with a child who does not collaborate (Melis, Altrichteer, & Tomasello, 2013).

Implications of the Free-Rider Problem for Education

What are some implications of the free-rider problem for educational settings? Educators are faced with the challenge of constructing meaningful group projects that foster cooperation and reduce the likelihood that individuals will be free-riders. Educators at every level, from preschool through graduate school, are seeking ways to introduce collaborative learning into their instruction. Collaborative projects have a number of benefits including teaching people how to work well in groups, expanding the range of information that can be gathered to address a problem, and introducing new and more diverse ideas into problem-solving efforts. Participants can learn from one another, stimulate one another to focus on the challenges of the topic, resolve conflicts, and motivate one another to achieve new levels of performance (Smith, 2006; Becker & Dwyer, 1998). Educational group work is expected to provide transferable skills that are becoming increasingly essential in the corporate environment where individuals are faced with complex problems that require collaboration across departments and areas of expertise (Caruso & Wooley, 2008).

Although group projects are thought to be educationally valuable, they are often less popular with students than they are with instructors. Group work may involve more time, more dependence on others, and the need to resolve a number of interpersonal problems in comparison to individual assignments. Whereas instructors may view these challenges as part of the benefit of group projects, students may view these challenges as an undesired use of their time and effort. This leads to the problem of the free-riders; students who decide that they do not really need to contribute to the group project but will still benefit from whatever grade the group project receives. Students typically have no way to make one another accountable and are reluctant to complain to the instructor about another student's lack of contribution.

The presence of free-riders in work groups has a number of negative consequences. Presumably, the collective effort will not be as great when some members of the group do not contribute. The realization that some people are not doing their fair share undermines the motivation of others, thereby lowering the overall efforts of the group. If free-riding has no negative consequences, this behavior is likely to be repeated in other group contexts. For the students who did contribute to the project, a sense of an unfair reward structure may prejudice them against engaging in future group efforts (Eberly Center for Teaching Excellence, 2014; Piezon & Donaldson, 2005).

A number of interventions and recommendations have been devised to support both in-class and distance learning group projects. These approaches help to minimize the likelihood of free-riding, and support positive group experiences (Kao, 2013). Features of these approaches include:

Designing group projects that really require contributions from each of the members.

Creating groups that are not too large.

Clearly defining the roles and responsibilities of each member and linking those to the group outcome.

Providing opportunities for group members to share their knowledge and experiences with one another.

Creating a timetable for project milestones so that participants and the instructor can monitor progress toward the end product. Part of the overall grade can be assigned based on meeting this timetable.

Using a computer-based format, like Wikipages, to monitor the time each participant gives to the project and their contributions.

Creating a transparent grading system that is a product of individual contributions, peer evaluation, and the quality of the group project.

HOW DOES EVOLUTIONARY THEORY ANSWER THE BASIC QUESTIONS THAT A THEORY OF HUMAN DEVELOPMENT IS EXPECTED TO ADDRESS?

1. *What is the direction of change over the life span? How well does the theory account for patterns of change and continuity?*

   The direction of development from infancy through adulthood is guided by genetic information that has evolved over thousands of years. All humans share a common direction of biological development including the maturation of the nervous system, motor capacities, and the reproductive system. Infants are born with certain instincts or reflexes that can be considered a product of natural selection. Over the course of infancy and childhood, these reflexes either drop away or come under voluntary control. The critical points in the life span include survival of infancy and childhood to achieve reproductive age, finding a mate, reproducing, and rearing one's young to their reproductive age.

   The process of natural selection focuses on species change over long periods of time. Change occurs as a gradual process of adaptation to changing environmental conditions over generations. Adaptation is a process by which living things develop structures and problem-solving mechanisms that enable them to thrive in a specific environment. However, the human genome and the basic physical structures of the human brain and body are a product of a very slow process of change, such that the physical nature of human growth and development that we observe today is quite similar to that of our historical ancestors of ten thousand years ago. From the perspective of the cosmic calendar, homo sapiens is a relatively young species that has not had much time to undergo species change.

2. *What are the mechanisms that account for growth? What are some testable hypotheses or predictions that emerge from this analysis?*
    The human **genome** includes a plan for the nature and direction of growth. This genetic plan is a product of thousands of years of evolution that links human beings to other mammals, especially the primates. The human genome, according to the theory of evolution, is a product of the mechanism of natural selection. The human beings that exist today, including their mind/brain, have evolved over time in the face of a repeated set of problems to solve, including the need to recognize edible from poisonous foods; protection from predators; the ability to attract a mate; preserving and safeguarding one's social connections; rearing and protecting one's young; and creating durable shelter.

    Testable hypotheses that emerge from this theory suggest that the human mind will approach specific adaptive problems with an eye toward how the solution contributes to their reproductive success or the success of the larger group of which they are a member. As an example, evolutionary psychology suggests that men and women have different reproductive goals. As a result, their preferences for mate selection will differ in order to support their reproductive goals.

    A multidisciplinary science of evolution contributes to the ongoing understanding of human behavior. Archeological evidence, biological studies, and experimental studies are providing evidence about the conditions under which humans evolved, the similarities and differences among humans in various geographic regions, and the ways environmental conditions may alter the human genome. Each of these fields proceeds through the use of testable hypotheses.

3. *How relevant are early experiences for later development? What evidence does the theory offer to support its view?*
    The concept of fitness includes the importance of the ability to survive the vulnerable period of infancy and childhood in order to reach reproductive age. For humans, the social and cognitive capacities that are established early in life have implications for subsequent ability to find a mate and rear one's children to reproductive age. The importance of the human brain for problem solving points to the significance of early childhood experiences, especially health, social interactions, and cognitive stimulation, for later survival and reproductive success. The theory has led to the investigation of attachment as a primary behavioral system through which parents and children establish a close emotional bond which facilitates the growth of children through the vulnerable periods of infancy and childhood. The study of attachment provides an evolutionary basis for conceptualizing how experiences in childhood may be translated into parenting practices in adulthood that support the safety and protection of the next generation of offspring. An enormous body of research evidence points to the contribution of the quality of attachment for later adaptive success, and cross-generational transmission of fitness.

4. *How do the environmental and social contexts affect individual development? What aspects of the environment does the theory suggest are especially important in shaping the direction of development?*

    The basic mechanism of evolutionary change is natural selection, which predicts that behavior is adapted to the environment in which it occurs. Over long periods of time, those members of a species that have a selective advantage in a particular environment are more likely to survive, mate, and produce offspring. The field of ethology is focused on the study of the functional significance of behaviors that appear to be innate and specific to a particular species which are expressed under particular environmental conditions. Both reflexes and fixed action patterns require certain environmental cues in order to be expressed. At the level of the individual, survival continues to reflect the ability to resolve adaptive problems, including: recognition of threat, the ability to acquire needed resources, the ability to find a suitable dwelling, the ability to collaborate in order to protect one's territory, or the ability to attract a mate. Solutions to these adaptive problems depend on the specific resources and demands of the specific environment in which one lives.

    Infants and families have co-evolved. Because of their relatively long period of dependence, infants require a context of protection and nurture for their survival. Families have evolved to serve this function, creating environments that provide food, shelter, social contact, and protection over a number of years. The nurturing environment of the family is intimately linked to the child's adaptive capacities for cognitive functioning, social competence, language and communication skills, self-regulation, emotional expressiveness, and physical and mental health. When the family environment is harsh, neglectful, or abusive, the child's physical and psychological development is compromised (Biglan, Flay, Embry, & Sandler, 2012).

    Families are embedded in cultures which shape developmental pathways. Cultures operate on human biodiversity by creating restrictions on mating practices and family formation over generations. Individuals from groups that are geographically close may still differ noticeably in their genetic features as a result of cultural forces that impact mate selection (Xing et al., 2009). For example, cultural rules regarding kinship may limit mating among certain levels of relation (e.g. first cousins can't marry). Culture may also influence mate selection by identifying appropriate or inappropriate relationships across tribal, caste, social class, or racial boundaries. These restrictions could be guided by informal social norms (e.g. families that urge their children to marry within their religious faith), or laws and sanctions that address violations of these restrictions.

5. *According to the theory, what factors place individuals at risk at specific periods of the life span?*

    Evolutionary theory is quite specific about the importance of critical issues that threaten survival across the life span. Over the life span, fitness is enhanced when the person is able to meet goals for health and safety, reproductive success, social allegiances, and the care and nurture of his or her offspring. In infancy, protection from harm is especially important, thus generating the extensive focus on attachment and the complementary parenting behavioral system. At each stage of the life span, social interaction is required to obtain the necessary resources from the environment. Factors that interfere with the achievement of social competence, including physical characteristics that might lead to social rejection, parental abuse or neglect, dominance by others, or social alienation, are all relevant risk factors. Evolutionary psychology focuses on the ability of the human mind to solve adaptive problems. Factors that interfere with the person's adaptive problem-solving capacity, including genetic anomalies, malnutrition, or lack of social or cognitive stimulation, could all place individuals at risk for survival.

The concept of inclusive fitness extends the notion of risk and protective factors to include the person's family and larger social group. Groups that lack access to resources or are exposed to chronic threat over many generations are vulnerable to extinction. Human history is replete with examples of cultural groups that flourish for periods of time and then are destroyed through a variety of risks including inbreeding, invasion by technically advanced groups, deaths due to infectious diseases, wars with competing tribes or nations, and targeted genocide.

6.   *What are some practical implications of this theory?*

Evolutionary theory is useful as a conceptual framework that ties together biology, ecology, archeology, anthropology, and medical and behavioral sciences. Artificial selection, or selective breeding, has been used for generations; but with the theory of evolution we have a greater understanding of how and why this process works, as well as new approaches to create and modify species. We also understand how certain strains of insects and bacteria become resistant to the drugs and chemicals that are used to eradicate them, leading to new approaches to management (Bull & Wichman, 2001).

Features of human sensory and motor capacities make certain stimuli and physical arrangements easier or more difficult to manage. For example, the nature of visual displays and lighting in the workplace can be arranged to complement the human visual system. Evolutionary theory can help to guide the design and creation of work environments to optimize functioning and reduce stress (Fostervold, Watten, & Volden, 2014).

Evolutionary psychology assumes that modern humans carry with them a mind/brain that has evolved in response to a specific set of survival challenges. The mental mechanisms that operate to assess dangers, respond to threat, evaluate a person's trustworthiness, or evoke feelings of attraction are all elements of this evolved adaptive capacity. Based on this theory, a wide range of human behaviors can be examined for their contributions to fitness and reproductive success. Advances in understanding the history and evolution of the human species can help to clarify the nature of the genetic similarities across groups and the interrelatedness of all humans, thereby guiding policy toward more inclusive approaches to the resolution of inter-group conflicts. A wide range of behaviors have been identified as having evolutionary origins including patterns of eating, physical appearance, cooperative and competitive behaviors, sexual behaviors, parenting behaviors, sibling rivalry, striving for status, the expression and meaning of emotions, the nature of morality and collective behavior, and in-group and out-group orientations.

CRITIQUE OF EVOLUTIONARY THEORY

From an evolutionary point of view, the future of a species depends on the capacity of its individual members to survive during infancy and childhood, mate, reproduce, and rear their young to reproductive age. The factors that contribute to the vigor and continuity of a species are the health of individual members when they attain reproductive capacity, an environment that is conducive to the formation of sexually mature dyads, and the capacity of sexually mature partners to rear their offspring. Among humans, the attachment-parenting systems are essential for an infant's survival and subsequent capacity to form enduring social bonds. During adolescence, when sexual activity emerges and attitudes about marriage and parenting are being formulated, the quality of life for young people of every cultural group is critical to the future of human beings. During adulthood, the ability to attract a mate, be fertile, and protect and nurture one's offspring are the signposts of fitness.

The focus of evolutionary psychology is on analyzing mental mechanisms that are primed to respond to specific cues or input. According to this theory, humans are not consciously striving for fitness or reproductive success. Their behavior is not guided by a general goal of wanting to ensure the continuation of their genetic material in future generations. Rather, their behavior is analyzed in terms of the natural or pre-adapted response of a mental mechanism to a specific cue: for example, the smell of meat stimulates salivation; the site of a beautiful face stimulates a positive attraction; the detection of cheating stimulates wariness. The environmental cues are proximal (immediate to the point of response), but the origins of the responses are distal (based on adaptive processes established in the ancient past).

Strengths

The evolutionary perspective draws attention to the interconnection between an individual's life history and the long-range history of the species. The theory provides one basic mechanism to account for change across species and time: principles of natural selection operate slowly over generations. However the reproductive success of individuals over the course of their own life span will determine whether their genetic material continues to be represented in the larger population. The application of evolutionary theory to human motivation, mental processes, and behavior integrates information and observations from many fields, including developmental biology, paleontology (including paleobiology and paleozoology), paleoanthropology, population genetics, social psychology, developmental psychology, cognitive psychology, medicine, and education.

Evolutionary theory and its extensions into ethology and evolutionary psychology have stimulated investigation of the universal nature of human thought and behavior as well as the adaptive nature of individual differences. Beginning with the assumption that contemporary human beings share a common human ancestry, the theory inspires the investigation of a wide variety of topics including shared cognitive problem-solving strategies, social competences, motives for mate selection and fidelity, reproductive strategies, and the role of emotions in guiding behavior. The theory has become a fertile heuristic in focusing inquiry on how humans assess critical features of their social environments and how they make use of that information to guide action.

Evolutionary theory offers explanations for widely shared human behaviors, such as the tendency of men to show more evidence of intrasexual competition than women, or the tendency of parents to prefer a norm of equal distribution of resources across their offspring while children tend to compete with one another for resources. Evolutionary psychologists and ethologists do not assume that concerns about fitness are conscious. However, they do assume that motivation toward fitness ultimately shapes behavior in systematic directions as a result of a conscious assessment of one's situation. Thus, the theory helps to explain why behaviors that may appear to be risky, dangerous, or self-destructive may be preferred under conditions of low resources or low status if those behaviors offer some opportunity for increasing one's reproductive opportunities or the reproductive opportunities of one's offspring (Daly & Wilson, 2001).

The evolutionary perspective also draws attention to the importance of variability for a species to survive. Individual differences contribute to the vigor of a species. Human beings are genetically designed to permit wide variations in size, body shape, coloration, strength, talent, intelligence, and personality. Although homo sapiens are a relatively new species, this variability should contribute to the capacity of some members of the species to adapt successfully to changing environmental conditions, thereby protecting the species as a whole from extinction.

Weaknesses

Evolutionary theory assumes that the human species that exists today is a product of the process of natural selection that took place over millions of years. Without denying the truth of that assumption, one is still left to puzzle about the adaptive requirements of life in that long-ago time. Evolutionary psychology suggests that mental mechanisms exist today because they solved problems our ancestors faced in the past. In identifying evolutionary hypotheses to explain contemporary behaviors, such as mate selection, risk taking, jealousy, cooperative behavior, free-riding, or cheating, evolutionary psychologists consider a likely human and environmental landscape that faced ancestors in a hunter-gatherer society.

The reconstruction of the nature of prehistoric life rests on evidence from paleontology and paleoanthropology. There are no written records of the conditions of life over the millions of years through which homo habilis, homo erectus, and homo sapiens evolved. Thus, the conceptualization of the specific conditions often referred to as the environmental stimuli to which the human mind had to adapt is the result of speculations drawn from fossil remains, the presence of tools and artifacts in the region where fossil skeletal remains were found, and the reconstruction of the landscape, climate, and plant and animal life likely to have lived at the same time. Assumptions about the kinds of problems men and women had to solve are based on an unverifiable construction of prehistoric life. This study of the challenges faced by human groups in prehistoric times is an ongoing investigation that is often modified as new information surfaces from the fossil discoveries. Although we do have skulls that indicate changes in brain size, we do not have any remaining evidence to compare the actual neural structures of prehistoric and modern brains.

Evolutionary theory views the human mind as comprised of a large number of small specialized mechanisms. These mechanisms are primed to recognize a particular type of input, evaluating it for the relevant information, and passing it on or integrating it with other information to produce actions. Most of this takes place outside of conscious awareness and yet is essential for adaptive functioning. This view of the mind, coupled with the assumption about adaptation to an ancient past, fails to incorporate the flexibility and adaptive capacity of human cognition. The modern human brain has evolved with remarkable capacities for symbolic representation, including language, symbolic drawing, and symbolic play, extensive capacities to learn through imitation, guided instruction, trial and error, and repetition, and capacities for creativity and abstract thinking, including analysis and synthesis. As a result, we are a product of what Julian Huxley (1941) referred to as **psychosocial evolution** as well as natural selection. According to Huxley, the adaptive mechanisms that humans bring to bear in coping with modern day life are a result of information that is passed down across recent generations from parents, teachers, books, religious leaders, lawmakers, and philosophers, as well as the mental mechanisms that may have been inherited through natural selection. Adaptive responses can include "unconscious" orientations as well as conscious rules and insights about the current situation.

The brain is not limited in its problem solving only to those mechanisms that may have been shaped by an ancient social and environmental landscape. It is also informed by information that is passed down from one generation to the next. The creative capacities of human minds allow individuals to invent modifications to environments (e.g. cities, water purification systems, central heating, electric lighting, air conditioning) and to human adaptive capacities (e.g. birth control, eye glasses, hip replacement) that can impact fitness of the species and be passed along from one generation to the next. Research into the human genome suggests that there may be a time in the near future when biomedical interventions can alter the genome, bypassing the long, slow process of evolution.

Evolutionary theory is primarily explanatory, not predictive. As Darwin noted in the quotation earlier in the chapter, the process of evolution is ongoing. Evolution can be altered by the emergence of mutations that are particularly suited to improve reproductive success in a specific environment, by some drastic environmental conditions that eliminate some variability from the gene pool, or by a prolonged physical separation of species (Gould, 2002). In modern times, the reproductive success of individuals can be altered through access to certain birthing practices, alternative reproductive technologies, genetic engineering, and genocide. The theory does not predict the direction of human evolution. Given the increasing capacity of humans to alter both the genome and the environment, one might ask whether the process of natural selection continues to be as relevant to the human species as it was in the distant past.

One might say that evolutionary theory focuses on all that is important. As a species, we are here as a result of evolution. The kind of humans we are, our structures, functions, and brains, are all a product of evolution. Yet, contemporary evolutionary psychology has focused more attention on the role of men in the evolutionary process, especially early men as hunters, men in the mate-selection process, and social/emotional aspects of men including jealousy, aggression, and cooperation/competition. The roles of women and children have received much less attention, with the exception of topics such as the importance of female attractiveness in the mate-selection process, and the theory of differential investment in offspring. Recent efforts to address this shortcoming include: new studies of the active role of women in the mate selection process; intra-female competition for partners; sexual fluidity among women; women's roles in food preparation and its implications for nutrition, health, and cooperative group behavior; and women's cooperative behaviors in childcare and childrearing (Sokol-Chang & Fisher, 2013). The emphasis on parental behavior has called into question earlier views about the role of men as primarily hunters with little investment in the childrearing process. Recent studies of contemporary hunter-gatherer cultures show that men often spend more time with their children than is the case in modern, post-industrial societies. These observations alter the scenario that is often presented in evolutionary theory about the differential tasks and challenges faced by men and women (Hewlett & Macfarlan, 2010). Table 2.2 summarizes the strengths and weaknesses of evolutionary theory as an approach to the study of human development.

CRITICAL THINKING QUESTIONS AND EXERCISES

1. How do the concepts of adaptation, natural selection, and evolution apply in modern life? How do these concepts help you understand individual development?
2. What are the implications of the human's ability to modify the environment for the theory of evolution? Describe three ways that the ability to modify the environment might impact fitness.
3. How might the issues of fitness and reproductive success be relevant for work in education, counseling, and human services?
4. How might the natural study of behavior in the classroom be used to improve learning environments? Using an evolutionary perspective, list four behaviors you would focus on in

this kind of research, and describe features of the behaviors that could be observed and coded in the classroom.

5. Think back to the case of Mark and Linda. What is the evolutionary theory's explanation for differences in the ways that men and women evaluate attractiveness? What evidence is there to support this view?

6. What next for Mark and Linda? What does evolutionary theory have to offer about what might account for a person's reproductive success in modern society?

Table 2.2 Strengths and weaknesses of evolutionary theory

Strengths	Weaknesses
Places individual development in the context of species development.	Assumptions regarding the challenges faced by human ancestors thousands of years ago are a matter of speculation.
Explains species development and the origins of species using the basic mechanism of natural selection.	The view of the human mind as pre-adapted to conditions of the evolutionary past fails to incorporate the adaptive and flexible nature of human cognition.
Integrates research from many fields.	The theory fails to integrate information that is transmitted from one generation to the next, which contributes to an individual's assessment of the environment and adaptive strategies.
Stimulates research into the adaptive value of individual differences.	Science and technology are co-evolving with the mechanism of natural selection to introduce new processes that may alter the human genome and are not incorporated into the theory.
Stimulates research into a wide range of human thought and behavior including: cognitive problem-solving strategies; social competence; motives for mate selection and fidelity; reproductive strategies; childrearing; the role of emotions in guiding behaviour.	The theory is primarily explanatory, not predictive. It does not offer hypotheses about new directions of human evolution.
Stimulates research into universal features of "human nature."	Evolutionary theory has highlighted the role of men more than the role of women in the adaptive process; that weakness is being addressed in current research.
Stimulates research about how humans assess critical features of their environments and make use of this information to guide action.	The focus on fitness and reproductive success, while important to species survival, does not encompass many other aspects of the social, cognitive, physical, and emotional development relevant for optimal growth over the life span.
Propositions generated by the theory are testable.	

KEY TERMS

adaptation
adaptive problems
attachment behavior system
caregiving
ethology
evolutionary psychology
extinction
fitness
free-rider

genome
human nature
inclusive fitness
innate behaviors
mutations
natural selection
parenting
psychosocial evolution
reflexes

RECOMMENDED RESOURCES

**AboutDarwin.com (www.aboutdarwin.com)
A website devoted to examining the life and times of Charles Darwin including photographs, maps, citations from diaries, and links to other sources.

**Applied Evolutionary Psychology Society. www.aepsociety.org/
An organization devoted to bringing ideas informed by evolutionary theory to a wide range of settings including policy-making, education, business administration, nutrition, medicine, and mental health.

**Buss, D.M. (2012). *Evolutionary psychology: The new science of the mind.* 4th ed. Upper Saddle River, NJ: Pearson.
A comprehensive overview of the field of evolutionary psychology written by a leader in the field.

**Cosmos: A Spacetime Odyssey (2014). *Episode 1: Standing up in the Milky Way. Episode 2: Some of the things molecules do.* National Geographic. Aired March 9, 2014.
The first two episodes in a new television series with an explanation of the cosmic calendar, placing human life in the timeframe since the big bang; an explanation of natural selection and its application to the domestication of dogs and the evolution of polar bears.

**Darwin, C. (1872/2009). *The expression of emotions in man and animals.* Reprinted New York: Penguin Classics.
This edition was published to commemorate the 200th anniversary of Darwin's birth. Illustrated with color photos. The book was widely read in its time and continues to influence the contemporary study of emotion.

**Feminist Evolutionary Psychology Society (FEPS) website: www.maryannefisher.com/feps/
FEPS supports research that: (a) is informed by a female perspective, (b) directly investigates the active role that females have had in human evolution, and/or (c) studies gender in the evolutionary context with scientific theory and methodology.

**Fisher, M.L., Garcia, J.R., & Sokol-Chang, R. (Eds.) (2013). *Evolution's empress: Darwinian perspectives on the nature of women.* New York: Oxford University Press.
Evolution's empress identifies women as active agents within the evolutionary process. The chapters in this volume focus on topics as diverse as female social interactions, mate competition and mating strategies, motherhood, women's health, sex differences in communication and motivation, sex discrimination, and women in literature.

**Fineberg, Harvey. "Are we ready for neo-evolution?" Ted Talks. www.ted.com/talks/harvey_fineberg_are_we_ready_for_neo_evolution
A lecture that provides an overview of the biological basis of human evolution, linking current scientific discoveries with scenarios about the future direction of human evolution based on selective choices about desired features and the features of our offspring.

**Smithsonian National Museum of Natural History (2014). What does it mean to be human? http://humanorigins.si.edu/evidence/human-fossils/species/homo-sapiens
A website devoted to the evolution of the human species with images of artifacts, videos, fossil evidence, and paleoarcheology.

REFERENCES

Ainsworth, M.D.S. (1973). The development of infant-mother attachment. In B.M. Caldwell and H.N. Ricciuti (Eds.), *Review of child development research: Vol. 3*. Chicago: University of Chicago Press.

Ainsworth, M.D.S. (1985). Patterns of infant–mother attachments: Antecedents and effects on development. *Bulletin of the New York Academy of Medicine, 61*, 771–791.

Ainsworth, M.D.S. (1989). Attachments beyond infancy. *American Psychologist, 44*, 709–716.

Ainsworth, M.D.S., Blehar, M.C., Waters, E., & Wall, S. (1978). *Patterns of attachment: A psychological study of the strange situation*. Hillsdale, NJ: Lawrence Erlbaum Associates.

Akhtar, N. & Gernsbacher, M.A. (2008). On privileging the role of gaze in infant social cognition. *Child Development Perspectives, 2*, 59–65.

Archer, J. (1991). Human sociobiology: Basic concepts and limitations. *Journal of Social Issues, 47*, 11–26.

Barlow, N. (Ed.) (1958). *The autobiography of Charles Darwin: 1809–1882*. New York: Norton.

Becker, D. & Dwyer, M. (1998). The impact of student verbal/visual learning style preference on implementing groupware in the classroom. *The Journal of Asynchronous Learning Networks, 2*, 61–69.

Belsky, J., Campbell, S.B., Cohn, J.F., & Moore, G. (1996). Instability of infant–parent attachment security. *Developmental Psychology, 32*, 921–924.

Biglan, A., Flay, B.R., Embry, D.D., & Sandler, I.N. (2012). The critical role of nurturing environments for promoting human well-being. *American Psychologist, 67*, 257–271.

Bowlby, J. (1958). The nature of the child's tie to his mother. *International Journal of Psychoanalysis, 39*, 350–373.

Bowlby, J. (1969/1982). *Attachment and loss: Vol. 1. Attachment*. New York: Basic Books.

Bowlby, J. (1988). *A secure base: Parent–child attachment and healthy human development*. New York: Basic Books.

Bretherton, I. (1990). Open communication and internal working models: Their role in the development of attachment relationships. In R. Dienstbier & R.A. Thompson (Eds.), *Nebraska Symposium on Motivation 1988: Vol. 36. Socioemotional Development* (pp. 57–113). Lincoln, NE: University of Nebraska Press.

Bull, J.J. & Wichman, H.A. (2001). Applied evolution. *Annual Review of Ecology and Systematics, 32*, 182–217.

Buss, D.M. (1995). Evolutionary psychology: A new paradigm for psychological science. *Psychological Inquiry, 6*, 1–30.

Buss, D.M. (2012). *Evolutionary psychology: The new science of the mind*. 4th ed. Upper Saddle River, NJ: Pearson.

Caruso, H.M. & Wooley, A.W. (2008). Harnessing the power of emergent interdependence to promote diverse team collaboration. *Diversity and Groups, 11*, 245–266.

Cassidy, J. (2008). The nature of the child's ties. In J. Cassidy & P.R. Shaver (Eds.), *Handbook of attachment: Theory, research, and clinical applications* (pp. 3–22). New York: Guilford Press.

Charlesworth, W.R. (1988). Resources and resource acquisition during ontogeny. In K.B. McDonald (Ed.), *Sociobiological perspectives on human behavior* (pp. 24–77). New York: Springer-Verlag.

Charlesworth, W.R. (1992). Darwin and developmental psychology: Past and present. *Developmental Psychology, 28*, 5–16.

Cosmides, L. & Tooby, J. (1997). Evolutionary Psychology: A primer. Retrieved on November 6, 2002, at http://psych.ucsb.edu

Cosmos: A Spacetime Odyssey (2014). *Episode 1: Standing up in the Milky Way*. National Geographic. Aired March 9, 2014.

Daly, M. & Wilson, M. (2001). Risk-taking, intrasexual competition, and homocide. In R.A. Dienstbier, J.A. French, A.C. Kamil, & D.W. Leger (Eds.), *Evolutionary psychology and motivation: Vol. 47. Nebraska Symposium on Motivation* (pp. 1–36). Lincoln, NE: University of Nebraska Press.

Darwin, C. (1979). *The illustrated "Origin of species."* Abridged and introduced by Richard E. Leakey. New York: Hill & Wang. (Original work published 1859)

Darwin, C. (2009). *The expression of the emotions in man and animals*. New York: Penguin Classics. (Original work published 1872)

Delton, A.W., Cosmides, L., Guemo, M., Robertson, T.E., & Tooby, J. (2012). The psychosemantics of free riding: Dissecting the architecture of a moral concept. *Journal of Personality and Social Psychology, 102,* 1252–1270.

Eberly Center for Teaching Excellence (2014). What are the benefits of group work. Retrieved at www.cmu.edu/teachingdesignteach/deisign/instructional strategies/

Edelstein, R.S., Alexander, K.W., Shaver, P.R., Schaaf, J.M., Quas, J.A., Lovas, G.S., et al. (2004). Adult attachment style and parental responsiveness during a stressful event. *Attachment and Human Development, 6,* 31–52.

Eibl-Eibesfeldt, I. (2007). *Human ethology.* Piscataway, NJ: Aldine Transaction.

Ein-Dor, T., Mikulincer, M., Doron, G., & Shaver, P.R. (2010). The attachment paradox: How can so many of us (the insecure ones) have no adaptive advantages? *Perspectives on Psychological Science, 5,* 123–141.

Fearon, R.P., Bakermans-Kranenburg, M.J., Van IJzendoorn, M.H., Lapsley, A., & Roisman, G.I. (2010). The significance of insecure attachment and disorganization in the development of children's externalizing behavior: A meta-analytic study. *Child Development, 81,* 435–456.

Feeney, J.A. (2008). Adult romantic attachment and couple relationships. In J. Cassidy & P.R. Shaver (Eds.), *Handbook of attachment: Theory, research, and clinical applications* (pp. 456–481). New York: Guilford Press.

Fogel, A., Hsu, H-C., Shapiro, A.F., Nelson-Goens, G.C., & Secrist, C. (2006). Effects of normal and perturbed social play on the duration and amplitude of different types of infant smiles. *Developmental Psychology, 42,* 459–473.

Fonagy, P. (2003). The development of psychopathology from infancy to adulthood: The mysterious unfolding of disturbance in time. *Infant Mental Health Journal, 24,* 212–239.

Fostervold, K., Watten, R.G., & Volden, F. (2014). Evolutionary adaptations: Theoretical and practical implications for visual ergonomics. *Work, 47,* 387–397.

George, C. & Solomon, J. (2008). Attachment and caregiving: The caregiving behavioral system. In J. Cassidy & P.R. Shaver (Eds.), *Handbook of attachment: Theory, research, and clinical applications.* 2nd ed. (pp. 833–856). New York: Guilford Press.

Gould, S.J. (2002). *The structure of evolutionary theory.* Cambridge, MA: Harvard University Press.

Hamilton, W.D. (1964). The genetical evolution of social behavior. *Journal of Theoretical Biology, 7,* 1–52.

Hardin, R. (2013). The free-rider problem. In E.N. Zalta (Ed.), *The Stanford Encyclopedia of Philosophy.* http://Plato.stanford.edu/archives/spr2013/entries/free-rider.

Hayden, T. (2009). What Darwin didn't know. *Smithsonian Magazine.* www.smithsonianmag.com/science-nature/what-darwin-didnt-know.

Hazan, C., Campa, M., & Gur-Yaish, N. (2006). Attachment across the lifespan. In P. Noller & J. Feeney (Eds.), *Close relationships: Functions, forms and processes* (pp. 189–209). Hove, England: Psychology Press.

Hazan, C. & Shaver, P.R. (1987). Attachment as an organizational framework for research on close relationships. *Journal of Personality and Social Psychology, 52,* 511–524.

Hewlett, B.S. & Macfarlan, S.J. (2010). Fathers' roles in hunter-gatherer and other small scale cultures. In M.E. Lamb (Ed.), *The role of the father in child development* (pp. 413–434). Malden, MA: Wiley.

Howes, C. & Spieker, S. (2008). Attachment relationships in the context of multiple caregivers. In J. Cassidy & P.R. Shaver (Eds.), *Handbook of attachment: Theory, research and clinical applications* (pp. 317–332). New York: Guilford Press.

Huxley, J. (1941). *The uniqueness of man.* London: Chatto & Windus.

Kanwisher, N. (2006). Neuroscience. What's in a face? *Science, 311,* 617–618.

Kao, G.Y-M. (2013). Enhancing the quality of peer review by reducing student "free-riding": Peer assessment interdependence. *British Journal of Educational Technology, 44,* 112–124.

LaFreniere, P.J. (2000). *Emotional development: A biosocial perspective.* Belmont, CA: Wadsworth.

Lewin, R. & Foley, R. (2004). *Principles of human evolution.* 2nd ed. Malden, MA: Blackwell.

Lorenz, K.Z. (1981). *The foundations of ethology* (K.Z. Lorenz & R.W. Kickert, Trans.). New York: Springer-Verlag. (Original work published 1935)

Lyell, C. (1833). *Principles of geology* (3 vols.). London: J. Murray. (Original work published 1830)

Lyons-Ruth, K., Lyubchik, A., Wolfe, R., & Bronfman, E. (2002). Parental depression and child attachment: Hostile and helpless profiles of parent and child behavior among families at risk. In S.H. Goodman & I.H. Gotlib (Eds.), *Children of depressed parents: Mechanisms of risk and implications for treatment* (pp. 89–120). Washington, DC: American Psychological Association.

Marvin, R.S. & Britner, P.A. (2008). Normative development: The ontogeny of attachment. In J. Cassidy & P.R. Shaver (Eds.), *Handbook of attachment: Theory, research and clinical applications* (pp. 269–294). New York: Guilford Press.

Mayr, E.W. (1991). *One long argument: Charles Darwin and the genesis of modern evolutionary thought.* Cambridge, MA: Harvard University Press.

Melis, A.P., Altrichter, K., & Tomasello, M. (2013). Allocation of resources to collaborators and free-riders in 3-year-olds. *Journal of Experimental Child Psychology, 114,* 364–370.

Mikulincer, M. & Shaver, P.R. (2012). An attachment perspective on psychopathology. *World Psychiatry, 11,* 11–15.

Neese, R.M. (2001). Motivation and melancholy: A Darwinian perspective. In R.A. Dienstbier, J.A. French, A.C. Kamil, & D.W. Leger (Eds.), *Evolutionary psychology and motivation: Vol. 47. Nebraska Symposium on Motivation* (pp. 179–204). Lincoln, NE: University of Nebraska Press.

O'Neil, D. (2013). Early modern homo sapiens. Retrieved on April 14, 2014 at http://anthro.palomar.edu/homo2/mod_homo_4.htm

Piezon, S.L. & Donaldson, R.L. (2005). Online groups and social loafing: Understanding student-group interactions. *Online Journal of Distance Learning Administration, 8,* 1–12.

Polar Bears International (2014). Retrieved on April 25, 2014 at www.polarbearsinternational.org/about-polar-bears/essentials/evolution

Renne, P.R., Deino, A.L., Hilgen, F.J. et al. (2013). Time scales of critical events around the Cretaceous-Paleogene boundary. *Science, 339,* 684–687.

Sagan, C. (1977/2012). *Dragons of Eden: Speculations on the evolution of human intelligence.* New York: Ballantine Books. Reprinted in 2012.

Schneider, B.H., Atkinson, L., & Tardif, C. (2001). Child–parent attachment and children's peer relations: A quantitative review. *Developmental Psychology, 37,* 86–100.

Simons, E.L. (1989). Human origins. *Science, 245,* 1343–1350.

Smith, A. (2006). Group work benefits pupils, study finds. *The Guardian.com.* Retrieved on April 25, 2014 at www.theguardian.com/education/2006/mar/31/schools.uk2

Sokol-Chang, R. & Fisher, M.L. (2013). Letter of purpose of the Feminist Evolutionary Psychology Society. *Journal of Social, Evolutionary and Cultural Psychology, 7,* 286–294.

Spencer, H. (1864). *Principles of biology: Vol. 1.* London: William & Norgate.

Tattersall, I. (2012). *Masters of the planet.* New York: Palgrave Macmillan.

Tinbergen, N. (1951). *The study of instinct.* Oxford: Clarendon Press.

Tracy, R.L. & Ainsworth, M.D.S. (1981). Maternal affectionate behavior and infant–mother attachment patterns. *Child Development, 52,* 1341–1343.

Tracy, J.L., Shaver, P.R., Albino, A.W., & Cooper, M.L. (2003). Attachment styles and adolescent sexuality. In P. Florsheim (Ed.), *Adolescent romantic relationships and sexual behavior: Theory, research, and practical implications* (pp. 137–159). New York; Psychology Press.

Trivers, R. (1972). Parental investment and sexual selection. In B. Campbell (Ed.), *Sexual selection and the descent of man: 1871–1971* (pp. 136–179). Chicago: Aldine.

Weinfield, N.S., Sroufe, L.A., Egeland, B., & Carlson, E.A. (2008). The nature of individual differences in infant-caregiver attachment. In J. Cassidy & P.R. Shaver (Eds.), *Handbook of attachment: Theory, research, and clinical applications.* 2nd ed. (pp. 78–101). New York: Guilford Press.

Wilson, E.O. (1975). *Sociobiology: The new synthesis.* Cambridge, MA: The Belknap Press.

Xing, J., Watkins, W.S., Witherspoon, D.J., Zhang, Y., Guthery, S.L., Thara, R., Mowry, B.J., Bulayeva, K., Weiss, R.B., & Jorde, L.B. (2009). Fine-scaled human genetic structure revealed by SNP microarrays. *Genome Research, 19,* 815–825.

3
Psychoanalytic Theory

CHAPTER OUTLINE

GUIDING QUESTIONS

- Explain the basic concepts of psychoanalytic theory. What is the direction of development from infancy to adulthood?
- What is the unconscious? What role does the unconscious play in shaping behavior in childhood, adolescence, and adulthood?
- What are defense mechanisms? How do they operate to support or undermine adaptive behavior?
- How does the theory characterize the differences between "normal" and "abnormal" behavior?
- What are some distinctions in the way development is portrayed in classical psychoanalytic theory, object relations theory, and ego psychology?

CASE VIGNETTE

"Tim (*who was four years old*) had a compulsive need to collect litter such as ice cream wrappers, stones, and cigarette butts. If someone tried to take the litter away from him or clean his room, he became furious and filled with anxiety. At night he often woke up in fear, and did not respond to any parental comfort. Constantly on alert, he continuously tracked the location of his parents in the apartment, and devised ways not to be left alone in his room. He had to go to the bathroom as often as every fifteen minutes, and had sudden, inexplicable outbursts of rage. At nursery school, Tim was provocative towards both children and staff. Over time, the staff found it more and more difficult to like him. In their frustrated efforts to help him, they felt disappointed, despairing and angry. When classmates occasionally attacked him, Tim made no attempt to defend himself, nor did he protest" (American Psychoanalytic Association, 2014). Eventually Tim's teachers and his parents agreed to have him start psychoanalysis.

Psychoanalytic theory combines a view of normal development with an approach to therapeutic intervention that helps to reduce symptoms associated with mental disorders. As you think about the case of Tim, you want to consider the view that psychoanalytic theory presents of children in the period of toddlerhood and early school age (2–4; 4–6). The theory incorporates ideas about the likely sources of anxiety and aggression; the role of symptoms for expressing psychological conflicts; and the importance of a child's relationship with parents and other adult authority figures. The case introduces issues of self-control, willfulness, anxiety, fear, and angry outbursts. These are normal concerns of the toddler and early-school-age period. However, the extreme nature of Tim's behavior, including the compulsive hoarding of litter, the anxiety associated with having his collection disturbed, the intensity and persistence of his fears, as well as the disruptive impact of these behaviors on Tim's experiences at home and school have led to the decision to seek psychoanalysis.

As you read more about psychoanalytic theory, you will appreciate a complex interplay between stages of life, drives or motives, levels of consciousness, and mental structures that combine to produce personality and interpersonal behavior. You may wonder what might be a successful or positive outcome for Tim through psychotherapy and how that outcome could be reached. You may also wonder what the long-term consequences might be for children who experience similar conflicts and fears in childhood but do not have the benefit of early intervention.

Evolutionary theory calls attention to the importance of the reproductive functions as they contribute to fitness and long-term species adaptation. In contrast, psychoanalytic theory focuses on the impact of sexual and aggressive drives on an individual's psychological functioning. It distinguishes between the impact of drives on mental activity and their effect on reproductive functions. The theory assumes that very young children have strong sexual and aggressive drives that find unique modes of expression through successive developmental stages. Throughout childhood, adolescence, and adult life, sexual and aggressive drives operate to direct aspects of one's fantasies, self-concept, problem-solving strategies, and social interactions as well as one's reproductive behavior.

A unique feature of psychoanalytic theory is the importance placed on childhood experiences for shaping adult thoughts, emotions and behavior. The theory focuses on both normative and pathological patterns of growth and development that result from the socialization pressures that act on biologically based drives within historical periods and cultural contexts. The theory highlights the relevance of certain primary social relationships, especially the mother–child and father–child dyads, for their role in determining the expression and gratification of needs and the internalization of moral standards. Freud's work inspired a vibrant community of theorists and analysts in Europe and the United States (Makari, 2008). Psychoanalytic theory continued to evolve with many new adaptations, both in the conceptualization of basic motives and needs, and the strategies for therapeutic intervention. Psychoanalytic theory continues to influence the study of development and approaches to understanding mental disorders.

HISTORICAL CONTEXT

Sigmund Freud was born in Freiberg (now Pribor), Czechoslovakia, in 1856. Both his grandfather and great-grandfather had been rabbis. He was the first son of his father Jacob's second or third marriage (Jahoda, 1977, p. 5). His family's business failed when he was 4 years old, and in 1860 his family moved to Vienna. In 1873, he entered the University of Vienna and in 1883 he graduated with a medical degree.

In school, he became interested in neurology and studied nerve tracts and the relationship of nerve cells. His early research focused on the functions of the medulla and the conduction of nerve impulses in the brain and spinal cord. He also did pioneering work in the use of cocaine as a local anesthetic, but he did not carry on with this work.

In 1885, Freud went to Paris to work with a French neurologist, Jean Martin Charcot, who specialized in treating hysteria using hypnosis. During his time in Paris, Freud became less interested in the physiological bases of neurological problems and more interested in their psychological bases. Freud began working on this problem in collaboration with a close friend and colleague, Josef Breuer. Freud and Breuer developed a theory of hysteria in which they attributed certain forms of paralysis to psychological conflict rather than to physiological damage (Breuer & Freud, 1893–95/1955).

In 1886, Freud returned to Vienna and opened up a private practice. He began using hypnosis as a therapeutic treatment. During this time he began to develop the idea that the human mind was made up of both conscious and unconscious components. He published *A case of successful treatment by hypnotism* in 1892–93 and *Studies on hysteria* in 1893–95. In the 1890s he stopped using hypnosis and began using free association as a way of reaching the unconscious mind. In this technique, the patient was aware of what he or she said. In an article published on the etiology of neuroses, Freud first used the term "psychoanalysis" instead of "suggestion" or "catharsis" to describe his methods (Sigmund Freud Chronology: 1896, 2014). The process of psychoanalysis focused on analyzing the material that was produced through association and areas of resistance to reveal the content of the unconscious.

In 1900, Freud published *The interpretation of dreams*, which includes substantial information from his own self-analysis. He believed that dreams gave more direct evidence of the contents of the unconscious mind than free associations even though the dream content was in symbolic form. Thus, free association and dream interpretation became established as two primary techniques of psychoanalysis.

In 1905, Freud published *Three essays on the theory of sexuality*, which articulated his view that sexual conflict and expression of impulses existed in infancy and young childhood and influenced the formation of the adult personality. His theory was formulated in part as a critique of the social conventions of the time in which sexual urges and the psychological representations of sexual drives were severely constrained. These ideas were met by a storm of anger, rejection, and protest by many within the medical community. His medical colleagues could not accept the idea of childhood sexuality. They considered his public lectures on the topic to be crude and distasteful. Freud was denied a professorial appointment at the University of Vienna primarily because of these lectures and writings. Even Breuer, his longtime colleague and collaborator, found Freud's preoccupation with sexual motives offensive and terminated their association.

But, at the same time, the new theory of infantile sexuality led a group of young followers to gather around Freud and pursue the implications of these ideas. Freud helped form the International Congress on Psychoanalysis. There, he developed his psychoanalytic theory and taught the principles of psychoanalysis to his followers. Freud demanded rather strict adherence to the basic principles and concepts of this theory, and some members of the analytic circle broke away to pursue their own versions of the theory. Most notable among these were Carl Jung and Alfred Adler, who broke with Freud in 1912 and founded their own schools of analytic thought that continue to be influential today.

Freud spent the last 25 years of his life lecturing, writing, teaching his theory to younger physicians, working with patients to gather supporting evidence for his theory, and conducting the business of the International Congress. He remained in Vienna during the rise of Nazism in Germany, but was spirited away to England by supporters in 1938 after the Nazis invaded Austria. In 1923, he developed cancer of the jaw, which was very painful. He underwent repeated surgeries and finally died of the disease in 1939.

Marie Jahoda (1977) noted that "there is virtually no aspect of Freud's work that has escaped becoming the subject of controversy; even some biographical details provided by him or his contemporaries are now open to doubt" (p. 5). Major biographers such as Jones (1953–57) and Ellenberger (1970) disagree about the facts of Freud's life and the factors that guided his thoughts and work. Freud was a very prolific writer and over the years he often revisited aspects of his theory and analytic techniques. Thus, when someone asks, "Did Freud believe this or that?" it is possible to find support for a variety of positions depending on which work one consults. This helps perpetuate the controversies over his ideas. However, there is no doubt that his ideas have been influential in determining how we think about the human psyche and the factors that shape it.

KEY CONCEPTS

Seven organizing concepts of psychoanalytic theory are discussed below: the domains of consciousness, the concept of drives, the idea that all behavior is motivated, the three basic structures of personality, five stages of development, the notion of defense mechanisms, and the processes of identification and transference.

Domains of Consciousness

One of the most enduring contributions of psychoanalytic theory is the analysis of the topography of mental activity (see Figure 3.1). Freud thought the human mind was like an iceberg. **Conscious** processes are the tip that protrudes out of the water; they make up only a small part of the mind. Our conscious thoughts are fleeting. We can have only a few of them at any one time. As soon as energy is diverted from a thought or image, it disappears from consciousness.

The **preconscious** is analogous to the part of the iceberg near the waterline. Material in the preconscious can be made conscious if attention is directed to it. Preconscious thoughts are readily accessible to consciousness through focused attention. You may not be thinking about your hometown or your favorite desserts right now, but if someone were to ask you about either of them, you could readily recall and discuss them.

The **unconscious**, like the rest of the iceberg, is hidden from view. It is a vast network of content and processes that are actively barred from consciousness. Freud hypothesized that the content of the unconscious, including wishes, fears, impulses, and repressed memories, plays

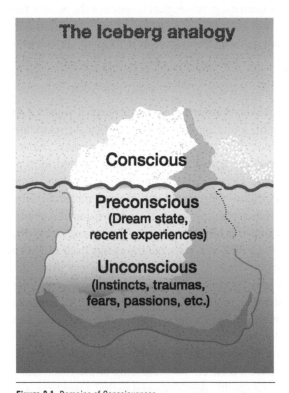

Figure 3.1 Domains of Consciousness

Source: Gerard Keegan, *Iceberg analogy.* www.gerardkeegan.co.uk/glossary/
gloss_i.htm. Reproduced with permission.

a major role in guiding behavior even though we cannot explain the connections consciously. Behaviors that are unusual or extremely intense may not make sense if they are explained only in terms of conscious motives. However, through certain techniques used in psychotherapy, the link between unconscious wishes and fears and overt behaviors often can be established.

The unconscious is a storehouse of powerful, primitive **motives** of which the person is unaware. Unconscious as well as conscious motives may motivate behavior simultaneously. Thus, behaviors that may appear to be somewhat unusual or extremely intense are described as **multiply determined**—that is, a single behavior expresses many motives, some of which the person can recognize and control and others that are guided by unconscious thought. One of the most controversial aspects of Freud's psychoanalytic theory was the central role he gave to the unconscious as the guide or force behind most aspects of human behavior.

> In the course of centuries the *naïve* self-love of men has had to submit to two major blows at the hands of science. The first was when they learnt that our earth was not the center of the universe but only a tiny fragment of a cosmic system of scarcely imaginable vastness. This is associated in our minds with the name of Copernicus, though something similar had already been asserted by Alexandrian science. The second blow fell when biological research destroyed man's supposedly privileged place in creation and proved his descent from the animal kingdom and his ineradicable animal nature. This revaluation has been accomplished in our own days by Darwin, Wallace, and their predecessors, though not without the most violent contemporary opposition. But human megalomania will have suffered its third and most wounding blow from the psychological research of the present time which seeks to prove to the ego that it is not even master in its own house, but must content itself with scanty information of what is going on unconsciously in its mind. (Freud, 1917/1955, pp. 1916–1917)

Drives

Freud's analysis of normal development as well as his explanations for specific forms of mental illness are derived from his understanding of the ways that the **sexual drive** and the **aggressive drive** press for expression and are inhibited or given various outlets in thoughts, dreams, behaviors, and symptoms. The term *drive* is sometimes referred to as psychic energy, tension, instincts, impulse, or *libido*. **Drives** can be thought of as sexual and aggressive forces that have a biological or somatic origin—they are a result of some metabolic function, but they are also intimately linked to psychological processes. Freud envisioned a model in which the energy behind the drives builds up as it seeks satisfaction. The psychic energy that is embodied in these drives can be expressed in a variety of ways, but the energy itself will not be destroyed.

Drives have a power or *force*. A person can experience a drive along a continuum from mild to strong. Drives have an *aim*—a desire to be satisfied that may be handled immediately, delayed, or possibly redirected so that it is only partly satisfied. When possible, drives are satisfied immediately to reduce tension and achieve a state of equilibrium. Drives have an *object*—a person or thing that allows the drive to achieve its aim. The object of the drive is closely linked to the specific environment in which the child functions. Thus, in order to understand how drives are satisfied one must have a concrete understanding of the social and physical resources that are available to a child at a specific developmental period. Over time, a person becomes able to delay the satisfaction of the drives and finds increasingly flexible and socially appropriate ways to achieve satisfaction.

All Behavior Is Motivated

Freud assumed that all behavior (except that resulting from fatigue) is motivated. He thought that all behavior has meaning; it does not occur randomly or without purpose. Many of the concepts of psychoanalytic theory attempt to describe the processes by which sexual drives and aggressive drives, most of which are unconscious, motivate behavior.

Here is an example of the complexity of the process. A patient of Freud's who had recently been married sometimes forgot his wife's name. Freud hypothesized that consciously the man felt he loved his wife and thought they were happy together. Freud thought that forgetting the wife's name provided a clue to the content of the man's unconscious. In his unconscious, the man had strong, negative feelings about his wife, feelings that were so unacceptable that they could not be allowed expression. By forgetting his wife's name, Freud reasoned that the young man could express some level of hostility toward her and, at the same time, punish himself for his unconscious anger toward her.

Three Structures of Personality

Freud (1933/1964) described three components of personality: the id, the ego, and the superego. In his writings about these structures, Freud suggested a developmental progression in which id exists alone at birth, ego emerges during infancy, and the superego takes shape in early childhood. In adulthood, the three structures must find an effective pattern of interaction in order to support adaptation.

Id. The **id** is the source of instincts and impulses. It is the primary source of psychic energy, and it exists from birth. Freud believed that newborn infants' mental processes were comprised completely of id impulses, and that the ego and superego emerged later, drawing their energy from the id.

The id expresses its demands according to the **pleasure principle**: People are motivated to seek pleasure and avoid pain. The pleasure principle does not take into account the feelings of others, society's norms, or agreements between people. Its rule is to achieve immediate satisfaction of impulses and discharge of energy. When you lie to a friend to protect your own image, or when you cut ahead of people in line so you won't have to wait, you are operating according to the pleasure principle.

The logic of the id is also the logic of dreams. This kind of thinking is called **primary process thought**. It is characterized by a lack of concern for the constraints of reality. In primary process thought, there are no negatives. Everything is yes. There is no time. Nothing happens in the past or in the future. Everything is now. Symbolism becomes flexible. One object may symbolize many things—the image of a house may be a symbol for one's mother, a lover, or the female genitalia, as well as for a house. Many different objects may mean the same thing—many male faces can all represent the father.

Ego. **Ego** is a term that has two related meanings. One is the idea of ego as a person's self including one's physical self, self-concept, self-esteem, and mental representations of the self in relation to others. This sense of ego emerges as psychic energy is directed toward the self—a process that is sometimes called *primary narcissism*. The idea is that the sense of self is born out of self-love, an enthusiasm and excitement for one's body, one's experiences, and one's emerging sense of agency.

The second meaning of ego refers to all mental functions that have to do with the person's relation to the environment. It includes a multitude of cognitive processes, such as perception, learning, memory, judgment, self-awareness, and language skills that allow a person to take in information, process it, assess its implications, and select a course of action. Freud thought the ego begins to develop in the first 6 or 8 months of life and is well established by the age of 2 or 3. Other scholars view the ego processes as present from birth. Of course, much change and growth occur over time as the ego responds to demands from the environment and finds strategies that support effective functioning. The ego also responds to the demands of the id and the superego and helps the person satisfy needs, live up to ideals and standards, and establish a healthy emotional balance.

The ego operates according to the **reality principle**. Under this principle, the ego strives to satisfy id impulses in ways that are safe, realistic and appropriate in the situation. The ego assesses the situation in order to decide what is appropriate, and makes a plan for how to satisfy the impulse in a way that will avoid negative consequences. In contrast to the pleasure principle, the reality principle often involves delaying until a socially acceptable form of expression or gratification can be found. Imagine that you are driving a car to reach an important destination. The pleasure principle tells you to go as fast as possible to reach your goal. As the driver, the reality principle helps you decide how fast to go in light of traffic, legal limits, and road conditions. You still reach your goal, but within the constraints of the demands and limits of the situation.

In the ego, primary process thought becomes subordinated to a more reality-oriented process, called secondary process thought. This process begins to dominate as the ego matures. **Secondary process thought** is the kind of logical, sequential thinking that we usually mean when we discuss thinking. It allows people to plan and act in order to engage the world and to achieve gratification in personally and socially acceptable ways. It enables people to delay gratification. It helps people assess plans by examining whether they will really work. This last process is called **reality testing**.

Superego. The **superego** includes both a punishing and a rewarding function. The **conscience**, which includes ideas about which behaviors and thoughts are improper, unacceptable, and wrong, carries out the punishing function. The ego ideal, which includes ideas about what behaviors and thoughts are admirable, acceptable, and worthy of praise, carries out the rewarding function. Freud's work led him to conclude that the superego does not begin to develop until the age of 5 or 6, and probably is not firmly established until several years later. Other theorists have suggested that the roots of the superego emerge in infancy as the child becomes differentiated from the caregiver and aware of the possibility of disrupting the close bond with this loving object (Klein, 1948).

Because it is formed during early childhood, the superego tends to be harsh and unrealistic in its demands. It is often just as illogical and unrelenting in its search for proper behavior as the id is in its search for pleasure. When a child thinks about behaving in a morally unacceptable way, the superego sends a warning by producing feelings of anxiety and guilt.

The superego is developed through a process called **identification**. Motivated by love, fear, and admiration, children actively imitate their parents' characteristics and internalize their parents' values. Through identification, parents' values become the ideals and aspirations of their children. In this way, the moral standards of a society are transmitted from one generation to the next.

The Relationship of Id, Ego, and Superego. In the mature person, ego processes work toward satisfying id impulses through thoughts and actions without generating strong feelings of guilt in the superego. In one sense, the ego processes serve both the id and the superego, striving to provide gratification, but in morally and socially acceptable ways. In another sense, ego is the executive of personality. The strength of the ego determines the person's effectiveness in meeting his or her needs, handling the demands of the superego, and dealing with the demands of reality. If the ego is strong and can establish a good balance among id, superego, and environmental demands, the person is satisfied and free from immobilizing guilt and feelings of worthlessness.

When id and superego are stronger than ego, the person may be tossed and turned psychologically by strong desires for pleasure and strong constraints against attaining those desires. When environmental demands are strong and the ego is weak, such as when an adolescent is confronted by strong pressures for peer conformity and the threat of peer rejection, a person may also be overwhelmed. According to psychoanalytic theory, it is the breakdown of the ego that leads to mental disorder.

Much of the relationship of the id, the ego, and the superego is played out at an unconscious level. In early childhood, aspects of basic drives and primary process thought are noticeable in a child's consciousness. This is an indication of the conscious presence of the id. As the ego grows stronger, it is able to push the id's desires and fantasies into the unconscious so the person can attend to the exploration and demands of the external world. Freud thought that the superego also operated mostly at the unconscious level, although the ego ideal is largely conscious. He thought the ego, however, functioned at both the conscious and unconscious levels.

The concept of achieving new levels of ego strength reflects the goal of development in psychoanalytic theory. Over time, the ego has to attend to pressures from the id and find acceptable outlets for drive satisfaction. The ego has to choose morally acceptable behaviors in order to avoid guilt from a punitive superego. Finally, the ego has to act in the real world, finding ways to protect the self and loved ones from real dangers as well as to find new sources of access to objects that will satisfy basic drives.

Stages of Psychosexual Development

Freud assumed that the most significant developments in personality take place during five life stages from infancy through adolescence, with the primary emphasis given to the first 5 or 6 years of life. After that time, according to Freud, the essential pattern for expressing and controlling impulses has been established. Later life serves only to uncover new modes of gratification and new sources of frustration.

The stages Freud described reflect his emphasis on **sexuality** and **aggression** as driving forces. Freud used the term sexuality broadly, referring to the full range of physical pleasure, from sucking to sexual intercourse. He also attached a positive, life-force symbolism to the concept of sexuality, suggesting that sexual impulses provide a thrust toward growth and renewal. Freud's view of aggression evolved from observations of angry, competitive and harmful behaviors directed toward the self and others. In later writings, he attached a symbolic meaning to aggressive impulses, linking them to the idea of a death instinct, a force that strives to return life to its inorganic form. Other theorists, such as Fenichel (1945, 1953) and Jones (1957), believed that this abstract view of life and death instincts is unnecessary. Rather, they consider sexuality and aggression to be basic instinctual drives that are observable in clinical practice.

At each stage, a particular body zone is of heightened sexual and aggressive importance. The shift in focus from one body zone to the next is due largely to the biologically based unfolding of physical maturation. The five stages Freud identified are the oral, anal, phallic, latent, and genital stages.

During the **oral stage**, in the first year of life, the mouth is the site of sexual and aggressive gratification. Babies use their mouths to explore the environment, to express tension, and to experience pleasure. Freud characterized infants as passive and dependent. They take things in, absorbing experience just as they swallow milk. As infants learn to delay gratification, the ego becomes more clearly differentiated and they become aware of the distinction between the self and others. With this awareness comes the realization that all wishes cannot be satisfied.

In the **anal stage**, during the second year of life, the anus is the most sexualized body part. With the development of the sphincter muscles, a child learns to expel or withhold feces at will. The conflict at this stage focuses on the subordination of the child's will to the demands of the culture (via parents) for appropriate toilet habits. A child's feelings of frustration or loss of control as parents attempt to impose toileting practices may result in new expressions of aggression toward others or self-harm.

The **phallic stage** begins during the third year of life and may last until the child is 6. It is a period of heightened genital sensitivity in the absence of the hormonal changes that accompany puberty. Freud described the behavior of children at this stage as bisexual. They direct sexualized activity toward both sexes and engage in self-stimulation. This is the stage during which the Oedipal or Electra complex is observed.

The **Oedipal complex** in boys and the **Electra complex** in girls result from ambivalence surrounding heightened sexuality. According to psychoanalytic theory, the child has a strong, sexualized attraction to the parent of the opposite sex. The child may desire to have the exclusive attention of that parent, and may fantasize that the other parent will leave, or perhaps die. In other words, the same-sex parent becomes a fantasied rival and a target of the child's aggression. At the same time, the child fears that amorous overtures toward the desired parent may result in hostility or retribution from the parent of the same sex. The child also worries that this beloved, same-sex parent will withdraw love. Parental threats intended to prevent the child from masturbating, and fantasies of the possibility of castration or bodily mutilation, may add to the child's fears that sexualized fantasies are going to result in punishment or withdrawal of love.

An important component of the Oedipal or Electra complex dynamic is the view of the young child as engaged in complex, conflicting sexual and aggressive wishes that involve the mother–father–child triad. Many competing impulses come into play: the conflict between wanting to satisfy sexual drives and the awareness that self-stimulation is not socially acceptable; the conflict between wanting to remain a child who is loved and cared for by both parents and the desire to assume a more mature role in the eyes of the opposite-sex parent; the anger and rivalry experienced toward the same-sex parent and the desire to preserve that parent's love and admiration; the pressures to embrace one's own gender identity and the envy one feels toward the opposite sex.

In a successful resolution of the Oedipal or Electra conflict, the superego emerges as a strong structure that aids the ego in controlling unacceptable impulses. Through a process of identification with one's parents' moral and ethical values, the child achieves a new level of autonomy, and at the same time receives the admiration and approval of both parents, who see the child moving in the direction of maturity and self-control. Most of the intense and painful conflicts of this period are repressed, and the ego emerges with a new degree of self-esteem and confidence about his or her place in the family structure (Tyson & Tyson, 1995).

Freud believed that once the Oedipal or Electra conflict is resolved, the child enters a period of **latency**. During this stage, which lasts from about 7 years until puberty, sexual development is slowed, and a process of repression ensues, cutting the person off from the conscious memories of the conflicts and wishes of earlier stages. The primary personality development during this period is the maturation of the ego, with sublimation of drives to new channels such as school work, hobbies, and friendships.

A final stage of development begins with the onset of puberty: the **genital stage**. During this period, the person finds ways of satisfying sexual impulses in mature, dyadic relationships. Adolescence brings about a reawakening of Oedipal or Electra conflicts and a reworking of earlier childhood identifications. Freud explained the tension of adolescence as the result of the sexual threat that the mature adolescent poses to the family unit. In an effort to avoid this threat, adolescents may withdraw from their families or temporarily devalue their parents. With the selection of a permanent sex partner, the threat of intimacy between young people and their parents diminishes. At the end of adolescence, a more autonomous relationship with one's parents becomes possible.

Freud believed that the psychological conflicts that arise during adolescence and adulthood result from a failure to satisfy or express specific childhood wishes. At any of the childhood stages, sexualized and aggressive impulses may have been so frustrated or overindulged that the person continues to seek their gratification at later stages of life. Freud used the term **fixation** to refer to continued use of pleasure-seeking or anxiety-reducing behaviors appropriate to an earlier stage of development.

Since no person can possibly satisfy all wishes at every life stage, normal development depends on the ability to channel the energy from those impulses into activities that either symbolize the impulses or express them in a socially acceptable form through a process called **sublimation**. During adolescence and early adulthood, patterns of impulse expression, fixation, and sublimation crystallize into a life orientation. From this point on, the content of the id, the regulating functions of the superego, and the executive functions of the ego rework the struggles of childhood through repeated episodes of engagement, conflict, and impulse gratification or frustration.

Defense Mechanisms

Much of the ego's work involves mediating the conflicts between the id's demands for gratification and the superego's demands for "good" behavior. This work is conducted outside the person's awareness. When unconscious conflicts threaten to break through into consciousness, the person experiences anxiety. If the ego functions effectively, it pushes these conflicts into the unconscious and thereby protects the person from unpleasant emotions. The ego proceeds to satisfy desires in acceptable ways by directing behavior and social interaction.

Strong, unresolved conflicts may leave a person in a state of constant anxiety and symptoms may emerge. A person who feels a desire that is judged to be very "bad," such as an unconscious wish to harm a parent or to be sexually intimate with a sibling, may experience anxiety without recognizing its source. The ungratified impulse continues to seek gratification. The superego continues to find the impulse unacceptable, and the conflict continues to produce anxiety in the person's conscious experience. The unpleasant emotional state may preoccupy the person and make it difficult to handle the normal demands of day-to-day life.

Defense mechanisms protect the person from anxiety so that effective functioning can be preserved. They distort, substitute, or completely block out the source of the conflict. They are usually initiated unconsciously. The defense mechanism used depends on a person's age and the intensity of the perceived threat. Younger children tend to use denial and repression (pushing thoughts from awareness). A more diverse set of defenses, requiring greater cognitive complexity, becomes available in the course of development. In situations of greatest threat, denial is often the initial defense used, regardless of age.

According to Freud, the basic defense mechanism is **repression**, a process whereby unacceptable impulses are pushed into the unconscious. It is as if a wall were constructed between the unconscious and the conscious mind so that anxiety-provoking thoughts and feelings cannot enter consciousness. With unacceptable thoughts and impulses far from awareness, the person is protected from uncomfortable feelings of anxiety and may devote the remaining psychic energy to interchange with the interpersonal and physical environments. This defensive strategy has two major costs. First, it takes energy to continue to protect the conscious mind from these thoughts, thereby reducing the amount of mental energy available to cope with other daily demands. Second, if too many thoughts and feelings are relegated to repression, the person loses the use of the emotional system as a means of monitoring and evaluating reality.

The following are some of the more common defense mechanisms:

Repression: Unacceptable wishes are barred from conscious thought.

Projection: Unacceptable wishes are attributed to someone else.

Acting out: Expressing in behavior (like having a tantrum or hitting someone) those thoughts and feelings that the person cannot reflect on or express in words; this releases some of the energy associated with the impulse and provides temporary relief of tension.

Reaction formation: Unacceptable feelings are expressed by the opposite feelings.

Regression: One avoids confronting conflicts and stresses by reverting to behaviors that were effective and comforting at an earlier life stage.

Displacement: Unacceptable impulses are expressed toward a substitute target.

Rationalization: Unacceptable feelings and actions are justified or given a more acceptable interpretation using logical or pseudo-logical explanations to avoid the more distressing or anxiety-provoking feelings.

Intellectualization: An overemphasis on thinking when confronted with an unacceptable impulse or situation, without addressing any emotions associated with the circumstance in order to distance the ego from the impulse.

Isolation: Feelings are separated from thoughts.

Denial: Parts of external reality are denied.

Dissociation: Under conditions of distress or threat, the ego seems to separate from time and place; the person may disconnect from the situation and live for a time in a different world that is not as unbearable.

Sublimation: Unacceptable wishes are channeled to socially acceptable behaviors.

According to psychoanalytic theory, all people resort to defense mechanisms at various times in their lives. These mechanisms not only reduce anxiety but may lead to positive social outcomes. Physicians who use isolation may be able to function effectively because they are able to apply their knowledge without being hindered by their feelings. Children who rationalize defeat may be able to protect their self-esteem by viewing themselves favorably. The child who projects angry feelings onto someone else may find that this technique stimulates a competitive orientation that enhances performance. Sublimation is considered a mature defense mechanism that allows people to refocus unacceptable drives into productive, creative, and socially acceptable forms. The person who has strong sexual and aggressive drives may become devoted to extreme sports that allow repeated investment in physical exertion and competition.

Regression is an especially important defense when considered from a developmental perspective. Many theorists suggest that development is a spiraling process in which forward movement and increased integration of complex functions may alternate with temporary backsliding or return to a more comfortable, less demanding position. In psychoanalytic theory, regression may occur when a person (child or adult) reverts to an earlier form of drive satisfaction, immature forms of relationships with others, lower moral standards, or more simplistic ways of thinking and solving problems. Anna Freud (1965) and Peter Blos (1967) both wrote about the idea that regression can serve ego development if it is not met with extreme disapproval. Sometimes it is necessary to return to an earlier mode of functioning in order to resolve conflicts that were inadequately resolved at that time, or to engage in a kind of playful childishness in order to achieve a new level of mastery. Most obviously, in the creative process, a certain amount of regressive fantasy thought can unlock possible associations that make sense according to primary process thinking but are censored in secondary process thinking (Tyson & Tyson, 1995).

Some people rely more on one or two defensive techniques than on the others. The resultant defensive style becomes part of an overall personality pattern. It permits one to regulate the impact of the environment and to perceive experiences in ways that are compatible with one's needs. When defense mechanisms are used to excess, however, they may indicate a deeper psychological problem. The use of defense mechanisms draws psychological energy from the ego. Energy that is used to prevent certain wishes from entering conscious thought is not available for other life activities. A person whose energy is devoted to defensive strategies may be unable to develop other ego functions and to use those functions adequately.

Identification and Transference

Psychoanalytic theory suggests that beginning in childhood and continuing through adulthood, we incorporate the observable characteristics and personal values of people whom we either love, admire, or fear. This process is referred to as **identification**. We form an internal representation of the self that is coordinated with the representation of the other that has been created through observations, interactions, and playful exchanges (Decety & Chaminade, 2003). Identification plays a key role in the process of ego development and socialization in early childhood. Through this process, significant components of gender identity and morality are incorporated into the self. Identification may begin in a wishful fantasy to become like someone else or to merge with a love object. However, over time the content of these identifications becomes integrated into the person's stable character. The source of the identification may become repressed or detached from its origin. A teenage boy who is trying to negotiate with his parents to let him go on a weekend trip with his friends may try to argue that by going away he will be showing his parents just how responsible he can be. He may be surprised when his mother tells him that he is acting just like his father in the approach he is taking to make his case.

Identification begins in early childhood and continues throughout life. It may be both a conscious and an unconscious process. For example, a young adult may perceive that a co-worker is especially successful in the work setting, and may begin to identify with some of that person's actions or attitudes, thinking "If I am more like my co-worker, perhaps I will be more highly valued in the work setting." The motivation to identify with the co-worker may also originate from unconscious anger or envy of the co-worker's success. In order to defend against these unacceptable aggressive drives, the person may take on characteristics of the co-worker. This conflicted motivation for identification may create anxiety for the person as he or she manifests attitudes and behaviors that are at some level attached to aggressive fantasies (Schafer, 1968; Abend & Porder, 1995).

In identification, a person incorporates characteristics of a valued object. In **transference**, a person projects the characteristics of an internalized identification onto another person. The person repeats feelings or desires that had been directed to an important object in an earlier time of life to a new, contemporary relationship. Transference is especially likely in situations where a person is in a differential power relationship, similar to that of a child to a parent. So, for example, a student may transfer characteristics of his or her mother onto a teacher, acting toward the teacher as if that person were his or her mother, and expecting the teacher to treat him or her the way the student's mother treated him or her. The motivation for the transference may be to satisfy an unfulfilled wish or to reconstruct an unfulfilled relationship. A contemporary object becomes a symbolic substitute for the person who was important in childhood. From the psychoanalytic perspective, some amount of transference becomes integrated into every adult's character. The unmet, repressed wishes toward significant childhood figures, including parents, siblings, teachers, or religious leaders, are carried forward into adulthood. Transference can occur when the contemporary relationship, such as a relationship with a lover, a supervisor, or a mentor, has some real or symbolic equivalence or resemblance to the earlier relationship.

The concepts of identification and transference are important not only because children and adults experience them, but because adults are often the objects for these processes in others. As teachers, community leaders, therapists, human service professionals, supervisors, intimate partners, and parents, adults are the significant others who provide the content for identification and may become the objects of transference.

NEW DIRECTIONS

In much of his writings on psychoanalytic theory, Freud concentrated on the nature of unconscious conflicts, their sources, the way they found expression, and the ways in which they operated to rob the ego of energy or disrupt adaptive functioning. One direction that emerged in the elaboration of psychoanalytic theory was the importance of the ego, including a more detailed description of ego development, ego functions, and the ability of the ego to assess and manage threats. This direction is referred to as **ego psychology**. Another direction focused on the centrality of early object relations, that is the interpersonal sphere in which self and other are co-constructed, as the context for ego development and as prototypes for shaping subsequent object relations. This direction is referred to as **object relations theory**.

Ego Psychology

In his structural theory, Freud introduced the concept of ego and its *executive* functions in managing the expression of impulses, negotiating between the id and the superego, striving to attain goals embedded in the ego ideal, and assessing reality. His daughter, Anna Freud, took these ideas further in her important book, *The ego and the mechanisms of defense* (1936/1946), outlining new ego capacities that emerge from infancy through adolescence. In this work, she highlighted the various threats that the id poses to the ego at each stage of development, and provided a classification of the defense mechanisms the ego uses to protect itself from unruly and unacceptable impulses.

Anna Freud gave special attention to the period of adolescence as a time of increased sexual and aggressive energy that is linked to the biological changes of puberty. At this time, children are likely to be overwhelmed by libidinal energy and the ego is more or less fighting for its life. Anger and aggression become more intense, sometimes to the point of getting out of hand. Appetites become enormous. Oral and anal interests come to the surface again expressed as pleasure in dirt and disorder, exhibitionistic tendencies, brutality, cruelty to animals, and enjoyment of various forms of vulgarity. In her clinical cases, Anna Freud observed that previously successful defense mechanisms threatened to fall to pieces as intense sexual impulses emerged. During this period, the ego may employ very rigid defenses in order to deny the instinctual drives. Adolescents may vacillate in their behavior from loving to mean, compliant to rebellious, or self-centered to altruistic, as the ego tries to assert itself in the midst of conflicting and newly energized libidinal forces.

Elaborating on Anna Freud's view of adolescent development, Peter Blos (1962) expanded the concept of ego and the mechanisms of defense by identifying the coping mechanisms that emerge in adolescence as young people find ways of adapting psychologically to the physical transitions of puberty. By the end of adolescence, those ego conflicts present at the beginning of puberty are transformed into more manageable aspects of identity construction and expression. Blos noted five major accomplishments of ego development for young people who navigate adolescence successfully:

1. Judgment, interests, intellect and other ego functions emerge that are specific to the individual and very stable.
2. The conflict-free area of the ego expands, allowing new people and experiences to acquire psychological importance.
3. An irreversible sexual identity is formed.
4. The egocentrism of the child is replaced by a balance between thoughts about one's self and thoughts about others.
5. A wall separating one's public and private selves is established.

The prominence of ego psychology was enhanced through the work of Heinz Hartmann. In his book, *Ego psychology and the problem of adaptation* (1939/1964), Hartmann suggested that not all aspects of the ego's functioning arise out of conflict with the id and the superego. He introduced the concept of the **conflict-free sphere of the ego**, including basic adaptive functions such as perception, recognition of objects, logical problem solving, motor development, and language. These functions help the person assess and adapt to reality.

Hartmann thought that the concepts of ego, id, and superego were more accurately viewed as three interrelated components of mental functioning that could expand or contract under the influence of one another. He offered a developmental picture of the ego beginning with early differentiation and distinction between id and ego, a process of growing clarity between self and the external reality, a shift from early narcissism to investment in others, and to the eventual achievement of adaptive, secondary process thinking (Boesky, 1995). Hartmann expanded the scope of interest within psychotherapy to include more attention on problem solving and the goal-oriented nature of thought and behavior.

Building on Hartmann's work, Edith Jacobson (1964) described how the self is shaped through identification with others and achieves new levels of autonomy through the incorporation of moral codes and ethical values. According to Jacobson, the superego is not always a threat to the ego. It can become a stimulus for new levels of ego development when anxiety or guilt signal a need for a new standard of moral behavior.

Charles Brenner, a leader in the psychoanalytic movement in the United States, went even further in his rejection of the distinctions between id, ego, and superego. Whereas Hartmann argued that there is a conflict-free sphere of the ego, Brenner (1994) viewed mental activity of all types as a product of ongoing conflict between underlying, instinctually based wishes and the defenses against them.

In their extension of the concept of ego, Rubin and Gertrude Blanck (1986) moved from a view of many ego functions to a more executive, integrated analysis of ego:

> We suggested that the ego is the overall organizing process. Instead of defining it by its functions (Hartmann), we proposed that it be defined by its function*ing*—that is, we now focus attention upon the total person who functions, rather than upon the separate functions. (Blanck & Blanck, 1986, p. 88)

Thus, ego psychology became a study of the development and differentiation of the ego as integrative, adaptive, and goal-directed. The ego is at once an intricate composite of multiple capacities, including planning, assessing, defending, coping, and mediating, and the integration of these with other aspects of self-concept, self-esteem, and personal identity that give the person substance, individuality, and location in the social world. The contemporary field of ego psychology has a developmental focus, addressing the emerging capacities of the infant to sense and organize experience, and to achieve self-regulation in the face of strong needs and drives.

Object Relations Theory

The relational paradigm emerged and has been consolidated within psychoanalytic thought over the past 70 years (Greenberg & Mitchell, 1983; Borden, 2000; Safran, 2012). Theorists such as W.R.D. Fairbairn, Melanie Klein, Harry Stack Sullivan, Donald Winnicott, and Heinz Kohut are forerunners in this perspective. They stress that humans have basic needs for connection, contact, and meaningful interpersonal relationships throughout life. According to this view, the self is formed in an interpersonal context, and emerges through interactions with others. These others are the *objects* to which the theory refers. Typically the mother or primary caregiver is the first object; followed by other significant relationships such as parents and siblings.

The path toward maturity requires that the person achieve a sense of vitality, stability, and inner cohesiveness which are formulated through interpersonal transactions. In the relational perspective, psychopathology or dysfunction arise when a person internalizes rigid, rejecting, or neglectful relational experiences built upon disturbances in relationships with early caregivers in infancy and early childhood. The person then uses these internalizations to anticipate or respond to real life social encounters. Since the internalized relational pattern is familiar and well learned, the person is reluctant to give it up even if it leads to feelings of isolation, anxiety, or self-loathing. The result is recurring maladaptive interpersonal relations which are evidenced in contemporary friendship, family, work, and intimate contexts, and are typically observed in the therapeutic relationship as well (Messer & Warren, 1995; Levinson, 2010). Object relations theories continue to recognize the unconscious as a source of wishes and related defense conflicts. However, they view these wishes and conflicts as arising from disturbances in early interpersonal relationships rather than from frustrated internal drives.

One of the leading theorists in the elaboration of object relations theory was Margaret Mahler. Her work grew out of the study of psychoses in children, especially infantile autism and what was referred to as symbiotic psychosis. In an effort to understand how the self emerges, she carried out detailed studies of mother–child dyads. Thus, her theory tends to emphasize the role of mothers;

however the concepts would apply equally to any other primary caregiver–infant relationship. Based on her observations, she identified three phases in the emergence of a balanced, integrated sense of self and other: the autistic phase, the symbiotic phase, and the separation–individuation phase. Underlying her theorizing is a view that the infant brings an innate capacity to engage and extract responses from the environment. At each period, Mahler observed evidence of the infant's drives, motor capacities, interests, and excitability as evoking reactions from the mother and the mother's reactions prompting the infant's reactions (Mahler & Furer, 1968; Mahler, Pine, & Bergman, 1975).

In the autistic phase, which was thought to take place during the first month or so of life, an infant is primarily focused on satisfying physical needs and achieving a state of biological equilibrium. Mother–infant interactions focus on meeting these needs and creating an appropriate state of physical comfort, wake–sleep cycles, and satisfaction of hunger. The infant's behavior is guided almost entirely by internal drives with little awareness of the mother as a separate person.

In the symbiotic phase, which lasts from about 2 to 6 months, the infant takes new pleasure in engaging in rhythmic interactions with the mother. This includes smiling, gazing, some forms of imitation, touching and tickling, and other forms of "dialogue." In this phase, the infant is thought to experience "blissful states of merger" with the mother (Kernberg, 1995, p. 459). The symbiotic phase provides the infant with a sense of confidence and predictability, which also serve as a template for subsequent forms of interpersonal communication. Implied in the term symbiotic is the idea that both the infant and the mother are dependent upon one another and derive satisfactions from their coordinated interactions.

The separation–individuation phase begins at around 4 or 5 months as the infant shows new interest in the world beyond the mother. Mahler viewed this phase as ongoing and open-ended (Mahler, 1972). In the first sub-phase, *differentiation*, the infant finds new satisfaction in exploration of other things and people, especially the father and siblings, and begins to be able to move away from the mother through creeping and crawling. Although the infant may move out beyond the mother, he or she frequently checks back to locate the mother and is more readily comforted by her. Many of the elements of this period are very similar to the attachment process described in Chapter 2.

The second step in the separation–individuation phase, called *practicing*, takes place between 11 and 16 months. This period is marked by walking; new excitement in exploration apart from the mother; and some evidence of aggressive behavior toward the mother, including scampering away, resisting her requests, and asserting a new degree of willfulness. In this phase, babies are thought to have a sense of unrealistic omnipotence. Their pleasure in their mother is not fully balanced by an appreciation of their dependence upon her.

The third step in the separation–individuation phase, called *rapprochement*, takes place between 18 months and the end of the third year. Toddlers show clinging, anxious behavior, manipulative demanding behavior, and a desire to control their mother. This phase is thought to be brought on in part by the child's own aggressive impulses and desire for new levels of autonomy coupled with a new realization of how small and vulnerable he or she is among the world of adults. Thus, the child's earlier narcissism and sense of power are diminished in the face of a new level of reality testing. The conflicts between needs for autonomy and security are frequent and the child finds himself or herself struggling with angry, resentful feelings and safe, loving feelings toward the mother. The intensity of this period is heightened if the mother has difficulty letting go of her enjoyment of the symbiotic phase, if the child's own aggressive drives result in harsh conflicts with the mother, or if traumatic events such as harsh punishment, object loss, or neglect cause a blow to the child's sense of self-worth.

The last phase of the separation–individuation process, referred to as *toward object constancy*, begins at about 24 months but is never completed. This concept has a lot in common with Piaget's notion of object constancy, which will be discussed in Chapter 4. The child is gradually able to integrate the frustrating, angry, and loving memories of his or her mother into a stable representation of self and other. The child achieves a greater tolerance for strains in the relationship with the mother, knowing that the basic bond is pleasurable and positive.

Over time, the representation of the integrated, loving, caring mother is internalized through identification, so that the child can use this representation to comfort himself or herself. At the same time, the internalization of the loving mother contributes positively to the child's sense of self-esteem. "I am someone who is safe, loved, and valued." The child not only experiences the stability of giving and receiving love in the interpersonal domain, but integrates a sense of being loveable into a component of the constant self. The process is viewed as ongoing since this representation may be altered through subsequent life events, and the internalized representation of the mother is never a complete substitute for the real mother's love (Tyson & Tyson, 1995).

This view of the development of normal object relations has important implications for caregiving. It acknowledges the lifelong struggle between autonomy and closeness that is inherent in the parent–child relationship. In order to foster a positive separation–individuation process, parents need to create a comforting, secure context for the child to discover both the self and the other. Parental attributes of comforting responsiveness, psychological availability, and calm reassurance are emphasized. Parents are encouraged to enjoy the symbiotic pleasure of the early phase, but to be willing to stand aside and give the child space to experience separateness as the child requires it.

Object relationship theory has been especially influential in shaping approaches to psychotherapy and parent education. However, increasing attention to the social nature of the classroom and the dynamics of teacher–student interactions suggest that object relations theory may have much to contribute to our understanding of the educative process. The theory suggests that interpersonal experiences impact the person's ability to form new, vital, creative relationships, their approach to teaching and learning, and the expression of maladaptive interpersonal behaviors such as bullying or cheating.

A RESEARCH EXAMPLE: THE REDISCOVERY OF THE UNCONSCIOUS

> Let us suppose … that every mental process … first exists in an unconscious state or phase, and only develops out of this into a conscious phase, much as a photograph is first a negative and then becomes a picture through the printing of the positive. But not every negative is made into a positive, and it is just as little necessary that every unconscious mental process should convert itself into a conscious one. It may be best expressed as follows: Each single process belongs in the first place to the unconscious psychical system; from this system it can under certain conditions proceed further into the conscious system. (Freud, 1924/1960, p. 305)

In the early twentieth century, two competing camps argued about mental functioning. The behaviorists discounted mental processes, suggesting that consciousness was irrelevant in the study of behavior. The psychoanalysts argued that unconscious mental processes were the primary source of information for understanding the meaning of behavior. By the 1950s, the strong behavioral and experimental nature of the study of psychology in the United States led to skepticism about the existence of the unconscious (Bruner, 1992). However, beginning in the 1980s, scholarly interest in cognitive processes has resulted in renewed attention to the notion of the cognitive unconscious, the range of mental structures and processes that operate outside awareness but play a significant role in conscious thought and action (Kihlstrom, 1987). Just as Freud argued, the iceberg model is accurate. Conscious thought, that is the task, emotions, or object-related thoughts of which one is aware, has limited capacity. Even if you are multi-tasking, driving your car, listening to music, and talking on the phone, you are only able to attend to a very limited number of thoughts at one time. It is evident that conscious thought accounts for only a small proportion of our capacities to identify, analyze, recall, and synthesize information (Dijksterhuis & Nordgren, 2006).

One model of the way humans process information suggests that there are a large number of processing units or modules, each devoted to a specific task or category, that operate in parallel (Rumelhart & McClelland, 1986; Gazzaniga, 1989). This approach is very similar to that proposed by evolutionary psychologists. Figure 3.2 provides a model of how the neural network might work to lead from stimulus to action (Greenwald, 1992). The model suggests that perception, attention, memory, and semantic processing may all be operating at the same time. Activity within the neural system moves from less complex to more complex levels of analysis—from recognition of a feature of a stimulus, to recognition of a complete image, to naming the stimulus and linking

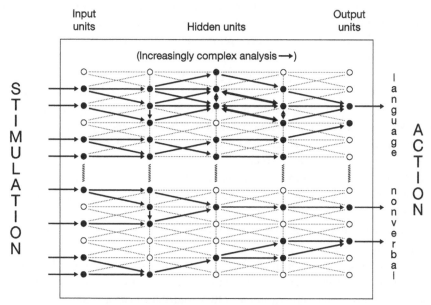

Note: Activity is represented by thickened links (arrows) and darkened nodes (circles). Resonant (i.e. sustained) high levels of activation within a subnetwork of hidden units (black arrows, interconnecting black dots) indicate the selective attention sense of conscious cognition. Connections from hidden units to language outputs provide a capacity of the network to report on its operations. Unconscious cognition in the sense of verbally unreportable cognition occurs to the extent that language outputs fail to report validly on network operation. (Nothing in the network structure guarantees validity of such self-conscious, or introspective, reports.) Unconscious cognition in the attentionless sense occurs in the form of activation of outputs other than those mediated by resonantly active subnets.

Figure 3.2 The Dynamic Organization of Neural Networks

Source: A.G. Greenwald (1992). New look 3: Unconscious cognition reclaimed. *American Psychologist, 47*, p. 774. Copyright © 1992 by the American Psychological Association, reproduced with permission.

it to other related stimuli. Activity also moves vertically across domains so that a stimulus may prompt awareness of shape, color, sound, and texture, all or part of which may lead to recognition of the stimulus and action. Activation of one unit may excite some units and inhibit others.

Information about an object may be found in a number of processing units. The stimulus of an apple, for instance, may be represented in units related to things that are red, fruits, teachers, health (an apple a day keeps the doctor away), and other more idiosyncratic units (such as a fear of bees that swarm around rotting apples, or a pleasant memory of the family picking apples, or the smell of apple sauce cooking in Mother's kitchen). Many mental functions, including language, memory, and planning, could be operating in response to the presentation of an apple as a stimulus, although most of them would be occurring unconsciously. Each time the network is used, connections are strengthened, as indicated by the darkened arrows and blackened circles. This view of the way the brain is organized gives a major role to unconscious processing, which accompanies all types of conscious activity.

Consider three implications of this model for an understanding of unconscious cognition. First, there are many *hidden units* of activity that lead to nonverbal rather than verbal outputs. The implication is that there are processes at work that a person cannot report verbally. Second, in addition to the darkened paths that lead to darkened circles, there are many light paths that lead to the same circles. In other words, there are both conscious and unconscious links between stimuli and action. Some links to output are weak but present and could be strengthened through repeated activation (such as through free association). Third, connections can move in both directions, toward more complex and less complex levels of analysis as well as across processing modes. Memory can alter perceptions, and perceptions can modify memories.

The nature of the connections that exist in the neural network is very individual. For people with a great depth of expertise in a specific area, such as writing news articles or solving math problems, many of the sub-networks of cognition are well developed and possibly relegated to the less complex area of functioning, leaving more conscious attention for the special problems and unique tasks. Each person's unconscious content will differ depending on the diversity of his or her experiences, the acuity and reliance on specific perceptual systems, and the depth or intensity of his or her special abilities (Bruner, 1992).

A variety of empirical studies provide evidence for the existence of mental processes that occur outside of awareness. Here, we are speaking not only about mental mechanisms such as attention and memory, but about the way information is recognized and interpreted. These are big, complex questions about the nature of the mind and how it functions (Greenwald, 1992; Cramer, 2000; Bassett & Gazzaniga, 2011).

Four examples will give a sense of the diversity of evidence. The research on the nature of unconscious cognition is ongoing. Each advance in methodology provides new insight into the capacities of unconscious mental activity, and how they contribute to adaptation.

Unconscious Perception

This research provides evidence that perceptions that occur outside of awareness can influence thoughts, attitudes, and behaviors. Among the early research was work by Bruner and Postman (1947; Postman & Bruner, 1948). Using the tachistoscope, an instrument used in studies of perception and memory that can display a stimulus for very brief intervals under a second, one could present a word at a speed that was below the threshold of verbal recognition. Early studies showed that the time it took to recognize a word depended in part on where it stood on a person's hierarchy of values. For example, a person who valued hard work as a means to success would recognize the word *effort* more readily than would a person for whom hard work was not an especially important value. In addition, they found that before participants could fully recognize a word, they would guess that the word was in a similar value domain to the word that had been flashed on the screen. Finally, they found that when they presented a word that was disturbing, reaction times were delayed. They called this *perceptual defense*. This line of research provided early evidence that some level of meaning was processed before a target word was consciously recognized (Bruner, 1992).

Recent studies demonstrate that **subliminal perception**, that is presenting words or images so rapidly that the person is not consciously aware of having perceived them, can influence attitudes and preferences. For example, participants in one study were subliminally primed with words related to cleanliness or dirtiness. Then participants were asked how much they needed a cleaning product, such as Ajax. Those participants who were primed with words related to dirtiness were more likely to say they needed Ajax than those who were primed with words related to cleanliness (Loersch, Durso, & Petty, 2013).

In a different study, the focus was on the use of priming to activate social categories that may modify aspects of the self-concept. Participants were primed with images of a social group, for example hippies or jocks, and then tested to determine the extent to which they modified their sense of self as incorporating features of the primed social category. Evidence from this research suggests that there is an unconscious process at work through which people modify salient features of their self-concept including personality and physical features to coordinate their sense of self with salient social categories (Kawakami, Phills, Greenwald, Simard et al., 2012). The authors explain this process as a component of a strong evolutionarily based need for belonging through which people unconsciously modify their self-concept in order to increase the sense of similarity with others, a process which is accompanied by heightened feelings of safety, security, and connection.

Selective Attention

Another line of research has focused on selective attention, particularly *dichotic listening*, in which a person wears headphones and different information is played into the two ears. Subjects are asked to focus on information coming into one ear while information is also coming into the other ear. Under these conditions, the subject is later tested for information from the secondary source. Results show that there is an ability to recognize features of this unattended auditory stimulus. This is sometimes called *attentionless unconscious cognition*. Although the kind of processing of this unattended information is usually limited to features such as pitch or loudness, if the information in the secondary channel is especially significant, word meaning can be retrieved (Johnston & Dark, 1986; Greenwald, 1992).

Neurological Damage

A third source of evidence about unconscious processing comes from clinical cases. In a very early case of anterograde amnesia (a condition in which people cannot remember events right after they have occurred), Claparede (1911) tested a woman's memory by hiding a pin in his hand and pricking the patient's hand. When he tried to grasp her hand again she would not let him, but she could not explain why she refused. Weiskrantz (1986/2009, 1997) described the condition called *blindsight*, in which patients have suffered damage to the cortex of the occipital lobes, thus losing their subjective experience of seeing. Upon presentation of visual stimuli, these patients can respond correctly to the presence or absence of an object as well as its location and movement, although they cannot provide information about color, form, or identity. In other clinical cases involving amnesia, subjects may have no recall of learning or being exposed to certain words, but they will use information about the word in subsequent learning tasks (Jacoby, Lindsay, & Toth, 1992). In a final example, Galin (1974) reported on the response of a patient in Roger Sperry's split-brain research who had her corpus callosum (the band of fibers that connects the two hemispheres of the brain) severed in an attempt to treat severe epilepsy (as cited in Levin, 1995).

> One film segment [of Sperry's research] shows a female patient being tested with a tachistoscope . . . In the series of neutral geometrical figures being presented at random to the right and left [visual] fields, a nude pinup was included and flashed to the right (nonverbal) hemisphere. The girl blushes and giggles. [The experimenter] asks 'What do you see?' She answers, 'Nothing, just a flash of light,' and giggles again, covering her mouth with her hand. 'Why are you laughing then?' [asks the experimenter], and she laughs again and says, 'Oh, doctor Sperry, you have some machine.' (p. 573)

These examples illustrate the capacity of the unconscious for implicit memory, memories that are formed without conscious awareness, which influence thoughts and behavior. The memories are intact in some sensory, motor, or affective form, and can survive over long periods to influence familiarity, preferences, and fears or worries.

Unconscious Insights

A contemporary view of cognition and neuroscience is that the unconscious can perform every basic cognitive function that is carried out in conscious thought (Hassin, 2013). The examples provided above suggest that there are unconscious processes that recognize stimuli, remember and categorize information, and link stimuli to related neural networks. These final examples move a bit closer to a view of the unconscious as capable of more complex processing that integrates information from various sources and influences decision making.

The first example focuses on the nature of mathematical insight. The premise of this research is that in the process of problem solving people may use an unconscious strategy that becomes conscious with repeated activation. The point at which the strategy becomes conscious is typically the moment of insight, but the unconscious is using the strategy as a shortcut even before the person is aware of its relevance. To illustrate this process, Siegler & Stern (1998) gave second grade children math problems to solve that involved inversion. The problems are of the type $A + B - B = A$. These problems can be solved mathematically by adding A and B, and then subtracting B. They can also be solved through insight by realizing that the answer is always the first number, A. Children were asked to solve these problems and then to explain how they solved them. The time it took to solve the problems was also measured. When the answer is arrived at through computation, it takes 8 seconds or more to solve these problems. When the answer is arrived at through insight, the solution takes 4 seconds or less.

The children were timed to see how long it took them to solve the problems, and they were interviewed to find out how they solved the problems; 90% of the children discovered the unconscious shortcut before they were able to explain the shortcut verbally. That is, through the speed of their response it was clear that they were using the shortcut even though in their verbal report they said they were using computation to solve the problems. The use of the unconscious shortcut affected the time to solve the problem immediately. In other words, there was an abrupt switch from an average response time of 12 seconds to an average response time of 2.7 seconds. After three or four trials where they used the unconscious strategy, many children reported using the shortcut as a strategy for solving the problem. However, not all the children who used the shortcut were able to explain it as a strategy (Siegler, 2000).

Siegler's research demonstrates that the unconscious integrates information to carry out problem solving. Another program of research has extended this view by illustrating that the unconscious can analyze and integrate information about a number of variables and arrive at conclusions that are more satisfactory than those arrived at through conscious thought. For example, participants were given information about four hypothetical apartments which were each described according to 12 features, for example Apartment A has a balcony; Apartment B has a newly renovated kitchen, etc. Then, they were asked to select the apartment they would prefer. In fact, there was an objectively "best" apartment that had more positive features and fewer negative features than the others. The participants were divided into three groups, those who had to give their choice immediately, those who were told to think about it for 3 minutes and then choose, and those who had to perform a distracting task for 3 minutes so that they could not think about it, and were then asked to choose. This latter group was viewed as making an unconscious choice since their conscious mind was preoccupied with the distracting task. Only this unconscious group reported a preference for the objectively most desirable apartment; the other two groups were not sure which apartment was best. The authors argue that when many variables are involved, the unconscious mind with its greater capacity and fewer predetermined rules and preferences is better able to reach a sound decision (Dijksterhuis & Nordgren, 2006). Thus, the age-old wisdom to "sleep on it" when you are faced with a complex and multi-dimensional decision appears to have empirical support. What you are actually doing is allowing the unconscious mind to integrate information, emotions, memories, and sense impressions to arrive at a direction for action.

The research summarized provides strong support for an unconscious component to cognition. The mind is a beautifully complex organ comprised of 80 to 100 billion nerve cells. It makes sense to think that many of the sensory, perceptual, and integrative functions necessary for adaptation are carried on outside awareness. As our methodological sophistication and ingenuity advance, we are certain to uncover more about the features that distinguish conscious from unconscious processing and the links between the two.

AN APPLICATION: PSYCHOANALYTIC THEORY AND PARENTING

Psychoanalytic theory, focusing as it does on the early experiences of childhood, has a strong influence on the conceptualization of parenting practices. Freud's theory addressed the experiences of infants and young children and the mental representations of those experiences. Implications from the theory have been used to emphasize the importance of parenting for the child's immediate day-to-day life, and for the impact of the parent–child relationship on subsequent personality development and adult behavior.

Freud characterized infancy as a period of oral dependency. This description of infants was extended in work by object relations theorists. Winnicott (1960) described a developmental process of ego emergence in the context of the infant–parent relationship. In the very earliest weeks of life, the infant and primary caregiver are like one system; the infant has a profound need for care and most caregivers have a strong desire to meet those needs by providing comfort and care. The infant has almost no control over the quality of care provided by the caregiver; his or her emerging being is totally dependent on the effective, calming, and responsive care that is provided. During this phase, Winnicott described the quality of early parenting that creates a foundational object relationship in which both physical and psychological needs are met. The essential qualities of this parenting behavior include the following characteristics:

The care meets the infant's physical needs.

The care is reliable, responding with empathy to the infant's changing states.

The care protects the infant as much as possible from harm or pain, through gentle holding, comforting, auditory stimulation, protection from extreme heat or cold, and from loss of support.

> The mental health of the individual, in the sense of freedom from psychosis or liability to psychosis, is laid down by this maternal care, which when it goes well is scarcely noticed. (Winnicott, 1960, p. 592)

From absolute dependence, Winnicott described the infant as emerging into a state of relative dependence. The infant becomes aware of the other person and the characteristics of their care. This period is similar to the stage of attachment formation described in Chapter 2, when the child begins to anticipate the kind of care he or she is likely to receive. Through a process of internalization, infants form a representation of the quality of care, their first emerging object relationship and its representation in mental life.

Winnicott described the third phase in this process as moving toward independence. Infants use their memories, their mental representations, and their repertoire of coping behaviors to reflect upon and, to an extent, evoke care. At the same time, the primary caregiver is able to recognize the emerging personality and temperamental characteristics of the infant, allowing for this separateness of being. In some cases, the caregiver is not able to identify with the infant in the initial phase, resulting in ineffective care and laying a foundation for mental health problems. In other cases, the caregiver is not able to let go of the early identification with the dependency of the infant–caregiver system, thereby thwarting the gradual emergence of the infant's separate sense of self.

Psychoanalytic theory presented a view of the developing child as experiencing strong sexual and aggressive impulses that shifted in focus from the oral to the anal to the genital body zones. The child's ability to manage and express these impulses was influenced by the reaction of parents, especially parents' restrictive or permissive responses, to the child's pleasure-seeking behaviors. Both overly harsh restriction of the expression of these impulses and overly permissive indulgence or stimulation of these impulses were thought to lead to fixations in a primitive mode of sexual gratification. Unconscious conflict about the gratification of these needs, resulting largely from parental reaction, was viewed as providing a framework for adult personality. In particular, Freud pointed to parenting behaviors related to sucking on the breast, toilet training, and masturbation as highly sensitive behaviors where conflict over the expression of sexual and aggressive impulses could become a focus for traumatic anxiety. In this context, psychoanalytic theory led to two important ideas about parenting:

1. Neuroses were produced by the response of parents or significant others to the expression of basic sexual or aggressive drives early in childhood.
2. Early traumatic childhood experiences would contribute to the formation of adult personality conflicts and behaviors that would be played out again in one's own parenting behaviors.

In addition to the role of parents in frustrating or indulging children's drives, psychoanalytic theory also viewed parents as playing a key role in the formation of the superego. During the phallic stage, a child's conflicting impulses toward his or her parents are resolved through the process of identification. As a result, the child internalizes the parents' values and moral standards. The child's superego is shaped through interactions with parents in which impulse expression and misbehaviors are met with acceptance or rejection, permissiveness or control, consistency or inconsistency. Those behaviors that parents accept and value or reject and repudiate become integrated into the child's superego. Since the superego is formed while the child is still young, there is little opportunity for critical reflection and comparative assessment about the content of these moral positions. Thus, when the child grows up and enacts the parent role, it is likely that the moral imperatives of childhood, incorporated into the superego, will guide the adult's initial approaches to discipline and child guidance. Many of the early empirical studies in developmental psychology focused on issues that derived from this theory, such as childrearing and discipline practices, moral development, and childhood aggression.

Several implications for parenting practices emerged from this theory. First, there was a strong emphasis on the early and long-lasting impact of parenting, especially mothering, on the child's development. In this regard, parents were urged to accept the child's sexual and aggressive behaviors as "normal" rather than dirty, sinful, or needing to be "stamped out." Parents were encouraged to avoid either overly harsh or overly permissive reactions to these behaviors. Rather, parents were advised to meet these behaviors with calm acceptance, imposing only those limits that were considered necessary for the child's social integration and physical health.

Second, parents were viewed as the primary source of values that formed the content of the superego. Children were thought to incorporate these values through observation and imitation. Thus, parents were encouraged to recognize that their children were observing their actions as well as listening to their words. Parents were advised to model positive behaviors, recognizing that children were often more impressed by the parents' actions than by their words.

Finally, parents were encouraged to support children's ego development through the use of inductions as a form of discipline. **Inductions** provide explanations for why the misbehavior is wrong, and point out the implications of the misbehavior for others. Inductions may also include suggestions for how the child ought to handle the situation in the future. (I know you want Robby's truck, but you can't just grab it away. Imagine how you would feel if someone grabbed your toy while you were playing with it. You can see how sad Robby feels when you grab his truck. Next time, why don't you ask Robby if you can have a turn with his truck.) The use of inductions supports the ego by giving reasons for controlling an aggressive impulse, and avoids shaming or threatening the ego, strategies which are more likely to result in a defensive reaction.

For psychoanalytic theory, parenting and the quality of parent–child interactions are the basic context for determining the person's ability to manage impulses, to get along with others, to establish adaptive or maladaptive behavior patterns, and to experience anxiety, guilt, or self-confidence and self-esteem. In analysis, the features of these early relationships are brought to life through transference. In some approaches, analysts strive to help clients move through their defenses and resistance to recognize and understand the problematic aspects of these early relationships. This awareness and the discussion that can ensue about early relationships allow the client to reflect upon and redefine contemporary relationships. In a different approach, the analyst assesses the maladaptive nature of the client's early object relations, and by modeling some new patterns of interaction the client experiences an alternative possibility which can be practiced in therapy and gradually exported into other relationships (Safran, 2012). In either case, the quality of parenting and the related fantasies, memories, and defenses that a person has about his or her parents or early caregivers are essential to the psychoanalytic therapy.

HOW DOES PSYCHOANALYTIC THEORY ANSWER THE BASIC QUESTIONS THAT A THEORY OF HUMAN DEVELOPMENT IS EXPECTED TO ADDRESS?

1. *What is the direction of change over the life span? How well does the theory account for patterns of change and continuity?*

   In the healthy personality, over time, the ego becomes increasingly successful in finding socially acceptable ways to satisfy sexual and aggressive drives. The direction of change is from a primarily libidinal orientation, expressed through primary process thought and guided by the pleasure principle, to a more balanced orientation, expressed through secondary process thought and guided by the reality principle.

   The direction of change is largely biologically programmed through five stages of psychosexual development. However, there are important personal experiences that influence how well a person adapts at each of those stages. Continuity occurs because unconscious drives and conflicts continue to seek expression in behavior. In the healthy personality, the ego finds acceptable expression through sublimation. For the neurotic personality, without the benefit of psychotherapy, certain primitive conflicts continue to require defensive control. Unfilled wishes may produce symptoms that are sources of anxiety or patterns of behavior that are troubling and cannot be regulated by voluntary efforts.

2. *What are the mechanisms that account for growth? What are some testable hypotheses or predictions that emerge from this analysis?*

   A certain amount of growth is expected as a result of maturation. The focus of the drives shifts from one body zone to the next. These changes occur in the context of socialization pressures to delay gratification or to redirect the aim of gratification to a more socially acceptable target. The conflict between innate drives and social constraints forces the ego to find new avenues for gratification. The ongoing tension between id and superego stimulates new ego development by forcing the ego to resolve this tension in acceptable ways. Growth can be disrupted if the id or the superego is so powerful that the ego cannot find ways of balancing them.

   The theory is more explanatory than predictive. However, some predictions can be inferred. First, over the first 5 or 6 years of childhood, one would observe a shift in the focus of pleasure seeking from the oral to the anal to the phallic body zone. Second, severe punishment for oral, anal, or phallic activities would result in repression of these impulses. Evidence of this repression would be observed in the repetition of symbolically related behaviors in adolescence or adulthood. Third, overindulgence of oral, anal, or phallic activities would result in the inappropriate reliance on these forms of gratification in adolescence and adulthood. Specific predictions are difficult because the object of drive satisfaction is closely linked to the environment and developmental time when the drive is seeking expression. Fourth, from object relations theory one would expect that early interactions with the primary caregivers will establish patterns that shape later interpersonal relationships.

3. *How relevant are early experiences for later development? What evidence does the theory offer to support its view?*

Early experiences are extremely relevant for later development. In fact, psychoanalytic theory suggests that basic patterns of personality, defensive style, and need gratification are formed by the age of 6 or 7. Theorists who continued to develop ego psychology and object relations theory suggest that basic patterns of self-organization and interpersonal relationships are established in infancy. These patterns form an orienting structure upon which subsequent experiences are based. Freud used the reports of his adult patients, including childhood memories, dream interpretation, and free association, as evidence of the importance of early childhood experiences. Analysts use material from the client's free associations, dreams, and interactions in therapy to raise hypotheses about the nature of these early childhood experiences. Some analysts such as Melanie Klein, Margaret Mahler, Donald Winnicott, and John Bowlby studied mother–infant interactions in order to gain greater insight into the nature and quality of these early bonds and their impact on subsequent development.

4. *How do the environmental and social contexts affect individual development? What aspects of the environment does the theory suggest are especially important in shaping the direction of development?*

Psychoanalytic theory assumes a basic tension between the individual's desire to satisfy drives, and the society's limitations for individual pleasure seeking. The theory views individuals as motivated by the pleasure principle, which, if left unchecked, would satisfy all of one's desires and disregard the needs of others. The role of the social environment is to establish guidelines in the form of laws, taboos, and moral standards that restrict the expression of drives, limit the object of drives, or determine the age at which drives can be satisfied. The social environment may also suggest positive directions for channeling drives through valued forms of sublimation.

In psychoanalytic theory, the most important aspect of the social environment is one's parents. They are the primary love objects. They are also a primary source of fear through their possible retaliation for the expression of unacceptable wishes. Children's ideas about the acceptability of various forms of drive satisfaction are thought to originate from the way parents react to their child's pleasure-seeking behaviors. Through identification with parents, children incorporate the social standards and moral principles of their community. Because of the dynamics of the Oedipal or Electra complex, children continue to seek a symbolic representation of their parents as they choose an adult partner.

In adulthood, a key feature of one's environment is the relationship with an adult love object. The love object provides a context for the expression of mature sexuality and a satisfying interpersonal relationship. Many of the problems that adults bring to therapy result from an inability to form this kind of satisfying relationship, or problems that arise in the context of these relationships.

Another central feature of an adult's environment is the work setting. In work, adults can find outlets for the expression of sexual and aggressive drives through sublimation. Work can provide support for the ego through opportunities for new learning, problem solving, and the expression of competence. Valued work can enhance the ego ideal. At the same time, work can become a context for conflict depending on the nature of the worker's drives and those of co-workers and supervisors.

5. *According to the theory, what factors place individuals at risk at specific periods of the life span?*

The first 6 or 7 years of life are viewed as the most critical for healthy development, with an additional period of vulnerability emerging during adolescence. A child is born with certain hereditary dispositions for strong or weak libidinal impulses in one drive area or another. The child then experiences appropriate parenting or dysfunctional parenting including: overly harsh parenting, overly indulgent parenting, overly sexualized parenting, neglectful parenting, or a high degree of inter-adult conflict. At each stage of psychosexual development, the combination of a child's biological predisposition, strong wishes for drive gratification, level of ego development, and experiences of parenting will determine whether the emerging adolescent or adult has a vulnerability to neurotic fixations and symptom formation. Ego development continues through adolescence and into adulthood. Particularly in adolescence, when libidinal drives are strengthened through pubertal maturation, some people may be especially vulnerable to being overwhelmed by their impulses.

At some point in adult life an unusual experience, a traumatic event, or an unexpected transition or loss can become symbolically connected with childhood. In some cases, the events of infancy and early childhood produce strong, unacceptable conflicts that appear to lie in wait in the unconscious until they are brought to life through events of adulthood. In other cases, unmanageable events of adulthood result in regression to a time of childhood when libidinal impulses were more easily gratified.

6. *What are some practical implications of this theory?*

Psychoanalytic theory is a big theory that addresses conscious and unconscious thought, emotions, family dynamics, problems in living, intrapsychic and interpersonal conflicts, and the symbolic and fantasy life of a person from infancy into adulthood. The primary application has been the development of "talk" therapy. Although its effectiveness is controversial, recent evidence suggests that it can be effective in the hands of skillful practitioners (Tracey, Wampold, Lichtenberg, & Goodyear, 2014). Even contemporary approaches to psychotherapy that do not follow the traditional psychoanalytic model continue to apply certain basic concepts from Freud's approach, including an assumption of unconscious motivation, defense mechanisms, resistance, and transference (Safran, 2012).

Psychoanalytic theory provides a view of mental life that links symptoms and problems to basic human needs and drives. For example, in the anal stage, children are preoccupied with holding and expelling urine and feces. Their control of bladder and bowel functions can be a source of physical pleasure. Subsequent preoccupations with order, control, cleanliness, and dirt are representations of this normal physical activity. In adult life, a certain preoccupation with order, cleanliness, and the accumulation of material goods can be successful ways to sublimate anal drives. However, anxiety over dirt, disorder, or loss of control can be expressed in obsessive or compulsive behaviors. Similar analyses can be useful in understanding the expression of oral and phallic drives. Thus, the theory has had the practical value of helping to understand the continuum from mental health to mental illness.

Freud's work had the practical implication of raising awareness of sexual and aggressive drives at a time when there were many societal restrictions on the discussion or expression of these drives. In general, the development of a model of the mind in which many motives, wishes, and fantasies are unconscious has become a mainstay in the modern view of mental life.

The psychoanalytic theory gives voice to the power of fantasy and symbolism. In a society that values science and evidence, it is important to remember that children and adults invent imagined worlds that can shape their thoughts and behaviors. Fantasies and the life of imagination provide a context for the expression and gratification of drives; a world that is exploited in movies, television, novels, casinos, and adventure theme parks.

CRITIQUE OF PSYCHOANALYTIC THEORY

Psychoanalytic theory offers a dynamic approach to understanding mental activity. It offers a model for explaining how drives, the ego, parental expectations, and the superego all interact to produce mental representations and behavior. The theory provides a model of the topography of the human mind and the interaction among structures across conscious and unconscious domains. Many domains of mental activity, including fantasies, dreams, primary process thoughts and symbols, and defense mechanisms, influence the way people derive meaning from their experiences. Through analysis, the analyst develops hypotheses about the meaning of these ideas and interprets them to the client, who, over time, comes to recognize their validity.

Strengths

Through the concept of the unconscious and the notion of primary process thought, the theory provides a way of making sense out of seemingly irrational or maladaptive behaviors. Psychoanalytic theory recognizes domains of thought that may not appear to be logical to the observer. The nature of the unconscious and its functions continues to be a focus of research in cognitive science, leading to new appreciation for its many adaptive capacities.

The theory emphasizes the importance of early childhood experiences and their influence on adult behavior. While this may seem obvious today, in Freud's time, this was not the accepted view. Children were viewed by some as miniature adults, to be treated as other adults. Another view was that children were blank slates to be shaped by parental teachings. A third view was that children were born in original sin and that their behaviors had to be shaped and punished in order to bring them into a state of acceptance. Freud's theory offered a new insight into the significance of early childhood experiences that were formed by the interaction of biological drives seeking expression in the context of specific socialization environments. Through the extension of object relations theory, a more nuanced appreciation for the significance of relationships with early caregivers has emerged.

In addition to emphasizing the importance of childhood experiences, the theory identifies stages of development. This view includes an emphasis on a qualitative shift in the child's needs and the kinds of interpersonal relationships that are necessary to meet those needs. The stage approach led the way to a new scientific study of child development that, when combined with the work of Piaget, provided a more detailed analysis of the patterns of cognitive, social, emotional, and self-concept development that emerged in the early months and years of life.

The theory acknowledges the role of sexual and aggressive motives and the challenges around managing their expression in ways that are socially acceptable. In his writings, Freud emphasized the link between infantile sexual and aggressive drives and drive reduction, and adult pathologies. He provided a way of conceptualizing adult neuroses as maladaptive expressions of normal drives. Whereas the healthy person is able to find socially acceptable sublimations for drive satisfaction, the neurotic person develops symptoms. This approach helped to reduce the psychological distance between mental illness and mental health, encouraging a more normalizing approach to the treatment of mental illness.

Psychoanalytic theory was highly influential in producing a new method of therapeutic intervention. Through techniques of free association, dream interpretation, and the analysis of transference, clients are supported in overcoming the resistance to recognizing these conflicts and identifying the origins of the conflicts. Over time, the client gains new understanding of the nature of the defense mechanisms that have been used to keep certain conflicts out of awareness, and of the conflicts themselves. By gaining insight into the defensive process, the conflicts, and the role of the symptoms, the client gains new ego strengths. Energy that had been used to keep conflicts out of consciousness is now available for more flexible, adaptive coping. Freud's creation of "talk therapy" stimulated numerous adaptations and modifications which are applied in the mental health field today, including play therapy with children, group therapies, and short-term or brief psychoanalysis.

Psychoanalytic theory was influential in stimulating new theories. Theory development grew in a number of directions. Many of those mentioned earlier in this chapter extended Freud's initial work by expanding the ideas of ego development and the importance of early object relations. A second group took issue with some of Freud's original ideas and wrote their own psychodynamic theories. Among the most famous were Alfred Adler, Carl Jung, and Harry Stack Sullivan.

Adler (1964) argued that a will to power was the basic organizing drive rather than sexual and aggressive drives. His theory focused on the initial physical inferiority of children in relation to adults and lifelong efforts to compensate, creating the concept of the *inferiority complex*. Other contributions focused on the nature of sibling relationships and the dynamics of power between first born and later born children. Jung (1953) viewed personality development as a product of goals and aspirations as well as needs. He saw the direction of development as a striving for unity and integration of the many opposing forces that comprise the self. Jung also introduced the idea that the content of the unconscious included archetypes that were part of the human *collective unconscious* as well as personal experiences.

Sullivan (1953) focused on interpersonal needs and problems in communication. When people become anxious, their communication is likely to be more closely monitored, idiosyncratic, and ineffective. Lack of effective communication increases social isolation and, as a result, increases anxiety.

Each of the theorists mentioned above suggested a new focus for therapeutic intervention. Psychoanalytic theory emerged out of medicine. However, it quickly expanded into the fields of psychology, education, social work, and nursing. Several of Freud's writings, especially *Moses and monotheism* (Freud, 1939/1967) and the interpretation of a childhood memory of Leonardo da Vinci (Freud, 1919/1964), suggested expansions of psychoanalytic theory into psychobiography and psychohistory. Ideas about the role of unconscious sexual and aggressive drives in guiding behavior, the importance of childhood conflicts, and the interpretation of dreams found expression in literature, art, and theater. There is probably not a single textbook about child development, whether in education, psychology, social work, pediatrics, or nursing, that does not refer to Freud's psychoanalytic theory.

The ideas introduced by psychoanalytic theory have led to numerous research directions. Although Freud did not introduce techniques for systematic measurement, his writings stimulated thinking about a vast array of topics that have become the focus of empirical inquiry including moral development, early infant–caregiver relationships, the nature of unconscious thought, identification, parenting practices, and studies of the therapeutic process.

Weaknesses

The approach to motivation offered in psychoanalytic theory has received wide criticism. Some critics argue that the theory oversimplifies motivation by reducing all behavior to an expression of sexual or aggressive drives. Among these critics are those who suggest a different set of basic, or primary needs that highlight the social-orientation of human beings and strong needs for connection, social affiliation, and power. Others, like Henry Murray, offer a comparatively large list of needs. Still others, like Gordon Allport, suggest that the motivational structure is flexible over the life span so that what might begin as a secondary need can take on greater salience based on experience and goals. Finally, some critics, such as Robert White, suggest that human behavior is more properly understood as competency and mastery-oriented, goal-oriented, and stimulus-seeking. Rather than searching for a calm state of equilibrium, human beings often strive to achieve new levels of competence by taking on new and difficult challenges.

Psychoanalytic theory assumes a universal, biological unfolding of the sensitivity of body zones that results in specific stages of development: the oral, anal, genital, latency, and phallic stages. At each stage, the drive for sexual or aggressive satisfaction is organized around specific avenues for gratification. At the same time, the nature of these modes of gratification is thought to bring the child into conflict with societally imposed sanctions and prohibitions which can produce unconscious conflicts.

Several criticisms have been offered about this view of development. The extent to which these body areas and their related functions become a focus of conflict varies across cultures. The theory, developed during the Victorian era, reflects a cultural context in which such activities as breast feeding, toilet training, and masturbation were treated with great privacy. Children's behaviors in these areas were likely to be targeted with harsh discipline and shaming. However, cultural practices and beliefs about these basic activities range widely from relative openness and permissiveness to strict control. In some cultures, infants are able to nurse at the breast of any one of a number of lactating women; children learn toileting practices from older siblings; and masturbation and sex play are openly accepted as a way for children to learn about reproduction. These cultural practices suggest that the issues Freud identified as organizing developmental stages may not be as universal as he suggested.

A particular criticism about the nature of the stages of development focuses on the Oedipal/Electra model and the process of superego formation. This construction of the origins of morality is viewed as incorrect on several counts. First, it places the formation of the conscience too late in childhood. More recent theorists suggest, as we discussed earlier in the chapter, that superego formation begins in infancy as the child forms an emotional bond with a loving caregiver. Second, it overemphasizes the role of the father as a fearful, threatening figure in the formation of conscience. Much of the research on moral development in childhood suggests that the father plays a modest role, partly because fathers have traditionally not been involved in the daily socialization activities of young children. In contrast, mothers play a major role, especially in the way they combine warmth and limit setting in their disciplinary strategy. Third, the Oedipal/Electra model is especially inadequate for accounting for moral development for girls, particularly the ideas of penis envy and blaming the mother for genital mutilation. Freud concluded that, because girls are less fearful of their mothers than boys are of their fathers, they are less likely to repress their Electra fantasies and would have a less punitive superego. In contrast, most research finds that girls are more conscientious about resisting temptation and obeying rules than boys. Finally, it is difficult to see how the constructions of the Oedipal or Electra conflicts contribute to moral development for children in single-parent families or families with two parents of the same sex.

Another criticism of the developmental stages is the notion of latency. The description of psychosexual stages presumes that the years from about age 6 or 7 until puberty are devoted primarily to ego development. However, other theorists have introduced views of this period of childhood that suggest key domains for personality and social maturation. Sullivan viewed these years as especially relevant for the formation of close, same-sex friendships. Erikson viewed these years as a time when self-concept was crystallized around issues of competence and worth. Piaget wrote about new capacities for understanding the nature of rules which influence moral development. Juvonen and others have documented the expression of aggressive drives through bullying, a widespread practice that appears to be deeply entrenched in the social fabric of middle childhood. The term "latency," which implies that sexual and aggressive drives are dormant, misses some of these significant aspects of development.

Another criticism is that the developmental stages do not continue into adulthood and later life. From a life-span view of development, some argue that psychoanalytic theory places an overemphasis on the role of childhood experiences in shaping adult behavior, and fails to suggest important new directions for growth in adulthood.

The stages of development and the processes of psychological tension between id, ego, and superego are based on evidence from Freud's clinical cases. As a result, much of what was inferred about normal development was drawn from observations and treatment of adults who had probably experienced childhood trauma. Freud did not develop a theory based on the longitudinal observation of individuals over the course of their lives from infancy through adulthood. The fields of behavioral genetics and cognitive neuroscience which guide our understanding of individual differences, sensitivity to environmental conditions, and the complexity of cognitive processes were not available to Freud. Thus, his insights into the human mind are more linear and unidirectional than is likely to be accurate. Contemporary human science views development as more probabilistic, with greater appreciation for the interactions of biology, environment, and individual agency in shaping the direction of life paths.

The theory offers explanations rather than predictions. In most of the cases, the analysis starts with the presenting symptoms and strives to find the explanations for these symptoms. The theory does not predict what the symptom will be. There is too much ambiguity in the path from a given conflict to specific symptoms, so it is not possible to test behavioral outcomes based on a known conflict. In the case of Little Hans, for example, Hans had a fear of horses and because of this he grew afraid to go outside. Freud eventually traced this fear to Hans's fear of his father and the related Oedipal conflict. However, Little Hans might just as well have developed a fear of a machine, or another kind of animal, or a fear of loud noises. The theory does not provide a way to predict which symptom might arise from particular early conflicts.

The theory is difficult to test empirically. Freud and many of his followers even argued that the theory could not be studied outside the context of psychoanalysis. For example, there are no guidelines for assessing restrictiveness or permissiveness in parenting and the conditions under which either of these two approaches will result in fixation. Freud was prolific in providing analytic interpretations for symptoms and for suggesting the possible path of a neurosis from childhood to the present. He did not provide any systematic strategies for assessing the strength of unconscious drives, the disruptive impact of childhood events, or the capacity of a person to benefit from psychotherapy. Table 3.1 summarizes the strengths and weaknesses of psychoanalytic theory as an approach for understanding human development.

Table 3.1 Strengths and weaknesses of psychoanalytic theory

Strengths	Weaknesses
The theory offered a view of the mind in which the domain of the unconscious was highlighted as a dominant force, both as a storehouse for wishes, drives, and fantasies, and as a source of influence on mental activities and behavior.	The theory's view of sexual and aggressive drives as the primary motivation for behavior has been criticized on a number of fronts. This view fails to highlight the social needs of humans; that many motives influence behavior; the motivational structure is flexible over the life span; and the nature of motivation is more competency- and mastery-based than is implied by the theory.
Highlights the significance of early childhood experiences, including relationships with primary caregivers, and their influences on adult behavior.	The theory is culturally ethnocentric, assuming a universal pattern of stages and conflicts which does not take into account the diversity of cultural practices that may influence the expression or control of sexual and aggressive impulses at each stage of development.
Describes stages of development in which there are qualitative shifts in the child's needs and the kinds of interpersonal relationships necessary to meet those needs.	Many criticisms have been directed to the Oedipal and Electra complex as a way of accounting for the emergence of conscience and morality in childhood. Empirical studies have shown the reasoning of this aspect of the theory to be faulty on several counts.
Highlights the importance of sexual and aggressive motives.	Freud thought that there was a period identified in the theory as "latency," when sexual and aggressive drives were dormant and little in the way of new gains in personality took place. However, subsequent research and theory has shown that a number of new domains emerge during this time.
Links the early expression of sexual and aggressive drives to adult pathologies, thereby establishing a continuum between adaptive and maladaptive behavior.	Overemphasizes the importance of early childhood and fails to address directions for new development in adulthood.
The theory was influential in producing a new method of therapeutic intervention using techniques of free association, dream interpretation, interpretations of transference, and overcoming resistance to recognizing conflicts.	The theory is based on clinical observations of adults in therapy from which a view of early childhood and structures of the mind was reconstructed. Current research suggests that the process of development is more probabilistic and less unidirectional than the theory suggests.
Big ideas from the theory were influential in stimulating new theories and an extensive body of research.	The theory is more explanatory than predictive.
	Specific propositions of the theory are difficult to test empirically.

CRITICAL THINKING QUESTIONS AND EXERCISES

1. What are some practical implications of the idea of the unconscious and the study of the unconscious for the educational environment? How might an understanding of unconscious processes contribute to fostering a more effective educational climate?

2. What are your own experiences with defense mechanisms? Which defenses have you observed in your interactions with others? Over the course of one week, pay attention to the situations that evoke a defensive reaction on your part. Make a list of these situations. What can you learn from this list about the relationship of the id, the ego, and the superego?

3. Given your own experiences and observations of young children, describe some examples of sexual and aggressive behaviors. What is your assessment of the importance of sexual and aggressive drives in shaping development?

4. What are some specific applications of psychoanalytic theory for parenting and parent education? Visit some websites that are intended to support effective or nurturant parenting. To what extent do they draw on or build upon concepts from psychoanalytic theory?

5. Think back to the case of Tim. Using the concepts from psychoanalytic theory, how would you explain Tim's behavior? Make a list of Tim's symptoms, and try to identify possible underlying causes of each symptom.

6. Imagine that Tim's parents brought him to you for therapy. How would you go about evaluating Tim and understanding his underlying concerns? Which ideas from psychoanalytic theory would be helpful in guiding the treatment?

KEY TERMS

aggression	multiply determined behavior
aggressive drive	object relations theory
anal stage	Oedipal complex
conflict-free sphere of the ego	oral stage
conscience	phallic stage
conscious	pleasure principle
defense mechanisms	preconscious
drives	primary process thought
ego	reality principle
ego ideal	reality testing
ego psychology	repression
Electra complex	secondary process thought
fixation	sexual drive
genital stage	sexuality
id	sublimation
identification	subliminal perception
inductions	superego
latency	transference
motive	unconscious

RECOMMENDED RESOURCES

**Sigmund Freud Chronology. 1856–1939. The Sigmund Freud Museum in Vienna. www.Freud/
Museum.at/Freud/chronolg/chrnlg-e.htm
A chronology of Sigmund Freud's life from birth to death with links to photos, family background, publications, and professional achievements.

**Sigmund Freud Documentary, in 3 parts. Part 1. www.youtube.com/watch?v=3q9IRY_VXPs
A discussion of Freud's contributions to psychology and psychotherapy in the context of his social and historical period and the contemporary approach to working with people with psychological problems. Many photos and brief videos of the times.

**Ericksonian hypnotherapy for an impulse problem* with Jeffrey K. Zeig (2007). APA video series.
A video prepared for the public by the American Psychological Association. The client is portrayed by an actor, based on real case material.

**Play therapy with a six-year-old* with Jane Annunziata (2007). APA video series.
A video prepared for the public by the American Psychological Association. The client is portrayed by an actor, based on real case material.

**Psychotherapy with children with conduct disorders using games and stories* with Richard A. Gardner (2006). APA video series.
A video prepared for the public by the American Psychological Association. The client is portrayed by an actor, based on real case material.

**Safran, J.D. (2012). *Psychoanalysis and psychoanalytic therapies.* Washington, DC: American Psychological Association.

***Psychoanalytic therapy over time* with Jerome D. Safran.
A video to accompany the above book in APA's therapeutic training series. As a companion to the book, the film helps to illustrate how the theory is applied in practice. The video has a brief introductory discussion reviewing the basic principles of the psychoanalytic techniques being demonstrated. This film covers sessions with an actual client in un-edited therapy sessions. Safran helps a client to recognize her own needs and strengths, and to feel more optimistic about the future. The video has a therapy commentary track in which the therapist explains his approach and his reasoning allowing students to gain insight into the therapist's thoughts and decisions. This video may not be available to the public, but may be acquired by qualified members of the American Psychological Association.

**Stoycheva, V., Weinberger, J., & Singer, E. (2014). The place of the normative unconscious in psychoanalytic theory and practice. *Psychoanalytic Psychology, 31,* 100–118.
The authors review five aspects of what they call normative unconscious processes: attribution, implicit memory, implicit learning, affective salience, and automaticity. These processes are all important features of adaptive behavior that are not driven by conflict and defense but have relevance for the behavior of clients and therapists.

**Viktor Frankl's lecture on believing in people's higher sense of meaning and purpose. www.ted.com/speakers/viktor_e_frankl
Viktor Frankl, a renowned psychotherapist and Holocaust survivor, explains his view about how important it is within a therapeutic relationship to believe in a person's higher capacities and sense of purpose, thereby supporting their optimal level of functioning.

REFERENCES

Abend, S.M. & Porder, M.S. (1995). Identification. In B.R. Moore & B.D. Fine (Eds.), *Psychoanalysis: The major concepts* (pp. 463–470). New Haven: Yale University Press.
Adler, A. (1964). *Social interest: A challenge to mankind.* New York: Putnam.

American Psychoanalytic Association (2014). Children in psychoanalysis: Their stories. Retrieved on April 29, 2014 at http://apsa.org/About_Psychoanalysis/Child_and_Adolescent_Psychoanalysis/Children_in_Psychoanalysis_Their_Stories.aspx

Bassett, D.S. & Gazzaniga, M.S. (2011). Understanding complexity in the human brain. *Trends in Cognitive Sciences, 15,* 200–209.

Blanck, R. & Blanck, G. (1986). *Beyond ego psychology.* New York: Columbia University Press.

Blos, P. (1962). *On adolescence: A psychoanalytic interpretation.* New York: Free Press.

Blos, P. (1967). The second individuation process of adolescence. *Psychoanalytic Study of the Child, 23,* 162–186.

Boesky, D. (1995). Structural theory. In B.R. Moore & B.D. Fine (Eds.), *Psychoanalysis: The major concepts* (pp. 494–507). New Haven: Yale University Press.

Borden, W. (2000). The relational paradigm in contemporary psychoanalysis: Toward a psychodynamically informed social work perspective. *Social Service Review, 74,* 352–380.

Brenner, C. (1994). The mind as conflict and compromise formation. *Journal of Clinical Psychoanalysis, 3,* 473–488.

Breuer, J. & Freud, S. (1955). Studies on hysteria. In J. Strachey (Ed.), *The standard edition of the complete psychological works of Sigmund Freud: Vol. 2.* London: Hogarth Press. (Original work published 1893–1895)

Bruner, J. (1992). Another look at New Look 1. *American Psychologist, 47,* 780–783.

Bruner, J. & Postman, L. (1947). Emotional selectivity in perception and reaction. *Journal of Personality, 16,* 69–77.

Claparede, E. (1911). Recognition and 'me-ness.' In D. Rapaport (Ed. & Trans.), *Organization and pathology of thought* (pp. 58–75). New York: Columbia University Press.

Cramer, P. (2000). Defense mechanisms in psychology today: Further processes for adaptation. *American Psychologist, 55,* 637–646.

Decety, J. & Chaminade, T. (2003). When the self represents the other: A new cognitive neuroscience view on psychological identification. *Consciousness and Cognition, 12,* 577–596.

Dijksterhuis, A. & Nordgren, L.F. (2006). A theory of unconscious thought. *Perspectives on Psychological Science, 1,* 95–109.

Ellenberger, H.F. (1970). *The discovery of the unconscious,* New York: Basic Books; London: Allen Lane.

Fenichel, O. (1945). *The psychoanalytic theory of neurosis.* New York: Norton.

Fenichel, O. (1953). *The collected papers of Otto Fenichel.* New York: Norton.

Freud, A. (1946). *The ego and mechanisms of defense.* New York: International Universities Press. (Original work published 1936)

Freud, A. (1965). Normality and pathology in childhood. In *Writings of Anna Freud: Vol. 6* (pp. 3–235). New York: International Universities Press.

Freud, S. (1892–1893). A case of successful treatment by hypnosis. In J. Strachey (Ed.), *The standard edition of the complete psychological works of Sigmund Freud: Vol. 1* (pp. 115–128). London: Hogarth Press.

Freud, S. (1953). The interpretation of dreams. In J. Strachey (Ed.), *The standard edition of the complete psychological works of Sigmund Freud: Vols. 4 & 5.* London: Hogarth Press. (Original work published 1900)

Freud, S. (1953). Three essays on the theory of sexuality. In J. Strachey (Ed.), *The standard edition of the complete psychological works of Sigmund Freud: Vol. 7.* London: Hogarth Press. (Original work published 1905)

Freud, S. (1955). Lecture XVIII—Fixation to Traumas—The Unconscious. In J. Strachey (Ed.), *The standard edition of the complete psychological works of Sigmund Freud: Vol. 16.* London: Hogarth Press (Original work published 1916–1917)

Freud, S. (1960). *A general introduction to psychoanalysis.* New York: Washington Square Press. (Original work published 1924)

Freud, S. (1964). *Leonardo da Vinci: A psychosexual study of infantile reminiscence.* New York: Norton. (Original work published 1919)

Freud, S. (1964). New introductory lectures on psychoanalysis. In J. Strachey (Ed.), *The standard edition of the complete psychological works of Sigmund Freud: Vol. 22.* London: Hogarth Press. (Original work published 1933)

Freud, S. (1967). *Moses and monotheism.* New York: Vintage Books. (Original work published 1939)

Gazzaniga, M.S. (1989, September). The organization of the human brain. *Science, 245,* 947–952.

Greenberg, J. & Mitchell, S.A. (1983). *Object relations in psychoanalytic theory.* Cambridge, MA: Harvard University Press.

Greenwald, A.G. (1992). Unconscious cognition reclaimed. *American Psychologist, 47,* 766–779.

Hartmann, H. (1964). *Ego psychology and the problem of adaptation*. New York: International Universities Press. (Original work published 1939)

Hassin, R.R. (2013). Yes it can: On the functional abilities of the human unconscious. *Perspectives on Psychological Science, 8*, 195–207.

Jacobson, E. (1964). *The self and the object world*. New York: International Universities Press.

Jacoby, L.L., Lindsay, D.S., & Toth, J.P. (1992). Unconscious influences revealed: Attention, awareness, and control. *American Psychologist, 47*, 802–809.

Jahoda, M. (1977). *Freud and the dilemmas of psychology*. Lincoln, NE: University of Nebraska Press.

Johnston, W.A. & Dark, V.J. (1986). Selective attention. *Annual Review of Psychology, 37*, 43–75.

Jones, E. (1953–1957). *Sigmund Freud, life and work: Vols. 1, 2, and 3*. London: Hogarth Press; New York: Basic Books.

Jones, E. (1957). *The life and work of Sigmund Freud: Vols. 1–3*. New York: Basic Books.

Jung, C.G. (1953). The psychology of the unconscious. In *Collected works: Vol. 7*. Princeton, NJ: Princeton University Press. (Original German edition published 1943)

Kawakami, K., Phills, C.E., Greenwald, A.G., Simard, D. et al. (2012). In perfect harmony: Synchronizing the self to activated social categories. *Journal of Personality and Social Psychology, 102*, 562–575.

Kernberg, O. (1995). Psychoanalytic object relations theory. In B.R. Moore & B.D. Fine (Eds.), *Psychoanalysis: The major concepts* (pp. 450–462). New Haven: Yale University Press.

Kihlstrom, J.L. (1987, September). The cognitive unconscious. *Science, 237*, 1445–1452.

Klein, M. (1948). *Contributions to psycho-analysis, 1921–1945*. London: Hogarth Press.

Levin, F.M. (1995). Psychoanalysis and the brain. In B.R. Moore & B.D. Fine (Eds.), *Psychoanalysis: The major concepts* (pp. 537–552). New Haven: Yale University Press.

Levinson, H. (2010). *Brief dynamic therapy*. Washington, DC: American Psychological Association.

Loersch, C., Durso, G.R.O., & Petty, R.E. (2013). Vicissitudes of desire: A matching mechanism for subliminal persuasion. *Social Psychological and Personality Science, 4*(5), 624–631.

Mahler, M.S. (1972). On the first three subphases of the separation–individuation process. *International Journal of Psychoanalysis, 53*, 333–338.

Mahler, M.S. & Furer, M. (1968). *On human symbiosis and the vicissitudes of individuation*. New York: International Universities Press.

Mahler, M.S., Pine, F., & Bergman, A. (1975). *The psychological birth of the human infant*. New York: Basic Books.

Makari, G. (2008). *Revolution in mind: The creation of psychoanalysis*. New York: Harper.

Messer, S. & Warren, S. (1995). *Models of brief psychodynamic therapy*. New York: Guilford Press.

Postman, L. & Bruner, J. (1948). Perception under stress. *Psychological Review, 55*, 314–323.

Rumelhart, D.E. & McClelland, J.L. (1986). *Parallel distributed processing: Vol. 1*. Cambridge, MA: MIT Press.

Safran, J.D. (2012). *Psychoanalysis and psychoanalytic therapies*. Washington, DC: American Psychological Association.

Schafer, R. (1968). *Aspects of internalization*. New York: International Universities Press.

Siegler, R.S. (2000). Unconscious insights. *Current Directions in Psychological Science, 9*, 79–83.

Siegler, R.S. & Stern, E. (1998). A microgenetic analysis of conscious and unconscious strategy discoveries. *Journal of Experimental Psychology: General, 127*, 377–397.

Sigmund Freud Chronology: 1896 (2014). The Sigmund Freud Museum, Vienna. Retrieved on April 30, 2014 at www.Freud-museum.at/freud/chronolg/1896-e.htm

Sullivan, H.S. (1953). *The interpersonal theory of psychiatry*. New York: Norton.

Tracey, T.J.G., Wampold, B.E., Lichtenberg, J.W., & Goodyear, R.K. (2014). Expertise in psychotherapy. *American Psychologist, 69*, 218–229.

Tyson, P. & Tyson, R.L. (1995). Development. In B.R. Moore & B.D. Fine (Eds.), *Psychoanalysis: The major concepts* (pp. 395–420). New Haven: Yale University Press.

Weiskranz, L. (1986). *Blindsight: A case study and implications*. Oxford: Clarendon Press.

Weiskranz, L. (1997). *Consciousness lost and found*. Oxford: Oxford University Press.

Weiskrantz, L. (2009). *Blindsight: A case spanning 35 years and new developments*. 2nd ed. Oxford: Oxford University Press.

Winnicott, D.W. (1960). The theory of the parent-infant relationship. *The International Journal of Psychoanalysis, 41*, 585–595.

4

Cognitive Developmental Theory

CHAPTER OUTLINE

GUIDING QUESTIONS

- What is cognition? How is it similar to or different from the concepts of conscious and unconscious thought discussed in Chapter 3?
- According to cognitive developmental theory, what is adaptation, and how does it promote new levels of cognition from infancy through adolescence?
- What is the difference between how children think and what children know? In education, how much effort should be given to enhancing the capacity for reasoning as compared to increasing knowledge?
- How has cognitive developmental theory informed our understanding about moral development and social competence?
- What are some diverse views about the biological versus the cultural basis of cognition?

CASE VIGNETTE

Every afternoon after preschool, Vivi, who is 3, watches about an hour of television, usually two episodes of *Dora the Explorer*. Her parents, Rona and Lewis, have been impressed by how much Vivi's language skills and pretend play have blossomed over the past few months, and they attribute much of this to her exposure to Dora. It's fun to see Vivi invent new adventures with her dolls, and talk back to the television when Dora gets into mischief. Now, Rona and Lewis have decided to let their 6-month-old infant Micky watch Dora along with Vivi. They think that Micky will start talking even earlier since he will have this enriched exposure to the television program as an infant.

Cognitive developmental theory provides insights into the quality of thought of infants, children, and adolescents, with consideration for the qualitative shifts in thinking and reasoning that take place at various stages. Decisions regarding television viewing are just one among many decisions that parents make about the kinds of toys, games, and other sources of stimulation that they bring into their children's lives. An assumption behind these decisions is that parents want to provide resources that will promote optimal development. However, without a theory about children's cognitive abilities and the experiences that promote cognitive growth, they are "shooting in the dark."

As you read about cognitive developmental theory, think about the kinds of daily experiences that are likely to promote thought and reasoning at various stages of life. What are children able to comprehend at various ages? What might be some changes in the kinds of experiences that will stimulate thought and reasoning at different ages? What role might television viewing play for the cognitive development of infants as compared to toddlers? Cognitive developmental theory offers some answers to these questions and directions that parents and teachers can consider to support the optimal growth of their children.

Cognition is the process of organizing and making meaning of experience. Interpreting a statement, solving a problem, synthesizing information, critically analyzing a complex task— all are cognitive activities. The modern approach to understanding cognitive development has been stimulated by the work of Jean Piaget. Piaget was trained as a biologist. He thought of the cognitive system as a biological system whose purpose, like other biological systems such as locomotion, respiration, or digestion, was to permit the organism to adapt and survive.

According to Piaget, every organism strives to achieve equilibrium. **Equilibrium** is a balance of organized structures, including motor, sensory, and cognitive. When these structures are in equilibrium, they provide effective ways of interacting with the environment. Whenever changes in the organism or in the environment require a revision of the basic structures, they are thrown into **disequilibrium** (Piaget, 1975/1985). Piaget discussed two types of equilibrium: first, equilibrium with the environment, which is achieved through the formation of schemes and operations that form systematic, logical structures for comprehending and analyzing experience; and second, equilibrium within the schemes and operations themselves.

In this theory, **knowing** is an active process of achieving and reachieving equilibrium, not a constant state (Miller, 2011). Knowing is a product of continuous interaction between the person and the environment. We approach new situations with expectations that have developed in the past. Each new experience changes those expectations somewhat. Our ability to understand and interpret experience is constantly changing because we encounter diversity and novelty in the environment that create disequilibrium and put pressure on the mind to return to equilibrium by trying to understand the experience.

HISTORICAL CONTEXT

Jean Piaget was born in Switzerland in 1896. Much like Darwin, he showed talent as a naturalist early in childhood. He observed and studied birds, fossils, and seashells, and at the age of 10 made a contribution to a scientific journal about the albino sparrow. While in high school he began to publish papers describing the characteristics of mollusks. His work in this area was so impressive that he was invited to become the curator of the mollusk collection at the Geneva Museum. He earned his doctorate from the University of Neuchatel in 1918; his dissertation was on the mollusks of Vallais.

The most direct consequence of Piaget's training as a naturalist for the study of cognitive development was his belief that the principles of biology could be used to explain the evolution of knowledge. The observational skills he acquired would serve him well as he developed his theory. Between 1918 and 1921, he worked in the laboratory of Theodore Lipps, whose research focused on the study of empathy and aesthetics. He spent some time working at Eugen Bleuler's psychiatric clinic near Zurich, where he learned the techniques of psychiatric interviewing.

He went to the Sorbonne in Paris, where he had the opportunity to work in the laboratory of Alfred Binet. Binet's laboratory was actually an elementary school in which studies on the nature of intelligence were being conducted. Here, Piaget investigated children's responses to reasoning tests. He devised an interview technique to determine how children arrived at their answers to reasoning problems. He became interested in the patterns of thought revealed by incorrect answers. In essence, Piaget focused on how children think rather than on how much they know.

Piaget's observations and interviews provided the basis for his first articles on the characteristics of children's thought processes. One of these articles brought him to the attention of the editor of *Psychological Archives*, who offered him the job of director of studies at the Institute Jean-Jacques Rousseau in Geneva. There, Piaget began to investigate children's moral judgments, theories about everyday events, and language. In 1923, Piaget married Valentine Châtenay who worked with him on the preparation of *The moral judgment of the child*. In the period from 1923 to 1929, Piaget conducted experiments and systematic observations with preverbal infants. In that work, he began to unravel the basic mysteries of the growth of logical thought. This work was significantly enriched by observations of his own children, Jacqueline, Lucienne, and Laurent.

While Piaget was working in Europe during the 1920s and 1930s, his work was largely unknown in the United States. It was not until the 1960s with John Flavell's publication, *The developmental psychology of Jean Piaget*, that Piaget's theory became accessible to the English-speaking academic community in the United States. By that time, learning theory and behaviorism were the dominant forces in American psychology (see Chapter 5) and shaped the way psychologists and educators thought about how children learn. This perspective focused on conditions under which stimuli and responses became associated with each other, and the ways that behavioral responses were altered depending on the consequences of those responses. Questions about how children come to know or understand what they know were largely ignored. The notion of intelligence was approached as a construct that could be understood primarily through the administration of standardized tests, based on the response of individuals to questions and tasks requiring verbal and mathematical reasoning. Little attention was paid to how children arrived at the answers to these questions; rather the focus was on comparing individuals' scores to norms that had been established using large samples. Against this context, Piaget's work revolutionized the way scholars and eventually educators thought about the development of knowing.

Piaget produced a massive quantity of research and theory about cognitive development, logic, the history of thought, education, and the theory of knowledge (epistemology). In 1969, the American Psychological Association gave Piaget the Distinguished Scientific Contribution Award for the work that had revolutionized our understanding of the nature of human knowledge and the development of intelligence. In 1970, a group of international, interdisciplinary scholars established the Jean Piaget Society (www.piaget.org) to stimulate and advance the study of the developmental construction of human knowledge. Piaget continued his work on the nature of children's cognitive development until his death in 1980, at the age of 84.

KEY CONCEPTS

Piaget assumed that the roots of cognition lie in the person's biological capacities. He hypothesized that logical thought unfolds in a series of biologically guided stages that emerge in a fixed sequence as the person engages and explores the environment. Five concepts form the basis of Piaget's theory: schemes, organization, adaptation, stages of development, and egocentrism.

Schemes

Piaget and Inhelder (1969) defined **scheme** as "the structure or organization of actions as they are transferred or generalized by repetition in similar or analogous circumstances" (p. 4). A scheme is any organized, meaningful grouping of interrelated actions, images, feelings, or ideas that determine how a person interacts with the environment. Piaget preferred the term *scheme* rather than *concept* because it can be used to describe interrelated groups of actions as well as ideas. He used the word to discuss the sensorimotor counterpart of concepts and conceptual networks during the period of infancy before language and other symbolic systems are developed.

Schemes begin to be formed during infancy through the repetition of regular sequences of action. Two kinds of schemes emerge in infancy. The first guides a particular action, such as grasping a rattle or sucking on a bottle. These generalize to patterns of actions for grasping and sucking a wide range of things in the environment. The second type of scheme links sequences of actions, such as climbing into the high chair in order to eat breakfast or crawling to the door to greet Daddy when he comes home (Uzgiris, 1983).

Infants form a wide array of schemes for people, objects, actions, and sequences of action. Infants are able to distinguish between people who are familiar and those who are unfamiliar. They differentiate between playful sounds, such as cooing and babbling, and sounds that will bring a caregiver, such as crying and screeching. They recognize foods they will eat readily and those they reject. These groupings suggest that schemes are developed by mental coordination processes that evolve over time through repeated actions with specific aspects of the environment. Schemes are created, modified, and organized continuously throughout life.

Organization

Piaget argued that all living organisms organize their various structures into a coordinated, integrated system. This is true at the physical and the psychological levels. The capacity for **organization** is an innate feature of living creatures. At the biological level, the respiratory, circulatory, and digestive systems are organized and integrated in order to sustain survival. At the psychological level, a person organizes visual, auditory, proprioceptive, and motor systems in order to move toward a goal. In early infancy, a child can see an object and grasp an object. They are two separate activities. After some time, the infant organizes these two systems in order to carry out visually guided reaching and grasping.

The tendency toward organization operates at the cognitive as well as the behavioral level. The idea of developing a category of objects, such as fruits or animals or family members, is an example of cognitive organization. A person identifies features that a variety of objects have in common, including perceptual features such as shape, smell, or color, and functions that the objects can serve such as something to sit on or something to eat. Cognitive organization serves an adaptive function by reducing the amount of information that is needed to respond to individual stimuli.

Adaptation

Piaget (1936/1952) viewed cognition as a continuously evolving process in which the content and diversity of experiences stimulate the formation of new schemes. People are constantly striving to attain equilibrium both with the environment and in the cognitive components of their mental structures. According to Piaget, knowledge is the result of **adaptation**, the gradual modification of existing schemes to take into account the novelty or uniqueness of each experience. You can see the similarity between this use of the term adaptation and its use in evolutionary theory. Piaget extended the concept of adaptation, suggesting that it works to produce modifications in the capacity for logical thought. "It is by adapting to things that thought organizes itself," he says, "and it is by organizing itself that it structures things" (1936/1952, pp. 7–8).

Adaptation is a two-part process in which the continuity of existing schemes and the possibility of altering existing schemes interact. One part of the adaptation process is **assimilation**—the tendency to interpret new experiences in terms of an existing scheme. Assimilation contributes to the continuity of knowing. For example, Karen thinks that anyone who goes to the private high school in her city is a snob. When she meets Gail, who attends the private school, she expects Gail to be a snob. After talking with Gail for 5 minutes, she concludes that Gail really is a snob. Here we see assimilation: Karen interprets her interactions with Gail in light of an existing scheme about the kinds of students who attend private schools.

The second part of the adaptation process is **accommodation**—the tendency to modify familiar schemes in order to account for new dimensions of the object or event that are revealed. For example, if Karen and Gail were to spend a little more time together, Karen might discover that Gail is not rich and is attending the private high school on a scholarship. She and Karen actually have a lot of common interests. Gail is quite friendly and wants to see Karen again. Karen decides that not everyone who goes to the private school is a snob. She realizes that she has to postpone judgment about people until she gets to know them a little better. Here we see accommodation: Karen is modifying her scheme about the students who attend private school in order to integrate the new information she is receiving.

Throughout life we gain knowledge gradually through the related processes of assimilation and accommodation. In order to have a new idea, we must be able to relate a new experience, thought, or event to some already existing scheme. Also, we must be able to modify our schemes in order to differentiate the novel from the familiar. At first, we ask if the element of the environment can be understood by using existing schemes to interpret it. We may even distort reality to make it fit existing schemes. When current schemes are inadequate to account for the new experiences, successful adaptation requires that we adjust them to take into account the demands of reality. According to Piaget, cognitive development proceeds through a sequence of stages through this back and forth process—comparing new experiences to what is already known, making modifications in what is known to take into account new information, and then using the revised schemes to guide subsequent encounters with the environment. Moderately discrepant experiences can be accommodated, but if discrepancies are too different from one's current level of understanding, cognitive adaptation is not likely to occur.

Stages of Development

Piaget's theory included a description of **stages of cognitive development**. He was working to describe a fundamental pattern of cognitive maturation, a universal path along which the human capacity for logical reasoning unfolds. Piaget spoke of a stage as a "structure of the whole," that is a structure with a unitary character (Piaget, 1955). At each stage, a set of mental operations form mental structures that underlie the sense of knowing. In infancy, these structures are referred to as schemes, repeatable, generalizable sequences of actions, that underlie the child's knowing. In later stages, the structures are organized mental operations that provide a foundation for organizing and interpreting experiences.

Table 4.1 Piaget's stages of cognitive development

Stage	Approximate age	Key features and emerging structures
Sensorimotor intelligence	Birth to 18 months	Sensory and motor adaptation Causal reasoning Understanding of objects including object permanence and categorization of objects
Preoperational thought	18 months to 5 or 6 years	Loose, egocentric logic Representation of actions using symbols and signs Language, fantasy play, symbolic imitation, symbolic drawing
Concrete operational thought	5 or 6 to 11 or 12 years	Mental operations involving the representation of objects and relationships among objects Coordination of mental structures including identity, reversibility, and reciprocity resulting in conservation of mass, number, weight, and volume Classification, including structures for class inclusion and class hierarchies
Formal operational thought	11 or 12 and onward	Mental operations that form a logical system which can be applied to hypothetical as well as to concrete or real-world problems Structures that permit coordination of multiple variables; probabilistic thinking; and reflection about one's thoughts and reasoning

The stages he described encompassed abstract processes that could be applied to many content areas and that could be observed at roughly the same chronological age periods across cultures. His theory focused on the epigenesis of logical thought—the development of new structures for thought—not on explanations for individual differences in knowledge and reasoning or on differences that might result from cultural and subcultural experiences. The stages emerge through times of disequilibrium and efforts to achieve new levels of equilibrium through the processes of constructing new mental structures and new strategies for gaining and evaluating information. Development involves periods of preparation or formation followed by periods of completion or equilibrium that bring a qualitatively distinctive organization to thought and problem solving (Piaget, 1955).

Most summaries of Piaget's theory highlight four stages of cognitive development: sensorimotor intelligence, preoperational thought, concrete operational thought, and formal operational thought. At each new stage, the competences of the earlier stages are not lost but are integrated into a qualitatively new approach to thinking and knowing. The key features of each of these stages are summarized in Table 4.1

Sensorimotor Intelligence

The first stage, **sensorimotor intelligence**, begins at birth and lasts until approximately 18 months of age. This stage is characterized by the formation of increasingly complex sensory and motor schemes such as reaching and grasping, following an object through its path of movement, and means–end relationships like kicking the cribside in order to get a mobile to wiggle. Sensorimotor schemes allow infants to organize and exercise increasing control over their environment.

What is sensorimotor intelligence? Think for a moment of a familiar experience, such as tying your shoelaces. The pattern of tying the shoelace unfolds with little, if any, language involved. In fact, the task of explaining to a young child how to tie a shoelace is particularly difficult because very few words or concepts are part of the process. This kind of motor routine is an example of sensorimotor intelligence. When infants begin to adapt their sucking reflex to make it more effective, or when they use different techniques of sucking for the breast and the bottle, they are demonstrating sensorimotor intelligence.

How do infants organize their experiences? According to Piaget's (1970) theory, the chief mechanism governing the growth of intelligence during infancy is sensorimotor adaptation. From the very earliest days of life, infants use their reflexes to explore their world. At the same time, they gradually alter their reflexes to take into account the unique properties of objects around them. Infants do not make use of the conventional symbolic systems of language and mental representation to organize experience. Rather, they form concepts through perception and direct investigation of the environment. Sensorimotor intelligence develops as a result of the elaboration and repetition of patterns of movement and sensory experiences that the child comes to recognize in association with specific environmental events. With each new challenge, a process of adaptation results in the revision of basic schemes to better predict and interpret experience (Gopnik & Meltzoff, 1997).

One of the most important components of sensorimotor intelligence is the capacity to anticipate that certain actions will have specific effects on objects in the environment. Infants develop an understanding of causality based largely on sensory and motor experience. Babies discover that if they cry, Mama or Papa will come to them; if they kick a chair, it will move; and if they let go of a spoon, it will fall to the floor. These predictable sequences are learned through repetition and experimentation. The predictability of the events depends on the child's initiation of the action and on the consistency with which objects in the world respond. Babies learn to associate specific actions with regularly occurring outcomes. They also experiment with their own actions to determine the variety of events that a single behavior may cause. Eventually they are able to work backward: they can select a desirable outcome and then perform the behavior that will produce it.

The Development of Causal Schemes. The achievement of complex, purposeful causal behavior develops gradually during the first 2 years of life. This achievement requires that infants have an understanding of the properties of objects in their environment and a variety of strategies for manipulating those objects. They must be able to select the most effective strategies for coordinating actions to achieve specific goals.

Piaget and Inhelder (1966/1969) described six stages in the development of **causal schemes**. Subsequent research and related theoretical revisions confirm these levels of cognitive development (Fischer & Silvern, 1985).

Stage 1: Reflexes. In stage 1, approximately birth to 1 month, cause and effect are linked through involuntary reflexive responses. The built-in stimulus-response systems of key reflexes are viewed as the genetic origin of intelligence. Babies suck, grasp, and root in response to specific types of stimulation. Piaget viewed the reflexes as adaptive learning systems. In detailed observations of his youngest child, Laurent, he noted daily changes in sucking behavior during the first month of life. Laurent became increasingly directed in groping for the breast, forming early associations between those situations in which he would be fed and those in which he would not (Piaget, 1936/1952).

The reflexes are exercised both in response to the evoking stimulus and as a part of generalized activity. For example, a newborn begins sucking when the breast is inserted in his or her mouth, but may lose contact and stop sucking. After a few days, the baby finds the nipple more easily, begins sucking more vigorously and can return to the nipple if it slips away. After a few weeks, it is not unusual to see an infant sucking even when there is no bottle or nipple, but purely to exercise this activity pattern.

Stage 2: First Habits. In the second stage, approximately 1 to 4 months, called first habits (sometimes called primary circular reactions), the reflexive responses are used to explore a wider range of stimuli. Often by chance, babies find their thumb or fingers near their mouth and begin to suck on them. Over time, they may try to find their hand with their mouth or stuff their whole fist in their mouth. Gradually, they are able to coordinate the movement of their hand or thumb to their mouth and stop or start sucking voluntarily. First habits typically involve actions restricted to the baby's own body like repeating vocalizations, sucking on fingers or toes, or deliberate kicking. The fact that babies can satisfy their own desires by starting or stopping a motor behavior is a very early form of purposive causal behavior.

Stage 3: Secondary Circular Reactions. The third and fourth stages involve coordination of means and ends, first with familiar situations and then with new ones. In the third stage, approximately 4 to 10 months, called secondary circular reactions, babies connect an action with an expected outcome. They shake a rattle and expect to hear a noise; they drop a spoon and expect to hear a noise when it hits the floor; they pull Daddy's beard and expect to hear an "ouch." They do not understand why a specific action leads to the expected outcome, but they show surprise when the expected outcome does not follow (Wentworth & Haith, 1992).

Stage 4: Coordination of Means and Ends. The fourth stage, from 10 to 12 months, called coordination of means and ends, marks the beginning of what we might recognize as true problem solving. Infants use familiar actions or means to achieve new outcomes. They may push away your hand to avoid a spoon of vegetables, shake a rattle to startle Mommy, or reach out their arms to be picked up. Rather than repeating the same action sequence over and over as in the third stage, the action is goal-oriented and the baby has to draw upon some existing scheme to reach the goal. There can be no question about the purposiveness of behavior at this point.

Stage 5: Experimentation with New Means. The fifth stage, experimentation with new means, sometimes called tertiary circular reactions, brings a new inventiveness to cognition. Around the age of 12 to 18 months, children begin to experiment with means to achieve new goals. When familiar strategies do not work, children will modify them in light of the situation. At this stage, infants are interested in the features of objects and in discrepancies from the familiar. They may experiment to see which of their toys they can push out through the bars of their crib or which blocks they can fit into their dump truck. One can think of this stage as sensorimotor problem solving.

Stage 6: Invention of New Means Through Insight. The sixth stage, from about 18 months to 2 years, called invention of new means through **insight**, is the last stage in the development of sensorimotor causality. It involves mental manipulation of means–end relationships. Instead of actually going through a variety of physical manipulations, children carry out trial-and-error problem-solving activities and planning in their minds, anticipating outcomes. They can sort out possible solutions and reject some without actually having to try them out. The result is insight. Mental experimentation brings the child to the best solution, which is the only one necessary to enact. Key features of the stages in the development of causality are summarized in Table. 4.2.

The capacity to perceive one's self as a causal agent and to predict the outcome of one's actions is essential to all subsequent experiences of mastery. This capacity is the cornerstone of the development of a sense of competence. It involves investigation of the environment, directed problem solving, and persistence toward a goal. Adults' abilities to formulate a plan, execute it, and evaluate its outcome depend on this skill (Kenward, Folke, Holmberg, Johansson, & Gredebäck, 2009; Barrett & Morgan, 1995).

Table 4.2 Six stages in the development of sensorimotor causality

Stage	Approximate age	Characteristic	Example
1. Reflexes	From birth to 1 month	Reflexive responses to specific stimuli	Grasp reflex
2. First habits	From 1 to 4 months	Use of reflexive responses to explore new stimuli	Grasp rattle
3. Circular reactions	From 4 to 10 months	Use of familiar actions to achieve new goals	Grasp rattle and make banging noise on table
4. Coordination of means and ends	From 10 to 12 months	Deliberate use of actions to achieve new goals	Grasp rattle and shake to play with dog
5. Experimentation with new means	From 12 to 18 months	Modifications of actions to reach goals	Use rattle to bang a drum
6. Insight	From 18 to 24 months	Mental recombination of means and ends	Use rattle and string to make a new toy

Source: Newman, B.M. & Newman, P.R. (2015). *Development through life: A psychosocial approach, 12th ed.* Stamford, CT: Cengage Learning, p. 154. © 2015 South-Western, a part of Cengage Learning, Inc. Reproduced by permission. www.cengage.com/permissions

Understanding the Nature of Objects. Through looking, manipulating, and examining, infants establish that objects have basic properties. Very young babies recognize the contours of objects and by 4 months, they seem to perceive objects just as adults would. That is, babies see objects as separate from each other, defined by boundaries, taking up space, having depth, and having certain attributes of weight, color, malleability, texture, and the capacity to contain something else or not. All of these properties influence the types of actions that infants use to explore the objects and the ways they are eventually woven into other actions (Xu, 2003).

Piaget (1954a) argued that understanding the properties of objects was one of the foundations of logical thought. One of the most carefully documented of these properties is **object permanence**—the concept that objects in the environment are permanent and do not cease to exist when they are out of reach or out of view. A permanent object retains its physical properties even when it cannot be seen (Cacchione, 2013).

Piaget suggested that initially, the infant is aware of only those objects that are in the immediate perceptual field. If a 6-month-old girl is playing with a rattle, it exists for her. If the rattle drops out of her hand or is taken away, she may show some immediate distress but will not pursue the rattle. The attainment of the concept of the permanent object frees children from reliance only on what they can see. The ability to hold the image of an object in the mind is a critical step in the emergence of complex representational thinking.

Piaget suggested that the capacity to understand that objects continue to exist requires a level of representational or symbolic thinking, which would permit an infant to hold the idea of the object in mind while it was hidden. It also requires a combination of sensorimotor capacities that permit the infant to become actively engaged in reaching, tracking, and uncovering hidden objects and learning about the spatial properties of objects in the environment. Thus, according to Piaget, the first real evidence that infants have the ability to pursue a hidden object could not really be observed much before 8 or 9 months of age, when babies begin to crawl; and the full confidence in an object's permanence could probably not emerge much before 16 to 18 months, when infants have access to representational thinking. By this age, infants can imagine various movements and displacements of objects without actually viewing them.

As the sensorimotor stage comes to a close, infants have the cognitive resources to expect stability and permanence of objects. The next stage of cognitive development adds new flexibility to mental operations as children acquire the capacity to represent objects and actions through symbols and signs.

Preoperational Thought

The second stage of cognitive development, **preoperational thought**, begins in toddlerhood, when a child begins to represent actions with mental images, and ends about age 5 or 6 with the beginning of concrete operational thought. During this stage, children develop the tools for representing schemes symbolically through language, imitation, mental imagery, symbolic play, and symbolic drawing. Their knowledge is still very much tied to their own perceptions but they are increasingly able to manipulate objects and actions mentally.

The stage of preoperational thought is a transitional period during which the schemes that were developed during infancy are represented internally. The most significant achievement of this new stage of cognitive development is the capacity for semiotic or representational thinking—understanding that one thing can stand for another (Miller, 2011). In semiotic thinking, children learn to recognize and use symbols and signs. **Symbols** are usually related in some way to the object for which they stand. The cross, for example, is a symbol of Christianity. **Signs** stand for things in a more abstract, arbitrary way. Words are signs; there is no direct relation between the word *dog* and the animal to which the word refers, yet the word stands for the object. For adults, it seems natural to use matchsticks or little squares of cardboard to represent people or buildings, but for children, the idea that a stick may be a car or a horse calls for a dramatic change in thinking that emerges gradually during the preoperational period.

Symbolization brings enormous flexibility to human thought. A symbol embodies an idea of something separate from the thing itself, as the cross represents a story of martyrdom, a belief system, and a group of people who share this belief system. Before the period of preoperational thought, children do not really pretend because they cannot let one thing stand for something else. Once the capacity for symbolic thought emerges, children become increasingly flexible in allowing an object to take on a wide variety of pretend identities. With the elaboration of various types of symbols, children can begin to recount events apart from the situation in which they occurred. They can invent worlds that never existed.

In the development of preoperational thought, children acquire five representational skills that support the mental manipulation of objects rather than relying solely on direct behavior: 1. imitation in the absence of the model, 2. mental images, 3. symbolic drawing, 4. symbolic play, and 5. language. Representational skills allow children to share their experiences with others and to create imagined experiences. These skills open up opportunities to communicate about the past or the future, as well as the present. Children can express relationships they may have observed in the past by imitating them, drawing them, talking about them, or acting them out in fantasy. They can portray events and relationships that they wish would occur or that they wish to alter. They can also experiment with solutions mentally, forming and altering strategies in their thoughts.

Preoperational thought is characterized by an animistic, egocentric loose logic. Children tend to reason from the basis of their own experiences, assuming that their experiences can explain events in the larger world. When speaking to young children on the phone, for example, they often assume that you can see what they can see, pointing or talking about things that are in their home or their room. When asked why it is dark at night, a preoperational child might say, "Because I sleep better in the dark." Or "So we can see the moon and stars better." When asked what makes clouds move, a preoperational child might say, "They move along to follow us." Or "They move so we can see the sky."

Grier (5½): What is rain?—*It's water.*—Where does it come from?—*The sky*—Is there water in the sky?—*God sends it down.*—How?—*He throws out buckets of water.*—Who told you that?—*No one.*—Where does he get the water from?—*In his tap.* (Piaget, 1951/1926)

Concrete Operational Thought

The third stage, **concrete operational thought**, begins about age 6 or 7 and ends around age 11 or 12. During this stage, children begin to appreciate the logic of certain causal relationships. They can manipulate categories, classification systems, and hierarchies in groups. The term *concrete* is used because children are more successful at solving problems that are clearly tied to physical reality than at generating hypotheses about purely philosophical or abstract concepts.

The word **operation** refers to an action that is performed on an object or a set of objects. A mental operation is a transformation that is carried out in thought rather than in action. Piaget argued that such transformations are built on some physical relationship that the younger child can perform but cannot articulate. For example, a toddler can arrange a graduated set of circles on a stick so that the largest circle is at the bottom of the stick and the smallest circle is at the top. The child does not have a verbal label for the ordering operation but can perform it. With the emergence of concrete operations, children begin to consider a variety of actions that can be performed on objects and can do so mentally without having to do them physically. Thus, a mental operation is an internal representation of an alteration in the relationships among objects.

Piaget (1972) used the term concrete to contrast this quality of thinking to the more hypothetical reasoning of adolescents and adults. The child reasons about objects and relations among them but has difficulty entertaining hypothetical statements or propositions. Thinking is typically focused on relationships among adjoining or related terms rather than among any two or more terms. For example, children can reason about problems involving grouping trees into different categories and identifying the features of these categories. It would be much more difficult, however, for them to identify variables that relate trees to other life forms such as bacteria, insects, and mammals.

During the stage of concrete operations, the two operational structures that have received the most attention are: (a) conservation and (b) classification. Over the period of middle childhood, children apply these skills to achieve a clearer understanding of the logic, order, and predictability of the physical world. As children take a new approach to problem solving through the use of the logical principles associated with concrete operational thought, they generalize these principles to their thinking about friendships, team play and other games with rules, and their own self-evaluation.

As the order of the physical world becomes more apparent, children begin to seek logic and order in the social and personal domains as well. Sometimes, this search for order is frustrated by the unpredictability of the social world. At other times, children use their enhanced capacities for reasoning to solve interpersonal problems and to arrange their daily life so that it better meets their interests and needs. A hallmark of this period is an increase in logical, focused problem solving. Children are able to consider two competing explanations, look at a problem from another person's point of view as well as their own, and, using this information, plan a strategy to reach a goal.

Conservation. The basic meaning of **conservation** is that physical matter does not magically appear or disappear despite changes in form or container. The concept of conservation can be applied to a variety of dimensions, including mass, weight, number, length, and volume.

Conservation is achieved gradually over the period, with conservation of mass and number occurring earlier than conservation of weight and volume. A child who conserves is able to resist perceptual cues that alter the form of an object, insisting that the quantity remains the same despite the change in form. One of the most common problems of this type that Piaget investigated involves conservation of mass. The child is presented with two clay balls and asked to tell whether or not they are equal (see Figure 4.1). Once the child is satisfied that the balls are equal, one of them is flattened out into a pancake. The child is then asked, "Which has more—this one [the pancake] or this one [the ball]?" Sometimes, the child is also asked whether the clay pieces are still the same. The child who does not conserve might say the pancake has more clay because it is a lot wider than the ball. This child is still in the preoperational stage of thought. He or she is using personal perceptions to make judgments. In contrast, the child who conserves knows that the two pieces of clay are still identical in mass and can explain why.

Conservation of number is achieved at around age 6 or 7 (Halford & Boyle, 1985). Once they have acquired the scheme for conservation of number, children understand that certain physical transformations will not alter the number of units in a set. If ten poker chips are lined up in a row, the number remains constant whether they are spread out, squeezed tightly together, or stacked. Sometime between the ages of 3 and 4, children can use counting to answer a "how many" question. For example, they can assign one number to each item in a set of four poker chips and tell you that there are four chips in all. However, young children have more difficulty selecting a set of six chips from a larger pile, or establishing that two sets of chips are equal in number. They also have trouble solving verbal story problems when no concrete objects are present (Jordan, Huttenlocher, & Levine, 1992; Sophian, 1988).

Combinatorial skills including addition, subtraction, multiplication, and division are all learned at this stage. Addition and subtraction are coordinated operations as are multiplication and division. They form an organized system of mental operations that bring logic and predictability to the physical and social worlds. Children learn to apply the same operations no matter what specific objects or quantities are involved. Piaget claimed that it is no coincidence that schools begin to instruct children in the basic skills of arithmetic at age 6. It is probably a strength of our schools that they meet an important aspect of cognitive readiness at the appropriate time.

Children eventually use the three concepts illustrated in Figure 4.1 to ascertain that equality in any physical dimension has not been altered. First, the child may explain that the pancake has the same amount of clay as the ball; no clay has been added or taken away. This is an example of the concept of **identity**: the pancake is still the *same* clay, and nothing has been changed except its shape. Second, the child may point out that the experimenter can turn the pancake back into a ball. This is an example of the concept of **reversibility**. The child becomes aware that operations can be reversed, so that their effects are nullified. Third, the child may notice that, although the pancake has a larger circumference, the ball is much thicker. When the child can simultaneously manipulate two dimensions, such as circumference and thickness, we observe the concept of **reciprocity**. In the clay ball example, change in one dimension is compensated for by change in another; the total mass remains the same. With consolidation of the concepts of identity, reversibility, and reciprocity, the child is able to conserve in any physical dimension. There appears to be a developmental sequence in the capacity to conserve. Children generally conserve mass and number earliest, weight later, and volume last.

Classification Skills. **Classification** is the ability to identify properties of categories, to relate categories or classes to one another, and to use categorical information to solve problems. An

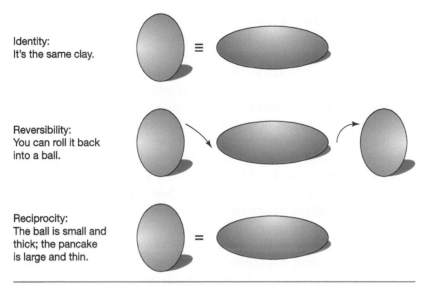

Figure 4.1 Three Concepts That Support the Scheme for Conservation

Source: From B.M. Newman & P.R. Newman (2015). *Development through life: A psychosocial approach.* 12th ed. Stamford, CT: Cengage Learning. © 2015 South-Western, a part of Cengage Learning, Inc. Reproduced by permission. www.cengage.com/permissions

adaptive benefit of categorization is that one can assume that whatever holds true for one member of a category is likely to hold true for other members as well. For example, if water and juice are both liquids, then if you can pour water, you can pour juice. Other substances classified as liquids should also have this property, even substances one has never seen.

From ages 6 to 12, children's knowledge of categories and of the information associated with them expands dramatically. What is more, children have a broad range of categories available into which to incorporate a novel observation. The value of classification skills is not purely to organize objects or experiences into classes, but to take advantage of what is known about these categories to make inferences about the characteristics and dynamics of members of the same categories, members of hierarchically related categories, and objects that are not members of a specific category.

One component of classification skills is the ability to group objects according to some dimension that they share. The other component is the ability to order subgroups hierarchically so that each new grouping will include all previous subgroups. Vygotsky (1934/1962) devised a method for studying classification in young children. Children are presented with a variety of wooden blocks that differ in shape, size, and color. Under each block is a nonsense syllable. The children are instructed to select all the blocks that have the same syllable, one at a time. The youngest children, who would be characterized as preoperational in Piaget's stage theory, tend to select blocks by their color. Their technique for grouping is highly associative. They choose each new block to match some characteristic of the previous selection, but they do not hold in mind a single concept that guides their choices.

Children who have entered the stage of concrete operations tend to focus on one dimension at first, perhaps shape, and continue to select blocks until they discover that they have made an incorrect choice. They use this discovery to change their hypothesis about which characteristics of the blocks are associated with the nonsense syllable. This classification task demonstrates the child's ability to hold a concept in mind and to make a series of decisions based on it. It also demonstrates that during the stage of concrete operations, children can use information from their mistakes to revise their problem-solving strategy.

Piaget studied reasoning about class hierarchies or inclusion by asking questions about whether a group of objects included more members of one subtype than of the group as a whole (Piaget, 1941/1952). Thus, when a set of pictures shows three ducks, six sparrows, and two robins, one might ask, "Are there more sparrows or more birds in these pictures?" This is an unusual kind of question, one that children are probably rarely asked. By the age of 8 or 9, however, many children can respond correctly because they recognize the distinction between classes and subclasses. In order to handle such problems, children have to inhibit their tendency to reinterpret the question in line with a more common comparison, such as, "Are there more sparrows than ducks?"

At about age 5 or 6, children's performance on tests of cognitive maturity is inconsistent. For example, children can conserve quantity but may make errors in conservation of weight, volume, or space. They may be able to perform a classification task correctly when they sort by one dimension, such as color, but may make errors when asked to sort objects that have more than one dimension in common. The process of classifying objects and the logic of conservation are not fully integrated until sometime during middle childhood and may not reach peak performance until adolescence or adulthood (Flavell, 1982a).

As concrete operational intelligence develops, the child gains insight into the regularities of the physical world and the principles that govern relationships among objects. Perceptions of reality become less convincing than a logical understanding of how the world is organized. For example, even though it looks as if the sun sinks into the water, children learn that what we see is a result of the earth's rotation on its axis.

Formal Operational Thought

At the earliest stage of development, children depend on their senses and motor skills to "know" the world. Each subsequent stage frees them somewhat from their dependence on sensation. Through repeated interactions with the environment, children and adolescents discover logical bases for organizing and interpreting experience. By adolescence, their thought processes become increasingly effective at logically analyzing and understanding experiences.

Just as the body undergoes significant changes during puberty, so too does mental activity. Adolescents begin to think about themselves and their world in new ways that reflect a broadening of consciousness. This includes greater introspection or monitoring of their thoughts, greater integration of information from various sources, and more focused planning and control of behaviors guided by goals and strategies. Young people are able to think about several dimensions at once rather than focusing on just one domain or issue at a time. They are able to generate hypotheses about events that they have never perceived and to use logical reasoning to evaluate evidence to support or disconfirm these hypotheses. These complex cognitive capacities have been described by Jean Piaget as **formal operational thought** (Inhelder & Piaget, 1958; Piaget, 1970, 1972).

Piaget proposed a qualitative shift in thinking during adolescence from concrete to formal operational thought. In the period of concrete operational thought, children use mental operations to explain changes in tangible objects and events. In the period of formal operational thought, young people use operations to manipulate and modify thoughts and other mental operations (Piaget, 1972). A central feature of formal operational reasoning is the ability to separate and distinguish between reality and possibility. For example, in thinking about trying to get a part-time job, adolescents may consider the number of hours they want to work, their access to transportation, the kind of work they want to do, and the kind of work they think they are qualified for before they start filling out applications. They are able to create different scenarios about working, based partly on what they want and partly on what they know. They are then able to modify their plan based on new information they obtain about available jobs.

Another important characteristic of formal operational thought is the ability to raise hypotheses to explain an event, and then to follow the logic that a particular hypothesis implies. Hypotheses are tentative propositions or possible explanations about the causes of events or the systematic associations among factors that explain events. One of the classic experiments that Piaget and Inhelder designed to demonstrate the development of **hypotheticodeductive reasoning** involves the explanation of the swing of a pendulum. The task is to find out what variable, or combination of variables, controls the speed of the swing. Four factors can be varied: the mass of the object, the height from which the pendulum is pushed, the force with which it is pushed, and the length of the string. To investigate this problem, it is necessary to begin by isolating the separate factors and then varying only one factor at a time while keeping the others constant. As it happens, only the length of the string influences the speed of the pendulum. The challenge then is to demonstrate that the length of the string accounts for the speed and that the other factors do not. Children in the stage of concrete operational thought have difficulty coordinating the interaction among four separate variables and may lose track of what is being varied and what is being held constant. After trying one or two strategies, they may simply give up. In contrast, being able to use formal operational thought, a child can create a matrix of variables and test each factor separately to evaluate its contribution (Inhelder & Piaget, 1958; Flavell, 1963).

Six Characteristics of Formal Operational Thought. Formal operational thought is not a specific skill or expertise; rather, it is a way of approaching and solving problems based on new capacities for abstract, probabilistic thinking. Six conceptual skills emerge during the stage of formal operations. Each one has implications for how adolescents approach interpersonal relationships and the formulation of personal plans and goals as well as for how they analyze scientific and mathematical information.

1. Adolescents are able to manipulate mentally more than two categories of variables at the same time; for example, they can consider the relationship of speed, distance, and time in planning a trip. They can draw upon many variables to explain their behavior as well as that of others.
2. Adolescents are able to think about things changing in the future. They can realize, for instance, that their current friendships may not remain the same in the years ahead.
3. Adolescents are able to hypothesize about a logical sequence of possible events. For example, they are able to predict college and occupational options that may be open to them, depending on how well they do in certain academic course work in high school.
4. Adolescents are able to anticipate consequences of their actions. For instance, they realize that if they drop out of school, certain career possibilities will be closed to them.
5. Adolescents have the capacity to detect the logical consistency or inconsistency in a set of statements. They can test the truth of a statement by finding evidence that supports or disproves it. They are troubled, for example, by the apparent contradictions between statements such as "All people are equal before the law" and the reality that people who have more money can

afford better legal representation and are likely to have different experiences with the legal system than those who are poor.

6. Adolescents are able to think in a relativistic way about themselves, other individuals, and their world. They know that they are expected to act in a particular way because of the norms of their community and culture. Adolescents also know that in other families, communities, and cultures different norms may govern the same behavior. As a result, the decision to behave in a culturally accepted manner becomes a more conscious commitment to the society. At the same time, it is easier for them to accept members of other cultures, because they realize that these people are the products of societies with different sets of rules and norms.

These qualities of thought reflect what is possible for adolescents rather than what is typical. Most adolescents and adults approach problem solving in practical, concrete ways in their common, daily functioning. However, under the most supportive conditions, more abstract, systematic, and self-reflective qualities of thought can be observed, capacities that bring a new perspective to the way adolescents approach the analysis of information and the acquisition of knowledge.

Egocentrism

The term **egocentrism** refers to the child's limited perspective at the beginning of each new phase of cognitive development (Piaget, 1926; Inhelder & Piaget, 1958). In the sensorimotor phase, egocentrism appears as an inability to separate one's actions from their effects on specific objects or people. As the scheme for causality is developed, the first process of decentering occurs. Infants recognize that certain actions have predictable consequences and that novel situations call for new, relevant behaviors. For example, one cannot turn the light on by turning the knob on the radio. At each developmental stage, **decentering** is a process that allows the person to approach situations from a more objective, analytic point of view.

In the phase of preoperational thought, egocentrism is manifested in an inability to separate one's own perspective from that of the listener. When a 4-year-old girl tells you about something that happened to her at the zoo, she may explain events as if you had seen them too. When a 3-year-old boy is explaining something to his grandmother over the phone, he may point to objects in the room, unaware that his grandmother cannot see over the phone line.

The third phase of heightened egocentrism occurs in the transition from concrete to formal operational thought. As children develop the capacity to formulate hypothetical systems, they begin to generate assumptions about their own and others' behavior that will fit into these systems. For example, an adolescent boy may insist that cooperation is a more desirable mode of interaction than competition. He argues that cooperation ought to benefit each participant and provide more resources for the group as a whole. This boy may become angry or disillusioned to discover that teachers, parents, and even peers seek competitive experiences and appear to enjoy them. He may think, "If the cooperative system is so superior, why do people persist in their illogical joy in triumphing over an opponent?" This kind of egocentrism reflects an inability to recognize that others may not share one's own hypothetical system.

In adolescence, decentering requires an ability to realize that one's ideals are not shared by all others. We live in a pluralistic society in which each person is likely to have distinct goals and aspirations. Adolescents gradually discover that their neat, logical life plans must be constantly adapted to the expectations and needs of others. As they develop the flexibility of thought that accompanies formal operational perspective taking, their egocentrism usually declines.

Innovative Research Methods

In addition to describing the characteristics of thought at various stages, Piaget contributed to the methodology of research with children. His theory of intelligence during infancy (sensorimotor intelligence) was based primarily on careful observations and slight manipulations of his own children's behavior (1936/1952). His theory of intelligence during toddlerhood (preoperational thought) was based on children's answers to questions about their dreams and familiar life events, such as what makes things alive and what causes day and night (1924/1952, 1926/1951). He carried out his research on characteristics of the school-age child's thought (concrete operations) and the adolescent's thought (formal operations) by posing a variety of problems, watching children solve them, and questioning them about their solutions (1941/1952, 1954b). The emphasis of these studies was on how the person arrived at the answer rather than on the answer itself. The children became collaborators, providing Piaget with insight as to the meaning of the problem and the path toward a solution from their own points of view.

NEW DIRECTIONS

Due to its central role in human adaptation, the development of the capacity for reasoning and knowing has understandably led to an enormous amount of theory and scholarly research. We now have an extensive literature that examines many of Piaget's concepts, and another body of literature that extends his theory in new directions. Evidence in support of qualitatively unique developmental levels of the sort Piaget described is quite impressive. The following sections take two somewhat different directions. In the first two, we examine areas where Piaget offered initial theorizing: moral reasoning and reasoning about the point of view of others. These two topics have been extended in theories of moral development and theories of social cognition. The third, fourth, and fifth sections present work that extends and elaborates Piaget's work, suggesting additional constructs for understanding the unfolding of logical thought: information processing, the theory of conceptual structures, and the theory of post-formal reasoning.

Moral Reasoning

Moral reasoning is the application of principles of logic to moral issues in order to decide which actions are right or wrong, just or unfair. Piaget (1932/1948) described the major transition in moral judgment as a shift from heteronomous to autonomous morality. In **heteronomous morality**, rules are understood as fixed, unchangeable aspects of social reality. Children's moral judgments reflect a sense of subordination to authority figures. An act is judged as right or wrong depending on the letter of the law, the amount of damage that was done, and whether or not the act was punished. In **autonomous morality**, children see rules as products of cooperative agreements. Moral judgments reflect a child's participation in a variety of social roles and in egalitarian relationships with friends. Give and take with peers highlights mutual respect and mutual benefit as rewards for holding to the terms of agreement or abiding by the law. Piaget posed situations like the following to young children in order to help clarify the difference between heteronomous and autonomous morality:

> Mark rushes into the kitchen, pushing open the door. Although he did not realize it, his mother had left a set of ten cups and saucers on a stool behind the door. When he pushed the door open, the cups and saucers fell off the stool and broke.

Matt was climbing up on the kitchen counter to reach some cookies that his mother told him he was not supposed to eat. While climbing on the counter, he broke one cup and saucer.

Who committed the more serious moral transgression? Which boy should be more severely punished?

Children operating with a heteronomous morality believe a child who breaks ten cups by accident has committed a much more serious transgression than the child who broke only one. Children who have achieved an autonomous morality believe that the child who disobeyed and violated his mother's trust committed the more serious transgression. Younger children are likely to judge the moral seriousness of an action based on the magnitude and nature of the consequences. If an action, no matter what the intent, produced harm, it should be punished. Older children are able to consider both the intention and the consequences in making a moral judgment. If an action was intended to harm and produced harm it should definitely be punished (Helwig, Zelazo, & Wilson, 2001).

Expanding on Piaget's distinction between heteronomous and autonomous morality, cognitive developmental theorists have described a sequence of stages of moral reasoning (Kohlberg, 1976; Damon, 1980; Gibbs, 2014). As children become increasingly skillful in evaluating the abstract and logical components of a moral dilemma, their moral judgments change. At the core of this change is the mechanism called **equilibration**. Stage changes in moral reasoning are associated with efforts to reconcile new perspectives and ideas about basic moral concepts, such as justice, intentionality, and social responsibility, with existing views about what is right and wrong. Children's reasoning may be thrown into disequilibrium by external sources, such as their parents' use of explanations and inductions regarding a moral dilemma or encounters with friends who reason differently about a moral conflict. In addition, children's own cognitive maturation, especially the ability to think abstractly and hypothetically about interrelated variables, determines how their reasoning about moral dilemmas will be structured (Piaget, 1975/1985; Walker, Gustafson, & Hennig, 2001).

Stages of Morality

Kohlberg (1969, 1976) described three levels of moral thought, each characterized by two stages of moral judgment. At Level I, **preconventional morality**, Stage 1 judgments of justice are based on whether a behavior is rewarded or punished. Stage 2 judgments are based on an instrumental view of whether the consequences will be good for "me and my family." The first, and to some degree the second, stages of Level I characterize children of early school age. Level II, **conventional morality**, is concerned with maintaining the approval of authorities at Stage 3 and with upholding the social order at Stage 4. Level III, **postconventional morality**, brings an acceptance of moral principles that are viewed as part of a person's own ideology, rather than simply being imposed by the social order. At Stage 5, justice and morality are determined by a democratically derived social contract. At Stage 6, a person develops a sense of universal ethical principles that apply across history and cultural contexts.

According to this theory, the stages form a logical hierarchy. At each new stage, individuals reorganize their view of morality, realizing the inadequacy of the stage below. For example, once a person sees morality in terms of a system that upholds and protects the social order (Stage 4), then reasoning that argues for an act as moral because it was rewarded or immoral because it was punished is seen as inadequate. The stages form an invariant sequence, moving from a very idiosyncratic, personal view of morality, to a view in which rules and laws are obeyed because they have been established by an authority or a society, and finally, to an understanding of rules and laws as created to uphold basic principles of fairness, justice, and humanity (Boom, Brugman, & van der Heijden, 2001).

Longitudinal studies in a variety of countries observe an evolution of moral thought much like that proposed by Kohlberg in which the reasoning shifts from an idiosyncratic to a more principled approach to evaluating moral conflicts (Gielen & Markoulis, 2001). Critics point out that there is a difference between moral reasoning and moral behavior. Often, moral behavior is based on a rapid emotional reaction to the situation followed by a slower process of reasoning. In addition, cultures and families differ in the content of their moral codes. The cognitive developmental focus is on the quality of the reasoning, not on the emotional reaction or the cultural content that may guide moral action (Arnold, 2000; Haidt, 2013).

Social Cognition

Another area of interest has been **social cognition,** the development of knowledge about the self and others. What do children understand about how others view the world? At what point do children understand that their point of view and that of another person may differ? You may appreciate the link between these questions and the issues raised by the object relations theorists. What do infants and children know about *"the other"* and how does their thinking about *the other* mature with age? These questions are central to the field of social cognition. Researchers have traced the development of the ability to take the point of view of another person by studying empathy and perspective taking. Empathy typically refers to the ability to identify and experience the emotional state of another person. **Perspective taking** refers to the cognitive capacity to consider a situation from the point of view of another person. This requires a recognition that someone else's point of view may differ from one's own. It also requires the ability to analyze the factors that may account for these differences (Flavell, 1974; Piaget, 1932/1948; Selman, 1971).

Piaget introduced the importance of perspective taking in his study of moral development and subsequently in his analysis of concrete operational reasoning. He posed problems in which children were asked to place objects on a mat to reflect how the person sitting across from them would see the objects. Young children have difficulty with this type of task; their own view of the situation is more convincing than the idea that someone else sees it differently. With development, children are increasingly able to coordinate multiple perspectives.

Imagine a child who wants to play with another child's toy. If the first child thinks, "If I had that toy, I would be happy, and if I am happy, everyone is happy," then she or he may take the toy without anticipating that the other child will be upset. Recognizing the differences between your own view of a situation and the view of others requires perspective taking. The capacity to take another person's perspective is achieved gradually through parental explanations called inductions, peer interactions, social pretend play, conflict, and role playing.

Theory of Mind

From ages 4 to 6, children become more aware that people have different points of view. Work on **theory of mind** focuses on the natural way children understand another person's behavior. The theory of mind suggests that people form a theory of others based on a view that beliefs, desires, and actions are logically linked. A person engages in some action because he or she believes that this action will satisfy a specific desire. For example, Jakob wants his father to take him to the toy store because he wants a new toy train and he believes that he can get one at the toy store. In trying to understand a person's actions, it is important to consider the interaction of beliefs and desires since they operate together to guide action (Wellman, 1990).

Research on theory of mind typically poses situations to children to see what they understand about someone else's beliefs and desires. For example, in the early research children watched a character named Maxi put a chocolate candy in one location. Then, when Maxi leaves, children watched while another character moved the chocolate to a new place. Children were asked what Maxi thinks or what Maxi will do when he comes back into the room. Where does Maxi believe the chocolate is located? Where will Maxi look (action) for the chocolate? Three-year-olds typically said that Maxi will look for the chocolate where they know it is, in the new location. Older children ages 4 and 5 realized that Maxi has an incorrect belief and predicted that Maxi will look for the chocolate in its old location (Wimmer & Perner, 1983; Wellman, Cross, & Watson, 2001).

Subsequent research using similar scenarios finds that children as young as 3 are very good at considering what a character wants, even if it is different from what they might want. However, they have trouble thinking about what someone else might believe, especially disconnecting their own knowledge of the situation from the point of view of another. By the time children are 5, however, they are quite skilled at detecting the possibility of false or incorrect beliefs. They can separate what they know about a situation from what someone else may know, and they expect that a character's actions will be based on the character's beliefs, even when those beliefs are incorrect (Ziv & Frye, 2003).

The ability to appreciate that what you know or believe to be true is different from what others know and believe to be true is a salient feature of social cognition. It allows children to begin to speculate about what others may think about them, and how their behavior may be understood or misunderstood.

As children interact with peers who see the world differently than they do, they begin to understand the limits of their own points of view. Piaget (1932/1948) suggested that peers have an important influence in diminishing one another's self-centered outlook precisely because they interact as equals. Children are not forced to accept one another's ideas in quite the same way as they are with adults. They argue, bargain, and eventually compromise in order to maintain friendships. The opportunity to function in peer groups for problem solving and for play leads children away from the egocentrism of early childhood and closer to the eventual flexibility of adult thought. The benefit of these interactions is most likely to occur when peers have differences in perspective that result in conflicts that must be resolved. The benefits are especially positive for children who interact with slightly more competent peers who can introduce more advanced or flexible approaches to problem solving (Tudge, 1992).

Social Perspective Taking

Building on Piaget's ideas about the maturing capacity for perspective taking, Robert Selman (1980) studied the process of social perspective taking by analyzing children's responses to peer conflicts. Children watched audiovisual filmstrips that depicted interpersonal conflicts. They were then asked to describe the motivation of each actor and the relationships among the various performers. Four levels of social perspective taking were described. At Level 1, the youngest children (4–6 years old) recognized different emotions in the various actors, but they assumed that all the actors viewed the situation much as they did. The children at Level 4 (about 10–12 years old) realized that two people were able to take each other's perspective into account before deciding how to act. Furthermore, they realized that each of those people may have viewed the situation differently from the way they did. Many moral dilemmas require that children subordinate their personal needs for someone else's sake. To resolve such situations, children must be able to separate their personal wants from the other person's. Selman's research suggested that children under 10 can rarely approach interpersonal conflicts with this kind of objectivity (Selman, 1994; Kwok & Selman, 2012).

The behavior of well-adjusted, competent children is maintained in part by a number of cognitive abilities, including social perspective taking, interpersonal problem solving, and reflection. These cognitive abilities foster a child's entry into successful peer interactions. At the same time, active participation with peers promotes the development of these social-cognitive abilities.

Information Processing

Information processing focuses on how individuals make sense of the great amount of information that is present in their environment, how they analyze tasks in order to perform them effectively, how they translate their analyses into plans for action, and how they implement their plans. The computer is the primary metaphor for this approach. Within a developmental perspective, studies have focused on six areas where aspects of information processing improve from childhood to adolescence: attention, working memory, long-term memory, processing speed, organizational strategies, and self-modification. Other aspects of information processing that are currently being studied include planning, decision making, goal setting, coping, and the relationship of motivation to these activities. Cognitive neuroscience is an emerging field that links these cognitive aspects of information processing to neurological processes, providing evidence for changes in neural networks as a result of experience, and the involvement of various aspects of the brain in different types of cognitive tasks (Rose, Feldman, & Jankowski, 2009; Keating, 2004; Demetriou, Christou, Spanoudis, & Platsidou, 2002).

Attention

The first step in information processing is **attention**. In order for something to be processed, the person has to attend to it. Every sensory system has a sensory register or a capacity to process a particular kind of sensory information. A person's attention can be directed to a stimulus through one or more of these sensory systems. Something comes to your attention because you hear it or smell it. Things can also come to one's attention through several systems at once—you smell and hear the stimulus. Information is held in the sensory register for a brief time, and then processed further in short-term memory. There is evidence that as a person gets older, development involves improvements in *selective attention*, where a person focuses on one kind of information and ignores others, and improvements in divided attention, where a person can stay focused on two different sources of information (Higgins & Turnure, 1984; Schiff & Knopf, 1985; Casteel, 1993). Reading and listening to music at the same time is an example of *divided attention*. Problems in the development of attention, such as Attention Deficit and Hyperactivity Disorder (ADHD), have become extremely prevalent in our society as we increase demands for information processing.

Short-Term Memory

Short-term memory is also called *working memory*. Once information has made an impact on the sensory register it is held for a brief time in the working memory. Adults can generally keep five to nine units of information in working memory for about 30 seconds. After that time, the information is either transferred to long-term memory by linking it to other knowledge and information, repeated in order to hold it in short-term memory, or lost from memory. When you meet a new person and ask their name, you can recall the name easily for 30 seconds. However, unless you take some steps to transfer the name into long-term storage, it is likely that you will forget the name once the next event catches your attention and makes an impression on the sensory register. Strategies for transferring the information from working memory to long-term memory can include repeating the information several times, putting the information in a familiar context, or connecting the information with a unique word or image that will help you retrieve it. The short-term memory can be used as a scratch pad for combining new information with information from long-term memory to perform calculations or other manipulations, such as planning. You can also call up information from the long-term memory to review it, build thoughts and concepts, and evaluate outcomes.

Long-Term Memory

Long-term memory is a complex network of information, concepts, and schemes related by associations, knowledge, and use. It is the storehouse of a lifetime of information. Studies of memory focus on different kinds of tasks, each with their own trajectory of growth and decline. *Semantic memory* focuses on basic knowledge such as recalling the meaning of words such as vegetable, democracy, or insect. Once learned, information in the semantic memory is very resistant to loss. *Episodic memory* focuses on specific situations and data. Studies of episodic memory may ask people to recall words from a list or to recall what they had for breakfast three days ago. Unless the events have some particular importance, they may not be encoded or they may be difficult to retrieve. *Prospective memory* is memory about events or actions that will take place in the future. An example would be remembering to take your medicine at 4 o'clock in the afternoon or remembering to go to class at 10 a.m. This type of memory requires that something needs to happen at a future time or under some future condition and also remembering what needs to be done.

Memory capacity appears to improve from infancy through adolescence due to several factors (Keating, 2004). With age, neurological development results in increased processing speed. This means that it takes less time to encode and retrieve information. There is also a process of neural pruning, resulting in stronger associations among neural networks. As children acquire more information, this permits more rapid storage of new information in connection with existing knowledge and results in a greater chance for retrieval. In studies of memory capacity in adulthood, short-term memory does not differ much between younger and older adults. However, older adults appear to have greater difficulty transferring new information from short-term to long-term storage, and then retrieving it upon demand. They also rely more on context and meaning for information storage and retrieval, and are not as effective as younger adults in recalling random numbers or nonsense syllables, especially when this type of information is presented rapidly (Zelinski & Lewis, 2003).

There are different types of memory for different kinds of activities. The more a child reads, the easier it is to recognize new words. Memory for words does not necessarily result in better memory for solving puzzles or computing arithmetic problems. Exposure to each area of knowledge is associated with a growing capacity to store information and retrieve it. In adulthood, effective coping requires that one directs attention on storing and retrieving the details of information that are most salient for success in work and family life.

Organizational Strategies

Over time, children become more proactive in imposing **organizational strategies** that help preserve and retrieve information, manage more information by chunking or grouping bits of information together, and by linking new information with information that has already been stored (Siegler & Alibali, 2005). For example, young children learn to whisper instructions to themselves, repeat information, give numbers or letters to a list of items, or make up rhymes to help them remember things. Improvement in using organizational capacities to manage information is associated with maturation of the prefrontal cortex, the site of a complex capacity often referred to as executive function (Miller, Freedman, & Wallis, 2003). Executive functions include working memory, planning and organizing, and the ability to resist distractions and inhibit inappropriate impulses. Individual differences in executive functions have been attributed to genetic factors, prenatal environment, and caregiving quality in infancy and toddlerhood (Leve, DeGarmo, Bridgett et al., 2013; Cuevas, Deater-Deckard, Kim-Spoon et al., 2014). Executive functions mature throughout childhood and adolescence into early adulthood, providing a neurological foundation for advances in scientific reasoning, logical problem solving, and planning.

The Theory of Central Conceptual Structures

In the 1970s and 1980s, scholars began to raise questions about the adequacy of Piaget's conceptual framework for describing cognitive development in children. A group of theorists, sometimes referred to as neo-Piagetian theorists, emerged (Morra, Gobbo, Marini, & Sheese, 2008; Young, 2011). The neo-Piagetians agreed with Piaget's characterization of development as stage-like rather than continuous. They also considered biological maturation as providing the basic constraints on cognition at any given age. And they agreed that children are developing internal mental structures that support logic and reasoning across problems. However, they argued that Piaget's broad characterization of stage-related mental structures was too general, that it did not take into consideration emerging evidence from neuroscience about the maturation of the brain, and that it did not consider the insights and skills derived from instruction and practice that can advance children's reasoning. Their work provided explanations for content-specific advances in reasoning, and explanations for individual differences based on education, socioeconomic background, and neurological development.

Robbie Case's theory of Central Conceptual Structures is an example of this neo-Piagetian perspective (Case, 1998). Case sought to integrate three fields of study to account for changes in cognitive functioning: the empiricist, the rationalist, and the sociohistoric perspectives. From the empiricist tradition, he drew on evidence about changes in processing speed, memory, and executive control to explain that as children get older they can keep more information in the mind at once, thereby allowing them to organize, coordinate, and compare data in order to solve problems. At the same time, he observed that children did not advance in their reasoning at the same rate across specific domains. The ability to coordinate dimensions related to number did not generalize to this same ability in problems involving spatial relations or interpersonal problems. This led him to hypothesize the emergence of **central conceptual structures** within task areas rather than across fields.

From the rationalist tradition, Case sought to characterize the qualitative shifts in reasoning that are observed as children approach similar problems. The rationalist tradition assumes that intelligence involves more than the ability to detect and remember information; it requires one to impose structures on information in order to organize and interpret it. Stages of reasoning emerge as a result of the maturing capacity for **executive control** through which children are able to represent and manipulate the relationships among elements of a problem. In the early phases, independent exploration and imitation provide support for structural development. The combination of biological maturation, instruction, and practice contribute to the child's increasing efficiency and systematic approach to problem solving.

The sociohistorical perspective focuses on the physical, historical, and social contexts in which learning takes place. What is known, what is considered valuable information, and how ideas are explained or taught differ across time and cultures. Case acknowledged the role of instruction through guided teaching, expanded opportunities for exploration, and encouragement for practice. Advances in reasoning emerge as operations become more and more efficient, a result of the integration of neurological maturation, independent exploration, practice, and instruction (Case, 1987).

The product of this approach was the theory of Central Conceptual Structures (Case & Okamoto, 1996). "Central conceptual structures were originally defined as networks of semantic modes and relations that have an extremely broad (but not system-wide) domain of application and that are central to children's functioning in that domain" (Case & Okamoto, 1996, p. 5). Through empirical study of children's understanding of number, Case provided an example of this idea of a conceptual structure. At the age of 4 many children can count to 5, and they can judge quantity when groups of items are presented to them in order to say which group has more. However, they are often incorrect in answering a question like: which is bigger 4 or 5? In other words, the central conceptual structure that links a number word, like two or four, to an idea of a set of items with a certain quantity, has not yet emerged. By the age of about 6, children understand that giving an item a new number tag or word is the same as changing its quantity. The conceptual structure of the relationship between numbers and quantity becomes a tool that can be used in many problems involving quantity such as assessing distance, or measuring length or weight.

Case suggested that structures, such as the one described here, depend upon the maturation of certain central processing capacities, especially processing speed and short-term memory storage, and the development of executive functions that support the integration of information, especially the ability to attend to and organize multiple elements. Once a central conceptual structure is formed, it provides a way of understanding a variety of situations within and across content areas. These central conceptual structures are the basic building blocks upon which more complex structures are based.

The specific conceptual structure differs from one domain to another. For example the basic understanding of the relationship of number words and quantity is a central conceptual structure for arithmetic, and may apply to other domains where measuring and counting are important. It is not the central conceptual structure for social understanding, for example that behaviors of another person may be intentional and motivated by needs and desires. Each domain has its own conceptual structure. However, the process of moving from labeling states to recognizing the link between states and then attributing causal or relational characteristics to these states is roughly the same. Thus, Case offers a model of cognitive development that is at once content-specific and developmentally general, suggesting a common path of development while also accounting for individual differences based on biological maturation, experience with problems in a particular domain, and practice.

The Theory of Post-Formal Reasoning

Cognitive theorists are beginning to document the direction of developmental changes during the stages of adulthood. Research on adult problem solving and reasoning has been inconclusive.

Some studies have shown that adults tend to be practical rather than hypothetical in their approach to tasks. Others have emphasized adults' increasing capacity to maintain opposing ideas and to find solutions that are adaptive in a given context (Labouvie-Vief, 1992).

Research based on the standard Piagetian tasks has been criticized for its lack of relevance and familiarity to older adults. The traditional tasks are dominated by the role of pure logic, disconnected from the situation. They emphasize problems that have a scientific rather than a pragmatic focus. Although the solution to most formal operational problems requires the manipulation of multiple variables, there is typically only one correct solution, as in the answer to the pendulum problem. In adult life, most problems involve multiple dimensions with changing or poorly defined variables and more than one solution. (For example, given my limited resources, should I buy more life insurance, put cash in a certificate of deposit, or invest in the stock and/ or bond market to best protect my family's financial future?) Much of the demand for systematic reasoning and decision making in daily life requires a person to think about several possible solutions, each one with potential costs as well as benefits. These problems are embedded in cultural and social circumstances so that a good answer or a "right" answer depends on one's point of view (Kincheloe & Steinberg, 1993; Berg & Strough, 2011).

As a result of these limitations or criticisms of formal operational reasoning, scholars have begun to formulate a view of postformal thought. Postformal thought has been characterized in the following ways (Commons & Richards, 2003):

A greater reliance on reflection on self, emotions, values, and the specific situation in addressing a problem.

A willingness to shift gears or take a different approach depending on the specific problem.

An ability to draw on personal knowledge to find pragmatic solutions.

An awareness of the contradictions in life and a willingness to try to include conflicting or contradictory thoughts, emotions, and experiences in finding a solution.

A flexible integration of cognition and emotion so that solutions are adaptive, reality-oriented, and emotionally satisfying.

An enthusiasm for seeking new questions, finding new frameworks for understanding experience.

People who operate with postformal thought do not do so in every situation. When a problem has clear parameters and needs a single solution, concrete or formal operations will work. However, when a problem is value-laden, ambiguous, or involving many inter-personal implications, postformal thinking comes into play (Sinnott & Cavanaugh, 1991; Labouvie-Vief, 1992). The cognitive processes associated with the roles of psychotherapist, diplomat, or community leader are all examples of the kinds of adult roles that require postformal thought.

A RESEARCH EXAMPLE: METACOGNITION

Metacognition refers to a range of processes and strategies used to assess and monitor knowledge. It includes the "feeling of knowing" that accompanies problem solving, the ability to distinguish ideas about which we are confident from those which we doubt (Tarricone, 2011). Piaget's study of children's intelligence included a method of inquiry in which he asked children to explain how they knew an answer to a problem. This approach led the way to early investigations of metacognition. Rather than being concerned solely with the exact answers children gave, he wanted to understand how they reasoned to arrive at their answers. Being able to tell someone else about your reasoning is a component of metacognition.

In his description of formal operational reasoning, Piaget emphasized the capacity for applying principles of logical reasoning to an analysis of one's own thoughts. Rather than operating on objects, as takes place during the stage of concrete operational thought, adolescents and adults can impose propositional logic on hypotheses, carrying out mental operations in order to assess the logic of relationships and propositions. This analysis of the developmental direction of cognition inspired new research on metacognition and executive control. This research suggests that during the second decade of life, the person is increasingly able to manage the focus and direction of his or her thoughts, deciding what to think about and how to evaluate knowledge (Kuhn, 2006). As they approach problem solving and new learning, adolescents are better able than younger children to monitor and manage their learning strategies, and to create effective approaches to gathering and evaluating information.

One element of the "feeling of knowing" is understanding the source of one's beliefs. For example, we can be told about sand, we can see pictures of sand, or we can feel and touch it. All three of these sources of information may coincide to create a single belief, or we may discover that there are inconsistencies between what someone says is true and what we perceive through sight or touch. By the ages of 4 and 5, children are able to understand how all three sources of information have contributed to their understanding of an experience (O'Neill & Gopnik, 1991).

Research on the emotion of *interest* highlights the role of metacognition in the process of knowledge acquisition and learning (Izard & Ackerman, 2000). People are likely to spend more time exploring something if it is interesting. They look longer at paintings that are interesting, spend more time trying to understand written materials that are interesting, and work harder at trying to solve problems that are interesting. The cognitive appraisal perspective suggests that emotions are associated with distinct patterns of appraisal. According to research by Paul Silvia (2005), the emotion we refer to as "interest" is a product of the interaction of two types of appraisals. First, when an event or stimulus occurs, a person makes a *novelty* appraisal. This appraisal assesses whether the event is new, complex, unexpected, mysterious, or in some other way creates disequilibrium in existing schema. Second, the person makes an appraisal of his or her *coping potential* with regard to the stimulus. This refers to an assessment of whether the person has the ability to understand the new stimulus. When a stimulus is appraised as both novel or complex and also understandable, interest is high.

In order to study this, Silvia (2005) asked students to react to an abstract, complex, and unfamiliar poem. For half the group, he provided instructions in which the following information was given:

> The following page has a poem by Scott MacLeod. Please read it, see how you feel about it, and then give your impressions and reactions on the following pages. This poem is entitled *The Whitest Parts of the Body* and it is from his book *The Life of Haifisch*.

The other half of the group received identical instructions except the following was added: "Haifisch" means "shark" in German. All of the poems in this book, including the poem that you will read, are about killer sharks.

People in the second group who had been given this clue about the poem rated their ability to understand the poem as higher than those who were not given the supplemental clue. Moreover, those in the second group found the poem more interesting than those in the first group. Other experiments support the proposition that the metacognitive process of appraising one's ability to understand something plays a key role in fostering interest or boredom. When complexity is high, as in abstract art or multidimensional problem solving, a person's appraised ability to understand the material will be associated with a greater sense of interest.

In addition to assessing one's ability to understand something, people use metacognition to review various strategies for approaching a problem in order to choose the one that is most likely to result in a solution. People monitor their comprehension of the material they have read and select strategies for increasing their comprehension (Currie, 1999). "I need to reread this section." "I need to underline and take notes to focus my attention on new information." "I need to talk about this with someone in order to understand it better."

Metacognition develops in parallel with other cognitive capacities. As children develop their ability to attend to more variables in their approach to problems, they simultaneously increase their capacity to take an "executive" posture in relation to cognitive tasks. They can detect uncertainty and introduce strategies to reduce it. They can learn study techniques that will enhance their ability to organize and recall information. These capacities continue to develop as the child becomes a more sophisticated learner (Veenman, Wilhelm, & Beishuizen, 2004). They are also quite amenable to training, both at home and at school.

Metacognition appears to be a natural component of cognitive development. However, just like first-level cognitive capacities, it is constructed in a social context. Interactions between children and adults or peers may nurture and stimulate metacognition by helping children to identify sources of information, talk about and recognize the differences between feelings of certainty and uncertainty in their knowledge, and devise effective strategies for increasing their "feelings of knowing" (Stright, Neitzel, Sears, & Hoke-Sinex, 2001).

AN APPLICATION: TEACHING LOGICO-MATHEMATICAL KNOWLEDGE

Piaget's approach to understanding the development of knowledge led to a new respect for the ways that young children make meaning of their experiences. Children are seen as building or constructing knowledge through active engagement with objects and exploration of physical relationships among objects. According to Piaget (1967/1971), there are three types of knowledge: physical knowledge, which refers to what one knows about the properties of the physical world (a ball is round, it rolls downhill); social conventional knowledge, which refers to the conventions people in a community use to refer to ideas (we use words like one, two, and three in English; in French those same concepts are un, deux, trois); and **logico-mathematical knowledge**, the internal schemes that are formed in a child's mind.

Constance Kamii (2000), one of the most influential scholars to apply Piaget's theory to educational settings, explains logico-mathematical knowledge with the following example. Imagine that a child is playing with pick-up sticks. Are two sticks similar or different? If the child focuses on the color of two sticks, one red and one green, then the child will view the sticks as different. If the child focuses on the shape and size of the two sticks, then the sticks are similar. The ideas of similar and different are examples of logico-mathematical knowledge, constructed on the basis of mental operations imposed on physical knowledge. While color, shape, and size are observable properties and the names we give to various colors and shapes are social conventional knowledge, the understanding of objects as similar or different is not directly observable, but is a product of mental operations (Kamii, Rummelsburg, & Kari, 2005).

One of the essential aspects of logico-mathematical knowledge is an understanding of number as a representation of quantity. Kamii has explored a variety of educational interventions in order to foster the logico-mathematical knowledge that underlies arithmetic competence in young children. Her premise is that children need to have ample time to gain physical knowledge in order to construct the underlying relationships that are essential for solving arithmetic problems. Simply giving children manipulatives, asking them to fill out workbook pages, or supplying them with counters are not sufficient for solving arithmetic problems when children do not bring logico-mathematical knowledge of number as a quantity, part–whole relationships, and sequential relationships to the tasks (Kamii, Lewis, & Kirkland, 2001).

In one study, a group of 26 low-performing, low-SES first graders were involved in physical-knowledge activities during their regular math class rather than typical math instruction. This group was compared to a similar group in another school who experienced traditional arithmetic instruction. The experimental group spent the first half of the year engaged in physical-knowledge activities. Examples of some of these activities included pick-up sticks, bowling, and balancing small construction pieces on a paper plate that was placed on the neck of a bottle. When they were ready for solving arithmetic problems, these children were shifted to an approach that emphasized arithmetic games and word problems in which children worked together and exchanged views on how to solve problems. The curriculum was built upon Piagetian principles, including the focus on direct involvement with physical objects, opportunities to solve problems in the context of play, and the opportunity to work with other age mates to invent strategies. This latter feature of the learning environment is thought to help reduce overly personal or egocentric understanding and fosters an appreciation for multiple views of a problem and its solution (DeLisi, 2002).

At the end of the school year, children in the two groups were compared on two types of math abilities: mental arithmetic problems (17 addition problems of the type 5 + 4, with 3 seconds for each answer); and four story problems. An example of a story problem was: "There were three children. There are six cookies for them to share. How many cookies will each child get?" Children in the experimental group did better on all but one of the mental arithmetic problems; their performance was significantly better on 8 of the 17 problems. More children in the experimental group solved the story problems than children in the traditional classrooms, and the differences were significant in two of the problems. In the example of the cookies problem, half the children in the experimental group solved it correctly; none of the children in the traditional group solved the problem.

In general, Kamii argues, when children are challenged in play-based contexts to think hard about solving problems requiring physical knowledge they build a strong logico-mathematical foundation that makes solving arithmetic problems easier. Understanding that parts make up a whole, for example, means that when faced with a problem such as 4 + 3, a child can move quickly, counting on 3 more from 4, rather than starting to count from 1. They can devise mental strategies to solve story problems, remembering the numerical facts of the problem and inventing ways to coordinate information to arrive at a solution.

According to cognitive developmental theory, asking children to memorize strategies such as *carrying* or *borrowing* to solve arithmetic problems relies on a type of social conventional knowledge that comes from outside the child (Kamii & Dominick, 2009). In order to foster mathematical problem solving, it is better to let children arrive at an understanding of ideas of quantity through constructivist abstraction (Kamii, Lewis, & Kirkland, 2001). Kamii and others have applied cognitive developmental theory to the creation of many strategies for the use of manipulatives and games that foster children's thinking about quantity, number, spatial, and sequential relationships (Kamii & Nagahiro, 2008; Ozaki, Yamamoto, & Kamii, 2008; Kamii & Rummelsburg, 2008).

HOW DOES COGNITIVE DEVELOPMENTAL THEORY ANSWER THE BASIC QUESTIONS THAT A THEORY OF HUMAN DEVELOPMENT IS EXPECTED TO ADDRESS?

1. *What is the direction of change over the life span? How well does the theory account for patterns of change and continuity?*

    Cognitive developmental theory proposes four stages of development. In infancy, knowledge is based primarily on action and direct investigation of objects in the environment. Actions become coordinated, and schemes or mental representations are formed that link actions into coordinated operations. In toddlerhood, new capacities emerge that allow the child to represent experience symbolically. This is a critical transformation, leading to an increased freedom from direct experience. In early and middle childhood logico-mathematical knowledge emerges. Children begin to understand that certain principles underlie the relationships among objects, and they can use these operations to solve problems. With development, cognition becomes increasingly abstract and multidimensional. Logical thought can be imposed on hypothetical propositions, rather than on concrete objects and relationships. Knowledge is always based on action. Thus, the direction of change over the life span is from direct sensorimotor actions on objects to mental actions on mental operations. At each more advanced stage, ways of knowing of earlier stages are integrated into new, more abstract and flexible approaches.

2. *What are the mechanisms that account for growth? What are some testable hypotheses or predictions that emerge from this analysis?*

    Cognition is an adaptive capacity that has its basis in evolution. The concept of cognitive adaptation includes a dialectical tension between two processes—assimilation and accommodation—the former a conservative tendency and the latter a progressive tendency. Assimilation operates to preserve existing structures by incorporating new information and confirming that what is already known is useful in making sense of experience. Accommodation operates to alter existing structures in the direction of new environmental demands, thereby creating a new basis for future assimilations (van Geert, 1998).

    According to cognitive developmental theory, cognition emerges in a predictable pattern as infants and young children encounter discrepancies between existing schemes and contemporary experiences. There is an assumption of a fundamental striving toward cognitive equilibrium, where one's schemes and structures match experience. New structures emerge when children have to concentrate on tasks that challenge their physical and social-conventional knowledge. Encounters with all types of novelty, especially experiences that are moderately distinct rather than widely different from what is already known, are important for advancing new ideas and new ways of organizing thought. Encounters with different opinions and ways of solving problems, especially through peer interactions, discussion, and problem solving, help reduce egocentrism and stimulate reflection on new ways of understanding the world.

    The theory predicts that there is a level of developmental readiness for movement from one stage to the next. According to this view, children will not be able to solve certain types of problems until they have attained a level of mental operations that supports the underlying concepts associated with the problem. For example, until children understand the concept of quantity, they will not be able to be successful in solving arithmetic problems. The theory also predicts that this level of understanding is best achieved through active engagement with objects rather than being taught rules and strategies for solving problems. Children who have constructed foundational principles through active engagement in the physical world will have a stronger, more immediate grasp of the logic underlying the organization of the mathematical, physical and social worlds.

3. *How relevant are early experiences for later development? What evidence does the theory offer to support its view?*
As the previous discussion suggests, cognition is an active, gradually changing process. New knowledge is based partly on the schemes that were formed earlier, and partly on encounters with new information. New information requires the reframing and reorganization of earlier schemes. At the same time, one's approach to problem solving becomes increasingly flexible and abstract. Once the child has reached the stage of concrete operational thought, knowledge about the physical world becomes more compelling than perceptions. In the conservation task, for example, the tall thin glass may "appear" to have more juice than the wide, short glass because the liquid level is higher, but children at the stage of concrete operational thought know that height and weight compensate for one another. Thus, their reasoning overrides their sensory knowledge. Some of Piaget's studies of memory illustrate this principle, showing that as children move from the preoperational to the concrete operational stage, they remember problems differently based on what they now "know" to be true.

4. *How do the environmental and social contexts affect development? What aspects of the environment does the theory suggest are especially important in shaping the direction of development?*
Cognitive theory views development as a product of a biologically guided plan for growth and change. The elements that make cognitive growth possible are all present in the genetic information that governs the growth of the brain and nervous system. However, the process of intellectual growth requires interaction with a diverse and responsive environment. Cognitive development is fostered by recognition of discrepancies between existing schemes and new experiences. Through the reciprocal processes of assimilation and accommodation, schemes are modified and integrated to form the basis for organizing and explaining experience.

According to this view knowledge emerges through active engagement with the environment. Children as well as adults select, explore, and experiment with objects and later with ideas. They create the basis of logical reasoning through encounters with novelty. The way the environment is structured, especially opportunities for exploration and investigation guided by a child's natural curiosity, will promote cognitive reasoning. At subsequent stages, especially during the period of formal operational reasoning, environments differ in the extent to which they encourage and evoke abstract, hypothetical reasoning. For example, in some cultures formal operational reasoning is observed only in a few of the leaders, not in all adults. Within the school environment, settings that place a greater emphasis on rote memorization will be less likely to support formal operational reasoning than settings that encourage active problem solving and project-based inquiry. Methods of instruction, beginning in preschool and continuing through college, can foster or inhibit the formulation of abstract conceptualization and executive functioning that Piaget suggests are possible.

The constraints that accompany unequal power between children and parents or teachers are considered potential impediments to learning, whereas the freedom that is associated with egalitarian peer relationships is considered a positive context for cognitive growth. Piaget's emphasis on the role of peer interaction suggests that children and adolescents benefit when they can engage in social exchange as part of the problem-solving process. Social interactions with peers are expected to help reduce egocentrism, and allow children and adolescents to consider multidimensional problems from alternative points of view.

5. *According to the theory, what factors place individuals at risk at specific periods of the life span?*
The theory assumes a biological unfolding of cognitive capacities in the context of a supportive environment. Any of a number of neurological challenges could place a person at risk for failure to develop the more advanced cognitive capacities. Because cognition unfolds in a sequential process, sensory and motor delays in infancy may interfere with later capacities for logical reasoning. A lack of physical stimulation and restrictions on exploration may place infants at risk for development. In the toddlerhood period, when representational skills are emerging, a lack of a communication partner and limited opportunities for verbal interaction as well as lack of encouragement or punishment for pretend play would place children at risk. In the period of concrete operational reasoning, undue emphasis on rote memorization and repetition as well as instruction in which children are given rules and strategies rather than having opportunities to invent or discover them weaken the foundation for logico-mathematical reasoning. This type of environment continues to impede cognitive growth in adolescence.

At later stages, a learning environment that is overly authoritarian and lacking in active, peer-based learning opportunities is likely to result in a rigid approach to rules rather than the desired deep level of understanding about the application of principles of logic to complex problems. Any environment that gives children answers or solutions in order to speed learning along rather than waiting for children to discover them takes away the positive emotions that accompany understanding. The learning environment should present problems at levels that are appropriately challenging, just discrepant enough from what is already known to engage interest but not overly complex to discourage the promise of successful solutions.

6. *What are some practical implications of this theory?*
Because cognitive development is based on action, children need many opportunities to investigate and experiment with objects in their environment. Beginning in infancy, babies need opportunities to use their sensory and motor abilities to explore a diverse array of objects, and to experience causal links between their actions and related consequences. In the preoperational stage, children require encouragement and freedom for engaging in representational thought including opportunities for pretense, many forms of language stimulation, and other forms of symbolic activity such as drawing and playing symbolic games. This time spent in imaginary play provides children with early experiences of freewheeling thought that can later be brought into the service of inventiveness, creative arts, and scientific discovery.

In the teaching and learning process, the theory suggests that it is better to give children time to discover principles through direct exploration rather than teaching them rules to solve problems. When children do not seem to discover basic structures in a timely fashion, it is better to try to invent games and projects that will allow children to "stumble on to the idea" rather than to give them the answer.

The theory presents a very trusting outlook on the child's eagerness and natural curiosity as the basis for cognitive growth. A premise of the theory is that children are using a kind of logic to understand their world, although this logic is not identical to an adult's reasoning. Thus, an understanding adult would not discount a child's explanations or questions, but try to understand their origins.

In the home and family environment, the theory would encourage parents to support inquiry by asking questions, engaging in conversations, and being an interested partner in the child's discovery of the natural and social worlds. As adults who are fostering a child's cognitive growth, parents and caregivers need to provide the array of stimuli and resources that may capture the child's attention, follow the child's interests, and build on those interests in supportive ways. Just having their trusted parent nearby provides many children with the sense of safety and support that is needed for them to explore and investigate. As children get older and begin to struggle with more complex problems, adults have to resist the tendency to jump in with answers, and continue to encourage children to try different strategies in search of solutions. Parents may need to intervene to protect inquisitive, self-motivated children from the domination of authoritarian teachers and bullying students who may try to intimidate them in the learning environment.

CRITIQUE OF COGNITIVE DEVELOPMENTAL THEORY

Strengths

Piaget's theory emphasized the importance of cognition in the study of development. In contrast to other developmental psychologists who focused on mechanisms of learning or individual differences in intelligence, motor development, or temperament, Piaget brought new attention to how children, including very young infants, acquire knowledge and approach problem solving. This focus on cognition had a dramatic and permanent impact on the field of developmental science leading to vast amounts of research on the way children make meaning.

Within this theoretical framework, Piaget took a new look at children's reasoning, highlighting distinctions in the way children of different ages approach problems and noting differences in the quality of children's thinking from that of adults. His work led to a new appreciation of the infant as actively constructing knowledge about objects and people in the environment, and a new respect for infant intelligence that went beyond the child's ability to imitate adult actions or respond to adult instructions.

Piaget's approach to the study of cognition, including the invention of a variety of unique tasks and the use of the interview technique to inquire about a child's reasoning, resulted in a rich body of descriptive data about how children behave and what they understand. This approach influenced inquiry into other fields, including moral development, social development, and metacognition.

From the point of view of characteristics of a "good theory," Piaget's work has had an enormous impact on subsequent research (Flavell, 1996). In the 1970s and 1980s, cognition dominated the field of developmental psychology, and most studies were designed to replicate, test, or extend Piaget's theories. Since that time, research and theory have emerged to address identified weaknesses in Piaget's theory, considering new ways to integrate research on information processing, the social contexts of cognition, and the neurological bases of cognitive functioning. Neurological studies of brain development have provided evidence to support the stage-like shifts in cognitive capacity that were first characterized by Piaget, although the nature of these new capacities is not identical to those he predicted (Gogtay et al., 2004; Giedd et al., 1999).

Weaknesses

Perhaps the strongest criticism of Piaget's theory focuses on his view of stages of development. Although qualitative changes in problem solving are observed, cognition is much more variable than a strict stage approach implies. Children and adolescents solve problems in different ways depending on the domain, and children within an age group are much more variable in their cognitive capacities than one might expect given Piaget's description of stages. Studies of brain functioning and information processing capacities suggest more diversity in the timing of emerging capacities and individual differences in ability at specific ages than is implied by Piaget's views (Giedd, Stockman, Weddle et al., 2010).

Piaget may have underestimated the cognitive capacities of infants and young children, and overestimated the capacities of adolescents. Piaget's view of development suggests that there is a period of maturational readiness for the application of logical operations to physical objects. Piaget argued that left to their own processes of exploration and experimentation, children would discover the regularities and operations that underlie conservation. Showing a child a conservation problem and then explaining and reinforcing the correct answer should not be very effective if the child is not ready to assimilate this information. However, research has shown that it is possible to train young children of preschool age to conserve (Brainerd, 1977). These training studies find that it is possible to introduce such concepts as identity and reversibility so that children as young as 4 can achieve conservation. Children also transfer conservation from the tasks involved in training to other materials and dimensions (Field, 1981; May & Norton, 1981).

Preschool and kindergarten age children can integrate and apply more abstract concepts than Piaget's theory predicted. For example, children as young as 3 and 4 have shown that they understand the idea that materials are made of tiny particles that retain their properties even when they are invisible. They can use this notion of particles to explain how a substance, such as sugar, continues to exist in a solution and retain its sweetness even when it is invisible (Au, Sidle, & Rollins, 1993; Rosen & Rozin, 1993). These examples illustrate the criticism that Piaget's theory underestimates the abstract reasoning abilities of the preoperational age child.

At the other end of the developmental continuum, the stage of formal operations may overestimate the way that most adolescents and adults approach problems. Although most researchers agree that formal operational thinking exists and does characterize mature, scientific reasoning, many studies show that adolescents and adults typically do not function at the formal operational level, and that their use of formal reasoning is inconsistent across problem areas (Bradmetz, 1999). For example, Neimark (1975) followed changes in the problem-solving strategies of adolescents over a three-and-a-half-year period. Even the oldest participants in her study who were 15 did not apply formal operational strategies across all problems.

A different criticism of Piaget's theory is that his descriptions of concrete and formal operational thought are too narrow and do not encompass the many dimensions along which cognitive functioning matures. Increases in speed, efficiency, and capacity of information storage and retrieval have been documented during the period from ages 11 to 16 (Kwon & Lawson, 2000; Kuhn, 2006). Improvements in logical reasoning are in part a result of being able to handle greater quantities of information more quickly and efficiently.

In addition to development in basic processes, there are gains in knowledge both as a result of schooling and as a result of experience. Knowledge in each specialized subject such as mathematics, language, or science expands, bringing not only increases in logic but increases in understanding the procedures or strategies that are most likely to work for a given problem. Complementing changes in specialized knowledge, adolescents demonstrate increases in self-monitoring, conscious control and guidance of mental activity, such as the ability to hold conclusions in abeyance while they examine alternative solutions or gather new information. These capacities for executive cognitive functioning and greater flexibility contribute to the potential for more mature solutions (Donald, 2001).

Piaget's search for universal patterns in the emergence of cognitive structures may have led him to underestimate the role of culture and social contexts on development. Development takes place in a social context. The theory does not provide a lens for characterizing the important features of the environment that may shape the path for cognitive growth. For example, in the most basic concept of attention, some cultures expect infants and young children to learn by watching and imitating, placing a high priority on the infant's ability to attend to multiple targets. Other cultures expect infants and young children to learn through investigation and manipulation, placing a high priority on the infant's ability to focus attention on one activity at a time. The way culture shapes knowing is not addressed in this theory.

A somewhat different criticism focuses on the lack of attention to the process of instruction. Piaget was optimistic about the child's natural capacity to discover basic schemes and structures. As a result, he was not especially interested in the instructional process as a way of improving, or speeding along the child's cognitive abilities. In fact, one might say that he mistrusted efforts to teach a child what the child could learn through discovery. However, many higher order principles might never be discovered without guidance from a more skilled or experienced teacher. Every culture has ways of transmitting knowledge from one generation to the next. It makes sense to expect that the mature emergence of cognition involves an integration of a person's natural capacity for adaptation with the symbolic systems, knowledge, teaching techniques, and beliefs of the culture.

Finally, some critics focus on the nature of Piaget's techniques and specific experiments as limiting the way he characterized young children's cognitive capacities. For example, in studying object permanence, Piaget relied on an infant's motor ability to pursue a hidden object as evidence that the child understood that the object continued to exist. Baillargeon (2004) has shown that by altering the experimental methods, one can demonstrate that young infants who do not yet crawl can anticipate an object's trajectory and can follow an object through different ways of hiding it. Others have pointed to similar problems in conservation tasks. If you ask a child to judge whether two balls of clay are the same, and then flatten one of the balls into a pancake and ask the question again, a child may assume that since you are asking the question again, something has changed. In one study, children ages 5 to 7 were asked how certain materials looked and how they really were. Giving the children this verbal distinction between appearance and reality led to increases in the number of children who gave the correct answer (Bijstra, van Geert, & Jackson, 1989). These examples illustrate that the limitations Piaget pointed out in children's cognitive functioning could be in part a result of the constraints imposed by his methods. The strengths and weaknesses of cognitive developmental theory are summarized in Table 4.3.

Table 4.3 Strengths and weaknesses of cognitive developmental theory

Strengths	Weaknesses
New attention to how infants and young children acquire knowledge and approach problem solving.	The characterization of stages is overly general; it does not adequately account for individual differences within age groups, differences in timing of emerging abilities, and differences in reasoning across task domains.
Major impact on the field of human development including expansion of research on children's thinking and reasoning.	The theory underestimates the abilities of infants and young children and overestimates the abilities of adolescents.
Inspired a new understanding of infant cognition and the ways that infants make meaning of their experiences.	The theory undervalues the role of instruction and guidance in promoting cognitive growth.
Brought a new understanding about differences in the quality of children's thinking at different stages of development, and contrasting this to adult reasoning.	Advances in cognitive capacity from childhood to adolescence include many more features than are incorporated into the stages of concrete operational and formal operational thought.
Identification of basic mechanisms of change including adaptation and equilibration.	Advances in education within specific fields provide new insights which can promote the revision and elaboration of cognitive structures.
Invention of new research methods to explore children's reasoning.	The specific tasks and problems used to evaluate cognition may place constraints on the kinds of responses children are able to make.
Principles of the theory have been applied to new domains including moral development, social reasoning, and metacognition.	The theory does not provide a lens for considering the impact of differences among cultures and social contexts on cognition.
Application of the theory to educational settings, especially early childhood education.	

CRITICAL THINKING QUESTIONS AND EXERCISES

1. What evidence have you seen of sensorimotor intelligence in infants? Make a list of five or six examples. How does sensorimotor intelligence contribute to your own day-to-day functioning?
2. What is your understanding of the concept of structures like object permanence, numbers as quantities, or class hierarchies? How do structures emerge? Can they be taught or do they have to be discovered through experience?
3. Explain the difference between concrete operational thought and formal operational thought. What differences have you observed in the ways that 8-year-olds and 15-year-olds solve problems that reflect these qualitative distinctions? Give three examples.
4. Compare the psychoanalytic view of ego and the cognitive developmental view of cognition. In what ways are they similar; in what ways are they different?
5. Reflect on the opening case. Watch an episode or two of *Dora the Explorer*. Based on your understanding of cognitive developmental theory, do you think that early exposure to that television program will have a benefit for Micky? Explain your reasoning.
6. Look into the recommendations regarding television viewing from the American Academy of Pediatrics. What recommendations do they have for infants, toddlers, and early school age children? To what extent are their recommendations based on cognitive developmental theory?

7. What ideas from cognitive developmental theory do you think would be helpful to share with parents of infants, toddlers, school age children and adolescents? Give two examples for each stage.

8. Based on what you have read, what do you consider to be the most significant weaknesses or limitations of cognitive developmental theory?

KEY TERMS

accommodation	knowing
adaptation	logico-mathematical knowledge
assimilation	long-term memory
attention	metacognition
autonomous morality	moral reasoning
causal schemes	object permanence
central conceptual structures	operation
classification	organization
combinatorial skills	organizational strategies
concrete operational thought	perspective taking
conservation	postconventional morality
conventional morality	preconventional morality
decentering	preoperational thought
disequilibrium	reciprocity
egocentrism	reversibility
equilibration	scheme
equilibrium	sensorimotor intelligence
executive control	short-term memory
formal operational thought	signs
heteronomous morality	social cognition
hypotheticodeductive reasoning	stages of cognitive development
identity	symbols
information processing	theory of mind
insight	

RECOMMENDED RESOURCES

**Jean Piaget Society: Society for the study of knowledge and development. Website: www.piaget. org
A website for a society that expands on Piaget's works including resources for scholars, published papers, free full-text versions of Piaget's books, and videos. The society sponsors conferences, a journal, and a newsletter.

** Piaget on Piaget, a four-part series. On YouTube. https://youtube.com/watch?v=11JWr4G8YLM
In this video, made in 1977, Piaget presents the basic ideas of his theory, with filmed examples from small experiments carried out with young children. In his narrative, Piaget explains the way

his ideas differ from those of other theoretical perspectives, and demonstrates the evidence he uses to support his conclusions.

***The growing mind: A Piagetian view of children.*
A DVD series. Four half-hour videos covering cognitive developmental topics relevant to the preoperational, transitional, and concrete operational stages. The videos include a variety of interviews with children, illustrating the Piagetian method of inquiry as well as the developmental constructs.

***Direct vs indirect ways of teaching number concepts at ages 4–6.* A video by Constance Kamii. This video lecture explains indirect ways of teaching number concepts by encouraging children to think. Recorded at the University of Alabama at Birmingham, November 2013. This video is on YouTube. www.youtube.com/watch?v=L06tFh4FSF4

***Kato, Y., Honda, M., & Kamii, C. (2006). Kindergarteners play "Lining up the 5's": A card game to encourage logico-mathematical reasoning. *Beyond the Journal; Young Children on the Web.* Retrieved on May 26, 2014 at www.naeyc.org/files/yc/file/200607/Kamii706BTJ.pdf
The article illustrates how a modified version of card dominoes, called Lining up the 5s, contributes to young children's mathematical reasoning with examples of how children at different ages and developmental levels play the game.

***Chick, N. (2014). Metacognition. Retrieved at http://cft.vanderbilt.edu/guides-sub-pages/metacognition/
An essay explaining the concept of metacognition, its importance for learning, and strategies for teaching metacognition.

REFERENCES

Arnold, M.L. (2000). Stage, sequence and sequels: Changing conceptions of morality post-Kohlberg. *Educational Psychology Review, 12,* 365–383.

Au, T.K., Sidle, A.L., & Rollins, K.B. (1993). Developing an intuitive understanding of conservation: Invisible particles as a plausible mechanism. *Developmental Psychology, 29,* 286–299.

Baillargeon, R. (2004). Infants' physical world. *Current Directions in Psychological Science, 13,* 89–94.

Barrett, K.C. & Morgan, G.A. (1995). Continuities and discontinuities in mastery motivation during infancy and toddlerhood: A conceptualization and review. In R.H. MacTurk & G.A. Morgan (Eds.), *Mastery motivation: Origins, conceptualizations and applications* (pp. 57–93). *Advances in Applied Developmental Psychology: Vol. 12.* Westport, CT: Ablex Publishing.

Berg, C.A. & Strough, J. (2011). Problem solving across the lifespan. In K.L. Fingerman, C.A. Berg, J. Smith, & T.C. Antonucci (Eds.), *Handbook of life-span development* (pp. 239–268). New York: Springer.

Bijstra, J., van Geert, P., & Jackson, S. (1989). Conservation and the appearance–reality distinction: What do children really know and what do they answer? *British Journal of Developmental Psychology, 7,* 43–53.

Boom, J., Brugman, D., & van der Heijden, P.G.M. (2001). Hierarchical structure of moral stages assessed by a sorting task. *Child Development, 72,* 535–548.

Bradmetz, J. (1999). Precursors of formal thought: A longitudinal study. *British Journal of Developmental Psychology, 17,* 61–81.

Brainerd, C.J. (1977). Cognitive development and concept learning: An interpretive review. *Psychological Bulletin, 84,* 919–939.

Cacchione, T. (2013). The foundations of object permanence: Does perceived cohesion determine infants' appreciation of the continuous existence of material objects? *Cognition, 128,* 397–406.

Case, R. (1987). The structure and process of intellectual development. *International Journal of Psychology, 22,* 571–607.

Case, R. (1998). The development of conceptual structures. In W. Damon (Ed.), *Handbook of child psychology: Vol. 2. Cognition, perception and language* (pp. 745–800). Hoboken, NJ: John Wiley and Sons.

Case, R. & Okamoto, Y. (1996). The role of central conceptual structures in the development of children's thought. *Monographs of the Society for Research in Child Development, 61,* whole.

Casteel, M. (1993). Effects of inference necessity and reading goal on children's inferential generation. *Developmental Psychology, 29,* 346–357.

Commons, M.L. & Richards, F.A. (2003). Four post formal stages. In J. Demick & C. Andreoletti (Eds.), *Handbook of adult development* (pp. 199–219). New York: Plenum.

Cuevas, K., Deater-Deckard, K., Kim-Spoon, J., Wang, Z., Morasch, K.C., & Bell, M.A. (2014). A longitudinal intergenerational analysis of executive functions during early childhood. *British Journal of Developmental Psychology, 32,* 50–64.

Currie, L.S. (1999). "Mr. Homunculus, the Reading Detective": A cognitive approach to improving reading comprehension. *Educational and Child Psychology, 16,* 37–42.

Damon, W. (1980). Patterns of change in children's social reasoning: A two-year longitudinal study. *Child Development, 51,* 1010–1017.

DeLisi, R. (2002). From marbles to instant messenger: Implications of Piaget's ideas about peer learning. *Theory into Practice, 41.* Retrieved March 28, 2006 at http://findarticles

Demetriou, A., Christou, C., Spanoudis, G., & Platsidou, M. (2002). The development of mental processing: Efficiency, working memory, and thinking. *Monographs of the Society for Research in Child Development, 67.*

Donald, M. (2001). *A mind so rare: The evolution of human consciousness.* New York: Norton.

Field, D. (1981). Can preschool children really learn to conserve? *Child Development, 52,* 326–334.

Fischer, K.W. & Silvern, L. (1985). Stages and individual differences in cognitive development. *Annual Review of Psychology, 36,* 613–648.

Flavell, J.H. (1963). *The developmental psychology of Jean Piaget.* Princeton, NJ: Van Nostrand.

Flavell, J.H. (1974). The development of inferences about others. In W. Mischel (Ed.), *Understanding other persons.* Oxford: Blackwell, Basil, & Mott.

Flavell, J.H. (1982a). On cognitive development. *Child Development, 53,* 1–10.

Flavell, J.H. (1982b). Structures, stages, and sequences in cognitive development. In W.A. Collins (Ed.), *The concept of development* (pp. 1–28). Hillsdale, NJ: Lawrence Erlbaum Associates.

Flavell, J.H. (1996). Piaget's legacy. *Psychological Science, 7,* 200–203.

Gibbs, J.C. (2014). *Moral development: Beyond the theories of Kohlberg, Hoffman, and Haidt.* 3rd ed. New York: Oxford University Press.

Giedd, J., Blumenthal, J., Jeffries, N., Castellanos, F., Lui, H., Zijdenbos, A. et al. (1999). Brain development during childhood and adolescence: A longitudinal MRI study. *Nature Neuroscience, 2,* 861–863.

Giedd, J.M., Stockman, M., Weddle, C. et al. (2010). Anatomic magnetic resonance imaging of the developing child and adolescent brain and effects of genetic variation. *Neuropsychology Review, 20,* 349–361.

Gielen, U.P. & Markoulis, D.C. (2001). Preference for principled moral reasoning: A developmental and cross-cultural perspective. In L.L Adler & U.P. Gielen (Eds.), *Cross-cultural topics in psychology.* 2nd ed. (pp. 81–101). Westport, CT: Praeger/Greenwood.

Gogtay, N., Giedd, J.N., Lusk, L. et al. (2004). Dynamic mapping of human cortical development during childhood through early adulthood. *Proceedings of the National Academy of Science of the United States of America (PNAS), 101,* 8174–8179.

Gopnik, A. & Meltzoff, A.N. (1997). *Words, thoughts, and theories.* Cambridge, MA: MIT Press.

Haidt, J. (2013). Moral psychology for the twenty-first century. *Journal of Moral Education, 42,* 281–297.

Halford, G.S. & Boyle, F.M. (1985). Do young children understand conservation of number? *Child Development, 56,* 165–176.

Helwig, C.C., Zelazo, P.D., & Wilson, M. (2001). Children's judgments of psychological harm in normal and noncanonical situations. *Child Development, 72,* 66–81.

Higgins, A. & Turnure, J. (1984). Distractability and concentration of attention in children's development. *Child Development, 44,* 1799–1810.

Inhelder, B. & Piaget, J. (1958). *The growth of logical thinking from childhood to adolescence.* New York: Basic Books.

Izard, C.E. & Ackerman, B.P. (2000). Motivational, organizational, and regulatory functions of discrete emotions. In M. Lewis & J.M. Haviland-Jones (Eds.), *Handbook of emotions*. 2nd ed. (pp. 253–264). New York: Guilford Press.

Jordan, N.C., Huttenlocher, J., & Levine, S.C. (1992). Differential calculation abilities in young children from middle and low-income families. *Developmental Psychology, 28*, 644–653.

Kamii, C. (2000). Teachers need more knowledge of how children learn mathematics. *Dialogues*. Retrieved March 18, 2006 at http://nctm.org

Kamii, C. & Dominick, A. (2009). The harmful effects of "carrying" and "borrowing." Retrieved on May 26, 2014 at https://sites.google.com/site/constancekamii/publications/

Kamii, C., Lewis, B.A., & Kirkland, L. (2001). Manipulatives: When are they useful? *Journal of Mathematical Behavior, 20*, 21–31.

Kamii, C. & Nagahiro, M. (2008). The educational value of Tac-Tac-Toe for four-to-six year olds. *Teaching Children Mathematics, 14*, 523–527.

Kamii, C. & Rummelsburg, J. (2008). Arithmetic for first graders lacking number concepts. *Teaching Children Mathematics, 14*, 389–394.

Kamii, C., Rummelsburg, J., & Kari, A. (2005). Teaching arithmetic to low-performing, low-SES first graders. *Journal of Mathematical Behavior, 24*, 39–50.

Keating, D.P. (2004). Cognitive and brain development. In R. Lerner & L. Steinberg (Eds.), *Handbook of adolescent psychology*. 2nd ed. (pp. 45–84). New York: Wiley.

Kenward, B., Folke, S., Holmberg, J., Johansson, A., & Gredebäck, G. (2009). Goal directedness and decision-making in infants. *Developmental Psychology, 45*, 809–819.

Kincheloe, J.L. & Steinberg, S.R. (1993). A tentative description of post-formal thinking: The critical confrontation with cognitive theory. *Harvard Educational Review, 63*, 296–321.

Kohlberg, L. (1969). Stage and sequence: The cognitive-developmental approach to socialization. In D.A. Goslin (Ed.), *Handbook of socialization theory and research*. Chicago: Rand McNally.

Kohlberg, L. (1976). Moral stages and moralization: The cognitive-developmental approach. In T. Lickona (Ed.), *Moral development and behavior* (pp. 31–53). New York: Holt, Rinehart & Winston.

Kuhn, D. (2006). Do cognitive changes accompany developments in the adolescent brain? *Perspectives on Psychological Science, 1*, 59–67.

Kwok, J. & Selman, R.L. (2012). Moral reasoning, moral motivation and informed social reflection. In K. Heinrichs, F. Oser, & T. Lovat (Eds.), *Handbook of moral motivation: Theories, models, applications* (pp 550–564). New York: Springer Science and Business Media.

Kwon, Y.-J. & Lawson, A.E. (2000). Linking brain growth with the development of scientific reasoning ability and conceptual change during adolescence. *Journal of Research in Science Teaching, 37*, 44–62.

Labouvie-Vief, G. (1992). A neo-Piagetian perspective on adult cognitive development. In R.J. Sternberg & C.A. Berg (Eds.), *Intellectual development* (pp. 197–228). New York: Cambridge University Press.

Leve, L.D., DeGarmo, D.S., Bridgett, D.J. et al. (2013). Using an adoption design to separate genetic, prenatal and temperament influences on toddler executive function. *Developmental Psychology, 49*, 1045–1057.

May, R.B. & Norton, J.M. (1981). Training-task orders and transfer in conservation. *Child Development, 52*, 904–913.

Miller, E.K., Freedman, D.J., & Wallis, J.D. (2003). The prefrontal cortex: Categories, concepts and cognition. In A. Parker, A. Derrington, & C. Blakemore (Eds.), *The physiology of cognitive processes* (pp. 252–273). New York: Oxford University Press.

Miller, P.H. (2011). *Theories of developmental psychology*. 5th ed. New York: Worth.

Morra, S., Gobbo, C., Marini, Z., & Sheese, R. (Eds.) (2008). *Cognitive development: Neo-Piagetian perspectives*. New York: Taylor and Francis Group/Erlbaum.

Neimark, E.D. (1975). Longitudinal development of formal operations thought. *Genetic Psychology Monographs, 91*, 171–225.

Newman, B.M. & Newman, P.R. (2015). *Development through life: A psychosocial approach*. 12th ed. Stamford, CT: Cengage Learning.

O'Neill, D.K. & Gopnik, A. (1991). Young children's ability to identify the sources of their beliefs. *Developmental Psychology, 27*, 390–397.

Ozaki, K., Yamamoto, N., & Kamii, C. (2008). What do children learn by trying to produce the Domino effect? *Young Children, 63*, 58–64.

Piaget, J. (1926). *The language and thought of the child.* New York: Harcourt Brace.

Piaget, J. (1948). *The moral judgment of the child.* Glencoe, IL: Free Press. (Original work published 1932)

Piaget, J. (1951). *The child's conception of the world.* New York: International Universities Press. (Original work published 1926)

Piaget, J. (1952). *Judgment and reasoning in the child.* New York: Humanities Press. (Original work published 1924)

Piaget, J. (1952). *The child's conception of number.* London: Kegan Paul, Trench, & Trubner. (Original work published 1941)

Piaget, J. (1952). *The origins of intelligence in children.* New York: International Universities Press. (Original work published 1936)

Piaget, J. (1954a). *The construction of reality in the child.* New York: Basic Books.

Piaget, J. (1954b). *The psychology of intelligence.* New York: Harcourt Brace.

Piaget, J. (1955). The stages of intellectual development in the child and the adolescent. In P. Osterrieth, J. Piaget, R. DeSaussure, J.M. Tanner, H. Wallon, R. Zazzo, et al. (Eds.), *Le problème des stades en psychologie de l'enfant* (pp. 33–42). Paris: Presses Universitaires de France.

Piaget, J. (1970). Piaget's theory. In P.H. Mussen (Ed.), *Carmichael's manual of child psychology: Vol. 1.* 3rd ed. (pp. 703–732). New York: Wiley.

Piaget, J. (1971). *Biology and knowledge.* Chicago: University of Chicago Press. (Original work published 1967)

Piaget, J. (1972). Intellectual evolution from adolescence to adulthood. *Human Development, 15,* 1–12.

Piaget, J. (1985). *The equilibration of cognitive structures.* Chicago: University of Chicago Press. (Original work published 1975)

Piaget, J. & Inhelder, B. (1969). *The psychology of the child.* New York: Basic Books. (Original work published 1966)

Rose, S.A., Feldman, J.A., & Jankowski, J.J. (2009). Information processing in toddlers: Continuity from infancy and persistence of pre-term deficits. *Intelligence, 37,* 311–320.

Rosen, A.B. & Rozin, P. (1993). Now you see it, now you don't: The preschool child's conception of invisible particles in the context of dissolving. *Developmental Psychology, 29,* 300–311.

Schiff, A. & Knopf, I. (1985). The effects of task demands on attention allocation in children of different ages. *Child Development, 56,* 621–630.

Selman, R.L. (1971). Taking another's perspective: Role-taking development in early childhood. *Child Development, 42,* 1721–1734.

Selman, R.L. (1980). *The growth of interpersonal understanding: Developmental and clinical analysis.* New York: Academic Press.

Selman, R.L. (1994). The relation of role taking to the development of moral judgment in children. In B. Puka (Ed.), *Fundamental research in moral development. Moral development: Vol. 2. A compendium* (pp. 87–99). New York: Garland.

Siegler, R.S. & Alibali, M.W. (2005). *Children's thinking.* 4th ed. Upper Saddle River, NJ: Prentice Hall.

Silvia, P.J. (2005). What is interesting? Exploring the appraisal structure of interest. *Emotion, 5,* 89–102.

Sinnott, J.D. & Cavanaugh, J.C. (1991). *Bridging paradigms: Positive development in adulthood and cognitive aging.* New York: Praeger.

Sophian, C. (1988). Limitations on preschool children's knowledge about counting: Using counting to compare two sets. *Developmental Psychology, 24,* 634–640.

Stright, A.D., Neitzel, C., Sears, K.G., & Hoke-Sinex, L. (2001). Instruction begins in the home: Relations between parental instruction and children's self-regulation in the classroom. *Journal of Educational Psychology, 93,* 456–466.

Tarricone, P. (2011). *The taxonomy of metacognition.* New York: Psychology Press.

Tudge, J.R.H. (1992). Processes and consequences of peer collaboration: A Vygotskian analysis. *Child Development, 63,* 1364–1379.

Uzgiris, I.C. (1983). The organization of sensorimotor intelligence. In M. Lewis (Ed.), *Origins of intelligence: Infancy and early childhood.* 2nd ed. (pp. 135–190). New York: Plenum/Springer.

van Geert, P. (1998). A dynamic systems model of basic developmental mechanisms: Piaget, Vygotsky and beyond. *Psychological Review, 105,* 634–677.

Veenman, M.V.J., Wilhelm, P., & Beishuizen, J.J. (2004). The relation between intellectual and metacognitive skills from a developmental perspective. *Learning and Instruction, 14,* 89–109.

Vygotsky, L.S. (1962). *Thought and language.* Cambridge, MA: MIT Press and Wiley. (Original work published 1934)

Walker, L.J., Gustafson, P., & Hennig, K.H. (2001). The consolidation/transition model in moral reasoning development. *Developmental Psychology, 37,* 187–197.

Wellman, H.M. (1990). *The child's theory of mind.* Cambridge, MA: MIT Press.

Wellman, H., Cross, D., & Watson, J. (2001). Meta-analysis of theory-of-mind development: The truth about false belief. *Child Development, 71,* 655–684.

Wentworth, N. & Haith, M.M. (1992). Event-specific expectations of 2- and 3-month-old infants. *Developmental Psychology, 28,* 842–850.

Wimmer, H.M. & Perner, J. (1983). Beliefs about beliefs: Representation and constraining function of wrong beliefs in young children's understanding of deception. *Cognition, 13,* 103–128.

Xu, F. (2003). The development of object individuation in infancy. In H. Hayne & J. Fagen (Eds.), *Progress in infancy research: Vol. 3* (pp. 150–192). Mahwah, NJ: Erlbaum.

Young, G. (2011). *Development and causality: Neo-Piagetian perspectives.* New York: Springer.

Zelinski, E.M. & Lewis, K.L. (2003). Adult age differences in multiple cognitive functions: Differentiation, dedifferentiation, or process-specific change. *Psychology and Aging, 18,* 727–745.

Ziv, M. & Frye, D. (2003). The relation between desire and false belief in children's theory of mind: No satisfaction? *Developmental Psychology, 39,* 859–876.

Part II
Theories That Emphasize Environmental Factors

One of the persistent controversies in the study of human development has been whether nature or nurture is more important in shaping the direction of development. The theories we reviewed in the preceding section fell more on the side of nature, emphasizing the role of a biologically based plan for development that guides the direction of maturation and growth. The theories we will review in this section fall more on the side of nurture. These theories take the position that development is essentially a product of the events that the person experiences. Returning to the analogy of a plant, one might say that given the general direction of development, which is guided by genetic information within a seed, all the environmental factors such as nutrients, sun, water, soil, and air temperature are exactly what will determine whether the plant flourishes.

Environmental factors are a source of enormous variation, including exposure to nutrition, health care, cognitive stimulation, interpersonal interactions, educational opportunities, financial resources, stressors, community resources, work settings, cultural artifacts and rituals, climate, and geographical conditions. These environmental factors produce differences in physical development, as well as individual thought and behavior; they shape expectations, which, in turn, shape individual goals and actions.

The three theories that are presented in this section, learning theories, social role theory, and life course theory, each operate at a different level of analysis. Learning theories examine links between stimuli and responses and day-to-day experiences; social role theory focuses on the impact of the integrated environmental framework of social roles; and life course theory addresses the broad scope of historical/social eras with their diverse opportunities and constraints. Each theory provides a distinct perspective on how to conceptualize the environment and the specific mechanisms that account for how environmental events alter or influence behavior.

The chapter on learning theories summarizes key concepts from four different approaches: classical conditioning; operant conditioning; social learning theory; and cognitive behaviorism. In contrast to cognitive developmental theories, which focus on the processes through which mental structures are formed, the learning theories highlight links between thought and behavior. These theories emphasize processes that account for modifications in behavior as a result of experience. They share a view of humans as adaptive and flexible in their ability to change their behaviors in light of exposure to changing environmental circumstances. Each theory highlights distinct mechanisms to account for these changes in behavior, and uses different experimental methods to test their propositions.

Social role theory emphasizes age-graded roles that guide the direction of development throughout life. Roles vary from one society to another. The behaviors associated with specific roles are defined by the norms and expectations within one's culture. For example, the role of mother may exist in many cultures, but what behaviors are expected to be performed in the role of mother and ideas about "good mothers" may differ from one culture to the next. Continuity is explained by the enactment of roles that endure over long periods, such as the roles of child or parent. Continuity is also explained by participation in reciprocal roles; one learns about the expectations of one's own role and the adjoining roles. Change is explained by the process of role gain, role loss, and entry into an increasing number of roles that produce new levels of societal engagement.

Life course theory expands the window on development by considering one's lifetime in an historical context. The theory describes maturation as taking place in the context of changes in historical events which can increase or restrict access to resources and opportunities. In the face of changing social and cultural contexts, such as war, economic recession, new technologies, or changing social values, individuals set goals and make decisions that shape the direction of their life trajectories.

The three theories have a common focus on the role of environments for shaping the direction of growth. As such, they highlight important sources of individual variability based on the effects of experience. They differ in the aspect of the environment that is emphasized. The learning theories draw attention to the micro level of moment-to-moment consequences of action. Social role theory considers the impact of social organization on guiding patterns of social interaction and self-definition. Life course theory takes the broadest view of the environment, bringing into focus intergenerational and cultural dimensions of the environment within which individuals interpret their experiences and project their futures.

5
Learning Theories

CHAPTER OUTLINE

GUIDING QUESTIONS

- What is learning? According to the theories presented in this chapter, what are the basic mechanisms that account for learning?
- What is the meaning of the term "learning" in these theories as compared to its meaning in the question: "What did you learn today?" In other words, what is the difference between learning as a process, and learning as content or knowledge?
- How are the theories presented in this chapter related to the concept of "behaviorism"?
- How might the theories presented in this chapter be used to influence marketing strategies or consumer behavior?
- What are some laws of human behavior that have emerged from the learning theories?
- What are some features of the learning theories that have resulted in their widespread application to a variety of contexts such as parenting practices, education, and mental health?
- How do the theories help explain behaviors that may appear to be illogical or a product of superstition?

CASE VIGNETTE

Molly is in the fifth grade. She and her family have just moved to this new neighborhood, so she is new to the school where most of the students have been together since kindergarten. Molly is a bit shy, and somewhat overweight, but she is an eager learner, and has been a very successful student. She has been studying violin for three years, and gives at least two hours to practice every day, something she truly enjoys.

On Monday in gym class, during a game of volleyball, three girls formed a circle around Molly and started to throw the ball at her. At first, she thought it was a game, but then they started aiming the ball at her head and laughing when she got hit. At one point, she fell down and twisted her hand. In her pain and embarrassment, she started to cry. The other girls just stared, and then one of them started laughing. Molly ran from the room.

That night, Molly's wrist started to swell so she couldn't practice the violin. She went to her room to start her homework and found that someone had posted a picture from gym class to their Instagram© account with the caption: "Fat Molly on her butt." After seeing that, Molly couldn't concentrate at all on her homework. She wanted to talk to her mother and father, but she was worried that they would get upset and make a scene at school, so she kept it to herself.

The next day, Molly was very nervous about going to school. She was late getting ready for school; she had not finished her homework; and she felt a bit dizzy. When she saw the girls from gym class coming toward her in the hall, she suddenly became nauseous. She ran to the bathroom and got sick. Then she went to the nurse and said she needed to go home.

Learning theories focus on changes in beliefs and behaviors that are associated with experience. Learning is a necessary capacity for survival, allowing living beings to recognize and adapt to changing conditions. In the current case, consider the confluence of events that could detract from Molly's positive outlook on school. In this example, several of the mechanisms that are presented in the learning theories converge to produce fear, avoidance, and physical symptoms. The learning theories offer explanations for how a few negative experiences might result in the modification of behavior.

As you read about the learning theories, try to consider the ways in which bullying may alter the behavior of bullies, victims, and bystanders. What concepts from classical conditioning help to understand how getting hit with the ball is linked to fear of the girls who threw the ball? What concepts from operant conditioning might suggest that there are reinforcements for the girls who carried out the bullying? What concepts from social learning theory suggest how bullying behavior might be imitated in other contexts? What concepts from cognitive behaviorism help account for the development of Molly's expectations about her self-concept and about the school environment? Try to break this case down into smaller elements in order to see how each event might contribute to Molly's reactions. Then consider how the theories might be useful in guiding interventions to support Molly and to reduce bullying behavior in the school.

Learning theories have proposed mechanisms to account for the relatively permanent changes in behavior that occur as a result of experience. This definition does not limit learning to the types of experiences we encounter in school. The outcomes of learning can include such varied behaviors as stopping at a red light, feeling hungry at 6 o'clock in the evening, figuring out how to use the online research database, and riding a bicycle. The changing and changeable nature of human behavior is largely due to human beings' extensive capacity for learning. Four theories of learning have made significant contributions to the study of human development: (a) classical conditioning, (b) operant conditioning, (c) social learning, and (d) cognitive behaviorism. The first two, classical conditioning and operant conditioning, began as theories that focused on exploring systematic relationships between stimuli that impinge on the organism and the organism's response. These theories focused on analyzing changes in behavior and became the basis for the field of behaviorism. In recent expansions of these theories, the neurological underpinnings of these kinds of learning are being discovered.

The second two, social learning theory and cognitive behaviorism, began as theories that focused on intervening variables, especially information and expectations, that might connect experiences with behaviors. These theories differentiate learning and performance, suggesting that there is a complex process in which the learner evaluates the conditions under which the learned response is relevant or appropriate. As you read about these theories, you will begin to appreciate that the term *learning* encompasses a wide variety of processes (Schunk, 2011).

HISTORICAL CONTEXT

The learning theories emerged in the later part of the nineteenth century and the first part of the twentieth century, as scholars began to apply the scientific process to an analysis of human behavior. Psychologists were looking for principles to explain human behavior that could be verified through systematic observation, objective measurement, and statistical probability, as opposed to reflection, intuition, introspection, and logic. They found ways to apply the experimental method to the study of learning and memory by isolating specific cause–effect links between stimuli and responses. In most of the learning theories, the person is viewed as largely malleable, able to adapt flexibly to the demands and rewards of the environment. Research and theory went hand in hand as psychologists invented new experimental contexts in which to identify the mechanisms through which experiences in the environment would alter and sustain changes in behavior (Ormrod, 2011).

Learning theories emerged from the work of many scholars including Ivan Pavlov, E.L. Thorndike, John Watson, B.F. Skinner, Clark Hull, Albert Bandura, Edward Tolman, and Walter Mischel. Along with sensation and perception, learning and memory were among the earliest concepts that psychologists studied. For the most part, they began their work to identify basic principles of learning, including laws that applied across species, rather than to account for developmental changes in learning. However, many of the ideas that are included as part of the broad field of learning theories have been applied to work with children and adolescents, including parenting and the socialization process, teaching and the management of classroom environments, and the creation of therapeutic environments. A bit more about the historical context of each of the four learning theories will be provided in the sections that follow.

KEY CONCEPTS OF FOUR THEORIES OF LEARNING

Classical Conditioning

Ivan Pavlov was a Russian physiologist whose early research focused on the relationship of the nervous system to the functioning of the heart. Between 1891 and 1900 he focused on the physiology of the digestive system. As part of this work, he developed a technique for inserting tubes that would allow him to monitor the functioning of various organs while the animal was still alive and engaged in normal digestive activities. This was a breakthrough in the science of physiology, allowing him to demonstrate the intimate link between the nervous system and the digestive system in living animals. He was awarded the Nobel Prize in 1904 for his work on the physiology of the digestive system.

Pavlov was studying the reflexive responses of digestion when food was placed in an animal's mouth. While he was working on this research, Pavlov noticed that events at a distance, such as the sight of food, the sight of a person delivering the food, or noises that occurred regularly in the room, produced digestive responses. Pavlov realized that the animals had learned to associate a reaction with a stimulus that one would not think would produce that reaction. He called these associations **conditioned reflexes**. The type of learning that Pavlov studied was called classical conditioning (Pavlov, 1927/2003).

In **classical conditioning**, a bond already exists between some stimulus in the environment and some physiological response of the learner. These naturally occurring stimulus–response bonds are called **reflexes**. Because of his interest in digestion, the reflexive response Pavlov was most interested in was the salivation response to food. In classical conditioning the stimulus that naturally produces a reflexive response is called the **unconditioned stimulus** (UCS). The natural reflexive response is called the **unconditioned response** (UCR). Examples of other UCS–UCR reflexive bonds in addition to that of the food-salivation reaction include: the reaction of the eye to threat (the eyeblink reflex); the reaction of the eye to different intensities of light (the pupillary reflex); and the reaction to a loud, sudden noise (the startle reflex).

Pavlov discovered that events happening regularly just before the events that trigger a reflexive response will also produce a version of the reflexive response. For example, sounds that occur regularly just before an animal is fed will eventually cause an animal's digestive system to secrete chemicals in the same way it does to food. These sounds are, in themselves, neutral. If they occur at other times of day and in other contexts they do not normally result in evoking the dog's salivation response. However, when they are linked in time over several days, they become "meaningful" signals that food is coming. As a result, these formerly neutral sounds begin to be associated with food and, as such, they evoke a conditioned salivation response.

The model for classical conditioning is seen in Figure 5.1. Before conditioning, the bell is a **neutral stimulus** (NS). It elicits a response of interest or attention, but nothing more. The sight and smell of food are unconditioned stimuli (UCS) that elicit salivation, the unconditioned response (UCR). During conditioning trials, the bell is rung shortly before the food appears. The dog is said to have been conditioned when it salivates to the sound of the bell, before the food is presented. The bell, therefore, comes to control the salivation response. It is now the **conditioned stimulus** (CS). Salivation that occurs in response to the bell alone is called the **conditioned response** (CR). The CR is usually not exactly identical to the UCR.

Let's consider a different stimulus-response situation that may be observed with human infants. A loud noise will produce a startle response, including tightening of muscles, rapid respiration, and heightened arousal. Let's imagine that whenever an infant is taken to the pediatrician for a check-up, she is startled by the sudden loud cries of other infants in the examination rooms. The loud cries are the UCS; the startle response is the UCR. After two or three visits, she begins to make a partial startle reaction as she enters the doctor's office. The doctor's waiting room becomes a CS for the startle response, CR. As she gets older, her mother tries to prepare her for visits to the doctor's office. The visits are very infrequent, but the child continues to show an anxiety reaction to the mere discussion of the doctor and the coming visit. The words and imagery associated with the doctor combine to maintain the CS–CR bond. The transfer of the CR from the waiting room to the discussion of the doctor's visit is called **higher order conditioning**.

Subsequent research on Pavlovian conditioning demonstrated that conditioning is a means by which the learner identifies structure in the environment (Gottlieb & Begej, 2014). The pairing of two events, such as the sound of a bell and the presentation of food, becomes significant because one stimulus turns into a signal for the other. Conditioning does not take place randomly between any two events linked in time. If there is no systematic relationship between the two, conditioning will not take place. The light may be on in the kitchen whenever the telephone rings, for example, but since there is no predictable relationship between the light and the telephone, the light does not become a signal that the telephone is going to ring. Conditioning is not an artificial paradigm; it is an actual process by which one stimulus provides information about another.

Furthermore, the CS itself is not totally neutral. A visual stimulus such as a colored light will prompt visual orienting, for instance, whereas an auditory stimulus may simply increase attention or arousal. In a conditioning experiment, the learner builds many associations simultaneously. Although the focus of a particular experiment may be on establishing a link between one CS and one UCS, the learner will build links among many elements of the environment—its visual, auditory, and olfactory components, including the UCS. Pavlovian conditioning provides a model for understanding how multiple associations can be established and triggered in the process of concept formation, memory, and problem solving (Lavond & Steinmetz, 2003).

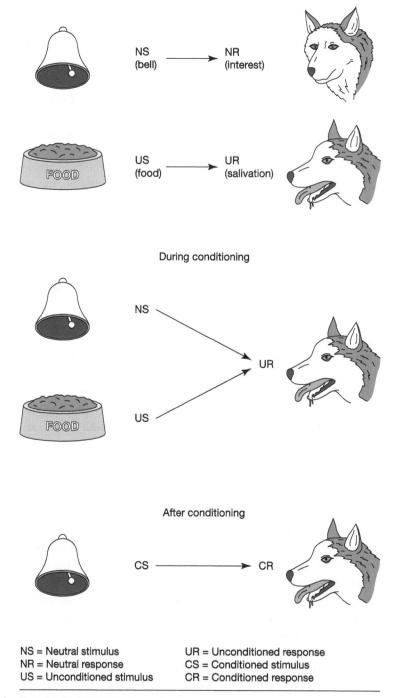

NS = Neutral stimulus   UR = Unconditioned response
NR = Neutral response   CS = Conditioned stimulus
US = Unconditioned stimulus   CR = Conditioned response

Figure 5.1 The Classical Conditioning Paradigm

Source: From B.M. Newman & P.R. Newman (2009). *Development through life: A psychosocial approach.* 10th ed. Stamford, CT: Cengage Learning. © 2009, South-Western, a part of Cengage Learning, Inc. Reproduced by permission. www.cengage.com/permissions

Extinction and Spontaneous Recovery. The formation of the CS–CR bond needs support in order to be maintained. When the CS is presented by itself for a number of trials without the UCS, the CR will be weakened and eventually eliminated. This process is called **extinction**. When a bell that used to signal food is no longer followed by food, the salivation response will eventually fade. In the laboratory, a CR may be extinguished on one day by repeatedly presenting the CS without the UCS. However, if you bring the animal back to the laboratory the next day and present the CS, the CR will occur. This is called **spontaneous recovery**. The response strength is not quite as great at the point of spontaneous recovery as it was at the peak of conditioning. After extinction, the response can either be readily reconditioned or extinction trials can eventually fully inhibit the response.

The phenomenon of spontaneous recovery demonstrates that extinction is different from forgetting. Once a CS–CR bond has been established, an inhibitory force must be developed to interfere with the learning. In extinction, we see another example of the adaptive nature of learning. A new response is maintained as long as it is an accurate reflection of environmental conditions. When conditions change, the learner is capable of revising its responses to reflect those changes. The phenomenon of spontaneous recovery shows that the learner will test the environment to confirm that conditions have permanently changed. If the conditions that were present during learning are reestablished, the learned response can be readily restored. However, if after several tests the conditions no longer support the original learning, the response is inhibited.

Over the course of development, a person confronts a variety of different environments. The meaningful connections between stimuli and responses may not be the same from one environment to the next. The process of extinction helps explain how responses that are not adaptive in a specific setting drop away, while new, meaningful responses are acquired.

Generalization. Another characteristic of learning is **generalization**. When a CS–CR bond is established, stimuli that are similar to but not exactly the same as the CS will also produce some measurable CR. The new response generalizes to stimuli that are similar to the original CS. The size or strength of the CR will depend upon the degree of similarity between the new stimulus and the conditioned stimulus. The more similar the CS and the new stimulus, the stronger the CR.

Generalization means that the same associations are not relearned in each new situation. When the stimuli in different situations are fairly similar, the learned associations or behaviors will be applied. We know that a red traffic light means stop, regardless of the exact shade of red that is used in the light. Generalization aids in managing the large amount of information we encounter in the environment by allowing the person to respond in the same way to stimuli that are approximately the same. Generalization may also help to explain stereotyped responses to social stimuli. If the learner has a negative response to one member of a group, these reactions may generalize to other members of the group who have similar features, or even to the label of that group through higher order conditioning.

Discrimination. The opposite of generalization is **discrimination**. In discrimination, the learner makes a response to a specific CS, but inhibits responding to stimuli that are similar to the CS. For example, the CS could be a red light, and other similar stimuli could be orange, pink, or reddish-orange lights. When the CS (red light) is presented it is always followed by food, the UCS. When a stimulus similar to the CS, for example, an orange light, is presented, it is never followed by food. Gradually, the animal learns to make the conditioned response to red, the stimulus that was followed by food, and not to make the conditioned response to orange, the stimulus that was not followed by food. You discriminate red from green at every stop light.

Pavlov explored the limits of discrimination learning. He conditioned a dog to distinguish between a circle and an ellipse. Once the dog could reliably differentiate the two, Pavlov began to alter the shape of the ellipse so it became more and more circular. After a number of modifications, the dog could not distinguish between the two stimuli even though one was followed by food (UCS) and the other was not. The dog's ability to discriminate grew worse. In addition, the dog's behavior in the experimental situation became disorganized. The dog barked and squealed; it tore at the apparatus and resisted being taken into the experimental room. After 3 weeks, when it was tested with the original circle and ellipse, the dog could no longer differentiate between them. Pavlov described this sequence of behaviors as a case of experimentally induced neurosis. He speculated that disorganization of behavior would be produced when the tendency to make a response and to inhibit that response are both present because the situation produces anxiety.

Classical conditioning can account for a great deal of the associational learning that occurs throughout life. When a specific symbol is paired with an image, emotional reaction, or object, that symbol takes on new meaning. The associations that are made through classical conditioning may involve labels and concepts, but they do not necessarily require language skills. During infancy and toddlerhood, a variety of positive and negative emotional reactions are conditioned to people, objects, and environments as the child develops attachments. Our reactions to the taste of a certain type of food or the feel of a particular material may be the result of conditioned learning that has persisted until adulthood.

Similarly, fears can be the results of classical conditioning. Fear can be conditioned to a specific cue, such as a sound, light, or smell, which signals the onset of a painful experience. It can also be conditioned to the context in which the painful event occurred (Kim & Jung, 2006; Fanselow & Ponnusamy, 2008). Fear conditioning is a powerful form of learning that has adaptive value in protecting individuals from danger or harm. However, it may become a source of anxiety when aroused in non-threatening situations, and may be difficult to extinguish. Many people recall at least one frightening experience, such as nearly drowning or falling from the top of a slide. The association of fear or pain with a specific target may lead to systematic avoidance of that object for the rest of one's life.

Operant Conditioning

E.L. Thorndike, an American psychologist, graduated from Wesleyan University, and then studied under William James at Harvard. He continued his doctoral studies at Columbia where he developed his approach to animal learning using puzzle boxes. He spent the majority of his career on the faculty of Teachers College at Columbia. As evidence of his long and productive career, he was elected to be president of the American Psychological Association in 1912, and head of the American Association for the Advancement of Science in 1934.

Trial-and-Error Learning. Thorndike (1898) studied a different type of learning at about the same time that Pavlov was working on classical conditioning. He observed cats as they figured out how to escape from a cage. Thorndike described a process of **trial-and-error learning** in which the cats made fewer and fewer random movements and increasingly directed their behavior to the correct solution (pulling a string to release a latch). Thorndike argued that the improvement in problem solving was not the result of learning an idea or an insight but the gradual association between a stimulus and a response. A **stimulus** is any event or energy source in the environment. It can also be an internal event like a pain or a thought. A **response** is any behavior that occurs in reaction to the stimulus.

Thorndike (1911/2012) proposed the **law of effect** to explain how specific stimuli are linked to specific responses. According to the law of effect, a bond is established between the situation and the reaction depending on the feeling state accompanying the reaction. Other things being equal, when a response is followed by a positive feeling state, it strengthens the bond between the stimulus and the response. When faced with a similar situation, the response is likely to recur. When a response is followed by a negative feeling state, it weakens the bond between the stimulus and the response. When faced with a similar situation, the response is less likely to recur.

Thorndike also proposed the **law of exercise**. In trial-and-error learning, the pattern of connections between the stimulus and responses is established by the consequences that follow the responses. Patterns are strengthened through repetition. The law of exercise states that the more frequently a stimulus–response connection is repeated, the stronger it becomes. The pattern is called a **habit** when it appears to be automatic.

Through the combination of the laws of effect and exercise, a specific response to a stimulus occurs immediately. Other possible responses do not occur. Complex behaviors can be established as the response from one stimulus becomes a stimulus for the next response. For example, think about your sequence of activities when you get up in the morning. You go to the bathroom, you wash your hands, brush your teeth, take a shower, get dressed, have breakfast, assemble your papers to get ready for your day, and leave the house. This sequence occurs every day in the same order with little planning or thought. It is a complex pattern of habits. Each step in the sequence can be thought of as a response and as a stimulus for the next step. Once a bond is formed between a stimulus and a response, learned behaviors can be very efficient and lead the way to complex habit sequences freeing the person to use their conscious thought for other tasks.

American psychologist B.F. Skinner had the benefit of reviewing Pavlov's work on classical conditioning and Thorndike's work on trial-and-error learning. In an early paper, Skinner (1935) summarized the essential differences between the two kinds of learning:

1. In classical conditioning, the conditioned reflex can begin at zero level; that is, it is not present at all. In trial-and-error learning, the response must be made if it is to be reinforced or strengthened.
2. In classical conditioning, the response is controlled by what precedes it. In trial-and-error learning, the response is controlled by what follows it.
3. Classical conditioning is most suitable for internal responses (emotional and glandular reactions). Trial-and-error learning is most suitable for external responses (muscle movements, verbal responses).

The Role of Reinforcement. Skinner's (1938/2006) work followed along the lines of Thorndike's. His focus was on the modification of voluntary behaviors as a result of the consequences of those behaviors, a type of learning referred to as **operant conditioning**. In the operant conditioning experiment, the researcher selects a response in advance and then waits until the desired response (or at least a partial response) occurs. Then the experimenter presents a reinforcement. **Reinforcement** is operationally defined as any stimulus that makes a repetition of the response more likely. There are two kinds of reinforcers. **Positive reinforcers**, such as food and smiles, increase the rate of response when they are present. **Negative reinforcers**, such as electric shock, increase the rate of response when they are removed.

Consider this example. A researcher places a rat in a cage. An electric grid in the floor of the cage is activated. As soon as the rat presses a bar, the electric shock is turned off. Soon the rat learns to press the bar quickly in order to turn off the shock. The shock is a negative reinforcer because its removal strengthens the response of bar pressing. Suppose a mother gets upset whenever she hears her baby cry. She may try a number of responses to stop the crying—rocking, feeding, talking, changing the baby's diaper. If one of these behaviors leads to an end to the noise, it is reinforced. The mother is more likely to try that behavior the next time. The baby's cry is a negative reinforcer because when it stops, the specific caregiving response is strengthened.

Shaping. One of the challenges of operant conditioning is the problem of getting the learner to make the desired response in the first place. This is especially problematic if the desired response is a complex behavior that the learner has never shown before. One means of developing a new complex response is **shaping**. Here the response is broken down into its major components. At first a response that is only an approximation of one element of the behavior is reinforced. Gradually new elements of the behavior are added, and a reinforcement is given only when two or three components of the response are linked together. Once the person makes a complete response, earlier approximations are no longer reinforced.

Parents often use the shaping process to teach their young children such complicated behaviors as using the toilet and caring for their belongings. For example, parents may begin toilet training by reinforcing children when they behave partially in the desired way, such as by telling the parents that they have to go to the bathroom. Eventually the children receive reinforcers only when they have completed the entire behavior sequence (including wiping, flushing, adjusting clothing, and washing hands).

Schedules of Reinforcement. Within the field of operant conditioning, research has been devoted to identifying which conditions of learning result in the strongest, longest-lasting habits. **Schedules of reinforcement** refer to the frequency and regularity with which reinforcements are given (Ferster & Skinner, 1957/1997). A new response is conditioned rapidly if reinforcement is given on every learning trial. This schedule is called continuous reinforcement. Responses that are established under conditions of **continuous reinforcement** are very vulnerable to **extinction**—that is, if the reinforcement is removed for several trials, performance deteriorates rapidly. Some schedules vary the amount of time or the number of trials between reinforcements. This procedure is called **intermittent reinforcement**. The learner responds on many occasions when no reinforcement is provided but does receive reinforcement every once in a while. Such schedules result in the most durable learning.

Intermittent reinforcement lengthens the time an operant behavior remains in the learner's repertoire after reinforcement has been permanently discontinued (Ferster & Culbertson, 1982; Shull & Grimes, 2003; Pierce & Cheney, 2013). Some form of intermittent reinforcement schedule is probably truer to real life. It would be very difficult for anyone to learn a behavior if every instance of it had to be reinforced. A person often exhibits a new response when no observers are present, when teachers are attending to other matters, or in the context of other behaviors that are followed by a negative consequence. Research on operant conditioning demonstrates that conditions of intermittent reinforcement are precisely those under which the longest-lasting habits are formed.

Extinction and Punishment. Positive and negative reinforcement are associated with trying to build up or increase the likelihood of a behavior. Operant conditioning also has concepts associated with damping out or reducing the likelihood of a behavior. **Extinction** is a process in which an expected reinforcer no longer occurs following the response. When parents or teachers are advised to ignore a child's undesirable behavior, they are using extinction as a means of eliminating the behavior. Theoretically, if the tendency to make a specific response can be strengthened through reinforcement, it can be weakened though extinction. **Punishment** refers to a noxious consequence that follows an undesirable behavior. In an experiment with animals, a behavior might be punished by administering an electric shock after the animal presses a bar. After a few trials, the animal will no longer press the bar. However, Skinner argued that punishment did not work any more quickly than extinction and often was accompanied by undesirable side effects.

Some students find the concepts of negative reinforcement and punishment confusing. In our two examples with rats described previously, in Example 1, bar pressing is learned when it stops the electric shock (negative reinforcer); in Example 2, bar pressing stops when it is followed by the electric shock (punishment).

The principles of operant conditioning apply whenever the environment sets up priorities for behavior and conditional rewards or punishments for approximating a desired behavior. Operant conditioning refers to the development of behavior patterns that are under the learner's voluntary control (Davey & Cullen, 1988; McSweeney & Murphy, 2014). The person can choose to make a response or not, depending on the consequences associated with the behavior. People change whenever their operant behaviors adapt to changes in environmental contingencies. The environment controls the process of adaptation through the role it plays in establishing and modifying contingencies (Skinner, 1987). Behavior can be modified in the desired direction as long as the person who is guiding the conditioning has control over the distribution of valued reinforcers.

These principles of learning are especially applicable during toddlerhood (2 to 4 years) and early school age (4 to 6). Children of these ages are unlikely to be able to conceptualize about the existing framework of reinforcement. Once individuals can analyze the reinforcement schedule, they may choose to adapt to it, resist it, or redefine the environment in order to discover new sources of reinforcement. There is no doubt that operant conditioning occurs at all ages. Reinforcement schedules set by work, spouse, and self operate on much of an adult's behavior. Reinforcement conditions determine the behaviors that will be performed. Conditions of learning influence how long a given behavior will persist once the reinforcement for it is removed.

Social Learning

The learning theorists all agree that changes in behavior are influenced by experiences. However, the two theories we discuss here, **social learning** theory and cognitive behaviorism, attend more to cognitive processes that intervene between the stimulus and the response. The concepts of **observational learning** or **vicarious learning** evolved from an awareness that much learning takes place because of the person's tendency to observe and imitate other people's behavior (Bandura & Walters, 1963). Albert Bandura described it this way: "Fortunately, most human behavior is learned observationally through modeling: from observing others, one forms an idea of how new behaviors are performed, and on later occasions this coded information serves as a guide for action" (Bandura, 1977, p. 22).

After receiving his Ph.D. in psychology from the University of Iowa, where behaviorism was a central theoretical framework, Bandura took a faculty position at Stanford in 1953. In a recent interview, Bandura reflected on his emerging dissatisfaction with the theoretical views of his time. "I looked around and I couldn't figure out how it is that all our complex competences and these complex social systems we created, how could all this be produced by trial and error learning and rewarding and punishing consequences?"

Commenting on his views about behavioral conditioning, Bandura offered this criticism: "Much of the early psychological theorizing was founded on behavioristic principles that embraced an input–output model linked by an internal conduit that makes behavior possible but exerts no influence on its own behavior" (Bandura, 2001, p. 2). Bandura's dissatisfaction with the principles of behaviorism led him to explore the ways that people learn through observation.

Bandura pointed out the distinction between learning and performance. He argued that the behaviorist concepts represent a theory of performance rather than a theory of learning. A boy may learn a great deal about how to play football by watching other children. He may also learn a great deal about how to play the game by watching adults on television. No one would realize that the child knows about football until there is an opportunity to play. The boy's learning would be cognitive, occurring without reinforcement of any overt behavior.

Modeling. In social learning theory, the people who are being observed are called models and the process of learning is called **modeling**. In one of the early modeling studies, nursery school children watched two adult models interact with a large inflated doll called Bobo. One group of children watched a model who ignored the doll and played with Tinker Toys. The other group of children watched a model who attacked the doll. The experimenter designed the attack so that it was unlike anything the children had done themselves or seen others do. A third group of children did not see a model. After observing, the children were placed in a situation with the Bobo doll. The children who had seen the model attack the doll showed much more aggressive behavior than children in either of the other two groups. Often the attacks were almost exact duplications of the attacks they had witnessed. They threw the doll into the air, pounded it with a mallet, kicked it, and shouted at it in the same way the model did (Bandura, Ross, & Ross, 1961).

In a subsequent study, children saw a film of an adult attacking a Bobo doll. One group of children saw the model rewarded after the attack, a second group saw the model punished, and a third group did not observe any consequences to the model after attacking the doll. A fourth group (the control group) saw no model and no attack. In the play period following the film, the children who had seen the model rewarded demonstrated the greatest amount of aggressive behavior. The group that observed the attack and no consequences demonstrated the second highest amount of aggressive behavior. The group who saw the attack and saw the model punished showed considerably less aggressive behavior than either of the first two groups. The least amount of aggression was displayed by the control group. Thus, it was shown that the consequences that follow the model's behavior influence whether it will be imitated and the degree of imitation (Bandura, 1965). Another implication of this research is that learning can occur through the observation of a symbolic or virtual environment. The events that can influence behavior do not necessarily have to take place in the learner's direct physical environment; and as the filmed condition of the experiment suggests, the events can be fictional.

Conditions That Influence the Imitation of a Model. A great deal of research has been devoted to identifying conditions that determine whether or not a child will imitate a model (Bandura,

1971/2006, 1977, 1986). A number of studies have shown that when children observe a model who is acting in a helpful or generous way, the children's generosity and sharing increase. In one study, children between the ages of 7 and 11 saw a model play a game and give away his winnings. Months later, the children played the same game with a different experimenter. Those children who had observed a generous model gave away more of their winnings than a control group who had not observed a generous model (Rushton, 1976). Under the right conditions, children will imitate aggressive, altruistic, helping, and stingy models. They are most likely to imitate models who are prestigious, who control resources, or who themselves are rewarded. The concept of social learning highlights the relevance of models' behavior and the observed consequences of the behavior in guiding the behavior of others. These models may include parents, older siblings, entertainment stars, or sports heroes.

The principles of social learning are assumed to operate in the same way throughout life. Observational learning may take place at any age. Insofar as exposure to new influential, powerful models who control resources may occur at any life stage, new learning through the modeling process is always possible. Exposure to a certain array of models and a certain pattern of rewards results in the encouragement to imitate some behaviors rather than others. The similarity in behavior among people of the same ages reflects their exposure to a common history of models and rewards.

Bandura's theory of social learning and the role of **imitation** in many aspects of learning was based on experimental studies of children's behavior in the presence of models. Subsequent research in neuroscience has provided validity to this theory through investigation of the mirror neuron system (Iacoboni & Dapretto, 2006). The **mirror neuron system** in humans is a coordinated network of three areas: one area gathers visual information; one recognizes and processes the motor components of the visual information; and one processes the goal of the action. Information from the goal-oriented area is sent back through the system to match up with the original visual information to guide motor behavior. The system supports sensory and motor integration while the person is observing others, imitating others, and being imitated by others. The mirror neuron system is considered to be a key to clarifying empathy and our ability to understand others through imitation of facial expressions, body posture, and gestures.

Cognitive Behaviorism

One objection that is frequently raised to classical and operant conditioning as theories of learning is that they have no language or concepts to describe events that occur in the learner's mind. In these approaches, learning is described as a relationship between environmental stimuli and individual responses. Edward Tolman (1932/1967, 1948) discussed the notion of **intervening variables**. He suggested that cognitions intervened between stimulus and response. He said that the learner develops a **cognitive map**, an internal mental representation of the learning environment. Individuals who perform a specific task in a certain environment attend primarily to that task, but they also form a representation of the rest of the setting. The cognitive map includes expectations about the reward system in operation, the existing spatial relationships within the setting, and the behaviors accorded highest priority. An individual's performance in a situation represents only part of the learning that has occurred. The fact that people respond to changes in the environment indicates that a complex mental map actually develops in the situation. Tolman emphasized the purposive aspects of behavior. This involves how people use information from the environment to direct their responses and how they use information following their responses to correct or modify their behavior in developing new responses.

Cognitive behaviorism is the study of the many internal mental activities that influence behavior. These theories of learning are included in this part of the book where environmental influences are emphasized because much of the focus is on what the learner comes to know and expect about the environment, and how this knowledge influences behavior. Nonetheless, the cognitive behaviorists bring to light the internal representation of the environment, which emerges as a result of experience, but is also influenced by the learner's level of cognitive complexity, attention, and motivation, all of which might be biologically based. Thus, the cognitive behavioral theories of learning are less mechanistic and less reliant upon environmental factors as the primary cause of behavior than is operant conditioning.

Cognitive and Emotional Factors That Influence Behavior. According to Walter Mischel (1973, 1979; Mischel & Shoda, 1995), six types of cognitive and emotional factors influence a person's behavior in a situation and account for continuity in how people respond across situations: encodings; expectancies and beliefs; affects (feelings and emotional responses); goals and values; competencies; and self-regulatory plans (see Figure 5.2). **Encodings** refer to constructs or schemes the person has about the self, the situation, and others in the situation. **Expectancies** refer to cognitive assessments about one's ability to perform, ideas about the consequences of one's behavior, and the meaning of events in one's environment.

Affects are the feelings and emotional reactions or physiological responses that are associated with a situation. Feelings of anger, fear, arousal, excitement, or jealousy might interact with expectancies and encodings to guide behavior. **Goals** and **values** are related to the relative importance one places on the outcomes of situations. One person may value high levels of task performance, whereas another may value success in social situations. One's behavior in a situation is influenced by how one values its possible outcomes. **Cognitive competences** consist of knowledge, skills, and abilities.

Self-regulatory plans are strategies for achieving one's goals, including techniques for managing internal emotional states, creating a plan and putting it into action (Kross, Mischel, & Shoda, 2010; Mischel, 2012). Self-regulation is especially important in situations where temptations, frustrations, or self-doubt threaten to pull one away from important goals (Mischel & Ayduk, 2002). As people become increasingly aware of the effects of stimuli on their behavior, they can learn to overcome, channel, or eliminate those influences that tempt them to abandon their goals.

Cognitive behaviorism draws on concepts presented in Chapter 4 associated with information processing, and concepts introduced in this chapter associated with learning theories. In any new situation, the learner's basic information processing capacities for attention, memory, and organizational strategies are required. Concepts such as encodings, affect, and cognitive competences all depend on these basic mental capacities which allow the learner to attend to relevant features of the environment, compare these features to prior experiences, and prepare for action. At the same time, according to cognitive behaviorism, the learner makes higher order assessments of the situation in order to guide behavior. These assessments are associated with expectancies, values, goals, and plans.

Self-efficacy. Of the six areas highlighted in Figure 5.2, one that has received considerable attention among those interested in learning and performance is expectancies. People's judgments about how well they expect to perform, and whether or not they expect to improve their performance with effort have a clear impact on their behavior. Albert Bandura (1982,

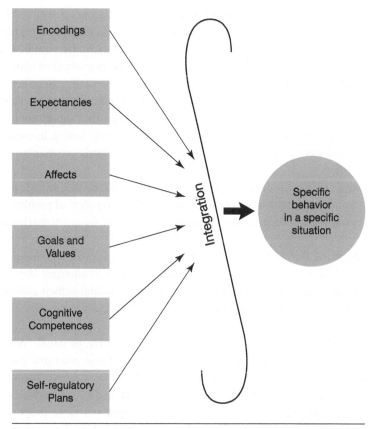

Figure 5.2 Six Cognitive and Affective Dimensions That Influence Behavior

Source: From B.M. Newman & P.R. Newman (2015). *Development through life: A psychosocial approach.* 12th ed. © 2015 South-Western, a part of Cengage Learning, Inc. Reproduced by permission. www.cengage.com/permissions

1989a) identified **self-efficacy** as a key element in the cognitive basis of behavior. Self-efficacy is defined as the sense of confidence that one can perform the behaviors demanded by a situation. According to Bandura, the decision to engage in a situation, as well as the intensity of effort expended in the situation, are dependent upon a person's confidence about success. A key feature of self-efficacy, according to this theory, is that it is domain-specific. A person can have confidence about performing well in one area, such as mathematics or public speaking, and lack confidence about success in another area (Bandura, 1997).

Bandura theorized that four sources of information contribute to judgments of self-efficacy. The first source is **enactive attainment**, or prior experiences of mastery in the kinds of tasks that are being confronted. Children's general assessment of their ability in any area (e.g. mathematics, writing, or gymnastics) is based on their past accomplishments in that area. Successful experiences increase perceived self-efficacy whereas repeated failures diminish it. Failure experiences are especially detrimental when they occur early in the process of trying to master a task. Many children are diverted from mastering such sports as tennis and baseball because they have made mistakes early in their participation. They develop doubts about their abilities which then prevent them from persisting in the task.

The second source of information is **vicarious information**. Seeing a person similar to oneself perform a task successfully may raise one's sense of self-efficacy; seeing a person similar to oneself fail at a task may lower it. **Verbal persuasion** is the third source. Children can be encouraged to believe in themselves to try a new task. Persuasion is likely to be most effective with children who already have confidence in their abilities and it helps boost their performance level. The fourth source of information that contributes to judgments of self-efficacy is **physical state**. People monitor their bodily states in making judgments about whether they can do well or not. When children feel too anxious or frightened they are likely to anticipate failure. In contrast, children who are excited and interested but not overly tense are more likely to perceive themselves as capable of succeeding.

Those who have a high sense of efficacy visualize success scenarios that provide positive guides for performance and they cognitively rehearse good solutions to potential problems. Those who judge themselves as inefficacious are more inclined to visualize failure scenarios and to dwell on how things will go wrong. Such inefficacious thinking weakens motivation and undermines performance (Bandura, 1989a). In the face of difficulty or failure, those who have confidence in their abilities and high self-efficacy will work harder to master challenges. They will attribute difficulties or failure to not trying hard enough, and they will redouble their efforts. Those who have a low sense of self-efficacy tend to give up in the face of difficulty because they attribute their failure to a basic lack of ability.

The level of self-efficacy also affects how individuals prepare to handle new challenges. In their thoughts, emotions, and preparation for action, those who are preoccupied by self-doubt differ from those who believe in the likelihood of success. Those armed with positive self-efficacy are more likely to set challenging goals, and to enact a variety of effective strategies that contribute to success such as finding the right setting to practice, organizing their time, and identifying ways to stay focused on the task (Bandura, Barbaranelli, Caprara, & Pastorelli, 1996).

Bandura pointed out that adjustment depends on one's judgment about the outcome of the situation. If a woman with a strong sense of self-efficacy is in an environment that is responsive and rewards good performance, she is likely to behave in a self-assured, competent way. If this same woman is in an environment that is unresponsive and does not reward accomplishment, she is likely to increase her effort and even try to change the environment. People who judge their efficacy to be low tend to give up and become apathetic in unresponsive environments. In responsive environments they may become more depressed and self-critical as they see others who appear to be similar to themselves succeeding. The concept of self-efficacy clarifies how people adapt when they enter new roles or new situations. The successes and failures we observe in others and the encouragement we receive from others influence our expectations.

Cognitive behaviorism suggests that through the processes of classical conditioning, operant conditioning, and observational learning, the learner acquires cognitive structures that influence subsequent learning and performance. We might say that the learner acquires an outlook on the learning situation. This outlook may influence the learner's feeling of familiarity with the task, motivation to undertake the task, optimism about performing the task successfully, and strategies for approaching the task. In addition to everything a parent, teacher, or supervisor might do to structure a learning environment, one must always take into account the outlook the learner brings to the task. Differences in judgments of self-efficacy, self-control strategies, values, and goals all influence the way people approach a learning situation.

NEW DIRECTIONS

The learning theories have led to several new directions in the study of development. The two that we focus on here are social cognitive theory, which emphasizes the active role of individuals in guiding the direction of their behavior, and experiential learning theory, which focuses on individual differences in how people approach the tasks of acquiring and using information.

Social Cognitive Theory

Social cognitive theory (SCT) emerged in the context of Albert Bandura's earlier work on social learning theory and self-efficacy. The theory takes issue with three ideas that emerged from classical and operant conditioning: 1. that people are shaped by their environments; 2. that biological capacities constrain or limit behavior; and 3. that the role of psychology is reductionistic, that is, to identify the elements upon which more complex behaviors are based. In contrast to these ideas, social cognitive theory proposes a dynamic view of learning and behavior produced by three interactive factors: internal personal factors including cognitive, emotional, and biological domains; behavioral patterns of action; and environmental influences including resources, constraints, and incentives.

The Sense of Agency. According to social cognitive theory, a core feature of human learning is the capacity for **agency**, actions that are intentional and carried out with forethought and purpose. The importance of agency in the theory emerged from Bandura's work on self-efficacy. According to SCT, a central factor in a person's motivation is a belief that one has the power and ability to have a desired impact through one's actions (Bandura, 1997). Without this belief, there would be no hope for a desired outcome. Efficacy beliefs influence the challenges people are willing to undertake, the amount of effort they are willing to expend, and the degree of persistence they exhibit in the face of difficulties or failures.

Cognitive Components of Agency. In addition to self-efficacy beliefs, agency involves cognitive components including intentionality, forethought, and self-reactiveness (Bandura, 2001). **Intentionality** involves the ability to represent a future and to plan a course of action toward that future. It requires the ability to visualize an outcome and to plan a series of steps to achieve that outcome. The outcome may or may not be achieved, but the notion behind intentionality is that the action has a purpose focused on an anticipated future goal.

People do more than set their sights on a future goal. They exercise **forethought**, that is they represent the future situation in their current thinking and anticipate some of the consequences of their actions. They guide and regulate their behavior by making an informed estimate of the consequences of their behaviors. The future cannot impact current behavior, but a cognitive representation of the future and associated expectations can influence behavior.

The third cognitive function, **self-reactiveness**, refers to the variety of processes through which a person evaluates and modifies actions. This can happen when performance is evaluated in comparison to standards and goals. Based on these comparisons, a person can be encouraged by feelings of pride and self-worth, or discouraged by feelings of dissatisfaction or shame. These self-reactive emotions can motivate new levels of striving, or they can undermine one's resolve. The person is able to use cognitive capacities to evaluate progress toward their intended goals, and to make modifications based on feedback from these assessments.

Emotional Components of Agency. In addition to the cognitive aspects of agency, there is an emotional feature that contributes to effective action (Bandura, 1989b). One aspect of this is the person's sensitivity to threats or positive encouragement in the environment that may impact motivation or confidence in one's ability to achieve one's goals. Another dimension is individual differences in the intensity of emotions such as depression or anxiety, and the ability to understand and control these emotions. People who are able to control or limit the thoughts that create strong feelings of anxiety or depression are better able to plan and revise strategies, and preserve flexibility in order to implement new directions to achieve a goal. A third emotional aspect of agency is the reinforcing nature of pride or satisfaction that accompanies progress toward a goal or goal achievement. This emotional state helps to focus attention, sustain motivation, and support perseverance.

Social and Environmental Components of Agency. SCT assumes a social feature to most human agency. Building on the early work of social learning theory, Bandura conceives of humans as social in nature whose capacity for learning is enhanced by the ability to observe and imitate others. The exercise of human agency often involves others, a concept that Bandura calls **collective agency**, "people's shared belief in their collective power to produce desired results" (Bandura, 1997). Through collective effort, individuals can achieve more ambitious goals by sharing their knowledge and skills, and by interacting in ways that advance the potential of the group.

A final feature of SCT is its differentiated view of the **environment**. According to SCT, environments have different degrees of modifiability. Some environments, like prisons or schools, are imposed; some, like cars, vacation spots, or places you choose to go to have lunch, are selected; and some, like the way you decorate your room or organize your study area, are constructed. Earlier theories of learning tended to view environments as imposed; but one of the unique features of human beings is their capacity to select and modify their environments.

> Through agentic action, people devise ways of adapting flexibly to remarkably diverse geographic, climatic and social environments; they figure out ways to circumvent physical and environmental constraints, redesign and construct environments to their liking, create styles of behavior that enable them to realize desired outcomes, and pass on the effective ones to others by social modeling and other experiential modes of influence. By these inventive means, people improve their odds in the fitness survival game. (Bandura, 2001, p. 22)

This view of environments, seen through the lens of human agency, leads to a dynamic revision of learning theories, highlighting the bidirectional nature of person and environment.

Experiential Learning Theory

Proponents of **experiential learning** theory (ELT) claim that the theory describes a model of the learning process as well as a model of adult development. Like other learning theories, ELT emphasizes the central role that experience plays in the learning process. However, the theory combines aspects of behavioral and cognitive learning theory by linking experience to both reflection and action (Kolb, 2014). The ELT model portrays two distinctly different ways of grasping experience—**concrete experience** (CE) and **abstract conceptualization** (AC). The first is knowledge you have because of your experiences; the second is knowledge you have because you read about it or were taught about it, but you did not necessarily experience it directly. There

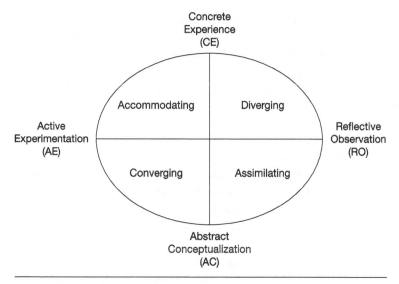

Figure 5.3 Experiential Learning Theory and Four Learning Styles

Source: From D.A. Kolb, R.E. Boyatzis, & C. Mainemelis (2001). Experiential learning theory: Previous research and new directions. In R.J. Sternberg & L.F. Zhang (Eds.), *Perspectives on thinking, learning and cognitive styles* (pp. 227–248). New York: Routledge. Reproduced by permission. Taylor and Francis Group LLC Books, Copyright © 2000, CCC Republication.

are also two opposing modes of making use of knowledge: **reflective observation** (RO) and **active experimentation** (AE). Knowledge gained either through concrete experience or through abstract conceptualization can result in reflective observation, that is, thinking more about the topic, asking new questions, or generating hypotheses about this knowledge. Similarly, knowledge gained either through concrete experience or through abstract conceptualization can result in active experimentation, trying out new behaviors that are based on the knowledge to see what benefit may result.

According to the four-stage learning cycle shown in Figure 5.3, ELT proposes a cycle of learning from CE through each of the subsequent stages to AE. Immediate or concrete experiences are the basis for observations and reflections. These reflections are assimilated and distilled into abstract concepts from which new implications for action can be drawn. These implications are actively tested and serve as guides in creating new experiences.

Although ELT suggests that all four processes are involved in learning, the theory also suggests that individuals have their preferred ways of gaining and using knowledge called *learning styles* (Kolb, Boyatzis, & Mainemelis, 2001). The learning styles shown in Figure 5.3 are likely combinations of one approach to knowing and one approach to transforming or using information. They are described as diverging, assimilating, converging, and accommodating. The following descriptions are adapted from Kolb et al. (2001).

Diverging. The dominant learning abilities are concrete experience (CE) and reflective observation (RO). Best at viewing concrete situations from many different points of view. Perform better in situations that call for generation of ideas, such as a "brainstorming." Have broad cultural interests, like to gather information, interested in people, tend to be imaginative and emotional, tend to specialize in the arts. Prefer to work in groups, listening with an open mind and receiving personalized feedback.

Assimilating. The dominant learning abilities are abstract conceptualization (AC) and reflective observation (RO). Best at understanding a wide range of information and putting it into concise, logical form. Less focused on people and more interested in ideas and abstract concepts. Value the logical soundness of a theory over its practical value. Important for effectiveness in information and science careers. Prefer readings, lectures, exploring analytical models, and having time to think things through.

Converging. The dominant learning abilities are abstract conceptualization (AC) and active experimentation (AE). Best at finding practical uses for ideas and theories. The ability to solve problems and make decisions based on finding solutions to questions or problems. Prefer to deal with technical tasks and problems rather than with social issues and interpersonal issues. Important for effectiveness in specialist and technology careers. Prefer to experiment with new ideas, simulations, laboratory assignments, and practical applications.

Accommodating. The dominant learning abilities are concrete experience (CE) and active experimentation (AE). The ability to learn from primarily "hands-on" experience. They enjoy carrying out plans and involving themselves in new and challenging experiences. Tendency to act on "gut" feelings rather than on logical analysis. In solving problems, rely more heavily on people for information than on their own technical analysis. Important for effectiveness in action-oriented careers, such as marketing or sales. Prefer to work with others to get assignments done, to set goals, to do field work, and to test out different approaches to completing a project.

Although it has its critics, ELT has been very influential in the field of adult education, guiding the way professional development courses are structured, and energizing the widespread emphasis on experiential learning as a component of academic course work at the undergraduate and graduate levels. ELT has inspired trainers and coaches in the corporate environment to integrate experiential activities, to increase sensory and emotional factors, and to encourage team building (Beard & Wilson, 2013).

Experiential learning theory focuses on the macro level, considering the big picture of how people change and grow as they reflect on their experiences, develop some general principles, and experiment to see if what they learned holds up in the next concrete situation. The theory has led to the description and measurement of learning styles, which has had a major impact on how teachers conceptualize the learning process in order to promote deeper levels of understanding across a diversity of learners.

A RESEARCH EXAMPLE: LEARNED HELPLESSNESS AND LEARNED RESOURCEFULNESS

Drawing upon the principles of classical conditioning and operant conditioning, Martin Seligman devised an experimental procedure to explore the pattern of learned responses when negative events are unavoidable. **Learned helplessness** is a term applied to the effects of uncontrollable negative events on later learning. In his early research, Seligman (1975) described the behavior of dogs who received shock that they could not escape from. One group of dogs (Group 1) was confined in a harness and trained to turn off a shock with their nose by pressing a panel. A second group of dogs (Group 2) experienced the same number of shocks in the same pattern and duration. However, nothing the dogs could do would end the shock. A third group of dogs (Group 3) were confined in the harness but no shocks were delivered.

Twenty-four hours after the dogs had been in the harness treatment, they were placed in an escape avoidance shuttle box. This box has two compartments with a barrier between. When the barrier is lifted, there is still a hurdle in the middle of the box. The dog has to jump the hurdle to move from one compartment to another. The floor of the box can be electrified. At first, a signal such as a sound or light is followed by an electric shock. The dog can escape the shock by leaping over the hurdle. In later trials, the dog can leap the hurdle in response to the signal and escape the shock completely. In the shuttle box, Group 1 that could control the shock when in the harness and Group 3 that was never shocked when in the harness quickly learned to jump over the barrier to avoid the shock. However, 6 of the 8 dogs that could not control the shock when they were in the harness never learned the escape response in the shuttle box.

Seligman proposed a theory of learned helplessness in humans that was based on the reactions of both animals and humans to uncontrollable stress. Helplessness is defined as an expectation that an outcome will not be influenced by any response that a learner makes. You might think of it as the opposite of Bandura's concept of efficacy or agency. Once this expectation is formed, it interferes with learning to respond effectively in situations where the outcomes are controllable. Learned helplessness interferes with new learning in three ways: (a) it reduces the motivation to control the outcome of events; (b) it interferes with learning that some responses do control events; and (c) under extreme stress, it produces fear for as long as the person is uncertain about the uncontrollability of the outcome. This prolonged fear leads to depression (Peterson, Maier, & Seligman, 1993).

In the typical experimental situation designed to study learned helplessness, a person is faced with a set of conditions where there is no effective or successful solution. Responses that would normally be effective in the situation do not work. In these conditions, one often observes efforts at self-regulation. For example, a person will strive to remain goal-directed, use some new planning or problem-solving approach, remain calm, or use reassuring verbalizations in order to stay focused. These are all efforts to continue to address the task effectively, even when nothing seems to work. This combination of self-regulatory or self-control strategies is called **learned resourcefulness**. If self-efficacy is an expectation that one can succeed in a demanding situation, learned resourcefulness is the repertoire of behaviors that contribute to that success.

As the term implies, resourcefulness in the face of stress can be learned and enhanced. A key feature of resourcefulness is the fostering of self-control strategies including: self-talk; recognizing the links between emotions and behavior; and developing planning strategies to reduce the impact of the stressful conditions. People differ in the extent to which they have acquired this repertoire of learned resourcefulness behaviors (Rosenbaum & Ben-Ari, 1985; Rosenbaum, 1990; Ronen & Rosenbaum, 2010).

In our stressful world, where people are often confronted by an uncontrollable influx of demands and stimuli, people who are high in learned resourcefulness are better able to cope. They are more capable of adopting health-related behaviors that require the kind of self-control that is directed at breaking habits in order to adopt new and more effective behaviors (Rosenbaum, 1989). Rather than emphasizing risk and vulnerability, research about learned resourcefulness has guided thinking about positive adaptations to stressful life events. Following along this line of research, Seligman and his colleagues fostered a focus on **positive psychology** (Seligman, Steen, Park, & Peterson, 2005; Seligman, 2011). Positive psychology emphasizes the pleasant emotions of happiness and joy, the cognitive outlooks of optimism and hopefulness, and the adaptive, creative behaviors that result in mastery and efficacy.

AN APPLICATION: COGNITIVE BEHAVIORAL THERAPY

Cognitive behavioral therapy (CBT) is a form of psychotherapy that integrates many of the principles of classical conditioning, operant conditioning, and cognitive learning theory (National Association of Cognitive-Behavioral Therapists, 2014). CBT is based on the scientifically supported assumption that most emotional and behavioral reactions are learned. Therefore, the goal of therapy is to help clients *unlearn* their problematic reactions and learn a new way of reacting. CBT is a form of psychotherapy that emphasizes the important role of thinking in how we feel and what we do. If we are experiencing unwanted feelings and behaviors, it is important to identify the thinking that is causing the feelings or behaviors and learn to replace this thinking with thoughts that lead to more desirable reactions. Although there are several different forms of CBT, most have the following characteristics, which are drawn from the website of the National Association of Cognitive-Behavioral Therapists (http://nacbt.org):

1. CBT is based on a cognitive model of emotional response, assuming that thoughts cause feelings and behaviors. The benefit of this assumption is that thoughts can be changed to help a person feel better or behave more effectively, even if the situation does not change. By revising their thinking, people may be able to behave in the situation in order to change it for the better. Even if the situation cannot be changed, the person can feel less distressed by taking a new view of it.

2. CBT is brief and time-limited, one of the "fastest" in terms of results obtained. The average number of sessions clients receive (across all types of problems) is 16. Other forms of therapy, like psychoanalysis, can take years. What enables CBT to be briefer is its highly instructional nature and the fact that it makes use of homework assignments. Because CBT is comparatively brief, it is also less expensive, thus bringing an effective form of psychotherapy within reach of a much larger number of people.

3. Learning to think differently is the focus of therapy. Some forms of therapy assume that the main reason people get better is because of the positive relationship between the therapist and client. Cognitive behavioral therapists believe it is important to have a trusting relationship with clients, but that is not enough. CBT therapists believe that the clients change when they learn to think differently; therefore, CBT therapists focus on teaching new rational thinking skills that the person can use when he or she is no longer in counseling.

4. CBT is a collaborative effort between the therapist and the client. CBT therapists seek to learn what their clients want out of life (their goals) and then help their clients achieve those goals. The therapist's role is to listen, teach, and encourage, while the client's role is to express concerns, learn, and implement that learning.

5. CBT is based on teaching how to minimize negative and upsetting emotions. CBT does not tell people how they should feel. However, most people seeking therapy want to change the way they feel. CBT teaches the benefits of feeling calm when confronted with undesirable situations. It also emphasizes the fact that people have undesirable situations. If people are upset about their problems, they have two problems—the problem, and their emotional state about it.

6. CBT therapists ask questions and teach clients to ask questions. CBT therapists want to gain a very good understanding of their clients' concerns. That is why they often ask questions. They

also encourage their clients to ask questions of themselves, such as, "How do I really know that I am boring someone?" Maybe the other person is yawning because he or she is overtired.

7. CBT is structured and directive. CBT therapists have a specific agenda for each session. Specific techniques and concepts are taught during each session. CBT focuses on helping clients achieve the goals they have set. When people understand how and why they are doing well, they can continue to practice what they have learned and apply it to new situations when the therapy has ended.

8. CBT theory and techniques rely on evaluating thoughts. Often, people upset themselves about things because they misinterpret the situation. Therefore, CBT encourages clients to treat their thoughts as hypotheses that can be questioned and tested. If they find that their hypotheses are incorrect, perhaps because they have new information, then they can change their thinking to be in line with their new understanding of the situation. This may result in a change in emotions that were a product of prior incorrect analysis of the situation.

9. Homework is a central feature of CBT. Goal achievement, if obtained, could take a very long time if a person were only to think about the techniques and topics taught for 1 hour per week. CBT therapists assign homework exercises and reading each week to encourage their clients to engage in the new learning frequently between therapy sessions, just as one would be encouraged to practice the piano between lessons. Through repetition, new techniques are acquired more quickly and supported by weekly reinforcement from the therapist. Figure 5.4

Where were you?	Emotion or feeling	Negative automatic thought	Evidence that supports the thought	Evidence that does not support the thought	Alternative thought	Emotion or feeling
Where were you? What were you doing? Whom were you with?	Emotions can be described with one word. Rate from 0–100%	What thoughts were going through your mind? Memories or images?	What facts support the truthfulness of this thought or image?	What experiences indicate that this thought is not completely true all of the time? If my best friend had this thought what would I tell him/her? Are there any small experiences that contradict this thought?	Write a new thought that takes into account the evidence for and against the original thought	How do you feel about the situation now? Rate from 0–100%

Figure 5.4 CBT Thought Record (a Sample Worksheet)

Source: Adapted from PsychologyTools.org. www.psychology.tools/cbt-thought-record.html

provides an example of a homework sheet that helps clients make an evaluation of their thoughts and experiment with the idea of entertaining an alternative hypothesis.

CBT is a product of several of the different types of theories we have discussed. It draws upon principles of classical conditioning to understand the association between thoughts and feelings. It also draws on the principles of operant conditioning, especially the focus on the way that habits are built based on the positive or negative consequences of one's behaviors. Finally, it takes into account the complex forms of thinking that intervene between stimulus and response as outlined in cognitive learning theory, especially expectations, values, and goals. The technique has grown rapidly over the past 30 years and has been applied to a wide array of mental health problems including depression, various forms of anxiety disorders, and social skill deficits. One meta-analysis of the effectiveness of CBT in treating generalized anxiety disorders reported that in comparison to waiting list or placebo control groups, CBT was more effective. Several studies also showed CBT to be more effective than pharmacotherapy, with the notable feature that individuals remained in therapy longer when in CBT than when being treated with drugs (Mitte, 2005).

CBT has also been shown to be effective in the treatment of depression, panic disorder, bulimia (an eating disorder), and post-traumatic stress disorder (Baker, McFall, & Shoham, 2009; Hofmann, 2012). Techniques of CBT have been applied to populations of children, for example socially rejected children, to teach them positive relationship skills and to overcome negative attribution biases that occur because they expect others to react negatively to them.

HOW DO THE LEARNING THEORIES ANSWER THE BASIC QUESTIONS THAT A THEORY OF HUMAN DEVELOPMENT IS EXPECTED TO ADDRESS?

1. *What is the direction of change over the life span? How well does the theory account for patterns of change and continuity?*

   Theories of learning do not suggest a direction for development over the life span. In contrast to the psychosexual or cognitive developmental theories, which offer a predictable sequence of stages, the learning theories assume that the adaptive learner will change his or her behavior in response to systematic changes in the environment. To the extent that environments remain the same, habits that are formed will continue to be expressed across settings. Ideas such as self-efficacy and expectations, which emerge from social learning theory and cognitive behaviorism, suggest that a person's beliefs about the self and the environment will contribute to continuity in behavior over time. According to the learning theories, the reason that people of a certain age behave in a similar way is due to the fact that they have encountered similar reinforcement schedules and have been rewarded for behaving in similar ways.

2. *What are the mechanisms that account for growth? What are some testable hypotheses or predictions that emerge from this analysis?*

   The learning theories offer a number of mechanisms that account for relatively permanent changes in behavior. These mechanisms are described in Table 5.1. More than many other theories discussed in this book, the learning theories offer testable hypotheses about the conditions under which change takes place. Testable hypotheses have focused on the timing and sequencing of associations; the effects of reinforcement and schedules of reinforcement on learning; generalizability of responses; the role of expectations and goals on learning;

the conditions under which models will be imitated; the role of memory in learning; the conditions under which something that has been learned will be observed in performance; and the conditions, including the learner's outlook about the nature of the task and the contingencies accompanying action, that foster a sense of agency.

Table 5.1 Mechanisms that account for change

Learning theory	Mechanism that accounts for change
Classical conditioning	Associational learning: The pairing of two events, such as the sound of a bell and the presentation of food, becomes significant because one stimulus becomes a signal for the other.
Operant conditioning	The law of effect: When a response is followed by a positive feeling state it strengthens the bond between the stimulus and the response. When faced with a similar situation, the response is likely to occur. When a response is followed by a negative feeling state, it weakens the bond between the stimulus and the response. When faced with a similar situation, the response is less likely to occur. The law of exercise: Patterns are strengthened through repetition; the more frequently a stimulus–response connection is repeated, the stronger it becomes. People change whenever their operant behaviors adapt to changes in the environmental contingencies.
Social learning	Modeling: New learning occurs through the observation and imitation of models. Those models who are perceived as powerful and who control resources are most likely to be imitated.
Cognitive behaviorism	Cognitions or mental representations are formed that intervene between the stimulus and the response. The learner acquires cognitive structures that influence subsequent learning and performance. Some of the most significant of these include a cognitive map of the environment, expectancies about the reward structure of the environment, a sense of self-efficacy, and goals.
Social cognitive theory	In addition to features of the environment that shape behavior, change occurs due to a person's sense of agency, based on a belief that one has the power and ability to have a desired impact through one's actions. In addition to this sense of efficacy, agency involves intentionality, forethought, and self-reactiveness. A number of emotional conditions influence effective action.
Experiential learning	Four factors influence learning: concrete experiences; abstract conceptualizations; reflective observations; and active experimentation.

3. *How relevant are early experiences for later development? What evidence does the theory offer to support its view?*
   Classical conditioning has the most to offer about how early experiences of infancy contribute to patterns of expectations. The meaningful links between sights, sounds, smells, and tactile stimulation that occur as part of an infant's daily care provide early structures that are connected to reflexive responses such as nursing, grasping, smiling, or clinging. Classical conditioning also suggests a mechanism through which signs and symbols come to have meaning through repeated association with the objects they represent. Operant conditioning offers a way of understanding the formation of early habits that are acquired in the context of systematic reinforcements such as food, social reinforcement, smiles, hugs, and kisses. As early habits are formed, certain behaviors become automatic and can be linked together to form more complex behaviors.

   Social learning theory introduces the notion that learning can happen rapidly; not as a chain of simple responses, but as a result of observing and then imitating entire behavior sequences. Most likely, many of the expressions, activities, and strategies children use are acquired in this way, and then used to achieve a child's own idiosyncratic goals. The role of imitation in child development has been widely studied, pointing to the conditions that make it most likely that a model will be imitated. This research has led to a widely held belief in the importance of models, and their potential impact on children who observe and emulate their behaviors.

As information processing theory suggests, the trajectory from novice to expert provides a way of conceptualizing the gradual transformation of early experiences, which may be isolated, discrete behaviors, into complex strategies for solving problems. The educational system is designed to encourage increasingly complex, efficient approaches to problem solving. At each age, society is organized to introduce the person to more information, to expect individuals to make use of new problem-solving strategies, and to build on these strategies in order to achieve new levels of expertise.

Social cognitive theory introduces the role of symbolic thought for representing goals, and anticipating the consequences of actions. The early nature of social connectedness provides the foundation for goal-directed behaviors which gradually mature into purposive, intentional actions. Early efforts at agency can be facilitated and encouraged or stymied and undermined, resulting in different beliefs about the possibility of one's actions having a desired outcome.

Experiential learning theory offers a potential developmental model for learning. Concrete experience based on sensorimotor exploration is the initial mode of learning. Although more reflective and analytic capacities emerge, the richness of one's concrete experiences and the joy in sensorimotor exploration provide the groundwork for all subsequent learning.

4. *How do the environmental and social contexts affect development? What aspects of the environment does the theory suggest are especially important in shaping the direction of development?*
As one might expect, this is a strength of the learning theories, in that these theories have done much to highlight salient aspects of the environment that influence behavior. The stimulus-response (S-R) theories emphasized the association of stimuli that occur close together in time. Learning was tied almost exclusively to stimuli in the environment and to the consequences of behavior. With social learning theory, the lens was widened to include more elaborate behavioral sequences that could be observed and imitated. The early learning theories were described as ignoring the mind entirely or referring to the mind as a "black box" that was unknowable. Subsequent theories, especially cognitive behaviorism, social cognitive theory, and experiential learning theory, focus more on cognitive capacities that allow the learner to make sense of the environment. They still assume that behavior is intimately shaped by the learner's transactions with the physical and social environments; however, more attention is given to the learner's beliefs, goals, and intentions as they influence both learning and performance.

In an interview with Albert Bandura, he discusses the need to rethink our understanding of the environment. The distinction between the person and the environment has become fuzzy. Given the rapid growth of digital technologies, individuals can carry their desired environments with them. Music, video, games, books and magazines, data and spreadsheets, and interpersonal communication can become immediately available as a person drives to work, walks in the park, or travels on a train or airplane. As a result, the person plays an increasingly powerful role in creating the features of his or her immediate social and sensory environments. The specific features of the physical environment can become a distant background for the selected environment.

5. *According to the theory, what factors place individuals at risk at specific periods of the life span?*
Several factors are known to interfere with learning. First, any neurological damage occurring prenatally as a result of exposure to teratogens or as a result of genetic anomalies, neurological damage due to accident or illness, drug use, or deterioration associated with the illnesses of aging can interfere with learning and memory. Second, the inability to manage strong emotions such as anxiety or depression, created through inconsistent or noncontingent reward and punishment, trauma, or harsh punishment, can interfere with the ability to learn. Third, fear of failure can produce undue cautiousness and an over-reliance on established habits which may not be adaptive to changing environmental contingencies. Fourth, a low sense of self-efficacy in a particular area can interfere with new learning. Those with low self-efficacy are more likely to assume that they will not be successful, and give up in the face of difficult challenges thereby missing the opportunity to reach new levels of competence.

Of particular relevance to the school environment is the documented impact of bullying as a risk for learning. Many of the principles of the learning theories apply. In many schools, the experience of being bullied can be likened to learned helplessness. Children who are bullied come to believe that nothing can be done to stop this behavior. Being a target of bullying has physical consequences including raising the blood level of C-reactive protein (CRP) which is a marker of systemic inflammation and associated risk factors for cardiovascular and other diseases (Copeland, Wolke, Lereya, Shanahan, Worthman, & Costello, 2014). In addition, being a victim of chronic bullying is associated with anxiety, headaches, stomach pain, sleep disturbances, appetite suppression, and other frequent illnesses. These somatic consequences are coupled with a reluctance to attend school, and difficulties in concentrating, all of which impair learning. Evidence of the accumulated risk of bullying was observed in a study of over 2,300 sixth graders. Over the course of middle school, those children who reported being victimized as well as children who were nominated by others as likely victims of bullying showed significant declines in grade point averages as well as declines in teachers' perceptions of their academic engagement (Juvonen, Wang, & Espinoza, 2011).

Bullying becomes a feature of the social environment. In support of a social learning theory perspective, upon entering middle school, children who perceived that peer-directed aggression was associated with high social status were more likely to increase their antisocial behavior toward peers in the subsequent school year (Juvonen & Ho, 2008). In some school environments, bullies are popular and admired, giving them more power to intimidate, and placing them in a visible role for imitation. Students who choose to support or defend victims have to have a high degree of self-efficacy and confidence in the benefits of their actions, since they are taking on a significant social risk in confronting a bully (Pöyhönen, Juvonen, & Salmivalli (2012).

6. *What are some practical implications of the learning theories?*
The learning theories have been widely applied to manage, control, and change behavior in diverse settings including school classroom management, work with autistic children, teaching children who have a variety of developmental delays, parenting practices, and management of difficult behaviors such as aggression or alcohol and drug use. The learning

theories provide the basis for therapeutic interventions as described in cognitive behavioral therapy. Experiential learning theory is used widely in the corporate environment, especially for team building and the enhancement of creative problem solving.

Simple notions of reinforcement are intricately embedded in a variety of marketing techniques including "reward points," priority privileges, and other incentives for using a product. Many of the computer games designed for young children incorporate principles of classical and operant conditioning to support continuing use and involvement with the game. More advanced games incorporate principles of cognitive behaviorism by establishing goals, incentives, and contingencies based on the player's past performances and moving the player to more advanced levels as learning takes place.

The learning theories lend themselves to applications in a "top down" context where someone or some group has a desired behavior or set of behaviors in mind. Under these conditions, the environment, including the physical and sensory environment, and the social and emotional signals, are selected to encourage some behaviors and to discourage others.

The application of learning theories can be used to manage traffic through the use of signals, signs, and contingent penalties; to stimulate shopping in a department store or grocery through the use of sounds, lighting, and social reinforcements; to encourage team work in a military unit through rewards and recognition; and to encourage competition among co-workers in a corporation through bonuses and merit pay.

CRITIQUE OF THE LEARNING THEORIES

The learning theories include several different views about how systematic changes in the environment produce relatively permanent changes in behavior. Classical conditioning and operant conditioning focus on relatively simple forms of learning which, when chained or linked together, can account for some complex behaviors. Social learning theory, cognitive behaviorism, social cognitive theory, and experiential learning theory examine the processes involved in relatively more complex types of learning, including learning of social behavior, the reward structure of situations, and the development of purposive, goal-oriented strategies for solving problems. Cognitive behaviorism and social cognitive theory also offer ways to think about self-correcting systems where information gathered from the consequences of action can be used to modify understanding of the situation and alter subsequent behavior.

Strengths

The learning theories draw attention to the way that even some minute, incidental events influence learning and produce change. The focus on reinforcement and its association with behavior have led to new ways of thinking about how to structure the environment in order to promote new learning, to alter unacceptable behaviors, and to encourage more desirable behaviors. The learning theories have provided ways of analyzing systematic features of environments and have highlighted the capacity of humans to detect and respond to those features. As a result, the learning theories have had widespread application in the design of educational, organizational, and therapeutic environments.

The emphasis on the environment leads to ideas about how a person might respond differently depending on the nature of the setting or situation and its reinforcing properties. In contrast to some of the theories discussed in Part I, which suggest that people at a certain stage of development are likely to behave similarly across settings, the learning theories predict that behavior is shaped by environmental contingencies, and that these contingencies are likely to vary from setting to setting. This approach to understanding behavior has led to a greater appreciation of contexts for learning and development.

More than many other theories discussed in this book, the learning theories evolved as a result of controlled experiments. Because the theories, especially classical conditioning, operant conditioning, and social learning, focused on conditions associated with changes in behavior, the constructs offered in these theories were systematically translated into observable behaviors such as salivation to the sound of a bell, bar pressing, or imitation of a model. These theories emerged through a step-by-step deductive process as experiments were carried out, results were examined, and general principles were formulated. More than many other theories of change, the learning theories have produced testable hypotheses about causal relationships between antecedents and consequences. Some of the basic laws of behavior, such as the notion that a behavior is likely to be repeated when it is followed by a positive consequence, have emerged through the experimental science associated with learning theories. As the learning theories took into account more cognitive and affective processes such as expectancies, emotions, values, goals, and plans, testing hypotheses became more difficult in the interest of addressing more complex features of learning.

All theories of development are expected to offer ideas about the direction of change and the processes that may account for change. The learning theories have contributed greatly to our understanding of the mechanisms of change, especially as they apply to the acquisition of new thoughts and behaviors, and the alteration of old habits. Basic concepts about mechanisms of change emerging from the learning theories include: the association of events in time, the effects of repetition, the effects of reinforcement, the speed of learning and resistance to extinction under various conditions of reinforcement, the salience of role models for learning new behaviors, the development of expectancies and the internal representation of environments as guides for behavior, and the feedback loop for modification of behavior.

These theories suggest that there is an incremental nature to change in which habits or responses become consolidated and strengthened through repetition. These theories also offer ideas about how change is maintained across situations, through the concept of generalization and the notion that schedules of reinforcement produce resistance to extinction. Bandura's concept of self-efficacy suggests a mechanism through which the learner comes to have confidence in the possibility of change and is willing to persist over the course of some failures in order to achieve a goal.

Weaknesses

The principles of learning theories emerged from controlled experimental situations that were designed to be able to test causal relationships. As a result, many of these experiments lacked ecological validity, that is they were conducted under conditions that were not really similar to the real-world environments where learning naturally occurs. Animals were placed in environments such as the T–maze, the Skinner box, or the Pavlovian harness. In fact, animal and human behavior takes place in complex settings where the learner has access to additional environmental cues that may contribute to learning. Studies of animal behavior in the natural environment have demonstrated that animals are capable of much more flexible and complex responses than were observed in the laboratory. Reliance on animal studies and the use of artificial learning conditions that are quite unlike the learner's natural environment raise questions and suggest limitations regarding the applicability of the learning principles to explain processes of learning for humans.

Both classical conditioning and operant conditioning experiments typically used deprivation to manipulate motivation. Animals were placed on a very restrictive feeding schedule in order to ensure that food would be a valued reinforcement. These theories do not address the orientation of organisms to learn about their environment because of exploratory motives such as curiosity or the desire to exercise mastery in the face of challenge. Cognitive behaviorism addressed this deficit by including concepts such as goals and values, suggesting that the learner has the capacity to impose an agenda on the direction of behavior change. As an example, in the process of career management, a person may decide to learn new skills in order to be successful in competing for a particular type of job, or to achieve a salary raise or promotion. The goal itself becomes a long-term reward that motivates behavior change.

The application of learning theory to behavioral control in environments such as prisons often involves the use of tokens to reward specific behaviors. These "token economies" keep people relatively deprived by establishing a strict regimen with few choices or privileges. The tokens become valuable in such an environment because they can purchase items that the person is deprived of or has no other way of obtaining. The application of these ideas with more typically developing children and adolescents may fail to consider the power of competence, curiosity, and mastery as motivations for learning. For example, you do not need to reward a child with a sticker for solving a problem or getting a good score on a test. You want children to enjoy the internal experience of mastery and the related feelings of competence, which are independent of an external reward. These internal reinforcements transcend environments and are important for guiding an individual's behavior over the life span.

In order to identify universal laws governing learning, the theories typically do not take into account individual differences including differences in ability, maturational level, or internal states. For example, the theory that learning takes place through observation and imitation of models does not address the fact that people differ in their observational skills. Cognitive behaviorism introduced a variety of variables such as expectancies, values, affects, and goals, along which individuals can differ. The strict application of principles of behaviorism often fails to address these differences.

A key feature of the learner is his or her developmental level which is a product of physical maturation, cognitive developmental level, emotional maturity, social relationships, previous learning, and the synthesis of complex habits. For example, a 2-year-old child may be motorically coordinated, demonstrate effective language skills, and enjoy play and social interaction. However, even with much social reinforcement, and the opportunity to observe and imitate his older brother, he cannot pedal a tricycle. His legs are not quite long enough and strong enough to make the needed pedal strokes. He does not quite understand the idea of steering with the handle bars, and he is likely to tip over when he tries to turn the tricycle around. By age 3, the child will most likely be able to accomplish this new task. Similar examples can be seen with 4- and 5-year-old children who are not developmentally ready to read, and seventh graders who do not have the formal operational reasoning and abstract conceptualization necessary to understand algebra.

Learning theories place emphasis on the structure of the environment and the ability of the learner to alter behavior in order to adapt to environmental regularities. The theories tend to view the environment as distinct from the person. Yet, we know that individuals can select and alter their environments, striving to create desirable contexts for behavior. The strengths and weaknesses of the learning theories are summarized in Table 5.2.

Table 5.2 Strengths and weaknesses of the learning theories

Strengths	Weaknesses
Highlight ways to structure the environment to promote new learning and behavior change.	Reliance on animal studies and studies of learning in experimentally created environments weakens generalizability to principles of learning in humans.
Widespread practical applications in educational, organizational, and therapeutic environments.	Reliance on deprivation to manipulate motivation in learning limits generalizability, and misses the importance of exploratory motives such as curiosity and mastery.
Contribute new understanding of how environmental contexts may differ, and as a result, promote changes in behavior.	Lack of attention to individual differences in ability, motives, skills, and maturity that influence learning.
Theoretical constructs closely tied to testable hypotheses and systematic experimentation.	Lack of framework to account for developmental differences in learning and performance.
Important contributions to our understanding of mechanisms of change.	The theories present a view of environments as separate from the person whereas individuals play an active role in selecting and designing their environments.
Important contributions to our understanding of mechanisms that support continuity and persistence in behavior.	
Cognitive behaviorism and social cognitive theory introduce constructs that address the diverse mental representations which accompany continuity and change in behaviors, including representations of the self and the environment.	

CRITICAL THINKING QUESTIONS AND EXERCISES

1. Explain four distinctions between the S-R theories of classical and operant conditioning and the theories that introduce intervening variables such as cognitive behaviorism and social cognitive theory. What similarities link these theories?
2. How do each of the learning theories help account for continuity and change in human development? Make a chart that highlights how each of the learning theories accounts for continuity, and how each accounts for change.
3. What examples of your own habits can be explained best by classical and operant conditioning?
4. What evidence do you have of the impact of modeling and principles of social learning on your behavior? Identify four behaviors that are a product of observational learning.
5. Explain the idea of self-efficacy. Can you identify some examples of how your own self-efficacy differs from one context to another? How well does the theory help account for these differences?
6. What is the unique contribution of Bandura's idea of agency to learning? How does this idea alter your view of the process through which learning takes place?
7. Think back to the opening case of Molly. What are some characteristics that make Molly a potential target for bullying? What are the concepts from the learning theories that contribute to an understanding of Molly's reactions including fear, physical nausea, avoidance of school, and difficulty concentrating?
8. What should Molly have done in this situation? What concepts from the learning theories have implications for understanding how the environment might be supporting bullying, and for how Molly might cope in this situation?

9. Bullying is prevalent in many school environments. What concepts from the learning theories might be useful in designing interventions that would help reduce the incidence of bullying, encourage students to stand up against bullies, and promote a climate that is more civil and respectful of differences? Visit some websites that focus on anti-bullying programs or anti-violence programs in schools. What principles from the learning theories have informed these programs?

KEY TERMS

Classical Conditioning
classical conditioning
conditioned reflexes
conditioned response (CR)
conditioned stimulus (CS)
discrimination
extinction (in classical conditioning)
generalization
higher order conditioning
neutral stimulus (NS)
reflexes
spontaneous recovery
unconditioned response (UCR)
unconditioned stimulus (UCS)
Operant Conditioning
continuous reinforcement
extinction (operant conditioning)
habit
intermittent reinforcement
law of effect
law of exercise
negative reinforcer
operant conditioning
positive reinforcer
punishment
reinforcement
response
schedules of reinforcement
shaping
stimulus
trial-and-error learning
Social Learning Theory
imitation
mirror neuron system
modeling
models

observational learning
social learning
vicarious learning
Cognitive Behaviorism
affects
cognitive behaviorism
cognitive competences
cognitive map
enactive attainment
encodings
expectancies
goals
intervening variable
physical state
self-efficacy
self-regulatory plans
values
verbal persuasion
vicarious information
Social Cognitive Theory
agency
collective agency
environment
forethought
intentionality
self-reactiveness
Experiential Learning Theory
abstract conceptualization
active experimentation
cognitive behavioral therapy
concrete experience
experiential learning
learned helplessness
learned resourcefulness
positive psychology
reflective observation

RECOMMENDED RESOURCES

**Beck, J.S. (2011). *Cognitive behavior therapy: Basics and beyond.* 2nd ed. New York: Guilford Press.
A highly regarded introductory text to the practice of CBT, including guidance for how to engage patients, plan treatment, and structure effective sessions. The book presents many case examples and vignettes to illustrate the methods of CBT. Reproducible clinical tools are included.

**Laufenberg, Diana. "How to learn? From mistakes". Ted Talks. www.ted.com/talks/diana_laufenberg_3_ways_to_teach
Diana Laufenberg talks about her experiences teaching middle school and high school students. She compares the information-rich environment of her students with that of her parents and grandparents, suggesting that the purpose of school and the activities one should experience there need to change. She emphasizes the importance of experiential learning which includes opportunities for students to make mistakes and learn from them.

**Inside the Psychologist's Studio with Albert Bandura. Published by the Association for Psychological Science, 2013. On YouTube. www.youtube.com/watch?v=-_U-pSZwHy8#t=40.
This is a 46-minute interview with Albert Bandura, covering his childhood, graduate school, the early period of his observational learning experiments, and his evolving theory of social cognitive behavior.

**National Association of Cognitive Behavioral Therapists. www.nacbt.org
This organization is devoted to supporting professionals and the general public by providing resources which explain the nature of cognitive behavioral therapy, therapeutic best practices, publications, and links to finding a certified CBT therapist.

**Social and emotional learning and bullying prevention. www.abqsafeschools.org/files/SEL_and_bullying.pdf
This report is an overview of the nature of bullying as a school-wide concern, and the use of a social and emotional learning framework for the prevention of bullying. Many principles of the learning theories reviewed in this chapter are incorporated into this approach as well as an explanation for why piecemeal interventions are unlikely to be successful. Prepared by Katharine Ragozzino and Mary Utne O'Brien for the Collaborative for Academic, Social, and Emotional Learning (CASEL) and the Social and Emotional Learning Research Group at the University of Illinois at Chicago. November 2009.

**The Chicken and the Queen of Hearts. www.youtube.com/watch?v=2F5kLv6ErOA
A YouTube video showing the use of classical conditioning and operant conditioning to teach a hen to select the Queen of Hearts playing card from an array of cards.

REFERENCES

Baker, T.B., McFall, R.M., & Shoham, V. (2009). Current status and future prospects of clinical psychology. *Psychological Science in the Public Interest, 9,* 67–103.

Bandura, A. (1965). Influence of model's reinforcement contingencies on the acquisition of imitative responses. *Journal of Personality and Social Psychology, 1,* 589–595.

Bandura, A. (1971/2006) *Psychological modeling: Conflicting theories.* Chicago: Aldine–Atherton. Reprinted New Brunswick, NJ: Aldine Transaction.

Bandura, A. (1977). *Social learning theory.* Englewood Cliffs, NJ: Prentice Hall.

Bandura, A. (1982). Self-efficacy mechanism in human agency. *American Psychologist, 37,* 122–147.

Bandura, A. (1986). *Social foundations of thought and action: A social cognitive theory.* Englewood Cliffs, NJ: Prentice Hall.

Bandura, A. (1989a). The regulation of cognitive processes through perceived self-efficacy. *Developmental Psychology, 25,* 729–735.

Bandura, A. (1989b). Human agency in social cognitive theory. *American Psychologist, 44,* 1175–1184.

Bandura, A. (1997). *Self-efficacy: The exercise of control.* New York: W.H. Freeman.

Bandura, A. (2001). Social cognitive theory: An agentic perspective. *Annual Review of Psychology, 52,* 1–26.

Bandura, A., Barbaranelli, C., Caprara, G.V., & Pastorelli, C. (1996). Multifaceted impact of self-efficacy beliefs on academic functioning. *Child Development, 67,* 1206–1222.

Bandura, A., Ross, D., & Ross, S.A. (1961). Transmission of aggression through imitation of aggressive models. *Journal of Abnormal and Social Psychology, 63,* 575–582.

Bandura, A. & Walters, R.H. (1963). *Social learning and personality development.* New York: Holt, Rinehart, and Winston.

Beard, C. & Wilson, J.P. (2013). *Experiential learning: A handbook for education, training and coaching.* 3rd ed. Philadelphia: Kogan Page Publishing.

Copeland, W.E., Wolke, D., Lereya, S.T., Shanahan, L., Worthman, C., & Costello, E.J. (2014). Childhood bullying involvement predicts low-grade systemic inflammation into adulthood. *Proceedings of the National Academy of Sciences of the United States of America, 111,* 7570–7575.

Davey, G. & Cullen, C. (1988). *Human operant conditioning and behavior modification.* New York: Wiley.

Fanselow, M.S. & Ponnusamy, R. (2008). The use of conditioning tasks to model fear and anxiety. In R.J. Blanchard, D.C. Blanchard, G. Griebel, & D. Nutt (Eds.), *Handbook of anxiety and fear. Handbook of behavioral neuroscience. Vol. 17* (pp. 29–48). San Diego, CA: Elsevier Academic Press.

Ferster, C.B. & Culbertson, S.A. (1982). *Behavior principles.* 3rd ed. Englewood Cliffs, NJ: Prentice Hall.

Ferster, C.B. & Skinner, B.F. (1957/1997). *Schedules of reinforcement.* New York: Appleton, Century, Crofts. Reprinted Acton, MA: Copley Publishing Group.

Gottlieb, D.A. & Begej, E.L (2014). Principles of Pavlovian conditioning: Description, content and function. In F.K. McSweeney & E.S. Murphy (Eds.), *The Wiley-Blackwell handbook of operant and classical conditioning* (pp. 1–25). Hoboken, NJ: Wiley-Blackwell.

Hofmann, S.G. (2012). The future of cognitive therapy and research is bright and clear. *Cognitive Therapy and Research, 36,* 259–260.

Iacoboni, M. & Dapretto, M. (2006). The mirror neuron system and the consequences of its dysfunction. *Nature Reviews/Neuroscience, 7,* 942–951. www.nature.com/reviews/neuro.

Juvonen, J. & Ho, A.Y. (2008). Social motives underlying antisocial behavior across middle school grades. *Journal of Youth and Adolescence, 37,* 747–756.

Juvonen, J., Wang, Y., & Espinoza, G. (2011). Bullying experiences and compromised academic performance across middle school grades. *The Journal of Early Adolescence, 31,* 152–173.

Kim, J.J. & Jung, M.W. (2006). Neural circuits and mechanisms involved in Pavlovian fear conditioning: A critical review. *Neuroscience Biobehavioral Review, 30,* 188–202.

Kolb, D.A. (2014). *Experiential learning: Experience as the source of learning and development.* 2nd ed. Upper Saddle River, NJ: Pearson FT Press.

Kolb, D.A., Boyatzis, R.E., & Mainemelis, C. (2001). Experiential learning theory: Previous research and new directions. In R.J. Sternberg & L.F. Zhang (Eds.), *Perspectives on thinking learning and cognitive styles* (pp. 227–248). New York: Routledge.

Kross, E., Mischel, W., & Shoda, Y. (2010). Enabling self-control: A cognitive-affective processing system approach to problematic behavior. In J.E. Maddux & J.P. Tangney (Eds.), *Social psychological foundations of clinical psychology* (pp. 375–394). New York: Guilford Press.

Lavond, D.G. & Steinmetz, J.E. (Eds.) (2003). *Handbook of classical conditioning.* Dordrecht, Netherlands: Kluwer.

McSweeney, F.K. & Murphy, E.S. (Eds.) (2014). *The Wiley-Blackwell handbook of operant and classical conditioning.* Oxford: John Wiley & Sons.

Mischel, W. (1973). Toward a cognitive social learning reconceptualization of personality. *Psychological Review, 80*, 252–283.

Mischel, W. (1979). On the interface of cognition and personality: Beyond the person–situation debate. *American Psychologist, 34*, 740–754.

Mischel, W. (2012). Self-control theory. In P.A.M. Van Lange, A.W. Kruglanski, & E.T. Higgins (Eds.), *Handbook of theories of social psychology: Vol. 2* (pp. 1–22). Thousand Oaks, CA: Sage.

Mischel, W. & Ayduk, O. (2002). Self-regulation in a cognitive-affective personality system: Attentional control in the service of the self. *Self and identity, 1*, 113–120.

Mischel, W. & Shoda, Y. (1995). A cognitive-affective system theory of personality: Reconceptualizing situations, dispositions, dynamics, and invariants in personality structure. *Psychological Review, 102*, 246–268.

Mitte, K. (2005). Meta analysis of cognitive behavioral treatments for generalized anxiety disorder: A comparison with pharmacotherapy. *Psychological Bulletin, 131*, 785–795.

National Association of Cognitive-Behavioral Therapists (2014). What is Cognitive Behavioral Therapy? Retrieved June 16, 2014 at http://nacbt.org

Newman, B.M. & Newman, P.R. (2006). *Development through life: A psychosocial approach.* 9th ed. Belmont, CA: Wadsworth.

Ormrod, J.E. (2011). *Human Learning.* 6th ed. Upper Saddle River, NJ: Pearson.

Pavlov, I.P. (1927/2003). *Conditioned reflexes.* (G.V. Anrep, Trans.) London: Oxford University Press. Reprinted Mineola, NY: Dover Publications.

Peterson, C., Maier, S.F., & Seligman, M.E.P. (1993). *Learned helplessness: A theory for the age of personal control.* New York: Oxford University Press.

Pierce, W.D. & Cheney, C.D. (2013). *Behavior analysis and learning.* 5th ed. New York: Psychology Press.

Pöyhönen, V., Juvonen, J., & Salmivalli, C. (2012). Standing up for a victim, siding with the bully, or standing by? Bystander responses in bullying situations. *Social Development, 21*, 722–741.

Ronen, T. & Rosenbaum, M. (2010). Developing learned resourcefulness in adolescents to help them reduce their aggressive behavior: Preliminary findings. *Research on Social Work Practice, 20*, 410–426.

Rosenbaum, M. (1989). Self control under stress: The role of learned resourcefulness. *Advances in Behavior Research and Therapy, 11*, 249–258.

Rosenbaum, M. (Ed.) (1990). *Learned resourcefulness: On coping skills, self-control, and adaptive behavior.* New York: Springer.

Rosenbaum, M. & Ben-Ari, K. (1985). Learned helplessness and learned resourcefulness: Effects of noncontingent success and failure on individuals differing in self-control skills. *Journal of Personality and Social Psychology, 48*, 198–215.

Rushton, J.P. (1976). Socialization and the altruistic behavior of children. *Psychological Bulletin, 83*, 898–913.

Schunk, D.H. (2011). *Learning theories: An educational perspective.* 6th ed. Upper Saddle River, NJ: Pearson.

Seligman, M.E.P. (1975). *Helplessness: On depression, development, and death.* San Francisco: W.H. Freeman.

Seligman, M.E.P. (2011). *Flourish: A visionary new understanding of happiness and well-being.* New York: Atria Books.

Seligman, M.E.P., Steen, T.A., Park, N., & Peterson, C. (2005). Positive psychology progress: Empirical validation of interventions. *American Psychologist, 60*, 410–421.

Shull, R.L. & Grimes, J.A. (2003). Bouts of responding from variable-interval reinforcement of lever pressing by rats. *Journal of Experimental Analysis of Behavior, 80*, 159–171.

Skinner, B.F. (1935). The generic nature of the concepts of stimulus and response. *Journal of Genetic Psychology, 12*, 40–65.

Skinner, B.F. (1938/2006). *The behavior of organisms.* New York: Appleton Century Crofts. Reprinted Acton, MA: Copley Publishing.

Skinner, B.F. (1987). Whatever happened to psychology as the science of behavior? *American Psychologist, 42*, 780–786.

Thorndike, E.L. (1898). Animal intelligence: An experimental study of the associative processes in animals. *Psychological Review Monograph Supplement, 2*, No. 8.

Thorndike, E.L. (1911/2012). *Animal intelligence.* New York: Macmillan. Reprinted London: Forgotten Books.

Tolman, E.C. (1948). Cognitive maps in rats and men. *Psychological Review, 55*, 189–208.

Tolman, E.C. (1967). *Purposive behavior in animals and men.* New York: Appleton, Century, Crofts. (Original work published 1932)

6
Social Role Theory

CHAPTER OUTLINE

GUIDING QUESTIONS

- What are social roles? What are some features of social roles that influence the ways they are enacted?
- How does social role theory provide a conceptual link between personal development and the social environment?
- What concepts from social role theory help account for continuity and change over the life span?
- What are the conditions that create role conflict? How might role conflict place individuals at risk? How might role conflict prompt adaptive responses?
- What are some similarities and differences in how learning theories and social role theory conceptualize the environment? What do the learning theories have to offer about how social roles are learned?
- How do social roles guide or constrain your behavior? Which of your roles are most salient in shaping your social identity?

CASE VIGNETTE

A person's social identity is formed through the enactment of a variety of social roles. The following narrative of Azhar, an 18-year-old, illustrates this idea.

> Basically I feel that there are three main facets of what I feel are priorities in my life. What shape my decisions. One being my Pakistani heritage. My father and mother are from Pakistan, and growing up I was really ingrained in Pakistani culture, meaning that I was always exposed to the music, the culture, the tradition, the poetry of Iqbal, the whole family style of being Pakistani ... Then there comes the American aspect of my identity. I love pop culture, I love watching Steven Colbert, and Jon Stewart on *The Daily Show*, I love rock music. I love being part of America in general. It gives you so much freedom to express your ideas in whatever ways you want. And then comes Islam, which ties into everything. And it sort of gives me a direction in which I look to. From the start, as far as I can remember, I was always ingrained in an Islamic household. My parents always emphasized that you should be a good Muslim. We should have strong moral values ... following the *sunnah* of the Prophet. And along with that came a lot of education. I was really involved in going to a lot of educational seminars. I was part of some Muslim youth organizations. (Sirin & Fine, 2008, p. 122).

Social role theory provides a way of thinking about the links between personal development and the social environment. Social roles are the building blocks of society; the defined positions that carry expectations for behavior by the members of groups to which one belongs. Social roles structure the path from childhood to adulthood by indicating the nature of the new and increasingly complex combination of roles one is expected to enact.

In the case of Azhar, we see a young man at a particular time in his life, later adolescence, when he is able to identify and articulate the nature of the three important aspects of his social identity—his Pakistani culture, his American identification, and his Islamic religion. He expresses a positive affection for the ways each of these forces has shaped his life, including his role in the family, his enjoyment of leisure, his sense of personal freedom, his moral outlook, and his education. Azhar appears to be comfortable with the expectations and demands of these three forces. However, in the years to come, as he emerges into young adulthood, he will encounter new roles, particularly those involved in work, family, and community. He will face new challenges in trying to integrate his social identity with these new roles. As we will discuss in Chapter 8 on psychosocial theory, some young people have difficulty integrating their multiple roles into a coherent social identity, leaving them in a state of role confusion.

A major question in the study of human development is how the immature child is transformed into a mature, well-integrated member of society. The learning theories point to moment-by-moment features of the environment that shape behaviors and form enduring habits. In contrast, social role theory focuses on how children, adolescents, and adults are able to locate their positions and status within the society, and how they learn the behaviors, feelings, and expectations that are associated with their roles. Social role theory traces the process of socialization and personality development as a person moves through life, occupying and enacting increasingly diverse and complex social roles.

HISTORICAL CONTEXT

The idea of describing patterns of human behavior as social roles emerged in several fields in the late 1920s and 1930s. Early scholars differed in the way they conceptualized roles and their functions in shaping social behavior (Biddle, 1979). Anthropologist Ralph Linton, for example, saw roles as units of culture and assumed that roles were consistent throughout a society (Linton, 1936, 1945). The sociologist Talcott Parsons (1951/2012) suggested that roles belonged to the social system. The fact that they resulted in common patterns of behavior across individuals was explained by the shared role expectations held by members of the social group. Parsons argued that common role behaviors were supported by shared sanctions. George Herbert Mead (1934) saw **role taking** as an essential socialization process through which the self-concept is formulated as the person identifies with and internalizes the goals and values of society.

Roles are thought to be a form of self-other system. As a person learns how to enact a role, he or she also learns what others expect. Thus, **social role** learning includes acquiring a patterned set of behaviors and an internalized understanding of how others will react to those behaviors. Building on these ideas, J.L. Moreno (1934/1953), the creator of *psychodrama*, applied the activity of role playing to education and psychotherapy. In the context of group therapy, a person might introduce an experience that was especially troubling. If the members of the group agree, they would re-enact the situation with the person involved taking the central role, and other members of the group acting out related parts. In psychodrama, the person would have an opportunity to reflect on his or her feelings, group members might suggest alternative responses, and the group might enact different alternative endings to the situation in order to help the person consider the situation from various perspectives. Because of the compelling premise that social roles shape key interactions that individuals have with others, the concept of social roles and associated processes gained momentum in the study of socialization, identity theory, interpersonal relationships, and the function of social organizations (Brim, 1966).

This perspective brought new insights to the field of development, which, in the early 1900s, had been dominated by a greater emphasis on maturation than socialization and more focused on descriptions of physical and cognitive maturation than social and interpersonal behavior (Brim, 1966). In the 1950s and 1960s a number of research directions emerged in the field of human development that grew out of assumptions closely tied to social role theory. Albert Bandura's social learning theory highlighted the concept of **role models**, suggesting that children observe and imitate individuals who play key roles in their lives, especially authority figures, peer leaders, and television or film heroes and heroines (Bandura & Walters, 1963). Eleanor Maccoby (1961) wrote about the importance of role taking, pointing out that children learn much about the complementary roles that are enacted by their parents as they coordinate their behaviors with those of their caregivers. As a result, internalization of societal expectations occurs in part through participation in complementary role relationships.

Scholars who were interested in adult development drew upon social role theory as a way of thinking about mechanisms of change. Bernice Neugarten (1963; Neugarten, Moore, & Lowe, 1965) introduced the idea of **age norms** and **age constraints**, suggesting that society has age-graded expectations for the timing of entry into or exit from key roles. Orville Brim, Jr. (1968) focused on the new expectations associated with continuing roles and entry into new roles requiring new learning as two mechanisms that accounted for development in adulthood. Thus, the study of development expanded to include analysis of adulthood largely through a conceptualization of the timing and nature of adult roles. Social role theory has provided a fruitful framework for the study of adolescent identity development, gender studies, work–family interactions, organizational systems, and life transitions related to marriage, parenting, divorce, retirement, and widowhood.

KEY CONCEPTS

A Definition of Social Roles

A **role** is any set of behaviors that has a socially agreed upon function and an accepted code of norms (Biddle, 1979; Biddle & Thomas, 1966; Brown, 1965). We are children, parents, teachers, friends, students, workers, citizens, competitors, and lovers. These and other roles refer to particular positions. Aspiring to enact certain roles, and feeling pressure from others for adequate role performance, make an impact on the consolidation of personality. Especially roles that endure across many life stages, including the roles of child, parent, and worker, carry certain norms for behavior that will be integrated into a personal conception of self. What is more, the acquisition of new roles is generally accompanied by internalized expectations, or values about how particular roles ought to be enacted. We come to define ourselves in terms of the primary roles we hold. Moreover, through the process of role enactment we internalize expectations for our own behavior and the behavior of others that shape subsequent interactions.

The term *role* was taken from the theater. In a play, actors' behaviors are distinct and predictable because each actor has a part to play and follows a script. Role theory uses the theatrical metaphor to explain the structure of society and the integration of the individual in social life (Biddle, 1986). Social roles serve as a bridge between the individual and the society. Every society has a range of roles, and individuals learn about the expectations associated with them. As people enter new roles, they modify their behavior to conform to these role expectations.

However, the theatrical metaphor should not be misunderstood to suggest that roles are a form of pretense. People experience their roles as meaningful, demanding, and compelling aspects of their identity. People may experience conflicts among their roles, or conflicts among role groups within societies that result in intense emotional stress.

An infant has few roles that have socially agreed upon functions. In our own culture, the roles of an infant may include that of child, sibling, and grandchild. At successive life stages, the person acquires a variety of roles within the family, as well as within the context of other social institutions, such as school, business, and community.

The concept of role highlights the importance of the social context in the developmental process. Individuals bring their own unique temperaments, skills, and values to bear on the interpretation and enactment of their roles. Nonetheless, most roles exist independently of the people who enact them. For example, our expectations about the role of a teacher guide our evaluation of each new teacher we meet. Those same expectations influence the way people who perform the role of teacher actually behave in this role. These expectations may relate to professional appearance, preparation, respectful interactions with students, and insight about the teaching-learning process. Knowledge of the functions and norms associated with any given role will influence both the performance of the person who assumes it and the responses of a whole network of people associated with the performer (Goffman, 1959; Biddle, 1979).

Dimensions of Social Roles

Social roles differ along four dimensions: the number of roles, intensity of involvement, time demands, and specificity of structure. First, one must ask about the number of roles in which a person is involved. As that number increases, the person's appreciation of the social system as a whole increases. Cognitive complexity, social perspective taking, and interpersonal problem-solving ability can be expected to increase with the number and diversity of social roles. In fact, Parsons (Parsons & Bales, 1955) argued that the process of socialization can best be understood as an outcome of participation in a growing number of increasingly diverse and complex social roles. People who resist involvement in new roles can be viewed as forestalling their development by closing off access to new responsibilities as well as new demands.

A second dimension along which roles vary is the intensity of involvement that they demand or that a person brings to them. Sarbin and Allen (1968) proposed an 8-point scale of role involvement, from zero, or noninvolvement, to 7, at which the self is indistinguishable from the role. At the low end, they give the example of a person whose membership in a club has lapsed for a number of years. Such a position holds no immediate expectations for behavior, although the person could resume involvement at any time. At the high end, they give the example of a person who believes he or she is the object of witchcraft. The total being is so involved in the role that death can result.

The more intense a person's role involvement is, the greater their investment of attention and energy in the role. The greater their emotional commitment to the role, the greater their anxiety about failure to meet role expectations. As a person becomes fused with a role, his or her personality comes increasingly to be influenced by the socialization pressures that are tied to it.

A third dimension of the social role is the amount of time the role demands. This dimension is important because a time-consuming role sets up the basic structure for many daily interactions. The role of gas station attendant, for example, may not involve high intensity, but it may require so many hours per day that the person has few opportunities to enact other roles. In fact, a low-intensity role may be a source of constant personal frustration if it continues to demand a large number of waking hours.

The fourth dimension of a role that influences its impact on personality is the degree of structure specified for it. Social roles vary in the extent to which expectations are specified and in the degree of consensus about how they should be performed. Some social roles, such as member of Congress, police officer, and college president, have written criteria for their enactment. Such public figures are generally held accountable for their performance of the services they were elected, hired, or appointed to provide. The role performer and the audience agree upon certain behaviors as being appropriate to the role. Even less public roles, such as secretary, bookkeeper, and salesperson, have written criteria stating a specified degree of structure. Like public figures, these workers are expected to perform the services for which they were hired.

Other roles are much less clearly articulated. They may be defined by cultural myths (for example, the role of explorer) or by community norms (such as the role of neighbor). Enactment of some roles is quite private—viewed only by members of the immediate family or a few close friends. In these instances, one is free to define and to enact the role as it suits the few people who are involved. Lovers, siblings, close friends, and marriage partners can develop relationships along a variety of paths without coming under the scrutiny of elaborate socialization pressures for specific role performances. This does not mean that no expectations accompany these roles; rather, they provide room for individual agreements and improvisation.

When roles are highly structured, the issue of person–role fit comes into question. Under conditions of lack of fit, a role occupant experiences continual frustration at the demands for behavior that are not compatible with his or her temperament, talents, or motives. In contrast, when the fit is comfortable, a highly structured role may provide the reassurance and support that come from knowing the expectations for behavior. Under conditions of person–role compatibility, a highly structured role may offer opportunities for the development of new competences that will contribute to a person's maturation and growth.

When there is less consensus about a role, the occupant generally has more opportunities to shape it to reflect personal predispositions. However, privately defined roles can generate considerable conflict if the people in reciprocal role positions cannot agree about how a role should be played. For example, although the roles of husband and wife offer considerable latitude for expressing personal preferences and values, if the partners cannot agree about the expectations that accompany these roles, the marriage will suffer from continual conflict and uncertainty.

Reciprocal Roles

Each role is usually linked to one or more related or **reciprocal roles**. The student and the teacher, the parent and the child, and the salesperson and the customer are in reciprocal roles. Each role is partly defined by the other roles that support it. The function of the role is determined in relation to the surrounding role groups to which it is allied. When you enact a role, you also learn about how the person in the reciprocal role is likely to behave. As in ballroom dancing, in order to perform the role well, it is necessary to anticipate and coordinate your actions with those in the complementary role.

Role Expectations and Norms

Social roles are characterized by certain **role expectations** for behavior including obligations the person is expected to carry out and privileges that are permitted to the person in the role (Gold & Douvan, 1997). These expectations are typically understood by the person in the role, by people in complementary or reciprocal roles, and by any audience of observers to the role enactment.

Norms are the shared beliefs held by members of a community, not just those involved in the role, about role expectations and related behaviors. For example, in the U.S., it is the norm for customers to leave a tip for their waiter or waitress at the end of a meal. This is expected by custom, but not required by law. Norms are an informal form of social control. People are influenced in their behavior by their perceptions about what others are doing. For example, in recent efforts to encourage energy-conscious practices, people are informed by their energy company about how their energy usage compares to that of their neighbors. This information, which can be considered a form of informal normative pressure, has the impact of encouraging consumers who are using comparatively more energy to look for ways of reducing their consumption. Today, there are many efforts to encourage people to alter their behaviors such as food consumption, energy consumption, physical exercise, and drug and alcohol use, by introducing information related to social norms that can operate as social pressures toward compliance (Cialdini, 2007).

Influence of Multiple Roles on Development

In general, the pattern of increased participation in a greater number of complex roles is viewed as a normal and positive experience. Social-role theorists argue that the underlying mechanism of development is the opportunity to expand one's repertoire of role enactments (Brim, 1966; Nye, 1976; Parsons & Bales, 1955). The increase in the number of simultaneous roles that a person plays comes with a demand to learn new skills of role playing, role differentiation, and role integration. With each new role, the person's self-definition changes, and his or her ability to influence the environment increases (Brim, 1976). Allport (1955, 1961) argued that the first criterion for a healthy personality is that the person demonstrate an extension of the self. This means that the person derives satisfaction and pleasure from diverse activities, participates in a variety of roles and activities, and shows involvement in meaningful relationships with others. This suggests that it is not only normal but growth-producing to participate in many roles simultaneously.

This is not to say that the experience of simultaneously occupying several roles is easy or free from stress. Quite the opposite may be true. There is often competition or conflict between the demands of two or more roles. Many college students experience difficulty managing the role expectations of their work and student roles. Young adults who are in an early phase of their occupational role find that they have trouble meeting the role expectations from work, family, friends, and intimate relationships. Particularly among dual-career couples, the intensity of role involvement at work may interfere with meeting role expectations of one's spouse or intimate partner. While part of role learning involves a widening of competences and relationships, another part involves balancing the conflicting responsibilities of simultaneous role expectations.

A case study of four Mexican-American boys illustrates the complexity of role enactments and how multiple roles provide knowledge, influence, and marginality all at the same time (Smith & Whitmore, 2006). These boys are sons and parents, living with family members who care about them. They are active members of the CRIP gang, which provides a peer group role and expectations for role enactment. As one consequence of their illegal gang activity, they are considered to be delinquents by the juvenile court with the associated definition, status, and

Figure 6.1 Adulthood Is a Period for the Accumulation of New and Complex Roles

expectations of this deviant role. Finally, they are tied to a school community as students and dropouts, viewed as "at risk" students in this context. These boys enact roles that are central to some social systems and marginal to others; they have insights about how to traverse multiple communities; and they illustrate how inadequate it is to categorize an individual on the basis of only one of the many roles a person plays.

Three concepts help to clarify the potential stressors associated with managing multiple roles: role overload, role conflict, and spillover (Nickols, 1994). **Role overload** occurs as a result of too many demands and expectations to handle in the time allowed. For example, a parent with three children ages 8, 11, and 15 may find that the demands of getting the children ready for school, attending functions at three different schools, picking children up and dropping them off at various places, and trying to be emotionally available for the "problem of the day" are exhausting. Role overload can be experienced in one or more adult roles.

Role conflict refers to ways that the demands and expectations of various roles conflict with each other. For example, role conflict occurs when a worker is expected to stay late at the job to finish a project, but that same night is a spouse's birthday or a child's performance.

Spillover occurs when the demands or preoccupations about one role interfere with the ability to carry out another role. For example, a person may be disrupted at work by worries about an ill parent or distracted at home by a work assignment that is due the next day.

Although the stresses from role conflict can be great, they may also be a force toward growth. When role demands conflict, the person must begin to set priorities about how much energy can be devoted to each role. In the process of bringing many diverse roles into balance, the person imposes his or her own value system on life's demands. There may be ways to bring diverse roles into harmony or to eliminate roles that are no longer meaningful. In adulthood, the challenges posed by role conflict or role overload may foster a reevaluation of personal goals, as well as an integration of role behaviors. In striving to resolve **role strain**, the person can achieve, in each of the roles, competences that can enhance the performance of other roles. Having achieved a workable balance of role commitments, one has the opportunity to function at new levels of effectiveness. We might even hypothesize that the ability to resolve role strain effectively may, in itself, generate energy that will allow the person to take on additional roles or to perform existing roles with increased vigor.

Ineffective efforts to resolve role conflict, however, may detract from role performance in several roles. Failure to resolve role conflict drains energy from the total system. The person who is unable to bring work and family expectations into balance may experience chronic tension, physical symptoms, and disruption in the performance of both the work and family roles. What is more, this cycle of role failure is self-perpetuating. Drained of energy, a person is likely to falter as an effective worker, which may lead to ostracism by other workers, lack of promotion, or being fired. Inability to perform the role of spouse effectively may lead to estrangement, dissolution of the marriage, or social rejection by the extended family or the community. Because many roles are so essential to the maintenance of social organizations, failure at role enactment generally has serious consequences.

The Contribution of Changing Social Roles to Development

Experiences of **role gain** and **role loss** across the life span have the potential for stimulating development. Four kinds of role changes are especially important to the process of reorganization of personality: movement through age roles; attainment of desired roles; abrupt entry into new roles; and role loss.

Movement through Age Roles. Successive **age roles** are part of every culture's organization. For example, in traditional Chinese culture (Ch'ing dynasty, AD 1644–AD 1911) development was differentiated into five periods: infancy (birth to age 3 or 4), childhood (4 to 15), adolescence (16 to marriage), fertile adulthood (marriage to about 55), and later adulthood (55 to death) (Levy, 1949). The notion of age roles reflects sequential changes in personal competences as well as changes in cultural expectations and demands. At each new stage, the person is able to function more effectively, master new tasks, and focus attention on new areas of concern. At the same time, the culture offers new opportunities, new areas of responsibility, and new restrictions (Newman & Newman, 2015).

Development at each new life stage can be understood as adaptation to both the opportunities and the restrictions of the new age role. Each age role brings a change in the person's status as well as a change in the range of behaviors that are expected. In order to meet these expectations, the person normally has to acquire new skills. Growth is promoted as the person tries to live up to the expectations for a new age role. The person is also usually expected to give up some of the earlier modes of behavior. The adolescent who threatens to tell his mother about a peer's misbehavior may be told to stop acting like a baby. The adult who is very moody, impulsive, and self-centered is described as acting like an adolescent. The older adult who decided to have a hair transplant and a facelift and to try out singles bars is criticized for refusing to "grow old gracefully." Consensus about the appropriate age for certain life attainments or activities seems to work as a prod to keep people moving along in their socialization as adults (Neugarten, Moore, & Lowe, 1965). Especially in middle and later adulthood, people tend to perceive age-related norms as motivating guidelines for behavior. Age norms about marriage, parenting, financial independence from parents, emotional independence from parents, and involvement with one's children force many people to give up old, familiar patterns in order to live up to the cultural expectations of a new age role.

Attainment of Desired Roles. The second important source of role change is the attainment of desired roles. Whereas age roles are attained as a function of chronological age, some roles are achieved through effort and skill. Examples of achieved roles to which a person might aspire are: leader of a student organization, leader of a gang, supervisor or executive in an organization, or elected official. Often, one's ideals are stated in terms of roles. A person may hope to improve the conditions for people in his or her neighborhood by running for city council or by becoming a social worker and establishing a social service agency. People may become deeply involved in attaining desired roles because many motives are being satisfied at the same time.

As a person strives to attain desired goals, a process of reality-oriented reevaluation takes place. If a desired goal is achieved, the person is encouraged about the attainment of goals and the possibility of success in subsequent effort. One also has an opportunity to evaluate whether these ideals are really satisfying. One might try to become a school leader and then discover that the role is less glamorous or less satisfying than one had expected. There is also a reality-oriented reevaluation that comes from failing to achieve desired roles. When goals are missed, the person begins to redefine personal aspirations so that they more adequately reflect existing competences. Or the person may be highly motivated to strengthen existing competences and try, once again, to attain the goal that is being sought.

Abrupt Entry into New Roles. A third kind of change in roles that prompts development is the relatively abrupt entry into new roles. There are some life experiences for which training or preparation is minimal. Some common examples are starting school or dating. Other examples occur in conditions of unexpected transition—a woman's husband is killed and she becomes a young widow and a single parent; a young man's father dies and he is now responsible for the support of his mother and younger siblings; a reservist is suddenly called up for active duty. Each of these experiences requires new learning on many levels at once. The role requires the development of many new skills, it generally involves increased uncertainty and anxiety, and there is considerable pressure from others in reciprocal roles to achieve effective enactment of the role. Because of the lack of training, one must draw on inner resources to cope with the uncertainty and social pressures tied to these new role positions. Effective coping will lead to the acquisition of new information, new strategies for responding to emerging demands, and the use of existing skills in new, more appropriate ways.

What may begin as an anxiety-producing new role can stimulate an important expansion of competence. The satisfactions of the new role eventually bring about greater identification with the functions and norms of the role until the new role becomes integrated into the self-concept. In many instances, the opportunities of a new role bring to the surface latent competences and predispositions of which the person was not aware. The new parent may for the first time identify his or her potential for nurturance or playfulness. The new retiree may discover a latent capacity for intellectual development or for mastery of a manual skill that had never been given the opportunity to flourish.

With each new role, the person changes in two ways. First, the person attempts to meet new demands by making use of existing skills, making the role an extension of what he or she already does well. Second, the person modifies existing skills or acquires new skills in order to function more effectively in the new role. Over time, the person understands the role more fully, plays the role more effectively, and views the role as a less alien part of his or her life pattern.

Some of the most important life roles persist through several stages. For example, we are someone's child from infancy until death, and we may be a partner in an intimate sexual relationship from adolescence through later adulthood. In each of these roles there is both continuity and change (Feldman & Feldman, 1975). The expectations for the role performance remain the same in some respects but change in others. We can begin to see how social roles provide a thread of consistency to life experience and how they prompt new learning.

Role Loss. Over the life span we also lose roles. The most dramatic instance comes with the death of a reciprocal role partner. When a parent, child, or spouse dies, we lose an important role. Graduation from school, divorce, loss of employment, and retirement are other transitions that result in role loss. Social role theory helps to explain the stressful nature of these changes by taking into account the time, emotional intensity, structure, and culturally shared meaning that are bound up in a single life role and the subsequent disorientation that is likely to follow its loss.

NEW DIRECTIONS

Gender Role Development

Gender is a critical element of one's identity. All cultures construct gender-differentiated roles, and these **gender roles** are associated with expectations to perform distinct tasks, have access to certain resources, and display certain powers and attributes. What is more, they form expectations of how men and women ought to act when they are together so that the distinctions between the genders are demarcated (Freud, 1994). One might consider these *sex stereotypes*. If you had no information about a person other than whether the person was male or female, what qualities would you attribute to that person? How would you expect the person to behave? **Gender role standards** tell us what the culture considers typical and admirable for girls and boys, men and women (Eagly, 2009). The study of gender roles expands social role theory by examining the complex interplay of socialization processes and self-concept development as they influence attitudes, values, emotional responses, preferences, and behavior. The study of gender roles includes an analysis of the demands and expectations associated with gender that operate at the group or social community level, as well as the ways individuals internalize these expectations such that the gender role standards influence individual behavior. In this section we present theoretical considerations about the influence of gender roles on behavior within a life-span perspective.

Gender is a basic cognitive category that organizes social relations and influences the interpretation of experiences (Leaper & Bigler, 2011). Children learn that people are grouped into two sexes—male and female. Once children learn this powerful category, they go about the business of figuring out how to apply it. They recognize people as men and women, boys and girls, and they identify themselves as members of one of these two groups. They form expectations based on this categorization—that certain toys, interests, and behaviors are appropriate for boys and others are appropriate for girls; that certain activities, dispositions, and occupations are appropriate for men and others for women. These expectations are generally reinforced by the beliefs of the older children and adults with whom children interact. Thus, the gender roles that are conceived during childhood play a significant part in guiding a child's daily activities and in shaping a preliminary vision of oneself in the future. Gender-based beliefs may become integrated into moral development, so that children begin to believe that it is morally right to adhere to certain gender role standards and morally wrong to violate these standards.

In the United States, gender role standards have been changing over the past 50 years. Nonetheless, young children continue to identify certain toys, activities, and occupations as appropriate for girls and others as appropriate for boys. A 4- to 6-year-old child's knowledge about gender role standards shapes the child's preferences and behaviors. For example, once children identify certain toys as more appropriate for girls and others as more appropriate for boys, their own toy preferences are guided by these standards. Conversely, when they like a toy that is not obviously sex-stereotyped, they are inclined to think that other children of their sex would like that toy as well (Martin, Eisenbud, & Rose, 1995).

Parental socialization is thought to influence children's understanding of gender roles, but the nature of parental influences is complex. Some parents believe that boys should be assertive and fight for their rights. Others believe that boys should think carefully about what is right and wrong and guide their actions by reason rather than by impulsive aggression. Each of these sets of parents has a conception of male attributes that is communicated to their sons by a variety of means over a long period. The toys that parents give their children, the experiences to which they expose them, and the activities in which they encourage their children's participation all reflect dimensions of the parents' gender role standards. By the time children reach school age, they have been encouraged to adopt those standards and may have been shamed or chided for what their parents have viewed as gender-inappropriate behavior. Young girls may be shamed for their assertiveness by being told that they are acting bossy, and young boys may be warned to stop acting like a sissy.

As the cognitive underpinnings related to the concept of gender mature, children form increasingly complex **gender schemes**, or personal theories about cultural expectations and stereotypes related to gender. Children look for clues about gender, seeking information from their social environment about what activities they should or should not engage in ("Boys don't dance," "Girls don't play with trucks," "Pink scooters are for girls; blue scooters are for boys"), whom they should play with, and what information is especially relevant for them as boys or girls. They use this information to organize their perceptions, focus their attention, and interpret information in such a way as to be consistent with their gender scheme. For example, when young children are placed in a situation where they are uncertain about how to use a certain piece of equipment or when they are trying to understand a new bit of information they are more likely to turn to an adult of their own gender to get new information (Martin & Ruble, 2004; Ma & Wooley, 2013).

As a child's understanding of gender role standards is clarified, a related set of attitudes is formed regarding a personal preference for the kinds of activities and attitudes associated with masculine or feminine roles. Preferences for gender-typed play activities and same-sex play companions have been observed among preschoolers as well as older children (Hoffmann & Powlishta, 2001). Egan and Perry (2001) conceived of **gender preference** as a combination of gender typicality and gender contentedness. **Gender typicality** refers to whether a child fits in with others of the same sex, likes to do the same kinds of things as others of the same sex, is good at the same kinds of things as others of the same sex, and in general displays the typical traits of being a girl or a boy. **Gender contentedness** means that a child likes being the sex proscribed at birth, does not think it would be more fun to be the opposite sex, and does not spend time wishing to do things that members of the opposite sex can do.

In their research, Egan and Perry found a strong and consistent relationship between gender typicality and measures of self-esteem, social competence, and acceptance from both male and female peers. With respect to gender contentedness, they found that the greater social pressure children felt to conform to gender role norms, the more important gender contentedness was in sustaining self-esteem and perceived social competence. Those children who were not content about being a boy or a girl and also perceived a lot of pressure to conform to gender stereotypes experienced lower self-esteem.

In the U.S., there is typically more latitude or flexibility around the behaviors that are viewed as acceptable for young girls than for young boys. Little boys are more frequently stigmatized for acting in what is considered girlish ways, and are more likely to experience peer rejection if their behaviors are deemed gender atypical. As a result, a nonconforming gender preference is more likely to be a source of distress for boys (Wallien, van Goozen, & Cohen-Kettenis, 2007; Hegarty, 2009).

Parental Preferences and Expectations

Gender preference can be influenced by environmental cues as to the value of one sex or the other. The cues may emanate from the family, ethnic and religious groups, the media, social institutions (such as schools), and other culture carriers. Many cultures have traditionally valued men more than women and have given men higher status. For example, among Japanese immigrants who came to the United States between the 1890s and early 1900s, a strong value was the commitment to a hierarchical and male-head-of-household view of the family (Ishii-Kuntz, 1997):

The Issei (*first-generation immigrant families*) customarily designated their eldest son the successor to the family business ... Accordingly, the eldest Nisei (*second-generation*) son usually received special treatment and privileges from his parents. In many Issei families, he was the second to be served at meals, after his father, and he was generally indulged by his mother . . . Younger siblings were instructed to obey his directions, and even older sisters were expected to defer to him. (Ishii-Kuntz, 1997, p. 138)

To the extent that a cultural preference for males is communicated to children, boys are likely to establish a firmer preference for their sex group, and girls are likely to experience some ambivalence toward if not rejection of their sex group. It is easier to be happy and content with oneself if one feels highly valued than if one feels less valued. Parental preference for one sex over the other can influence the quality of parent–child interactions and the resources, interactions, and opportunities available to boys and girls as they are growing up. The attainment of gender preference is a more complex and dynamic accomplishment than might be imagined. In fact, one's gender preference may fluctuate at different stages of life particularly as one perceives gender-based changes in access to roles, resources, and social status (Maccoby, 2002).

Expanding on the relationship between gender role bias and the socialization of children's competencies and interests, Eccles (1993) proposed the following model:

The evidence suggests that general (parental) gender role beliefs influence perceptions of individual children's competencies and interests, which in turn affect the kinds of experiences parents provide . . . Essentially, we believe that parents' gender role stereotypes, in interaction with their children's sex, affect the following mediators: (1) parents' causal attributions for the children's performance; (2) parents' emotional reaction to their children's performance in various activities; (3) the importance parents attach to their children acquiring various skills; (4) the advice parents provide their children regarding involvement in various skills; and (5) the activities and toys parents provide. In turn, we predict that these subtle and explicit mediators influence the development of the following child outcomes across the various gender-role-stereotyped activity domains: (1) children's confidence in their ability; (2) children's interest in mastering various skills; (3) children's affective reaction to participating in various activities, and as a consequence of these self and task perceptions, (4) the amount of time and type of effort the children devote to mastering and demonstrating various skills. (p. 170)

A number of studies support the underlying dynamics of this model. Parents' beliefs and behaviors, often influenced by gender stereotypes and social norms, influence their expectations for their children's academic futures (Davis-Kean, 2005). Independent of actual gender differences in specific domains, including math, sports, or English, parents' stereotypes about which gender is more talented in a particular area influence their perceptions of their own child's competence in that area. Parents' perceptions of competence are directly related to their children's perceptions of competence.

Reevaluating Earlier Gender Role Standards and Learning New Ones in Adolescence and Young Adulthood

Gender role expectations exist at the cultural, institutional, interpersonal, and individual levels. As later adolescents learn about these expectations, they must integrate and synthesize them with their assessments of their personal needs and goals. The content of gender role standards—that is, the cultural and subcultural expectations concerning the appropriate behavior of male and female individuals—is different for later adolescents than for young children. This content changes as a result of changing age-related expectations and social change. For a 6- or 7-year-old boy, it may have been important to learn to be tough and not to cry or whimper, to stand up for himself, and not to hit girls. For a 6- or 7-year-old girl, on the other hand, the emphasis may have been on taking turns, not being too bossy, and staying clean. In contrast, young men and women begin to develop an analysis of what it takes to get ahead in their social world, whether success is defined as finding a mate, getting a good job, being a good parent, or being popular. They may learn to be more flexible in their interpersonal behavior, modifying their strategy to suit their goals. They discover that such traits as assertiveness, goal-directed behavior, competitiveness, being a good communication partner, personal disclosure, and negotiation are all required in social situations, and they learn to develop and apply them as required. In previous generations, some of the aforementioned traits were considered masculine and some feminine. Today, however, they are perceived as helpful to both men and women to be able to succeed in work and family life.

Changing Gender Role Standards

Gender role standards may change from one generation to the next, so that parents who are socializing their children may have grown up with one set of gender role expectations, but their children may enter later adolescence with a very different set of norms and expectations. For example, in a national survey of college freshmen, students were asked to respond to a number of statements about attitudes and values. One of those statements was, "Activities of married women are best confined to home and family." In 1970, 48% of freshmen agreed with that statement; 34 years later, in 2004, only 21% of freshmen agreed (U.S. Census Bureau, 1996; *Chronicle of Higher Education*, 2005). One could speculate that many of the parents who were college freshmen in the 1970s had more traditional gender role attitudes than their children currently have. Societal changes related to education, employment, views about marriage and childbearing combine to modify the outlook of both men and women on their appropriate and normative roles.

The U.S. culture is moving toward more flexible standards. It is normative for women, even married women with young children, to be in the labor market. The prevalence of dual-earner couples, combined with the increased educational attainment of women, has led to increases in career achievement and leadership roles for women in many fields. As a result, young women have numerous role models of women who are assertive, competitive, and achievement-oriented. Young men have numerous role models of men who are effectively combining career and family life roles, and who take pride in their ability to nurture and mentor their own children as well as younger workers. Many gender-stereotyped expectations about behaviors that are appropriate for men or women have been relaxed and replaced by a greater diversity of behavior that is considered acceptable for both men and women in our society.

The greatest impact of this revision of gender roles is on the later adolescent population as they formulate their gender identities. There are more options, choices, and goals, and fewer obstacles to expressing personal preferences. Nonetheless, later adolescents do incorporate gender role standards and expectations into their self-concept, and these internalized standards guide their behavior. Research with college-age students demonstrates how gender role standards serve a regulatory function. Students report increases in self-esteem and positive emotions when they behave in ways that conform to their own gender role standards, and more distress when they behave in ways that conflict with these standards (Witt & Wood, 2010).

Even as gender role standards are becoming more flexible in the U.S., certain ethnic groups face new conflicts between adhering to traditional cultural expectations and embracing gender roles that are less scripted. For example, Mexican-American women experience a strong cultural emphasis on the role of women as mothers who are nurturing, virtuous, and devoted to their husbands and children. This gender role standard places pressure on them to restrict their occupational aspirations and to remain close to their family of origin, particularly when it comes to thinking about going to college or planning a career (Wright, Mindel, Tran, & Habenstein, 2012). In later adolescence, however, these young women may review these expectations, weighing the benefits from this kind of close, attentive mothering with their own desire for higher levels of educational and occupational attainment. For some young women, this conflict results in psychological distress as they struggle to balance their commitments to home and family with their desires for challenging and rewarding careers. As economic demands and educational opportunities have expanded, Mexican-American women are seeking ways to satisfy their community's traditional expectations while still claiming some space for their own personal goals (Denner & Dunbar, 2004). This example illustrates the impact of role conflict emanating from the tension between traditional and modern views of gender roles.

Gender Role Socialization and Career Choice. **Gender role socialization** shapes career decisions through two significant psychological factors: (1) perceptions of ability, and (2) career-related values and goals. First, as a result of socialization, men and women are likely to form different expectations about their ability to succeed at various career-related skills. Self-expectancies about the ability to fulfill the educational requirements and the job duties of specific careers are a major factor in determining career choices. Recall the discussion of parents' expectations about their children's competence in certain skill areas and its relation to the child's own perceptions of competence. In a longitudinal study, mothers' gender-stereotyped beliefs about their young child's math and science abilities predicted their child's self-perceptions of math and science self-efficacy 2 years after high school. Mothers' prediction of their child's ability to succeed in a math-oriented career was a significant predictor of their college-age child's career choice (Bleeker & Jacobs, 2004).

In the process of career decision making, strong gender-typed conceptualizations of the job demands of specific careers intervene to screen out some alternatives and highlight others. For example, there is a clear path from belief in one's competence in math to aspirations about careers in math, science, and engineering (Correll, 2001). Gendered beliefs about mathematics competence, influenced in part by parental expectations, teachers' evaluations, and career guidance advisors, may contribute to the persistent gender divide with respect to women enrolling in university and graduate programs in mathematics, physics, and engineering. A national survey of students entering college in 2012 asked freshmen to rate their ability in a variety of areas. Even though women are now more likely than men to enter college and graduate, entering female students were less confident about their academic ability, less confident about their computer skills, and less confident about their mathematical abilities than entering male students (CIRP, 2012). Based in part on the implications from social role theory that gender role standards can be altered by exposure to role models and mentors, a growing number of supportive groups, many funded in part by the National Science Foundation, have formed to encourage young women who have ability in mathematics to pursue college majors and occupations in the fields of science, mathematics, and technology.

Second, as a result of socialization, women and men are likely to establish different value hierarchies, reflecting different long-range life goals. Among college students, young men have been found to prefer "jobs characterized by high salaries, power or influence over others, opportunities for advancement or achievement, risk taking, challenging tasks, a high level of responsibility, and a high level of prestige" (Weisgram, Bigler, & Liben, 2010, p. 779). Young women have been found to prefer "jobs that allow them to work with or help others, develop their knowledge or skills, and spend time with family" (Weisgram et al., 2010, p. 779). The internalization of gender-related goals is directly related to how motivated a young man or woman is in pursuing a career that promises to allow him or her to attain those goals (Evans & Diekman, 2009).

The Concept of Gender Role Convergence in Adulthood. The idea of **gender role convergence** suggests a transformation of gender role orientation at both the societal and the personal levels. At the societal level, it suggests a fading of differentiated expectations about how men and women ought to behave, and an equalizing of the opportunities open to men and women in key domains including work, family, community, religion, and government (Monahan Lang & Risman, 2006). At the personal level, gender role convergence suggests that men and women embrace similar attitudes and values and strive for similar life goals (Gutmann, 1987).

The extent to which gender role convergence is taking place is a subject of controversy (Blau, Brinton, & Grusky, 2006). Progress toward equalization of pay and equality of opportunity in employment in the U.S. has been substantial over the past 50 years, yet differences in these areas still exist. Women hold top leadership positions in many large and successful U.S. corporations including IBM, General Motors, and PepsiCo; however, the overall percentage of women CEOs in the Fortune 1000 companies is 5% (Catalyst, 2014). Studies of leadership continue to find a masculine bias, evidenced in the association of leadership qualities with masculine characteristics and traits. These values are held especially strongly by men who, in turn, control many decisions related to hiring and promotion (Koenig, Eagly, Mitchell, & Ristikari, 2011).

Within the domain of family life, the dual-earner breadwinner family has contributed to a gradual convergence of family roles in which men spend more time and women spend less on housework; men are increasingly involved in childcare and childrearing; and families are smaller, thereby requiring less time overall for men and women in the active parenting role (Chesters, 2013). Nonetheless, the gender role expectations associated with parenthood continue to be a more salient aspect of women's identity, influencing their decisions regarding career choice, and their experiences of role strain when work and family demands conflict (Simon, 1992).

A RESEARCH EXAMPLE: BALANCING WORK AND FAMILY ROLES

Almost everyone manages a career while juggling commitments to spouse, children, parents, other household members, and friends. A decision to assume more authority, work longer hours, accept an offer with another company, quit a job, accept a transfer to a new location, or start up one's own business will touch the lives of other household and family members.

The combination of role overload, role conflict, and spillover can lead to reduced satisfaction at work and in family roles, and a decline in the person's sense of well-being (Kinnunen, Feldt, Mauno, & Rantanen, 2010). On the other hand, multiple role involvement has been shown to contribute to well-being. Spousal support for the partner's involvement in work can increase work satisfaction, and feelings of success and pride in one's accomplishments at work can contribute to marital satisfaction (Dreman, 1997).

Work–Family Conflict

The domains of work and family, both central to adult lives across cultures, are likely to conflict under certain circumstances. In order to understand the nature of this conflict, researchers have identified the elements of work and the elements of family roles that appear to be most central to this conflict. The basic assumption is that there are role pressures from work and family that are mutually incompatible, so that meeting the expectations in one domain makes it very difficult to meet expectations in the other. Moreover, there may be interactions such that conflicts from work make it difficult to meet role expectations in the family, but then the disruptions in the family make it difficult to meet role expectations at work (Frone, 2003). Despite these tensions between work and family obligations, people strive to find ways for the two roles to work together (work–family fit), which leads to greater job satisfaction. Job flexibility is viewed as a factor that can contribute to this successful adaptation. This model is presented in Figure 6.2.

In a study of the interface between work and family roles, the model just described was tested in 48 countries (Hill, Yang, Hawkins, & Ferris, 2004). The characteristics of a job that were identified as producing **work–family conflict** were: job responsibility, job workload, and job travel. The characteristics of the family that were identified as producing family–work conflict were: responsibility for children, responsibility for elders, and being married. The model was tested by analyzing survey responses of more than 25,000 IBM workers, whose average age was 39. The countries were divided into one group of Eastern countries with a collectivist orientation, and three groups of countries with a more individualist orientation: Western developing countries, Western affluent countries, and the United States.

The results of this study showed that the model was a good fit for all four groups of countries. The three job characteristics were significantly related to work–family conflict across all 48 countries, although the strength of the relationship was greater in the three individualist groups of countries.

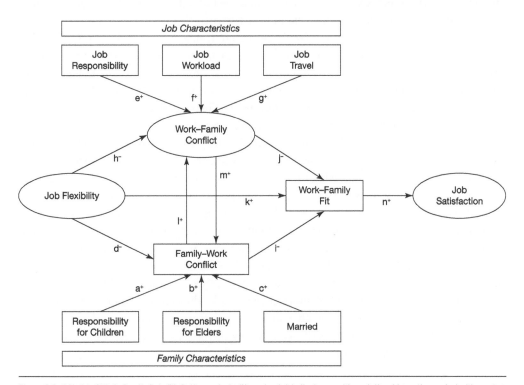

Figure 6.2 A Model of Work–Family Role Fit. Paths marked with a *plus* (+) indicate a positive relationship; paths marked with a *minus* (–) indicate a negative relationship.

Source: Reproduced with permission from E.J. Hill, C. Yang, A.J. Hawkins, & M. Ferris (2004). A cross-cultural test of the work-family interface in 48 countries. *Journal of Marriage and the Family, 66,* No. 5, Figure 1, p. 1302. Copyright © 2004, John Wiley and Sons.

Responsibility for children and elders was related to family–work conflict across all the countries, but this relationship was stronger for women than for men. Contrary to expectations, marriage was related to less family–work conflict across all the countries. Job flexibility was associated with work–family conflict in the Eastern countries and the Western developing countries but not in the Western affluent countries or the United States. Across all the countries, work was much more likely to create conflict in family life than family life was to be disruptive for work. The general model was a good predictor of job satisfaction across very different work environments. One might ask whether the global corporate environment of IBM might have smoothed out some of the cultural variations that might have been observed had workers been drawn from a greater diversity of businesses. However, this research is an exciting beginning to understanding the dynamics of work–family role interactions at a global level.

The cross-national study adds to a growing literature documenting that women are more distressed by family–work conflict, possibly because responsibilities for household and childcare continue to rest more on the shoulders of employed women than on those of employed men (Voydanoff, 2004). Nonetheless, trends in the United States are moving toward a more egalitarian model. Men and women increasingly agree about the value of having women in the labor market and the importance of family-friendly workplace policies. Employed men are spending an increasing amount of time on household and childcare tasks, both on workdays and non-workdays. Between 1977 and 2002, the gap between the amount of time women and men spent on household tasks decreased from 3 hours to 1 hour on non-workdays, and from 2.5 hours to 1 hour on workdays. As men spend more time on childcare tasks, the result is that children actually have more time with a parent than they did in 1977 (Barnett, 2004).

Adaptations to balancing work and family life are not simple. We are looking at the interface of multiple, interacting systems—each partner's work environment, each partner's role demands within the family, and the partners' relationships with one another and with their children. One example of this dynamic interaction was highlighted in research about the link between work-related stress and its impact on children's adjustment. When mothers worked long hours and felt overloaded, they were less warm and accepting toward their adolescent children. When fathers worked long hours and felt overloaded, they experienced more conflict with their adolescent children. In addition, husbands' negative work-related stressors also increased their wives' sense of overload, beyond what the wives were experiencing because of their own work situation (Crouter & Bumpus, 2001). Another example of the impact of work–family conflict on the family system focused on the mental health of the parents. In a study of dual-earner families with children living at home, perceptions by one partner that the other partner was experiencing work-to-family conflict increased the person's own experiences of family-to-work conflict. In other words, worrying about one's partner's difficulties at work and observing the way the demands of the work role impacted his or her family life had a measurable impact on that person's ability to concentrate and be productive at work. The combination of perceiving that one's spouse experienced work-to-family conflict and one's own family-to-work conflicts was a strong predictor of psychological distress including increased anxiety, depression, and anger (Young, Schieman, & Milkie, 2014).

Work–Family Facilitation

The ability to bring positive energy from work to family is a product of individual and workplace characteristics. Voydandoff (2004) referred to this as **work–family facilitation**. Although people experience many types of work–family conflict, they may also find that experiences in the workplace increase their sense of self-worth, competence, and fulfillment, resulting in a more positive outlook on their interpersonal relationships at home. Voydanoff (2004) suggested that work–family facilitation is supported when the workplace revises its expectations for the worker role to include a greater consideration of the fact that most workers are also striving to meet pressing family role expectations within the scope of their daily lives. For example, policies that allow workers to take family-related leave without risking their job security, or to take time off during the day to take a child to the doctor or meet with a teacher, reduce work–family conflict. In one study of a workplace initiative, employees could control their work schedule and location without permission from a supervisor. This new degree of autonomy over when and where they worked, which placed greater emphasis on work-related results, was associated with reduced work-to-family conflict and substantially reduced employee turnover (Moen, Kelly, & Hill, 2011). A supportive work climate in which supervisors help workers feel comfortable about using these family-flexible policies and accommodating significant family obligations contributes to work–family facilitation. The implication of this research is that responsibility for success in achieving an effective balance between work and family roles should fall not only on the coping strategies of individuals but on the policies and climate of the work setting that support efforts to integrate the demands of multiple roles.

Workplace Policies

Unfortunately, U.S. workplace policies have not kept pace with the realities of contemporary U.S. families. The U.S. policies impacting work and family life reflect a view that is more in harmony with work and family roles for the middle class in the 1960s. The major piece of supportive federal family-work legislation passed in the last 20 years, the Family and Medical Leave Act passed in 1993, only covers half the labor force, those working in companies of 50 employees or more (Williams & Boushey, 2010). Work–family conflict is a growing national concern, resulting in childrearing difficulties, marital conflict, and mental health and physical health problems (Greenhaus, Allen, & Spector, 2006).

There are many dual-career arrangements, each involving the negotiation of roles and responsibilities to meet the convergence of work and family needs. A major issue in coping with the dual-career pattern seems to be each partner's capacity to revise basic expectations for his or her own behavior and his or her spouse's behavior. This is not easy. It touches on deep emotional commitments to central life roles including one's view of one's self as a man or a woman, a husband or a wife, and a mother or a father. It also affects the enactment of one's worker role, including values about being a breadwinner, and making significant work-related accomplishments. Because workplace policies are slow to change, the burden of role enactment and resolution of work–family role conflict rests almost entirely on individuals and families.

AN APPLICATION: SUPPORTING REFUGEE FAMILIES AND YOUTH

Imagine growing up in a country and suddenly finding that people of your ethnic, religious, or racial group were a target of systematic extermination. You and your family decide to flee, to find safe haven in another country where you believe you would be free from persecution. Concepts from social role theory are especially helpful in thinking about how best to support refugee families and youth as they cope with the many aspects of cultural and social change. Refugee families, especially those who are forced to migrate due to political persecution or wartime violence, experience the collision of multiple roles: life before the violence or war; life during the violence, sometimes accompanied by imprisonment or life in refugee camps; and life as a new immigrant. For those who immigrate to the United States, refugees try to enact adult roles as parents, spouses, extended family members, members of a religious community, and workers, trying to forge some kind of meaningful accommodation to the different role expectations and cultural norms of their new home. Typically, they experience varying degrees of role conflict as they try to preserve essential cultural beliefs and values associated with the key life roles from the past while striving to ensure safety, economic and educational opportunities, and a hopeful future for their children in the new social environment.

In a qualitative study of Bosnian refugees in the Chicago community, researchers noted that Bosnian families expressed intense concern about problems experienced by their adolescent children. These problems included school-related difficulties, such as underachievement, school failure, and dropping out of school; family conflict; and association with delinquent youth (Weine et al., 2006). This research team wanted to learn more about how the trauma associated with war and genocide, forced migration, and life in exile in a major U.S. urban center might be contributing to these problems. Twenty-one families, including fathers, mothers, and adolescent children, participated in a guided 7-week discussion program facilitated by Bosnian refugees trained and supervised by university researchers. Themes from the discussion groups were coded to reveal basic family beliefs, homeland factors, and refugee factors that were influencing the families' adaptation and youth behavior. Through this work, four ideas associated with role theory emerged:

1. Parents held role expectations for themselves and their children that reflected their Bosnian traditions before the war. These included the view that families should be together and spend time together; children should respect their elders; and the family should stay connected to the extended family. They believed that the enactment of certain traditions, such as drinking coffee together, practicing the Muslim religion, and speaking the Bosnian language, was important.
2. Parents had clear role expectations for the worker role; they believed in working hard and striving to achieve economic stability. They believed that their children should apply this same work ethic to their school work and to earning money when they were old enough to work.
3. Parents saw their refugee status in the United States as a way of ensuring a better life for their children. Many believed that their own adult future was lost; their work roles were menial and their status within Bosnian society was lost. This meant that they were more deeply invested in the parent role than they might have been had they remained in Bosnia. Their hope was for a life of peace, happiness, and possibilities for their children that could not be attained for them in their home country.
4. Parents had grave concerns over the negative influence of American culture on their children. They believed that their children were being drawn into the youth culture too quickly. They saw pressures toward individualism, materialism, lack of discipline, exposure to crime, sex, and drugs, and delinquent peer associations. Parents recalled a time in Bosnia before the war, when they did not have to worry as much about their children and their children were free to be independent. Now, they found themselves redefining their parent role in order to limit their children's exposure to the undesirable influences of American life. The idea that the United States is a culture that could provide new roles and related opportunities and unwanted loss of one's cultural identity is not uncommon among refugee populations.

Each of these sets of role expectations posed some challenges for youth. The first set of expectations regarding family togetherness and family traditions was difficult for many Bosnian adolescents to satisfy given that they were trying to enact new role expectations conveyed by parents, peers, and teachers in their school and neighborhood. They wanted to have time to explore their community and to take advantage of new opportunities, such as after-school activities and community programs. They found their parents to be judgmental and critical of the way they spent their time. With parents working long hours, and often multiple shifts, and many youth also working, they were not able to spend as much time with their parents as they might have liked.

Youth and parents expressed concerns about the school environment. Adolescents reported being bored; some said they did not get the kind of counseling or advice they had hoped for from teachers about how to adjust to U.S. social and cultural life. Parents believed that the schools were not challenging their children. There was some disappointment in the way U.S. teachers enacted the teacher role, with parents saying they believed the teachers should use a more strict form of discipline and insist on greater respect from students. Unfamiliar with the U.S. school system, the parents did not know how to communicate their expectations. Often, their disapproval was directed to their children who became increasingly disengaged from the student role.

Youth tended to have two different ways of coping with the intense investment that their parents were making in their future. Some believed that they could find a promising future in the United States by attending school, planning for college, working, and spending time with their parents and their relatives. They explored their new environment but tried not to worry their parents.

Others felt that they had been victimized by the Serbs and the war; displaced from their home; and misunderstood by their family, teachers, and peers. They experienced an irreconcilable role conflict between their parents' expectations for them to succeed in school and to prosper in the American community, and their parents' mistrust of American values and disappointment in American schools. They saw their parents as trying to guard them against a culture they had brought them to. As a result, they experienced the role loss of the trusting, harmonious parent–child relationship of their past, and hopelessness about the possibilities for meaningful role enactment as a student, child, or friend in their new culture.

In many of the narratives of immigrants resettling in the U.S., one finds evidence of efforts to continue some ties to the culture and language of the home country (Historical Society of Pennsylvania, 2014). This may be expressed in membership in culturally based social organizations, contribution to websites focusing on their home language or culture, working toward increasing awareness of the needs of people in their home country, and sending money and resources to family members left behind. Not all immigrants are able to establish full citizenship, thus creating an ambiguous role as "undocumented" or "illegal aliens." Social role theory is especially useful as a lens to help understand the array of role conflicts and role strain that might accompany this ambiguous status.

HOW DOES SOCIAL ROLE THEORY ANSWER THE BASIC QUESTIONS THAT A THEORY OF HUMAN DEVELOPMENT IS EXPECTED TO ADDRESS?

1. *What is the direction of change over the life span? How well does the theory account for patterns of change and continuity?*
   Societies have a series of age-graded roles that guide the direction of development throughout life. The roles vary from one society to another. In societies where there is cultural continuity,

roles may remain quite constant from age to age, with new levels of mastery expected at each age. In societies where there is cultural discontinuity, childhood roles are very distinct from adult roles, and one must go through certain rites of passage or training to enter the adult roles. Continuity is explained by the enactment of roles that endure over long periods, such as child or parent. Continuity is also explained by participation in reciprocal roles; one learns about the expectations of one's own role and the adjoining roles. Change is explained by the process of role gain, role loss, and entry into an increasing number of roles that produce new levels of societal engagement.

2. *What are the mechanisms that account for growth? What are some testable hypotheses or predictions that emerge from this analysis?*
Role norms and expectations, as well as the norms for reciprocal roles, are mechanisms that guide development. Individuals learn the norms of the roles they enact and the norms for the roles they expect to enact in the future. The idea of a role model suggests that individuals can observe, emulate, and internalize the behaviors of others so that they are able to enact these roles effectively at the appropriate time.

One testable hypothesis is that people who occupy the same role will demonstrate common behaviors, which reflect the norms and shared expectations for people in that role.

A second testable hypothesis is that the way a person enacts a role, such as teacher, is influenced by the expectations of those in reciprocal roles, such as students. In other words, a teacher's behaviors are shaped in part by his or her students' expectations and the students' behaviors are influenced by teachers' expectations.

A third testable hypothesis is that role enactment is guided by salient role models. For example, as one enacts the parent role, one is guided by the observations of one's own parents, and other adults one has observed in the parenting role.

3. *How relevant are early experiences for later development? What evidence does the theory offer to support its view?*
Early experiences are relevant for later development in several ways. First, children have opportunities to enact a variety of roles that provide insight into the point of view of others, especially through role taking, as in fantasy play or team sports. Second, family roles and roles in school, religious settings, and communities provide avenues for social participation that can provide a positive foundation for later social integration. Third, through the enactment of certain roles, children gain insight into the reciprocal roles that complement their own. This gives them ideas about what will be expected of them in adulthood. In the role of student, the child learns about teachers. If he or she becomes a teacher, the person has ideas about how teachers behave based on how he or she experienced teachers while in the student role. A parent who is interacting with a child's teacher has ideas about what teachers should be like based on his or her own experience with teachers in childhood.

In contrast to these ways that early experience can influence adult development, role theory also offers many ideas about new learning and new paths for development in adulthood. Many new roles open up in adulthood that require new learning. Experiences of role loss and role gain require flexible adaptations. Expectations about the timing and sequencing of adult roles, and the need to balance competing roles, are challenges that are associated with new growth in adulthood. As society changes, role expectations change and new roles may emerge that were not available during one's childhood. This is especially true in the world of work. New technologies may introduce new roles, such as online dating partner, sperm-donating father, surrogate mother, or blogger. Role theory offers a way to think about new opportunities and demands for adaptation, and a supportive structure for personal development.

4. *How do the environmental and social contexts affect development? What aspects of the environment does the theory suggest are especially important in shaping the direction of development?*

   Social roles are a key component of the environment. The direction of development is shaped largely by the roles that are available at each period of life, the demands and expectations for those roles, and the sanctions associated with role enactment. People are influenced by the roles they play, the reciprocal roles linked to these roles, and the roles they aspire to in the future.

   As discussed in the section on work–family balance, there are many ways in which the role expectations in one domain can impact role enactment in another domain. Organizations can create structures and expectations for the work role that either support or conflict with one's family roles. Partners can have expectations for one another that can support or interfere with enactment of the worker role.

5. *According to social role theory, what factors place individuals at risk at specific periods of the life span?*

   Social role theory offers several ideas about factors that may place individuals at risk. First, individuals may be unable to meet role expectations due to physical, cognitive, or emotional limitations. For example, role expectations for students in the elementary grades may include sitting quietly, taking turns, focusing attention, listening attentively to others, and completing tasks. Children who have been diagnosed with Attention Deficit and Hyperactivity Disorder have six or more symptoms of inattention or impulsivity that make these role expectations very difficult to achieve.

   A second factor that may place individuals at risk is the possibility of role conflict, role overload, or role strain. Especially in adulthood, individuals experience many highly demanding roles. When these roles are particularly salient, as with parenting and work roles, a person may find that he or she simply cannot meet all the expectations of each role adequately. Role strain is a form of stress that can result in physical and mental health problems.

   A third factor that may result in risk is uncontrolled or unwanted role loss, like unemployment, widowhood, or nonvoluntary retirement. To the extent that a social role provides a structure for personal identity and social integration, role loss can bring serious problems of alienation and social isolation.

6. *What are some practical implications of social role theory?*

   Social role theory has been widely applied in organizational settings. You might think of an organizational chart as a map of social roles, with positions, functions, and lines of authority or supervision reflecting the nature of the organization's roles.

   The literature on work and family draws heavily on social role theory, including ideas about how policies and informal norms support or impede a person's ability to balance work, parental, spousal, and filial roles. Some organizations have offices devoted to helping people understand and manage the demands of competing roles, especially issues such as caring for aging parents, coping with family members who have chronic illnesses, or coordinating dual careers. These same issues may be addressed by workshops offered through religious organizations, mental health centers, and other social service agencies.

The concept of role gain or entry into a new role has particular relevance as a "teachable moment." When people are about to take on a new role, they are especially open to learning about the expectations of the role and to acquiring new skills that will help them in efforts to be effective in their role enactment. Colleges and universities often provide special workshops and programs for "first generation" students in which they clarify the role expectations for student success. Programs in marriage preparation and preparation for parenting are two other examples. The concept of "student teaching" can be viewed as preparation for entry into the new role of novice teacher. Many teacher preparation programs have a list of the attributes and behaviors expected of student teachers. Students and cooperating teachers are made aware of these role expectations and students are evaluated for how well they conform to these role expectations.

Role playing can be a useful technique for problem solving and conflict resolution in therapy groups, work groups, team building, or family contexts. Role playing typically involves assuming coordinated or complementary roles and exploring various possible scenarios in which the actors try out different approaches to their conflict. Observers may comment on the dynamics, thereby providing the players with feedback about the impact of their behavior on one another. An assumption of role playing is that social roles can be modified through feedback in order to achieve more harmonious or effective interactions.

Social role theory can be viewed as a source of inspiration for social change. Over the past 30 years, valued social roles have been identified for historically culturally devalued groups. For example, in 1990, the Americans with Disabilities Act was passed, which opened up the notion that full role enactment in the workplace and the community was a right of persons with disabilities. In 1995, the woman who was named Miss America was hearing impaired. Michael J. Fox, who suffers from Parkinson's disease, continues to perform as an actor in televison comedy and drama. These examples illustrate a shift in openness to highly visible social roles for persons with disabilities. Over time, as more and more people become aware of changing role expectations, attitudes toward previously undervalued groups are transformed.

CRITIQUE OF SOCIAL ROLE THEORY

Strengths

Social role theory offers a way of linking the individual and the social world. The concepts of social roles and the process of role enactment suggest a mechanism for socialization, a framework for relationships, and a structure for adult life. Social roles are not only the positions that the person observes to exist in society; they are the lens through which people guide their own behaviors as they enact specific roles. In societies where individualism is prized, the construct of social roles offers a way of understanding how people may experience a sense of autonomy and self-directed goal attainment by choosing to enter certain roles, and still behave in ways that are similar to others who occupy similar roles.

As societies change, new institutions emerge offering new roles. These new roles are mechanisms that recruit people for the operation of the new institutions and at the same time provide new scripts for how people interact and work together effectively in the new or changing institution. For example, with the emergence of public education in the late nineteenth century came the professionalization of the teacher role; roles for faculty in colleges specifically designed to prepare teachers; a hierarchy of administrative roles related to the organization of school districts and schools; roles for state and federal officials who established funding and credentialing of teachers; new expectations for children in the student role; and new expectations for parents to support their children's education by encouraging school attendance and engagement rather than by educating their children themselves.

Social role theory helps explain how identity becomes focused in adulthood and how it continues to change through role gain, role loss, and the integration of multiple roles. In contrast to many other developmental theories that do not deal with adult development, social role theory has provided a rich and fruitful framework for conceptualizing continuity and change in adulthood. Much of the research on managing work and family life, career development, transition to parenthood, retirement, widowhood, and grandparenthood uses concepts from social role theory as an organizing framework.

The theory is specific enough to offer testable hypotheses. Many studies have demonstrated that constructs from the theory such as role strain, role conflict, spillover, and role loss can be measured and that they are salient sources of stress that can interfere with mental and physical health. The research on gender roles illustrates the premise that a role can shape one's attitudes and behaviors as well as one's interactions with others.

Social role theory uses a language of terms that is readily understood and the concepts have been applied widely across contexts including organizations, public policy, education, mental health, and families.

Weaknesses

One assumption of social role theory is that individuals are attuned to the expectations of others in order to guide their role enactment. The theory does not elaborate the mechanisms through which individuals learn and internalize role expectations. We do not know how people at different stages of life read or interpret the expectations of others. Young children may be less aware than adolescents or adults of others' expectations. Role expectations may vary in how strongly held they are and how clearly they are communicated. The theory does not provide guidance about how these variations influence role commitment or role enactment.

Another assumption of social role theory is that societies are structured by roles that have agreed upon norms, expectations, and sanctions for violating these expectations. In modern, post-industrialized society, there appears to be less consensus around role norms and expectations. There is increasing variability in whether individuals choose to enact significant roles, such as marriage partner or parent. If a person does choose one of these roles, there are also fewer agreed upon norms for associated expectations. Accompanying these changes in shared expectations, there is also a decline in associated sanctions for violating role expectations. The legal system may continue to operate to enforce specific types of role enactment, but the informal community mechanisms of social control appear to have weakened. As a result, one might say that the theory is less applicable to development in contemporary post-industrial life where individual expression is more highly prized than preservation or protection of the social group.

Social roles change as societal norms and values change. The theory does not provide explanatory mechanisms for how individuals incorporate these changing norms. In a lifetime of

80 years, people have seen dramatic shifts in family formation, involvement of men and women in the labor market, diversity in gender roles, and views about the treatment of various conditions such as mental illness, alcoholism, child abuse, and developmental disabilities, just to name a few. How do these changes impact a person's role enactment or their expectations for others? The theory assumes that social roles are flexible, but it does not offer explanations for how social changes are integrated into a person's role expectations for themselves or others.

The theory does not provide much guidance about how role loss, role gain, or role conflict operate to alter development. One needs additional constructs tied to identity, self-directed goal attainment, and self-actualization in order to understand how role acquisition or loss impacts the person. Roles may be salient or relatively unimportant. Role loss may be voluntary or involuntary. The meaning of the role and its place in the person's worldview will influence how changes in the role will impact subsequent adjustment. The theory is limited by the lack of an integrated developmental perspective that links role acquisition and enactment to other aspects of the self theory. Table 6.1 summarizes the strengths and weaknesses of social role theory.

Table 6.1 Strengths and weaknesses of social role theory

Strengths	Weaknesses
Links the individual and the social world.	No clear explanation for how individuals learn role expectations; the theory is missing a developmental perspective on the process of role awareness and internalization of role-related expectations.
A mechanism for socialization.	The theory may be less applicable in post-modern societies where norms and constraints regarding role enactment are variable and less widely shared.
A framework for considering the pattern of adult life, including continuity and change.	No clear explanation for how individuals incorporate changing social norms and social roles into role expectations for themselves and others.
A concept for thinking about how changes in society are linked to changes at the individual level.	A need for clearer testable mechanisms to explain how role gain or role loss is linked to self-concept and identity.
New roles are mechanisms that recruit people for the operation of new institutions and provide new scripts for how people are to interact and work together in new or changing institutions.	
Testable hypotheses emerge from the theory.	
Offers a language that is readily understood and broadly applicable across contexts.	

CRITICAL THINKING QUESTIONS AND EXERCISES

1. How does social role theory advance your thinking about the environment beyond the ideas introduced in the chapter on the learning theories?
2. List three or four social roles you play. What are the norms and expectations associated with each of these roles? Are any of these expectations in conflict with each other? How do you cope with this conflict?
3. Looking to the future, what new roles do you hope to enact? What steps do you need to take to attain these roles? Once you have added these new roles, what new challenges will you face with regard to balancing roles?

4. Thinking about gender roles, how would you compare the way you think about your gender role and the way your parents think of their gender roles? Describe the changes that have taken place from one generation to the next with respect to gender role expectations. How do you account for similarities and/or differences in these outlooks?

5. Look back to the opening case. How might the three forces in Azhar's life influence his gender role? What aspects of Pakistani culture, American culture, and Islamic beliefs and values have a bearing on this question? You may need to do some research about Pakistani culture, American culture, and the religion of Islam to answer this question.

6. Looking ahead, how might the three influences guide his future roles? How might these influences create role conflict for Azhar? How might they support role enactment?

7. What are two or three practical applications of social role theory in your own professional development? Give two or three examples of role gain and/or role loss you have experienced that shape your emerging professional identity.

KEY TERMS

age constraints	role
age norms	role conflict
age roles	role expectations
gender contentedness	role gain
gender preference	role loss
gender role	role models
gender role convergence	role overload
gender role socialization	role strain
gender role standards	role taking
gender schemes	social role
gender typicality	spillover
norms	work–family conflict
reciprocal roles	work–family facilitation

RECOMMENDED RESOURCES

**Blau, F.D., Brinton, M.C., & Grusky, D.B. (Eds.) (2006). *The declining significance of gender?* New York: Russell Sage Foundation.
An edited volume that explores both optimistic and pessimistic views regarding the cultural, economic, political, and organizational factors that contribute to changes in the nature of gender role expectations.

**Goffman, E. (1959). *The presentation of self in everyday life.* New York: Doubleday.
A classic analysis of the nature of social interaction using the metaphor of the theater including performance, roles, and the front stage and back stage environments, to describe how people present themselves to others, and how others respond.

**Historical Society of Pennsylvania (2014). Exploring diversity through Pennsylvania ethnic history. Retrieved on June 28, 2014 at www.hsp.org/education/unit-plans/africanimmigration/african-immigrant-family-case-studies
Brief case studies of African immigrants and their efforts to preserve their cultural links through a variety of educational, service, and community roles.

**Marsh, Nigel (2010). "How to make work-life balance work." Ted Talks. www.ted.com/talks/nigel_marsh_how_to_make_work_life_balance_work
Nigel Marsh describes his experiences in trying to balance work and family life, and shares four big ideas about why this is so difficult and what a person needs to do to bring life into better balance.

**Obejas, A. & Bayles, M. (Eds.) (2014). *Immigrant voices: 21st century stories.* Chicago: Great Books Foundation.
Eighteen short stories that explore the personal and interpersonal experiences of new immigrants to the United States. These stories illustrate the complex nature of social roles in cultural and cross-cultural contexts.

**Voydanoff, P. (2005). Consequences of boundary spanning demands and resources for work to family conflict and perceived stress. *Journal of Occupational Health Psychology, 10,* 491–503.
This study examines the workplace demands, such as bringing work home, and resources, such as time off for family responsibilities, that are associated with work-to-family conflicts and associated stress. Data are based on responses from over 2,000 participants in the 2002 National Study of the Changing Workforce.

REFERENCES

Allport, G.W. (1955). *Becoming: Basic considerations for a psychology of personality.* New Haven, CT: Yale University Press.

Allport, G.W. (1961). *Pattern and growth in personality.* New York: Holt, Rinehart, and Winston.

Bandura, A. & Walters, R.H. (1963). *Social learning and personality development.* New York: Holt, Rinehart, and Winston.

Barnett, R.C. (2004). Preface: Women and work: Where are we, where did we come from, and where are we going? *Journal of Social Issues, 60,* 667–674.

Biddle, B.J. (1979). *Role theory: Expectations, identities, and behaviors.* New York: Academic Press.

Biddle, B.J. (1986). Recent developments in role theory. In R.H. Turner & S.F. Short, Jr. (Eds.), *Annual Review of Sociology, 12* (pp. 67–92). Palo Alto, CA: Annual Reviews.

Biddle, B.J. & Thomas, E.J. (1966). *Role theory: Concepts and research.* New York: Wiley.

Blau, F.D., Brinton, M.C., & Grusky, D.B. (2006). The declining significance of gender. In F.D. Blau, M.C. Brinton, & D.B. Grusky (Eds.). *The declining significance of gender?* (pp. 215–244). New York: Russell Sage Foundation.

Bleeker, M.M. & Jacobs, J.E. (2004). Achievement in math and science: Do mothers' beliefs matter 12 years later? *Journal of Educational Psychology, 96,* 97–109.

Brim, O.G., Jr. (1966). Socialization through the life cycle. In O.G. Brim & S. Wheeler (Eds.), *Socialization after childhood: Two essays* (pp. 1–49). New York: Wiley.

Brim, O.G., Jr. (1968). Adult socialization. In J. Clausen (Ed.), *Socialization and society* (pp. 183–226). Boston: Little, Brown.

Brim, O.G., Jr. (1976). Life-span development of the theory of oneself: Implications for child development. In H.W. Reese (Ed.), *Advances in child development and behavior: Vol. 11* (pp. 241–251). New York: Academic Press.

Brown, R. (1965). *Social psychology.* New York: Free Press.

Catalyst (2014). Women CEO's of the Fortune 1000. Retrieved on June 26, 2014 at www.catalyst.org/knowledge/women-ceos-fortune-1000.

Chesters, J. (2013). Gender convergence in core housework hours: Assessing the relevance of earlier approaches for explaining current trends. *Journal of Sociology, 49,* 78–96.

Chronicle of Higher Education (2005). Life objectives considered essential or very important by college freshmen, 2004. *Almanac issue,* August 26, 14–18.

Cialdini, R.B. (2007). Descriptive social norms as underappreciated sources of social control. *Psychometrika, 72,* 263–268.

CIRP (2012). *The American Freshmen: National norms for fall, 2012.* Retrieved on May 23, 2013 at http://heri.ucla.edu/monographs/TheAmericanFreshman2012.pdf

Correll, S.J. (2001). Gender and the career choice process: The role of biased self-assessments. *American Journal of Sociology, 106,* 1691–1730.

Crouter, A.C. & Bumpus, M.F. (2001). Linking parents' work stress to children's and adolescents' psychological adjustment. *Current Directions in Psychological Science, 10,* 156–159.

Davis-Kean, P.E. (2005). The influence of parent education and family income on child achievement: The indirect role of parental expectations and the home environment. *Journal of Family Psychology, 19,* 294–304.

Denner, J. & Dunbar, N. (2004). Negotiating femininity: Power and strategies of Mexican-American girls. *Sex Roles, 50,* 301–314.

Dreman, S. (1997). *The family on the threshold of the 21st century: Trends and implications.* New York: Psychology Press.

Eagly, A.H. (2009). The his and hers of prosocial behavior: An examination of the social psychology of gender. *American Psychologist, 64,* 644–658.

Eccles, J.S. (1993). School and family effects on the ontogeny of children's interests, self-perceptions and activity choices. In J.E. Jacobs (Ed.), *Developmental perspectives on motivation: Nebraska Symposium on Motivation, 1992* (pp. 145–208). Lincoln, NE: University of Nebraska.

Egan, S. & Perry, D. (2001). Gender identity: A multidimensional analysis with implications for psychosocial adjustment. *Developmental Psychology, 37,* 451–463.

Evans, C.D. & Diekman, A.B. (2009). On motivated role selection: Gender beliefs, distant goals, and career interests. *Psychology of Women Quarterly, 33,* 235–249.

Feldman, H. & Feldman, M. (1975). The family life cycle: Some suggestions for recycling. *Journal of Marriage and the Family, 37,* 277–284.

Freud, S. (1994). The social construction of gender. *Journal of Adult Development, 1,* 37–46.

Frone, M.R. (2003). Work–family balance. In J.C. Quick & L.E. Tetrick (Eds.), *Handbook of occupational health psychology* (pp. 143–162). Washington, DC: American Psychological Association.

Goffman, E. (1959). *The presentation of self in everyday life.* Garden City, NY: Doubleday Anchor Books.

Gold, M. & Douvan, E. (1997). *A new outline of social psychology.* Washington, DC: American Psychological Association.

Greenhaus, J.H., Allen, T.D., & Spector, P.E. (2006). Health consequences of work-family conflict: The dark side of the work-family interface. In P.L. Perrewée & D.C. Genster (Eds.), *Employee health, coping and methodologies: Research in occupational stress and well-being: Vol. 5* (pp. 61–98). Bingley, England: Emerald Group Publishing.

Gutmann, D. (1987). *Reclaimed powers: Toward a new psychology of men and women in later life.* New York: Basic Books.

Hegarty, P. (2009). Toward an LGBT-informed paradigm for children who break gender norms: Comment on Drummond et al., 2008 and Rieger et al., 2008. *Developmental Psychology, 45,* 895–900.

Hill, E.J., Yang, C., Hawkins, A.J., & Ferris, M. (2004). A cross-cultural test of the work–family interface in 48 countries. *Journal of Marriage and the Family, 66,* 1300–1316.

Historical Society of Pennsylvania (2014). Exploring diversity through Pennsylvania ethnic history. Retrieved on June 28, 2014 at www.hsp.org/education/unit-plans/africanimmigration/african-immigrant-family-case-studies.

Hoffmann, M.L. & Powlishta, K.K. (2001). Gender segregation in childhood: A test of the Interaction Style Theory. *Journal of Genetic Psychology, 162,* 298–313.

Ishii-Kuntz, M. (1997). Japanese American families. In M.K. DeGenova (Ed.), *Families in cultural context: Strengths and challenges in diversity* (pp. 131–153). Mountain View, CA: Mayfield.

Kinnunen, U., Feldt, T., Mauno, S., & Rantanen, J. (2010). Interface between work and family: A longitudinal, individual, and cross-over perspective. *Journal of Occupational and Organizational Psychology, 83,* 119–137.

Koenig, A.M., Eagly, A.H., Mitchell, A.A., & Ristikari, T. (2011). Are leader stereotypes masculine? A meta-analysis of three research paradigms. *Psychological Bulletin, 137,* 616–642.

Leaper, C. & Bigler, R.S. (2011). Gender. In M.K. Underwood & L.H. Rosen (Eds.), *Social development: Relationships in infancy, childhood and adolescence* (pp. 289–315). New York: Guilford Press.

Lemay, R. (1999). Roles, identities, and expectancies: Positive contributions of role theory to normalization and social role valorization. In R.J. Flynn & R.A. Lamay (Eds.), *Quarter-century of normalization and social role valorization: Evolution and impact* (pp. 219–240). Ottawa, Ont.: University of Ottawa Press.

Levy, M.J., Jr. (1949). *The family revolution in modern China.* Cambridge, MA: Harvard University Press.

Linton, R. (1936). *The study of man.* New York: Appleton Century.

Linton, R. (1945). *The cultural background of personality.* New York: Appleton Century.

Ma, L. & Wooley, J.D. (2013). Young children's sensitivity to speaker gender when learning from others. *Journal of Cognition and Development, 14,* 100–119.

Maccoby, E.E. (1961). The taking of adult roles in middle childhood. *Journal of Abnormal and Social Psychology, 63,* 493–503.

Maccoby, E.E. (2002). Perspectives on gender development. In W.W. Hartup & R.K. Silbereisen (Eds.), *Growing points in developmental psychology* (pp. 202–222). New York: Psychology Press.

Martin, C.L., Eisenbud, L., & Rose, H. (1995). Children's gender-based reasoning about toys. *Child Development, 66,* 1453–1471.

Martin, C.L. & Ruble, D.N. (2004). Children's search for gender cues: Cognitive perspectives on gender development. *Current Directions in Psychological Science, 13,* 67–70.

Mead, G.H. (1934). *Mind, self and society.* Chicago: University of Chicago Press.

Moen, P., Kelly, E.L., & Hill, R. (2011). Does enhancing work-time control and flexibility reduce turnover? A naturally occurring experiment. *Social Problems, 58,* 69–98.

Monahan Lang, M. & Risman, B. (2006). Blending into equality: Family diversity and gender convergence. In K. Davis, M. Evans, & J. Lorber (Eds.), *Handbook of gender and women's studies* (pp. 287–305). London: Sage Publications Ltd.

Moreno, J.L. (1953). *Who shall survive?* Rev. ed. Washington, DC: Nervous and Mental Disease Publication New York: Beacon House. (Original work published 1934)

Neugarten, B.L. (1963). Personality changes during the adult years. In R.J. Kuhlen (Ed.), *Psychological background of adult education* (pp. 43–76). Chicago: Chicago Center for the Study of Liberal Education for Adults.

Neugarten, B.L., Moore, J.W., & Lowe, J.C. (1965). Age norms, age constraints, and adult socialization. *American Journal of Sociology, 70,* 710–717.

Newman, B.M. & Newman, P.R. (2015). *Development through life: A psychosocial approach.* 12th ed. Stamford, CT: Cengage Learning.

Nickols, S.Y. (1994). Work/family stresses. In P.C. McKenry & S.J. Price (Eds.), *Families and change: Coping with stressful events* (pp. 66–87). Thousand Oaks, CA: Sage.

Nye, I. (1976). *Role structure and analysis of the family.* Beverly Hills, CA: Sage.

Parsons, T. (1951/2012). *The social system.* Glencoe, IL: Free Press. Reprinted New Orleans, LA: Quid Pro Books

Parsons, T. & Bales, R.F. (Eds.) (1955). *Family socialization and interaction process.* Glencoe, IL: Free Press.

Sarbin, T.R. & Allen, V.L. (1968). Role theory. In G. Lindzey & E. Aronson (Eds.), *Handbook of social psychology: Vol. 1.* 2nd ed. Reading, MA: Addison-Wesley.

Simon, R.W. (1992). Parental role strains, salience of parental identity and gender differences in psychological distress. *Journal of Health and Social Behavior, 33,* 25–35.

Simons, E.L. (1989). Human origins. *Science, 245,* 1343–1350.

Sirin, S.R. & Fine, M. (2008). *Muslim American youth: Understanding hyphenated identities through multiple methods.* New York: New York University Press.

Smith, D. & Whitmore, K.F. (2006). *Literacy and advocacy in adolescent family, gang, school, and juvenile court communities.* New York: Routledge.

U.S. Census Bureau (1996). *Statistical abstract of the United States, 1996.* Washington, DC: U.S. Government Printing Office.

Voydanoff, P. (2004). The effects of work demands and resources on work-to-family conflict and facilitation. *Journal of Marriage and the Family, 66,* 398–412.

Wallien, M.S.C., van Goozen, S.H.M., & Cohen-Kettenis, P.T. (2007). Physiological correlates of anxiety in children with gender identity disorder. *European Child and Adolescent Psychiatry, 16,* 309–315.

Weine, S., Feetham, S., Kulauzovic, Y., Knafl, K., Besic, S., Klebic, M., Muvagic, A., Muzurovic, J., Spahovic, D., Pavkovik, I. (2006). A family beliefs framework for socially and culturally specific preventive interventions with refugee youth and families. *American Journal of Orthopsychiatry, 76,* 1–9.

Weisgram, E.S., Bigler, R.S., & Liben, L.S. (2010). Gender, values, and occupational interests among children, adolescents and adults. *Child Development, 81,* 778–796.

Williams, J.C. & Boushey, H. (2010). *The three faces of work-family conflict: The poor, the professionals and the missing middle.* Report published by the Center for American Progress. Retrieved on June 27, 2014 at http://americanprogress.org/issues/labor/report/2010/01/25/7194.

Witt, M.G. & Wood, W. (2010). Self-regulation of gendered behavior in everyday life. *Sex Roles, 62,* 635–646.

Wright, R.H., Jr., Mindel, C.H., Tran, T.V., & Habenstein, R.W. (2012). *Ethnic families in America: Patterns and variations.* 5th ed. Upper Saddle River, NJ: Pearson.

Young, M., Schieman, S., & Milkie, M.A. (2014). Spouse's work-to-family conflict, family stressors, and mental health among dual-earner mothers and fathers. *Society and Mental Health, 4,* 1–20.

7

Life Course Theory

GUIDING QUESTIONS

- What are the similarities and differences between social role theory and life course theory?
- What are some examples of cultural and historical factors that might shape the direction of development?
- How does the concept of agency fit into the life course theory? How much control do you think people have over the direction of their lives?
- Think about the domains of education, work, and family. What are the key transitions in these domains? How might they converge or conflict?
- What might be the impact if two or more transitions take place at once?
- How does the concept of timing fit into life course theory? What kinds of evidence are needed to evaluate whether early or late timing has an impact on developmental outcomes?

CASE VIGNETTE

Jeff was an average to below average high school student from a loving family. His mother was a real estate agent; his father was a railroad engineer. He grew up in an upper middle-class community where most of his friends were college bound. A boy with little ambition, and no obvious talent in math or science, he graduated from high school in 1989 and joined the Navy. After basic training, he was assigned to a destroyer, and served in the Persian Gulf War. This was a time when the Navy was accelerating its investment in land attack missiles. Suddenly, Jeff found himself in a position of adventure and excitement. This was an historically successful military operation in which the Navy played a central role. In 2009, Jeff retired from the military with 20 years of service. He opened his own security company, providing bodyguards and security for events including technology conventions, rock concerts, and festivals. Jeff made use of his military training, his experience with combat conditions, and his love of adventure to create a successful business.

Jeff's story has to be understood as one of a developing person in a specific historical and cultural context. As he approached the end of high school, Jeff and his parents recognized that he was not on any kind of clear pathway into adulthood. His interests and talents had not crystallized. The typical decision of his high school friends to enroll in college did not seem to make much sense for Jeff. Jeff felt supported by his parents in choosing an option that was quite different from that of most of his friends and neighbors. Volunteering for the Navy turned out to be a very positive alternative for Jeff. He did well in the highly disciplined environment of naval training. He was given positions of responsibility; his worldview expanded; and the experiences in combat were sobering but meaningful. Jeff's life in the Navy helped to solidify his sense of identity and facilitated a successful transition into adulthood. His position in the Navy was a point of pride for his family, and when he retired, he was able to use his experiences and contacts to build a successful second career.

The **life course** perspective offers a framework for understanding and explaining how changing societal conditions and social forces influence development through life. The term *life course* refers to the integration and sequencing of phases of education, work, and family life over time. Glen H. Elder, Jr. (1985, 1995), a leader in the elaboration of the life course perspective, has created a way of thinking about individual lives embedded in developmental and historical time as well as the linking of interdependent lives over time.

HISTORICAL CONTEXT

In the late 1920s and early 1930s, Harold and Mary Jones, Jean MacFarlane, and Nancy Bayley launched their pioneering **longitudinal research** studies of children, from the Berkeley Institute of Child Welfare (now called the Institute for the Study of Human Development). There were few other projects engaged in studying children over time. Harold and Mary Jones established the Oakland Growth study with a group of children born in 1920–1922. The Berkeley Guidance sample included children born in 1928–1929. Initially these studies were not intended to examine development beyond childhood. However, opportunities arose to allow investigators to continue to study these participants through the Depression, World War II, and the postwar period. Data gathered through these studies offered a window into the transformation of children of the Depression into adolescents, adults, parents, and workers (Elder, 1974, 1999; Elder & Caspi, 1988).

Glen Elder is the Howard W. Odum Distinguished Research Professor of Sociology and a fellow of the Carolina Population Center at the University of North Carolina, Chapel Hill. He received his B.S. degree from Pennsylvania State University, his M.S. degree from Kent State University in Ohio, and his Ph.D. from the University of North Carolina, Chapel Hill. His first faculty appointment was at the University of California, Berkeley in the sociology department and the Institute for Human Development. This is where he first became acquainted with data from the Berkeley Guidance study and the Oakland Growth study which allowed him to examine the impact of periods of marked historical change including the Great Depression and the Second World War on patterns of coping and adaptation in adolescence and adulthood. He also explored how relative economic deprivation during the Depression altered marital and parent–child relations. He studied how the economic depression of the 1930s affected the subsequent development of children who had grown up in middle- and working-class families before the economic collapse. Elder described the impact of these data on his own thinking about development.

> The archival data from year to year broadened my vision of lives and revealed the dramatic instability of families under changing economic conditions, the Great Depression. A good many study members could say that they were once "well off" and then "quite poor." Institute records noted frequent changes of residence and jobs. A child in an economically deprived family who seemed "old beyond his time" recovered his youthful spirit when family income improved. Overall, the Depression children who did well in their adult years left many puzzles behind. (Elder, 1998, p. 1)

These observations focused Elder's attention on new ways of thinking about social change, life pathways, and individual development. In his view, these pathways refer to the social trajectories of education, work, and family that are followed by individuals and groups through society. He hypothesized that the multiple pathways of individuals and the developmental implications of these pathways are basic elements of the "life course," which could be conceptualized in research and theory. At the time, the field of life-span development was newly emerging. Few theories offered ways of thinking about change over time that recognized the impact of historical context on development, the interconnections of multiple roles, and the processes through which events that impacted adults might alter the developmental experiences of children and adolescents.

Elder's conceptualization of life course theory was influenced by five theoretical traditions (Elder, 1996). First, Charlotte Buhler's (1935) study of individual lives through biographies provided close-up and detailed analyses of the development of individuals and an appreciation for mechanisms of personal change in response to key life events. The second tradition is exemplified by the work of Thomas and Znaniecki (1918–1920/1974) who wrote life history studies of Polish peasants in Europe and the United States. Typically, childhood socialization prepares children to enter adult roles. The experiences of immigration illustrate the disruptions in the life course that can occur when the lessons of childhood are no longer appropriate preparation for the roles available in adult life. Thomas (as cited in Volkart, 1951, p. 593) emphasized that priority should be given to the longitudinal approach to life history: "Studies should explore many types of individuals with regard to their experiences in various past periods of life in different situations and follow groups of individuals into the future getting a continuous record of experiences as they occur."

The third tradition examined the meanings of age in accounts of birth cohorts (Elder, 1974, 1999; Ryder, 1965; Riley, Johnson, & Foner, 1972). Ryder's essay about the importance of the **cohort** in the study of social change pointed out that people who grow through time together in a society experience historical events at specific age-stages and these experiences may influence the development of people in a certain stage in specific ways. Ryder's idea of a cohort provides a way of linking historical time and individual time. It also points out a problem with cross-sectional research designs. Studies that compare people of different ages typically overlook the historical contexts of each age group. Behaviors, attitudes, or coping strategies that appear to characterize people of different ages could be a result of the different historical events to which each cohort was exposed as well as a result of developmental maturation.

The fourth tradition that influenced Elder was the study of culture and intergenerational models (Kertzer & Keith, 1984). Generations of a family are interdependent. Children are influenced by the changing realities of their family environments. Families are changed by the changing capacities and resources of individual family members. As children mature and form families of their own, they bring some of the experiences they have had as young children into their relationships as marital partners and parents. For example, children who have problems with impulse control, emotional regulation, and aggressiveness may find that their adult intimate relationships are unstable and characterized by negativity. Children raised in such families are more likely to experience emotional problems of their own, thus transmitting the parents' problem behaviors to the next generation of children.

This kind of model of **intergenerational transmission** is especially relevant for thinking about the process through which cultural values, beliefs, and practices influence the life course. Early childhood socialization includes cultural socialization into a worldview about age roles, gender roles, family, occupational goals and ambitions, and moral values. Historical factors may frustrate or facilitate these cultural aspirations and commitments. For example, in the United States, a common cultural view is that people who work hard and are competent will be able to earn money and support their families. In the Great Depression, many adults lost their jobs, were unable to find work, and experienced depression, irritability, and interpersonal strain. Many young boys whose families lost their economic base developed a sense of low self-worth, low social competence, and impaired goal orientation. These psychosocial disadvantages persisted into adulthood with evidence of heavy drinking, low energy, and discouraged attitudes about work (Elder, 1979). Thus, in many families, a historical event disrupted the intergenerational transmission of cultural values.

Finally, the fifth influential tradition was the broad area of personality development and life-span psychology (Baltes, 1987; Funder, Parke, Tomlinson-Keasey, & Widaman, 1993). This perspective emphasizes the importance of viewing development across the full life span from infancy through very old age (Newman & Newman, 2015). Although considerable attention is given to how events of early childhood and adolescence impact the transitions into adulthood, it has become increasingly evident that decisions of adult life influence the resources and adaptive capacities of later adulthood and aging. Role transitions, disruptions in pathways, and interrelationships across multiple roles can occur at many points in the life span, and can have an impact on subsequent adaptation. What is more, childhood socialization is carried out in the context of a view of the life span, in an effort to prepare children to be successful in the cultural contexts they will encounter in early and middle adulthood. The changing person is adapting to changing cultural and historical contexts over the full life span, accumulating resources, encountering risks, and exercising personal agency within a framework of personal and social ambitions and expectations.

KEY CONCEPTS

Trajectories and Transitions

Two central themes in life course theory are trajectories and transitions. A **trajectory** is the long-term path of one's life experiences in a specific domain, particularly education, work, and family life. The family trajectory might include the following sequence: marriage, parenthood, grandparenthood, and widowhood. A **transition** is a component within the trajectory marked by the beginning or close of an event, role relationship, or developmental stage. In a person's work trajectory, for example, transitions might include: getting one's first job, being laid off, and going back to school for an advanced degree. Life course theory analyzes the impact of social change on individual lives by observing evidence of fluctuations in trajectories and transitions that are associated with specific historical periods.

Historical Time and Place

Human development takes place in **historical time** and place. Most theories of development focus on the individual as if he or she was living in an historical vacuum. In contrast, life course theory emphasizes that periods of significant historical change will differentiate the developmental trajectories of specific cohorts.

You cannot separate the story of development from the historical context during which the life unfolds. The life course of a man who was born in 1900 and died in 1975, including the ages of entry into marriage, completion of educational attainment, work, and retirement, would look quite different from that of a man born in 1925 and reaching age 75 in 2000. The two people would have gone through the same chronological ages and stages of life, but during different periods of history with different opportunities, expectations, and challenges. The person born in 1900 would have been 30 at the time of the Great Depression, with the possibility that economic downturn disrupted his work life and the financial stability of his family. The person born in

1925 would have been 5 at the time of the Great Depression, experiencing the impact of sudden poverty and family conflict as a young child.

Cultural expectations for the timing of the transitions as well as the pattern of the family and work trajectories changed dramatically over the twentieth century. As a specific example, Stewart and Ostrove (1998) described two groups of women who were in their mid-twenties; a sample of Radcliffe College graduates from 1964 and one from 1975. At comparable ages, about two-thirds of the older cohort were married and 16% had children; 13% of the younger cohort were married and none had children. The majority of the younger cohort of women were in the labor force or enrolled in graduate school. Thus, even though the women may have had many common social, intellectual, and economic characteristics leading up to college enrollment, the landscape of their early adulthood roles looked remarkably different, reflecting changes in cultural norms.

Differences in medical advances, occupational opportunities, educational resources, and the number of people in the cohort are four factors that may affect the pattern of life events. In addition, major crises, such as war, famine, and political unrest, may alter a trajectory by introducing unanticipated transitions—for example, closing off certain activities, as when young men interrupt their education to go to war, and opening up new opportunities, as when women enter the labor market because many of the men are in the military (Elder, Caspi, & Downey, 1986; Elder, 1987; Elder, Shanahan, & Clipp, 1994).

For the baby boom generation of women, who reached later adolescence and early adulthood during the women's movement and the civil rights movement, the political and social transitions of the time had a significant impact. Participation in these movements had consequences for their political participation and also for their role enactment at later points in life. Stewart, Settles, and Winter (1998) reported the way these experiences were woven into women's public and private lives:

> the women's movement led (me) to feel 'freer to leave my husband for a more fulfilling sex life' and another who said that the movement generally 'made the whole free-thinking, autonomous style of my life possible, both then and now' (Stewart & Ostrove, 1998, p. 1192)

Agency

People operate with a sense of **agency** in their own behalf, choosing among the opportunities that are available in their time and society. People make choices that become building blocks of their life course transitions and trajectories, such as choosing to be married or to leave a marriage, deciding to become a parent, and choosing career directions from among the options available. Within a cohort, the choices people make contribute to individual differences. Consider the decision about going to medical school in the 1960s.

Reflecting back on her early adulthood, one woman who was in college in the 1960s expressed regret about decisions she made then: "When I was in college I considered a career in medicine. Due to lack of support from family members and future husband, I didn't pursue it. I would have at least tried it if I were 20 today" (Stewart & Ostrove, 1998, p. 1188). In the first half of the twentieth century, very few women enrolled in medical school. Today, almost half of the graduates of U.S. medical schools (48%) are women (AAMC, 2012).

Timing of Lives

The timing of lives, particularly social time and the social meaning of age, gives structure to the life course. **Social time** focuses on the entry and exit from age-graded social roles, the sequencing of these roles, and the social and cultural meaning or expectations associated with these roles. One form of cultural expectation is what Bernice Neugarten and her colleagues (Neugarten, Moore, & Lowe, 1965) termed the **social clock**. This term refers to "age norms and age expectations [that] operate as prods and brakes upon behavior, in some instances hastening behavior and in some instances delaying it" (p. 710). Neugarten and her associates suggested that social class groups tend to agree on the appropriate age for significant life events, such as marriage, childrearing, and retirement.

This consensus exerts social pressure on individuals, pushing them to assume a particular role at an expected age. Age norms may also suppress behaviors that are considered inappropriate for one's age. Adults are aware of existing norms regarding the timing of certain behaviors and evaluate their own behaviors as being "on time" or "too soon" or "too late." The social clock is constantly being reset as people confront the challenges, demands, and new structures of modern society. In contemporary society, with the lengthening of the life expectancy and the increasing vitality of older adults, there are fewer and fewer domains in which a person is considered "too old" to participate (Neugarten, 1990).

Implied in the notion of the social clock are expectations about the sequencing of entry into new roles. For example, European American adults in the United States tend to view an ideal sequence as work, marriage, and parenting in that order. Research indicates that for women, following this sequence is associated with better mental health, including less depression and greater happiness in adulthood. Among African Americans, however, the sequence of work, parenting, and then marriage is associated with less depression and greater happiness (Jackson, 2004). This suggests that different social norms for **role sequencing** may be operating in the respective ethnic communities.

A unique contribution of life course theory is to place developmental stage and social time into a historical timeframe. Historical, cultural, and societal changes may disrupt opportunities, making it impossible to enact the transitions expected by the social clock. Or these changes may introduce new opportunities and resources that allow individuals to break out of socially expected patterns and invent new pathways. The principle of the timing of lives must be framed in a societal context which takes into account the scope of resources, opportunities, and constraints that impinge on people at particular periods in their personal development.

Linked or Interdependent Lives

Lives are linked through social relationships and influenced by the social regulation, social support, and patterning that occur through these relationships. The principle of **linked lives** is very important for explaining how the events happening for parents impact their children. For example, when parents experience economic strain, they may become more irritable and depressed. This can disrupt their marital relationship and result in harsh parenting or withdrawal from parenting. Both of these are known to have negative effects on children. Two other examples are the sense of filial obligation of adult children to their aging parents and the disruption of friendship networks as a result of divorce.

Within an individual life course, the trajectories and transitions within trajectories are linked and influence one another. For example, life course theory focuses on the age-linked changes in occupational and family careers. You can map the convergence of transitions across the occupational and family trajectories over time, highlighting periods of potential harmony and conflict between the demands in the two trajectories. Imagine two different scenarios: 1. A woman extends her educational preparation to include a master's degree, works before marriage, marries at age 32, and has her first child at age 38. She drops out of the labor market for 5 years, then returns to work to help pay for the college education of her children, and retires at age 68. 2. A woman marries right after high school, begins having children at age 20, works throughout her adulthood from age 18 to age 62, and retires at age 62. The interlocking of occupational and family careers would look quite different for these two women, entering and leaving roles at different ages and making commitments to certain roles over others.

Mechanisms that Link Changing Times and Individual Lives

The following five mechanisms were proposed as ways to understand the links between the societal, historical, and cultural levels of change and the individual level (Elder, 1996).

1. The Life Stage Principle. The influence of a historical event depends upon the stage of life at which a person experiences the event. Rather than assuming that a historical event has the same impact on everyone who is alive at the time, this principle suggests that the transforming nature of the event depends on the person's developmental stage. Developmental **life stages** can be viewed as socially defined positions, such as child, adolescent, or adult. These age statuses may be linked to specific expectations for behavior, rights, and responsibilities. Developmental life stages may also be viewed theoretically, as in Piaget's stage of concrete operational thought or Freud's genital stage. Within a life course perspective, it is important to consider a person's developmental stage in trying to speculate about how historical events or cultural change might make an impact on individual lives. The transforming nature of events will vary depending upon the way individuals make meaning, their degree of dependence or interdependence on others, their commitment to certain social relationships, their personal and financial resources, and their aspirations and goals, all of which change at various stages of the life span.

Stewart and Healy (1989) offered a model of how to think about the differential impact of historical events or cultural change depending upon a person's stage of development. In their model, events that occur during childhood are most likely to shape a person's "assumptions about life and the world," thus guiding core values. Events that occur during late adolescence are most likely to shape a person's "conscious identity," guiding decisions about life roles and lifestyle choices. Events that occur during the phases of early, middle, and later adulthood are likely to influence "opportunities that are open to them" rather than their values or identities.

This model is finding support in the field of political psychology. Political generations are forged as individuals in late adolescence and early adulthood encounter salient events, such as war, depression, and social unrest. According to Donald Kinder (2006), "people command more vivid memories and deeper knowledge for events that take place during their late adolescence and early adulthood" (p. 1906). Those young people who are working on identity issues at the time of major historical or cultural transitions, such as the Great Depression, World War II, the civil rights movement, and the Vietnam War, know more about these events and tend to apply the lessons they learned about government, policies, and politics during that time to their contemporary political outlook. These views, once established, are stable but not unchanging. According to Kinder, key role transitions, including entry into marriage, parenthood, the military, homeowner, and neighbor, are times when people may change their views.

*2. The Principle of **Interdependent Lives**.* The life course perspective emphasizes the interlocking of lives. Psychosocial development depends heavily on being embedded in a supportive, effective network of relationships where individuals, whether they are children, adolescents, or adults, experience a sense of being valued. Historical events that disrupt social relationships rob individuals of social capital, the benefits that derive from a person's network of people who provide information flow, skills, recognition, and support. For example, in the wake of Hurricane Katrina, thousands of people in New Orleans lost their homes. As many as 250,000 migrated to Houston, Texas. These events resulted in the disruption of kinship networks, disruption of employment and schooling, the need for new medical and mental health services, and the need to form new community ties. There were many different ways of adapting—some adapted well to their new environment; some returned home as soon as possible; and some continued to suffer from experiences related to the multiple losses associated with the disaster (Hamilton, 2010).

*3. The Principle of the **Control Cycle**.* When a person loses control, or when personal freedoms are threatened, there is generally an attempt to preserve or regain control. Historical events can influence individual behavior by eliminating or threatening the elimination of freedoms and resources. In reaction to this loss or threat of loss, the person takes steps to preserve control through a wide range of possible coping strategies. Under conditions of sudden political revolution, as in Cuba in 1959, many of those with resources left the country in order to retain their resources and preserve their cultural style of life. In the U.S., Cuban exiles have formed a strong community, especially in Florida, where they have established a vibrant cultural, economic, and political presence. Even in the context of imprisonment, an extreme condition of loss of control, inmates strive to preserve control by developing their physical strength through exercise, by dominating weaker prisoners, or by taking on roles as trustees who assume important functions in the operation of the prison.

*4. The Principle of the **Situational Imperative**.* Every situation has certain demand properties or requirements. If the situation changes, new behaviors are required. For example, the behaviors that are necessary to be successful in college are different from those necessary to be successful in manual labor. During the Cultural Revolution in China, colleges were all closed and college-age youth were sent into the rural areas to assist with the farming. Survival and success depended on the ability to refocus energy from scholarly pursuits to physical activities. There were many young people who might have been successful in the college environment, but who were not able to thrive under the harsh conditions and physical demands of farm labor. When conditions are so extreme that there is no way to exercise control or adapt successfully, people may be reduced to learned helplessness, a concept that was introduced in Chapter 5.

*5. The **Accentuation Principle**.* Under conditions of crisis or critical transition, the person's most prominent personality characteristics and coping strategies will be accentuated. Given the notion of a situational imperative, people will cope with a changing situation by trying to regain control through the exercise of their most enduring, well-learned habits. This principle suggests that people try to cope with change by remaining as consistent as possible.

People who have a tendency toward anxiety will become more anxious; those who are temperamentally withdrawn will become more withdrawn. People who cope by planning and setting goals will strive to use that strategy under conditions of uncertainty. Those who have had experience taking action or providing leadership are likely to exercise leadership in times of crisis.

Table 7.1 Mechanisms that link changing times and changing lives

Principle	Impact
Life stage principle	The impact of a historical event or cultural change depends on the stage of life at which a person experiences the event.
Principle of interdependent lives	People are embedded in important social networks and support systems, which can be disrupted by historical events, thereby altering developmental trajectories.
Principle of control cycle	In the face of events that create uncertainty, people strive to maintain or exert control.
Principle of situational imperative	Situations have demand properties and requirements. When situations change, new behaviors are required.
Accentuation principle	Under conditions of crisis or transition, a person's most prominent personality characteristics or coping strategies are most likely to be expressed.

In a study of Navajo women, Schulz (1998) described the strength that could be gained from successfully coping with life's adversities: to be Navajo is "to be able to handle any problem—even if we get to a place where we can't go forward, we always find a way" (p. 347).

Table 7.1 summarizes the five mechanisms that help explain how social, cultural, and historical change impact individual development. Life course theory links individual, social, and historical time. Each person's life course can be thought of as a pattern of adaptations to the configuration of cultural expectations, resources, and barriers experienced during a particular historical period.

NEW DIRECTIONS

Life course theory has opened up many new directions in the study of development. In contrast to the study of typical or modal patterns, life course theory leads to an examination of differences among cohorts, differences within cohorts across locations, and differences within cohorts depending on social capital and human agency.

The Consequences of Political Turmoil

The theory has been useful in guiding international investigations and cross-national comparisons, especially where social change has impacted military service, work and family roles, educational opportunities, and the timing of marriage and childbearing. Research on life experiences following the destabilization of the Soviet Union, and pathways for young men and women whose lives were affected by the Cultural Revolution in China, has inspired investigations of the impact of cultural and societal upheaval on education, family, and career trajectories (Elder, Wu, & Yuan, 1993; Titma & Tuma, 2000; Schaie & Elder, 2005).

The Role of Linked Lives

The principle of linked lives has influenced thinking about how events of childhood or adolescence may influence the life course of adults and the elderly; how life transitions for children and grandchildren may influence the parent and grandparent generations; and how grandparents contribute to the well-being of their grandchildren (Danielsbacka & Tanskanen, 2012; Taylor, Uhlenberg, Elder, & McDonald, 2013). In a study of disasters, Cohan and Cole (2002) examined the impact of Hurricane Hugo on subsequent patterns of marriage, childbirth, and divorce in the countries hardest hit by the storm. The concept of linked lives led investigators to consider that disasters not only disrupt individual lives, but they play a role in altering decisions for couples and families.

The Accumulation of Advantage or Disadvantage

The idea of transitions and trajectories introduced a new way of conceptualizing life by linking discrete events, such as entry into parenthood, into a larger framework with implications of timing and sequencing for personal well-being and subsequent opportunities. This perspective led to new ways of thinking about the accumulation of advantages and disadvantages over the life course (O'Rand, 1996). On the one hand, there is growing evidence across many domains of a positive feedback loop in which advantages produce subsequent advantages. Being in a favorable position within a system, whether it is schooling, physical health, financial resources, or social status, often becomes a resource that results in additional advantages (Rigney, 2010; DiPrete & Eirich, 2006). Within a life course perspective, it is important to recognize social and historical events that might provide new advantages to certain groups, or access to resources such as employment, education, or health care, which they had previously been denied. Examples from U.S. policies include social security benefits, the GI Bill, and the Affordable Health Care Act.

On the other hand, there is evidence of weathering or allostatic load, the accumulating costs of repeated or chronic stressors. The body enlists neural, neuroendocrine, and neuroendocrine-immune mechanisms in efforts to adapt to stressors. Under normal conditions, these responses are part of healthy functioning. However, when the person faces frequent stressors, or when, for some reason, the responses to stress are not adequately turned off, the wear and tear on physical systems may result in disease (McEwen & Stellar, 1993; McEwen, 1998). From a life course perspective, the concept of allostatic load requires longitudinal study of the personal and sociocultural contexts which may result in continuous exposure to stressful life events.

Turning Points

The notion of intra-cohort differences led to consideration of the concept of **turning points**, or unique life events that may result in significant reorganization or reframing of one's life trajectory (Rutter, 1996). Examples might include immigration, military service, substantial economic gain or loss, death of a close friend or family member, or falling in love. Turning points involve new opportunities and a sense of agency to take advantage of these opportunities in order to separate oneself from an earlier trajectory in order to pursue a new path. The study of turning points is often pursued through personal narratives, Although there is no single mechanism to account for turning points, they are an important feature of life course development in that they illustrate the possibility for trajectories to be altered through chance events or voluntary effort.

The Impact of Social Policies on Individuals and Cohorts

The life course perspective has increased our attention to the impact of social policies on development for certain cohorts. This is illustrated by studies of the impact of changes in U.S. social welfare policies on individuals and families, particularly single mothers and their children. It has led to a more contextualized analysis of basic developmental processes, such as friendship formation, academic achievement, and parent–child relationships, by exploring how changes in family, school, and community resources may impact the formation and survival of essential social networks.

An area of current application of life course theory to social policy is in the field of maternal and child health. A growing body of evidence shows that the conditions that impact the health of women prior to and during pregnancy have consequences for infants that endure throughout their childhood, adolescence, and into adult life. Drawing on this empirical portrait of cumulative impact over stages of life, Fine and Kotelchuck (2010) offered five key concepts from life course theory that need to be integrated into a reconceptualization of health care programs:

1. Timeline: today's experiences and exposures influence tomorrow's health.
2. Timing: health trajectories are particularly affected during critical or sensitive periods.
3. Environment: the broader community environment—biological, physical, and social—strongly affects the capacity to be healthy.
4. Equity: while genetic make-up offers both protective and risk factors for disease conditions, inequality in health reflects more than genetics and personal choice.
5. Lifelong intervention: throughout life and at all stages, risk factors can be reduced and protective factors enhanced, to improve current and subsequent health and well-being. (Fine & Kotelchuck, 2010, pp. 4–5)

These principles and their implications for practice are being embedded into maternal and health care education and training as well as the reorganization of local community service delivery and practice (Ramos, 2013; Brady & Johnson, 2014; Cheng & Solomon, 2014).

A RESEARCH EXAMPLE: WORK AND FAMILY TRADE-OFFS IN THREE COHORTS

In Chapter 6, on social role theory, we described the results of cross-national research that examined the nature of work and family roles, and the dimensions of these roles that are most likely to contribute to work–family conflict or work–family facilitation (Hill, Yang, Hawkins, & Ferris, 2004). The research was carried out in 48 countries with IBM workers whose average age was 39. The current research example also focuses on the general theme of balancing work and family life, but places this inquiry in the context of the historical period to highlight the life course theory perspective.

Since World War II, there have been dramatic changes that have altered social norms about married women in the workplace and men involved in family and household obligations. Over this time, there have also been marked changes in the nature of the labor market, with fewer manufacturing jobs and more jobs in the service, information, health care, and computer-technology sectors. Norms have changed from expectations of gender role specialization, with women focusing on family tasks and men focusing on labor-market tasks, to a less differentiated view of men's and women's work and family roles.

The research described here was undertaken to explore two basic questions. First, when men and women decide to pull back from or step out of the labor market in order to meet the demands of their family roles (work–family trade-offs), does this affect their sense of their occupational opportunities and their self-acceptance? Second, if there are work–family trade-off effects, do they differ by birth cohort, life stage, and/or gender?

Data were taken from the Midlife Development in the United States (MIDUS) survey of 3,000 adults who were ages 25 through 74 in 1995 (Carr, 2002). With this broad age span, the study was able to focus on three historical cohorts: those born between 1931 and 1943 (during the Depression); those born between 1944 and 1959 (baby boom generation); and those born between 1960 and 1970 (baby bust generation). The investigator argued that over the three historical periods, role expectations shifted from a norm for a clear gender-specialized division of labor to a view that men and women will engage equally in the employee and parent roles. The first wave of this shift, from the oldest to the middle cohort, emphasized the increasing participation of women in the labor market. The second wave of this shift, from the middle to the youngest cohort, emphasized the increasing participation of men in childrearing and household management. Thus, the impact of social change could be thought to have a greater impact on women in the middle cohort where the shift was toward greater expectations for labor force participation; and on men in the youngest cohort where the shift was toward greater expectations for family participation.

Work–family trade-offs were assessed based on whether people adjusted their work life in order to meet family responsibilities, especially responsibilities for childrearing. These adjustments were defined by asking about three possible modifications: (a) you stopped working at a job to stay home and care for the children; (b) you cut back on the number of hours worked at a job to care for the children; and (c) you switched to a different job that was less demanding or more flexible to be available to the children. Each person was assessed for whether they had made any of these three adjustments and for the specific adjustments they made.

In order to assess the impact of work–family trade-offs, Carr chose to measure two variables: perceptions of work opportunities and self-acceptance. The first relates to whether people who made work–family trade-offs believe that they have had the same opportunities for employment and good quality jobs as others who did not make these trade-offs. The second relates to whether people who made work–family trade-offs have the same level of self-acceptance as those who did not make these trade-offs.

The data on reported trade-offs provided three notable patterns. First, looking at the entire sample, women were much more likely to report some type of work–family trade-off than were men (53% versus 14%).

Second, over the three cohorts men showed a steady increase in the percentage who said they had made some type of work–family trade-off. More men in the youngest cohort (25%) than in the middle cohort (20%) and the oldest cohort (10%) made decisions to work less or change their job in order to spend more time with their families.

Third, for women the change across cohorts was noted in the percentage who said they left the workforce altogether in order to meet family responsibilities. Roughly two-thirds of all women said they made some type of work–family trade-off in each cohort, but the percentage who said they left the labor market declined from 58% in the oldest cohort to 47% in the middle cohort, and 38% in the youngest cohort. The youngest cohort shows the highest degree of gender similarity in seeking coping strategies that support work–family integration.

There is an assumption that when people are conforming to the social norms of their time, they will experience social approval and other types of reinforcement, which should contribute to their own self-acceptance. Thus, one would expect to see a change in the relationship between making work–family trade-offs and self-acceptance depending on the social norms of the period. For example, among the oldest cohort, women who continued to work while raising a family and men who modified their labor force participation in order to meet childrearing responsibilities could be expected to have lower self-acceptance because these behaviors were contrary to the social norms of their time. Figures 7.1 and 7.2 show the relationship of self-acceptance to making work–family trade-offs for the three cohorts of women and men.

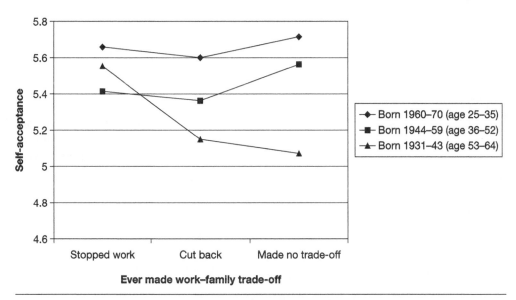

Figure 7.1 Self-Acceptance: Women of MIDUS, 1995

Source: Reprinted with permission from the American Sociological Association and Deborah Carr, "The Psychological Consequences of Work-Family Trade-Offs for Three Cohorts of Men and Women." *Social Psychology Quarterly, 65*, No. 2 (June, 2002), p. 117, Fig. 1.

Among the women, three groups were compared: those who stopped working, those who cut back, and those who continued working with no trade-offs. The clearest pattern is for the oldest cohort. Those who stopped working had significantly higher self-acceptance than those who cut back or continued working without any trade-offs. In comparison, for the middle and youngest cohorts, those who continued working had slightly higher levels of self-acceptance than those who stopped working or cut back. Among men, the comparison was made between those who made some type of trade-off and those who made no trade-off. The contrast is sharpest between the oldest and the youngest cohorts. For the oldest men, self-acceptance was lower among those who made trade-offs than among those who made no trade-offs. Among the youngest cohort the pattern was reversed; self-acceptance was lower among those who made no trade-offs.

The results of this study illustrate several of the key concepts of life course theory: (a) human development takes place in historical time and place; (b) people operate as agents in their own behalf choosing among the opportunities that are available in their time and society; and (c) within an individual life course, the trajectories and transitions within trajectories are linked and influence one another. The study supports the idea that the impact of certain life decisions on personal development depends on the interaction of the decision and the social meaning of that decision within a specific historical context.

AN APPLICATION: LIFE COURSE THEORY AND TRAJECTORIES OF CRIMINAL BEHAVIOR

In the field of criminology, considerable emphasis is given to trying to understand the developmental course of criminal behavior. When and why do adolescents begin to perform criminal acts? Do patterns of criminal activity persist from adolescence into young and middle adulthood? Are there differences between those who commit violent crimes as compared to crimes against property or "white collar" crimes? One can imagine at least four different

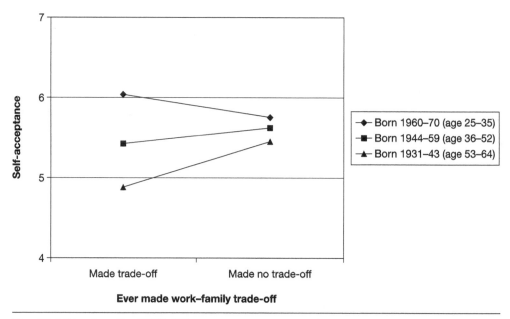

Figure 7.2 Self-Acceptance: Men of MIDUS, 1995

Source: Reprinted with permission from the American Sociological Association and Deborah Carr, "The Psychological Consequences of Work-Family Trade-Offs for Three Cohorts of Men and Women." *Social Psychology Quarterly, 65,* No. 2 (June, 2002), p. 117, Fig. 2.

trajectories with respect to criminal behavior: (a) those who are never involved in crime; (b) those who are involved in crime as children or adolescents but not as adults; (c) those who are involved in crime as adults, but not as children or adolescents; and (d) those who are persistently involved in crime from childhood and adolescence well into their adulthood. Are there different explanatory factors that account for these life trajectories? The concepts of life course theory have begun to be applied to an understanding of criminal trajectories.

Sampson and Laub (2004) developed their application of life course theory to criminal behavior on data gathered in a historic study of 500 delinquent and 500 non-delinquent boys studied over three time periods when their average ages were 14, 25, and 32. These boys were initially studied by Sheldon and Eleanor Glueck and the study included a vast amount of quantitative and qualitative data, including interviews with teachers, neighbors, and employers, psychiatric assessments, and agency records (Glueck & Glueck, 1950, 1968). After a long period of data reconstruction and analysis, Sampson and Laub (1993; Laub & Sampson, 2004) were able to analyze the continuities and changes in the lives of these boys into their adulthood. Eventually, they added new sources of data, which allowed them to examine a 50-year window on the persistence and desistance from crime from childhood into later life (Laub & Sampson, 2004).

The basic idea in this work is that the same principles can help to explain both the persistence or continuation of criminal behavior and the desistance or discontinuation of criminal behavior over the life course. Three basic causal mechanisms were identified: social controls, routine activities, and human agency (Sampson & Laub, 2004, 2005).

Family, school, and peer relationships provide the contexts through which social controls impact young children. Exposure to low levels of parental supervision, inconsistent and harsh punishment, and weak or insecure parental attachment are three aspects of family life that are consistently associated with delinquent behavior. In addition, a lack of a sense of school belonging or school engagement is associated with delinquent behavior. And attachment to delinquent friends is also independently associated with delinquent behavior. Taken together, these three sources of social control appear to be the processes through which structural factors such as poverty or neighborhood make their impact on children and adolescents.

However, when one takes a longer-term view of the life course trajectory of criminal behavior, patterns diverge. Some adults who had little or weak social control in childhood and adolescence find new sources of social control and stabilizing social structures in adulthood. Three of the most important of these are marriage, job stability, and military service. Social bonds that are formed in these three contexts are linked to disengagement from criminal activity. On the other hand, job instability and marital conflict, weak marital attachment, or absence of a marriage partner are associated with an increased likelihood of criminal involvement. Thus, the life course view offers a picture of the possibility of both continuity and change in the criminal life trajectory depending on positive involvement with key social institutions and the formal and informal social controls, social ties, and daily routines they provide.

Sampson and Laub (2004) were able to identify important turning points in the lives of adult men leading away from criminal behavior. These new situations, which often included marriage, the military, reform school, work, or neighborhood change, operated to split or "knife off" the past from the present. These new situations provided supervision and monitoring, new routines, new opportunities for social support, and new opportunities to revise their identities.

Within the context of these new situations, however, those who turned away from crime made active efforts to do so. In comparison, those who persisted in criminal activity also acknowledged responsibility for their actions. The principle of human agency figured heavily into this analysis, making predictions about individuals and their trajectories very difficult. The men did not seem to passively fall into or out of criminal behavior. Based on the interview data, it appears that the men made deliberate decisions to give up crime in order to be a hard worker, a family man, or a good provider. Others deliberately persisted in criminal activity, often for the perceived rewards of crime, to defy authority, or to stand in opposition to a system that they viewed as corrupt and unfair.

In order to understand the life trajectory of criminal behavior, one needs to understand the timing and opportunities for social connections, but this is not sufficient. One must also consider the importance of human agency and the extent to which a person is willing to make a commitment to a life of crime or to resist this life. Especially for those who have had an earlier life marked by weak or absent social bonds and social controls, the prolonged periods of unemployment, institutionalization, and social rejection may make the formation of social bonds in adulthood more difficult to envision or establish.

HOW DOES LIFE COURSE THEORY ANSWER THE BASIC QUESTIONS THAT A THEORY OF HUMAN DEVELOPMENT IS EXPECTED TO ADDRESS?

1. *What is the direction of change over the life span? How well does the theory account for patterns of change and continuity?*
    The life course is defined as "a sequence of socially defined events and roles that the individual enacts over time" (Giele & Elder, 1998, p. 22). The sequence is comprised of trajectories and transitions within these trajectories. There may also be turning points—critical experiences that lead to a new direction, such as a decision to become more invested in religion, or that terminate a trajectory, such as deciding to give up criminal behavior. The theory does not offer a universal view about the direction of change. The direction of change is a product of

social norms regarding timing and sequencing in interaction with personal agency regarding choices and decisions within the range of existing opportunities. Lives become increasingly diverse with age; for some the direction of change is toward an increasing sense of agency and well-being; for others the direction is one of discouragement and loss.

2. *What are the mechanisms that account for growth? What are some testable hypotheses or predictions that emerge from this analysis?*

The theory assumes that change is a result of age-graded social expectations, roles and the sequencing of roles, the linking of lives, the impact of human agency or choice, and the influence of historical events that open up or close certain opportunities that can alter one or more trajectories. Every situation has certain demand properties or requirements. If the situation changes, new demand properties emerge and new behaviors are required.

Stability can be expected when the demand properties of the situation remain unchanged. Stability is also a product of the constraints placed on the person through his or her embeddedness in a network of interdependent relationships. The stronger and more positive these relationships, the greater their influence to guide and stabilize development. Under conditions of uncertainty or crisis, people tend to rely on behaviors that are well established.

The following four testable hypotheses emerge from this theory:

1. The influence of a historical event depends upon the stage of life at which a person experiences the event. For example, an important technical innovation such as the internet, which began to be widely available on a commercial basis in the 1990s, might be predicted to have a different impact on individuals who first had access to the internet as young children as compared to those who first had access to the internet in middle adulthood.

2. Lives are interdependent. Positive psychosocial development is predicted to occur for those who are embedded in a supportive, effective network of relationships where they are able to experience positive social bonds. Negative psychosocial development is predicted for those who are unable to establish and participate in a supportive network of relationships.

3. When a person loses control, or when personal freedoms are threatened, there is generally an attempt to preserve or regain control.

4. Under conditions of crisis or critical transition, the person's most prominent personality characteristics and coping strategies will be accentuated. This hypothesis addresses stability of behavior, suggesting that when the person confronts sudden and dramatic environmental change, the initial response is to rely on behaviors that were well established in the past.

3. *How relevant are early experiences for later development? What evidence does the theory offer to support its view?*

The theory suggests that early life decisions, opportunities, and conditions affect later outcomes. There is an accumulated benefit to early advantage and an accumulated cost to early disadvantage. However, subsequent events and the response to these events can alter these trajectories. For example, dropping out of school can initiate a chain of events that have negative economic, occupational, and interpersonal consequences as well as consequences for one's physical and mental health. However, the cumulative disadvantage may be disrupted if a person encounters a new opportunity, for example, through military service or a community action initiative, to complete his or her GED and gain valued technical training. For some, trajectories can be altered through new opportunities, social support, and personal choice.

4. *How do the environmental and social contexts affect development? What aspects of the environment does the theory suggest are especially important in shaping the direction of development?*
   The theory has highlighted features of the social context that had been largely ignored in other theories.

   First, the theory emphasizes social change and the impact of historical periods in shaping the trajectories and transitions of the life course.

   Second, the theory points to social expectations or norms and the degree to which these shape entry, exit, and sequencing of social roles.

   Third, the theory highlights the interconnections among lives and the ways that people are affected by the quality of these linkages as well as the changes in the lives of those close to them.

   Fourth, the theory recognizes the importance of social institutions and social structures, such as schools, families, the military, and business organizations, in so far as these provide opportunities for the formation of social bonds and support for effective behavior in key roles. Institutions can create a framework for the life course; for example, where businesses offer professional development training, a promotional ladder, and a pension or other retirement benefits. These same institutions can disrupt the life course trajectory by overworking employees, creating work–family conflict, imposing large layoffs, shifting from full-time to part-time employment, relocating workers to new communities, or recalculating or reducing retirement benefits.

5. *According to the theory, what factors place individuals at risk at specific periods of the life span?*
   A central premise of life course theory is that the impact of critical events depends upon the stage of life when the events occur. A crisis or dramatic social change places individuals at risk when a person loses control, or when personal freedoms are threatened. The theory would then guide us to consider how a critical event might threaten the sense of control or personal freedom for individuals at various points in development. For example, in his work on the Great Depression, Elder found that the younger children experienced a greater disruption in their development than did the adolescents when their parents lost their jobs or faced dramatic financial losses (Elder, Caspi, & Downey, 1986). The younger children relied more on their parents to provide stability and security in their lives than did the adolescents. Parents who became psychologically distant, irritable, and inconsistent or harsh in their discipline transmitted their own sense of loss of control or threat to their children. Adolescents, on the other hand, were able to preserve some sense of control and even reduce their parents' distress by helping out at home, finding some ways to earn a bit of money, and taking care of themselves. We can hypothesize that the economic downturn of 2007–2008 (the Great Recession) may have put many children and families at similar risk.

   A second source of risk is the absence or disruption of social bonds. The theory emphasizes the importance of linked lives. Over the life course, individuals who care about each other provide social capital. At any point in the life course, the absence or loss of social bonds can increase a person's vulnerability. Examples include: the relationship of a lack of parent–child attachment and the absence of parental monitoring and supervision to the emergence of delinquent behavior and poor self-regulation in the early phase of life; the loss of employment or divorce and their consequences for social isolation; or the relationship of social isolation and the absence of kinship support to poor physical and mental health in later adulthood.

A third source of risk is being "off-time" or "off-sequence" in entry or exit from social roles. The assumption of life course theory is that there is an ideal or optimal sequence of transitions in a work, educational, or family trajectory, which is shaped by the norms of the community during a particular historical period. Conformity to the timing norms of the community provides social reassurance and should result in positive self-appraisal. Those who are off-time or out of sequence may experience social rejection, ridicule, or find themselves closed out of important opportunities. One of the most widely studied of these off-time events is early entry into parenthood (under age 18) which, for certain groups, is associated with family rejection or scorn, reduced educational attainment, low income, larger family size, and mental health problems.

6. *What are some practical implications of life course theory?*
    The theory is being used to provide a framework for rethinking maternal and child health, opening up a wider view of the links between early experiences, family support, community services, health care policies, and personal agency. The theory is also being used to guide new thinking about the nature of delinquency and its links to later criminal behavior in adulthood. This work has identified experiences that can consolidate criminal trajectories or lead people to reject criminal behavior in order to strengthen new relationships or attain new life goals. The theory has pointed to the significant impact of certain historical events and natural disasters on people at different age stages, an insight which has proven useful in counseling and mental health intervention.

    The theory sheds light on the role of culture in shaping lives through concepts including the social clock, age norms and age constraints, and optimal sequencing. These ideas are especially important in working with people who are in the midst of cultural change, including new immigrants and the children of immigrants. The social clock in one generation may not apply in a new cultural context. When historical conditions or uncontrolled events disrupt opportunities, the desire to meet closely held social expectations may not be satisfied.

    The concept of linked lives highlights the importance of social capital for the well-being of the members of a social network. Events that impact parents cascade to their children; resources that accrue to children can enhance the lives of parents and grandparents. One of the essential features of the impact of historical or cultural change is the extent to which events strengthen or disrupt access to the social capital of the interdependent network of relationships.

    Looking ahead, the theory offers a lens for considering how major changes in social policy or organizational structure may influence people in different cohorts or age stages. Policies can have intended and unintended consequences for the life trajectories of individuals, depending on the impact of those policies on **linked trajectories** and linked lives.

CRITIQUE OF LIFE COURSE THEORY

Strengths

Life course theory has provided a unique lens for exploring the impact of the macro social environment on development, especially changes in social, cultural, and economic conditions. In this respect it has increased awareness of the relevance of the historical context for interpreting patterns of behavior and behavior change.

The life course perspective encourages a long-term outlook on development. As a result, it has encouraged research on the relationship of earlier periods of childhood and adolescence to adulthood and aging. It has also stimulated the study of intergenerational influences, both downward from older to younger generations, and upward from younger generations to older. For example, the life course perspective has led to studies of how grandchildren influence the outlook of their grandparents and how divorce among adult children influences the caregiving received by aging parents. It has offered a way of thinking about the transmission of patterns of behavior and family practices from one generation to the next. This long-term perspective has also provided theoretical justification for investing in long-term longitudinal research, and for reanalysis of existing longitudinal data from a life course perspective.

Life course theory has provided a rich set of concepts for studying adulthood. It recognizes the central focus of adult life on a few trajectories, especially work and family life, and examines the interconnections among roles. It highlights the significance of the social bonds and social network that surround and support life trajectories, and the potential negative consequences when these bonds are disrupted.

The theory also integrates the idea of agency and personal decision making, which results in a view of adulthood as shaped but not wholly determined by social forces. Thus, it helps us understand how individual lives are both patterned and increasingly unique over time. Because of its focus on linking historical change with individual development, life course theory has become increasingly useful in guiding research on cross-national comparisons when people of similar age groups are faced with distinct social conditions and historical events. It has also been useful in inspiring focus on personal narratives which allow us to appreciate how individuals differ in the ways they make meaning out of similar life experiences.

Life course theory has been useful in helping to understand the impact of crises and traumatic events on the long-term adaptation of individuals and families. Concepts including transitions, turning points, role sequences, and linked lives are all useful in helping to clarify how a significant event can have long-range consequences for well-being.

The theory provides a way of understanding the pattern of increasing inequality across generations. By considering the impact of societal policies and organizational pressures on cohorts, and the nature of linked lives, one begins to appreciate the cascading pattern of advantage and disadvantage transmitted from one generation to the next.

Weaknesses

Life course theory has been viewed by some as more of a perspective than a theory. While it is useful in pointing out the importance of social factors in shaping development, it does not offer specific causal hypotheses. There is no agreed on set of predictions about which types of social change at particular life stage periods will result in specific consequences. The theory does not specify what historical changes are most likely to impact a cohort. This process appears to be empirically derived, based on knowledge of history and social change.

Similarly, the theory predicts that the effects of historical change will differ depending on the stage of life at which a person experiences it. However, the theory has a limited framework for predicting which aspects of development are most likely to be vulnerable to social change at particular stages. Without this type of developmental component the impact of social change would be studied differently, depending on each researcher's decision about what outcomes are considered important.

Although the theory acknowledges the increasing diversity of individuals over the life course, it does not offer many ideas about the source of these differences. For example, in thinking about the interconnections among roles and trajectories, the theory does not address the reality that people differ in the salience of particular roles and their motivation for sustaining or abandoning these roles. As another example, the theory emphasizes the importance of human agency, especially at key turning points, but does not offer explanations for individual differences in agency. The theory does not account for the fact that some people are more passive and others more assertive in the face of change. The theory lacks concepts to explain why some people have a greater tolerance for change and are more flexible while others are more stressed by change.

The theory can be most useful when combined with other theories of development that would help account for the biological and psychosocial correlates of agency, and the domains of likely vulnerability and growth in the context of social change. The strengths and weaknesses of life course theory are summarized in Table 7.2.

Table 7.2 Summary of strengths and weaknesses of life course theory

Strengths	Weaknesses
Highlights the impact of historical contexts on development.	Lacks causal hypotheses about which types of social change will result in specific alterations of the life course.
Encourages a long-term outlook on development; the relationship of early periods of childhood and adolescence to adulthood and aging.	Limited framework for predicting which aspects of development will be influenced by social change at particular stages of life.
Stimulated research on intergenerational influences of linked lives.	Few explanatory concepts for accounting for individual differences in dimensions such as salience of roles, flexibility, or agency.
Provided theoretical justification for investment in longitudinal studies and reanalysis of existing longitudinal data.	Lack of a biopsychosocial approach that would help connect the historical, cultural, and social framework with concepts of development, vulnerability, and resilience.
Provides concepts for the study of adulthood and aging including trajectories, transitions, and turning points.	
Highlights the positive effects of social bonds that support trajectories and the negative effects when these bonds are disrupted.	
With the concept of agency, it helps explain how lives are both patterned and increasingly unique over time.	
Useful in guiding research on cross-national comparisons.	
Useful in stimulating research on personal narratives.	
Becoming increasingly useful as a guiding framework for health care policy and practice.	
Useful in helping to account for the pattern of increasing inequality across generations.	
Useful in helping to understand the impact of crisis on individual and family adjustment.	

CRITICAL THINKING QUESTIONS AND EXERCISES

1. Imagine that you are creating a televised panel discussion among the following theorists: Charles Darwin, Jean Piaget, Sigmund Freud, Albert Bandura, and Glen Elder. Professor Elder presents the main ideas of life course theory. How will each of the other theorists react to his model? What are their contributions or criticisms of his theory?

2. Consider the first 15 years of the twenty-first century. What historical event(s) would you consider important enough to serve as a focus for a life course research project? What are some hypotheses about how the event might impact people differently at different life stages? How would you examine the principle of linked lives within this study?

3. Review the model of research on work–family trade-offs presented in the chapter. What are some changes in the norms about education, work, marriage, and parenting for men and women born in the period 1980–1990 that might influence their decisions about how to coordinate work and family roles?

4. Consider the concept of turning points in the opening case of Jeff. How might military service and training have provided a context for Jeff to alter or direct the course of his life? How did it enable him to move from a situation of low performance expectations to a view of himself as disciplined, hard-working, and self-directed?

5. What are some aspects of the social/historical context in the period from 1989 to 2009 when Jeff was in the military that may have been operating to facilitate Jeff's positive trajectory?

KEY TERMS

accentuation principle	linked trajectories
agency	longitudinal research
cohort	role sequencing
control cycle	situational imperative
historical time	social clock
interdependent lives	social time
intergenerational transmission	trajectory
life course	transition
life stages	turning points
linked lives	work–family trade-offs

RECOMMENDED RESOURCES

**Clark, G. (2014). *The son also rises: Surnames and the history of social mobility.* Princeton, NJ: Princeton University Press.

An analysis of the persistence of socioeconomic status over many generations in more than 20 societies. Tracing surnames from historical records, Clark demonstrates that movement up or down the social ladder is slow; much slower than a belief in a merit-based society might suggest. To learn more about Professor Clark and his research, visit his homepage at www.econ.ucdavis.edu/faculty/gclark/index.html

**Laub, J.H. and Sampson, R. (2012). YouTube interview. www.youtube.com/watch?v=PmaY OnotyuI
Laub and Sampson, winners of the Stockholm Prize in Criminology, discuss their discovery of the Glueck data archives and their decision to analyze these data using modern statistical techniques to test an age-graded theory of pathways and turning points in criminal behavior.

**Life course perspectives on health. An open access course available at http://ocw.jhsph.edu/ index.cfm/go/viewCourse/course/LifeCoursePerspectiveOnHealth/coursePage/index/
This open access course prepared by faculty at Johns Hopkins School of Public Health reviews the life course perspective on public health with an emphasis on developmental stages from infancy through later life. The website provides a syllabus, slides, readings, and assignments.

**Matteson, M. (2003). The first turning point of my life. NPR Radio podcast transcript. www.Snapjudgment.org/first-turning-point-my-life
This is a first person narrative describing a young girl's experiences at the time of her father's death. She explains how the sudden death of her father has led to commitments for her future career path and the formation of supportive relationships.

**Pudrovska, T. (2014). Early-life socioeconomic status and mortality at three life course stages: An increasing within-cohort inequality. *Journal of Health and Social Behavior, 55*, 181–195.
Analysis of data from the Wisconsin longitudinal study for participants covering the period from 1957 to 2011. The results indicate that higher socioeconomic status at age 18 is related to lower mortality at each subsequent period of life. The process results in increasing inequality in mortality rates, with early advantage having stronger benefits for women than for men.

**Ramos, D.E. (2013). Life course perspective: An approach to improving maternal, child and adolescent health. A PowerPoint presentation for the Los Angeles County Office of Public Health. Retrieved on July 6, 2014, at www.marchofdimes.com/pdf/california/CA_Life_Course_ Perspective.pdf
A PowerPoint slide presentation that provides an overview of the application of the life course theory perspective for training and service delivery in maternal, child, and adolescent health in Los Angeles County.

REFERENCES

AAMC (2012). U.S. medical school applicants and students 1982–1983 to 2011–2012. Retrieved on July 3, 2014 at www.aamc.org/data/facts/enrollmentgraduate/148670/total-grads-by-school-gender.html

Baltes, P.B. (1987). Theoretical propositions of life-span developmental psychology: On the dynamics between growth and decline. *Developmental Psychology, 231*, 611–626.

Brady, C. & Johnson, F. (2014). Integrating the life course into MCH service delivery: From theory to practice. *Maternal and Child Health Journal, 18*, 380–388.

Buhler, C. (1935). The curve of life as studied in biographies. *Journal of Applied Psychology, 19*, 405–409.

Carr, D. (2002). The psychological consequences of work–family trade-offs for three cohorts of men and women. *Social Psychology Quarterly, 65*, 103–124.

Cheng, T.L. & Solomon, B.S. (2014). Translating life course theory to clinical practice to address health disparities. *Maternal and Child Health Journal, 18*, 389–395.

Cohan, C.L. & Cole, S.W. (2002). Life course transitions and natural disaster: Marriage, birth, and divorce following Hurricane Hugo. *Journal of Family Psychology, 16*(1), 14–25.

Danielsbacka, M. & Tanskanen, A.O. (2012). Adolescent grandchildren's perceptions of grandparents' involvement in U.K.: An interpretation from life course and evolutionary theory perspectives. *European Journal of Ageing, 9*, 329–341.

DiPrete, T.A. & Eirich, G.M. (2006). Cumulative advantage as a mechanism for inequality: A review of theoretical and empirical developments. *Annual Review of Sociology, 32*, 271–297.

Elder, G.H., Jr. (1974). *Children of the Great Depression: Social change in life experience.* Chicago: Chicago University Press.

Elder, G.H., Jr. (1979). Historical change in life patterns and personality. In P.B. Baltes & O.G. Brim, Jr. (Eds.), *Life-span development and behavior: Vol. 2* (pp. 117–159). New York: Academic Press.

Elder, G.H., Jr. (1985). *Life course dynamics: Trajectories and transitions, 1968–1980.* Ithaca, NY: Cornell University Press.

Elder, G.H., Jr. (1987). War mobilization and the life course: A cohort of World War II veterans. *Sociological Forum, 2*, 449–472.

Elder, G.H., Jr. (1995). The life course paradigm: Social change and individual development. In P. Moen, G.H. Elder, Jr., & K. Lüscher (Eds.), *Examining lives in context: Perspectives on the ecology of human development* (pp. 101–139). Washington, DC: APA Press.

Elder, G.H., Jr. (1996). Human lives in changing societies: Life course and developmental insights. In R.B. Cairns, G.H. Elder, Jr., & E.J. Costello (Eds.), *Developmental Science* (pp. 31–62). Cambridge, UK: Cambridge University Press.

Elder, G.H., Jr. (1998). The life course as developmental theory. *Child Development, 69*, 1–12.

Elder, G.H., Jr. (1999). *Children of the Great Depression: Social change in life experience. 25th anniversary edition.* Boulder, CO: Westview Press.

Elder, G.H., Jr. & Caspi, A. (1988). Human development and social change: An emerging perspective on the life course. In N. Bolger, A. Caspi, G. Downey, & M. Moorehouse (Eds.), *Persons in context: Developmental processes* (pp. 77–113). New York: Cambridge University Press.

Elder, G.H., Jr., Caspi, A., & Downey, G. (1986). Problem behavior and family relationships: Life course and intergenerational themes. In A.B. Sorensen, F.E. Weinart, & L.R. Sherrod (Eds.), *Human development and the life course: Multidisciplinary perspectives* (pp. 293–340). New York: Psychology Press.

Elder, G.H., Jr., Shanahan, M.J., & Clipp, E.C. (1994). When war comes to men's lives: Life course patterns in family, work, and health. *Psychology and Aging, 9*, 5–16.

Elder, G.H., Jr., Wu, W., & Yuan, J. (1993). State-initiated change and the life course in Shanghai, China. Unpublished project report.

Fine, A. & Kotelchuck, M. (2010) (Under contract with U.S. Department of Health and Human Services, Health Resources and Services Administration). Rethinking MCH: The life course model as an organizing framework. Concept paper. Version 1.1. November, 2010. Available from: http://mchb.hrsa.gov/lifecourse/rethinkingmchlifecourse.pdf

Funder, D.C., Parke, R.D., Tomlinson-Keasey, C., & Widaman, K. (1993). *Studying lives through time: Personality and development.* Washington, DC: American Psychological Association Press.

Giele, J.Z. & Elder, G.H., Jr. (1998). *Methods of life course research: Qualitative and quantitative approaches.* Thousand Oaks, CA: Sage.

Glueck, S. & Glueck, E. (1950). *Unraveling juvenile delinquency.* New York: The Commonwealth Fund.

Glueck, S. & Glueck, E. (1968). *Delinquents and nondelinquents in perspective.* Cambridge, MA: Harvard University Press.

Hamilton, R. (2010). Five years later, Houstonians conflicted about Katrina. *The Texas Tribune*, August 30. Retrieved on July 4, 2014, at www.texastribune.org/2010/08/30/five-years-houstonians-conflicted-about-katrina/

Hill, E.J., Yang, C., Hawkins, A.J., & Ferris, M. (2004). A cross-cultural test of the work–family interface in 48 countries. *Journal of Marriage and the Family, 66*, 1300–1316.

Jackson, P.B. (2004). Role sequencing: Does order matter for mental health? *Journal of Health and Social Behavior, 45*, 132–154.

Kertzer, D.I. & Keith, J. (Eds.) (1984). *Age and anthropological theory.* Ithaca, NY: Cornell University Press.

Kinder, D.R. (2006). Politics and the life cycle. *Science, 312*, 1905–1907.

Laub, J.H. & Sampson, R.J. (1993). Turning points in the life course: Why change matters to the study of crime. *Criminology, 31*, 301–325.

Laub, J.H. & Sampson, R.J. (2004). *Shared beginnings, divergent lives: Delinquent boys to age 70*. Cambridge, MA: Harvard University Press.

McEwen, B.S. (1998). Stress, adaptation and disease: Allostasis and allostatic load. *Annals of the New York Academy of Sciences, 840*, 33–44.

McEwen, B.S. & Stellar, E. (1993). Stress and the individual: Mechanisms leading to disease. *Archives of Internal Medicine, 153*, 2093–2101.

Neugarten, B.L. (1990). The changing meaning of age. In M. Bergener & S.I. Finkel (Eds.), *Clinical and scientific psychogeriatrics: Vol. 1. The holistic approaches* (pp. 1–6). New York: Springer-Verlag.

Neugarten, B.L., Moore, J.W., & Lowe, J.C. (1965). Age norms, age constraints, and adult socialization. *American Journal of Sociology, 70*, 710–717.

Newman, B.M. & Newman, P.R. (2015). *Development through life: A psychosocial approach*. 12th edn. Stamford, CT: Cengage Learning.

O'Rand, A.M. (1996). The precious and the precocious: Understanding cumulative disadvantage and cumulative advantage over the life course. *The Gerontologist, 36*, 230–238.

Ramos, D.E. (2013). Life course perspective: An approach to improving maternal, child and adolescent health. A PowerPoint presentation for the Los Angeles County Office of Public Health. Retrieved on July 6, 2014, at www.marchofdimes.com/pdf/california/CA_Life_Course_Perspective.pdf

Rigney, D. (2010). *The Matthew effect: How advantage begets further advantage*. New York: Columbia University Press.

Riley, M.W., Johnson, M.E., & Foner, A. (Eds.) (1972). *Aging and society: Vol. 3. A sociology of age stratification*. New York: Russell Sage Foundation.

Rutter, M. (1996). Transitions and turning points in developmental psychopathology: As applied to the age span between childhood and mid-adulthood. *International Journal of Behavioral Development, 19*, 603–626.

Ryder, N.B. (1965). The cohort as a concept in the study of social change. *American Sociological Review, 30*, 843–861.

Sampson, R.J. & Laub, J.H. (1993). *Crime in the making: Pathways and turning points through life*. Cambridge, MA: Harvard University Press.

Sampson, R.J. & Laub, J.H. (2004). A general age-graded theory of crime: Lessons learned and the future of life-course criminology. In D. Farrington (Ed.), *Advances in criminological theory: Vol. 14. Integrated developmental and life course theories of offending* (pp. 165–182). Somerset, NJ: Transaction Publishers.

Sampson, R.J. & Laub, J.H. (2005). A life-course view of the development of crime. *The Annals of the Academy of Political and Social Science, 602*, 12–45.

Schaie, K.W. & Elder, G. (Eds.) (2005). *Historical influences on lives and aging*. New York: Springer.

Schulz, A.J. (1998). Navajo women and the politics of identities. *Social Problems, 45*, 336–355.

Stewart, A.J. & Healy, J.M., Jr. (1989). Linking individual development and social changes. *American Psychologist, 44*, 30–42.

Stewart, A.J. & Ostrove, J.M. (1998). Women's personality in middle age: Gender, history, and midcourse corrections. *American Psychologist, 53*, 1185–1194.

Stewart, A.J., Settles, I.H., & Winter, N.J.G. (1998). Women and the social movements of the 1960s: Activists, engaged observers and nonparticipants. *Political Psychology, 19*, 63–94.

Taylor, M.G., Uhlenberg, P., Elder, G.H., Jr., & McDonald, S. (2013). The role of grandparents in the transition to adulthood: Grandparents as "very important" adults in the lives of adolescents. In M. Silverstein & R. Giarrusso (Eds.), *Kinship and cohort in an aging society: From generation to generation* (pp. 104–130). Baltimore, MD: Johns Hopkins University Press.

Thomas, W.I. & Znaniecki, F. (1974). *The Polish peasant in Europe and America: Vols. 1–2*. Urbana: University of Illinois Press. (Original work published 1918–1920, New York: Octagon Press)

Titma, M. & Tuma, N.B. (2000). *Modern Russia*. Boston: McGraw-Hill.

Volkart, E.H. (1951). *Social behavior and personality: Contributions of W. I. Thomas to theory and social research*. New York: Social Science Research Council.

Part III
Theories That Emphasize the Interaction Between the Person and the Environment

The theories presented in the first section of the book highlighted biologically based patterns or directions of development that unfold in the context of adaptation to varied environments. The theories presented in the second section of the book highlighted the impact of varied environments in shaping thought and action. The theories covered in this final section view development as a product of ongoing interaction between the person and the environment. The distinction between person and environment is less clear in these theories. A few examples might help to illustrate this perspective.

When a baby emits babbling and cooing noises, these noises become part of the baby's auditory environment. Thus, the infant is producing his or her environment. At later phases of development, individuals make choices about toys to play with, friends, books to read, places to live, activities and so on that reflect the person's temperament, skills, interests, and needs. In this sense, a person's environment is, in part, an expression of the person.

On the other hand, the environment is integrated into the person and guides action. For example, an infant will use a different mode of locomotion on a flat surface, an incline, or on steps. The kind of motor pattern you observe includes the infant's adaptation to the environment. Action is context-specific. The behaviors you may observe when a person meets you for the first time are not the same behaviors you would observe if the person knows you well. The person modifies his or her behavior to adapt to the context. Knowledge of the environment and past experiences in similar situations influence a person's expectations and subsequent actions.

These examples illustrate the bidirectional influences of person and environment, and suggest the need for new ways of thinking about the interpenetration of person and environment as they contribute to development.

The theories that illustrate this perspective are psychosocial theory, cognitive social-historical theory, bioecological theory, and dynamic systems theory. Each of these theories offers a way of thinking about the ongoing interaction of individuals and their environments over time. Psychosocial theory focuses on the development of personality, self-understanding, and a worldview that guides a person's orientation toward self and others over the life course.

Psychosocial theory highlights the cultural context within which the person is maturing. Cognitive social-historical theory focuses on the development of thought and language, meaning, and the interconnections between learning and development. Bioecological theory examines individual development in the context of multiple layers of interacting systems that are changing over time. Dynamic systems theory offers a framework for exploring the mechanisms of continuity and change in any type of living system. The theory has been applied to human development in a variety of domains including motor development, skill development, parent–child relationships, and cognition.

Psychosocial theory grew from roots in psychosexual theory, cultural anthropology, and psychosocial evolution. The theory defines human development as a product of the ongoing interaction of an individual's biological and psychological needs and abilities on the one hand, and societal expectations on the other. Psychosocial theory predicts an orderly sequence of change in ego development and social relationships from infancy through late life. At each stage, new abilities and coping strategies emerge for engaging in social relationships and for meeting the demands of an ever-changing, increasingly complex social world.

Cognitive social-historical theory was developed in the time shortly after the Russian Revolution. The theory suggests that development begins in a social relationship between mother and child. The components of this relationship are internalized by the child and guide his or her behavior. Over the course of development, cognition advances from sources external to the child (intermental) to internalized thinking (intramental). The child learns best when a responsive adult or more skilled peer poses problems and guides solutions that are slightly beyond a child's current level of functioning. The child learns to guide his or her own behavior by developing an inner voice or inner speech that is a product of this social support and guidance.

Bioecological theory provides a model for thinking about the changing person in a web of interconnected environments, some of which the person can influence directly, and others which impinge on the person through their influence on related family members, important institutions, cultural norms, and governmental policies. Both personal characteristics, such as temperament or intelligence, and specific behaviors, such as crying or helping someone, can modify the environment and alter its subsequent impact. Similar to life course theory, bioecological theory widens our view about the diversity of relevant environments, and also introduces new ideas about the ongoing interactions of persons and settings.

Dynamic systems theory has its roots in the fields of mathematics, physics, chemistry, and biology. It was initially applied to the study of human development through the analysis of motor behavior. Development is understood as the result of multiple, mutual and continuous interactions among all levels of a developing system from the molecular to the cultural. The premise is that development is not guided by an executive, hierarchical plan either at the biological or the environmental level. Rather, new organizational patterns emerge as a result of the coordination and integration of recurring actions on many levels at once. The theory offers a way of linking the substantial variability of individual behaviors with the emergence of patterns and qualitative shifts in behavior over time.

8
Psychosocial Theory

CHAPTER OUTLINE

GUIDING QUESTIONS

- How would you characterize the similarities and differences between psychoanalytic theory and psychosocial theory? How are they related? What are four or five important distinctions between these theories?
- What is the direction of development in psychosocial theory? How would you characterize the path or pattern of maturity in this theory?
- What are some possible consequences of positive and negative development?
- How does this theory incorporate the role of culture? What are some mechanisms through which culture influences development at each stage of life?
- Each stage of life is viewed as presenting a unique set of conflicting forces. Which stages do you consider to be the most difficult in contemporary U.S. culture? Why?
- Looking back over your life, identify some examples of experiences that support the central concept of a psychosocial crisis at each stage of life.

CASE VIGNETTE

It is 1965 in Columbus, Ohio. Lillian has graduated from college where she majored in English. She is hoping to marry her steady boyfriend, Michael, who has a degree in engineering. Her desire to form a close, loving bond with a caring, ambitious partner who will be able to provide a comfortable life is central to her life plan. Lillian's friends and family are enthusiastic about the relationship, and after a year-long courtship, Lillian and Michael are married. Their life is a pleasant blend of household management, social life with neighbors, periodic visits with family members, and some travel. At this point, the work of forming a satisfying, cooperative close relationship is very satisfying. It meets their personal needs and fits well into the expectations of their friends and family.

Now fast forward to 1985. Lillian is 42. Michael is a senior partner in his engineering firm, experiencing the positive rewards of leadership, community status, and financial success. He comes home after work, expecting Lillian to have a nice dinner ready. After dinner, he reads the paper, watches the sports channel on television, has a glass or two of wine, kisses Lillian goodnight, and goes to bed.

In the afternoons, Lillian has been going to a consciousness-raising group at the community center. She and her neighbors have been thinking about the meaning of their lives, the nature of their relationships, and the way they spend their days. She still admires Michael, but is starting to feel stifled by the routine of their life together, and the limits of her ability to "make a difference" in the world. Lillian wants to know how she can contribute to something beyond her own immediate family. When she talks to Michael about her feelings, he seems impatient, feeling that the life they have built together over the past 20 years is very satisfying. "I still love you, just as I did when we met. And I don't want anything to change." But Lillian has a strong sense that something has to change if she is going to continue to keep growing as a person.

Psychosocial theory is unique in giving us a look at the inner world of thoughts, feelings, and desires that create a sense of self in the society. The theory introduces a picture of a dynamic tension or dialectic between opposing forces that shift from one stage of life to the next. Within this framework, the theory sketches out the signposts of an interdependent process through which societies direct the paths of maturity, and individuals struggle to resolve conflicts that will enable them to achieve new levels of maturity. At each stage of life, the process of growth results from the interaction of individuals' drives, goals, and abilities, and the expectations and demands of the culture. In order for the society to thrive, individuals must be able to make their way along a path of ethical, interpersonal, and intrapersonal challenges. In order for individuals to thrive, societies must be structured to recognize and support these emerging capacities. The theory shines a light on the inner world of the person, who is striving to find a sense of balance and purpose over a long life in a changing world.

In the case presented above, we see the dynamic interplay between personal development and societal change for Lillian and Michael. In their early adulthood, the primary psychosocial theme was the desire for a sense of intimacy, which they achieve within a normative social context for marriage, while emphasizing a culturally approved pattern in which men were the primary breadwinners, and women were primarily responsible for the care of home and family. Twenty years later, the developmental issues shift toward concerns for personal meaning in life, and a goal of experiencing a generative impact on others. Within this developmental context, we see a situation in which Lillian and Michael no longer share the same, harmonious expression of their developmental needs, brought about in part by the rapid changes in social, economic, and cultural conditions especially related to the opening up of new roles for women in education and the labor market. Questions emerge about how Lillian and Michael will resolve this interpersonal tension. Can Lillian spur Michael into a more coordinated, growth-directed life path? Will Lillian become disillusioned in her marriage and strive to establish a more independent, authentic path toward generativity on her own? Or is their future likely to drift along toward stagnation, protecting what they have but withdrawing from the risks that are associated with change?

Psychosocial theory seeks to explain changes in self-understanding, social relationships, and one's relationship to society as a product of interactions among **biological, psychological, and societal systems**. Changes in one of the three systems (biological, psychological, or societal) generally bring about changes in the others. From the psychosocial perspective, development results from the continuous interaction of the individual and the social environment. At each period of life, people spend much of their time mastering a unique group of psychological tasks that are essential for social adaptation within their society. Each life stage brings a normative crisis, which can be viewed as a tension between one's competencies and the new demands of society. People strive to reduce this tension by using a variety of familiar coping strategies and by learning new ones. A positive resolution of each crisis provides a new set of social abilities that enhance a person's capacity to adapt successfully in the succeeding stages. A negative resolution of a crisis typically results in defensiveness, rigidity, or withdrawal, which decreases a person's ability to adapt successfully in succeeding stages.

HISTORICAL CONTEXT

The person who is identified with the development of psychosocial theory is Erik Erikson. He and his wife Joan worked together to formulate the first presentation of the theory and its eight stages of development in 1950 (Erikson, J.M., 1988). Erik Erikson was born in Frankfurt, Germany, in 1902. His mother was unmarried, and he never knew the identity of his biological father. Erikson's Danish mother, Karla Abrahamsen, married a Jewish stockbroker before Erikson's birth, but the marriage did not last. Before Erik's third birthday, his mother married a German-Jewish pediatrician, Theodor Homburger, who gave Erik his surname. In his detailed biography of Erikson, Lawrence Friedman (1999) described Erikson's continuing efforts to unravel the mysteries of his origin, and the convergence of this personal dilemma with Erikson's emphasis on identity and the identity crisis.

Erikson was not a very good student and had trouble settling on a vocation. At age 18, after completing gymnasium (German secondary school that prepares students to study at a university), Erikson traveled around Europe for a year, spending several months on the shores of Lake Constance, reading, writing, and enjoying the beauty of the setting. When he returned home, he enrolled in art school and pursued this study for the next few years. After traveling to Florence, Italy, where he concluded that he was not going to succeed as an artist, he and some of his friends, including Peter Blos, wandered around for a time searching for a sense of themselves and their personal resources (Coles, 1970).

Erikson and Blos accepted an invitation to teach at a private school that had been founded by Anna Freud for the children of students at the Vienna Psychoanalytic Society. Erikson proved to be so talented in working with children that he was selected to be a full member of the society, where he studied the techniques of psychoanalysis and underwent a training analysis with Anna Freud. His decision to become an analyst was encouraged by the supportive, influential analysts of the Vienna Psychoanalytic Society who were eager to help promising people enter the field they had created. Erikson's admission to training was unusual in that he had neither a university nor a medical degree.

In 1933, after analytic training and marriage to Joan, whom he met in Vienna, he set off to the United States. He became one of the first child analysts in Boston, and began collaborating with Henry Murray at Harvard. By 1935, he went to Yale, and 2 years after that he went off to study the Sioux Indians in South Dakota. He benefited from the support and encouragement of a number of cultural anthropologists and sociologists who encouraged his interest in the integration of psychoanalysis and sociocultural processes.

After completing his research about the Sioux, he opened a clinical practice in San Francisco. During this time, he also became a faculty member at the University of California at Berkeley. In 1950, Erikson left Berkeley and became an analyst on the staff of the Austin Riggs Center in Stockbridge, Massachusetts. In the late 1950s he became a professor of human development at Harvard, and he retained this position until his retirement. Erikson's major theoretical work, *Childhood and society*, was synthesized while he was at Berkeley and published in 1950 when he was 48. In this work, Erikson presented his psychosocial theory of development. A revised edition was published in 1963, and he expanded and revised his theory in many other books and papers.

His thinking was influenced by a variety of sources. His training as an analyst was very influential in his view of an epigenetic, stage view of development. He viewed development as a progression in which the orientation or outlook acquired in earlier stages influenced one's approach to subsequent stages. Erikson's theory is often grouped with other psychoanalytic theories. However, his theory contributed a number of novel ideas that place it in a category of its own. The theory extends the view of development beyond adolescence into early, middle, and later adulthood. In comparison to the psychoanalytic tradition, which is focused on psychosexual development, Erikson became increasingly interested in the emergence of the skills necessary to participate in social life and to be meaningfully integrated into one's society. He focused on the emergence of ego strengths and competences rather than on the vulnerabilities and defenses that crystallize when needs are not gratified. Nonetheless, by casting his view of development as a dialectic tension between positive and negative forces, his theory offers a conception of vulnerabilities as well as strengths. The theory places culture in a central position, opening the way to thinking about the possibility of universal directions for development embedded in unique and varied cultural pathways.

Erikson's observations of American Indian tribes were guided by current research in cultural anthropology, and awakened his understanding of the way cultural norms and values are transmitted through childrearing and the socialization of children. He was a careful observer of daily behaviors such as nursing, toilet training, play, discipline, and other forms of adult–child interaction. In contrast to Freud's theory which relied on reports from adult patients about recollections of their childhood, Erikson's ideas were based more on the direct observation of children.

The fact that he was not trained in a specific intellectual field at the university level meant that Erikson was open to a variety of intellectual traditions. He was able to conceptualize aspects of social life that he observed but that were not yet part of traditional disciplines, such as psychology or psychoanalysis. For example, he corresponded with Julian Huxley, who was an evolutionary theorist. Huxley used the term **psychosocial evolution** to refer to those human abilities that have allowed people to gather knowledge from their ancestors and transmit it to their descendants. Childrearing practices, education, and modes of communication transmit information and ways of thinking from one generation to the next. At the same time, people learn how to acquire new information, ways of thinking, and ways of teaching their discoveries to others. In Huxley's thinking, psychosocial evolution proceeded at a rapid pace, bringing with it changes in technology and ideology that have allowed people to create and modify the physical and social environments in which they live (Huxley, 1941, 1942/1974).

In one of his letters to Erikson, Huxley asked how we could account for certain higher-level social concepts, such as intimacy, identity, generativity, and wisdom. His point was that these are some of the finest aspects of human capacity, but they were not really addressed in the existing psychological theories. Much of Erikson's theoretical focus was on trying to account for the emergence of these higher order capacities in adolescence and adulthood.

During this time, other theorists also were focusing on the development of mature competences that help support advanced functioning over the life course. Scholars such as Bernice Neugarten (1968), Robert Havighurst (1953, 1948/1972), and Robert White (1960) were building a framework for the study of personality development, competence, and mastery in adulthood. In the 1970s, theorists, including Daniel Levinson (1977; Levinson, Darrow, Klein, Levinson, & McKee, 1978), Roger Gould (1972), and George Vaillant (1977), developed related ideas about stages or phases of adult life, with a particular emphasis on the search for meaning that accompanies shifts in work, family, parenting, and self-understanding. The focus of this chapter is on Erikson's construction of psychosocial theory, with a recognition that his ideas converged with those of others working at about the same time.

KEY CONCEPTS

As proposed by Erik Erikson, psychosocial theory accounts for systematic change over the life span through five basic concepts: (a) stages of development, (b) psychosocial crises, (c) a radius of significant relationships, (d) prime adaptive ego qualities, and (e) core pathologies.

Stages of Development

A **developmental stage** is a period of life that is characterized by a specific underlying organization. At every stage, some characteristics differentiate it from the preceding and succeeding stages. Stage theories propose a specific direction for development. At each stage, the accomplishments from the previous stages provide resources for mastering the new challenges. Each stage is unique and leads to the acquisition of new skills related to new capabilities (Davison, King, Kitchener, & Parker, 1980; Flavell, 1982; Levin, 1986). Within the framework of psychosocial theory the concept of stages of development refers to patterns of changes in self-concept and a coordinated sense of self in society based on new cognitive capacities, new learning, and new relationship skills. At each stage, the biological, psychological, and societal systems converge around a set of defining challenges that require a new view of the self in society and a new way of relating to others (Whitbourne, Sneed, & Sayer, 2009; Newman and Newman, 2015).

Erikson (1950/1963) proposed that the stages of development follow the **epigenetic principle**, a biological plan for growth that allows each function to emerge systematically until the fully functioning organism has developed. An assumption of this and other stage theories is that the stages form a sequence. Although one can anticipate challenges that will occur at a later stage, one passes through the stages in an orderly pattern of growth. In the logic of psychosocial theory, the entire life span is required for all the functions of psychosocial development to appear and become integrated. There is no going back to an earlier stage because experience makes retreat impossible. In contrast to other stage theories, however, Erikson suggested that one can review and reinterpret previous stages in the light of new insight and/or new experiences. In addition, the themes of earlier stages may reemerge at any point, bringing a new meaning or a new resolution to an earlier conflict. Joan Erikson reflects on the fluidity and hopefulness in this perspective:

> This sequential growth ... is now known to be more influenced by the social milieu than was in previous years considered possible ... Where a strength is not adequately developed according to the given sequence for its scheduled period of critical resolution, the supports of the environment may bring it into appropriate balance at a later period. Hope remains constant throughout life that more sturdy resolutions of the basic confrontation may be realized. (Erikson, 1988, pp. 74–75)

Erikson (1950/1963) proposed eight stages of psychosocial development. The conception of these stages can be traced in part to the stages of psychosexual development proposed by Freud and in part to Erikson's own observations and rich mode of thinking.

Figure 8.1 is the chart Erikson produced in *Childhood and society* to describe the stages of psychosocial development. The diagonal boxes identify the main psychosocial ego conflicts of each stage. These ego conflicts produce new ego skills. In Erikson's original model, you will note that the periods of life are given names, such as *oral-sensory* or *puberty and adolescence*, but no ages. This approach reflected Erikson's emphasis on an individual timetable for development, guided by both biological maturation and cultural expectations.

	1	2	3	4	5	6	7	8
1. Oral–sensory	Basic trust vs. Mistrust							
2. Muscular–anal		Autonomy vs. Shame, doubt						
3. Locomotor–genital			Initiative vs. Guilt					
4. Latency				Industry vs. Inferiority				
5. Puberty and adolecence					Identity vs. Role confusion			
6. Young adulthood						Intimacy vs. Isolation		
7. Adulthood							Generativity vs. Stagnation	
8. Maturity								Ego integrity vs. Despair

Figure 8.1 Erikson's Model of the Psychosocial Stages of Development

Source: From *Childhood and society* by Erik H. Erikson. Copyright © 1950, © 1963 by W. W. Norton & Company, renewed ©1978, 1991, by Erik H. Erikson. Used by permission of W. W. Norton & Company, Inc.

The concept of life stages permits us to consider the various aspects of development such as physical growth, social relationships, and cognitive capacities at a given period of life and to speculate about their interrelation. It also encourages a focus on the experiences that are unique to each life period—experiences that deserve to be understood both in their own right and for their contribution to subsequent development.

One must avoid thinking of stages as pigeonholes. Just because a person is described as being at a given stage does not mean that he or she cannot function at other levels. It is not unusual for people to anticipate later challenges before they become dominant. Many children of toddler (muscular-anal) and preschool (locomotor-genital) age, for example, play house, envisioning having a husband or a wife and children. You might say that, in this play, they are anticipating the issues of intimacy and generativity that lie ahead. The experience of having a child, whether this occurs at age 18, 25, or 35, is likely to raise issues of generativity, even if the theory suggests that this theme is not in its peak ascendancy until middle adulthood (McAdams & de St. Aubin, 1998). While some elements of each psychosocial theme can be observed at all ages, the intensity with which they are expressed at certain times marks their importance in the definition of a developmental stage. Erikson, Erikson, and Kivnick (1986) put it this way:

The epigenetic chart also rightly suggests that the individual is never struggling only with the tension that is focal at the time. Rather, at every successive developmental stage, the individual is also increasingly engaged in the anticipation of tensions that have yet to become focal and in reexperiencing those tensions that were inadequately integrated when they were focal; similarly engaged are those whose age-appropriate integration was then, but is no longer, adequate. (p. 39)

As one leaves a stage, the achievements of that period are neither lost nor irrelevant to later stages. Although the theory suggests that important ego strengths emerge from the successful resolution of conflicts at every stage, one should not assume that these strengths, once established, are never challenged or shaken. Events may take place later in life that call into question the essential beliefs established in an earlier period.

For example, the psychosocial conflict during early school age (locomotor-genital stage) is initiative versus guilt. Its positive outcome, a sense of initiative, is a joy in innovation and experimentation and a willingness to take risks in order to learn more about the world. Once achieved, the sense of initiative provides a positive platform for the formation of social relationships as well as for further creative intellectual inquiry and discovery. However, experiences in a highly authoritarian school environment or in a very judgmental, shaming personal relationship may cause one to inhibit this sense of initiative or to mask it with a facade of indifference.

The idea of life stages highlights the changing orientations toward one's self and others that dominate periods of the life span. Movement from one stage to the next is the result of changes in several major systems at approximately the same time. The new mixture of needs, capabilities, and expectations is what produces the new orientation toward experience at each stage.

Psychosocial Crisis

A **psychosocial crisis** refers to a state of tension that results from the discrepancies between the person's competences at the beginning of a stage and the society's expectations for behavior at that period of life (Erikson, 1950/1963). The psychosocial crisis arises because one must make psychological efforts to adjust to the demands of the social environment at each stage of development (Erikson, 1950/1963). The word *crisis* in this context refers to a normal set of stresses and strains rather than to an extraordinary set of events. Societal demands vary from stage to stage. People experience these demands as mild but persistent expectations for behavior. They may be demands for greater self-control, further development of skills, or a stronger commitment to goals. Before the end of each stage of development, the individual tries to achieve a resolution, to adjust to society's demands, and at the same time to translate those demands into personal terms. This process produces a state of tension that the individual must reduce in order to proceed to the next stage.

Psychosocial Crises of the Life Stages. Figure 8.1 lists the psychosocial crisis at each stage of development from infancy (oral-sensory) through later adulthood (maturity). This scheme, derived from Erikson's model, expresses the crises as polarities—for example, trust versus mistrust, and autonomy versus shame and doubt. These contrasting conditions suggest the underlying dimensions along which each psychosocial crisis is resolved. According to psychosocial theory, most people experience both positive and negative ends of the continuum. The inevitable discrepancy between one's level of development at the beginning of a stage and society's push for a new level of functioning by the end of it creates at least a mild degree of the negative condition. Even within a loving, caring family environment that promotes trust, an infant will experience some moments of frustration or disappointment that result in mistrust. The outcome of the crisis at each stage is a balance or integration of the two opposing forces. For each person, the relative frequency and significance of positive and negative experiences will contribute to a resolution of the crisis that lies along a continuum from extremely positive to extremely negative.

The likelihood of a completely positive or a completely negative resolution is small. Most individuals resolve the crises in a generally positive direction, supported by a combination of positive experiences combined with natural maturational tendencies. At each successive stage, however, the likelihood of a negative resolution increases as societal demands become more complex and the chances of encountering societal barriers to development increase. A positive resolution of each crisis provides new ego strengths that help the person meet the demands of the next stage. A negative resolution contributes to withdrawal and rigidity that make it more difficult to meet the new demands of the next stage.

To understand the process of growth at each life stage, we have to consider the negative as well as the positive pole of each crisis. The dynamic tension between the positive and negative forces respects and reflects the struggles we all encounter to restrain unbridled impulses, to overcome fears and doubts, and to look past our own needs to consider the needs of others. The negative poles offer insight into basic areas of human vulnerability. Experienced in moderation, the negative forces result in a clarification of ego positions, individuation, and moral integrity. While a steady diet of mistrust is undesirable, for example, it is important that a trusting person be able to evaluate situations and people for their trustworthiness and to discern cues about safety or danger in any encounter. In every psychosocial crisis, experiences at both the positive and the negative poles contribute to the total range of a person's adaptive capacities.

The term *crisis* implies that normal development does not proceed smoothly. The theory hypothesizes that tension and conflict are necessary to the developmental process. Crisis and its resolution are basic, biologically based components of life experience at every stage. In fact, they are what drives the ego system to develop new capacities.

The term *psychosocial* draws attention to the fact that the psychosocial crises are, in part, the result of cultural pressures and expectations. As part of normal development, individuals will experience tension because of the culture's need to socialize and integrate its members. The concept acknowledges the dynamic conflicts between individuality and group membership at each period of life.

The exact nature of the conflict is not the same at each stage. For example, few cultural limits are placed on infants. The outcome of the infancy stage depends greatly on the skill of the caregiver. At early school age, the culture stands in fairly direct opposition to the child's initiative in some matters by discouraging curiosity or questioning about certain topics, and offers abundant encouragement to a child's initiative in others. In young adulthood, the dominant cultural push is toward the establishment of intimate relationships; yet an individual may be unable to attain intimacy because of the lack of time to cultivate intimate relationships, competing pressures from the workplace, cultural norms against certain expressions of intimacy, or restrictions against certain types of unions.

As reflected in the epigenetic principle, the succession of crises occurs in a predictable sequence over the life course. Although Erikson did not specify the exact ages for each crisis, the theory hypothesizes an age-related progression in which each crisis has its time of special ascendancy. The combination of biological, psychological, and societal forces that operate to bring about change has a degree of regularity within society that places each psychosocial crisis at a particular period of life.

Radius of Significant Relationships

The third organizing principle of psychosocial theory is the **radius of significant relationships** (Erikson, 1982, p. 31). These relationships are thought to be the vehicle or channel through which age-related cultural and community expectations are communicated. A person's ego includes a social processing system that is sensitive to social expectations. Initially, a person focuses on a small number of relationships, beginning with the primary caregivers, siblings, and other close family members. During childhood, adolescence, and early adulthood, the number of relationships expands and the quality of these relationships takes on greater variety in depth and in intensity. In later adulthood, the person often returns to a smaller number of extremely important relationships that provide opportunities for great depth and intimacy.

At each stage of life, this network of relationships determines the demands that will be made on the person, the way he or she will be taken care of, and the meaning that the person will derive from the relationships. The relationship network varies from person to person, but each person has a network of significant relationships and an increasing readiness to enter into more complex social life (Vanzetti & Duck, 1996). The quality of these relationships and the norms for interaction influence the way the psychosocial crisis of the stage is experienced, and the interpersonal context in which it is resolved.

Prime Adaptive Ego Qualities

According to psychosocial theory, at each stage of life, consistent efforts to face and cope with the psychosocial crisis of the period result in the formation of basic adaptive capacities referred to as the **prime adaptive ego qualities**. When coping is unsuccessful and the challenges of the period are not adequately mastered, individuals are likely to form maladaptive orientations, referred to as the **core pathologies**.

Erikson (1978) postulated prime adaptive ego qualities that develop from the positive resolution of the psychosocial crisis of a given stage and provide resources for coping with the next. Drawing upon his concept of an epigenetic principle, Erikson viewed the prime adaptive ego qualities as guided by evolution and embedded into the developmental blueprint for human maturation. "Without them, and their re-emergence from generation to generation, all other and more changeable systems of human values lose their spirit and their relevance" (Erikson, 1950/1963, p. 274).

When the psychosocial crisis is resolved with a favorable balance between the positive and the negative poles, an enduring strength emerges. Erikson described these qualities as mental states that form a basic orientation toward the interpretation of life experiences. A sense of competence, for example, permits a person to feel free to exercise his or her wits to solve problems without being weighed down by a sense of inferiority.

The prime adaptive ego qualities and their definitions are: (a) infancy–hope, which is an enduring belief that one can attain one's deep and essential wishes; (b) toddlerhood–will, which is a determination to exercise free choice and self-control; (c) early school age–purpose, which is the courage to imagine and pursue valued goals; (d) middle childhood–competence, which is the free exercise of skill and intelligence in the completion of tasks; (e) early adolescence–fidelity to others, which is the ability freely to pledge and sustain loyalty to others; (f) later adolescence–fidelity to values, which is the ability freely to pledge and sustain loyalty to values and ideologies; (g) early adulthood–love, which is a capacity for mutuality that transcends childhood dependency; (h) middle adulthood–care, which is a commitment to concern about what has been generated; and (i) later adulthood–wisdom, which is a detached yet active concern with life itself in the face of death.

These ego qualities contribute to the person's dominant worldview, which is continuously reformulated to accommodate new ego qualities. The importance of many of the prime adaptive ego qualities has been verified by research. For example, hope has been identified as a significant factor in allowing people to cope with adversity as well as to organize their actions to achieve difficult goals (Snyder, 1994). People with a hopeful attitude have a better chance of maintaining their spirits and strength in the face of crisis than people who are pessimistic. In interviews with people in very old age, Erikson and his colleagues found that those who were hopeful about their own future as well as that of their children were more intellectually vigorous and psychologically resilient than those not characterized by this orientation (Erikson et al., 1986).

Core Pathologies

Although most people develop the prime adaptive ego qualities, a potential core pathology or destructive force may also develop as a result of ineffective, negatively balanced crisis resolution at each stage (Erikson, 1982). The core pathologies and their definitions are: (a) infancy–withdrawal, social and emotional detachment; (b) toddlerhood–compulsion, repetitive behaviors motivated by impulse or by restrictions against the expression of impulse; (c) early school age–inhibition, a psychological restraint that prevents freedom of thought, expression, and activity; (d) middle childhood–inertia, a paralysis of action and thought that prevents productive work; (e) early adolescence–dissociation, an inability to connect with others; (f) later adolescence–repudiation, rejection of most roles and values because they are viewed as alien to oneself; (g) early adulthood–exclusivity, an elitist shutting out of others; (h) middle adulthood–rejectivity, unwillingness to include certain others or groups of others in one's generative concern; and (i) later adulthood–disdain, a feeling of scorn for the weakness and frailty of oneself and others.

The core pathologies also serve as guiding orientations for behavior. These pathologies move people away from others, tend to prevent further exploration of interpersonal relations, and obstruct the resolution of subsequent psychosocial crises. The energy that would normally be directed toward mastering the developmental tasks of a stage is directed instead toward resisting or avoiding change. The core pathologies are not simply passive limitations or barriers to growth. They are energized worldviews leading to strategies that protect people from further unwanted association with the social system and its persistent, tension-producing demands. Figure 8.2 illustrates the mechanism for positive and negative psychosocial development at each stage.

NEW DIRECTIONS

Psychosocial theory has been expanded and elaborated upon as a framework for studying development across the life span (Newman & Newman, 1975, 2015). This perspective integrates two additional constructs: developmental tasks, and a central process for resolving the psychosocial crisis. It also expands the number of life stages and the related psychosocial crises. The three additional stages are prenatal development, early adolescence, and elderhood.

Additional Psychosocial Stages

The addition of three new stages provides a good demonstration of the process of theory construction. Theories of human development emerge and change within a cultural and historical

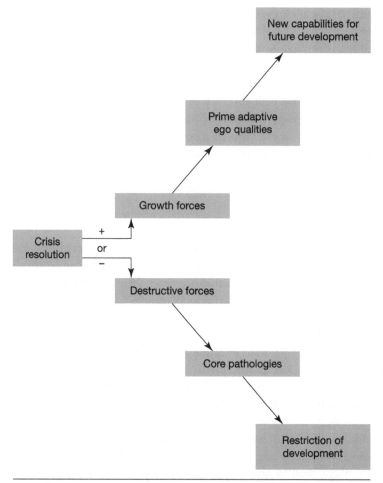

Figure 8.2 Mechanism for Positive and Negative Psychosocial Development

Source: From B.M. Newman & P.R. Newman (2015). *Development through life: A psychosocial approach*. 12th ed. © 2015 South-Western, a part of Cengage Learning, Inc. Reproduced by permission. www.cengage.com/permissions

context. Patterns of biological and psychosocial evolution occur within a cultural frame of reference. The prenatal stage is added to the stages of psychosocial development in the context of a growing body of research that illuminates the dynamic interaction of the genetically guided plan for fetal development and the fetal environment. This fetal environment is further influenced by features of the social and cultural contexts within which pregnancy occurs. Thus, the status of the fetus at birth is already a product of a psychosocial dynamic.

The division of the adolescent period into two psychosocial stages is a product of changes in the timing of onset of puberty in modern society, the expanding need for education and training before entry into the world of work, related changes in the structure of the educational system, and the variety of the available life choices in work, marriage, parenting, and ideology. The period of later adolescence, which is described in many of Erikson's writings as characterized by its focus on individual **identity**, is an effort to find a meaningful integration of one's roles that is acceptable and valued by society. Recent research has linked this capacity for self-reflection and the capacity to integrate diverse information into a complex, abstract sense of oneself with the continuing maturation of the prefrontal cortex tied to decision making, planning, and goal setting (Steinberg, 2005). The idea of later adolescence as a distinct stage of development has been supported by a growing body of research summarized by Jeffrey Arnett (1998, 2000, 2004). Arnett refers to this stage of life as *emerging adulthood.*

The period of early adolescence is characterized by its focus on social or group identity and its ties to the psychosocial transitions associated with pubertal change. The psychosocial crisis of this stage is group identity versus alienation. This crisis captures the tension between feeling that one is meaningfully connected to a valued social group and a sense of social estrangement. The prime adaptive ego quality is *fidelity to others*, a willingness to pledge one's loyalties to others and to sustain one's commitments to them. The core pathology is *dissociation*, a sense of separateness, withdrawal, and a reluctance to make the types of enduring commitments to others that foster long-term friendships (Newman and Newman, 1976, 2015).

The addition of a period of elderhood was stimulated by interest in the adaptive strategies that characterize people who have exceeded the life expectancy of their birth cohort. In the United States, those 85 and older are the fastest growing age group, expected to reach 7.2 million by 2020. Erikson hinted at this final stage in his book, *Vital involvements in old age* (Erikson et al., 1986). A psychosocial stage beyond maturity reflects the courage, vitality, and innovative coping strategies that are observed in this group, as well as the impact of advanced age on one's self-concept and one's outlook on mortality. The psychosocial crisis of elderhood is immortality versus extinction (Newman & Newman, 2015). This crisis reflects a tension between a view of life as transcending mortality through a symbolic, societal, or spiritual continuity, and the sense that death brings a final and permanent end to one's existence and one's impact. The prime adaptive ego quality is *confidence*, a trust in one's self and the meaningfulness of life. The core pathology is *diffidence*, an inability to act because of overwhelming self-doubt.

The need to differentiate the period of elderhood from later adulthood was confirmed in the writings of Joan Erikson who proposed a ninth stage of the life cycle (Erikson & Erikson, 1997). Joan Erikson wrote about this stage of life in the years after Erik died, while she was in her nineties. As a result of physical decline, social isolation, the loss of loved ones, and cultural neglect or disregard, Erikson suggested that the dystonic or negative poles of the eight psychosocial stages become newly salient. In addition, she distinguished the sense of despair in the eighth stage of the theory, which was despair over past opportunities and regret over past decisions, from a new kind of despair over the mounting disintegration and loss of capacities resulting from the physical declines of very old age. She wrote of the failure of society to find an appropriate strategy or program to embrace the realities of advanced aging that permits older adults to remain engaged, in touch, and integrated into social life.

The counter force to this process of decline and despair is what Joan Erikson described as *gerotranscendence.*

To reach for gerotranscendence is to rise above, exceed, outdo, go beyond, independent of the universe and time. It involves surpassing all human knowledge and experience. How, for heaven's sake, is this to be accomplished? I am persuaded that only by doing and making do we become. Transcendence need not be limited solely to experiences of withdrawal. In touching, we make contact with one another and with our planet. Transcendence may be a regaining of lost skills, including play, activity, joy, and song, and, above all, a major leap above and beyond the fear of death. It provides an opening forward into the unknown with a trusting leap. Oddly enough, this all demands of us an honest and steadfast humility. These are wonderful words, words that wind us up into involvement. Transcendence—that's it, of course! And it moves. It's one of the arts, it's alive, sings, and makes music, and I hug myself because of the truth it whispers to my soul. No wonder writing has been so difficult. Transcendence calls forth the languages of the arts; nothing else speaks so deeply and meaningfully to our hearts and souls. The great dance of life can transport us into all realms of making and doing with every item of body, mind, and spirit involved. I am profoundly moved, for I am growing old and feel shabby, and suddenly great riches present themselves and enlighten every part of my body and reach out to beauty everywhere. (Erikson & Erikson, 1997, p. 127)

Integration of Developmental Tasks

At each stage of development, one faces a new set of **developmental tasks** consisting of skills and competencies that contribute to increased mastery over one's environment. These tasks reflect areas of accomplishment in physical, cognitive, social, and emotional development, as well as development of the self-concept. The tasks define what is healthy, normal development at each age in a particular society. Success in learning the tasks of one stage leads to development and a greater chance of success in learning the tasks of later stages. Failure at the tasks of one stage leads to greater difficulty with later tasks or may even make later tasks impossible to master.

Robert J. Havighurst (1948/1972), who used the concept of developmental tasks in thinking and teaching about human development and education, believed that human development is a process in which people attempt to learn the tasks required of them by the society to which they are adapting. These tasks change with age because each society has age-graded expectations for behavior. "Living in a modern society is a long series of tasks to learn" (Havighurst, 1948/1972, p. 2). The person who learns well receives satisfaction and reward; the person who does not suffers unhappiness and social disapproval.

Havighurst credits Erik Erikson's psychosocial theory as playing a major role in his use of the concept of developmental tasks. It is a concept that bridges the individual and the society, assuming an active learner who is interacting with an active social environment. Although Havighurst's view of development emphasizes the guiding role of society in determining which skills need to be acquired at a certain age, he believed that there are sensitive periods for learning developmental tasks—that is, times when the person is most ready and most likely to expend effort to acquire a new ability. Havighurst called these periods *teachable moments*. Most people learn developmental tasks at the time and in the sequence appropriate in their society. If a particular task is not learned during the sensitive period, learning may be much more difficult later on.

A relatively small number of major developmental tasks dominate a person's problem-solving efforts and learning during a given stage. Keep in mind that one is changing on several levels at once during each period of life. Tasks involving physical, emotional, intellectual, and social growth, as well as growth in the self-concept, all contribute to one's resources for coping with the challenges of life. As these tasks are mastered, new competencies enhance the person's ability to engage in more complex planning, decision making, and relationship building. Successful cultures provide opportunities for their members to learn what they need to know at each age, for both their own survival and that of the group.

Mastery of the developmental tasks is influenced by the resolution of the psychosocial crisis of the previous stage, and it is this resolution that leads to the development of new social capabilities.

These capabilities orient the person toward new experiences, a new aptitude for relationships, and new feelings of personal worth as he or she confronts the challenges of the developmental tasks of the next stage. In turn, the skills learned during a particular stage as a result of work on its developmental tasks provide the tools for the resolution of the psychosocial crisis of that stage. Task accomplishment and crisis resolution interact to produce individual life stories.

The Central Process for Resolving the Psychosocial Crisis

Every psychosocial crisis reflects some discrepancy between the person's developmental competencies at the beginning of the stage and new societal pressures for more effective, integrated functioning. How is the discrepancy resolved? What experiences or processes permit the person to interpret the expectations and demands of society and internalize them in order to support change? The **central process** suggests a way that the person takes in or makes sense of cultural expectations and undergoes adaptive modifications of the self (Newman and Newman, 1975, 2015). The term *process* suggests a means by which the person recognizes new social pressures and expectations, gives these expectations personal meaning, and gradually changes. The process, unfolding over time, results in a new relationship between self and society. The central process might be compared to the physical phenomenon of absorption and evaporation through which moisture enters the body, is used and transformed, and leaves the body. At each life stage, specific modes of psychological work and social interaction must occur if a person is to continue to grow.

For example, in toddlerhood, the psychosocial crisis raises the question of how children increase their sense of autonomy without risking too many experiences that provoke a sense of shame and doubt. Imitation is the central process for psychosocial growth during toddlerhood (ages 2 and 3). Children expand their range of skills by imitating adults, siblings, television models, playmates, and even animals. Imitation provides toddlers with enormous satisfaction. As they increase the similarity between themselves and admired members of their social groups through imitation, they begin to experience the world as other people and animals experience it. They exercise some control over potentially frightening or confusing events by imitating elements of those occurrences in their play.

The movement toward a sense of autonomy in toddlerhood is facilitated by the child's readiness to imitate and by the variety of models available for observation. Imitation expands children's range of behavior, and through persistent imitative activity, children expand their sense of self-initiated behavior and control over their actions. Repetitive experiences of this kind lead to the development of a sense of personal autonomy.

The central process for coping with the challenges of each life stage provides both personal and societal mechanisms for taking in new information and reorganizing existing information. It also suggests the means that are most likely to lead to a revision of the psychological system so that the crisis of a particular stage may be resolved. Each central process results in an intensive reworking of the psychological system, including a reorganization of boundaries, values, and images of one's self and others. The central processes that lead to the acquisition of new skills, the resolution of the psychosocial crisis, and successful coping at each life stage are: (a) infancy–mutuality with a caregiver; (b) toddlerhood–imitation; (c) early school age–identification; (d) middle childhood–education; (e) early adolescence–peer pressure; (f) later adolescence–role experimentation; (g) early adulthood–mutuality among peers; (h) middle adulthood–person/environment fit and creativity; (i) later adulthood–introspection; and (j) elderhood–social support.

A RESEARCH EXAMPLE: INDIVIDUAL IDENTITY

Many themes identified in psychosocial theory have become the focus of research, including trust, autonomy, shame and doubt, intimacy, isolation and loneliness, and generativity. One of the most extensively studied concepts is the topic of personal or individual identity. Erik Erikson provided a comprehensive treatment of the meaning and functions of individual identity, from his inclusion of this concept in the theory of psychosocial development in 1950 to his analysis of American identity in 1974. His notion of identity involves the merging of past identifications, future aspirations, and contemporary cultural issues. The major works in which he discussed identity are the article "The problem of ego identity" (1959) and the book *Identity: Youth and crisis* (1968).

Later adolescents are preoccupied with questions about their essential character in much the same way that early school-age children are preoccupied with questions about their origins. In their efforts to define themselves, later adolescents must take into account the bonds that have been built between them and others in the past as well as the direction they hope to take in the future. In later adolescence, the identity process includes: examining alternatives; selecting goals in valued domains such as occupation, religion, intimacy, family life, and education; making personal and interpersonal commitments to achieve these goals; and taking the active steps to achieve them (Nurmi, 2004). Identity serves as an anchor point, providing the person an essential experience of continuity in social relationships. Identity achievement is associated with an internal sense of individual uniqueness and direction accompanied by a social or community validation about the direction one has chosen.

Identity Status

One of the most widely used conceptual frameworks for assessing identity status was devised by James Marcia (1980, 1993, 2007). Using Erikson's concepts, Marcia assessed identity status on the basis of two criteria: *crisis* and *commitment*. Crisis consists of a period of questioning, role experimentation, and active decision making among alternative choices. Commitment consists of a demonstration of personal involvement in activities and relationships that reflect one's beliefs and values in the areas of occupational choice, religion, political ideology, and interpersonal bonds. On the basis of Marcia's interview, one can determine a young person's progress in clarifying values, goals, and commitments. The status of one's identity development is assessed as either identity achieved, foreclosed, moratorium, or diffused (see Table 8.1.).

People who are classified as **identity achieved** have already experienced a time of questioning and exploration, and have made occupational and ideological commitments. People who are classified as **foreclosed** have not experienced a crisis but demonstrate strong occupational and ideological commitments. Their occupational and ideological beliefs appear to be close to those of their parents. The foreclosed identity is deceptive. A young person of 18 or 19 who can say exactly what he or she wants in life and who has selected an occupational goal, may appear to be mature. This kind of clarity of vision may impress peers and adults as evidence of a high level of self-insight. However, if this solution has been formulated through the wholesale adoption of a script that was devised by the young person's family, it may not actually reflect much depth of self-understanding.

People who are classified as being in a state of **psychosocial moratorium** are involved in an ongoing crisis. They are in a period of questioning, exploration, and experimentation; they have not yet made commitments. The moratorium status is typically an active, open time for gathering

Table 8.1 The relationship of crisis and commitment to identity status

Identity status	Crisis	Commitment
Achievement	+	+
Foreclosure	-	+
Moratorium	+	
Diffusion	+/-	-

information and figuring out how one fits in certain roles. Finally, people who are classified as **identity diffused** may or may not have experienced a crisis, and they demonstrate a complete lack of commitment. Marcia described several types of identify diffusion including people who have a rather cavalier, "party" attitude, and others who are more acutely confused and might be experiencing more serious psychopathology.

A significant body of research has shown patterns of personal characteristics associated with the four identity statuses that are consistent with Erikson's theory. Those who are classified as identity achieved show greater ego strength. They have higher levels of achievement motivation, moral reasoning, intimacy with peers, and career maturity. Those in the moratorium status are more anxious and have conflict over issues of authority. They are more flexible and less authoritarian than the other groups. Those in the foreclosed status are the most authoritarian; they are the least autonomous and have the greatest need for social approval (Berzonsky & Adams, 1999; Waterman, 1999a, 1999b; Zimmermann & Becker-Stoll, 2002).

The most maladaptive resolution of the crisis is identity diffusion. Individuals in this status have been shown to have low self-esteem; they are more likely than those in the other statuses to be influenced by peer pressures toward conformity; and they approach problem solving with tendencies toward procrastination and avoidance which contribute to difficulties in adjusting to the college environment (Berzonsky & Kuk, 2000; Kroger, 2003). In comparison to the moratorium group, young people in the diffused status are less conscientious, more likely to experience negative emotions, and more disagreeable (Clancy & Dollinger, 1993). They are generally not outgoing; rather, they describe themselves as self-conscious and likely to feel depressed. Their relationship with their parents is described as distant or rejecting. Several studies have found that young people who are characterized as identity diffused have had a history of early and frequent involvement with drug use and abuse (Jones, 1992). Difficulties in resolving earlier psychosocial crises, especially conflicts related to autonomy versus shame and doubt and initiative versus guilt, leave some young people with deficits in ego formation that interfere with the kind of energy and playful self-assertiveness that are necessary in the process of identity achievement (Marcia, 2006).

Developmental Progression of Identity Statuses

The theoretical construct of identity status assumes a developmental progression from diffusion to foreclosure, moratorium, and finally achievement. Identity diffusion reflects the least defined status. Movement from any other status to diffusion suggests regression. A person who has achieved identity at one period may conceivably return to a period of moratorium. However, those who are in a moratorium or achieved status can never be accurately described as foreclosed, since by definition they have already experienced some degree of crisis (Waterman, 1982; Meeus, 1996).

A number of studies, both cross-sectional and longitudinal, show evidence of identity maturation, including higher levels of exploration and commitment with age. Over time more young people are characterized as having the identity statuses of moratorium and achievement, and fewer are in foreclosure or identity diffusion (Kroger, Martinussen, & Marcia, 2010). When transitions in identity status occur, they are typically in the direction from moratorium to achievement. However, studies report diverse patterns of status transitions from diffusion or moratorium to foreclosure or achievement; and some studies find that many individuals do not change their identity status over the period of later adolescence and early adulthood (Meeus, 2011). Identity commitments provide stability and direction. Certain life events such as job loss, death of a loved one, or loss of a love relationship, can destabilize these commitments, resulting in a form of identity regression. For example, a person might move from achievement to moratorium or from foreclosure to diffusion (Marcia, 2010; Marcia & Simon, 2003). One implication is that the statuses are better thought of as self-theories or ways of linking information about the self and the world rather than formal stages that evolve in a strict sequence from one level to the next (Berzonsky, 2003).

AN APPLICATION: THE ROLE OF HOPE IN COPING AND PROBLEM SOLVING

Erikson (1982) theorized that the positive resolution of the psychosocial crisis of trust versus mistrust leads to the adaptive ego quality of **hope**. The prime adaptive ego qualities shape a person's outlook on life in the direction of greater openness to experience and information, greater capacity to identify a variety of pathways to achieve one's goals, more willingness to assert the self and to express one's wishes and views, and a positive approach to the formation of close relationships. Even in the face of difficulties and stressful life events, these qualities contribute to higher levels of functioning and well-being (Peterson & Seligman, 2003).

As the first of the prime adaptive ego qualities, hope pervades the entire life story. It is a global, cognitive orientation that one's goals and dreams can be attained and that events will turn out for the best. As Erikson described it:

> Hope bestows on the anticipated future a sense of leeway inviting expectant leaps, either in preparatory imagination or in small initiating actions. And such daring must count on basic trust in the sense of a trustfulness that must be, literally and figuratively, nourished by maternal care and—when endangered by all-too-desperate discomfort—must be restored by competent consolidation. (1982, p. 60)

Hopefulness combines the ability to think of one or more paths to achieve a goal with a belief in one's ability to move along that pathway toward the goal (Snyder, Cheavens, & Sympson, 1997). The roots of hopefulness lie in the infant's understanding of the self as a causal agent. Each time a baby takes an action to achieve an outcome, the sense of hope grows. When babies encounter obstacles or barriers to their goals, sensitive caregivers find ways to remove the obstacles or lead them along a new path toward the goal. The infant's sense of self as a causal agent combined with the caregiver's sensitivity create the context for the emergence of hope.

Research with adults shows that people who have a hopeful, optimistic outlook about the future have different achievement beliefs and emotional reactions in response to actual achievement than do people who have a pessimistic outlook (Dweck, 1992; Seligman, 2011). People who have higher levels of hopefulness undertake a larger number of goals across life areas and select tasks that are more difficult. Hopefulness is generally associated with higher goals, higher levels of confidence that the goals will be reached, and greater persistence in the face of barriers to goal attainment, thus leading to higher overall levels of performance (Snyder, 2002).

Feelings of hope have been shown to help people deal with their most difficult challenges, including serious illness, injury, bereavement, and facing the end of life (Sullivan, 2003). In the face of many difficulties as a result of separation from their mothers, poverty, and disruptive home environments, children who have higher levels of hope have been found to have fewer emotional and behavioral problems. These children are more likely to have ideas about how to overcome challenges in their lives rather than to be overwhelmed by the problems they face (Hagen, Myers, & Macintosh, 2005).

In studies of college students, hope has been found to be closely linked with academic success (Snyder, Shorey, Cheavens, Pulvers, Adams, & Wiklund, 2002). In a 6-year longitudinal study, students who were more hopeful had better grades and were more likely to graduate from college. Students' hopefulness was associated with having more clearly identified goals based on internal standards. Their goals served to energize their behavior and increase efforts to perform well. Hopeful students were more focused on their goals and less likely to be distracted by self-deprecating thoughts or negative emotions that undermined their efforts. Finally, students who were hopeful were able to identify several different paths toward their goals. If one path was blocked, they would use the information to find another alternative. In contrast, students low in hopefulness tended to stick with one strategy even when it was not working and, as a result, became more passive and disengaged.

Hope plays a key role in the therapeutic process (Snyder & Taylor, 2000). An assumption of counseling is that the client and the therapist can imagine a better future and that together they will explore pathways toward that future. Counselors nurture hope by helping clients to identify new possibilities for their future, clarify their goals, devise strategies or paths to achieve these goals, and increase their sense of **agency** about being able to enact these strategies. By modeling confidence and reassurance, the counselor creates an environment in which the client can begin to experience hopefulness about the future (Snyder & McDermott, 1999; Egan, 2013).

HOW DOES PSYCHOSOCIAL THEORY ANSWER THE BASIC QUESTIONS THAT A THEORY OF HUMAN DEVELOPMENT IS EXPECTED TO ADDRESS?

1. *What is the direction of change over the life span? How well does the theory account for patterns of change and continuity?*

   Psychosocial theory attempts to explain human development across the life span—especially patterned changes in **ego development**, which is reflected in self-understanding, identity formation, social relationships, and worldview. The theory defines human development as a product of the ongoing interaction of an individual's biological and psychological needs and abilities on the one hand, and societal expectations on the other hand. Psychosocial theory predicts an orderly sequence of change in ego development and social relationships from infancy through late life. At each stage, new abilities and coping strategies emerge for engaging in social relationships and for meeting the demands of an ever-changing, increasingly complex social world.

   Meaning is created out of efforts to interpret and integrate the experiences of the biological, psychological, and societal systems. A primary focus of this meaning making is the search for identity. Humans struggle to define themselves—to achieve an identity—through a sense of connectedness with certain other people and groups, and through feelings of distinctiveness from others. We establish categories that define whom we are connected to, whom we care about, and which of our own qualities we admire. We also establish categories that define those to whom we are not connected, those whom we do not care about, and those qualities of our own that we reject or deny. These categories provide us with an orientation toward certain kinds of people and away from others, toward certain life choices and away from others. The psychosocial perspective brings to light the dynamic interplay of the roles of the self and the others, the I and the We, as they contribute to the emergence of identity over the life course.

Psychosocial theory addresses issues of continuity and change over the life course. At each stage of life, the resolution of the psychosocial crisis results in the attainment of certain prime adaptive ego strengths or core pathologies. At each stage of life, one is embedded in a radius of significant relationships. These factors, carried forward into the next stage, as well as the tendency to anticipate the issues of the stages ahead, contribute to continuity in development. At the same time, the epigenetic principle assumes an unfolding of new capacities in the context of changing social expectations. As a result, one can expect new ways of understanding the relationship of self and other, and new facets of one's identity, to emerge over the life span. Although there is no going back to earlier stages of life, there is a capacity for reflection and revisitation through which the resolution of earlier crises may be reconfigured.

2. *What are the mechanisms that account for growth? What are some testable hypotheses or predictions that emerge from this analysis?*
The basic mechanism that accounts for growth is the psychosocial crisis. The crises arise as a result of the epigenetic principle through which tension is created due to the discrepancy between one's competencies at each stage and the new demands of society. People strive to reduce this tension by using a variety of familiar coping strategies and by learning new ones. The following testable hypotheses emerge from the theory:

1. A normal crisis arises at each stage of development, and a central process operates to resolve this crisis. The resolution of the crisis at each stage determines one's coping resources, with a positive resolution contributing to ego strengths and a negative resolution contributing to core pathologies.
2. Each stage of development is accompanied by a specific psychosocial crisis. Issues of later stages can be previewed at an earlier time, but each issue has its period of ascendance. It takes the entire life course, from the prenatal period through elderhood, for all aspects of the ego's potential to be realized.
3. Each person is part of an expanding network of significant relationships that convey society's expectations and demands. These relationships also provide encouragement and support in the face of challenges.
4. Development will be optimal if a person can create new behaviors and relationships as a result of skill acquisition through mastery of the developmental tasks and successful crisis resolution during each stage of growth. Lack of development and core pathologies result from tendencies that restrict behavior (especially social behavior) in general and new behavior in particular.

3. *How relevant are early experiences for later development? What evidence does the theory offer to support its view?*
Early experiences are highly relevant for subsequent development. The strengths and skills acquired through mastery of the developmental tasks and the resolution of earlier crises

are important for resolving later crises. The prime adaptive ego qualities of early life stages prepare a person to approach subsequent crises with an outlook of hope, determination, and empowerment. Similarly, crises that are resolved toward the negative pole contribute to a more cautious, inhibited, or withdrawn outlook. What is more, psychosocial theory suggests that each life crisis is foreshadowed in earlier stages, and that each crisis is played out in a more complex way at later stages. Thus, all of life is a tapestry in which the issues of the past are expressed in new forms at later stages, and issues of later stages are anticipated in less mature forms in earlier stages.

4. *How do the environmental and social contexts affect development? What aspects of the environment does the theory suggest are especially important in shaping the direction of development?*
   As its name implies, psychosocial theory emphasizes the ongoing interaction of the individual and society. An assumption of this theory is that the development of the person and the continued adaptive functioning of society are interdependent. Societies shape development through the messages that are conveyed to individuals through the radius of significant relationships, beginning with the first caregivers and expanding outward to siblings, grandparents, other family members, friends, co-workers, admired role models, intimate partners, children, grandchildren and so on. As the radius of significant relationships expands, people engage in an increasingly complex set of roles with more diverse individuals. With advanced age, the number of relationships may decline, but the ego development that was stimulated through this complex set of relationships continues to be expressed through characteristics of integrity and wisdom or despair.

   Societies differ. Prevailing cultural, religious, economic, and political factors have implications for the nature of interpersonal relationships, opportunities for social mobility, economic prosperity, and educational attainment, just to name a few. In societies where people are governed through intimidation and children are encouraged to embrace messages of inter-group hatred, the resolution of the psychosocial crises will likely be influenced by these conditions toward withdrawal, shame, and self-doubt. In societies where people are encouraged to value self-expression and agency, the resolution of the psychosocial crises will likely be influenced by these conditions toward more trust, autonomy, and initiative.

   Individuals shape societies through the ways they establish and preserve relationships, make commitments to work, family, and ideologies, and nurture future generations through their generative actions. Individuals and groups of individuals can bring about cultural and political change, creating more open, caring communities that support psychosocial well-being.

5. *According to the theory, what factors place individuals at risk at specific periods of the life span?*
   The theory offers a stage-based guide to experiences that place individuals at risk. At each stage, the negative pole of the psychosocial crisis suggests a potentially high risk outcome for that period of life—mistrust, shame and doubt, guilt, inferiority, etc. When the psychosocial crisis is resolved with a balance in the direction of the negative pole, the result is likely to be the emergence of a related core pathology. These core pathologies interfere with the formation of new relationships, produce defensiveness and withdrawal, interfere with the creation of new, flexible coping strategies, and leave the ego vulnerable to sentiments of resentment and despair. Even when earlier psychosocial crises have been resolved in the

direction of a positive pole, each new stage can bring a period of vulnerability, especially if life events converge to undermine resources or destabilize the social support system as a person strives to resolve the new crisis.

From a societal perspective, the early ego development of the child and the likelihood of a positive resolution of the psychosocial crises of infancy, toddlerhood, early and middle childhood are heavily dependent on the ego maturity and well-being of the caregivers. In that regard, societal conditions that undermine the financial, physical, or emotional well-being of caregivers, or that disrupt the social support for caregivers, can be considered risk factors for children.

Poverty is a major obstacle to optimal development. Under conditions of poverty, individuals have fewer options and less opportunity to escape or avoid other forms of societal oppression such as racism, sexism, or homophobia. It is well documented that poverty increases the risks that individuals face, including risks associated with malnutrition, poor quality health care, living in a hazardous or dangerous neighborhood, and attending ineffective schools. Poverty and prolonged economic strain tend to erode the self-esteem of caregivers, resulting in harsh parenting, parent conflict, and emotional withdrawal. Beyond childhood, poverty is linked with reduced access to the basic resources associated with survival. To the extent that poverty is stigmatized and associated with demeaning social treatment it has potentially powerful and pervasive effects on psychosocial development across the life span.

6. *What are some practical implications of psychosocial theory?*
One of the unique features of psychosocial theory is that it identifies key issues and themes for each period of life from infancy through late life. As a result, the theory has wide-ranging implications for parenting, education, counseling, intergenerational programs, adult education, organizational and leadership training, and social/community interventions. A few examples are provided here.

The theory identifies specific themes for each stage of life that can guide intervention. For example, in infancy, the crisis of trust versus mistrust has clear implications for the importance of sensitive, responsive, psychologically attuned parenting. In toddlerhood, the crisis of autonomy versus shame and doubt has implications for family and early childhood settings, encouraging adults to provide opportunities for choice, self-expression, and the fostering of self-regulation while limiting a child's experiences of humiliation and blame. Each psychosocial crisis suggests directions for positive development as well as potential aspects of vulnerability.

In the counseling context, the theory not only indicates potential areas of contemporary conflict, but suggests a way to think about how earlier periods of life might result in core pathologies that contribute to current difficulties. The framework of psychosocial crises, developmental tasks, prime adaptive ego strengths, and core pathologies has been used in counseling and social work settings to guide assessment of clients and provide directions for therapeutic interventions.

Psychosocial theory has inspired programs in mentoring and leadership development within corporations, adult education programs, and professional training. The concepts of generativity versus stagnation and integrity versus despair, the related ego strengths of care and wisdom, and the core pathologies of rejectivity and disdain, offer guiding principles for thinking about the relationship of supervisors and managers to both younger and older co-workers.

The theory offers a distinct perspective on the interaction of the person and society. As such, it suggests features of a community or larger society that may support or inhibit optimal well-being. As an example, in political science, the notion of trust versus mistrust has been applied to inter-group relations as the underpinning of diplomacy and conflict resolution. The concept of personal identity has been expanded to include ethnic group and national identity. As individuals move across national boundaries they face challenges associated with conflicting cultural identities. Communities can be viewed as supportive or hostile to the psychosocial adaptation of groups with diverse social identities.

CRITIQUE OF PSYCHOSOCIAL THEORY

Strengths

Psychosocial theory provides a broad, integrative context within which to study life-span development (Hopkins, 1995; Kiston, 1994). The theory links the process of child development to the stages of adult life, individual development to the nature of culture and society, and the personal and historical past to the personal and societal future. Although many scholars agree that such a broad perspective is necessary, few other theories attempt to address the dynamic interplay between individual development and society (Miller, 2011).

The emphasis of psychosocial theory on ego development and ego processes provides insight into the directions of healthy development throughout life. The theory provides a framework for tracing the process through which self-concept, self-esteem, and ego boundaries become integrated into a positive, adaptive, socially engaged person (Hamachek, 1985, 1994). Emphasizing the normal, hopeful, and creative aspects of coping and adaptation, the theory has taken the study of development beyond the deterministic position of psychosexual theory or the mechanistic view of behaviorism, providing an essential conceptual framework for the emergence of positive psychology.

At one time, some argued that a weakness of psychosocial theory was that its basic concepts were presented in language that is abstract and difficult to examine empirically (Crain, 2011; Miller, 2011). However, over the past 20 years, such terms as hope, inhibition, autonomy, personal identity, intimacy, generativity, and integrity—to name a few—have been operationalized (Bohlin, Bengtsgard, & Andersson, 2000; Christiansen & Palkovitz, 1998; de St. Aubin, McAdams, & Kim 2003; Kroger, 2007; Lopez & Snyder, 2003; Marcia, 2002; McAdams & de St. Aubin, 1998; Snyder, 2002). Concepts central to the theory—such as trust, autonomy, identity achievement, coping, well-being, social support, and intergenerational interdependence—have become thoroughly integrated into contemporary human development scholarship. Researchers have developed instruments to trace the emergence of psychosocial crises and their resolution in samples varying in age from adolescence to later adulthood (Constantinople, 1969; Darling-Fisher & Leidy, 1988; Domino & Affonso, 1990; Hawley, 1988; Waterman & Whitbourne, 1981; Whitbourne, Sneed, & Sayer, 2009).

Unlike some other stage theories, psychosocial theory identifies tensions that may disrupt development at each life stage, providing a useful framework for considering individual differences in development. The positive and negative poles of each psychosocial crisis offer a way of thinking about differences in ego development at each stage of life as well as a model for considering cumulative differences across the life span. This matrix of crises and stages also provides a useful tool for approaching psychotherapy and counseling.

The concept of normative psychosocial crises is a creative contribution that identifies predictable tensions between socialization and maturation throughout life. Societies, with their structures, laws, roles, rituals, and sanctions, are organized to guide individual growth toward a particular ideal of mature adulthood. However, every society faces problems when it attempts to balance the needs of the individual with the needs of the group. All individuals face some strains as they attempt to experience their individuality while maintaining the support of their groups and attempting to fit into their society. Psychosocial theory gives us concepts for exploring these natural tensions.

Longitudinal research using psychosocial theory as a framework for studying patterns of personality change and ego development has found support for many of its basic concepts. Changes in psychological outlook that reflect the major themes of the theory—such as industry, identity, intimacy, and generativity—appear to emerge and become consolidated over time (Whitbourne et al., 2009). There is also evidence of a preview of themes prior to their period of maximum ascendancy (Peterson & Stewart, 1993) and evidence for the notion of revisitation through which adults are stimulated to rework and reorganize the resolutions of earlier issues (Shibley, 2000).

Weaknesses

One weakness of psychosocial theory is that the explanations about the mechanisms for resolving crises and moving from one stage to the next are not well developed (Miller, 2011). The theory does not offer a universal mechanism for crisis resolution, nor a detailed picture of the kinds of experiences that are necessary at each stage if one is to cope successfully with the crisis of that stage.

The specific number of stages and their link to a biologically based plan for development have been criticized. The nature and number of stages of life is arguably highly culturally specific. For example, in some societies, the transition from childhood to adulthood is swift, leaving little time or expectation for identity exploration. In many traditional societies, parents choose one's marital partner, there are few occupational choices, and one is guided toward one's vocation from an early age. Thus, although there is always a biological period of pubescence, there may be little experience of the psychosocial processes of adolescence (Thomas & Schwarzbaum, 2006). In contrast, in our highly technological society, adolescence appears to be extended for some, especially as the age at first marriage is delayed and the complexity of preparing for and entering the labor market increases.

Along this same line of criticism, other human development scholars have taken a more differentiated view of the stages of adulthood and later life. In later life, health status, life circumstances, and culture interact to produce increasing variation in life stories. In a growing line of research, distinctions are being made between the "young-old" and the "old-old." These distinctions are sometimes based on health status and the person's capacity to manage tasks of daily life (Aldwin, Spiro, & Park, 2006; Poon & Harrington, 2006).

In other research, distinctions are made on the basis of chronological age. For example, Leonard Poon has written extensively about the differences between centenarians (people who are 100 or more), octogenarians (people in their eighties), and sexagenarians (people in their sixties). Each cohort of older adults has been exposed to different historical crises, educational, health and occupational opportunities, and shifting societal values. Therefore, it is likely that the normative patterns used to describe development in adulthood and later life will become dated and need reexamination (Randall, Martin, Bishop, Johnson, & Poon, 2012; Siegler, Poon, Madden, & Welsh, 1996). The increasing life expectancy, accompanied by a longer period of healthy later life and the elaboration of lifestyles, makes it difficult to chart a normative life course from early adulthood into very old age.

Finally, the psychosocial theory and related research have been criticized as being dominated by a male, Eurocentric, individualistic perspective that emphasizes **agency**—the ability to originate plans and take action—over connection and **communion**—the commitment to and consideration for the well-being of others (Abele & Wojciszke, 2007). The themes of autonomy, initiative, industry, and personal identity all emphasize the process of individuation. Critics have argued that ego development, separateness from family, autonomy, and self-directed goal attainment have been equated with psychological maturity, and that relatively little attention has been given to the development of interpersonal connection and social relatedness. These latter themes have been identified as central for an understanding of the psychosocial maturity of girls and young women. They also emerge in the study of collectively oriented ethnic groups— cultures in which maturity is equated with one's ability to support and sustain the success of the family or the extended family group rather than with one's own achievement of status, wealth, or recognition (Boykin, 1994; Josselson, Lieblich, & McAdams, 2007).

In our view, this last criticism is possibly overstated given the orientation of psychosocial theory toward the ongoing dynamic interaction of the individual and society. Within the framework of psychosocial theory, the theme of connection is addressed directly through the first psychosocial crisis of trust versus mistrust in infancy, and in subsequent psychosocial stages of early adolescence, early and middle adulthood, when group identity, intimacy, and generativity highlight the critical links that individuals build with others. The concept of the radius of significant relationships helps to maintain the perspective of the person interwoven in a tapestry of relationships, focusing especially on family and friends in childhood; the family, peer group, love relationships, and close friends in early and later adolescence; and intimate partners, family, friends, and co-workers in adult life. A basic premise of psychosocial theory is that the ego is taking shape in constant interaction with the community (Schlein, 1987, 2007). The strengths and weaknesses of psychosocial theory are summarized in Table 8.2.

Table 8.2 Strengths and weaknesses of psychosocial theory

Strengths	Weaknesses
Provides a broad, integrative framework within which to study the life span.	Explanations for the mechanisms of crisis resolution and process of moving from one stage to the next need to be developed more fully.
Provides insight into the directions of healthy development across the life span.	The idea of a specific number of stages of life and their link to a genetic plan for development is disputed.
Many of the basic ideas of the theory have been operationalized using traditional and novel approaches to assessment.	
The concept of psychosocial crises, including the positive and negative poles of the crisis, offers a model for considering individual differences within a framework of normal development.	The theory and much of its supporting research have been dominated by a male, Eurocentric perspective that gives too much emphasis to individuality and not enough attention to connection and social relatedness.
The concept of the psychosocial crisis identifies predictable tensions between socialization and maturation.	The specific ways that culture encourages or inhibits development at each stage of life are not clearly elaborated.
Longitudinal studies support the general direction of development hypothesized by the theory.	

CRITICAL THINKING QUESTIONS AND EXERCISES

1. How does psychosocial theory explain the interaction of societal forces and individual development?

2. Imagine that you are a school guidance counselor, a social worker, or a human relations specialist in an organization. You will be dealing with different age groups and populations. What are the implications of viewing development as a product of a tension between positive and negative poles at each stage of life for supporting optimal development in your work setting?

3. How do the negative poles of each crisis contribute to adaptive functioning? Give one or two examples for each psychosocial stage.

4. Consider the idea of a radius of significant relationships. Draw a map of your significant relationships; how do they influence the resolution of the psychosocial crisis of your current life stage?

5. The concept of personal identity is central to psychosocial theory. How might wider societal factors including social media, sports figures, celebrities, and political or religious leaders contribute to the process of identity formation?

6. Reflect on the case of Lillian and Michael. What life stages are they in? How does psychosocial theory help account for the change in Lillian's outlook from her twenties to her forties?

7. How would you assess the resolution of the crisis of intimacy versus isolation for Lillian and Michael? How would that resolution impact the way Lillian and Michael resolve their current psychosocial crisis?

8. In comparison to Lillian, who is looking for new meaning in her life, Michael appears to be in a state of complacency and stagnation. How does the theory help explain how two adults might approach a similar life stage with very different outlooks and worldviews?

9. Think about social change from the 1960s to the 1980s in the U.S. How might societal factors contribute to the resolution of the psychosocial crisis of generativity versus stagnation for people of that historical period? What about today? How might current social and economic trends influence the resolution of the crisis of generativity versus stagnation?

KEY TERMS

agency	identity
biological system	identity achieved
central process	identity diffused
communion	prime adaptive ego qualities
core pathologies	psychological system
developmental stage	psychosocial crisis
developmental tasks	psychosocial evolution
ego development	psychosocial moratorium
epigenetic principle	radius of significant relationships
foreclosed	societal system
hope	

RECOMMENDED RESOURCES

**Egan, G. (2013). *The skilled helper: A problem-management and opportunity-development approach to helping.* 10th ed. Stamford, CT: Cengage Learning.
An introduction to a person-centered approach to counseling with many illustrative examples and exercises.

**Erikson, E.H. (1963). *Childhood and society.* 2nd ed. New York: Norton. (Original work published 1950)
The classic book in which Erikson develops psychosocial theory including the eight stages of life as well as essays that illustrate the way he thinks about the role of culture in shaping ego development.

**Erik H. Erikson. YouTube video. www.youtube.com/watch?v=b1Nfhyqt2L0
A brief presentation of Erikson's early experiences in Vienna, his work with the Freuds, his marriage to Joan, and his initial experience studying the Sioux Indians.

**Goleman, D. (1988). Erikson in his own old age, expands his view of life. *New York Times Books.*
www.nytimes.com/books/99/08/22/specials/erikson-old.html
An interview with Erik and Joan Erikson in which they talk about their books, *Vital Involvements in Old Age* and *Wisdom and the Senses.*

**Kolar, R. How to apply Erikson's theory in instruction. www.ehow.com/how_8400675_apply-eriksons-theory-instruction.html
A guide for teachers to think about the way they approach the teaching and learning process in the three developmental stages: early childhood (initiative vs. guilt); middle childhood (industry vs. inferiority); and adolescence (identity vs. role confusion).

REFERENCES

Abele, A.E. & Wojciszke, B. (2007). Agency and communion from the perspective of self and others. *Journal of Personality and Social Psychology, 93,* 751–763.

Aldwin, C.M., Spiro, III, A., & Park, C.L. (2006). Health behavior and optimal aging: A lifespan developmental perspective. In J.E. Birren & K.W. Schaie (Eds.), *Handbook of the psychology of aging.* 6th ed. (pp. 77–104). San Diego, CA: Elsevier.

Arnett, J.J. (1998). Learning to stand alone: The contemporary American transition to adulthood in cultural and historical context. *Human Development, 41,* 295–315.

Arnett, J.J. (2000). Emerging adulthood: A theory of development from the late teens through the twenties. *American Psychologist, 55,* 469–480.

Arnett, J.J. (2004). *Adolescence and emerging adulthood: A cultural approach.* 2nd ed. Upper Saddle River, NJ: Prentice Hall.

Berzonsky, M.D. (2003). The structure of identity: Commentary on Jane Kroger's view of identity status transition. *Identity, 3,* 231–245.

Berzonsky, M. & Adams, G. (1999). Commentary: Reevaluating the identity status paradigm: Still useful after 35 years. *Developmental Review, 19,* 557–590.

Berzonsky, M.D. & Kuk, L.S. (2000). Identity status, identity processing style, and the transition to university. *Journal of Adolescent Research, 15,* 81–98.

Bohlin, G., Bengtsgard, K., & Andersson, K. (2000). Social inhibition and overfriendliness as related to socioemotional functioning in 7- and 8-year-old children. *Journal of Clinical Child Psychology, 29,* 414–423.

Boykin, A.W. (1994). Harvesting talent and culture. In R.J. Rossi (Ed.), *Schools and students at risk: Context and framework for positive change* (pp. 116–138). New York: Teachers College Press.

Christiansen, S.L. & Palkovitz, R. (1998). Exploring Erikson's psychosocial theory of development: Generativity and its relationship to paternal identity, intimacy, and involvement in childcare. *Journal of Men's Studies, 7*, 133–156.

Clancy, S.M. & Dollinger, S.J. (1993). Identity, self, and personality: 1. Identity status and the five-factor model of personality. *Journal of Research on Adolescence, 3*, 227–246.

Coles, R. (1970). *Erik H. Erikson: The growth of his work*. Boston: Atlantic–Little, Brown.

Constantinople, A. (1969). An Eriksonian measure of personality development in college students. *Developmental Psychology, 1*, 357–372.

Crain, W.C. (2011). *Theories of development: Concepts and applications*. 6th ed. Upper Saddle River, NJ: Prentice Hall.

Darling-Fisher, C.S. & Leidy, N.K. (1988). Measuring Eriksonian development in the adult: The Modified Erikson Psychosocial Stage Inventory. *Psychological Reports, 62*, 747–754.

Davison, M.L., King, P.M., Kitchener, K.S., & Parker, C.A. (1980). The stage sequence concept in cognitive and social development. *Developmental Psychology, 16*, 121–131.

de St. Aubin, E., McAdams, D.P., & Kim, T. (2003). *The generative society: Caring for future generations*. Washington, DC: American Psychological Association.

Domino, G. & Affonso, D.D. (1990). Erikson's life stages: The Inventory of Psychosocial Balance. *Journal of Personality Assessment, 54*, 576–588.

Dweck, C.S. (1992). The study of goals in psychology. *Psychological Science, 3*, 165–167.

Egan, G. (2013). *The skilled helper: A problem-management and opportunity-development approach to helping*. 10th ed. Stamford, CT: Cengage Learning.

Erikson, E.H. (1959). The problem of ego identity. *Psychological Issues, 1*, 101–164.

Erikson, E.H. (1963). *Childhood and society*. 2nd ed. New York: Norton. (Original work published 1950)

Erikson, E.H. (1968). *Identity: Youth and crisis*. New York: Norton.

Erikson, E.H. (1978). Reflections on Dr. Borg's life cycle. In E.H. Erikson (Ed.), *Adulthood* (pp. 1–31). New York: Norton.

Erikson, E.H. (1982). *The life cycle completed: A review*. New York: Norton.

Erikson, E.H. & Erikson, J. (1997). *The life cycle completed. An expanded version*. New York: Norton.

Erikson, E.H., Erikson, J.M., & Kivnick, H.Q. (1986). *Vital involvement in old age*. New York: Norton.

Erikson, J.M. (1988). *Wisdom and the senses: The way of creativity*. New York: Norton.

Flavell, J.H. (1982). Structures, stages, and sequences in cognitive development. In W.A. Collins (Ed.), *The concept of development* (pp. 1–28). Hillsdale, NJ: Lawrence Erlbaum Associates.

Friedman, L.J. (1999). *Identity's architect: A biography of Erik H. Erikson*. New York: Scribner.

Gould, R.L. (1972). The phases of adult life: A study in developmental psychology. *American Journal of Psychiatry, 129*, 521–531.

Hagen, K.A., Myers, B.J., & Macintosh, V.H. (2005). Hope, social support, and behavioral problems in at-risk children. *American Journal of Orthopsychiatry, 75*, 211–219.

Hamachek, D. (1985). The self's development and ego growth: Conceptual analysis and implications for counselors. *Journal of Counseling and Development, 64*, 136–142.

Hamachek, D. (1994). Changes in the self from a developmental/psychosocial perspective. In T.M. Brinthaupt & R.P. Lipka (Eds.), *Changing the self: Philosophies, techniques, and experiences* (pp. 21–68). Albany: State University of New York Press.

Havighurst, R.J. (1953). *Human development and education*. New York: Longmans.

Havighurst, R.J. (1972). *Developmental tasks and education*. 3rd ed. New York: David McKay. (Original work published 1948)

Hawley, G.A. (1988). *Measures of psychosocial development*. Odessa, FL: Psychological Assessment Resources.

Hopkins, J.R. (1995). Erik Homburger Erikson (1902–1994). *American Psychologist, 50*, 796–797.

Huxley, J. (1941). *The uniqueness of man*. London: Chatto & Windus.

Huxley, J. (1942/1974) *Evolution: The modern synthesis*. New York: Harper. Reissued New South Wales, Australia: Allen & Unwin.

Jones, R.M. (1992). Ego identity and adolescent problem behavior. In G.R. Adams, T.P. Gullota, & R. Montemayor (Eds.), *Adolescent identity formation* (pp. 216–233). Newbury Park, CA: Sage.

Josselson, R., Lieblich, A., & McAdams, D.P. (Eds.) (2007). *The meaning of others: Narrative studies of relationships.* Washington, DC: American Psychological Association.

Kiston, J.M. (1994). Contemporary Eriksonian theory: A psychobiographical illustration. *Gerontology and Geriatrics Education, 14,* 81–91.

Kroger, J. (2003). Identity development during adolescence. In G.R. Adams & M.D. Berzonsky (Eds.), *Blackwell handbook of adolescence* (pp. 205–226). Malden, MA: Blackwell.

Kroger, J. (2007). *Identity development: Adolescence through adulthood.* 2nd ed. Thousand Oaks, CA: Sage.

Kroger, J., Martinussen, M., & Marcia, J.E. (2010). Identity status change during adolescence and young adulthood: A meta-analysis. *Journal of Adolescence, 33,* 683–698.

Levin, I. (1986). *Stage and structure: Reopening the debate.* Norwood, NJ: Ablex.

Levinson, D.J. (1977). The midlife transition: A period in adult psychosocial development. *Psychiatry, 40,* 99–112.

Levinson, D.J., Darrow, C.M., Klein, A.B., Levinson, M.H., & McKee, B. (1978). *The seasons of a man's life.* New York: Knopf.

Lopez, S.J. & Snyder, C.R. (2003). *Positive psychological assessment: A handbook of models and measures.* Washington, DC: American Psychological Association.

Marcia, J.E. (1980). Identity in adolescence. In J. Adelson (Ed.), *Handbook of adolescent psychology* (pp. 159–187). New York: Wiley.

Marcia, J.E. (1993). The relational roots of identity. In J. Kroger (Ed.), *Discussions on ego identity* (pp. 101–120). Hillsdale, NJ: Erlbaum.

Marcia, J.E. (2002). Identity and psychosocial development in adulthood. *Identity, 2,* 7–28.

Marcia, J.E. (2006). Ego identity and personality disorders. *Journal of Personality Disorders, 20,* 577–596.

Marcia, J.E. (2007). Theory and measure: The identity status interview. In M. Watzlawik & A. Born (Eds.), *Capturing identity: Quantitative and qualitative methods* (pp. 186–214). Lanham, MD: University Press of America.

Marcia, J.E. (2010). Life transitions and stress in the context of psychosocial development. In T.W. Miller (Ed.), *Handbook of stressful transitions across the lifespan* (pp. 19–34). New York: Springer.

Marcia, J.E. & Simon, F.U. (2003). Treading fearlessly: A commentary on personal persistence, identity development, and suicide. *Monographs of the Society for Research in Child Development, 68,* 131–138.

McAdams, D.P. & de St. Aubin, E. (Eds.) (1998). *Generativity and adult development: Psychosocial perspectives on caring for and contributing to the next generation* (pp. 367–389). Washington, DC: American Psychological Association.

Meeus, W. (1996). Studies on identity development in adolescence: An overview of research and some new data. *Journal of Youth and Adolescence, 25,* 569–598.

Meeus, W. (2011). The study of adolescent identity formation 2000–2010: A review of longitudinal research. *Journal of Research on Adolescence, 21,* 75–94.

Miller, P.H. (2011). *Theories of developmental psychology.* 5th ed. New York: Worth.

Neugarten, B.L. (1968). Adult personality: Toward a psychology of the life cycle. In B. Neugarten (Ed.), *Middle age and aging* (pp. 137–147). Chicago: University of Chicago Press.

Newman, B.M. & Newman, P.R. (1975). *Development through life: A psychosocial approach.* 1st ed. Homewood, IL: Dorsey Press.

Newman, P.R. & Newman, B.M. (1976). Early adolescence and its conflict: Group identity versus alienation. *Adolescence, 11,* 261–274.

Newman, B.M. & Newman, P.R. (2015). *Development through life: A psychosocial approach.* 12th ed. Stamford, CT: Cengage Learning.

Nurmi, J.E. (2004). Socialization and self-development: Channeling, selection, adjustment, and reflection. In R.M. Lerner & L. Steinberg (Eds.), *Handbook of adolescent psychology.* 2nd ed. (pp. 85–124). New York: Wiley.

Peterson, C. & Seligman, M.E.P. (2003). Character strengths before and after September 11. *Psychological Science, 14,* 381–384.

Peterson, B.E. & Stewart, A.J. (1993). Generativity and social motives in young adults. *Journal of Personality and Social Psychology, 65,* 186–198.

Poon, L.W. & Harrington, C.A. (2006). Communalities in aging- and fitness-related impact on cognition. In L.W. Poon, W. Chodzko-Zajko, & P.D. Thomporowski (Eds.), *Activity, cognitive functioning and aging: Vol. 1* (pp. 33–50). Champaign, IL: Human Kinetics.

Randall, G.K., Martin, P., Bishop, A.J., Johnson, M.A., & Poon, L.W. (2012). Social resources and change in functional health: Comparing three age groups. *The International Journal of Aging and Development, 75,* 1–29.

Schlein, S. (1987). *A way of looking at things: Selected papers from 1930 to 1980. Erik H. Erikson.* New York: Norton.

Schlein, S. (2007, Summer). Dimensions of relatedness, activation and engagement: Erikson's interpersonal-relational method of psychoanalysis. *Psychologist-Psychoanalyst Newsletter, 59.*

Seligman, M.E.P. (2011). *Flourish: A visionary new understanding of happiness and well-being.* New York: Atria Books.

Shibley, P.K. (2000). The concept of revisitation and the transition to parenthood. Unpublished doctoral dissertation, Ohio State University.

Siegler, I.C., Poon, L.W., Madden, D.J., & Welsh, K.A. (1996). Psychological aspects of normal aging. In E.W. Busse & D.G. Blazer (Eds.), *The American Psychiatric Press textbook of geriatric psychiatry* (pp. 105–127). Washington, DC: American Psychiatric Press.

Snyder, C.R. (1994). *The psychology of hope: You can get there from here.* New York: Free Press.

Snyder, C.R. (2002). Hope theory: Rainbows in the mind. *Psychological Inquiry, 13,* 249–275.

Snyder, C.R., Cheavens, J., & Sympson, S.C. (1997). Hope: An individual motive for social commerce. *Group Dynamics: Theory, Research, and Practice, 1,* 107–118.

Snyder, C.R. & McDermott, D. (1999). *Making hope happen.* Oakland/San Francisco: New Harbinger Press.

Snyder, C.R., Shorey, H.S., Cheavens, J., Pulvers, K.M., Adams, V.H., III, & Wiklund, C. (2002). Hope and academic success in college. *Journal of Educational Psychology, 94,* 820–826.

Snyder, C.R. & Taylor, J.D. (2000). Hope as a common factor across psychotherapy approaches: A lesson from the dodo's verdict. In C.R. Snyder (Ed.), *The handbook of hope: Theory, measures, and applications* (pp. 89–108). San Diego, CA: Academic Press.

Steinberg, L. (2005). Cognitive and affective development in adolescence. *Trends in Cognitive Sciences, 9,* 69–74.

Sullivan, M.D. (2003). Hope and hopelessness at the end of life. *American Journal of Geriatric Psychiatry, 11,* 393–405.

Thomas, A.J. & Schwarzbaum, S. (2006). *Culture and identity: Life stories for counselors and therapists.* Thousand Oaks, CA: Sage.

Vaillant, G. (1977). *Adaptation to life.* Boston: Little, Brown.

Vanzetti, N. & Duck, S. (1996). *A lifetime of relationships.* Pacific Grove, CA: Brooks/Cole.

Waterman, A.S. (1982). Identity development from adolescence to adulthood: An extension of theory and a review of research. *Developmental Psychology, 18,* 341–358.

Waterman, A.S. (1999a). Commentary: Identity, the identity statuses, and identity status development: A contemporary statement. *Developmental Review, 19,* 591–621.

Waterman, A.S. (1999b). Issues of identity formation revisited: United States and the Netherlands. *Developmental Review, 19,* 462–479.

Waterman, A.S. & Whitbourne, S.K. (1981). The inventory of psychosocial development. *Journal Supplement Abstract Service: Catalog of Selected Documents in Psychology, 11* (Ms. No. 2179).

Whitbourne, S.K., Sneed, J.R., & Sayer, A. (2009). Psychosocial development from college to midlife: A 34-year sequential study. *Developmental Psychology, 45,* 1328–1340.

White, R.W. (1960). Competence and the psychosexual stages of development. In M.R. Jones (Ed.), *Nebraska Symposium on Motivation* (pp. 97–141). Lincoln, NE: University of Nebraska Press.

Zimmermann, P. & Becker-Stoll, F. (2002). Stability of attachment representations during adolescence: The influence of ego-identity status. *Journal of Adolescence, 25,* 107–124.

Cognitive Social-Historical Theory

GUIDING QUESTIONS

- What are some similarities and differences between cognitive social-historical theory and the theories introduced in Chapter 4, including: cognitive developmental theory, information processing, and the theory of central conceptual structures?
- How is cognitive social-historical theory similar to life course theory? What might be some valuable insights achieved by linking these two theories?
- What leads to the transformation from the intermental to the intramental?
- Why does Vygotsky place so much emphasis on language as a key tool for shaping higher order mental processes?
- What are some distinctions between the natural or lower mental processes, especially those discussed in Chapter 5 on learning theories, and the higher mental processes?
- What are some practical implications of cognitive social-historical theory for education, human services, and mental health?

CASE VIGNETTE

It's 7:30 at night. Jasmine, who is 3½, is playing with her Lego, building a big birthday cake. Her daddy says, "Jasmine, it's a 5-minute warning for bedtime."

"I'm busy," says Jasmine.
"Yes, but it's getting time for bed," says Daddy.
"Why?" says Jasmine.
"Because you need your rest," says Daddy.
"Why?" says Jasmine.
"Because you have had a busy day and now you need to rest," says Daddy.
"Why?" says Jasmine.
"Because your body needs to rest so you can have a great time tomorrow," says Daddy.
"What are we doing tomorrow?" asks Jasmine.
"We are going to take a trip to see your grandma and grandpa," says Daddy.
"Why?" says Jasmine.

According to cognitive social-historical theory, higher order mental processes emerge in an interpersonal context as children interact with others. The child is born into an existing cultural context replete with tools, customs, language, and other symbolic systems. In the early years, advances in the child's thinking depend on conversations and encouragement from and modeling of these more knowledgeable others.

The case vignette illustrates several features of the cognitive social-historical view about how higher order mental processes emerge in a cultural context. Jasmine uses the word "why" to achieve several goals. First, it stimulates social conversation with her dad. Second, it allows her to delay bedtime. Third, it provides a verbal tool for gaining more information. Often, that tool leads to uncovering new questions. Sometimes the answers are not fully understood. This depends on the skill and knowledge of the other. However, the pattern of interaction creates a model for the child about how to pursue information. The use of "why" in modern society is an accepted approach for problem solving. It leads one to examine possible explanations and seek new sources of information. You can imagine a society in which a child is not expected or encouraged to ask "why." Children in that social-historical context would have a different experience with their parents, possibly learning a different approach to information gathering that relies more on observation and imitation, and less on conversation and inquiry.

Piaget's focus on cognitive development emphasized a process in which children investigate, explore, discover, and rediscover meaning in their world. Although Piaget acknowledged the significance of social factors, especially parents and peers, in the cognitive process, his theory focused on what he believed to be universal processes and stages in the maturation of cognition from infancy through adolescence. In contrast, Vygotsky, often referred to as an interactionist, argued that development can only be understood within a social-cultural-historical framework. At the heart of his work is a focus on thinking, especially in childhood, which he links to the development of language and speech.

> The development of the child's thinking depends on his mastery of the social means of thinking, that is, on mastery of speech ... This thesis stems from our *comparison* of the development of inner speech and verbal thinking in man with the development of speech and intellect as it occurs in the animal world and the earliest stages of childhood. This comparison demonstrates that the former does not represent a simple continuation of the latter. The very type of development changes. It changes from a biological form of development to a socio-historical form of development. (Vygotsky, 1987a, p. 120)

Vygotsky, like many other theorists and philosophers of his time, was trying to account for the development of higher mental processes from their simpler forms. He saw development as following a continuous path from other animals to humans, and also a discontinuous path. This was captured in his view of *natural* or *lower mental processes*, and *higher mental processes*. **Lower mental processes**, which could be observed in animal behavior and the problem-solving behaviors of infants and very young children, are reflected in the types of learning described in Chapter 4 as classical conditioning, trial and error learning, and operant conditioning. **Higher mental processes** arise as children encounter and master the cultural tools of their society. Vygotsky viewed human beings across cultures as both similar to the extent that they shared basic physical characteristics and natural psychological processes, and substantially different depending upon the cultural **symbol systems** to which they are exposed, and how those systems shape thinking and behavior.

Higher mental processes, particularly language and meaning, emerge from the child's ongoing interactions within social, historical, and cultural contexts, as well as from the child's biological maturation. The child and the culture are intricately interwoven through the process of social interaction. New levels of understanding begin at an interpersonal level as two individuals, initially an infant and an adult, coordinate their interactions. Eventually interpersonal collaboration becomes internalized to make up the child's internal mental framework. Through continuous interaction with others, especially adults and older children, a child revises and advances his or her levels of understanding. Over time, it is the mastery of these cultural tools or symbol systems that permit individuals to alter their environments and guide, regulate, and redefine themselves.

HISTORICAL CONTEXT

Lev Semyonovich Vygotsky lived a brief but extremely productive life. Born in 1896 (the same year as Jean Piaget) to a professional family, his father was a banking executive and his mother was a teacher. In a family of eight children, family life was interesting with many evenings spent in lively conversation and debate. As a teenager, Vygotsky became known as the "little professor" because he liked to organize debates and mock trials where friends took the roles of historical figures such as Aristotle and Napoleon (Wertsch, 1985). He loved to read history, literature, and poetry. In 1917 he graduated from Moscow University with a specialization in literature. Later, he wrote a dissertation on Shakespeare's *Hamlet*. From 1917 to 1923, he taught literature and psychology at a teachers' college in Gomel, where he had attended school as an adolescent.

In 1924 Vygotsky gave an inspiring talk on the link between conditioned reflexes and conscious behavior. He deeply impressed Alexander Luria, a researcher at the Moscow Institute of Psychology, who later became a founder of the field of neuropsychology. Luria recommended Vygotsky for a position at the Institute. This began Vygotsky's intensive career as a researcher, educator, and clinical practitioner. Along with Luria and Alexei Nikolaivitch Leontiev, he dedicated his efforts to the formulation of an integrated theory of psychology that would be compatible with the broad principles of Marx's and Engels's political philosophy.

Vygotsky contracted tuberculosis sometime during his return to Gomel, and died in 1934. Some of his works were published shortly after his death, but from 1936 to 1956 his works were banned by the Communist Party. As a result, many of his theoretical ideas were slow in reaching a broader Western audience. His first book, *Thought and language*, was published in Russia in 1934, but was not translated into English until 1962.

Vygotsky entered the field of psychology at a time when there was a divide between those who were studying the physiology of the brain, reflexes, and sensory systems (psychology as a "natural science") and those in the Gestalt school who were studying higher order mental processes, especially the integrative capacities of meaning making and interpretation (psychology as a "mental science") (Cole & Scribner, 1978). He was an avid reader, and actively formed international connections with scholars whose work informed his own thinking. He knew of the works of Darwin, Piaget, and Freud and often compared his own concepts to theirs. In the formulation of his work, he built on the research of: zoologists, who studied the relationship of instincts and intellect; ethnographers, who studied the thoughts and practices of people in traditional societies; and comparative psychologists, who created experimental demonstrations of animal problem-solving behaviors (van der Veer & Valsiner, 1991).

Vygotsky was also deeply influenced by the writings of Marx and Engels. Marx's theory of historical materialism argued that changes in human consciousness and behavior are a result of changes in society and material life (Marx, 1844/1988). He was especially interested in the human capacity for tool use and production. He claimed that production was an inherently social process wherein people collaborate in order to grow things, build things, or sustain and protect their territory. He thought that people's values and ideas, their higher order cognitive processes, were a product of their material life, that is the way they live, work, produce, and exchange goods. Marx's theory suggested that history reflects a dialectical process—the conditions of production change over time. New tools and technologies come into conflict with existing patterns of production. As a result, new social and economic systems emerge that lead to new beliefs and values. He maintained that all phenomena should be considered as being in a process of change, influenced by historical changes in society and material or technological life. In order to understand contemporary behavior, one must reconstruct the origins of that behavior and the course of development from its simplest to its more complex expressions. Thus, Marx's contributions to Vygotsky's thinking included a commitment to a developmental analysis embedded in social and historical contexts.

Extending Marx's focus on the importance of tools as a means of production, Engels (1925/1940) wrote about the relationship of tools and evolution. He suggested that tool use led to the expansion of human consciousness. With the earliest invention of tools, human beings were prompted to new ways of examining the objects in their environment in order to assess their compatibility with existing tools or the ways that their tools could alter these objects. Tools led to new needs for communication and social interaction. And, tools brought about a new view of the environment as something that could be altered to meet human needs. The capacity to clear land, plant crops, and harvest them brought new cognitive capacities for planning and anticipating future needs. According to Engels, new tools led to new cognitive capacities. "The tool specifically symbolizes human activity, man's transformation of nature: production" (Marx & Engels, 1953, p. 63). From this critical insight, Vygotsky pursued the idea of "cultural tools," such as language, writing, and number systems which, once acquired, also alter and advance complex cognitive capacities. Symbolic tools are initially external to the person and a product of human culture. However, these tools gradually become internalized, changing the person and his or her way of thinking. "But tools affect their users: language, used first as a communicative tool, finally shapes the minds of those who adapt to its use" (Bruner, 1987, p. 3).

Vygotsky worked to create an integrated psychology of cognitive behavior that recognized the interaction of neurological mechanisms, a developmental history of cognition from its simple to its more complex forms, and the role of the society in influencing the ways higher order cognitive capacities emerge (Vygotsky, 1978a). His work placed an especially strong emphasis on language as a cultural tool that allows the person to modify the stimulus situation as part of the process of responding to it. He devoted a substantial part of his professional life to the conceptualization of educational strategies to reduce illiteracy and to support language functioning among children and adults who suffered from mental and physical disabilities.

Much like the works of Sigmund Freud, Vygotsky's writings continue to be embedded in controversy. Critics have argued that many of his writings have been edited, censored, misinterpreted, or mistranslated so that Western interpretations are inaccurate. What is more, Vygotsky continued to modify and revise his thinking, but due to his illness and early death, many papers were unfinished. Some were completed by colleagues and editors without clear acknowledgement of their incomplete state. As you read about the basic concepts of the theory, you need to consider the social-cultural-historical contexts of the scientific communities in which Vygotsky's work originated in the 1920s and 1930s, emerged through translation into U.S. scholarship and pedagogy in the 1970s and 1980s, and is now being revised and critiqued in Russia, Europe, and the U.S. (Daniels, 2005; van der Veer & Yasnitsky, 2011).

KEY CONCEPTS

Four concepts in Vygotsky's theory are introduced here: culture as a mediator of cognitive structuring, movement from the intermental to the intramental, inner speech, and the zone of proximal development.

Culture as a Mediator of Cognitive Structuring

Culture consists of physical settings; tools and technologies; and a patterned system of customs, beliefs, information, and social relationships. Within broad cultural groups, subcultures also exist with unique but shared patterns of behavior, values, and goals. When Vygotsky argues that cognitive development can only be understood in the context of culture, he is bringing our attention to this pervasive sense of culture. Think for a moment about the many ways that culture shapes the content of thought and the processes through which ideas are developed. A simple conversation between a mother and a child or a situation in which an older sibling is trying to instruct a younger sibling include layers of cultural beliefs and strategies—beliefs about what children think about; the skills they are encouraged to attain; the sources of information that are available to them; the ways that information is shared; the kinds of activities that children, adolescents, and adults are permitted to engage in; and the limits that are placed on participation in certain settings or certain forms of interaction. Bakhurst (1996) provides a helpful summary of Vygotsky's model:

> The human child enters the world endowed by nature with only elementary mental capacities. The higher mental functions constitutive of human consciousness are, however, embodied in the social practices of the child's community. Just as the child's physical functions are at first maintained only through connection with an autonomous system beyond the child, so his or her psychological life is created only through inauguration into a set of external practices. Only as the child internalizes or masters those practices is he or she transformed into a conscious subject of thought and experience. (p. 202)

Of the many elements of culture that shape cognition, one that was of special interest to Vygotsky was the idea of **tools** and signs as human inventions that shape thought. **Technical tools**, such as plows, cars, and weapons, and **signs**, sometimes referred to as **psychological tools**, such as symbolic systems, counting systems, and strategies for remembering, modify the child's relationship to the environment. Through the use of tools, humans change the way they organize and think about the world. Vygotsky viewed tools as a means through which the human mind is shaped and modified over the course of history.

Based on a variety of experimental demonstrations in the areas of memory, categorization, and attention, Vygotsky was able to show that children follow a common path in the development of higher order thinking.

- First, in the early years, they do not make any systematic use of **cultural tools** such as words, pictures, or other symbols to help in their problem solving.
- In the second phase, they are able to make use of cultural tools—for example, the use of a picture that has been given to them to recall a word—but they are not able to impose or actively create a symbolic aid if it has not already been provided.
- In the third phase, children can create their own links between pictures and words to be remembered, or find new strategies to help them remember words or categorize objects.
- In the final stage, the child internalizes these prompts or clues, no longer relying on the physical device to aid in their work. The cultural tools eventually mediate the task, supporting new levels of behavior that appear more integrated and automatic (Vygotsky, 1928, as referenced in van der Veer & Valsiner, 1991).

In particular, Vygotsky emphasized **language** as a sign system that dramatically alters human cognition. Language, which begins as a primarily social process linking individuals, becomes a tool that guides mental activity. Through language, children can recall the past, create problem-solving strategies, organize and categorize experiences, and talk and plan for the future. Vygostky argued: "The most significant moment in the course of intellectual development, which gives birth to the purely human forms of practical and abstract intelligence, occurs when speech and practical activity, two previously completely independent lines of development, converge" (Vygotsky, 1978a, p. 24).

Vygotsky eventually came to the conclusion that **word meaning** was the single unit of analysis that could link speech and thought. It is both speech and thinking. A word without meaning is not a word, just a sound. At the same time, any meaningful word is a concept. Thus, word meaning is both speech and cognition; it is an irreducible reflection of reality.

> The consciousness of sensation and thinking are characterized by different modes of reflecting reality. They are different types of consciousness. Therefore, *thinking and speech are the key to understanding the nature of human consciousness.* If language is as ancient as consciousness itself, if language is consciousness that exists in practice for other people and therefore for myself, then it is not only the development of thought but the development of consciousness as a whole that is connected with the development of the word ... The word is the most direct manifestation of the historical nature of human consciousness. (Vygotsky, 1987c, p. 285)

This idea of words as units that integrate speech and thought and that reflect human consciousness illustrates the interactionist perspective of Vygotsky's theory. The word unites the inner world and the interpersonal world; it unites the historical past and the present. The word has a developmental history as it emerges from actions that become socially meaningful and can be named.

From Intermental to Intramental

Perhaps contrary to common sense, Vygotsky argued that higher mental processes begin in external activity that is gradually reconstructed and internalized. He gave the example of pointing. Initially an infant will reach toward an object that is out of reach stretching the hand in the direction of the object and making grasping motions with the fingers. This is a movement directed to the object. But as soon as the mother recognizes that the child wants the object and is able to satisfy the child's request, the child begins to modify the reaching and grasping motion into a socially meaningful gesture—pointing. The mother's understanding of the gesture and **intermental** coordination between mother and infant result in an **intramental** process for the infant, an understanding of the special relationship in this case between the desired goal, the mother as mediator, and the pointing as a meaningful sign. According to Vygotsky:

> Every function in the child's cultural development appears twice: first on the social level, and later, on the individual level; first, between people (interpsychological), and then inside the child (intrapsychological). This applies equally to voluntary attention, to logical memory, and to the formation of concepts. All the higher functions originate as actual relations between human individuals. (Vygotsky, 1978b, p. 57)

Vygotsky's view is that society and its psychological tools precede individual development. Development begins at the intermental or interpersonal system level. Interpersonal interactions are the context within which subsequent higher mental processes emerge.

Infants and young children are part of a structured social unit in which individuals participate in coordinated interactions facilitated by a shared symbol system of language and other psychological tools. Once the infant's behavior is recognized and interpreted by others, the meaning of the behavior can gradually be internalized. The child's subsequent behavior is a product of the meaning that has been given in previous interactions. With the advantage of the tool of language, children can describe and analyze a given situation, draw upon their accumulation of past experiences, and decide how to act. All higher mental functioning, including planning, decision making, evaluation of information, and reflection or metacognition, begins in the intermental or interpersonal domain and is gradually integrated into the person's cognition.

Vygotsky emphasized the role of speech for influencing social interactions. As a first step, the adult uses speech to guide, inform, or redirect a child's behavior. Mother says, "No, don't touch that, it might break!" Subsequently, the child begins to use the word *no* to control the actions of his mother, a sibling, or a friend. "No, don't touch, Mine!" Eventually, the command "No, don't touch" becomes internalized and is used in the form of inner speech to guide the child's own behavior.

The more complicated the cognitive demands of a task, the more a child is likely to use spoken language to guide problem solving. The child uses the tool of language, which is normally thought of as functioning in the social system, to help focus and structure their intramental functioning. Thus, Vygotsky became especially interested in the mediating role of egocentric or **inner speech** as it contributed to the emergence of new concepts (cognition) and ideas about the self (metacognition).

> The specifically human capacity for language enables children to provide for auxiliary tools in the solution of difficult tasks, to overcome impulsive action, to plan a solution to a problem prior to its execution, and to master their own behavior. (Vygotsky, 1978a, p. 28)

Inner Speech

Vygotsky (1978a) argued that speech plays a central role in **self-regulation**, self-directed goal attainment, and practical problem solving. He described the problem-solving behaviors of toddlers as involving both speech and action. Toddlers use what was described by Piaget (1952) as egocentric speech to accompany their behavior. They talk out loud, but do not seem to be concerned about whether anyone can hear them or understand them. Piaget described the talk as egocentric because it did not seem to have any social intention. He suggested that the development of communication began with inner thinking of a very private, nonsocialized nature. He viewed egocentric speech in toddlerhood as evidence of the relative absence of social life and the great extent of nonsocialized thoughts that the child is unable to express.

Vygotsky (1987a) proposed a completely different developmental pathway to account for egocentric speech and its function. He represented the scheme as:

Social speech → egocentric speech → inner speech

As discussed above, Vygotsky viewed speech as beginning in the social interactions between children and adults or other children. The first and foremost function of speech is social. Egocentric speech is a transformation of this social speech inward. The child uses speech that was initially acquired through interactions with others to guide his or her own behaviors. It does not have a social intention; rather, it is a tool that helps to guide problem solving. Vygotsky

Table 9.1 Piaget's and Vygotsky's analysis of inner speech

Theoretical view	Piaget	Vygotsky
Origins of inner speech	Non-socialized private thought	Social communication with adults → egocentric speech → inner speech
Path of development	Declines as children form schemes and mental operations, and become more skilled at the use of language for communication	Use of inner speech increases as children confront more difficult and complex problems; eventually transforms into private thought
Function	No social intention; language of an egocentric nature	A tool that helps regulate, plan, and guide problem-solving and behavior

viewed egocentric speech and actions as part of the same problem-solving function. The more difficult the problem, the more speech is necessary for the child to find a solution. "Children solve practical tasks with the help of their speech, as well as their eyes and hands" (Vygotsky, 1978a, p. 26). Eventually, the egocentric speech of an audible nature dwindles (but does not disappear entirely) and becomes inner speech. Table 9.1 compares Piaget's and Vygotsky's concepts of the development and function of inner speech.

Inner speech gives children a new degree of freedom, flexibility, and control in approaching tasks and working toward a goal. They can use words to call to mind tools that are not visible. They can plan steps toward a goal and repeat them to guide their actions. They can use words such as *slowly*, *be careful*, or *hold tight* for self-regulation, to control their behavior as they work on a task. Language skills and self-control operate together to help children inhibit negative emotions and disruptive behavior during times of frustration (Lynam & Henry, 2001; Fernyhough & Fradley, 2005).

The private speech that guides problem solving emerges from the social speech that characterizes children's interactions with adults and eventually becomes inner speech. Often, when young children try to figure out how to work something or how to get something that is out of reach, they turn to adults for help. Vygotsky suggested that the kind of talk that adults use as they guide young children is then used by the children themselves to support and guide their own behavior. (That is the idea of movement from intermental to intramental.) He referred to this process as the "internalization of social speech." In a sense, a child's capacity for self-directed goal attainment depends on what he or she has taken in of the spoken, practical advice and guidance given by adults and older peers who have tried to help the child solve problems in the past. In adulthood, these speech-like cognitions are not typically audible; they are experienced as inner talk or self-talk, an inner voice that helps organize complex tasks (e.g. first make an outline), encourage persistence (e.g. concentrate, stay focused), or review and revise (e.g. doesn't fit, try the bigger one).

The Zone of Proximal Development

Taking the idea of **internalization** a step further, Vygotsky proposed the concept of the **zone of proximal development** to help explain the relationship of learning and development. Each child can be described as functioning at a certain mental age and as having the potential to function at a more advanced mental age. The zone of proximal development is "the distance between the actual developmental level as determined by independent problem solving and the level of potential development as determined through problem solving under adult guidance or in collaboration with more capable peers" (Vygotsky, 1978c, p. 86).

We have all experienced a situation in which we were unable to solve a task by ourselves, but with the assistance and advice of someone else we were able to be successful. The typical efforts of parents to help a child put together a jigsaw puzzle by suggesting strategies, such as selecting all the straight-edged pieces first to make the border, or sorting the many pieces into those with a similar color, is an example of how learning takes place within the zone. Children watch older children perform a task and they copy the strategy; children ask their parents or teachers for help when they get stuck in a task; teachers give children suggestions about how to organize a task or how to use resources that will help them complete an assignment. In these and many other instances, we recognize the variety of ways that children expand the level of their independent problem-solving capacities by drawing upon the expertise of others.

Vygotsky suggested that the level of functioning a child can reach when taking advantage of the guidance of others reflects the functions that are in the process of maturation, as compared to those that have already matured. What is more, recognizing and validating this social context in which learning takes place illustrates that cognitive development grows in the direction of the intellectual characteristics of those who populate the child's world. "Human learning presupposes a specific social nature and a process by which children grow into the intellectual life of those around them" (Vygotsky, 1978c, p. 88).

Contrary to the thinking of the time, Vygotsky argued that development lags behind learning. When children are exposed to new ideas beyond what they already know or understand, the child is stimulated to engage these new ideas and, as a result, development moves forward. In a very immediate and direct way, as children function in their zone, culture and the social context guide the direction in which learning promotes development. Learning within the zone of proximal development sets into motion the reorganization and internalization of existing developmental competences which then become synthesized at a new and higher intramental level.

Vygotsky used the term zone of proximal development to refer to a range of potential performance. When trying to assess a child's developmental level, it is important to understand not only what the child already knows and can already perform, but also the domains that are "in progress," so to speak, the areas that are emerging as new fields of mastery. Normally adults, especially parents and teachers, and more advanced peers promote development by engaging children in activities and problem-solving tasks that draw children into the new directions along which their capacities are maturing. This idea has been very influential in guiding educational instructional strategies. Effective instructional strategies not only move children from their current developmental level to their potential level, but, as the concepts are acquired, the zone itself expands upward (van Geert, 1998).

A unique contribution of Vygotsky's concept of the zone of proximal development is the notion of the interplay between two concurrent developmental levels, one that could be considered the child's actual or baseline level of cognitive functioning, and the other that is the child's potential level of functioning given appropriate instruction, support, and encouragement. According to Vygotsky, both of these levels exist within the zone for each domain of knowledge. If properly structured, educational settings create a zone of proximal development for specific school subjects.

A creative insight offered by Vygotsky is that movement within the zone can be prompted not only by instruction but in the child's own play. In play, Vygotsky saw a cognitive process that in and of itself captures a preshadowing of the child's next higher level of functioning. Vygotsky (1978d) captured a unique feature of fantasy play:

Play creates a zone of proximal development of the child. In play a child always behaves beyond his average age, above his daily behavior; in play it is as though he were a head taller than himself. As in the focus of a magnifying glass, play contains all developmental tendencies in a condensed form and is itself a major source of development. (p. 102)

In pretend play, children address areas where they do not yet feel competent in their lives and try to act as if they are competent. They set rules for their performance, and commit themselves to function according to them. So if a child is pretending to be a good mother, she brings forward all the ideas she has about how to be a good mother and applies them to the pretend situation. Similarly, if a child is pretending to be a superhero, she imposes all the rules of power, goodness, and helpfulness that she knows of and tries to limit her actions to those rules. Vygotsky regarded fantasy play as a window into the areas of competence that the child is striving to master but are still out of reach.

Although the zone of proximal development is usually thought to refer to children learning from older peers or adults, the concept need not be limited in this way. Anyone can learn from a more knowledgeable person. For example, parents may turn to their children to learn about new technologies, or new mathematical or scientific advances. Aging parents may learn from their adult children about new business, investment, or health care resources. The concept suggests that the capacity for development in any particular domain is advanced when a person has opportunities to learn from a more knowledgeable other.

NEW DIRECTIONS

Vygotsky's theory has had enormous influence on the cross-cultural study of development. Before Vygotsky's theory became well known, cross-cultural psychology of the 1960s and 1970s focused largely on exploring how children in different cultures would approach tasks and problems that had been developed in Europe or the United States. Many scholars were interested in determining, for example, whether the Piagetian stages of concrete operational and formal operational thought would be observed at about the same age, and in the same sequence, among children in traditional societies as they were in industrial societies (Rogoff & Chavajay, 1995). Tasks involving conservation, manipulation of multiple variables, logic, classification, and memory were modified for presentation to children in different cultures.

As the results of these studies were summarized and compared, several themes became clear. First, the tasks were not as readily generalizable across cultures as researchers had expected. Children who performed poorly in some of these tasks were observed to function in quite complex ways when engaging in activities natural to their everyday lives (Cole & Scribner, 1977). Second, the extent to which children were exposed to a Western type of schooling influenced their approach to these tasks. Variations in schooling across cultural groups substantially altered the ways that children approached specific tasks, including their understanding of the testing situation, as well as their ability and willingness to engage in the abstract tasks presented by the researchers (Cole, 1990).

Cultural Historical Activity Theory (CHAT)

Influenced by Vygotsky's theory, scholars began to move away from treating culture as a static variable within which individuals develop. In many of his writings, Vygotsky implied that cognition is culturally situated. However he did not have time to explore specific dimensions of cultural variation in detail. He pointed to language, instructional strategies, the nature of social interaction, and the social expectations adults had about children, as factors that might influence cognitive development. Contemporary extensions of Vygotsky's theory, sometimes called cultural historical activity theory (CHAT), are seeking new and varied ways of conceptualizing a process through which a child's cognitive development is intricately intertwined with the activities in which a child participates, the other people who engage in the activities with the child, and the cultural practices, artifacts, and institutional structures that provide the context for the activities. Rather than thinking of the individual and the society as distinct, the cultural historical approach attempts to contextualize development at every step (Cole, 2010).

One of the primary strategies for achieving this integration of person and society is to focus on activities or events as the unit of analysis. "The **activity** or event is a unit of analysis that focuses on people engaged in sociocultural endeavors with other people; working with and extending cultural tools and practices inherited from previous generations" (Rogoff & Chavajay, 1995, p. 871).

Doing Mathematics. As an example, one can think of "doing mathematics" as an activity. Studies have found that Japanese children perform better on mathematics problems than do children in the U.S. (Trends in International Mathematics and Science Study, 2004; Provasnik, Kastberg, Ferraro, Lemanski, Roey, & Jenkins, 2012). This is true even though there do not appear to be differences in intelligence between children in these cultures. A **sociocultural** approach to understanding learning and development helps to account for this difference in performance by highlighting the following features of Japanese culture.

First, Japanese parents believe that mathematics competence is a result of hard work and persistence whereas U.S. parents tend to view mathematics competence as largely a result of ability. When children have difficulties in math, a belief in trying harder is more likely to lead to improvement than a belief in ability.

Second, U.S. parents tend to overestimate their child's mathematical abilities, perhaps as part of their desire to see their child as unique or special. U.S. parents are basically satisfied with the level of mathematics ability their children have achieved. In contrast, Japanese mothers tend to keep encouraging their children to improve, focusing on wanting their children to fit in with their group. Children whose parents and teachers set high standards are more likely to continue to strive than children whose parents and teachers have lower expectations for their performance (Stevenson, Chen, & Lee, 1993).

Third, the Japanese language places special emphasis on the quantitative aspect of the environment with different words for counting different types of objects such as people, birds, broad thin objects such as paper, and long thin objects such as sticks. Japanese parents frequently play counting and number games with their children as a way of encouraging young children's attention to quantity (Hatano, as cited in Siegler, 1998).

Finally, mathematics instruction in Japanese classrooms is very different from instruction in U.S. classrooms. In Japan, teachers spend more time introducing new concepts and less time reviewing previous concepts. They focus more on complex problems that require four or more steps to reach a solution and spend more time on problems that are mathematically related but not simply a repetition of previous problems. There are usually two teachers in the classroom, one who can assist students who are having difficulty so that the class can move along together to the next level of work. Within this context, Japanese students also spend substantially more time on homework out of class than U.S. students. As a result, their mathematics understanding matures at a faster rate, they are able to become involved in more interesting problems, and they have greater confidence about their ability to master mathematics, a confidence that is supported by parental expectations, well-designed classroom experiences, and prior successes (National Center for Education Statistics, 2004).

Integration of the Individual, Interpersonal, and Cultural Levels of Analysis

In contrast to considering the impact of culture on individual development, researchers using the sociocultural approach view the individual, the interpersonal, and the cultural levels as operating together in an integrated fashion (Rogoff, 1995, 2003). One can focus on one of these three as the target and the others as background, but one cannot fully understand development without considering all three levels and their interactions.

Zinacanteco Childrearing. For example, among the Zinacantecos of southeastern Mexico, newborn infants are draped in a long skirt held in place by a belt or wrap. Zinacanteco babies are rarely on the floor. Rather, they are held in the mother's lap, in her arms, or carried on her back. In contrast to U.S. parents, Zinacanteco mothers rarely urge their babies to perform new motor behaviors and show no special recognition or excitement when a new behavior is accomplished. Zinacanteco babies are quieter and less demanding than typical U.S. babies. They lag behind U.S. babies by about 1 month in motor development, but they show about the same pattern of motor skill over the first year of life.

Cognition is nurtured through observation and imitation rather than through direct exploration and manipulation, as is the case among U.S. babies. The childrearing practices of the Zinacanteco instill two culturally valued characteristics: restrained movement and a tendency to observe and respond rather than to initiate behavior. These qualities, transmitted from one generation to the next through consistent childrearing practices, provide a source of continuity in cognition and behavior from infancy into adulthood, and across generations (Greenfield & Childs, 1991; Brazelton, Robey, & Collier, 1969). The example illustrates the integration of individual, interpersonal, and cultural processes in even the earliest development of motor skills.

In the **sociohistorical** study of cognition, variation is assumed rather than similarity or generality (Rogoff & Chavajay, 1995). Since development is thought to occur in specific contexts at particular periods of time, one focuses on how people in a particular cultural community engage with one another to achieve a specific goal. The learning that takes place or the growth in understanding that occurs cannot be generalized across individuals within a community, across communities, or across activities in various settings. As a result, the findings from any empirical study cannot be widely generalized. Rather, the field grows slowly through multiple, contextualized observations. Over time, one hopes to gain insight into how individuals integrate existing cultural understanding and produce new understanding, how participation in activities or events alters cognitive processes, and how shared cognitions across individuals and generations alter the practices of a culture.

Scientific Reasoning among the Schooled and the Nonschooled. Finally, the sociohistorical perspective has led to a greater awareness of the way in which the tools and methods of scientific inquiry are themselves culturally situated. As an example, in research on logical thinking, Luria (1976) asked schooled and nonschooled adults to solve a problem of logic: "In the Far North, where there is snow, all bears are white. Novaya Zemlya is in the Far North and there is always snow there. What color are the bears there?" Nonschooled peasants would not answer this kind of question, arguing that they have never been to Novaya Zemlya, so they could not speak about the color of the bears who lived there. "We always speak only of what we see; we don't talk about what we haven't seen" (as cited in Rogoff & Chavajay, 1995, p. 861). Other researchers have observed this similar tendency in other cultural groups to trust only what they have experienced or what someone who is greatly respected may have experienced. This does not mean that people from these cultural groups cannot reason logically; they are perfectly able to evaluate someone else's reasoning and conclusions as logical or inconsistent, but they are unwilling to reach a conclusion about a premise that they cannot verify (Scribner, 1977; Rogoff & Chavajay, 1995; Rogoff, 2003).

Vygotsky's insights about the cultural nature of symbolic tools extend to the tools of measurement and experimentation. Scholars in this field have become more attuned to the sociocultural and historical assumptions that underlie their research questions and their methods. They are increasingly striving to design approaches to inquiry that are appropriate to the worldview of the community being studied.

A RESEARCH EXAMPLE: CULTURAL MANAGEMENT OF ATTENTION

The principle that individual development is integrated with culture is illustrated in research on the management of attention described here. Attention is a basic process that has been investigated starting in the early study of sensation, perception, and cognition. Beginning with the early experiments in psychophysics, scientists asked questions about the level of stimulation required to cause a change in attention. In the study of infant perception, the process of habituation was used to explore sensory thresholds. Measures of attention, including gazing time, were used as operational definitions of preference. In the field of information processing, research was carried out to examine the limits of the capacity for attending to competing sources of information. Studies have found that with maturation from childhood to adolescence, there is improvement in both selective attention, the ability to screen out interfering information in order to focus on the primary task, and divided attention, the ability to attend to two tasks at the same time. In general, there has been an assumption in the field that the ability to attend to several stimuli or events at once is limited by some type of neural "bottle neck." As a result, the ability to function at an optimal level is impaired or delayed when the situation requires attention to competing demands. The research led to the conclusion that attention was a basic, universal process that functions in the same way across cultures (Pashler, 1999; Serences & Kastner, 2014).

Vygotsky contributed to this body of knowledge by pointing to the school-age child's development of voluntary memory and voluntary attention (Vygotsky, 1987b). The component elements of conscious awareness, sensation, perception, memory, and attention, become increasingly differentiated in toddlerhood and early childhood. By school age, memory and attention are sufficiently developed that the child can begin to be aware of them, permitting the child to direct attention purposefully.

The dissemination of Vygotsky's ideas led Barbara Rogoff and her colleagues to suspect that the emphasis on sequential, focused attention might be a result of the researchers' cultural preference. Ethnographic and anecdotal reports suggested that there were people from cultural groups who were especially skilled at managing attention to multiple tasks while sustaining a high level of functioning. For example, Ochs (1988) found that Samoan transcribers were able to listen to audio tapes and follow the conversations of three or four different people who were talking at once.

In order to pursue the idea that some cultural communities value and nurture the coordination of attention to multiple events, systematic studies were conducted that compared Guatemalan Mayan mothers and their toddlers from San Pedro with mothers and toddlers from Salt Lake City, Utah (Rogoff, Mistry, Göncü, & Mosier, 1993; Chavajay & Rogoff, 1999). Sixteen mothers and their toddlers (mean age = 17 months) from each community were interviewed at home. All the toddlers had older siblings who were 3 to 5 years old and who were home during the interview. At one point, mothers were given a number of novel objects and asked to involve their toddler with the objects one at a time. This segment was videotaped for 10 minutes; when the interview resumed, 10 more minutes of adult-focused interview time were videotaped. Both segments were coded, looking at how adults and toddlers managed instances of competing events. Thus, the study considered how mothers and toddlers in two communities managed instances of competing attention during a child-focused interaction (mother helping child play with a new object) and during an adult-focused interaction (mother responding to interviewer's questions).

The San Pedro mothers and their toddlers were more likely to attend to competing events simultaneously than the Salt Lake City mothers and their toddlers. The Salt Lake City mothers and their toddlers were more likely to shift their attention from one event to the next than the San Pedro mothers and their toddlers. The San Pedro toddlers were more likely to attend to events simultaneously than the Salt Lake City mothers, suggesting an early and pervasive preference for simultaneous attention in the Mayan community. The Mayan preference for simultaneous attention was shown across toddler-focused and adult-focused interactions, and was unrelated to the number of years of schooling experienced by the Mayan mothers.

Recent studies have documented cultural differences in how children attend to and learn from interactions that are directed to others. In communities where children are expected to learn by observing others and to contribute as needed to adult activities, children are more likely to watch and remember even when they are not the direct target of instruction. For example, in an experimental study, older siblings were told to wait while their younger sibling was being taught how to make a toy. The older siblings were told that they would make a different toy in a little while. In comparison to the European, middle-class children, children from the indigenous culture (Guatemalan Mayan children) were more likely to watch what their younger sibling was doing, and one week later they were better able to make the toy that their younger sibling had been making (Rogoff, Correa-Chavez, & Silva, 2011).

The results of this research suggest that there are patterns of managing attention that differ in the communities under study. One implication is that focused, selective attention is not the preferred or optimal cognitive strategy across communities. Rather, as hypothesized by Vygotsky, cognitive processes are varied and develop in cultural context. A second implication is that very young children can become skilled at managing their attention to competing events if the social community encourages this kind of coordinated attention. This illustrates the operation of the zone of proximal development.

A third implication is that cultural preferences about attention may be linked to patterns and expectations for social interaction. For example, the European idea of *dyadic intimacy*, in which we encourage mother and child to set aside all other tasks in order to interact with each other, is not necessarily the only way to achieve intimacy. In some communities, closeness is achieved when a group of people, including children and adults, interact around a variety of tasks in each other's presence. The comparison of attention strategies across cultural communities can highlight the tie between cognition and human interaction. This validates Vygotsky's ideas about the bond between the individual and society.

A fourth implication is that children can gain a lot of information by including them in the activities of the larger, more diverse social community. The idea of observational learning that was discussed in Chapter 4 is extended in this perspective to consider the larger cultural community in which children may participate. We may unintentionally deprive children of opportunities for learning by so narrowly separating them by age in the Western approach to schooling (Rogoff, Morelli, & Chavajay, 2010).

Finally, in the modern world, the demand to attend to multiple sources of information appears to be increasing. The strong cultural pressure in the European or Western communities toward focused attention on one event at a time may be in conflict with the growing technological pressure toward "multitasking." This may be an unrecognized source of cultural stress in Western societies.

AN APPLICATION: IMPLICATIONS OF VYGOTSKY'S THEORY FOR INSTRUCTION

Vygotsky's theory has influenced educational practices in the United States and in Russia. Fundamental to this application is Vygotsky's concept of the zone of proximal development. According to Vygotsky, school instruction should move ahead of development. This requires that the teacher create socially mediated opportunities for learning in which students draw on prior knowledge and abilities, but also incorporate new skills, information, and strategies in order to foster a reconceptualization or reorganization of their knowledge (Cole, 2010).

As you might expect given the sociocultural perspective introduced earlier in the chapter, the application of the theory has taken somewhat different forms in these two countries. In the United States, the theory has contributed to strategies for promoting **metacognition**, that is, interventions that are intended to increase children's responsibility for planning, directing, monitoring, checking, and evaluating their learning. The approach is referred to as **mediated learning**, or **reciprocal learning** (Haywood, 1996; Palincsar, Brown, & Campione, 1993). In Russia, the theory has contributed to approaches to promote the understanding of scientific knowledge by linking knowledge about concepts with knowledge about procedures. The approach is referred to as **theoretical learning** (Davydov, 1972; Karpov & Haywood, 1998).

Mediated Learning

According to Vygotsky's theory, complex cognitive capacities emerge first in social interaction and are gradually internalized through their use in guiding the behaviors of self and others. This idea has been translated into the educational domain by creating instructional experiences where students and teachers share responsibility for teaching. The mediated learning environment is structured as a community of learners where teachers model certain strategies for planning, summarizing, clarifying, and questioning the problem-solving process, and gradually turn these responsibilities over to the students. Consider the following example which addresses early experiences in learning to read (Cole, 2010).

Children and the teacher participate in a small group reading activity. Each person is given a specific role on an index card and each group member is responsible for enacting at least one role. The roles are:

- The person who asks about words that are hard to say
- The person who asks about words that are hard to say what they mean

- The person who asks a question about the main idea of the passage being read
- The person who picks the person who has to answer the question at hand
- The person who asks about what is going to happen next in the text.

The group members are instructed to read the passage and to jot down notes about the words or phrases they are reading, especially those related to their role. In this way, the group is involved in a question-asking type of reading. All the children and the teacher work together to come up with ideas about the meaning of the text, including some children who do not yet read with adequate comprehension. In this way, the teacher becomes aware of the aspects of reading that are challenging for each child, and the children learn from the teacher and one another about approaches to reading for meaning. Instead of viewing reading as an isolated activity for which each child is responsible, reading becomes a collective effort which advances the children at their own pace through the benefit of socially mediated interactions.

Students cooperate and share in the mutual regulation and control of the learning process, taking turns in observing, helping, and evaluating each other's work. This method of involving students in each other's learning and achievements creates an environment of social support for complex learning as well as creating opportunities for children to learn from both the teacher and the other students. Over time, the metacognitive skills of monitoring, planning, and evaluating are transferred to other academic domains, especially in learning environments where teachers invite students to engage in active discourse and critical analysis in order to think and make meaning of course content (Rogoff, Turkanis, & Bartlett, 2001; Forman & Cazden, 1985).

Theoretical Learning

Vygotsky distinguished between two types of concepts: *spontaneous concepts* and *scientific concepts*. **Spontaneous concepts** are similar to the kinds of schemes that Piaget described as emerging during the sensorimotor and preoperational stages; they are generalizations drawn from daily, personal, direct experiences. Spontaneous concepts form the basis of knowledge that has not been guided by systematic instruction or explanation from more experienced adults.

Scientific concepts are the ideas, laws, and information that have been accumulated over generations as a result of systematic research, philosophy, and shared, historical experience. According to Vygotsky, scientific concepts cannot be expected to be discovered or reinvented in the course of a single child's education, and therefore require knowledge transfer through a process of instruction. Once these ideas are internalized, they can be used to mediate new experiences and to create new applications or discover new scientific concepts.

However, the Russians found that the simple didactic presentation of scientific knowledge was not effective in helping students to achieve mastery of these concepts. They recognized that students needed to understand the procedures that are used to gain this knowledge as well as the concepts themselves in order to use the ideas for further problem solving. Theoretical learning is the approach they created in order to integrate knowledge of the signs and symbols of scientific concepts with the procedures that are used to generate these concepts. Theoretical learning involves teaching children a method or model for organizing and analyzing information appropriate to the subject matter, and then helping children use that method to solve new problems. The term **scaffolding** is sometimes used to describe this process. Through scaffolding, the student is able to master complex skills by taking advantage of strategies and guides from a more experienced learner. The approach is to simplify the learner's role in a way that allows the learner to complete the complex task with support, and then ultimately to internalize these supports and apply them to other tasks.

For example, in a high school science class, a teacher might first give students detailed guides to carrying out experiments; then give them brief guides to help structure experiments; and finally ask students to design and conduct experiments on their own (Slavin, 2011). Experiencing success in problem solving through the application of a particular strategy gives students the idea that other complicated problems may have a method or approach that will help them find the solution. Once children have had the opportunity to experience success by applying a procedure to solve a problem, they are likely to anticipate that there are other procedures that would be helpful in solving other types of problems (Davydov, 1986).

In their analysis of the application of Vygotsky's theory to education, Karpov and Haywood (1998) suggested that the integration of theoretical learning and mediated learning might be optimally effective. Theoretical learning does not exploit the power of the learning community. Both the verbal knowledge and the procedural knowledge first come from the teacher, and then are expected to be internalized by students without the benefit of social exchange or mutual instruction. Mediated learning focuses on the metacognitive processes of observing, planning, checking, and evaluating that should increase motivation and self-directed learning. However, it does not include a process for engaging students in mastery of the signs and symbols or procedures that create scientific knowledge. By integrating the two approaches, students could be asked to master the scientific concepts and procedures of a field, and then work together in order to solve problems using these strategies. Some students would attempt to solve a problem, while others would check and evaluate the work; then they would switch roles so that the metacognitive capacities and scientific knowledge would advance together.

HOW DOES COGNITIVE SOCIAL-HISTORICAL THEORY ANSWER THE BASIC QUESTIONS THAT A THEORY OF HUMAN DEVELOPMENT IS EXPECTED TO ADDRESS?

1. *What is the direction of change over the life span? How well does the theory account for patterns of change and continuity?*

   The direction of change is from intermental to intramental—from social speech, to egocentric speech, to inner speech. The theory suggests that major transitions in cognitive complexity are observed twice, first at the interpersonal or social level and then as internalized concepts. The direction of change is toward increasing cognitive complexity guided by the scientific knowledge and cultural values about intelligence that shape the sociohistorical context. A particular focus of the theory is on increasing capacities for metacognition and self-regulation which occur as the child internalizes guiding strategies for monitoring, analyzing, and evaluating problem-solving efforts that were initially provided by more skilled adults or knowledgeable others.

2. *What are the mechanisms that account for growth? What are some testable hypotheses or predictions that emerge from this analysis?*

   Vygotsky asked how the developing child incorporates the tools and scientific concepts of his or her culture in order to function as a contributing member of the culture and possibly to contribute to what is known through his or her own innovative problem solving. He was interested in conceptualizing how the intrinsic, biologically guided forces interact with cultural forces to produce new levels of cognitive functioning.

Tools or artifacts are central to understanding the emergence of higher order thinking (Cole, 2003). Tools can be both concrete or material (e.g. a hammer or a cell phone) and symbolic or conceptual (e.g. a story or a value). Tools combine an action and a goal; they merge the use to which they are directed with the capacity of the person using them. As such, tools are mechanisms that contribute to the development of thought and behavior. In Vygotsky's social-historical theory, tools are a mechanism that brings the external cultural world into the inner world of thought and goal-directed action.

A second mechanism that Vygotsky offered to account for growth is participation in collaborative problem solving with adults and more skilled peers. Children learn new strategies, use those strategies to regulate their own behavior and those of others, and eventually internalize those strategies for application in subsequent problem-solving situations.

A related mechanism is the concept of the zone of proximal development. The concept links development and learning, suggesting how instruction and interactions with more knowledgeable others can advance development. Children bring a spontaneous capacity for understanding and problem solving to each new situation. However, they also have the potential for a higher or more cognitively complex level of functioning that can be prompted through guidance by more skilled participants. Teachers and peers can foster new levels of cognitive functioning by introducing signs, symbols, and procedures that the child can learn to apply in new situations.

One testable hypothesis is that as children acquire the symbolic tool of language, inner speech can be used to help regulate attention and behavior. Children can be expected to rely on inner speech more heavily when the problems are more demanding.

Another testable hypothesis is that cultural orientations toward individualism or interdependence, shaped by symbolic and psychological tools, will contribute to the nature of attention, memory, and higher order problem solving.

Drawing on the concept of a zone of proximal development, one can predict that with the right amount of help or guidance, children should be able to solve more difficult problems than they can solve independently. The challenge is to identify problems that are "within the zone" and to provide the level of help that preserves the child's continued interest and motivation to engage the problem. Presumably, when a child is given a clue or strategy for solving a problem that is within the zone, the solution should come rather easily and the child should exhibit enthusiasm and interest in working on the task. If the problem is beyond the zone, the same clue or strategy will not result in a successful solution, and the child may experience a sense of confusion or disinterest. Thus, the ability to locate where a child is in his or her zone of proximal development depends upon the developmental level of the child, the nature of the activity or problem, and the nature of the guidance or support that the child is receiving. All of these factors interact to influence the child's success.

3. *How relevant are early experiences for later development? What evidence does the theory offer to support its view?*

    According to Vygotsky's social-historical perspective, cognition emerges from social interactions and the use of cultural tools which are gradually internalized. As a result, early social experiences of communication with caregivers, exposure to the social community and the cultural environment, and experiences of nurturing and care are all critical for the formation of early cognitions. Early in development, children hear and use words that have been used in adult speech. Although the child may understand the word in a more concrete form, and the adult understands it in a more abstract form, the child is able to coordinate his or her word use in a way that corresponds with the adult's understanding; by recognizing the child's use of a word, the adult supports the child's language use. This early coordination of language use is central to subsequent concept development.

As illustrated earlier in the chapter, early experiences shape the way children attend to events around them. Exposure to verbal and nonverbal cues provides additional tools for conceptualizing events. Patterns of teaching and evaluating knowledge that are characteristic of a culture become internalized and mediate the way children come to interpret new information. Thus, early experiences are critical for shaping the direction of subsequent development.

At the same time, at each new phase of life, individuals may participate in new social contexts that may introduce new ways of thinking. Schooling, for example, will introduce children to new procedures and tools, such as experimentation, which may lead to new kinds of scientific knowledge. As individuals mature, they may find ways to enter new zones of proximal development, by seeking out more challenging apprenticeships, educational settings, or training so that their earlier learning is transformed, and possibly replaced by new knowledge.

4. *How do the environmental and social contexts affect development? What aspects of the environment does the theory suggest are especially important in shaping the direction of development?*
In this theory, cognition is not located in the individual or in the society but in the specific meaning of a child's actions in context. Activities are socially constructed and have cultural meaning and value. Vygotsky argued against the idea of conceptualizing the environment as separate from the child. He placed greater attention on a child's *experiences* which are a product of a functional relationship between the individual and the environment. "Experience is a unit of personality and environment as they exist in development. Experience must be understood as the internal relationship of the child as an individual to a given aspect of reality" (1984, p. 382).

For example, in U.S. culture, there is a great value attached to an infant's transition from crawling to walking. Parents and other adults attribute considerable importance to walking, and view a child's age at walking as an indication of maturation. Cultural tools such as the "walker" have been invented to support or facilitate early walking. Thus, in the United States, walking is an activity that symbolizes maturity and readiness for the child to achieve a new level of autonomy and distance from the caregivers.

However, walking may be viewed differently in different subcultures, and may be regarded differently for boys and girls. In some families, walking at an early age may be a sign of athletic promise—a future football player, a soccer player, or a runner. In other families, early walking may be viewed as a sign that the child is on a path toward getting into difficulty—"We really need to keep our eye on this one; he's going to be a trouble maker." In other families, walking may be a worry because now the baby needs shoes and shoes are expensive. In still other families, as the baby begins to walk, the parents begin to "baby proof" the house, locking cabinets, moving items to new, higher locations, and installing covers on electrical outlets. All of these different reactions to walking illustrate how the biologically based capacity for walking interacts with the social and cultural context to give the activity specific meaning. Walking provides a basis for qualitatively different kinds of activities in the setting, and the meaning of those activities will differ depending on the sociocultural context.

5. *According to the theory, what factors place individuals at risk at specific periods of the life span?*

A primary source of risk would be the relative absence of interactions with caregivers and other caring adults. Because of the importance given to the role of social interaction which mediates culture, conditions that restrict a child's participation in social interaction would result in impoverished language and cognition. Given the importance placed on the role of skilled adults and peers who introduce the child to problem-solving strategies, new information, and new procedures for gaining knowledge, the lack of access to effective schooling or alienation from the world of more knowledgeable others would also place a child at risk with respect to achieving more advanced cognitive functioning. Each culture has its own tools and mechanisms for transmitting knowledge from one generation to the next. Individuals who, for whatever reason, lose their access to these resources will be at risk. This might result from poverty, war, natural disasters, homelessness, servitude or slavery, or other crises that disconnect a person from family, friends, school, and community.

According to this theory, learning and development scaffold each other. As children mature, they are able to learn new and more complex information, and to explore new procedures. This new learning stimulates new levels of cognitive awareness, provides alternative approaches to problem solving, and helps the child conceptualize problems from new perspectives. The child's new insights may lead to a desire for more information, which once again propels the child toward increasingly complex levels of cognitive functioning. At any point in this process, the child's further development can be inhibited if new opportunities for learning are restricted.

6. *What are some practical implications of cognitive social-historical theory?*

Perhaps the most well-known implications are related to applications in the field of education. Four concepts from the theory have been applied to educational settings:

1. Learning is a social/cultural process. Culture is present in every aspect of a social institution, including schools, and the tools and artifacts of culture mediate the learning process. This idea informs the teaching/learning activity and suggests the need to examine and reflect upon the cultural context of the school environment.
2. The idea of a zone of proximal development suggests that each learner has a current and a potential capacity. The teaching/learning process can be enhanced by introducing activities and strategies that will scaffold the learner from their current to their more advanced level. It is important to select tasks and activities that are within the zone.
3. The idea of socially mediated learning suggests that collaboration and modeling are important features of the learning process. Students at any level can benefit from observing and imitating more knowledgeable partners. One way of allowing this to happen is for the teacher or model to talk aloud, sharing their problem-solving strategies so that the learner can benefit from the thought processes of the more skilled partner.
4. The idea of scaffolding itself is an important implication in any effort to promote more advanced or complex thought. In scaffolding, the goal is to provide supports and guidance for the learner, thus making early efforts more successful. Scaffolding requires analysis of the task so that one can place fewer demands on the learner, while preserving the complexity of the task itself.

The theoretical focus on activities as a unit of analysis has implications for any context in which behavior change is desired. This focus has been applied to work with children with disabilities, to organizational behavior, and to inter-agency collaboration (Daniels, 2012). The theory provides insights into how people and organizations learn to do something new. It points to the importance of analyzing the language and communication that surround specific tasks, the impact of both material and symbolic tools, and the social/communicative nature of the workplace.

CRITIQUE OF COGNITIVE SOCIAL-HISTORICAL THEORY

Strengths

Vygotsky did more than bring our attention to the social, cultural, and historical contexts of development. He introduced an entirely new perspective on cognition, locating it at the interface of the person and the culture. The idea that the higher mental functions begin outside the person in the social environment and become internalized offered a unique perspective about the boundary of the self and the society and the direction of development. With this insight, one is able to appreciate that people in different cultures have different ways of representing their experiences and different preferences for higher order problem solving. Emerging from these ideas is a new excitement about ways of looking at development as a product of continuous and fluid exchanges between maturation, environmental opportunities and resources, and cultural tools.

The idea that higher order mental constructs begin outside the child, in the "intermental" social/cultural milieu, and are gradually internalized places new emphasis on the importance of an interactive, interpersonal learning environment. Achieving new levels of cognitive complexity is not the sole responsibility of the learner nor the teacher. Rather cognitive complexity advances as a product of activities in context mediated by social interactions. This idea brings new focus to the processes of collaboration and shared responsibility for learning.

Vygotsky took on big ideas including the nature of consciousness, identifying words as basic units of psychological analysis, the interrelationships of mental functions to create integrated experiences of thought, and the integration of thought and behavior. He resisted tendencies toward reductionism and was constantly reminding us to look at the big picture.

Vygotsky provided a new way of understanding the relationship of learning and development by introducing the concept of the zone of proximal development. The child has both a current mental age and a mental age potential. Through the processes of play and/or instruction, the child's insights about a subject advance, thus promoting new levels of cognitive development.

Vygotsky's view about the role of instruction in development is gaining popularity within educational circles. A child has strong internal motivation to experiment and explore. However, according to Vygotsky, the child's intrinsic interest and curiosity will not be adequate for learning the scope of knowledge that is required to function in adult life. What is more, in order for children to acquire scientific knowledge, they need to be taught about the systematic tools and procedures of their culture. Vygotsky's concept of the zone of proximal development gives a specific role to teachers to guide children to new, more complex levels of functioning by giving them just the right amount of help at just the right time.

Vygotsky was devoted to an analysis of development. His many experimental demonstrations were designed to simulate the emergence of a new mental capacity, from its early origins to its more advanced, culturally informed level. He designed experiments that he thought would provide an opportunity for learning and development for those children who participated. His work with traditional cultures, with children who were developmentally delayed, and his interest in primate research all preserved the focus on describing and explaining the transformation of capacities from lower to higher forms.

In many developmental theories, the focus has been on identifying general principles or patterns of growth. In contrast, Vygotsky emphasized diversity in development, an idea which has become increasingly integrated into the current study of development and its application to education. Consideration of varieties of learning styles, rates of development, types of intelligence, and temperament has become prominent in studies of cognition. Similarly appreciation for varieties of instructional strategies, tasks, and cultural values and contexts for learning has become a priority in understanding the educative process. Finally, the meaning of behavior is expected to vary depending on the setting in which the behavior takes place. This emphasis on specific contexts gives credit to the child who detects the expectations of others within a setting, and to the culture, which operates to encourage certain types of behaviors in certain settings.

Weaknesses

Vygotsky, who was remarkably productive in his brief lifetime, explored many ideas that he and his students and colleagues did not have time to develop. This was due in part to his untimely death, and in part to the suppression of his work. As a result, many of his ideas reemerged in the later part of the twentieth century in partial translation, and without adequate experimental or empirical evidence to support them.

The concept of the zone of proximal development, which has probably been the most widely accepted concept from his theory, has been criticized on several fronts. There are multiple definitions of the zone resulting in a lack of agreement about ways to operationalize this idea. Some interpretations focus on the difference between what a child can do alone and with some help. Some interpretations focus on the difference between the child's everyday knowledge and the scientific or mature knowledge that exists in the culture. Some interpretations focus on the ability of an individual and the socially constructed knowledge of the larger community (Lave & Wenger, 2005).

The width of the zone, that is how far a child can progress with help, differs for different kinds of problems, and for different children. The concept does not provide guidance for how much help a person should give or what type of help a person should give to foster movement in the zone. It is unclear if movement in the zone is long-lasting once the help is removed, or if one should expect improvement in the zone for one domain of learning to generalize to other domains. Finally, children enter the zone at different levels of expertise. There may be more room for growth for children who are at the beginning or novice level than for children who are more advanced in their competence. Researchers in the field have not arrived at an agreed on method for establishing a zone of proximal development or for measuring movement in the zone.

Although the theory of the zone of proximal development implies that children differ in their developmental capacities, the theory does not offer a description of normative developmental levels or hypotheses about how children of different ages/stages will function. Given that cultures may have differing expectations for children at different ages, a theory of development should be expected to provide some framework for age-related developmental differences.

Vygotsky placed a major emphasis on the cultural tools of speech and language as shaping mental processes. Some cognitive scientists might view this argument as an overstatement of the way speech and thought interact. As the work on the cognitive unconscious suggests, there are integrative aspects of higher mental functioning that are not consciously regulated by language. Moreover, capacities for the perception of auditory, visual, olfactory, and tactile stimulation are not limited by language. In other words, even if the language does not have a specific word for the smell of horse, hay, and dust mixed together, a person can still detect these smells and recognize that they are associated with a barn or a stable.

The theory was developed in the context of a powerful social/political philosophy of Marxism. As such, it emphasized that the mind is born from participation in the community:

> Vygotsky and his colleagues wanted to change citizens' thinking from a feudal (landlords and serfs) mentality of helplessness and alienation to a socialistic mentality of self-directed activity and commitment to a larger social unit based on sharing, cooperation, and support. In the new Soviet view, each person was responsible for the progress of the whole society. (Miller, 2011, p. 168)

The theory is based on the premise that the conditions of economic production influence the nature of working conditions and interpersonal interactions, and that these interactions influence cognition. "The hand shapes the mind." The value of shared goods was translated into the notion of shared knowledge, with the idea that it was the responsibility of those who were trained and educated to transmit this information to others in order to advance the society. As such, the theory is much more of a collectivist than an individualist view of cognition. To some extent, this balances the individualist emphasis of many of the other theories. The idea that the societal/historical/cultural environment provides the tools, attitudes, values, and knowledge that shape learning is a powerful insight. However, the theory did not provide a template for how to identify the key features of social/historical events that might influence higher order mental processes. This perspective has proven very difficult to translate into research.

Moreover, social and historical events of the past 25 years suggest that the marriage of the two traditions, Marxist philosophy and cognitive science, may be flawed. After the fall of the Soviet Union, it turned out that many deeply held ethnic and subcultural traditions and values that had been suppressed for several generations resurfaced. The training, instruction, and socialization of the Soviet regime did not succeed in becoming fully internalized as one might have expected. Vygotsky may have placed too much faith on the willingness of teachers and parents to encourage movement through the zone through gentle encouragement and hints rather than by insistence on a specific approach to problem solving. The theory is naïve in assuming that the powerful members of society will willingly share the full extent of their knowledge in order to promote the advancement of all its children. At the same time, the theory underestimates the presence of "free-riders" who will take advantage of group resources, but who will not collaborate fully in the efforts of the group.

The theory underestimates the willingness of communities to communicate multiple value systems that remain part of the intuitive knowledge base and are not displaced by the more formal, scientific knowledge base of those in power. The theory underestimates the contribution of the individual mind that may achieve a greater degree of independence from societal values and teachings once the tools of language and other symbolic resources have been mastered.

Individuals and groups differ in their motivation to achieve new levels of mastery. Given the importance that the theory places on mediated or collaborative learning, the theory does not offer any concepts to help predict the conditions that foster persistence and striving. Table 9.2 provides a summary of the strengths and weaknesses of Cognitive Social-Historical Theory.

Table 9.2 Strengths and weaknesses of cognitive social-historical theory

Strengths	Weaknesses
A novel view of cognitive development which states that higher mental functions begin outside the person in the social environment and become internalized.	Concept of zone of proximal development has multiple definitions which impedes operationalization.
New focus on the role of collaboration and shared responsibility for learning in the process of cognitive development.	Lack of clear guidance about how much help or what type of help one should give to promote movement through the zone for different types of tasks.
The concept of the zone of proximal development provides a novel way of thinking about the relationship of development and learning.	Lack of theoretical clarity about how much movement is to be expected for children of different levels of ability.
The theory provides a wealth of implications for educational application and practice.	No clear framework for normative age-related abilities or cognitive capacities.
Emphasis on diversity in development, including diversity of abilities, activities, cultural contexts, and settings.	The theory overstates the role of language in shaping cognition and higher mental processes.
Particular focus on culture, including material and symbolic cultural tools that shape thought and behavior.	Despite emphasis on the importance of the social/cultural/historical context, no framework to help identify features of this context that can be expected to impact higher order mental processes.
The meaning of behavior is expected to vary depending on the setting in which the behavior takes place.	The theory overestimates the beneficent nature of the collective, and underestimates the enduring power of separate cultures that may resist pressures for acculturation.
New emphasis on activities in context mediated by social interactions. Gives recognition to the child's ability to detect social expectations in the setting that will inform thought and behavior.	The theory underestimates the power of individual minds to achieve new levels of independence from societal values and beliefs.
	No concepts to help account for individual and group differences in persistence and striving.

CRITICAL THINKING QUESTIONS AND EXERCISES

1. Give three reasons that cognitive social-historical theory is viewed as an example of an interactionist theory. How does the theory characterize the interaction of the person and the environment in accounting for higher order mental functions?
2. Thinking back to cognitive developmental theory (Chapter 4) and the learning theories (Chapter 5), what are four new ideas that cognitive social-historical theory contributes to our understanding of cognitive development and learning?
3. Identify three or four material tools that you use in your daily life (for example your cell phone or your dishwasher). How do these tools shape your thinking? How do they influence your approach to problem solving or to the formation of plans and goals? To what extent does your own life experience with tools of your culture validate cognitive social-historical theory?

4. Identify three or four symbolic or psychological tools that you use in daily life (for example your understanding of the scientific process or your beliefs about health). How do these tools shape your thinking? How do they influence your approach to problem solving or to the formation of plans and goals? Trace the path from the intermental to the intramental for these tools. Where did they originate? How did they become part of your own way of thinking?

5. Can you identify some ways that the historical period may alter cognitive processes? For example, how might the dissolution of the Soviet Union in the early 1990s and the reemergence of the individual identities of the former member countries have altered or influenced the cognitive functioning of children growing up in this era of transition?

6. Going back to the case of Jasmine, what do you think she learns from this interaction? How does the case illustrate the theoretical idea of socially mediated cognition?

7. In the case of Jasmine, her father responds amiably to her repeated questioning, "Why?" Extend this interaction to the school environment. How should teachers respond to students' questions? What does the theory suggest about how teachers and other more knowledgeable adults can scaffold and support inquiry?

8. What can be achieved by creating a collaborative environment for student learning and development? Describe how you might transfer leadership for new learning from the teacher to the students in a collaborative learning environment.

KEY TERMS

activity	scaffolding
cultural tools	scientific concepts
culture	self-regulation
higher mental processes	sign
inner speech	sociocultural
intermental	sociohistorical
internalization	spontaneous concepts
intramental	symbol systems
language	technical tools
lower mental processes	theoretical learning
mediated learning	tools
metacognition	word meaning
psychological tools	zone of proximal development
reciprocal learning	

RECOMMENDED RESOURCES

**Cole, M. (1996). Interactive minds in a life-span perspective: A cultural-historical approach to culture and cognitive development. In P.B. Baltes & U.M. Staudinger (Eds.), *Interactive minds: Life-span perspectives on the social foundations of cognition* (pp. 59–88). New York: Cambridge University Press. http://lchc.ucsd.edu/People/MCole/InteractiveMinds0001.pdf

A book chapter which explores the unique role of culture in the way human minds interact over the life span. The chapter builds on Cole's ongoing interest in a cultural historical approach to development.

**Lev Vygotsky: A documentary.* A DVD from Lowe productions. PHD Lowe Productions #188-PO Box 8000, Abbotsford, B.C., V25 6H1, Canada. Phone: 604-854-8130, email: phd-lowe@shaw.ca
There are two versions: a 1 hour 53 minute documentary divided into three sections: life, theory, and Vygotskian concepts in practice; and a 35 minute summary of life, theory, and practice. Combines narration, archive photos, film footage, and interviews with family members, researchers, and educators.

**Play: A Vygotskian approach* (with Ph.D.s Elena Bodrova and Deborah J. Leong). A Davidson film. This film provides a comparison of Freudian, Eriksonian, Piagetian, and Vygotskian theoretical views on play. The film reviews traditional ways of studying play, highlights Vygotksy's theoretical views about how fantasy play contributes to development, and gives practical suggestions for fostering high-level play in early childhood settings. (Note: this film is available for purchase with a special discount rate by calling Davidson films at 888-437-4200. Check your university film resources to see if the film is already part of the film library.)

**Rogoff, B. (2003). *The cultural nature of human development.* New York: Oxford University Press.
This book received the William James Book Award from the American Psychological Association. The book provides research and theory to account for how culture matters in guiding and shaping child development through daily interactions and ongoing use of cultural tools.

**Vygotsky vs Piaget. A YouTube video. www.youtube.com/watch?v=Axi7xctulbM.
This is an animated video in which Vygotsky and Piaget argue about who has the more accurate view of cognitive development and learning.

**Vygotsky, L.S. (1978). Internalization of higher psychological functions. In M. Cole, V. John-Steiner, S. Scribner, & E. Souberman (Eds.), *Mind in society: The development of higher psychological processes* (pp. 52–57). Cambridge, MA: Harvard University Press.
In this paper, Vygotsky outlines a theory of cognitive development. The mind and higher order mental abilities emerge through interaction with the tools and communication of the surrounding society. Through their designs and functions, tools alter a person's inner world as well as the outer world. Societies provide individuals with technologies that can be used to shape the private processes of mind.

REFERENCES

Bakhurst, D. (1996). Social memory in Soviet thought. In H. Daniels (Ed.), *An introduction to Vygotsky* (pp. 196–218). London: Routledge. (Original work published 1990)

Brazelton, T.B., Robey, J.S., & Collier, G.A. (1969). Infant development in the Zinacanteco Indians of Southern Mexico. *Pediatrics, 44,* 274–290.

Bruner, J. (1987). In R.W. Rieber & A.S. Carton (Eds.), Prologue to the English edition. *Vol. 1. Problems of general psychology* (pp. 1–16). New York: Plenum.

Chavajay, P. & Rogoff, B. (1999). Cultural variation in management of attention by children and their caregivers. *Developmental Psychology, 35,* 1079–1090.

Cole, M. (1990). Cognitive development and formal schooling: The evidence from cross-cultural research. In L.C. Moll (Ed.), *Vygotsky and education* (pp. 89–110). Cambridge, England: Cambridge University Press.

Cole, M. (2003). Culture and cognitive science. *Outlines, 1,* 3–15.

Cole, M. (2010). Cultural-historical activity theory. Laboratory for Comparative Human Cognition, UCSD. Retrieved on July 30, 2014 at www.lchc.ucsd.edu/people/mcole

Cole, M. & Scribner, S. (1977). Cross cultural studies of memory and cognition. In R.V. Kail, Jr. & J.W. Hagen (Eds.), *Perspectives on the development of memory and cognition* (pp. 239–271). Hillsdale, NJ: Lawrence Erlbaum Associates.

Cole, M. & Scribner, S. (1978). Introduction. In M. Cole, V. John-Steiner, S. Scribner, & E. Souberman (Eds.), *Mind in society: The development of higher psychological processes. L. S. Vygotsky* (pp. 1–14). Cambridge, MA: Harvard University Press.

Daniels, H. (2005). *Introduction to Vygotsky.* 2nd ed. New York: Routledge.

Daniels, H. (2012). Institutional culture, social interaction and learning. *Learning, culture and social interaction, 1,* 2–11.

Davydov, V.V. (1972). *Types of generalization in learning.* Moscow: Pedagogika.

Davydov, V.V. (1986). *Problems of development-generating learning.* Moscow: Pedagogika.

Engels, F. (1940). *Dialectics of nature.* New York: International Publishers. (Original work published 1925)

Fernyhough, C. & Fradley, E. (2005). Private speech on an executive task: Relations with task difficulty and task performance. *Cognitive Development, 20,* 103–120.

Forman, E.A. & Cazden, C.B. (1985). Exploring Vygotskian perspectives in education: The cognitive value of peer interaction. In J.V. Wertsch (Ed.), *Culture, communication and cognition: Vygotskian perspectives* (pp. 323–347). New York: Cambridge University Press.

Greenfield, P.M. & Childs, C.P. (1991). Developmental continuity in biocultural context. In R. Cohen & A.W. Siegel (Eds.), *Context and development* (pp. 135–159). Hillsdale, NJ: Lawrence Erlbaum Associates.

Haywood, H.C. (1996). Cognitive early education: A key to school success. In S. Molina-Garcia & M. Fandos-Igado (Eds.), *Educación cognitiva* (pp. 167–192). Zaragoza, Spain: MIRA.

Karpov, Y.V. & Haywood, H.C. (1998). Two ways to elaborate Vygotsky's concept of mediation. *American Psychologist, 53,* 27–36.

Lave, J. & Wenger, E. (2005). Practice, person, social world. In H. Daniels (Ed.), *An introduction to Vygotsky.* 2nd ed. (pp. 145–152). London: Routledge.

Luria, A.R. (1976). *Cognitive development: Its cultural and social foundations.* Cambridge, MA: Harvard University Press.

Lynam, D.R. & Henry, G. (2001). The role of neuropsychological deficits in conduct disorders. In J. Hill & B. Maughan (Eds.), *Conduct disorders in childhood and adolescence* (pp. 235–263). New York: Cambridge University Press.

Marx, K. (1988). *Economic and political manuscripts of 1844 and The Communist Manifesto* (Martin Milligan, Trans.). Amherst, NY: Prometheus Books. (Original work published 1844)

Marx, K. & Engels, F. (1953). *Selected works.* Moscow.

Miller, P.H. (2011). *Theories of developmental psychology.* 5th ed. New York: Worth

National Center for Education Statistics (2004). *Highlights from the TIMSS 1999 video study of eighth-grade mathematics teaching study.* Retrieved on November 20, 2004, at nces.ed.gov.

Ochs, E. (1988). *Culture and language development: Language acquisition and language socialization in a Samoan village.* Cambridge, England: Cambridge University Press.

Palincsar, A.S., Brown, A.L., & Campione, J.C. (1993). First grade dialogues for knowledge acquisition and use. In E.A. Forman, N. Minick, & C.A. Stone (Eds.), *Contexts for learning: Sociocultural dynamics in children's development* (pp. 43–57). New York: Oxford University Press.

Pashler, H. (1999). *The psychology of attention.* Cambridge, MA: MIT Press.

Piaget, J. (1952). *The language and thought of the child.* London: Routledge & Kegan Paul. (Originally published in 1926)

Provasnik, S., Kastberg, D., Ferraro, D., Lemanski, N., Roey, S., & Jenkins, E. (2012). *Highlights from TIMMSS 2011: Mathematics and science achievement of U.S. fourth and eighth grade students in an international context. (NCES 2013-009).* National Center for Educational Statistics, Institute of Education Sciences, U.S. Department of Education. Washington, DC.

Rogoff, B. (1995). Observing sociocultural activity on three planes: Participatory appropriation, guided participation, and apprenticeship. In J.V. Wertsch, P. del Rio, & A. Alvarez (Eds.), *Sociocultural studies of mind* (pp. 139–164). Cambridge, England: Cambridge University Press.

Rogoff, B. (2003). *The cultural nature of human development*. New York: Oxford University Press.

Rogoff, B. & Chavajay, P. (1995). What's become of research on the cultural basis of cognitive development? *American Psychologist, 50*, 859–877.

Rogoff, B., Correa-Chavez, M., & Silva, K.G. (2011). Cultural variation in children's attention and learning. In M.A. Gernsbacher, R. Pew, L.M. Hough, & J.R. Pomerantz (Eds.), *Psychology in the real world: Essays illustrating fundamental contributions to society* (pp. 154–163). New York: Worth Publishers.

Rogoff, B., Mistry, J., Göncü, A., & Mosier, C. (1993). Guided participation in cultural activity by toddlers and caregivers. *Monographs of the Society for Research in Child Development, 58* (Serial No. 236).

Rogoff, B., Morelli, G.A., & Chavajay, P. (2010). Children's integration in communities and segregation of differing ages. *Perspectives on Psychological Science, 5*, 431–440.

Rogoff, B., Turkanis, C.G., & Bartlett, L. (2001). *Learning together: Children and adults in a school community*. New York: Oxford University Press.

Scribner, S. (1977). Modes of thinking and ways of speaking: Culture and logic reconsidered. In P.N. Johnson-Laird & P.C Wason (Eds.), *Thinking* (pp. 483–500). Cambridge, England: Cambridge University Press.

Serences, J.T. & Kastner, S. (2014). A multilevel account of selective attention. In K. Nobre & S. Kastner (Eds.), *The Oxford handbook of attention* (pp. 76–104). Oxford: Oxford University Press.

Siegler, R.S. (1998). *Children's thinking*. 3rd ed. Upper Saddle River, NJ: Prentice Hall.

Slavin, R.E. (2011). *Educational psychology: Theory and practice*. 10th ed. Upper Saddle River, NJ: Pearson.

Stevenson, H.W., Chen, C., & Lee, S. (1993). Mathematics achievement of Chinese, Japanese, and American children: Ten years later. *Science, 259*, 53–58.

Trends in International Mathematics and Science Study (2004). *TIMSS results*. Retrieved on November 20, 2004, at nces.ed.gov/timss

van der Veer, R. & Valsiner, J. (1991). *Understanding Vygotsky: A quest for synthesis*. Oxford: Blackwell.

van der Veer, R. & Yasnitsky, A. (2011). Vygotsky in English: What needs to be done. *Integrative Psychological and Behavioral Science, 45*, 475–493.

van Geert, P. (1998). A dynamic systems model of basic developmental mechanisms: Piaget, Vygotsky and beyond. *Psychological Review, 105*, 634–677.

Vygotsky, L.S. (1962). *Thought and language*. Cambridge, MA: MIT Press and Wiley. (Original work published 1934)

Vygotsky, L.S. (1978a). Tool and symbol in child development. In M. Cole, V. John-Steiner, S. Scribner, & E. Souberman (Eds.), *Mind in society: The development of higher psychological processes* (pp. 19–30). Cambridge, MA: Harvard University Press.

Vygotsky, L.S. (1978b). Internalization of higher psychological functions. In M. Cole, V. John-Steiner, S. Scribner, & E. Souberman (Eds.), *Mind in society: The development of higher psychological processes* (pp. 52–57). Cambridge, MA: Harvard University Press.

Vygotsky, L.S. (1978c). Interaction between learning and development. In M. Cole, V. John-Steiner, S. Scribner, & E. Souberman (Eds.), *Mind in society: The development of higher psychological processes* (pp. 79–92). Cambridge, MA: Harvard University Press.

Vygotsky, L.S. (1978d). The role of play in development. In M. Cole, V. John-Steiner, S. Scribner, & E. Souberman (Eds.), *Mind in society: The development of higher psychological processes* (pp. 92–105). Cambridge, MA: Harvard University Press.

Vygotsky, L.S. (1984). The crisis of seven years. In L.S. Vygotsky, *Collected works: Child psychology: Vol. 4*. Moscow: Pedagogika.

Vygotsky, L.S. (1987a). Genetic roots of thinking and speech. In R.W. Rieber & A.S. Carton (Eds.), *The collected works of L. S. Vygotsky: Vol. 1. Problems of general psychology* (pp. 101–120). New York: Plenum.

Vygotsky, L.S. (1987b). The development of scientific concepts in childhood. In R.W. Rieber & A.S. Carton (Eds.), *The collected works of L. S. Vygotsky: Vol. 1. Problems of general psychology* (pp. 167–241). New York: Plenum.

Vygotsky, L.S. (1987c). Thought and word. In R.W. Rieber & A.S. Carton (Eds.), *The collected works of L. S. Vygotsky: Vol. 1. Problems of general psychology* (pp. 242–291). New York: Plenum.

Wertsch, J.V. (1985). *Vygotsky and the social formation of mind*. Cambridge, MA: Harvard University Press.

10
Bioecological Theory

CHAPTER OUTLINE

GUIDING QUESTIONS

- How does bioecological theory differ from the theories presented in Part II, theories that focus on the environment, in its treatment of the environment?
- Define proximal processes. What are some examples? Evaluate the premise that proximal processes are the key forces that influence development in light of the full PPCT model.
- Reflect on the nature of the macrosystem in the culture of your childhood. What features of the macrosystem might have had important consequences for the patterns of childrearing and family life you experienced?
- Building on life course theory, how might historical time influence development within the framework of the bioecological model?
- Think about the idea of personXenvironment interaction. What does the theory predict about how developmental outcomes might differ depending on the interaction of processes and person characteristics in specific settings?
- What features make a context chaotic? How might chaotic environments contribute to dysfunction? What steps could be taken to intervene to reduce chaos or to minimize its disruptive impact?

CASE VIGNETTE

Marie is 93 years old. Up until last year, she had been active and independent; surrounding herself with family and friends from the neighborhood. She worked two days a week as a volunteer at the local museum giving tours of the "old mansion" and sharing her memories of the days when the building was the home of a leading family in the town. After work, she walked next door to the café where she visited with the owner before calling the Senior van that took her back home to the west side of town.

Marie was known in the family and neighborhood as being a wonderful cook. She had a vegetable and herb garden outside her kitchen door and always included fresh vegetables, herbs, garlic, and other spices in the dishes she was preparing. People were always dropping in for a taste of what was bubbling in the kitchen and a little bit of conversation. She looked forward to these visits.

Just last year she moved into an assisted living facility called Wakefield Meadows. She told her friends and family that her house was too big, and she wanted to lighten the burden of grocery shopping, cooking, cleaning the house, doing laundry, and washing up the dishes. She decided to rent her house to her great-nephew, Philip, and his family, and take advantage of the services that were offered in the assisted living complex. Her family was surprised with this decision, and a bit disappointed that the delicious meals from "Marvelous Marie's Diner" would come to an end. Marie claimed that she was tired and wanted to relax more. She thought this transition would make life a lot easier for her.

However, she was finding that the decision had not worked out as well as she expected. The meals at Wakefield Meadows were bland and lacked variety, and she missed her garden.

Marie was disappointed by the condescending tone of the staff at the complex and their insistence on doing many of the things that she was capable of doing for herself. She found that many of the other residents needed much more care than she did, and she was not used to being so passive. She missed unexpected visits from family and friends. Over time, Marie became increasingly depressed.

When Philip visited, he noticed the change. While they sat and talked, Philip suggested that Marie move back home to her house. There was enough room for all of them. Marie could continue to be active in her garden, and Philip and his family could provide help with meals and house cleaning. Marie gave notice at Wakefield Meadows, and the following month, she moved back home to a celebratory dinner.

The bioecological model of development emphasizes the interaction of four elements: process, person, contexts, and time. The activities and experiences that take place on a regular basis are the critical mechanisms that drive development. These activities and experiences are shaped in part by the demands and resources of the environment, and in part by the characteristics of individuals, including their physical, psychological, and social competences. Over time, people become adept at managing the demands of increasingly complex settings. Certain processes are thought to promote optimal developmental outcomes, resulting in new levels of competence; other processes lead to dysfunction, undermining competence.

In this case, the demands of Marie's life in her home stretch her physical energy to its limit. At the same time, all these demands keep her physically active, provide satisfying social interactions, engage her in creative work in her garden and kitchen, and connect her to other meaningful settings in the community. The bioecological theory provides a lens for thinking about how people's lives are supported by their physical contexts; and how the processes that contribute to development are intimately bound up with the settings in which activity takes place.

In the case of Marie, we see that people are active agents in creating, modifying, and changing their environments. However, we may not be entirely aware of the many ways that processes operate in a setting to sustain or foster optimal functioning. It is possible that the symbolic cultural and societal contexts associated with advanced age, including the availability of assisted living environments and the promotion of these settings for the elderly through television and community marketing, were macrosystem forces steering Marie into a decision that was not a good fit with her personal characteristics and psychosocial needs.

The bioecological theory of human development grew out of a concern that the research and theory of the time lacked a nuanced view of the interdependence of individuals and their environments. Bronfenbrenner defined the ecology of human development as follows:

The ecology of human development involves the scientific study of the progressive, mutual accommodation between an active, growing human being and the changing properties of the immediate settings in which the developing person lives, as this process is effected by relations between these settings and by the larger contexts in which these settings are embedded. (Bronfenbrenner, 1979, p. 21)

Bronfenbrenner believed that the study of development should combine systematic, scientific research with practical application. To that end, he argued that it was important to situate research in real-life contexts, and to understand how people made meaning of the settings in which they function. In the definition above, one can find the seeds of the bioecological theory: the person is active and changing, the settings are changing, the person is assumed to be functioning in more than one setting, and the settings themselves are impacted by forces in larger, community, cultural, and even societal contexts. Over time, the person comes to appreciate the larger, complex nature of his or her environments and the way forces push and pull behavior, while at the same time, identifying his or her own personal objectives and goals.

HISTORICAL CONTEXT

As the name suggests, bioecological theory builds upon the concept of ecology, the scientific study of the interaction of organisms in their environments. The term "ecology" has roots in the Greek word *oikos*, meaning house, dwelling place, or habitation. Descriptions of characteristics of the natural world date back to ancient authors including Hippocrates and Aristotle, who wrote about natural history. Pliny the Elder published an encyclopedia of natural history in the period AD 77 to 79.

The modern science of ecology emerged in the middle of the nineteenth century, heavily influenced by the writings of Charles Darwin and the theory of evolution (see Chapter 2). Although Darwin did not use the term, two concepts from this theory, adaptation and natural selection, point to the importance of understanding how organisms interact with their environments. One of Darwin's most enthusiastic proponents was the German zoologist, Ernst Haeckel (1866), who first coined the term ecology. He defined the term as follows:

By ecology, we mean the whole science of the relations of the organism to the environment including, in the broad sense, all the "conditions of existence." These are partly organic, partly inorganic in nature; both, as we have shown, are of the greatest significance for the form of organisms, for they force them to become adapted.

Building on these ideas, contemporary **ecology** explores the diversity, distribution, population, and competition between and within organisms within a setting (Egerton, 2013). The concept of ecosystems suggests the need to observe and analyze all the interacting features of a natural environment, including the organisms, the communities they form, and the non-living aspects of the environment with which they interact. From the field of ecology, we have inherited terms such as ecological niche or habitat, and processes such as recycling of resources, sustainability, and succession (the way organisms reproduce and pass along resources to the next generation).

In the United States, the field of home economics emerged toward the end of the nineteenth century. The field, influenced by the concepts of ecology, sought to apply the latest findings in science and economics to the home and household management. One can think of the home as an **ecological niche**. All the features of life in the home, including efficient use of resources, food preparation, the safety of the physical environment, childcare, clothing, and the appropriate use of emerging technologies, as well as the relationship of the home and family to adjoining community environments, were considered aspects of home management (Bubolz & Sontag, 1993). The field of home economics flourished in the early part of the twentieth century. The American Home Economics Association, which was established in 1909, grew to a membership of 50,000 in the mid-1960s, but declined to around 5,000 in 2012 under its new title: The American Association of Family and Consumer Sciences (AAFCS, 2012).

The field of home economics was intimately linked with colleges of agriculture, the agricultural research experiment stations, and the cooperative extension service. These programs were established through the Morrill Land Grant Acts (1862 and 1890), the Hatch Act (1887), and the Smith Lever Act (1914), which were intended to teach subject matter related to agriculture and mechanical arts (engineering) at the post-secondary level; foster agricultural research; and provide education and services to agricultural industries and farming families. Eventually, 70 colleges and universities in the United States were established through funding from these federal sources. The field of child development owes much to these land grant colleges and universities where the study of child development, parenting, and associated laboratory preschools were located. Among the land grant colleges and universities that offered courses for credit in home and family life was Cornell University. In 1907, the College of Agriculture at Cornell established the department of Home Economics. By 1925, the state of New York created the College of Home Economics (Cornell University, 2014). It was in the context of the College of Home Economics at Cornell that Uri Bronfenbrenner developed the research program that informed bioecological theory.

Uri Bronfenbrenner was born in 1917 in Moscow. He and his parents moved to the United States when he was 6, living first in Pittsburgh, and then in upstate New York. His father was a neuropathologist who worked as a physician at an institution for the developmentally disabled. As an adolescent, Uri worked at the institution as a male attendant. He and his father would discuss the cases, with his father encouraging him to look for patterns in a person's behavior that might relate to brain functions. His father was also his first teacher about the impact of the environment on development. Sometimes, the court would send a child of normal intelligence to the institution.

> My father had taken it on himself to examine each child on admission, and he had a way with kids. But before he could unwind the necessary red tape to have them released, it would be too late. After a few weeks in one of those cottages, their scores on the Stanford-Binet, given routinely by the staff psychologist, would prove the courts to have been right in the first place. By then, the children's IQs showed them to be mentally retarded. (Bronfenbrenner, 1995, p. 600)

In addition to family, Bronfenbrenner acknowledged the important role of his peer group, first in a working-class neighborhood of Pittsburgh, and then in upstate New York. This peer group provided the foundation for his American identity. He was part of a diverse group of friends who offered companionship, acceptance, and valuable information about American customs. When he or his parents had questions about some puzzling aspect of community life, he often checked with his friends to see if they would confirm his understanding.

Bronfenbrenner benefited from exposure to a diverse group of scholars who influenced his thinking. As an undergraduate psychology major at Cornell in the 1930s, he first encountered Titchener, who established psychology as a laboratory science for the study of sensation and perception. Later, he studied with Ogden and Freeman, two psychologists who studied psychological processes from a Gestalt perspective, looking for patterns and configurations. Upon graduation from Cornell, he went to Harvard for a master's degree, where he studied with Walter Fenno Dearborn and Clark Hull. In this context, he learned more about approaches to experimental design and the value of experimentation for both verifying hypotheses and disproving them.

He went to the University of Michigan for his Ph.D., where he identified his special focus on child development, and added new expertise in mathematical statistics. His doctoral dissertation focused on the development of young children's peer groups and friendship patterns, a topic that aligns well with his recollections of the important role his friends played in his own personal development (Bronfenbrenner, 1995).

But one of the richest opportunities for intellectual development in his early adulthood came right after completion of his degree, when he was inducted into the U.S. Army as a private. He was assigned to a unit of the Office of Strategic Services (OSS) where he came in contact with a group of psychologists, sociologists, and anthropologists who were to become leaders in the behavioral and social sciences. Among the most influential were Kurt Lewin and Edward Tolman. After his service, he eventually accepted a position at Cornell, one-quarter time in the department of psychology, and three-quarters time in the College of Home Economics. In 1965, the college changed its name to the College of Human Ecology, in part as a recognition of the lifetime impact of Uri Bronfenbrenner's theory and research on the field of human development.

Thirty years of scholarly work characterized by a combination of laboratory experiments, natural experiments, and cross-cultural research contributed to the formulation of Bronfenbrenner's initial theory, outlined in his book, *The ecology of human development* (1979), which is sometimes referred to as ecological systems theory. The theory presented propositions and testable hypotheses to account for

> the progressive, mutual accommodation between an active, growing human being and the changing properties of the immediate settings in which the developing person lives, as this process is affected by relations between these settings, and by the larger contexts in which the settings are embedded. (p. 21)

The ideas in this work led to a wide-ranging shift in the field of developmental science toward greater inclusion of setting characteristics, examination of behaviors across settings, and features of cultural contexts as well as social policies and practices that impact development. The theory provided an analysis of the nested environments that impact development and the features of those environments that are most salient for influencing developmental processes. Even now, many studies that refer to Bronfenbrenner's theory are primarily focusing on the demands, constraints, and resources of primary environments.

However, shortly after the publication of *The ecology of human development*, Bronfenbrenner was already modifying the theory, including a greater emphasis on time and changes over time as well as characteristics of the person and the role of the individual as an active agent in the developmental process (Rosa & Tudge, 2013). In handbook chapters published in 1998 and 2006, Bronfenbrenner revised and elaborated his views on development to formulate the bioecological theory of human development (Bronfenbrenner & Morris, 1998, 2006), which incorporates the four essential features of process, person, contexts, and time. This is the theoretical framework that is presented in the current chapter.

KEY CONCEPTS

Four key concepts are introduced below which constitute the focus of bioecological theory: process, person, contexts, and time (P-P-C-T). In addition, we discuss Bronfenbrenner's contributions to the research methods that have advanced the bioecological study of behavior and development.

Process

Bronfenbrenner used the term **process** to refer to any of a wide range of interactions between a person and the environment. These processes are viewed as the basic mechanisms that connect the active, growing person with the people, objects, and symbolic representations in the environment. To have an impact on development, these processes must take place frequently or regularly over relatively long periods of time. In general, Bronfenbrenner saw these processes as activity-based, much like the CHAT focus discussed in Chapter 9. The processes typically have an evolving quality. Over time, the maturing person may become engaged in the process in new ways, and the process itself may be modified to become more complex. Think about the process of reading bedtime books. In infancy, even before a baby can talk, a parent might read a book or two before bed. The process of reading has begun as a time for shared attention, physical closeness, and comfort. With advancing developmental competence, the infant can grab the books, turn the pages, and point or imitate sounds from the story. Reading becomes a physical process. After some months, the baby remembers parts of the stories and recognizes the books by the covers. Some books become favorites. The process of reading has transformed from something initiated by the adult to something sought after and cherished by the infant.

Person

The way processes influence development varies depending upon characteristics of the person. Bronfenbrenner acknowledged the biological basis of personal characteristics. But he was especially interested in any features of the **person** that might influence the way the person engaged in a setting, the kinds of resources or opportunities that the setting might provide due to these characteristics, or barriers that the person might encounter as a result of certain characteristics. Three features of a person were identified.

Demand Features. Age, gender, skin color, physical disability, and body type are all examples of **demand features** of a person. Demand features can invite or discourage interactions, depending on the expectations of the other participants in the setting. Cultural, community, and family beliefs and preferences about certain demand characteristics can alter the nature of proximal processes in a setting. In some classroom contexts, for example, teachers are more interested in what boys have to say and encourage boys to participate more than girls. The process of participating in classroom conversation is different for boys and girls, due largely to the demand feature of gender. Whereas demand features are often visible, dispositions and resources are less obvious.

Dispositions. Temperament, motivation, and persistence are all examples of **dispositions**, features of a person that can alter the way a person engages a setting. The discussion of self-efficacy, presented in Chapter 4, is an example of a disposition that is associated with persistence. Two children in the same school setting may experience very different kinds of social processes depending on whether they appear to be striving and trying hard to succeed, or appear to be giving up and withdrawing from the task.

Resources. Effective functioning requires an array of cognitive, emotional, physical, and social **resources**. Knowledge, past experiences, certain skills and talents, self-regulation and emotional control, a sense of humor, and a flexible approach to problem solving are all examples of psychological resources that have been associated with life satisfaction and well-being. In addition, material resources, including a healthy diet, access to quality health care, and a safe home, can influence the way a person engages in activities at a particular developmental stage.

As the theory evolved, Bronfenbrenner indicated that there were important ways that individuals influenced their environments (Bronfenbrenner & Morris, 2006). Both personal characteristics, such as intelligence, temperament, or physical appearance, and activities in which the person engages, such as social interactions, physical activities, or maintenance tasks, can modify the environment and alter its impact. Bronfenbrenner pointed out that some people are more intentional than others in trying to alter their environments. Repeated efforts to alter one's environment may improve a person's ability to effect change.

Contexts

The bioecological theory views the environment as a set of nested **contexts**, from the immediate, face-to-face settings to the broad, encompassing features of culture and society. The term **setting** refers to any place where people can engage in face-to-face interactions. Settings typically involve some kind of activity. For example, in the library setting people may be reading, studying, or looking for information. In the bar, people may be drinking, socializing, playing video games or pool, or eating. The concept of settings suggests activity in context. If you want to understand the nature of behavior, the theory suggests that you need to pay attention to features of the setting where the behavior takes place. Four levels of context are defined in the theory: microsystem, mesosystem, exosystem, and macrosystem (see Figure 10.1).

Microsystem. A **microsystem** is a setting with particular physical characteristics and resources. Microsystems are characterized by patterns of activities, roles, and interpersonal relations experienced by the developing person. A key feature of this definition is the word *experience.* A microsystem is not only defined by the features that might be noted by an objective observer, but by how a person perceives the setting and his or her role in it.

A person may function in multiple microsystems such as a family, workplace, friendship group, and religious or community social group. One might expect that as people mature they become involved in a larger number of microsystems with varying patterns of resources and expectations for behavior. Moreover, in many societies, as people mature they have increasing control over the choice of microsystems in which they participate. Personal dispositions and resources as well as demand features of the person may contribute to the kinds of settings in which the person functions, thereby increasing the bidirectional influences of persons and settings.

Mesosystem. A **mesosystem** comprises the interrelations among two or more settings in which the developing person actively participates. For example, for a child the relations among home, school, and neighborhood peer group; for an adult the relations among family, work, and social life. The demands of one setting, such as work, may require so much time and effort that the person is not able to meet expectations in another setting. This is similar to the idea of role strain we presented in Chapter 6, on social role theory. Or the rewards of one setting are so highly valued that the person begins to neglect responsibilities in another setting.

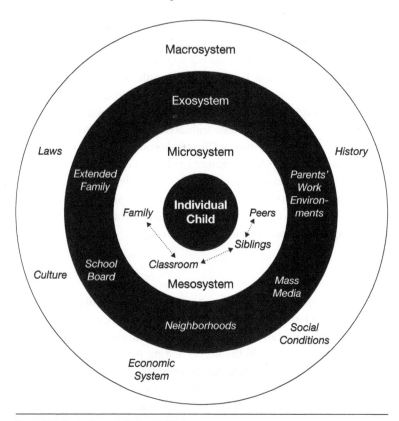

Figure 10.1 Bronfenbrenner's Ecological Model

Source: Urie Bronfenbrenner's ecological systems theory model. BioMed Central. www.biomedcentral.com/content/
figures/1471-2458-8-223-1-l.jpg

The concept of the mesosystem provides a way of thinking about social networks. People are linked to others through the variety of settings in which they participate. Through these related settings, people come to understand the norms and expectations for behavior across settings and can be helpful to newcomers who are entering the setting. Social and instrumental support can be acquired by activating contacts across the mesosystem.

Through a process of participation in a growth-enhancing mesosystem, a person's worldview expands, leading to new levels of cognitive complexity. Knowledge about the resources, activities, and expectations of different settings contributes to a comparative view of one's world. For example, a child may notice that at home he reads books, but at his friend Mark's house they watch TV. At the same time, the sense of oneself is being constructed through the patterns of activities and interpersonal relationships that take place across one's mesosystem.

Exosystem. An **exosystem** refers to one or more settings that do not involve the developing person as an active participant, but in which events occur that affect—or are affected by—what happens in the setting containing the developing person. For example, a woman gets a promotion at work which means more travel and time at corporate conferences. As a result, her partner has to spend more time at home caring for the children and the children have fewer opportunities with their mother. The partner and the children have no contact with the woman's work setting, but decisions made there have an impact on their lives.

The concept of the exosystem contributes to the metaphor of the nested systems. Conditions that may influence one or more members of a person's network of significant relationships can also influence the developing person. The influence can also go in the other direction. Something can happen at the level of the microsystem that trickles up into settings where the person is not involved. For example, a child who is riding in the front seat of a car is seriously injured in an accident. The impact of this event transcends the family, and becomes the focus of new laws that require young children to be placed in car seats behind the first row of seats. The child and the family are not directly involved in this decision, but are a stimulus for the new laws.

Macrosystem. The **macrosystem** refers to the culture or society that frames the structures and relationships among the systems. The macrosystem has laws and law enforcement practices, government agencies, political parties, social policies, health care resources, economic systems, educational resources, media, and many values and symbolic forms of influence that create the social, political, and financial contexts for development (Bronfenbrenner, 1979, pp. 22, 25, 26). For example in 2007–2008, the United States experienced a major financial crisis. Many people lost their retirement savings. Companies laid off tens of thousands of their employees. Thousands of people experienced foreclosure on their homes. These events, brought about by mismanagement and greed at the macrosystem level, led to dramatic disruption at the family and community levels. The extreme and sudden nature of the financial losses required people to cope with conditions that were outside their control and beyond the spheres of their mesosystem.

Time

Both the individual and the systems in which the person is embedded change over **time**. What is more, the relationships among the systems change over time. Some of these changes are patterned, developmental transformations, such as the changes in a child's capacity for coordinated movement and voluntary goal-directed actions. Other changes are initiated at the societal level, such as a community decision to restructure a school system, to make sidewalks and buildings more accessible to people with disabilities, or to pass a law that restricts voting to people who have a government-issued photo ID. Finally, some changes reflect the decline or improvement in resources over time, as when a neighborhood becomes transformed through urban development.

In later writings, Bronfenbrenner addressed the way time related to each level of context (Bronfenbrenner & Morris, 2006). Micro time refers to the timing and duration of activities in microsystems, for example the length of time that a father and child play together, or the time children spend watching television. Meso time refers to activities that take place with some consistency across settings, like the hours spent in childcare each week. Macro time reflects the idea that development takes place in a historical context. As historical events unfold, like the economic recession referred to above, children of parents who lost their jobs are influenced in different ways depending on their own developmental stage. Macro time may be a period of war, a time of famine, a time of peace and economic growth, or a time of governmental reorganization.

Research Design and Bioecological Theory

Building on his academic training, as well as his father's encouraging approach to observation and question-raising, Bronfenbrenner argued that theory development and the research process must advance hand in hand. In the early phases of theory building, the research process takes the form of what Bronfenbrenner and Morris (2006) called the *discovery mode*, rather than the *verification* or confirmation mode. In the discovery mode, research must allow for the generation of successive studies in which the exact nature of the relationships among the process, person, and contexts is examined over time. The specific nature of the proximal process to be studied depends on the outcomes of interest; and the timing for observations depends on the particular transitions or transformations under consideration.

An assumption of the theory is that proximal processes are the most powerful forces that shape behavior, but that their impact will vary depending on characteristics of the person and features of the context. At the very least, the research design has to lend itself to statistical techniques that will unveil or reveal interactions among these levels. For example, the process of nurturing parent–infant interactions may have a general positive benefit for infant mental health; however, nurturing interactions may have a somewhat greater benefit for babies with a difficult temperament than for babies with an easy temperament; and nurturing interactions may have greater benefit for babies in single-parent homes as compared to babies in two-parent homes. The benefit of parental nurture may be more obvious in the outcomes measured in infancy and toddlerhood, and may be less salient as other features of parenting, such as effective communication or parental monitoring, become more relevant to children's psychosocial development. The research design that will advance bioecological theory must be formulated to include process contrasts across contexts, persons, and time.

NEW DIRECTIONS

In the most mature form of the bioecological theory, Bronfenbrenner emphasized the central role of proximal processes as the basic engines that account for development (Bronfenbrenner & Morris, 1998). His concern was that enthusiasm for studying the contexts of development and comparing behaviors across contexts, which was inspired in part by his earlier writings, failed to incorporate the important features of process, person, and time. New directions of the theory strive to examine specific proximal processes in order to understand how they operate in interaction with characteristics of the person in various contexts to account for developmental outcomes over time. For example, many studies have examined processes within family contexts, such as the coordination of positive, playful interactions between infants and parents; communication synchrony, mismatch, and repair; and strategies for soothing, comforting, and reducing distress. All of these processes are associated with enhanced developmental outcomes (Newman & Newman, 2015). A growing body of research is examining the bidirectional nature of parents' mental health and infant behavior, with emphasis on the social support available to adults, the nature of community resources, and the timing of intervention as factors that can impact developmental outcomes (Bornstein & Tamis-LaMonda, 2010).

The theory can be applied to development across the life span, incorporating bidirectional influences of individual development and their contexts over time. The model emphasizes the importance of the people one interacts with in key settings, especially the family, educational, neighborhood, and work settings. These settings and the quality of interactions within them are vulnerable to decisions and policies made in more distant contexts, but the heart of the theory is discovering how roles, activities, and interactions within settings contribute to optimal or dysfunctional outcomes (Bronfenbrenner & Morris, 2006). Three principles of the theory can be summarized in the following way:

Put the person at the center of the model.

Focus on the person's experiences since they are the engines of development.

Attend to the nature of relationships and experiences within and across settings.

Relatively few empirical studies have attempted to incorporate all four features of the model (Tudge, Mokrova, Hatfield, & Karnik, 2009). However, those that do include at least three of the elements are discovering the validity of the approach. First, social categories such as gender, race, or poverty are less meaningful than the detailed nature of activities and processes the person experiences on a regular basis. Second, different processes contribute to optimal versus dysfunctional outcomes. For example, harsh parenting is associated with dysfunctional outcomes; whereas responsive, synchronized parenting is associated with optimal outcomes. Third, the processes operate in distinct ways depending upon the stage of life of the person and his or her characteristics. This has led to greater exploration of the model as it applies to people of different life stages, including infants, young children, adolescents, adults, and elders (Hoare, 2009).

Bronfenbrenner urged a greater clarification of the concept of **developmental outcomes**. He suggested that ambiguity around the meaning of this term has led to confusion about the focus of life course research and stands in the way of future theory development. For example, behaviors such as graduating from high school, or being promoted to a more responsible position at work, may be indicators of life course progress, but are they appropriate indicators of development? To address this problem, Bronfenbrenner (2005/1988) offered the following features of developmental outcomes:

Psychological development is characterized by patterns of mental organization and content.

A developmental outcome is inferred from a combination of subjective experiences including mental representations, and objective behaviors. There is a functional relationship between these two aspects.

A developmental outcome implies change over time, as well as some emerging stability following the change. This relationship between a prior state, change, and an emerging new stable pattern must be demonstrated.

One or more processes must be identified that can account for the change in both subjective experience and the related behaviors. (pp. 87–88)

By offering this clarification about the nature of developmental outcomes, Bronfenbrenner hoped to guide the future direction of the theory. What is more, he suggested three aspects of research design that he expected would be essential for further clarification of the model: a contrast between at least two groups of people across at least two settings; observations of developmental outcomes over two or more points in time; and measures of both subjective as well as behavioral outcomes and their relationships. As you read further in the field of developmental science, you will find an increasing emphasis on these ideas as they inform research and intervention.

A RESEARCH EXAMPLE: SENSITIVE CARE IN TWO CULTURES

Attachment is a widely accepted developmental outcome that emerges over the period of infancy. A primary assumption of attachment theory is that the quality of the attachment depends largely on the nature of the proximal processes associated with caregiving (De Wolff & van Ijzendoorn, 1997). Sensitive, synchronous care is associated with secure attachment outcomes; unpredictable, harsh, and neglectful care is associated with insecure attachment outcomes. However, the behavioral components of sensitive caregiving and how it might be expressed in various cultures have not been explored in great detail. A study by German Posada and colleagues which contrasted maternal care in two middle-class samples, one in Denver, Colorado, and the other in Bogota, Colombia, was designed to clarify this topic (Posada et al., 2002). The study illustrates three of the key concepts of bioecological theory: process, person, and context. In this study, process is examined through observations of the qualities associated with mother–infant interactions. Person is controlled by focusing on middle-class families and infants of about the same ages, roughly 9 to 11 months. Context is reflected at the micro level by observing family interactions at home, and at the macro level by contrasting the Denver and Bogota cultural environments.

Although men's and women's roles are changing in Latin America, especially among the urban middle class, the Colombian culture is considered more collectivistic and interdependent than the U.S. culture, which is viewed as more individualistic and independent. Two questions guided the research: 1. Are the features outlined in the attachment literature that define sensitive care descriptive of care in both cultures? and 2. Are there features of care that might be unique to the specific cultures that are related to attachment security?

The researchers used an ethnographic methodology to formulate categories of maternal behaviors. Two researchers observed mother–infant pairs at home for two 2-hour visits. Following the visits, the observers used a Q-sort technique to describe the mothers' behaviors. This technique involved sorting 90 cards that describe maternal behavior into three piles: characteristic, neither characteristic nor uncharacteristic, and uncharacteristic. Each of the three piles is then further sorted into categories rated from 1 (most uncharacteristic) to 9 (most characteristic).

From this rating process, eight categories of care were identified. Four of these categories were very similar to features of sensitive care outlined in the basic attachment research: 1. sensitive responding to infant signals and communication; 2. accessibility, which reflects a mother's ability to consider the baby's needs despite other competing demands; 3. acceptance of the infant, which is reflected in the mother's positive emotional tone while interacting with the baby; and 4. interference, a mother's intrusive or non-coordinated interactions with the baby. Two categories were observed that had not been captured in the literature as related to sensitive care: active, energetic interactions with the baby; and creating an interesting environment for the baby. One category was observed in each cultural group that was unique to that culture: for the U.S. mothers it was close intimate interactions involving cuddling and close affectionate touching; for the Colombian mothers it was concern with the baby's physical appearance, including concern that the baby was getting messy during feeding and that the baby was messy or soiled during play.

Mothers from the United States and Colombia were very similar in their scores on sensitive responding, accessibility, and acceptance, and all these dimensions were predictive of infants' secure attachments. However, there were differences in the patterns of mother–infant interactions in the two cultures. Mothers from Colombia were less interfering and more active and energetic in their interactions than the U.S. mothers. Mothers from the United States were more interfering and scored higher on creating an interesting environment for the baby. Of these three dimensions, interfering was negatively related to secure attachment for the U.S. sample, but not for the Colombian sample, and being active and energetic was positively related to secure attachment for the Colombian sample but not for the U.S. sample.

The results of this study highlight several points that illustrate the value of the bioecological model. First, as the theory suggests, one needs to observe behaviors in their settings in order to appreciate the specific features of proximal processes. In this study, the abstract concept of "sensitive care" has been deconstructed to reveal the particular qualities of care that can be experienced by mothers and infants in their day-to-day interactions.

Second, certain of these proximal processes appear to have beneficial consequences for infants in both cultures. When combined with results from many other studies, these features are becoming accepted as universally supportive of the attachment process—attuned response to the infant's signals, accessibility in the face of competing demands, and acceptance—the positive emotional tone of mother–infant interactions.

Third, some proximal processes of parenting are associated with attachment outcomes in one cultural context, but not in another. In this study, being active and energetic was positively associated with a secure attachment outcome for the Colombian sample, but not for the U.S. sample. Interfering was associated with an insecure attachment outcome for the U.S. sample, but not for the Colombian sample.

Finally, some features of parenting may be culturally or contextually specific and, while important for early socialization, may not be relevant for the formation of a secure attachment. In this study, creating an interesting environment for the infant and concern for the infant's physical appearance are two examples.

Relatively few studies fully capture the four dimensions of the bioecological model. In the example provided here, two salient aspects of the theory are illustrated: process and contexts. In order to fully test the model, person variables might have been added, such as comparing the caregiving processes for infants of easy or difficult temperament. Time could be included by relating the processes to the emergence of attachment behaviors over the period from 6 to 12 months, when the mental representation of the attachment relationship is expected to crystallize.

AN APPLICATION: EVALUATING THE IMPACT OF EARLY CHILDHOOD CARE ON DEVELOPMENTAL OUTCOMES

From his early research and analysis of the literature, Bronfenbrenner was concerned about the challenges faced by children in low-income families as they entered primary school. In 1964, he testified at a congressional hearing about an antipoverty bill, arguing that initiatives to reduce the negative impact of poverty should be directed to children through the establishment of quality childcare programs. He was invited to join a panel of 13 professionals to design a school readiness program for children of poor families, in the hopes that this intervention would put children on an equal footing with those from wealthier families as they started school. The panel eventually designed the framework for the national Head Start program which began in 1965. Bronfenbrenner was effective in convincing the panel that the intervention needed to incorporate family and community contexts as well as preschool experiences. Although parent involvement in school administration and operations was uncommon at that time, it became a central feature of Head Start. The model reflects Bronfenbrenner's theoretical view, highlighting the interplay across microsystems (the mesosystem) as well as the emphasis on proximal processes that nurture physical, cognitive, social, and emotional development in early childhood (American Psychological Association, 2004).

Given the goals of Head Start, a burgeoning literature has focused on the question of how early childcare experiences impact developmental outcomes. The National Institute of Child Health and Human Development (NICHD) began a longitudinal study of the effects of early childcare in 1991 (National Institutes of Health, 2000). The primary aim of the study was to learn what impact childcare has on developmental outcomes above and beyond the influence of family and home environments. In this study, 1,300 children under 1 month of age and their families were identified as participants from ten sites across the United States. The study followed children into early adolescence, ages 14 and 15. Families varied by race, income, family structure, mother's education and employment status, and the number of hours children spent in non-parental care. The kinds of care included: care provided by grandparents and other relatives; by a non-relative in the home; in a home-based setting; and in a center. The quality of care was measured with a focus on caregiver interactions that are expected to promote positive emotions, social competence, and cognitive and language skills.

Positive caregiving was measured by observing and documenting the frequency of interaction, and then rating the quality of the interaction. The childcare settings were also measured both in terms of the guidelines recommended by governments, such as group size, child to adult ratio, and physical environment; and the caregiver's characteristics, such as formal education, specialized training, childcare experience, and beliefs about childrearing.

Drawing from these data, a recent study was able to illustrate that children with different temperaments were differentially susceptible to parenting and childcare experiences (Pluess & Belsky, 2010). The results of this research illustrate the usefulness of the P-P-C-T model for evaluating the impact of early childhood care, including Head Start and other preschool programs, for emerging developmental outcomes. In this analysis, Process is the quality of parental care and setting care. Person is the temperamental negativity of the child. Children in the NICHD sample were assessed at 6 months for differences in temperament. Children who were characterized as having a difficult temperament in infancy, especially high levels of negativity and irritability at 6 months, were compared to children who were characterized as low in negativity at 6 months. Context is the comparison of home and out-of-home settings. Time is the period from 6 months through grade 6.

In 6th grade, these two groups of children were rated by teachers on behavior problems and teacher–child conflicts. For the children who had low levels of negativity, there was no relationship between their experiences in high- or low-quality childcare and the way teachers rated their behavior in 6th grade. For the children who had high levels of negativity as infants, the experiences in high- or low-quality childcare made a big difference. If these children who had a more difficult temperament also experienced low-quality childcare in toddlerhood, they had many more behavior problems and teacher–child conflicts. If the children who had a more difficult temperament were in high-quality childcare, they had fewer behavior problems and teacher conflicts than the low-negative children, even those who had been in high-quality care. As predicted by the bioecological model, the study revealed an interaction between person and process variables. When evaluating the long-term consequences of early childcare experiences, it is important to take into account variations in children's susceptibility to environmental conditions.

HOW DOES BIOECOLOGICAL THEORY ANSWER THE BASIC QUESTIONS THAT A THEORY OF HUMAN DEVELOPMENT IS EXPECTED TO ADDRESS?

1. *What is the direction of change over the life span? How well does the theory account for patterns of change and continuity?*
    The theory suggests that the direction of development is toward increasingly complex reciprocal interactions between an active, developing person and the people, objects, and symbols that the person experiences in the immediate environment.

Patterns of change are explained by the ongoing interactions among progressively competent, skillful individuals, environments which become more diverse and challenging, and engagement with a growing network of diverse, competent, and socially demanding relationships. As the child's capacities advance, parents and other caregivers introduce new and more interesting activities, conversations, and symbolic materials that stimulate further advances.

Continuity can be explained at three levels. First, biological patterns of development typically comprise periods of stability as well as periods of change. Whether the focus is on physical development, motor skills, cognitive capacities, emotional regulation, language, or social competence, one expects to find times of equilibrium when skills are consolidating. Second, continuity can arise during periods when the mesosystem is relatively stable; these are times when there are no significant changes in the structure and demands of the combination of microsystems in which the child is participating. Finally, continuity can be viewed as the content of prior learning that is carried forward into each new activity and setting. A person's knowledge, skills, and ability to exercise control become tools that can be applied in the face of new, complex conditions. Thus, continuity might be considered a higher order feature of the way a person typically conceptualizes and experiences new activities based on memories and accomplishments from the past.

2. *What are the mechanisms that account for growth? What are some testable hypotheses or predictions that emerge from this analysis?*
   Proximal processes are the basic mechanisms that account for growth. Proximal processes are associated with activities. The following testable hypotheses are proposed (Bronfenbrenner & Morris, 2006, p. 798):

   - To be effective, the activity must take place often over an extended period.
   - To be effective in stimulating development, activities and the related proximal processes must continue long enough to become increasingly more complex.
   - The proximal process must be bidirectional; to effect development there must be influence in both directions. In interpersonal interactions, the parties must engage in reciprocal communication.
   - Proximal processes can occur with objects and symbols as well as with people. In order for these activities to promote development, the objects and symbols must hold the child's interest, and allow exploration, manipulation, elaboration, and imagination.
   - As the child's developmental competences advance, the corresponding proximal processes must become more complex in order to foster the emergence of future potential.
   - As the child matures, the intervals between increasingly complex activities can become longer and still provide appropriate stimulation for development; but they must continue to occur on some relatively regular and frequent schedule. Otherwise, development may stagnate, or possibly regress.

3. *How relevant are early experiences for later development? What evidence does the theory offer to support its view?*
   The family is the first context in which proximal processes such as feeding, comforting, playing, talking, and reading aloud take place. In order to be optimally effective, a child needs to experience a strong, positive emotional attachment to one or more adults. The formation

of emotional ties with loving adults leads to the internalization of a representation of self and other. This idea of an attachment model was explained in the section on attachment theory in Chapter 2. At the same time, this affectionate tie with a caring person contributes to the child's enthusiasm and motivation to engage in the activities that have provided the basis for the reciprocal interactions. Thus, the proximal processes, experienced in the earliest context of affection and care, become the basis for new and more complex forms of investigation and exploration.

4. *How do the environmental and social contexts affect development? What aspects of the environment does the theory suggest are especially important in shaping the direction of development?*

   Bioecological theory gives context a central role in contributing to development. The theory directs attention to the diverse settings in which a developing person participates as well as to the interconnections among settings, and the larger cultural, community, and societal contexts that influence the lives of adults and the children in their care.

   For children, the family and early caregivers are the first microsystem and most essential context. The quality of proximal processes and the nature of the close, affectionate relationships that a child experiences in the family provide the initial context for development. As the child matures, new relationships with extended family members, neighbors, peers, and childcare/school adults contribute to the complexity of activities and settings that promote development. The theory draws our attention to the question of the harmony or conflict in values, expectations, and opportunities for activity among the settings (mesosystem) and how this synergy might impact developmental outcomes.

   Beyond the settings in which the individual participates directly, the theory considers the exosystem, the contexts that impact important figures in a person's life. Stressors from the workplace, for example, may make parents less psychologically available. A change in the health status of aging parents may require more attention by adult children, thus taking time away from their parenting activities. Finally, the macrosystem, including broad societal policies and laws, social class, culture, and ethnic or religious norms and practices, is relevant for understanding the larger contexts in which development takes place.

   Human beings are remarkably adaptive, able to thrive and grow in a diversity of contexts. They can create and modify their environments. What is more, the idea of personXenvironment interaction suggests that individuals differ in their sensitivity to certain features of the environment; and that some features of environments are more facilitative for certain individuals than for others. These ideas have been influential in encouraging research that examines behavior in natural settings as well as in the laboratory, and for examining individual differences in behavior within and across settings.

5. *According to the theory, what factors place individuals at risk at specific periods of the life span?*

   Bronfenbrenner uses the term **dysfunction** to discuss the issue of risk. He defines dysfunction as follows: "The term *dysfunction* refers to the recurrent manifestation of difficulties on the part of the developing person in maintaining control and integration of behavior across situations" (Bronfenbrenner & Morris, 2006, p. 803). He contrasts dysfunction with the idea of competence, suggesting that when the person faces considerable risks, the capacity for new cognitive, physical, and socioemotional growth is restricted.

A wide range of conditions are associated with risks for dysfunction. Disruptive factors can be identified in each aspect of the model—the person, the processes, the contexts, and time. And according to the model, disruption in any one of these can produce a dynamic cascade of difficulties. Bronfenbrenner viewed certain environments as especially disruptive. He characterized them as **chaotic systems**, environments that involve frenetic activity, lack of structure and routine, unpredictability, and high levels of background stimulation that interfere with or interrupt proximal processes (Bronfenbrenner & Evans, 2000). He saw these chaotic systems operating in families, neighborhoods, schools, and work settings to undermine the optimal path of developmental competence.

Bronfenbrenner was especially concerned about the disadvantages associated with poverty and low-resource families. Conditions associated with poverty during pregnancy are likely to result in low birth weight and abnormalities which increase the risks of dysfunction. These are disruptions at the level of the person. In his view, parents in low-resource families have to devote more effort and energy to offset the risks that can lead to further dysfunction, for example poor nutrition, lack of social capital in the community, poor quality housing, and poor health care. These are risks at the level of the macrosystem which fails to provide adequate resources for low-income families. Beyond these environmental conditions, stressors in the workplace, job loss, or harsh working conditions can result in harsh or neglectful parenting which is known to be a proximal process associated with dysfunction. Other risk factors, especially violence and conflict among adults in the home, drug and alcohol abuse, and lack of social support, increase the likelihood of dysfunction.

Bronfenbrenner's enthusiasm for Head Start stemmed from the belief that policies were not likely to eradicate poverty or dramatically alter the home environment. Rather, one could provide children with a resource-rich setting that could promote competence and, at the same time, introduce parents and their children to alternative patterns of interaction that might influence the quality of proximal processes at home. Subsequent extensions of Head Start, called Early Head Start, have directed intervention to infants and toddlers under age 3, their parents, and pregnant women in poverty, to provide evidence-based, developmentally enriching care.

6. *What are some practical implications of bioecological theory?*
One of Bronfenbrenner's early lessons about science came from Walter Fenno Dearborn who told him, "Bronfenbrenner, if you want to understand something, try to change it" (Bronfenbrenner, 1995, p. 606). This wisdom is at the heart of the practical implications of bioecological theory. Once you decide on the behavior you wish to change, for example reducing bullying in school or promoting civil behavior among students, the theory guides the direction of planning and intervention by raising the following questions: What are the key processes involved? What person characteristics evoke the behaviors in question? Where does the behavior take place? How do contexts support or discourage the behavior? What other related systems, such as family, neighborhood, religious, peer group, or employment systems, influence the behavior? What kinds of changes can you observe in the behavior over time—both historical changes in the long term and moment-to-moment changes over a day or week? Answers to these questions will help guide the design of interventions.

From its beginnings, the theory has been situated in concerns about real-life experiences including parenting, early childcare, education, and peer group relationships. The theory now informs professional development in a diverse range of fields including education, social work, family therapy, counseling, nursing, organizational development, human resources, and management training. The theory guides the design of interventions to consider the way environments influence a person's experiences, the interaction of person characteristics and environmental demands, and change over personal and historical time. In preparing individuals for transitions, such as the move from preschool to kindergarten, from high school to college, or promotion to management, the bioecological model is useful for helping to orient the person for shifts in proximal processes and context-related changes in resources and demands.

CRITIQUE OF BIOECOLOGICAL THEORY

Strengths

Bioecological theory made a significant impact on the study of development, especially child development. The theory laid out an expanded map of the environments in which activity takes place, as well as the more remote environments that might affect adults who are providing care. What is more, this perspective of "nested environments" led to greater attention to the congruence or tension across environments, and the notion that individuals adapt their behavior to multiple contexts.

As he worked on and revised the theory, Bronfenbrenner identified four components that interact: the process, the person, the contexts, and the timeframe, including both developmental time and historical time. This analysis addresses the reciprocal interactions between children and their caregivers. The analysis was expanded to address other reciprocal relationships, such as workers and supervisors, or students and teachers, where experiences and activities become the central engines that support or impede development. This model is both simple and complex; simple in identifying just four components that account for development, and complex in that each of the four components can have a great diversity of variables which create the possibility of complex interactions and multiple developmental pathways.

The model highlights the importance of looking at experiences within settings. Just naming contexts, like home, school, or work, is not adequate. One must begin to identify the specific proximal processes that take place, with the assumption that these processes might occur in settings that have the same name (like classroom or neighborhood) but differ greatly in their social characteristics, patterns of interactions, and organizational rules for behavior.

In early writings, Bronfenbrenner argued strongly for the importance of observing behavior in natural settings. Behavior observed in the laboratory cannot be generalized to other settings, such as home or school. This does not mean that laboratory research has no place in the study of development, but that it should be complemented by observations of similar processes in real-life contexts.

The view of the person changing and encountering changing contexts over time inspired new efforts to conduct large-scale longitudinal studies, such as the NICHD longitudinal study of early childcare, the national longitudinal surveys (NLS) of labor market activities and other life events from high school to adulthood, and the longitudinal studies of aging (LSOA), a multicohort study of persons 70 years of age and over designed to measure changes in health, functional status, living arrangements, and the use of health services. These and other studies have been guided by the PPCT framework to consider how transitions across time and contexts are navigated by people at different points in development.

The theory has had great appeal for its practical value in informing intervention and guiding professional training in fields of social work and counseling practice. Sensitivity to issues of personXenvironment interaction has proven to be a key feature of counselor training. Unfortunately, the implications of the theory for considering how policies and practices in one setting impact the processes in other related settings have not been integrated into many of the key contexts such as work–family, or school–home. The home and family settings continue to be vulnerable to larger corporations, agencies, and institutions that, through their egocentric goals, often ignore the negative consequences of their policies and practices on the equilibrium of family life.

The theory deals with relatively large areas of science, bringing together concepts from psychology, sociology, history, and anthropology. The theory is stated in testable propositions. Bronfenbrenner's concepts are frequently cited as a framework for research, although the full PPCT model is not often tested.

Weaknesses

In the PPCT model, the construct of Person is not very fully elaborated. In contrast to other theories, such as evolutionary theory, psychoanalytic theory, or psychosocial theory, bioecological theory is limited in detail about the motives, inner mental life, or worldview that might influence a person's ability to cope with environments. In contrast to cognitive developmental theory or cognitive social-historical theory, this theory does not offer a guide about the direction of normative changes in self-understanding, reasoning, or other aspects of competence over time.

A similar criticism can be directed to the concept of Process. Despite the emphasis on the importance of proximal processes as the driving force in the model, the theory leaves the exact nature of these processes open to investigation. For a theory of development, one expects to see more specific targeting of central mechanisms that contribute to advancing competence in one or more domains. Of all the possible activities and experiences one can imagine, which ones are most essential to promoting developmental outcomes at a particular time of life?

The variable of time is also left unspecified. The theory suggests that in order for proximal processes to influence development they must occur on a regular basis over a relatively long period of time. However, the theory does not specify any approach to considering time or timing. This is especially significant when the goal is to understand patterns of continuity and change.

Although the theory builds on the term "ecology," it does not incorporate many of the ideas that are part of biological ecology or ecological psychology in characterizing settings. For example, concepts such as population density/crowding, diversity of activities permitted in a setting, population turnover, adequacy of resources and cycling of resources, or boundaries and access to settings are not discussed. At the level of the mesosystem, the theory does not address the fact that some contexts are more powerful or influential than others. For example, the early childcare research has found that parenting practices and family environment are consistently more important predictors of behavioral outcomes than quality of childcare settings.

Given the comprehensive nature of the theory, relatively few studies have been designed to explore the interactive features of the full model. Even within the idea of contexts, few studies have examined the interrelationships among the multiple microsystems in which a person functions, and the consequences of continuity or discontinuity within the mesosystem. Table 10.1 summarizes the strengths and weaknesses of bioecological theory.

Table 10.1 Strengths and weaknesses of bioecological theory

Strengths	Weaknesses
Major influence on the study of child development, especially by providing a new perspective on contexts of development and nested environments.	The construct of Person is not fully elaborated. Limited detail about the nature of important psychological processes such as motivation, emotion, and goals.
The concept of proximal process captures the importance of reciprocal interactions among individuals and the people, objects, and symbols in their environments.	The theory does not provide a guide about the direction of development with respect to cognition, reasoning, or self-understanding.
The model is both simple (four basic factors) and complex (each factor can encompass a diverse array of variables).	Lack of clear specification about the essential proximal processes for supporting developmental outcomes at particular periods of life.
Highlights the importance of describing the proximal processes that take place within settings. These processes may differ across settings that have the same name or label (e.g. classroom or workplace).	Although time is a key factor in the model, the variable of time lacks specificity. Issues such as the importance of timing in relation to emerging competence, or the amount of time needed for experiences to have their desired impact, are not addressed.
Emphasizes the importance and value of observing behavior in natural settings.	The theory fails to incorporate many ideas from biological ecology and psychological ecology that are useful in characterizing the nature of environments.
The model inspired new initiatives in longitudinal studies that focus on development in changing contexts.	The theory lacks any way of evaluating the relative importance of one setting over others in the mesosystem.
Practical value in guiding the design of interventions and professional training across many fields.	Relatively few studies have been designed to examine the full model and the interaction among factors.
Integrates ideas from many fields.	
Ideas are stated in the language of testable hypotheses.	
The model is frequently cited as a framework for research in human development.	

CRITICAL THINKING QUESTIONS AND EXERCISES

1. Compare the discovery approach to research to the verification approach. What are two examples of when the discovery approach might be preferred, and two examples of when the verification approach might be preferred?

2. Design a study that takes into account all four components of the PPCT model. What developmental outcome would you focus on? How would you identify the critical process variables and the significant time periods for this outcome? Try to be specific about the nature of the contexts and person variables as well.

3. The theory assumes that individuals are in multiple microsystems (mesosytem). In immigrant families, it is not uncommon for parents to have traditional expectations from their culture of origin that are different from expectations for behavior that are operating in the neighborhood, peer group, or school. What are the consequences for developmental outcomes when these environments have conflicting expectations for behavior? Under what conditions might competing or conflicting demands and expectations in the mesosystem promote competence and cognitive complexity? Under what conditions might competing demands and expectations in the mesosystem contribute to dysfunction?

4. Head Start is a large, national program that is conceptually consistent with the basic PPCT model. Can you think of any other programs, not necessarily directed at early childhood, that might be consistent with this model? The program does not necessarily have to be operating at the national level; it might be a community, religious, college, or work-related initiative. It might be a program that strives to offset disadvantage, or one that strives to build new or enhanced strengths. Identify the elements of the program that fit the PPCT model and the developmental outcomes the program is intended to address.

5. Thinking about the case of Marie, how could you use the components of the bioecological theory to evaluate and inform a decision about whether an aging adult should remain in his or her home, or move to an assisted living environment?

6. If you were designing an assisted living facility, how would the bioecological model inform decisions about the physical environment, staff training, daily programming, and services? Sketch out a plan for an assisted living facility that addresses each of these issues from a bioecological perspective.

KEY TERMS

chaotic systems	macrosystem
context	mesosystem
demand features	microsystem
developmental outcomes	person
dispositions	process
dysfunction	resources
ecological niche	setting
ecology	time
exosystem	

RECOMMENDED RESOURCES

**Bronfenbrenner, U. (2005). *Making human beings human: Bioecological perspectives on human development*. Thousand Oaks, CA: Sage.
An edited volume of many of Bronfenbrenner's papers over his career, from 1942 to 2001.

**Bronfenbrenner, U. (1995). The bioecological model from a life course perspective: Reflections of a participant observer. In P. Moen, G.H. Elder, & K. Luscher (Eds.), *Examining lives in context: Perspectives on the ecology of human development* (pp. 599–618). Washington, DC: American Psychological Association.
Bronfenbrenner reflects on the features of his own life including childhood, education, military experiences, and early work experiences as they influenced his development as a scientist and the formation of his theory.

** U. Bronfenbrenner interview. The SRCD oral history project. This interview can be downloaded from www.srcd.org/sites/default/files/documents/bronfenbrenner_urie_interview.pdf

Glen Elder interviewed Uri Bronfenbrenner in 1998 as part of the SRCD oral history project. This is a transcript of the interview, covering many aspects of his personal experiences and the way they influenced his thinking.

REFERENCES

American Association of Family and Consumer Sciences (2012). AAFCS Fast Facts. History. Retrieved on August 31, 2014 at http://us1.campaign-archive2.com/?u=bee11993ef54296c205934b97&id=d267c11ab2#member

American Psychological Association (2004). Early intervention can improve low-income children's cognitive skills and academic achievement. Retrieved on September 12, 2014 at www.apa.org/research/action/early.aspx

Bornstein, M.H. & Tamis-LaMonda, C.S. (2010). Parent-infant interaction. In J.G. Bremner & T.D. Wachs (Eds.), *Wiley-Blackwell handbook of infant development: Vol. 1. Basic research* (pp. 458–482). Malden, MA: Blackwell Publishing.

Bronfenbrenner, U. (1979). *The ecology of human development: Experiments by nature and design*. Cambridge, MA: Harvard University Press.

Bronfenbrenner, U. (1995). The bioecological model from a life course perspective: Reflections of a participant observer. In P. Moen, G.H. Elder, & K. Luscher (Eds.), *Examining lives in context: Perspectives on the ecology of human development* (pp. 599–618). Washington, DC: American Psychological Association.

Bronfenbrenner, U. (2005). Interacting systems in human development. In U. Bronfenbrenner (Ed.), *Making human beings human: Bioecological perspectives on human development* (pp. 67–93). Thousand Oaks, CA: Sage. (Originally published in 1988 in N. Bolger, A. Caspi, G. Downey, & M. Moorehouse (Eds.), *Persons in context: Developmental processes* (pp. 25–49). New York: Cambridge University Press)

Bronfenbrenner, U. & Evans, G.W. (2000). Developmental science in the 21st century: Emerging theoretical models, research designs, and empirical findings. *Social Development, 9,* 115–125.

Bronfenbrenner, U. & Morris, P.A. (1998). The ecology of developmental processes. In W. Damon & R.M. Lerner (Eds.), *Handbook of child psychology: Vol. 1. Theoretical models of human development*. 5th ed. (pp. 993–1028). Hoboken, NJ: John Wiley & Sons.

Bronfenbrenner, U. & Morris, P.A. (2006). The bioecological model of human development. In R.M. Lerner & W. Damon (Eds.), *Handbook of child psychology*. 6th ed. Vol. 1. *Theoretical models of human development* (pp. 793–828). Hoboken, NJ: John Wiley & Sons.

Bubolz, M.M. & Sontag, M.S. (1993). Human ecology theory. In P.G. Boss, W.J. Doherty, R. LaRossa, W.R. Schumm, & S.K. Steinmetz (Eds.), *Sourcebook of family theories and methods: A contextual approach* (pp. 419–450). New York: Springer.

Cornell University (2014). Cornell University College of Human Ecology, History. Retrieved on August 30, 2014 at www.human.cornell.edu/about-our-college/facts/history.cfm

De Wolff, M.S. & van Ijzendoorn, M.H. (1997). Sensitivity and attachment: A meta-analysis on parental antecedents of infant attachment. *Child Development, 68,* 571–591.

Egerton, F.N. (2013). Contributions: History of ecological sciences, part 47: Ernst Haeckel's ecology. *Bulletin of the Ecological Society of America, 94,* 222–244.

Haeckel, E.H.P.A. (1866). *Generelle Morphologie der Organismen. Allgemeine Grundzüge der organischen Formen-Wissenschaft, mechanische Begründet durch die von Charles Darwin reformirte Descendenz-Theorie. Vol. II: Alllgemeine Entwickelungsgeschichte der Organismen*. Berlin, Germany: GeorgReimer.

Hoare, C. (2009). Models of adult development in Bronfenbrenner's bioecological theory and Erikson's biopsychosocial life stage theory: Moving to a more complete 3-model view. In M.C. Smith & N. DeFrates-Densch (Eds.), *Handbook of research on adult learning and development* (pp. 68–102). New York: Routledge.

National Institutes of Health (2000). The relation of child care to cognitive and language development. *Child Development, 71,* 960–980.

Newman, B.M. & Newman, P.R. (2015). *Development through life: A psychosocial approach*. 12th ed. Stamford, CT: Cengage Learning.

Pluess, M. & Belsky, J. (2010). Differential susceptibility to parenting and quality child care. *Developmental Psychology, 46,* 379–390.

Posada, G., Jacobs, A., Richmond, M.K., Carbonell, O.A., Alzate, G., Bustamante, M.R., & Quiceno, J. (2002). Maternal caregiving and infant security in two cultures. *Developmental Psychology, 38,* 67–78.

Rosa, E.M. & Tudge, J. (2013). Urie Bronfenbrenner's theory of human development: Its evolution from ecology to bioecology. *Journal of Family Theory & Review, 5,* 243–258.

Tudge, J.R.H., Mokrova, I., Hatfield, B.E., & Karnik, R.B. (2009). Uses and misuses of Bronfenbrenner's bioecological theory of human development. *Journal of Family Theory and Review, 1,* 198–210.

11

Dynamic Systems Theory

CHAPTER OUTLINE

GUIDING QUESTIONS

- What is a system? What are some properties of systems that allow them to adapt to changing environmental conditions?
- What is meant by openness of a system? How would you characterize the degree of openness of a system? How is this related to the process and capacity for change?
- What are some similarities and differences between dynamic systems theory and bioecological theory?
- What is meant by the idea of attractor states? How is this idea relevant to the study of development?
- What is unique in the explanation of development in dynamic systems theory that leads to the use of terms such as emergence and probabilistic epigenesis? What are three basic principles of change embodied in the concept of emergence? How do they help account for how new outcomes come into being from preexisting components and subsystems?
- What conditions prompt or promote adaptive self-organization?

CASE VIGNETTE

Robbie just turned 13. Throughout middle childhood, he had been very interested in baseball. He spent hours with his father developing his throwing and batting skills, and learning the subtleties of the game. He loves to read the sports pages and knows a lot about the major league teams and players. One of his most cherished activities is to go to the major league games with his dad where he proudly sports his team shirt and cap.

To everyone's surprise, recently, Robbie has become involved in musical theater. One of his friends encouraged him to try out for a community production, and he discovered that he was very good at it. What is more, he really likes the group of kids who are involved and the way they all encourage and support each other. One of the girls in the acting group began to take an interest in him. She texted him frequently, made plans to hang out after rehearsals, and invited him to go to the movies with a group of friends. For two months, Robbie thought they were "dating" but then on St. Patrick's Day, she "dumped" him. This was a surprise to Robbie, and although it did make him feel bad it didn't dim his enthusiasm for musical theater. He is rethinking his desire to play baseball in 8th grade, and has tried out for the drama program at his school.

In the last few months, Robbie has begun to spend more time alone in his room, responding with some intensity when his younger brother wants to come in to borrow something or just hang out. He has trouble falling asleep, and gets drawn into online games late into the night. In the last 3 months, he has grown 2 inches, and his mother has noticed that he is developing other signs of physical maturation—body odor, pubic hair, and muscle cramps.

Lately, he has been experiencing some conflicts about his desire for independence and his continued desire to remain close to his mother and father. His friends seem to be much more carefree and ready to loosen their ties to their parents. In his community it seems that kids gather at one another's houses after school when no adults are home, but Robbie still wants to be home with his family when they are there. He knows he is growing up; but he wonders if he is ready for everything that the world of teenage life is going to send his way.

Dynamic systems theory introduces the idea of **emergence**, a view that development is a probabilistic outcome of the interaction of processes at many levels and many systems. The theory encourages a view of development as shaped by forces both within and outside the person merging and influencing each other to produce new capacities and behaviors. Rather than seeking origins or causes for behavior, the theory broadens the explanatory landscape by examining the interplay of micro level (e.g. cellular or hormonal factors) and macro level systems (e.g. beliefs, parenting styles, or community norms) that play a role in an emerging capacity.

The case of Robbie illustrates the dynamic systems associated with puberty. New interests and talents surface at the same time as Robbie is experiencing pubertal growth. Changes in peer relationships and family dynamics are accompanied by changes in physical growth, sexual maturation, and emotional expression. Robbie's transition into puberty can be appreciated as a product of biological, psychological, family, peer group, and community factors, each contributing to the experiences of this time of life. One can imagine that the nature of pubertal transformations would differ for each person, depending on such factors as timing, sequencing, family dynamics, and community or cultural support. The qualitative changes of puberty are both normative and highly individual, shaped by genetic factors, hormonal levels, family and peer contexts, as well as cultural and community norms.

Over the course of development, there is both continuous and qualitative change. Continuous change can be seen, for example, in the increase in the number of words in a child's vocabulary, or the increase in height as a child grows in inches. Qualitative change can be seen as an infant's locomotor abilities change from slithering or crawling to walking; as gestures, babbling, and one-word utterances are integrated into grammatically correct sentences; and as visual and motor information are integrated in order to perform effective reaching and grasping. Dynamic systems theory (DST) attempts to explain how new, complex patterns or properties of behavior come into existence as a result of simpler components or processes that are already part of a system. It also seeks to address the reality of both variability and pattern in development. The theory can be applied to all systems from the microscopic level of cells to the macroscopic level of societies. Development is understood as the result of multiple, mutual, and continuous interactions among all levels of a developing system from the molecular to the cultural. A unique feature of the dynamic systems perspective is the premise that development is not guided by an executive, hierarchical plan either at the biological or the environmental level, but emerges as a result of moment-by-moment actions on many levels at once.

Whereas most students who have studied development come to understand that you need to take many variables into account in order to explain behavior, dynamic systems theory goes beyond this notion. It claims that the processes that may account for behavior, such as a child's genetic potential, neurological processes, physical characteristics, parenting strategies, family structure, and personal goals and motives, are inseparable; they are not independent causal factors in development. For example, the theory suggests that you cannot separate a child's characteristics and his or her parents' parenting strategies as distinct causal factors in the development of behaviors. We will discuss this idea further in the review of research about antisocial behavior. This notion of the ongoing interplay among related factors is why the approach is nonreductionistic and nonlinear. As such it challenges many deeply held views about the processes that account for change. The idea of interdependence across many levels and domains, and the probabilistic nature of developmental outcomes, will be illustrated in the chapter through a variety of concepts and examples.

HISTORICAL CONTEXT

Dynamic systems theory has roots in several fields. Systems theory, which explores the dynamic interrelationships among components of a system, was first elaborated by Ludwig von Bertalanffy in his book, *General Systems Theory*, in 1968. Von Bertalanffy acknowledged his historical debt to philosophers of the 1600s as well as to scientists working in the field of cybernetics in the 1940s and 1950s. One of the key concepts of dynamic systems theory is **self-organization**, the idea that the organization of an open system will transform itself into a more complex, effective system without guidance by outside forces. This idea was first presented by Descartes (1637), who suggested that the ordinary laws of nature tend to produce organization. The concept was expanded by naturalists of the eighteenth century and revived by modern scientists who noted that there are laws of physics and chemistry that guide the form and growth of biological systems.

The term *self-organizing* was introduced by W. Ross Ashby in 1947 and became linked to general system theory as a way of characterizing how systems emerge from simpler to more complex forms or patterns of behavior. The process of self-organization has been noted in physics, chemistry, mathematics, and in both the biological and social sciences (Kauffman, 1993). Within the study of development, Esther Thelen has been recognized as explicitly applying dynamic systems theory to the analysis of motor development, particularly in her analysis of infant stepping and walking. This work then led to a consideration of principles from dynamic systems theory that could be applied to cognitive development (Smith & Thelen, 1993; Thelen & Smith, 1994; Thelen, Schöner, Scheier, & Smith, 2001).

The application of dynamic systems theory to cognitive development was also undertaken by Kurt W. Fischer and Thomas R. Bidell in the 1980s and 1990s (Fischer, 1980; Fischer & Bidell, 1998). They criticized the field of cognitive science that dominated the literature at the time, citing the lack of theoretical concepts to account for the wide variability in age of acquisition of certain concepts, variability in the sequence of acquisition of concepts, and the tendency to want to explain action and thought through a reductionistic focus on lower-level systems including genes, neural networks, or biochemical process. Fischer and Bidell offered an alternative approach to understanding cognition as comprised of organized structures that are both active and adaptive as they manage the variability that is present in the environment. Cognition emerges like a web in which

> the strands are not fixed in a determined order but are the joint product of the web builder's constructive activity and the supportive context in which it is built . . . The separate strands in a web represent the various pathways along which a person develops. (Fischer & Bidell, 1998, p. 473)

Thus, dynamic systems theory offers a view of cognition as both structured and variable, a product of action adapted to the constraints and affordances of the environment.

Gilbert Gottlieb (1991, 1998) was one of the leading scholars who provided an integrated view of developmental systems theory, introducing the term **probabilistic epigenesis**, which considers the "mutually influential relations among genes, behavior, and contexts" (Hood, Halpern, Greenberg, & Lerner, 2010). Trained in a combined Ph.D. program in psychology and zoology at Duke University, his work has inspired a burgeoning approach to collaboration among biologists, ecologists, and psychologists. Gottlieb proposed that development occurs as a product of influences on many levels at once including the genetic, neural, behavioral, and the physical, social, and cultural environments. These forces are bidirectional and coactional. Drawing on a wide range of evidence from diverse fields, Gottlieb illustrated that development is not predetermined but highly variable and influenced by ongoing adaptations across levels.

At present, many subfields in human development are looking to dynamic systems theory to provide an overarching explanatory framework to help organize disparate observations about developmental change. Beyond the areas of motor development and cognition, the perspective has been applied to executive functions, infant language, emotion and personality development, moral development, temperament, parenting, and developmental psychopathology (Lewis, 2000; Lerner and Fisher, 2013). The hope for developmental systems theory is that it can lead to more accurate analysis of the points or periods of development, and characteristics of individuals that are especially sensitive to particular environmental characteristics, resulting in alterations in the emergence of capacities in order to promote optimal functioning.

KEY CONCEPTS

In this creative new approach to understanding development, four big ideas are signposts that help to illuminate a highly complex framework: *systems* and the nature of open systems; *emergence*; *self-organization*; and *nested timescales*. The following section provides a discussion of these ideas and the implications of these ideas for approaching the study of development.

Systems

Any **system**, whether it is a molecule, a neuron, an organ, an individual, a family, or a corporation, is composed of **interdependent elements** that share some common goals, interrelated functions, boundaries, and an identity. The system cannot be wholly understood by identifying each of the component parts. The processes and relationships of those parts make for a larger coherent entity; the whole is more than the sum of its parts. The language system, for example, is more than the capacity to make vocal utterances, use grammar, and acquire vocabulary. It is the coordination of these elements in a useful way within a context of shared meaning. Similarly, a family system is more than the sum of the characteristics and competences of the individual family members. Families are a composite of a sense of common destiny and the genetic heritage of the spouses and their developing children. As spouses develop or create their own composite heritage, this "we-ness" of communication patterns and reciprocal role relationships identifies the family. Common destiny, genetic heritage, patterns of communication, and reciprocal role relationships may be modified and elaborated as a family attempts to survive and undergo transformations.

A **dynamic system** is one that continuously changes in order to carry out its functions and to preserve its equilibrium or balance. A goal of dynamic systems theory is to understand the many interconnected relationships within the system and between the system and other living and nonliving systems that can explain the variability and direction of change over time. Fischer and

Rose (1999) described the assumptions that underlie the approach of dynamic systems theory as a lens for understanding the development of human activity.

> First, many influences come together to form the emergent properties of human action and thought. Second, a person is a self-organizing system who regulates these combinations based on feedback from both the immediate world in which the activities are embedded and his or her previous experiences and activities, especially those immediately preceding the activity to be explained. In other words, a person constructs activities, regulating the combination of influences that produce those activities through dynamic processes that centrally involve feedback from the immediate world and prior experience. (Fischer & Rose, 1999, pp. 198–199)

Taking a systems perspective on human development, one must think of the many domains that contribute to individual functioning including: biological; cognitive; personality and temperament; values, attitudes, beliefs, and expectations; knowledge and skills; and social relationships. One must also consider these domains as they contribute to the behavior of the other significant individuals (each also a system in his or her own right) with whom the individual interacts. These individuals are then embedded in a variety of systems, and surrounded by systems that have an impact on the individual and his or her network of relationships.

Figure 11.1 offers a developmental systems perspective for a single child–parent relationship. The individual child and the individual parent form a relationship that can be viewed as a system. The individuals and their relationship are embedded in and influenced by specific community, societal, cultural, and designed and natural environments all changing over time (Lerner, 2002, p. 211). This diagram of a child–parent system is intended to give you a glimpse of the comprehensive view of development that is implied by the dynamic systems perspective. What you cannot discern from the figure is that the individuals and the adjoining systems as well as society and culture are all changing over time, and they are changing at different rates. What is more, they are influencing each other to varying degrees.

The challenges of dynamic systems theory for development are: 1. to trace a pathway from one point in time, when the individual is functioning at a less mature level, to a later point when the individual is functioning at a more mature level; and 2. to identify the salient factors in the comprehensive array of interrelated systems that play the most significant roles in accounting for this change. This requires a detailed analysis of the many aspects of the behaviors in question, and an investigation into which aspects of each component are changing at specific times that may contribute to reorganization and growth.

A system cannot violate laws that govern the functioning of the parts, but at the same time it cannot be explained solely by those laws. Biological functioning cannot violate the laws of physics and chemistry, but the laws of physics and chemistry do not fully explain biological functioning. Similarly, children's capacities for cognitive growth cannot violate the laws of biological functioning, but biological growth does not fully explain quality of thought or the nature of action. A unique consideration of dynamic systems theory is a focus on the structure that provides organization and stability among the components within a system. This theory strives to resist tendencies toward reductionism, arguing that complex human thought and action cannot be adequately understood by compartmentalizing the components and analyzing them separately.

For example, a child's attempt to engage a parent in conversation cannot be understood by looking separately at verbal skills, purposive behavior, parental identification, and attachment.

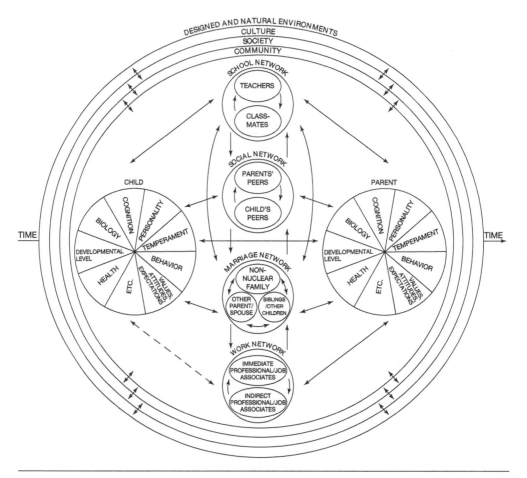

Figure 11.1 A Developmental Contextual View of Parent–Child Relations

Source: Copyright ©2001, CCC Republication. Lerner, R.M. (2002). *Concepts and theories of human development*. 3rd ed. Taylor and Francis Group LLC Books. Reprinted by permission.

The idea of a conversation is in itself a dynamic process that does not reside in either the child or the parent, but is part of their relational system. What is more, the quality of a conversation is influenced by the language, culture, and norms of the family as well as by the neurological, physical, and cognitive capacities of the partners and their motivations and goals for interaction. Even a brief conversation is supported by an enormous barrage of neural activity that occurs outside of awareness. This neural activity permits individuals to attend to, understand, and respond to one another. Each word or phrase in a conversation is itself an event that contributes to the next, thereby leading to an emergent structure of communication and shared meaning.

Open Systems. As we think about individuals, families, communities, schools, and societies, we are dealing with open systems. Ludwig von Bertalanffy (1950, 1968) defined **open systems** as structures that maintain their organization even though their parts constantly change. Just as the water in a river is constantly changing while the river itself retains its boundaries and course, so the molecules of human cells are constantly changing while the various biological systems retain their coordinated functions. Extending this analogy, as we think about human development, we strive to understand how it is that the psychology of the person is constantly changing, yet development follows a patterned course and the person retains a sense of self-sameness from moment to moment.

Open systems share certain properties. They take in energy from the environment; they transform this energy into some type of product that is characteristic of the system; they export the product into the environment; and they draw upon new sources of energy from the environment to continue to thrive (Katz & Kahn, 1966). This process requires an open boundary through which energy (or information) can pass and products (or waste) can be exported. The more open the boundary, the more vigorously the process operates. Each specific system has a unique set of processes that are appropriate to the particular forms of energy, product, and transformations relevant to that system.

In a family, for example, an open or permeable family boundary is responsive to stimulation and information from within and outside the family. This openness allows the family to use input for healthy adaptive growth and change. A closed family boundary does not allow for interchange and adaptive responses to the environment. In the analysis of systems, one focuses more on the processes and relationships among the parts that permit a system to take in and transform energy in order to survive and grow rather than on the characteristics of the parts themselves.

Properties of Open Systems. Open systems are, by their very nature, always in a process of change. Open systems move in the direction of adjusting to or incorporating more and more of the environment into themselves in order to prevent disorganization as a result of environmental fluctuations (Sameroff, 1982). Systems theory attempts to identify processes that help to explain how a system retains its functions while continuing to integrate new information from the environment and adjoining systems. Ervin Laszlo (1972) proposed four properties that help explain how systems balance stability and change:

1. *The whole is comprised of relationships among component parts.* The parts themselves do not comprise the whole; rather, it is the relationships and interactions among the parts that create the identifiable whole.
2. *There is a tendency for systems to resist change and to retain their identity and functions.* The property of **adaptive self-stabilization** addresses the ability of a system to make internal modifications of the relationships among component parts in response to changes in the environment.
3. *All systems exist in relationships with their environment.* Under conditions of **homeostasis**, the system and the environment are in balance. Changes in the environment are monitored by the system, internal relationships are modified, and the system's functions are preserved.
4. *Systems have **feedback** mechanisms that allow them to reduce the impact of wide variations in the environment on the internal balance of the system's components.* The more information the system is required to monitor in the environment—for example, changes in temperature, visual information, auditory information, and interpersonal communications—the more internal adjustments are required. The complexity becomes even greater when there is an interdependence among the components or subsystems—for example, when feedback from visual information, auditory cues, and olfactory cues are all needed in order to assess the safety of an environment.

Basic Open System Model

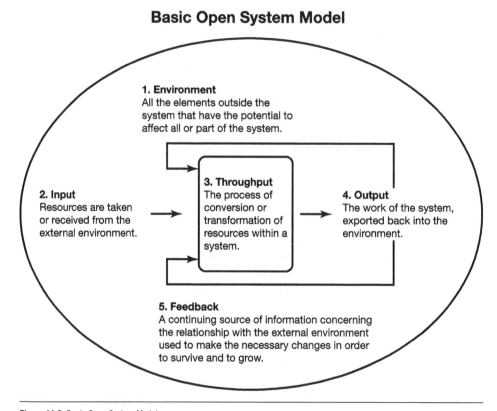

Figure 11.2 Basic Open System Model

Source: Helen Maupin, Basic open system model. www.rightojoy.com. Retrieved on August 20, 2014. Reproduced with permission.

Complex systems are especially vulnerable to environmental changes that might disturb the homeostasis. As a result, sensitive regulatory mechanisms, referred to as positive and negative feedback, are needed to preserve the relationship of the system and the environment. **Positive feedback** amplifies a variation and contributes to accelerated change in the same direction. For example, if a person is making a presentation and you say, "I can't hear you," the person will speak louder. If you say, "I still can't hear you," the person will speak even louder. Saying "I can't hear you" provides positive feedback to increase the speaker's volume. **Negative feedback** reduces deviations from the norm and supports stability. For example, when the oxygen level of the environment is reduced, you tend to grow sleepy. While you sleep, your breathing slows and you use less oxygen.

Some examples of adaptive self-stabilization are managed unconsciously by the organization of biological systems. Others are managed more deliberately by efforts to minimize the effects of environmental changes. Most systems have a capacity for storing or saving resources so that temporary shortages do not disrupt their operations. The process of self-stabilization allows the system to resist changes in the environment, and return to a desirable steady state.

Whereas self-stabilization describes a process of resisting environmental change, **adaptive self-organization** is a process of emerging changes in response to new external conditions. To the extent that the system cannot assimilate new information or buffer the subsystems from environmental changes, new subsystem relationships or new subsystem functions must emerge.

Organization is essential in order to sustain life. Consider the steps involved in performing simple tasks such as getting dressed or making a meal. One plans, selects necessary resources, implements the plan, monitors the progress, and makes minor changes based on feedback. This level of organization allows for goals to be achieved with efficiency and minimal effort. Human beings are active, adaptive organisms that are able to create new forms of organization when existing structures prove to be ineffective.

System Hierarchies and Attractor States.   Two features of systems' adaptive self-organization are **system hierarchies** and attractor states. Systems will develop in the direction of an increasingly hierarchical structure in which subsystems are organized into stable, specialized functions. The higher levels of the system have greater diversity of function, each one being comprised of subsystems that have more limited functions. One can think about spoken language as a hierarchical system that is comprised of subsystems including phonetics, syntax, grammar, and pragmatics. The system of spoken language and its subsystems work in a close interrelationship where the higher-level system draws on all the sources of meaning in the subsystems to produce meaningful communication.

Dynamic systems theory uses the term **attractors** to refer to recurrent patterns or stable states that emerge through the coordination of lower-level system elements into higher order organizations. These attractors are the organized patterns toward which change is likely to move. They are a result of many processes operating together that constrain and support each other in a given and recurring direction. Attractors are emergent processes that do not rely on a biological plan; they are likely but not fixed directions of change.

Living organisms have multiple attractors. For example, in the study of parent–child relationships, one might characterize a relationship as having four attractor states: positive playful, neutral question and answer or information sharing, negative conflictual, or disengaged. Over the course of many thousands of interactions, one could trace the amount of time spent in these four attractor states, the frequency and time spent in these states under various conditions, and the probability that time spent in one of these states at Time 1 would predict time spent in that same state at Time 2. As a relationship develops over time, some attractor states may become deeper, less vulnerable to environmental influences, and as a result, constrain future interactions (Granic & Patterson, 2006). One of the contributions of dynamic systems theory is the idea of considering an individual or a relationship system as having multiple attractor states rather than characterizing a person or a relationship as being of one type or another.

Emergence

In contrast to theories that use terms such as *learning, growth,* or *construction,* dynamic systems theory uses the term **emergence** to characterize the process of developmental change. The theory focuses on how new forms or properties come into existence as a result of ongoing processes that are found within the system itself. Larger patterns or capacities arise through interactions among smaller or simpler forms that do not have these properties themselves. The resulting emergent property or structure is novel, and cannot be reduced to the features of the simpler forms (Kelso, 2000; Clayton & Davies, 2006).

Developmental change is viewed as probabilistic rather than fully predictable. Human beings are always in action and always in a dynamic relationship with a changing environment. Even in sleep, mental activity, motor activity, sensation, and perception are functioning and reactive to changing environmental conditions. Human beings also have complex capacities for memory, including motor memory, sensory memory, narrative memory, spatial memory, and memory for specific information. Finally, humans have a variety of strategies for gaining information about the environment including sensory/perceptual systems, emotional reactions, verbal and nonverbal communication, information processing capacities, tools and measurement devices. In the course of planning and executing any action, there is ongoing feedback between multiple, interacting levels of information. The emergent or qualitatively new behavior is a result of the interaction of these levels over time.

The study of motor development has led the way in illustrating the usefulness of a dynamic systems model for the study of the emergence of new motor behaviors (Metzger, 1997). Although the normative patterns of motor development suggest a sequence of stages that is heavily guided by genetics and neural structures, research on the process of motor development has challenged this view. The regularities in motor behavior are better understood as a result of a dynamic process of exploration in which infants coordinate their physical actions with the demands and opportunities of the situation. Perception and action work hand in hand, giving the infant information about the physical properties of the situation and feedback about the consequences of specific motor strategies. Over time and with practice in similar situations, the infant discovers the combination of action, intensity, direction, and speed that will create the desired outcome. With additional practice, this pattern then becomes more likely and increasingly efficient (Thelen, 1995).

Principles of Change. The process of emergence is guided by three underlying observations about change (Miller & Coyle, 1999):

1. In the early phase of an emergent process, small differences or effects can have consequences that result in large differences or effects later.
2. A small change causes changes throughout the system.
3. The accumulation of small quantitative changes can lead to qualitative change as one of a number of related skills passes a certain threshold and contributes to the integration of what seems to be a qualitatively different skill.

An observational study of the emergence of infant crawling illustrates these points (Goldfield, 1989). Crawling requires coordination of head and shoulder movement, reaching, kicking, alternation of arms and legs over various types of surfaces, and ongoing feedback from each preceding action to guide the subsequent action. Fifteen infants were observed as they made the transition to crawling. Most babies reach a point when they rock in a stationary position on all fours before they can crawl. But at some point, they are able to move from a seated position to crawling. Illustrating the three ideas above, researchers found that the establishment of a strong hand preference was needed and had to occur before the system of crawling behaviors could unfold. This small change in the use of one hand over the other, which one might not intuitively associate with the emergence of a new locomotive skill, actually contributed substantially to the new behavior. This illustrates the idea that change in one component of the system will bring about changes throughout the system. When infants fell from a seated position onto their hands, they tended to fall onto their nonpreferred hand so that the preferred hand was available to reach out and begin crawling. Confidence in being able to maintain one's body weight on one arm and two legs while reaching out with the preferred hand was part of the motor sequence necessary for forward crawling. The gradual strengthening of hand preference was eventually integrated with other motor skills which resulted in the new behavior of crawling.

Each new motor capacity permits exploration in a more varied environment. As a result, infants have to be able to make immediate assessments of the relationship between their physical abilities and the environmental conditions in order to decide whether to avoid action, take familiar actions, or try to invent some new, adapted action. Evidence for this flexibility can be seen in a study of ways that babies experiment with moving along a descending slope or slide. Some try going down headfirst and then roll over onto their backs; others try to go down with a crab-like crawl and then switch over to their bottoms; and others refuse to go down the slope, waiting for someone to carry them off the device (Adolph & Eppler, 2002). From a dynamic systems approach, knowing how to cope with a new environmental challenge is a convergence of perceiving, moving, and remembering as each of these processes evolves over time in response to the specific properties of the task and its match with the person's current physical capacities (Thelen et al., 2001).

Self-Organization

As discussed above, adaptive self-organization is one of the central characteristics of a dynamic system, and perhaps the most essential concept relevant for explaining the emergence of qualitatively new behaviors.

> Dynamic systems theorists claim that all developmental outcomes can be explained as the spontaneous emergence of coherent, higher-order forms through recursive interactions among simpler components. This process is called *self-organization*, and it accounts for growth and novelty throughout the natural world from organisms to societies to ecosystems to the biosphere itself. According to principles of self-organization, these entities achieve their patterned structure without pre-specification by internal rules or determination by their environments. (Lewis, 2000, p. 36)

No single theory about how self-organization operates is accepted across disciplines or within the field of human development. However, the concept has been used to consider the spontaneous emergence of order and new levels of complexity in physics, chemistry, mathematics, biology, psychology, economics, and the study of human social groups (Lewis, 2000; Kauffman, 1993; Kelso, 1995). In efforts to define and study self-organization, three criteria should be considered: 1. The level of organization should be different before and after self-organization has taken place; 2. The level of complexity in the system should increase, that is, more information is required to predict the behavior of the system after a process of self-organization has occurred; and 3. It should be possible to demonstrate that the new organization is internally caused, not purely a consequence of some external force or requirement (Eoyang & Conway, 1999; Shalizi, Shalizi, & Haslinger, 2004).

Certain conditions appear to prompt or initiate self-organization. When systems are in a state of **disequilibrium**, or disorganization, there is a tendency for the overall organization of the system to change. The concept of disequilibrium suggests that there are circumstances when the adaptive functions of the system are not adequate to address current fluctuations either internal to the system (e.g. a breakdown in the coordination of components) or external to the system (e.g. novel conditions, or sudden depletion of resources). When an open system is in disequilibrium, a process takes place that directs energy to the elements of the system in order to achieve a new order or relationship. When this new arrangement has the impact of moving the system toward equilibrium, it is amplified through positive feedback and repeated at higher system levels. The overall organization of the system increases, achieving new levels of complexity and the emergence of new behaviors. New patterns at the level of the components or subsystems and new patterns at the larger system level reinforce or maintain each other, creating a condition in which the qualitatively new behavior is sustained from the "bottom up" and from the "top down" (Lewis, 2000).

Life is a process of periods of equilibrium and disequilibrium. At every level, from the firing of neurons to efforts to perform purposeful work, thousands of actions and reactions internal to the human system are being coordinated with events in the ever-changing environment. It is easy to consider how readily this complex being might encounter disequilibrium (Shalizi, 2010).

Humans are active, goal-oriented life forms (Swenson, 1997). Disequilibrium is often produced as a result of this active, goal-striving nature, and is resolved by this same characteristic. Disequilibrium can be experienced at the physical level, as when a child's desire to ride a tricycle is incompatible with his leg length and muscle strength. Disequilibrium can be experienced at the cognitive level, as when a child's concept or scheme does not adequately match real-world experiences or help to predict the consequences of action. Disequilibrium can be experienced at the interpersonal level when a teenager wants to be included in a group that does not offer membership. Disequilibrium can be experienced at the level of identity, when the roles that are available to the young adult are not a match with the person's values, goals, and beliefs. At each point, a process of change is set in motion in order to reestablish equilibrium in the system. Often, this results in the establishment of a new pattern of behavioral or cognitive organization.

Not all self-organization is preserved; sometimes it is the stimulus for the next step in self-organization. As systems become more complex, they become more sensitive to environmental variations and require more finely tuned internal mechanisms in order to preserve equilibrium (Sameroff, 1982). For most human beings, the result of self-organization is a more flexible, efficient way of functioning. However, in some cases the new organization is not effective. It cannot be sustained by lower-level components, requires more energy or resources than are available, or may interfere with the person's ability to manage daily tasks and sustain interpersonal relationships. Over time, this may interfere with other systems and subsystems (Sameroff, 1995).

Nested Timescales

In a dynamic system comprised of numerous subsystems, change takes place in different timescales (Smith & Thelen, 2003). On average, neurons may fire once every 5 milliseconds, but recognition of a stimulus may require hundredths of a second. A simple arithmetic problem might be solved in a few seconds, but the analysis of an algebra problem may require several minutes or longer. Development of skilled behaviors may advance slowly over days or months, with many years devoted to the eventual accomplishment of high levels of expertise. In the study of various aspects of behavior, one is likely to consider change within a specific timescale. For example, development of stimulus recognition and response in hundredths of seconds, or development of reaching and grasping in the weeks and months of early infancy. But for the organism, these timescales must be integrated and nested within one another, from the fastest and most frequent changes at the neural and cellular levels to the slowest processes required for the maturing self-understanding and wisdom.

Social interactions, which may last hours or longer, include individual behaviours, such as language, which occur over the course of seconds to minutes. Behaviours are driven by cognitive mechanisms like memory and categorization, which operate on sub-second time scales. These cognitive mechanisms are implemented in the brain, where neurons operate on a time scale of milliseconds. (Garzón, Laakso, & Gomila, 2008, p. 143)

In dynamic systems theory, the study of emergence has to consider the interactions of systems that function at different timescales, each of which can impact the others.

The concept of **nested timescales** has been incorporated into studies of emotional flexibility and rigidity. Hollenstein and his colleagues describe three timescales for emotional flexibility: 1. Micro flexibility, which is the moment-to-moment fluctuations in emotion; 2. Meso flexibility, which refers to emotional changes in response to changes in the situation or context; and 3. Macro flexibility, which reflects flexibility over months or years as a product of developmental regulation, biological maturation, and life events (Hollenstein, Lichtwarck-Aschoff, & Potworowski, 2013). In the study of deviant behavior, evidence suggests that emotional rigidity may be a precursor to developmental psychopathology. Emotional rigidity may be associated with an insensitivity to changing environmental demands. Moreover, children who are unable to express and regulate a flexible range of emotions may experience a limited range of coping behaviors (Granic, 2005).

NEW DIRECTIONS

Dynamic systems theory lays out a complex, multidimensional framework for explaining both variability and patterns or order in the developing system. Kurt W. Fischer and his colleagues have extended the theory with a focus on examining the development of thought and action as they emerge within physical contexts and social relationships (Fischer & Yan, 2002). Over the past 30 years, their work has evolved to guide new research and application. Among the many new insights he and his colleagues have brought to the study of development, three constructs are highlighted here: a new metaphor for conceptualizing the development of dynamic structures underlying thought and action—the constructive web; a focus on a new unit of analysis—the dynamic skill; and a way of measuring both long-term development and short-term change—a scale of behavioral complexity.

The Constructive Web

Fischer and Bidell (2006) begin with a focus on the variability of human thought and action. They argue that people understand their experiences through action that has many components and occurs in a specific physical, social, and cultural context. This perspective shares many features introduced in Chapter 9 in the discussion of cultural historical activity theory (CHAT). In order to capture the variability, flexibility, and change that are characteristics of human behavior, one needs a model of psychological structures that is equally dynamic.

Fischer and Bidell (2006) suggest that in many theories of development, psychological structure is conceptualized as a ladder with a fixed set of steps arranged in a fixed sequence. Development is characterized as movement "up" the ladder from one level of organization to the next. The problem with this view is that the metaphor of the ladder does not capture the observed variability in human behavior, both within a single individual across tasks, conditions, and settings, and across individuals and cultural groups. The metaphor of the ladder also suggests that there is a predetermined series of steps with little room to account for emergent or novel structures. Recall from Chapter 4 that Robbie Case struggled with this similar problem of how to incorporate both diversity and pattern in cognitive development. His solution was to introduce the idea of central conceptual structures which vary across domains.

In contrast to the metaphor of a ladder, Fischer and Bidell offer the metaphor of the **constructive web** as a way of thinking about the underlying structure of development (Fischer & Bidell, 2006). The value of the web metaphor is that it helps to conceptualize the many possible trajectories for development both within and across individuals. A web is constructed through the active, goal-oriented efforts of the actor in conjunction with the supportive structure of the physical and social contexts. Just as a spider adapts its web to the convenient edges of a bench, a doorway, or a branch, the developing pattern of dynamic skills is a result of actions adapted to a specific context.

The separate strands of a web suggest different components of development, with some strands interlocking with others thereby supporting or strengthening each other. For example, the skills of reading and the skills of mathematics are distinct and develop though different trajectories. However, when children have to comprehend written instructions in order to complete a mathematics assignment or solve word problems, reading skills and mathematics skills are both required and may strengthen each other.

The strands of a web may start and end at many points in the web. The strands representing one developmental component may emerge at different times and in a different order than the strands of another component. The idea of multiple trajectories suggests that children may start out along different pathways and end up at the same point. For example, children begin crawling and pulling to a standing position at different ages and in different sequences. In some cultures, exploratory crawling is not permitted. Thus, children may arrive at upright walking through different pathways and using different motor strategies. Similarly, two children growing up in very different family and community environments, one in the suburbs and one in a very poor urban center, may arrive at the same college and be roommates.

The web metaphor also suggests diverging pathways. Two children may grow up in very similar, low-resource communities, play together and spend a lot of time together in childhood, and attend the same elementary school. Yet, they can experience very different academic pathways— one dropping out of school before graduating from high school and the other going on to college.

A strand may be fragile in its first construction, and be strengthened through repetition or adding of fibers. It may be strong in its initial construction and be weakened as a result of isolation from other related strands or build-up of strands in another part of the web. This view of development helps to conceptualize the idea of *possible selves*. People can imagine possible outcomes and directions, and elect to pursue a direction by strengthening certain skills, ignoring some aspects of the self in order to enhance others, and modifying the structure in light of new opportunities or goals. The strength of the web is supported by underlying patterns of organization including the symmetry in shape, spatial relations among the strands, and effective connectivity to its context. "The web highlights integration, specificity, multiple pathways, active construction, and other central properties of skill development" (Fischer & Bidell, 2006, p. 325).

Dynamic Skill

One way that theories make their contribution to the study of human development is by focusing on specific behaviors that illustrate the processes that are central to the theory. Freud drew attention to free association, dreams, and slips of the tongue as behaviors that provide insight into the unconscious. Social role theory highlights the concept of social roles as constructs that link individuals' expectations, goals, and behaviors with those of their community. Erikson described a state of tension between the competences of the developing person and the demands of the environment that led to a psychosocial crisis. Vygotsky focused on the word as a way of linking the person and the social environment, as well as thinking and speech. Following in this line of theory building, Fischer introduced the idea of **dynamic skill** as a way of integrating the many features of dynamic systems theory (Fischer, 1980). "Skill is the capacity to act in an organized way in a specific context. Skills are thus both action-based and context specific" (Fischer & Bidell, 2006, p. 321).

The study of skills provides a framework for exploring many of the principles of dynamic systems theory. Skills are actions that take place in specific contexts. One uses the skill of manipulating a fork for eating, not to type on a computer. Skills can be of varying levels of complexity, from carrying a tune to playing poker. In each case, they have a developmental trajectory—the skill begins in some rudimentary form of action which may mature to increasingly high levels of performance. Skills are both context-specific and culturally guided. The skill of managing a fork for eating is valued in most Western cultures; however, chopsticks are the preferred tool in many Eastern cultures.

The term *dynamic skills* suggests that skills are changing as they become more advanced; they are also integrated with other skills which may permit new, more complex skills. Each skill is comprised of systems that must work together in order for the skill to be effective. For example, the use of a fork for eating requires hand–eye–mouth coordination; judgments about the consistency and size of the food; and understanding cultural practices for eating. Once the basic skill of using a fork becomes well established, it can be integrated into more complex skills such as cutting food with a knife and a fork; or the use of a fork in food preparation. The systems that contribute to one skill, such as hand–eye coordination, may contribute to more than one skill; and these contributing skills may develop at different rates, thus explaining why a skill may change slowly and then seem to advance to a new level rather suddenly.

Skills are self-organizing. Skills, by their very nature, are goal-oriented actions designed to perform specific functions in a particular environment. They depend for their effective functioning on the interpenetration or integration of several components that regulate each other. As the goals or the contexts for skill performance change, the skills may be modified or integrated with other skills to produce new behavior. For example, think about playing the piano as a skill. The original goal is to create music through the use of this specific instrument. Many components are required in order to play, including: memory, auditory perception, manual dexterity, rhythm, and the ability to read music. As one area improves, the level of playing may improve so that the notes are smoother, more rhythmic, and more "musical." At some point, simple tunes are replaced by more complex compositions requiring new fingering, more complex rhythms, faster speed, and coordinated use of right and left hands.

As the technical challenges of playing the piano are mastered, the person begins to build a repertoire of pieces and introduces emotion, interpretation, liveliness, and a personal voice into the music. Now, the skill of playing the piano becomes a means of self-expression, and the entertainment of others. People gather round to hear the playing; the person is invited to parties to entertain others; and perhaps the person begins to think that playing the piano is a skill that could be lucrative. Piano playing is combined with other business-related skills in order to schedule gigs, advertise, and record music for sale. The person has self-organized the activity, integrating the original skill for playing the piano with other entertainment skills and entrepreneurial skills that form the basis of a musical career.

Scale of Behavioral Complexity

Fischer and Bidell point out that in order for developmental science to advance, researchers need a common scale along which to measure change. The classic examples for measurement in the physical world are the Centigrade and Fahrenheit scales for measuring temperature. These scales can be used for measuring the temperature of a wide range of substances—such as water, air, and the human body. Fischer and Bidell (2006) created a scale for the measurement of **behavioral complexity** that could be applied across many types of skills. This common scale permits one to distinguish small continuous changes as well as growth spurts; and it suggests the direction of growth across three tiers, from action to representation to abstraction. The use of such a scale requires frequent measurements that can capture the shape of a growth curve, including the possibility of capturing both smooth growth and sudden jumps or shifts.

The scale is presented in Figure 11.3. It provides a way of thinking about dynamic skill development as comprised of three tiers and ten levels. The tiers are quite similar to Piaget's stages of sensorimotor, preoperational, and formal operational thought. The first tier of any skill begins with actions. Within the action tier, there are three levels: single actions, mapping, and systems. As a system of action is created, it is transformed into a single representation of the action that then is mapped to other representations and forms a system of representations. This system is transformed into an abstraction which is mapped to other abstractions and forms a system of abstractions, much like the operations involved in Piaget's formal operational reasoning.

Let's look at an example. As an infant, Donny uses his fingers to pick up little Cheerios from a bowl and put them in his mouth. His mother uses a spoon to put food into his mouth, and he experiments with using a spoon to pick up little Cheerios from the bowl. The actions of self-feeding with fingers and spoon-feeding are mapped on each other. This leads to a system of using

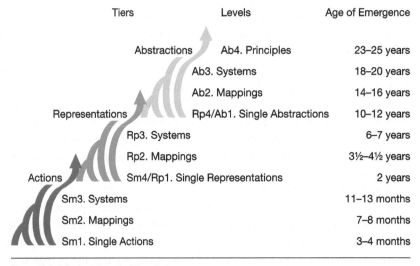

Figure 11.3 A Scale of Behavioral Complexity

Source: K.W. Fischer and T.R. Bidell (2006). Dynamic development of action and thought. In W. Damon & R.M. Lerner (Eds.), *Handbook of child psychology: Theoretical models of human development: Vol. 1.* 6th ed. (pp. 313–399). New York: Wiley. Copyright © 2006, John Wiley and Sons.

a spoon to feed himself. This system of self-feeding brings the action tier to a close. Now Donny has a dynamic skill for self-feeding that can be represented through speech, and imaginary activities.

Let's say that Donny has a dog. He observes that the dog eats from a bowl on the floor without a spoon. He now pretends to eat from a bowl on the floor. He has mapped the idea of his own eating behaviors and the dog's eating behaviors. He begins to understand that he eats, his mother and father eat, and his dog eats. There is a system of representations about eating that is emerging as the child connects the actions of eating and the representations about eating to an abstract idea about the requirement that living things must eat. This leads to observations and interests in how various living things eat, with the opportunity to read about eating behaviors among various animals and to study the ethology of eating.

As a young adult, Donny may become interested in the possibility of conducting research about the conditions that influence eating behaviors. He identifies a set of interrelated domains that influence eating, including sensory, perceptual, motor, cultural, and interpersonal dimensions that create a system of eating behaviors. Within this system, Donny recognizes the importance of the early experiences of self-feeding in infancy as a factor that guides subsequent eating behavior. He goes on to discover new principles about eating behavior, based on his own eating skills, his observational skills, and his research skills.

The **behavioral complexity scale** includes a three-step structure that is repeated at each tier. Skills merge with other skills or interpenetrate other skills to form new systems. One can imagine a person as having a wide variety of skills, some at the early tier of action and others more fully developed at the tier of representation or abstraction. At the tier of abstraction, a person may decide that new skills are required in order to move from the level of a single abstraction to a system of abstractions. Thus, skills can be deliberately nurtured in the service of other skills. The principle of self-organization is reflected in the transformation of the skill from a single action to a system of actions, from a single representation to a system of representations, and from a single abstraction to a system of abstractions. At each point, the system may look qualitatively distinct from the single level from which it emerged.

A RESEARCH EXAMPLE: THE A-NOT-B ERROR

Students of child development will readily recognize the game that Piaget (1954) described in *The construction of reality in the child*, that has become the prototype for the study of the **A-not-B task**. An adult hides a toy in location A. After some repetitions, an 8- to 10-month-old infant will successfully retrieve the toy at location A. Then, the adult hides the toy at a nearby location, B, while the infant watches. After a brief delay, infants are given the chance to retrieve the toy. At 8 months, infants will reach for the toy at location A even though they saw it being hidden at location B. By 12 months, infants search for the toy at location B. The task has been studied repeatedly with similar findings—12-month-old infants appear to know something about objects and retrieval of objects that 8-month-old infants do not. Piaget suggested that this capacity was related to mental representation of objects, and he linked the successful retrieval to his concept of object permanence.

Using the perspective of dynamic systems theory, Esther Thelen and her colleagues explain how the A-not-B error is an "emergent product of multiple causes interacting over nested timescales" (Smith & Thelen, 2003; Thelen et al., 2001). Their approach requires a detailed analysis of the components of the task, including looking, reaching, and remembering. It also integrates assumptions about neural activation of perceptual cues and the memory traces associated with each trial. On the first trial, even before the toy has been hidden, the infant is aware of the toy and the hiding locations. When the experimenter places the toy in location A, neurons associated with spatial location are activated. When the infant reaches toward location A, neurons associated with that spatial location are activated, along with a new memory of the action. Over each trial, the activation of location A is strengthened as a result of both the hiding cues provided by the experimenter and the memory of the previous reaching and finding efforts. Thus, for younger infants, the decision to reach to location A becomes self-stabilizing. For older infants, the activation of spatial location neurons at location B are just a bit stronger, allowing them to override the neural memories of location A over the slight delay in searching.

Now the experimenter provides a cue to indicate that the toy is going to be hidden in a new spot. If the infant is required to wait a bit before searching, the memory of actions at A become stronger than the perception of the toy being hidden at B and the infant searches at A. However, Thelen and her colleagues have shown that if the infant is able to search at once, without any delay, they do not make the error. What is more, a variety of manipulations can make the error come and go for infants at 8 or 12 months. For example, 8- to 10-month-old infants who sat down during the first phase of the experiment were supported to a standing position to watch the hiding at location B. These infants did not make the error; they went right for the toy at location B. In another experiment, infants wore heavy wrist weights while reaching on the A trials and light wrist weights on the B trials. These infants did not make the A-not-B error.

The research illustrates several principles from dynamic systems theory. First, just a small difference in the activation of spatial location neurons and memory can make a difference in the perseveration of reaching in this task. Second, the changes in behavior are a product of changes at many levels including spatial memory, experiences with various objects in the environment, and even real-life searching and finding. Third, a behavior that may appear to be stable can be modified by real-world variations. Finally, the sequence of everyday activities, such as reaching and retrieving an object, contributes a history of actions that impact the next actions.

The A-not-B task and its analysis have important implications for other, more complex aspects of cognitive problem solving including the study of spatial cognition (Spencer, Austin, & Schutte, 2012). Think about the last time you tried to recall where you left something—your keys, a notebook, or your cell phone. Many subsystems are involved in efforts to locate an object: visual memory of the object; a cognitive map of the environment relative to your own body and movements; some kind of working memory of the last time you had the object; and some way of updating or revising your search process as you move from one location to the next until the object is found. The search process is often accompanied by emotions, possibly anxiety, anger, or frustration, which may increase arousal or interfere with concentration.

And suppose that you have misplaced this item in the past. You have learned from past experience where you were most likely to have left the item as well as some search strategies that have worked before. So prior learning, which builds up slowly over time, contributes to current perception and search strategies. When you are successful in finding the item, you may experience relief or joy which further strengthens your memory of this process and its outcome. From the dynamic systems perspective, the emergence of new capacities for complex problem solving is a product of real-time, moment-by-moment events nested in longer-time learning trajectories which may look very uneven and variable as they unfold (Schutte & Spencer, 2010).

AN APPLICATION: A DYNAMIC SYSTEMS MODEL OF ANTISOCIAL DEVELOPMENT

An extensive literature addresses the etiology of antisocial behavior including the study of individual, family, and community contexts that give rise to aggressive and antisocial development, how **antisocial behavior** is maintained and transformed over time, and clinical approaches to prevention and intervention. Studies of bullying, externalizing behaviors, peer violence, peer rejection, harsh parenting, and child abuse and neglect are just a few areas that focus on the causes or consequences of antisocial development. A well-established line of research in this field is the work of Gerald Patterson on **coercion theory**, a model of how parents and children train each other through sequences of interactions so that the child's behavior is likely to become increasingly antisocial and aggressive, and the parents become increasingly unable to manage or regulate their child's aggressive behavior (Patterson, 1982; Reid, Patterson, & Snyder, 2002).

Isabela Granic and Gerald Patterson (2006) applied the dynamic systems theory perspective to an understanding of the etiology of antisocial behavior, extending coercion theory and providing new ideas about how to identify young children who are at risk for the establishment of antisocial behavior patterns. Several ideas from dynamic systems theory guided their research. First, they explore the process through which day-to-day, ongoing interactions contribute to the emergence of more complex systems of behavior. Second, they use the idea of attractors to characterize several types of stable patterns of parent–child interaction. Third, they introduce the idea of cascading constraints. This term refers to the fact that once behaviors are organized as attractors, these attractors become structured and resist change. Therefore they serve to constrain future behaviors. This idea captures the reality that an attractor is both the result of interactions that occur before the behavior has stabilized and the cause of behaviors that occur once the attractor has been formed.

You can think of parent–child interactions as creating a landscape of attractors, that is, the preferred patterns of interaction. Parents and their children typically have a variety of patterns of interaction that can be observed in different settings and for different purposes. For example, parents and children might be observed to be playful and humorous, engaged in some kind of problem solving, mutually supportive and encouraging, hostile, or disengaged. Each of these patterns is a possible attractor, depending on the specific nature of the parent–child dyad. Under normal conditions, parents and their children shift from attractor to attractor depending on the circumstances. Granic and Patterson (2006) hypothesized that interactions that were mutually hostile would be a strong attractor for children who are at risk for antisocial behavior, and that the parent–child interactions in these dyads would be more rigid than those of nonaggressive dyads.

To test these hypotheses, Granic and Lamey (2002) observed parents and their clinically referred children during 6 minutes. In their first 4 minutes, the parent and child were asked to discuss a difficult problem. Then there was a knock on the door and the parent and child were asked to use the next 2 minutes to wrap up their discussion and try to end on a positive note. The parent's and child's behaviors were marked on a coordinated grid. Every second, each partner's behavior was coded as hostile, negative, neutral, or positive. Using this method, one could trace the coordinated trajectory of the discussion as the pair moved from one type of interaction to another. For example, both the parent and the child could be hostile, the child could be negative and the parent could be neutral, or both the parent and the child could be positive. This type of interaction grid allows one to characterize the trajectory of interactions as well as the most frequent types of interactions over a fixed period of time. In this study, shifts in the quality of interaction before the intrusion of the knock on the door and after were observed. Granic and Lamey (2002) found that children who had been referred with externalizing problems, that is, tendencies to blame others, act aggressively to others or see the cause of their problems as due to people outside themselves, had parent–child interactions that tended to settle into two main attractors: hostile (child hostile–parent hostile) and permissive (child hostile–parent neutral or positive).

The second phase of this research linked the day-to-day quality of interactions to an emerging pattern of antisocial behavior. Researchers hypothesized that for those children who were on a path toward antisocial behavior, the hostile attractors would begin to constrain the interactions, and that parents and children would become more rigid and less able to adapt to changing environmental conditions (Hollenstein, Granic, Stoolmiller, & Snyder, 2004). This is the application of the idea of a cascading constraint to parent–child relationships.

Kindergarten children at risk for externalizing problems and their parents were observed for 2 hours in a variety of contexts including having snacks, playing games, solving academic problems, and talking about conflicts. The interactions were coded as positive engagement (humor, affection), neutral (talking, asking or answering questions), negative disengagement (sadness or fear), and negative engagement (anger or contempt) (Granic & Patterson, 2006). Interaction grids were created for each dyad and the following two indicators of rigidity were established: the number of times the dyad moved from one cell or characteristic type of interaction to another; and the mean length of time the dyad spent in each type of interaction. The more rigid parent–child dyads showed less frequent changes in their patterns of interaction and spent more time overall in specific types of interaction.

In order to link these data on moment-to-moment interactions with the emergence of developmental trends, teachers' reports of the child's antisocial behavior were collected at the beginning of kindergarten, the end of kindergarten, the beginning of first grade, and the end of first grade. Children whose externalizing scores were in the top 10% of the group at each time period were compared to the remaining 90%. There were no differences in rigidity scores between the top 10% of children and the remaining 90% at the first measurement. However, at each subsequent measurement, rigidity in parent–child interactions significantly predicted which children were rated in the top 10% of externalizing problems. What is more, the children whose externalizing scores were high and remained high or whose externalizing scores increased over the 2 years of kindergarten and first grade had more rigid parent–child interactions than those whose scores declined or were low and remained low.

As predicted by dynamic systems theory, the research was able to link the micro-level analysis of patterns of rigid parent–child interaction with an increasingly stable orientation toward externalizing problems. The results demonstrated that the tendency toward antisocial behavior was not a product of genes, personality traits, bad parenting, etc. One cannot separate the child and the parent as causal factors. Antisocial behavior is a product of ongoing interactions of parents and children that rely on complex systems of behavior comprised of stable patterns of interactions such as negative-negative or negative-neutral. Once the attractors emerge, they become increasingly structured and resist change, predisposing the child toward similar kinds of interactions in other kinds of social relationships.

The research suggests a potential approach for early intervention. A system-based intervention, described as the Family Check-Up (FCU), has been found to effectively reduce family conflict and increase parental support (Gill, Dishion, & Shaw, 2014). As a result, the intervention reduces parents' reports of children's problem behavior among young children as well as adolescents' reports of antisocial behavior (Dishion, Brennan, Shaw, McEachern, Wilson, & Jo, 2014; Smith,

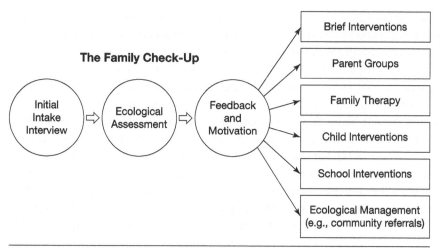

Figure 11.4 The Family Check-Up

Source: Child and Family Center, University of Oregon. Retrieved on August 24, 2014 at http://cfc.uoregon.edu/intervention-fcu.htm

Knoble, Zerr, Dishion, & Stormshak, 2014). The FCU is comprised of three elements: 1. An initial interview in which the consultant learns about the family's needs, acknowledges the individuality of each family member, and begins to clarify the family's concerns in order to evaluate how they can best serve the family; 2. An ecological assessment involving a home visit and an assessment of the child's adjustment to school; and 3. Feedback and motivation to guide future services and action including areas of family practice and behaviors that are strengths as well as areas that may benefit from services (see Figure 11.4).

HOW DOES DYNAMIC SYSTEMS THEORY ANSWER THE BASIC QUESTIONS THAT A THEORY OF HUMAN DEVELOPMENT IS EXPECTED TO ADDRESS?

1. *What is the direction of change over the life span? How well does the theory account for patterns of change and continuity?*

   The direction of change is toward increasing complexity as higher-level systems emerge from lower-level components. One of the central contributions of the theory is its ability to account for both continuous and discontinuous change. The system has a capacity for self-stabilization that supports continuity. When the system is in an attractor state, it is buffered from minor alterations or modifications that might result in change. However, under conditions of significant disequilibrium, the system also has a capacity for self-organization through which new, more adaptive characteristics emerge. The theory assumes that the nature of development involves many systems interacting in a coordinated way all of which are changing over time. This view promises a more detailed and subtle view of continuity and change than many other theories of development.

2. *What are the mechanisms that account for growth? What are some testable hypotheses or predictions that emerge from this analysis?*

   All living systems are characterized by a capacity for self-organization, the spontaneous emergence of coherent, higher order forms through recursive interactions among simpler components. The individual person is influenced by participation in other systems including relationships, families, communities, schools, and work settings. Thus, the tendency toward self-organization in any one or more of these systems can be a factor in stimulating the process of self-organization of the individual.

A central hypothesis of dynamic systems theory is that new forms of organization can be accounted for by understanding the interactions among components of the system that are precursors or forerunners of the eventual new behavior. Even in behaviors that might be viewed as stable, like walking or talking, differences can be observed in moment-by-moment interactions. These differences, though slight, can become the basis for developmental change (Fogel, 2011). For example, a child's gait, that is the pattern of moving forward, may be considered a stable feature. However, in observing children walking, one can see that every step is not the same; gait will vary depending on the type of surface, the incline, and whether the child is trying to carry something or push or pull something. From these variations, one can see the seeds of new forms of locomotion, like running, hopping, skipping, and jumping.

The combination of action and task demands, with feedback between expectancies and outcomes, brings about change. One does not need to rely on a preexisting, genetically guided plan or an environmentally orchestrated goal in order to account for change. One simply needs to identify the critical parameters along which change is taking place and the changes in essential limit-setting components that will bring about a phase shift.

One can think of a person as a maturing system with multiple attractors or organized patterns of cognitions and behaviors that change over time. Each attractor provides a model or forecast of what will happen following an action. With multiple forecasts and outcomes emerging from various attractors, there is an opportunity to observe which forecasts are most accurate and which are followed by discrepancies. When the events following an expectation are discrepant from the forecast, the person experiences surprise, an emotion that can produce the energy needed to move away from one attractor and toward another attractor (Metzger, 1997). Continuous feedback among expectations, actions, and the consequences of action contributes to the process of growth and patterns of change.

3. *How relevant are early experiences for later development? What evidence does the theory offer to support its view?*

The theory assumes that complex behaviors and new patterns of behavior emerge from preexisting components which are undergoing change. Early experiences are critically relevant for later development in three different ways. First, the theory assumes that each new action is influenced in part by the memory of previous actions. If the task and the context remain the same, the preceding action will most likely be repeated. Second, early experiences provide the elements or system components from which more complex behaviors emerge. In the example of crawling cited earlier in the chapter, hand preference is an early component of infant crawling. The timing of a clear hand preference will influence the onset of crawling. Complex behaviors are a result of the coordinative interaction of many subsystems. One or more of them must reach a certain level of maturation or functioning in order for the more complex behavior to emerge.

Third, the notion of attractor states suggests that some patterns or organizations of behavior become more stable and likely than others. Whether one is focusing on language, motor behavior, concept development, or relationships, once the child or the parent–child system establishes a few stable attractor states, these states become the most likely forms of behavioral organization, thus constraining subsequent behaviors. The theory does not specify which parameters or components are the critical precursors for each subsequent new behavior; nor does it specify the nature of attractor states across domains since those are not fixed, but emergent. However, it suggests that early experiences will hold the key for understanding each step in subsequent behavioral organization.

An illustration of this process is provided in the discussion of antisocial behavior and parent-child interactions. In families where the attractor states are both hostile and permissive, children are observed to exhibit more problem behaviors. Particularly in families where these attractor states become rigid, they constrain subsequent behavior, leading to an increase in antisocial behavior over time. However, with intervention such as the family check-up, the attractor state is reconstituted through the introduction of new information, emphasis on family strengths, and alternative parenting strategies. Alternative attractor states, especially positive interactions, become more likely, parent–child conflict decreases, and antisocial behavior decreases.

4. *How do the environmental and social contexts affect development? What aspects of the environment does the theory suggest are especially important in shaping the direction of development?*
According to dynamic systems theory, all actions take place in some context. Dynamic skill development, for example, is effective action that is adapted, through feedback processes, to the changing demands of the situation. New behaviors emerge when certain components needed for the expression of the behavior move beyond a critical value or level. The slowest or last component to reach a critical value is called the **control parameter**. In walking, a control parameter might be the muscle strength needed to lift one leg off the ground overcoming the forces of gravity. In driving a car, a control parameter might be the community's decision to require drivers to reach the age of 16 before qualifying for a driver's license. The goal is to understand the control parameters, the way they are integrated and mutually constrain each other, and the key changes in the required components that result in qualitatively new actions. There is no formal difference between control parameters that originate in the individual or in the environment.

The emphasis on moment-to-moment behavior as it takes place must consider the nature of the environment or setting in which the behavior occurs. Infant walking is adapted to the surface on which the steps are taking place. Parent–child interactions are constrained by the setting and the other people who are present. Communication between couples will differ depending on whether it is face-to-face, on the phone, or through email. One of the challenges in studying behavior change is to consider the specific features of the environment that may constrain or facilitate behavior.

Our typical approach to characterizing environments—for example, saying that behaviors take place in school, at home, or at the childcare center—may be too general or global to capture the important features of the environment that serve as control parameters for a particular behavior. Just as individuals can be thought of as being comprised of multiple, interacting systems, so are environments multidimensional. Schools, businesses, and governments are all complex dynamic systems which can be investigated using the principles of dynamic systems theory.

5. *According to the theory, what factors place individuals at risk at specific periods of the life span?*
In infancy, neurological impairments, sensory and motor impairments, and lack of access to diverse sensory and motor experiences are all potential risk factors. At the same time, parents

play a key role in supporting and scaffolding infant development such that factors including unresponsive, harsh, erratic, or neglectful parenting can be conditions of risk. The parent–child relationship is highlighted as a dynamic system that provides the early context for physical, cognitive, emotional, and social development. Any factors that introduce rigidity in this relationship or that disrupt the relationship can create substantial disequilibrium for the developing child.

At each period of life, phase transitions or periods of disequilibrium are times when the person is more vulnerable to fluctuations in adjoining systems that can influence the organization or stability of behavior. These transitions include entry into childcare, school transitions, moving to a new community, birth of a sibling, puberty, job change, marriage, entry into parenthood, death of a parent or loved one, or serious illness. At any of these times, existing attractors are likely to be inadequate for guiding subsequent actions, bringing the possibility for continued growth or for more rigid self-stabilization.

An interesting example of this vulnerability is the well-documented decline in student performance and school attachment associated with the transition to middle school or junior high school. Kim, Schwartz, Cappella, and Seidman (2014) have provided an analysis of the school social climate which helps to account for this change in students' perceptions. In comparison to teachers and administrators in the more traditional K-8 elementary schools, teachers in the middle and junior high schools perceived greater school chaos, more student conduct problems, less emphasis on professionalism, less school spirit, less of a sense of agency in their teaching role, and a greater despair about their students' ability to learn or succeed. These features of the school's social climate were associated with students' school attachment, including whether they felt they fit in, felt close to their classmates, felt close to teachers, enjoyed being at school, and felt safe at school.

The analysis helps to explain how features of the adults' perceptions of the school environment can disrupt the students' eagerness to learn, resulting in declines in academic performance and disengagement from school. One might say that the structural organization of middle schools and junior high schools produces new levels of chaos or disorder into which young people, who are in the midst of significant physical, cognitive, emotional, and social transformations, are thrown. The consequence at the individual level is one of heightened internalizing and externalizing problems and reduced peer values for academic goals.

Phase transitions that place individuals in negative environments can result in increased risk to move to more rigid, maladaptive attractor states. The theory would suggest that the response of individuals is not completely predictable. Even a harsh or undermining environment may offer opportunities for self-organization that can lead to new, more complex and creative levels of self-understanding, new relationships, or new skills. With maturity and a lifetime of experiences of moving in and out of periods of equilibrium and disequilibrium, adulthood brings new phases of brain development coupled with new ways of thinking. However, phase transitions may also result in self-stabilization in which the person resists change in order to retain the stability of the well-established patterns of organization even though they are inadequate to fully cope with the requirements of the new situation.

6. *What are some practical implications of dynamic systems theory?*
Dynamic systems theory provides a way to explore change within complex systems. Every system, from DNA molecules to government agencies, can be described in terms of dynamic

variations in moment-to-moment states which can provide the potential for the emergence of new features and behaviors. The emphasis on the coordination of stability and change across levels and among adjoining systems has practical implications for addressing a wide range of developmental issues, especially where the goal is to support behavior change (Fogel, King, & Shanker, 2008). The following examples illustrate this view:

- An analysis of the way neural networks communicate in order to achieve pattern recognition is being applied to the design of microchips that will handle complex tasks of pattern and voice recognition.
- An analysis of epigenetics, especially the way particular environmental stressors mark and modify genes which are passed on to offspring, is being applied to the technology of gene editing.
- A dynamic systems analysis of social networks is leading to a better understanding of social network behaviors, including goal striving, goal preventing, and system support, all of which can influence the use of social networks for organizational and individual change.
- An analysis of moment-by-moment parent–child interactions is being applied to interventions in parenting, supporting improved family communication and the reduction of family conflict.
- Within the field of counseling, dynamic systems theory is being used to understand pathways from stress and trauma to coping and resilience.
- The theory is being applied to second language learning, including both social and cognitive subsystems as they interact and constrain each other.
- Applications in cognition and education include the development of executive functions, dynamics of the teaching-learning process, and educational system transformations.

CRITIQUE OF DYNAMIC SYSTEMS THEORY

Strengths

Dynamic systems theory promises to advance the study of the development of patterns, change, and novelty in human behavior. Like evolutionary theory, it provides a lens or framework that links the study of human development to other fields of science including mathematics, physics, chemistry, and biology. It offers a more complex view of development than many other theories, recognizing the ongoing interactions among multiple systems as well as individual variability.

The theory focuses on the emergence of new organized patterns of behavior, acknowledging that many variables changing at different rates are required to account for these patterns. Thus, the theory offers a more authentic, nonlinear, nonreductionistic account of development. The theory provides a way of explaining both continuous, moment-to-moment changes, and qualitatively new patterns of organization, thereby accounting for what has been observed in other theories as stages of development. At the same time, these stages are viewed as emerging directly from the integration of existing components of the system in action, which helps to account for observed variability in the timing, sequencing, and level of performance that is achieved.

With its attention to variability within individuals as they repeat the same action over time, the theory helps to make sense of observations that may be viewed in other theories as aberrations, measurement error, or atypical variation. The theory suggests that even within developmentally stable patterns, one can expect to observe variations in behavior that may contribute to emerging capacities as these variations become integrated into new, more complex functions.

The theory lends itself to simulations and mathematical modeling. This allows one to explore modifications in control parameters, the timing of perturbations in the system, variations in the parameter estimates, and unlimited replications in order to explore the likely transformation of a given behavior over time. This type of modeling permits one to demonstrate how small changes in some variables early in a sequence of events can result in qualitatively different paths or emergent behaviors later (Schöner & Thelen, 2006).

Dynamic systems theory has wide applicability across fields. It has proven to be especially useful in accounting for changes in motor development, displacing earlier accounts of the emergence, and loss of certain motor patterns (Metzger, 1997). In the areas of cognitive development, communication, and parent–child relationships, the theory offers a promising new lens. The idea of self-organization inspires researchers to reject dualisms, such as person versus environment, brain versus behavior, perception versus cognition, or learning versus development, in order to consider the coordinated contributions of multiple processes to produce complex and changing behaviors. As research continues, it promises to provide a way of integrating neurological, psychological, and social processes as coordinated systems which account for the emergence of new behaviors.

The theory has inspired new methodologies including quantitative and qualitative microgenetic research methods in which many observations are made over periods of time when transitions or transformations are likely. These methods have been supported by new statistical techniques, especially hierarchical linear modeling, in order to evaluate the contribution of many variables to unifying constructs and their change over time (Fogel, 2011).

Weaknesses

As an emerging theoretical framework, dynamic systems theory suffers from disparities in terminology making it difficult to summarize and to apply. Many theorists who embrace the framework use different terms and different definitions for similar terms. For example, the idea of self-organization is central to the theory; however, there is no agreement about the definition of self-organization.

The idea of attractor states is fundamental to the theory, but the process through which attractor states emerge, and the conditions that support stability or flexibility of these states, are not readily explained by the theory. In each domain and at each system level, attractor states must be identified through empirical methods.

Those theorists who embrace dynamic systems theory agree that there is no hierarchical plan for development, either internal or external to the organism. They view behavior as the emerging product of the interactions of many systems and subsystems. The theory rejects a reductionist or dualistic approach to the study of development. At the same time, it does not provide guidance about which components or parameters of a system are the critical ones or how to identify these control parameters in a particular behavioral domain. A dynamic systems analysis of a particular behavior rests largely on the expertise of the investigators and their intimate understanding of the components and subsystems that have a possible bearing on the behavior under study.

There is disagreement among researchers about the appropriate methods for investigating development. Some researchers rely largely on simulations and mathematical models; others conduct observational research; others integrate data from experiments into models. There may be a need to invent new methodologies in order to capture the dynamic nature of the theory—both new observational and experimental techniques for multiple observations over time, and new mathematical techniques for modeling change across nested timescales, from neural firing to organized actions and long-term developmental periods. There are scholars at work to address these challenges, creating new tools for studying intensive observational data and for analyzing data from multiple systems over diverse timescales (Peck, 2009; Fogel, 2011; Hollenstein, 2013). A summary of the strengths and weaknesses of dynamic systems theory is presented in Table 11.1.

Table 11.1 Strengths and weaknesses of dynamic systems theory

Strengths	Weaknesses
Focus on patterns, change, and novelty in human behavior.	Disparities in definitions of key concepts across scholars who embrace the theory.
Links to other fields of science.	Lack of theoretical constructs to account for the specific nature of attractor states and their stability or change within systems.
A complex view of development, including the ongoing interaction among systems and the nature of individual variability.	No guidance in the theory about which aspects of a behavior or subsystem are especially relevant for influencing or constraining subsequent change.
A nonlinear, nonreductionistic view of development.	Lack of agreement about appropriate methods and adequacy of these methods for studying multi-system interactions across nested timescales.
Integrates moment-to-moment changes with qualitatively new patterns.	
Stages of development are viewed as emerging from existing components of the system in action which helps to account for variability in timing, sequencing, and level of performance that is achieved.	
Integrates individual variability into explanations for new behaviors.	
Has been explored through computer simulations and mathematical models.	
Wide applicability across fields to consider change in complex systems.	
Inspired new research methods and statistical techniques.	

CRITICAL THINKING QUESTIONS AND EXERCISES

1. How does dynamic systems theory explain the emergence of new behaviors?
2. What does dynamic systems theory have in common with the three other theories presented in this section of the text: psychosocial theory, cognitive social-historical theory, and bioecological theory? What are the unique contributions of this theory?
3. Identify a system of interest to you. How would you go about documenting the process of adaptive self-organization within that system? First, identify a timeframe that is appropriate for thinking about change in the system. Second, trace evidence of change over time. Third, consider factors both within and outside the system that might contribute to the process of change.

4. Compare and contrast Fischer's model of dynamic skill development with Vygotsky's concept of the zone of proximal development. What are the similarities and differences in the ways these theories explain how more advanced abilities emerge from less competent or complex forms?

5. In the case of Robbie, what are the systems and subsystems you can identify that are operating to influence his thoughts, feelings, and relationships?

6. Imagine that you are a school counselor. How would you use dynamic systems theory to help Robbie understand and cope with the changes he is experiencing?

7. How typical is it for new interests to emerge during early adolescence? How would dynamic systems theory explain this? What is the relationship of the emergence of these new interests to the concepts of attractor states and adaptive self-organization?

8. If you were Robbie's parents, what steps would you take to address some of the issues in this case, including Robbie's increasing desire to spend time alone; his irritability with his younger sibling; his difficulty sleeping; his late night involvement with online games; and his conflicts about independence and closeness?

KEY TERMS

A-not-B task	dynamic systems theory
adaptive self-organization	emergence
adaptive self-stabilization	feedback
antisocial behavior	homeostasis
attractors	interdependent elements
behavioral complexity	negative feedback
behavioral complexity scale	nested timescales
coercion theory	open system
constructive web	positive feedback
control parameter	probabilistic epigenesis
disequilibrium	self-organization
dynamic skill	system
dynamic system	system hierarchy

RECOMMENDED RESOURCES

**Baby Body Sense. A YouTube video of early motor development. http://youtu.be/RI3t_hsFzX0v A 10-minute video that illustrates principles of dynamic systems theory as they apply to early motor development.

**Child and Family Center (2014). The family check-up. Retrieved on August 24, 2014 at http://cfc.uoregon.edu/aboutus01.htm
Based on a dynamic systems approach to family interaction, this is an evidence-based intervention to increase family support and decrease family conflict.

**Conflict resolution in action: Applying dynamic systems theory. A YouTube video. www.youtube.com/watch?v=c7PrLXSIt3o

A workshop that illustrates how dynamic systems theory principles can be applied in helping people address inter-group conflicts. The video uses the case of a multi-party conflict in Nigeria as the point of focus.

**Fogel, A. (2011). Theoretical and applied dynamic systems research in developmental science. *Child Development Perspectives, 5,* 267–272.
A summary of some basic features of dynamic systems theory, a description of microgenetic methods for studying change over time, and examples of how the theory has been applied to a diverse range of topics in developmental science.

**Smith, L.B. & Thelen, E. (2003). Development as a dynamic system. *Trends in Cognitive Science, 7,* 343–348.
An overview of major ideas in dynamic systems theory, introducing the idea of nested timescales, and applying the theory to the A-not-B problem.

REFERENCES

Adolph, K.E. & Eppler, M.A. (2002). Flexibility and specificity in infant motor skill acquisition. In J.W. Fagen & H. Hayne (Eds.), *Progress in infancy research: Vol. 2* (pp. 121–167). Mahwah, NJ: Lawrence Erlbaum Associates.

Ashby, W.R. (1947). Principles of the self-organizing dynamic system. *Journal of General Psychology, 37,* 125–128.

Clayton, P. & Davies, P. (Eds.) (2006). *The reemergence of emergence: The emergentist hypothesis from science to religion.* Oxford: Oxford University Press.

Descartes, R. (1637). *Discourse on the method of rightly conducting one's reason and of seeking truth in the sciences. (Discours de la method pour bien conduire sa raison, et chercher la verité dans les sciences.)* Leiden, Netherlands.

Dishion, T.J., Brennan, L.M., Shaw, D.S., McEachern, A.D., Wilson, M.N., & Jo, B. (2014). Prevention of problem behavior through annual family check-ups in early childhood: Intervention effects from home to early elementary school. *Journal of Abnormal Child Psychology, 42,* 343–354.

Eoyang, G. & Conway, D.J. (1999). Conditions that support self-organization in a complex adaptive system. Retrieved on August 21, 2014 at http://amauta-international.com/iaf99/Thread1/conway.html

Fischer, K.W. (1980). A theory of cognitive development: The control and construction of hierarchies of skills. *Psychological Review, 87,* 477–531.

Fischer, K.W. & Bidell, T.R. (1998). Dynamic development of psychological structures in action and thought. In W. Damon (Series Ed.) & R.M. Lerner (Vol. Ed.), *Handbook of child psychology: Vol. 1. Theoretical models of human development.* 5th ed. (pp. 467– 561). New York: Wiley.

Fischer, K.W. & Bidell, T.R. (2006). Dynamic development of action and thought. In W. Damon & R.M. Lerner (Eds.), *Handbook of child psychology: Theoretical models of human development: Vol. 1.* 6th ed. (pp. 313–399). New York: Wiley.

Fischer, K.W. & Rose, S.P. (1999). Rulers, models, and nonlinear dynamics: Measurement and method in developmental research. In G. Savelsbergh, H. van der Maas, & P. van Geert (Eds.), *Nonlinear developmental processes* (pp. 197–212). Amsterdam: Royal Netherlands Academy of Arts and Sciences.

Fischer, K.W. & Yan, Z. (2002). The development of dynamic skill theory. In D.J. Lewkowicz & R. Lickliter (Eds.), *Conceptions of development: Lessons from the laboratory* (pp. 279–312). New York: Psychology Press.

Fogel, A. (2011). Theoretical and applied dynamic systems research in developmental science. *Child Development Perspectives, 5,* 267–272.

Fogel, A., King, B.J., & Shanker, S. (2008). *Human development in the 21st century: Visionary policy ideas from systems scientists.* Cambridge, UK: Cambridge University Press.

Garzón, P.C., Laakso, A., & Gomila, T. (2008). Dynamics and psychology, *New Ideas in Psychology, 26,* 143–145.

Gill, A.M., Dishion, T.J., & Shaw, D.S. (2014). The family check-up: A tailored approach to intervention with high-risk families. In S.H. Landry & C.L. Cooper (Eds.), *Wellbeing in children and families: Vol. 1. Wellbeing: A complete reference guide* (pp. 385–405). Hoboken, NJ: Wiley/Blackwell.

Goldfield, E.C. (1989). Transition from rocking to crawling: Postural constraints on infant movement. *Developmental Psychology, 25,* 913–919.

Gottlieb, G. (1991). Experiential canalization of behavioral development: Theory. *Developmental Psychology, 27,* 4–13.

Gottlieb, G. (1998). Normally occurring environmental influences on gene activity: From central dogma to probabilistic epigenesis. *Psychological Review, 105,* 792–802.

Granic, I. (2005). Timing is everything: Developmental psychopathology from a dynamic systems perspective. *Developmental Review, 25,* 386–407.

Granic, I. & Lamey, A.K. (2002). Combining dynamic systems and multivariate analyses to compare the mother–child interactions of externalizing subtypes. *Journal of Abnormal Child Psychology, 30,* 265–283.

Granic, I. & Patterson, G.R. (2006). Toward a comprehensive model of antisocial development: A dynamic systems approach. *Psychological Review, 113,* 101–131.

Hollentstein, T. (2013). *State space grids: Depicting dynamics across development.* New York: Springer.

Hollenstein, T., Granic, I., Stoolmiller, M., & Snyder, J. (2004). Rigidity in parent–child interactions and the development of externalizing and internalizing behavior in early childhood. *Journal of Abnormal Child Psychology, 32,* 595–607.

Hollenstein, T., Lichtwarck-Aschoff, A., & Potworowski, G. (2013). A model of socioemotional flexibility at three timescales. *Emotion Review, 5,* 397–405.

Hood, K.E., Halpern, C.T., Greenberg, G., & Lerner, R.M. (Eds.) (2010). *Handbook of developmental science, behavior, and genetics.* Malden, MA: Blackwell Publishing.

Katz, D. & Kahn, R.L. (1966). *The social psychology of organizations.* New York: Wiley.

Kauffman, S. (1993). *Origins of order: Self-organization and selection in evolution.* New York: Oxford University Press.

Kelso, J.A.S. (1995). *Dynamic patterns: The self-organization of brain and behavior.* Cambridge, MA: Bradford/MIT Press.

Kelso, J.A.S. (2000). Principles of dynamic pattern formation and change for a science of human behavior. In L.R. Bergman, R.B. Cairns, N. Lars-Goran, & L. Nystedt (Eds.), *Developmental science and the holistic approach* (pp. 63–83). New York: Psychology Press.

Kim, H.Y., Schwartz, K., Cappella, E., & Seidman, E. (2014). Navigating middle grades: Role of social contexts in middle grade school climate. *American Journal of Community Psychology, 54,* 28–45.

Laszlo, E. (1972). *Introduction to systems philosophy: Toward a new paradigm of contemporary thought.* New York: Taylor and Francis.

Lerner, R.M. (2002). *Concepts and theories of human development.* 3rd ed. New York: Taylor and Francis.

Lerner, R.M. & Fisher, C.B. (2013). Evolution, epigenetics and application in developmental science. *Applied Developmental Science, 17,* 169–173.

Lewis, M.D. (2000). The promise of dynamic systems approaches for an integrated account of human development. *Child Development, 71,* 36–43.

Metzger, M.A. (1997). Applications of nonlinear dynamic systems theory in developmental psychology: Motor and cognitive development. *Nonlinear Dynamics, Psychology, and Life Sciences, 1,* 55–67.

Miller, P.H. & Coyle, T.R. (1999). Developmental change: Lessons from microgenesis. In E.K. Scholnick, K. Nelson, S.A. Gelman, & P.H. Miller (Eds.), *Conceptual development: Piaget's legacy* (pp. 209–239). New York: Psychology Press.

Patterson, G.R. (1982). *Coercive family processes.* Eugene, OR: Castalia.

Peck, S.C. (2009). Using multilevel systems theory to integrate dynamic person-in-context systems. *Journal of Research in Personality, 43,* 262–263.

Piaget, J. (1954). *The construction of reality in the child.* New York: Basic Books.

Reid, J.B., Patterson, G.R., & Snyder, J. (2002). *Antisocial behavior in children and adolescents: A developmental analysis and model for intervention.* Washington, DC: American Psychological Association.

Sameroff, A.J. (1982). Development and the dialectic: The need for a systems approach. In W.A. Collins (Ed.), *The concept of development: The Minnesota Symposia on Child Psychology: Vol. 15* (pp. 83–103). Hillsdale, NJ: Lawrence Erlbaum Associates.

Sameroff, A. (1995). General systems theories and developmental psychopathology. In D. Cicchetti & D.J. Cohen (Eds.), *Developmental psychopathology: Theory and methods* (pp. 659–695). Wiley Series on Personality Processes: Vol. 1. New York: Wiley.

Schöner, G. & Thelen, E. (2006). Using dynamic field theory to rethink infant habituation. *Psychological Review*, *113*, 273–299.

Schutte, A.R. & Spencer, J.P. (2010). Filling the gap on developmental change: Tests of a dynamic field theory of spatial cognition. *Journal of Cognition and Development, 11*, 1–27.

Shalizi, C.R. (2010). Self-organization. Notebooks. December 3, 2010. Retrieved on August 21, 2014 at http://vserver1.cscs.lsa.umich.edu/~crshalizi/notebooks/self-organization.html.

Shalizi, C.R., Shalizi, K.L., & Haslinger, R. (2004). Quantifying self-organization with optimal predictors. *Physical Review Letters, 93*, 1–4.

Smith, J.D., Knoble, N.B., Zerr, A.A., Dishion, T.J., & Stormshak, E.A. (2014). Family check-up effects across diverse ethnic groups: Reducing early-adolescents' antisocial behavior by reducing family conflict. *Journal of Clinical Child and Adolescent Psychology, 43*, 400–414.

Smith, L.B. & Thelen, E. (Eds.) (1993). *A dynamic systems approach to development: Applications*. Cambridge, MA: MIT Press.

Smith, L.B. & Thelen, E. (2003). Development as a dynamic system. *Trends in Cognitive Science, 7*, 343–348.

Spencer, J.P., Austin, A., & Schutte, A.R. (2012). Contributions of dynamic systems theory to cognitive development. *Cognitive Development, 27*, 401–418.

Swenson, R. (1997). *Spontaneous order, evolution, and natural law: An introduction to the physical basis for an ecological psychology*. Hillsdale, NJ: Lawrence Erlbaum Associates.

Thelen, E. (1995). Time scale dynamics and the development of embodied cognition. In R. E. Port & T. van Gelder (Eds.), *Mind as motion* (pp. 69–100). Cambridge, MA: MIT Press.

Thelen, E., Schöner, G., Scheier, C., & Smith, L.B. (2001). The dynamics of embodiment: A field theory of infant perseverative reaching. *Behavioral and Brain Sciences, 24*, 1–86.

Thelen, E. & Smith, L.B. (1994). *A dynamic systems approach to the development of cognition and action*. Cambridge, MA: MIT Press.

von Bertalanffy, L. (1950). The theory of open systems in physics and biology. *Science, 111*, 23–28.

von Bertalanffy, L. (1968). *General systems theory*. Rev. ed. New York: Braziller.

12
Epilogue

CHAPTER OUTLINE

The ten theories presented in this book are still flourishing, stimulating research, and inspiring practice and intervention in fields of human development including education, counseling, organizational planning, human service delivery, and social policy. Each one has made unique contributions by altering the ways we explain development, and as a result, expanding efforts to improve the quality of life for children, youth, adults, the elderly and their families and communities. At the same time, each theory is a work in progress. New technologies, new statistical techniques, advances in the fields of genetics and neuroscience, changing approaches to the process of scientific inquiry, and expanding concerns about diverse cultures and communities will, over time, lead to extensions and elaborations of the theories.

Several of the theories reviewed here were striving to identify universal patterns of development and universal mechanisms or processes of change. In contemporary developmental science much more attention is being given to both individual differences in adaptive capacities, and cultural/community differences in beliefs and practices that influence development. Theorists and researchers are already striving to integrate concepts from several theories in order to more adequately account for this diversity, providing a more comprehensive analysis of development within and across cultures, levels of behavior, and dimensions of time.

We have three goals for this epilogue: to examine the same case through the lens of each of the ten theories; to contrast key features of the ten theories; and to address the issue of their usefulness as you pursue further study, research, and practice in the field of human development.

CASE VIGNETTE AND ANALYSIS

Case Vignette

Clara is a 40-year-old African American woman with two children. Her husband left her when the youngest was 2, and she has raised her family on her own, with the help of her mother and her church. For the past 20 years, Clara has been cleaning houses for a living. She runs her own home with clear rules: honesty, hard work, high expectations, and a belief in God. Her children are her treasures, and she hopes to see both of them graduate from college and become respected professionals. To that end, she has been saving whatever she can to help pay for college. Of course, she hopes for them to marry and have children, but in due time—no rush.

Clara's son, Deshawn, is a sophomore at a big, state university. He has a football scholarship which covers tuition, room and board. And Clara helps with other expenses, especially books and lab fees, medical insurance, clothes, and transportation. They have talked about his plans, and Deshawn has promised his mother that he will keep up his academics, and stay focused on the goal of graduating. But now, in the middle of his sophomore year, he is having a change of heart.

"Mom, I just can't keep playing football. It's not right. The coaches make millions, and my scholarship doesn't even cover all my expenses. I have to spend weekends traveling, and hours and hours in training which makes doing well in my classes practically impossible. Some of the players take the really easy courses, but I don't want that. I want to go on to get my MBA, and I need to do well to qualify. Some of my teammates have suffered broken bones, back injuries, and concussions. So far I'm fine and I'm in great shape, but you just don't know what might happen. The team doctors, who are paid by the university, often send the boys back to play even after they are injured. And when they can't play any longer, they lose their scholarships."

At first, Clara was upset with her son's decision. "We're not quitters," she tells him. "You made a promise and you took their scholarship money, so you need to see this through. And besides, how are we going to pay for your college without the athletic scholarship?" But Clara listened, she prayed about it, she talked to her pastor, and she began to understand Deshawn's concerns.

Deshawn's younger sister, Keisha, is a junior in high school. She is shocked by Deshawn's decision. He was such a hero to her and her friends all through middle school and high school. She went to all his high school games, kept track of his accomplishments, and bragged to her friends about his college and its winning record. How could she explain to her friends that Deshawn was going to quit the team?

As Deshawn continued to make his case, Clara could see that he was looking at the big picture. Many of the promises that were made to her and Deshawn by the college recruiter did not seem to be holding up for other players. She had trusted the recruiters that they would look after her son and be committed to his overall well-being. But she can see that this is not necessarily true. In spite of her worries, she is proud of Deshawn, and the young man he is becoming.

Case Analysis

The goal for this analysis is to appreciate how the same situation might be examined differently depending on one's theoretical focus. What might each theory point out about the issues facing Clara, Keisha, and Deshawn, and how to account for their behavior? We will offer some ideas, but we urge you to take on this exercise in your own way, using what you know about the theories to explore possible insights into the case.

Evolutionary Theory. Evolutionary theory focuses on long-term adaptation, building on the concept of fitness. From this perspective, Clara is directing her resources to ensure her children's best chances to find a mate and reproduce by investing in their education and encouraging them to set goals for a professional career. At first, she is concerned that Deshawn may be harming his success, but she realizes that he is making decisions that will support his long-term survival. Deshawn recognizes that the best interests of the university and the team may not be in his own best interests for his physical safety, his educational goals, and adaptation to the demands of the adult environment to which he aspires. Keisha is reacting to the threat to her status and her standing in her social group that might take place if Deshawn leaves the team. Social status is an important feature for reproductive success, but since high school is not an optimal time for mating, Clara will try to urge Keisha to talk to Deshawn and understand his decision.

Psychoanalytic Theory. The psychoanalytic theory highlights the central role of sexual and aggressive drives in shaping behavior. One can think of the game of football, and its elaboration in competitive sports, as a socially acceptable sublimation of these drives, allowing both intimate physical closeness and aggressive behavior to be expressed by young men under controlled conditions. In this single-parent home, despite working long hours and having limited financial resources, Clara managed to provide security, consistency, and affection in order to support ego and superego development for her children.

One might imagine that Clara and Deshawn formed a very close bond, in which Deshawn felt some pressure to assume the male role. His masculinity is expressed and validated through football, and his relationship with coaches may have satisfied his need to feel close to a father figure. Now, new ego strengths combined with some unconscious processes that contribute to adaptive problem solving are fostering his ability to differentiate himself from his relationship with his mother. He can see a path toward a more mature adult ego identity that is shaped around different ideals about masculinity and a more independent relationship with his mother.

Growing up in a female-headed family with an older brother, it is likely that Keisha saw Deshawn as a father figure, even though he was only a few years older. Her admiration and affection for him can be interpreted through the lens of the Electra complex. Now, with Deshawn taking a new path, it may create an opportunity for Keisha to distance herself from this relationship, and give her new space for individuation, both in relation to Deshawn and in relation to her mother.

Cognitive Developmental Theory. Deshawn is increasingly able to reason about the consequences of his academic performance for his future career goals. One feature of formal operational reasoning is the capacity to think in a probabilistic way about one's future. Here we see Deshawn, beginning to envision his desired future, and to think about whether the demands of playing football might put that future at risk. His ability to consider the interactions among several variables including the classes he is taking, the time involved in practice and games, the risk of injury, and the financial burden on his mother is being applied to his current situation. As he thinks about disengaging from football, he will need to draw on his advanced problem-solving abilities to figure out how to cover his college expenses and continue to achieve his goals.

Deshawn's cognitive developmental maturity is evidenced as well in his increasing intolerance for the inequities of his situation. He is able to recognize the inconsistencies between what was promised by the recruiters and what is actually happening for him and his teammates. He is able to evaluate the inequity of how hard his mother works for her living, what the coaches are paid, and what the players receive for their efforts. We can see evidence of conventional morality in Clara's initial position that one should uphold the agreements made with people in authority. And we see evidence of postconventional reasoning as Deshawn argues that some situations are basically exploitive and unfair.

Learning Theories. The basic principles of operant conditioning, that is repetition and reward, observational learning by watching the actions of others, and classical conditioning, especially response to cues and signals, are basic strategies for skill building in football as well as other sports. We can assume that Deshawn has excelled in all these forms of learning to reach the level of competence he has attained in being recruited for the university team.

Now, in the university environment, Deshawn is engaging in more complex learning, requiring new levels of analysis. The university environment is quite different from high school. Although being a football player may have some status, it is not the salient source of recognition and reward that it was in high school. In contrast, the university environment introduces Deshawn to a much wider range of ideas about possible futures than he had ever considered in high school. As suggested in the learning theories, including cognitive behaviorism, social cognitive theory, and experiential learning theory, there is a new kind of learning going on for Deshawn, one which integrates a personal sense of agency and intentionality with real-life experiences, new information, and abstract reasoning. Deshawn's own values and goals are drawing him into more rigorous academic challenges. He is using his capacity to observe and reflect in order to consider the implications of the current situation. He is asking himself whether the rewards and benefits of his participation in football are worth the possible risks to himself, through injury, or to his future professional career. Deshawn is reevaluating his goals and altering his behavior to achieve these goals.

Social Role Theory. Clara, Deshawn, and Keisha are all experiencing role transitions. Clara, who has invested years of effort and energy in her parent role, has wanted Deshawn to go to college. She has tried to structure her parent role around a few basic norms: honesty, hard work, high expectations, and a belief in God. She is proud of Deshawn, and sees his success as evidence of her effectiveness as a mother. His decision to leave football may undermine one of her primary ambitions for him. Now, as she listens to Deshawn's reasoning, she realizes that she has to revise her parent role. She never went to college, she never played football, and she isn't completely sure what an MBA is. She is still Deshawn's mother and realizes that he needs her support and approval. She is confident that he has learned the values she has emphasized, and that he will make good decisions, but she can no longer guide him as she did when he was young. However, she still needs to consider her role with regard to Keisha who continues to need her mother's guidance and encouragement especially during these high school years.

Deshawn is balancing several roles as a son, a student, an older brother, and a member of the football team. One concept from social role theory that is particularly relevant in this case is role loss. His role as a football player provides Deshawn with a social identity within the college environment. It is time-intensive, requires a lot of emotional energy as well as physical demands, and has a clear structure that impacts his daily life. If he gives up this role, he may also experience some hostility and social exclusion from peers, both team members and other friends, as well as some negative response from coaches. Deshawn will need to find ways to establish alternative roles within the college environment, possibly through his major, through co-curricular activities, or in his social network, to replace the many ways that the football team membership contributed to his life.

Keisha thinks that her role in her peer network will be affected by Deshawn's decision. She has attained a degree of social status based on Deshawn's athletic success. She may suffer a kind of reflected role loss if Deshawn leaves the team. Keisha is also troubled to hear her brother voice feelings of disillusionment with college and college sports. These conversations raise new doubts for Keisha about her own role as a student and her mother's plan for her to go to college. Clara may need to increase her support of Keisha, helping her to understand Deshawn's decision, and encouraging her to find friends and activities that build on her own strengths rather than those of her brother.

Life Course Theory. Life course theory highlights the idea of trajectories and transitions. Certainly, going to college can be viewed as a major transition in the educational trajectory. In this case, football promised to provide some continuity for Deshawn in his transition from high school to college. Now, as he exercises his sense of agency in shaping the direction of his educational trajectory, he is prepared to make another transition away from football and toward other academic and career goals.

The theory also introduces the concept of linked lives. In this case, Deshawn's decision raises concerns for Clara and for Keisha. We can imagine that Clara was hoping that her aspirations for Deshawn's education would be fulfilled through the football scholarship. Now, in her forties, instead of feeling some relief she may be worrying more about Deshawn's well-being. She may be wondering if she will have to take on more clients or a second job in order to continue to pay for his education. But if this decision increases Deshawn's likelihood of graduating from college, she can see the wisdom.

Deshawn's decision is also creating turmoil for Keisha. If Clara ends up working more hours, she will be less available to monitor Keisha. And if Keisha is correct about the importance of her brother's reputation for her own social status, she may find that she has lost her friendship group at the same time that her mother is less available to her. On the other hand Deshawn's decision to become more invested in his academic goals may inspire Keisha to find her own path, to reevaluate her friendship group, and to become more agentic about her own future.

Life course theory also places development in a historical context. In this case, one theme is the increased documentation about the risks associated with head injuries experienced in football. Whereas previous generations may not have been as concerned or aware of the negative consequences of the sport, recent studies show that brain trauma resulting in cognitive deficits affects almost one out of three retired professional players. Playing football increases the risks of developing long-term neurological impairment. Awareness of these risks may play a part in Deshawn's reasoning.

Psychosocial Theory. Psychosocial theory highlights the idea that each of the main characters in this case is at a different stage of development: Clara in middle adulthood; Deshawn in later adolescence; and Keisha in early adolescence. As such, this theory points to the different psychosocial crises that are at the center of their preoccupations. We speculate that Clara is struggling with issues of generativity versus stagnation. She wants to ensure the well-being of her children, prepare them for their future, and provide them with the support that will allow them to flourish well after she has passed on. As she thinks about Deshawn's decision, she struggles with her great desire to know that this decision will be the best for him and his future. She relies on members of her radius of significant relationships, especially her pastor and other members of her church, to help her understand and come to peace with this issue.

Deshawn's psychosocial crisis is personal identity versus role diffusion. The decision to leave the football team places some aspects of his identity in disequilibrium. He probably still thinks of himself as a student-athlete, a social identity that is reinforced by his friendship group at college. As he disengages from this role, he will need to redefine his identity in line with occupational and other personal goals. This might take place through some form of role experimentation, for example by joining a young professionals club, seeking an internship with a start-up company, or working as a research assistant for a professor in the business college. During this period of moratorium and exploration, Deshawn might feel a bit of tension or anxiety as he strives to crystallize his sense of self moving into a desired but not fully known future.

For Keisha, the psychosocial crisis is group identity versus alienation. The tension she faces is to establish and sustain a connection with a group in which she experiences a reciprocal sense of valuing others and being valued. Deshawn's decision to drop football may create some disequilibrium for her to the extent that her social network and peer reputation are linked to his status and reputation in the school and community. The situation may give her an opportunity to evaluate the basis of her friendships. Some of the relationships may be more about her link to Deshawn and the college team members; others may be more authentic friendships based on her own qualities. As she hears more about the decisions Deshawn is making, she may begin to think more concretely about her own future educational and career goals. She knows her mother wants her to go to college, but few of her friends have this goal. This may place her at odds with her friendship group and lead to efforts to connect with other peers who will support her ambitions. Keisha may begin to find satisfaction in other groups outside of school, possibly the church youth group or a community service group, or a school club based on her own talents and interests (e.g. the yearbook, the drama club, or the Spanish language club).

Cognitive Social-Historical Theory. A central idea in cognitive social-historical theory is that culture is a mediator of cognitive structuring. This concept can be applied to the broad landscape of occupational opportunities in the U.S. As skilled labor jobs have diminished, a greater and greater emphasis is being placed on the importance of a college education for a good-paying, stable career. If you place the case in a cultural context, you can see that families in low-resource communities are looking at a college education as a path out of poverty. What is more, for many African American youth, sports heroes are cultural icons whose salaries and fame inspire dreams of athletics as a life goal. Athletic scholarships are a cultural tool that creates a pathway for some young people from their childhood sports experiences into and through college. The idea of "student-athlete" starts out at the intermental level, as a socially meaningful role that becomes internalized.

In this case, Deshawn goes to college as a student-athlete. From the time he was young, the idea of going to college was communicated through his mother's encouragement, and the idea of being a student-athlete, which will allow him to achieve this goal, has been a driving force that focused his efforts and skill. This internalized cognitive structure is supported by encouragement from family, coaches, friends, and eventually from college recruiters.

What many people fail to recognize is that college is a new zone for development. The demands for performance in athletics increase. The diversity of peers typically expands beyond what was experienced in high school. New courses with greater intellectual demands, new ideas and approaches to scientific reasoning, and new requirements for oral and written communication, are all aspects of the college experience. In addition, college brings new demands for independence. This environment has the potential for scaffolding students to more and more advanced reasoning as well as new ambitions and goals. In this case, college creates a zone of proximal development for Deshawn. His experiences in the classroom with faculty and peers are stimulating a new, independent outlook and critical assessment of his own situation, and his view of the future.

Bioecological Theory. The PPCT model gives us a lot to consider in this case. The case highlights three microsystems for Deshawn, his family, his football team, and his other college academic courses. In each one of these, unique processes are at work, shaping his thoughts and ideas about his future. His mother's childrearing philosophy has emphasized honesty and hard work. These values have obviously contributed to Deshawn's success in athletics and as a student. Within the football team microsystem, key processes might include physical workouts, practice, games, social interactions with other players, and guidance from coaches. Within the classroom, processes might include reading new and interesting articles and texts, writing papers, giving oral presentations, and doing research for class assignments. In this case, we can imagine that Deshawn's mesosytem, that is, the interactions across microsystems, is contributing to some new insights about his choices, his life direction, and his ability to shape his future through a growing sense of agency.

The biological focus of the model suggests that we need to understand Deshawn's physical abilities as a part of this case. He probably enjoys the physical demands of participation in the sport and takes pride in his strength and fitness. However, Deshawn may be sensing a growing unease about the physical risks associated with football, and the realization that continued participation in the sport might result in both short-term acute injury as well as long-term cognitive deterioration.

The complex view of nested systems also adds a dimension to our understanding of this situation. Many of the policies that impact college football players are taking place in the exosystem. The NCAA has rules about how many credits a student has to be enrolled in in order to be eligible to play. They also have rules restricting scholarships, student employment, and other benefits to student athletes. The university has policies about health care coverage, year to year awards of scholarships, and salary schedules for coaches and assistant coaches, all of which might influence Deshawn's thinking about his situation, but over which he has no control.

The macrosystem creates an umbrella of values and mythology about the sport of football, as well as a reality about how few college players actually end up as professional players. At the same time, the macrosystem offers a wide range of career paths that are accessible with a college degree. Over the two years of college, Deshawn has become increasingly aware of the discrepancy between the mythology and the complex reality. With this insight, he is better able to consider how decisions he is making now will allow him to have greater control over life circumstances in the future.

Dynamic Systems Theory. Dynamic systems theory strives to answer the question: How do we get more from less? In other words, how do more complex, integrated actions, thoughts, or systems emerge from the more rudimentary elements that preceded them? In this case, we can focus on Deshawn's emerging desire to redirect his energy to academic goals and to strive toward a graduate degree in business. The theory guides us to look for the answer to this question at many levels at once. Origins of the desire to excel, whether at sports or in school, can be found in his home environment, including his mother's emphasis on honesty, hard work, high expectations, and a belief in God. His current exposure to hard work and high expectations as part of the football team supports this orientation. At the same time, the college environment opens up new potential paths toward adulthood that Deshawn may not have considered before. Feedback from instructors about his academic potential and the quality of his work, and information from the media and other sources about the risks of football are contributing to a revision of his thinking. And Deshawn is maturing. Cognitive capacities for analytic thinking, hypothetical reasoning, and probabilistic thinking about the future fuel this revision about what he wants out of a college education and how it fits in with his plans for the future.

Deshawn is undergoing adaptive self-organization. For a time, multiple attractor states may operate to compete in Deshawn's energy and effort, including a goal to please his mother, a goal to be loyal to his team members and coaches, and a goal to have a desirable and achievable career. Old goals are being abandoned as attractor states related to career goals become more compelling. Events that take place each day, including injuries experienced by teammates, controversies on campus about salaries paid to coaches, feedback on an assignment, support from friends, or an invitation from a mentor to apply for a special summer program, could each result in strengthening Deshawn's emerging commitment to one attractor state and weaken others. The theory suggests that small changes in one or another domain can ripple through the system, resulting in reorganization and transformation.

A vision of one's future self is a creative product of the interaction of the person and the environment over time. This process emerges for many students as they encounter the complex environment of the college including new ideas, new settings, and feedback from adults and peers about their strengths and limitations. College students are biological organisms that are undergoing physical, cognitive, social, and emotional changes. Their capacities for planning, organizing, and directing actions toward goals are advancing, and, at the same time, the environment is urging them to make commitments to their future by choosing a major, engaging in internships and field experiences, and looking for employment opportunities. Deshawn is a perfect example of a developing system that is undergoing reorganization toward a new, higher order goal.

WHY SO MANY THEORIES?

In Chapter 1, we raised the questions: Why so many theories? Which one shall I choose? Having read the case and the case analysis, you can appreciate that each theory sheds a somewhat different light on the issues facing the members of the family and leads to different explanations for their behavior. No single theory completely captures the complexity of development. Each theory has its range of applicability, impact, and limitations. In thinking about which theory to choose, it is helpful to compare and contrast them along a few basic dimensions:

Basic process concepts (how the theory accounts for change);
Periods of life (an emphasis on certain life stages);
Universal versus contextual emphasis (the extent to which the theory offers ideas that operate across contexts and time, or emphasizes social, cultural, and historical contexts);
Units and periods of time (over what length of time is change expected to take place). (See Table 12.1.)

Basic Process Concepts

Evolutionary theory accounts for change in adaptive capacities through the process of natural selection. Stemming from this approach, the issue of adaptive capacity can be traced through its expression in other theories. Cognitive developmental theory accounts for adaptation through the processes of assimilation and accommodation as infants and young children actively explore their environments. The learning theories also emphasize the adaptive capacities of the learner, introducing several mechanisms to account for change including conditioning, reinforcement, repetition and practice, observation, and the formation of expectations. Cognitive social-historical theory highlights the role of cultural tools, especially language and other symbolic systems, as shaping the direction of higher order mental processes which start first at the societal level and are gradually internalized. Psychoanalytic theory focuses on the expression and management of sexual and aggressive drives, self-control, and the symbolic representations of drives and wishes in mental life. Social role theory examines the ways societies structure development through the norms, expectations, and reciprocal relationships of roles over the life span. Psychosocial theory integrates this view with a psychoanalytic perspective, identifying the tension between developmental competence and societal expectations through the construct of psychosocial crises. Life course theory examines adaptation in broad strokes, focusing on trajectories and transitions in basic roles over the life span, with consideration for how events in one role influence the others. The bioecological theory takes a closer look within contexts at the dynamic interaction of person characteristics and processes that shape experiences. Finally, dynamic systems theory focuses on the moment-by-moment changes, across many internal and external levels at once, that account for shifts in the quality of behavior.

Periods of Life

Evolutionary theory highlights certain key periods of life as central to the idea of fitness: the mate selection period, reproductive years, and childrearing to the point when offspring can find a mate and reproduce. Psychoanalytic theory gives special attention to the early childhood years, especially infancy through about age 6 or 7. Within this framework, object relations theory emphasizes the quality of experiences in infancy; ego development theory places attention on the adolescent years. These theories focus on the impact of early experiences for adult development and behavior. One of the early directions of dynamic systems theory was also focused on infancy, especially the topic of how more complex behavior emerges from much less coordinated behaviors. However, the theory has been applied to many other periods of life, including adolescence, adult couples, and families. Cognitive developmental theory is mainly focused on infancy, childhood, and adolescence. In contrast, the learning theories are applicable across the life span. Cognitive social-historical theory has a primary emphasis on the emergence of higher order mental processes that take place through the internalization of social interactions beginning with language development in toddlerhood and continuing through childhood and adolescence. The remaining theories—social role theory, life course theory, psychosocial theory, and bioecological theory—are all life-span theories.

Universal versus Contextual Analysis

Some theories suggest that there are universal mechanisms that account for development across contexts. Other theories suggest that context must be taken into account in order to understand the patterns and direction of development. The theories that offer a more universal view include: evolutionary theory, psychoanalytic theory, cognitive developmental theory, the learning theories, and social role theory. The theories that integrate context more specifically into their frameworks are: life course theory, psychosocial theory, cognitive social-historical theory, and bioecological theory. The dynamic systems theory seems to have both universal and contextual features: certain characteristics of open systems are universal, but the process of change assumes transactions across system boundaries with specific adjoining systems.

Units and Periods of Time

Where should we start looking for explanations of development? Some theories focus on micro analysis of moment-to-moment experiences which gradually accumulate over time to create patterns of expectations, and new thoughts or behaviors. Examples are the learning theories, cognitive social-historical theory, bioecological theory, and dynamic systems theory. In the case of dynamic systems theory, these moment-by-moment events are viewed as nested in other timescales. Other theories suggest intermediate time intervals over weeks or months during which repeated processes may contribute to the emergence of new thoughts and behaviors. Examples include cognitive developmental theory, psychoanalytic theory, social role theory, and bioecological theory. Still other theories focus on macro analysis of longer, culturally sculpted processes and periods of time, including evolutionary theory, psychosocial theory, and life course theory.

Four of the theories incorporate the idea that singular events can occur at any time that can alter the course of development. In evolutionary theory, mutations can alter the nature of species adaptation. In social role theory, sudden role gain or role loss can prompt new demands and revision of one's self-concept. Life course theory draws attention to historical events, like war, economic recession, or a natural disaster, which can redirect a person's developmental trajectory. Dynamic systems theory considers the likelihood that one among many interacting factors could suddenly change, thereby altering the relationship of elements within a system and leading to reorganization.

Table 12.1 Comparison of key features of ten theories

Theory	Basic process	Periods of life	Universal vs. contextual	Units of time
Evolutionary theory	Adaptive capacities in biological, cognitive, emotional, and social domains that emerge through natural selection	Key periods central to fitness: mate selection, reproduction, and childrearing to the point when offspring mate and reproduce	Universal	Long-term change over generations
Psychoanalytic theory	Sexual and aggressive drives, self-control, symbolic representation of drives and wishes in unconscious and conscious mental life	Infancy through about age 6 or 7, with extension to adolescence, and implications of early experiences for adult functioning	Universal	Intermediate time intervals
Cognitive developmental theory	Cognitive capacities that advance through the adaptive processes of assimilation and accommodation	Infancy, childhood, and adolescence	Universal	Intermediate time intervals
Learning theories	Cognitive, emotional, and behavioral patterns that emerge through conditioning, reinforcement, repetition, practice, observation, and the formation of expectations	Applicable across the life span	Universal	Moment-to-moment experiences
Social role theory	Norms, expectations, and reciprocal expectations of social roles	Life span	Universal	Intermediate time intervals
Life course theory	Trajectories and transitions in life roles, and interconnections among roles	Life span	Contextual	Long-term over the life span
Psychosocial theory	Patterns of self-understanding and social adaptation that result from resolution of each psychosocial crisis	Life span	Contextual	Long-term over the life span
Cognitive social-historical theory	Higher order mental abilities develop through social experiences from intermental to intramental with particular focus on language as a tool that shapes thought	Emergence of higher order mental processes beginning in toddlerhood through childhood and adolescence	Contextual	Moment-to-moment social interactions
Bioecological theory	Dynamic interaction of personal characteristics and processes within contexts	Life span	Bioecological	Moment-to-moment experiences
Dynamic systems theory	The nature of systems and moment-to-moment changes across many levels both internal and external that account for continuity and change	Early focus on infancy; has been applied across life span	Both universal and contextual	Moment-to-moment experiences; nested timescales

WHICH ONE SHALL I CHOOSE?

It's not a matter of choosing one theory, but of thinking about how to make use of the various ideas from these theories to inform your work. The problems facing human development scholars are complex and multidimensional. For example, in trying to understand factors associated with academic success, educators are recognizing that the process of teaching and learning is social, emotional, and cognitive. What is more, learning is embodied in physical actions supported by neural pathways and motor patterns. Learning takes place in an interpersonal context nested in organizational, community, and cultural environments. The teaching and learning process is a dynamic interaction that requires an understanding of the developmental level of students, the peer environment, the psychosocial maturity of teachers, the nature of family interactions that support or detract from learning, and the social, historical, and cultural constraints and resources associated with schooling. If you hope to intervene in the teaching and learning process, you need to be able to use concepts from many theories.

The same point can be made about change in many contexts including health care, counseling, social services, and organizational development. The decision about the most appropriate theories to apply depends in part on how you have defined the situation and your goals for change. However, you may also find that the theories inspire you to look at the situation in a new light. In order to understand and guide the process of change, we need a rich basket of ideas that includes: understanding of the inner life of the person including drives, emotions, cognitions, and goals; the person's capacity for learning and adaptation; the quality of social relationships that support or constrain change; the demands and resources of settings; and the economic, cultural, and historical contexts that create the framework within which change is taking place. Having read about the theories, including their implications for practice as well as their strengths and weaknesses, you will undoubtedly find that some provide a clearer guide for your purposes than others. However, as a reflective practitioner we expect that you will draw from this basket of theories for self-understanding, for the capacity to relate to and empathize with others, as well as to design and implement interventions.

Glossary

A-not-B task: a problem in cognitive development involving the search for a hidden object in which the object is moved from one location to another

Abstract conceptualization: knowledge gained by reading about it or being taught about it, not necessarily through direct experience

Accentuation principle: in life course theory, under conditions of crisis or critical transition, the person's most prominent personality characteristics and coping strategies will be accentuated

Accommodation: in cognitive developmental theory, the process of changing existing schemes in order to account for novel elements in the object or event

Active experimentation: in experiential learning theory, trying out new behaviors that are based on the knowledge to see what benefit may result

Activity: in cultural activity theory, a unit of analysis that links thought, action, tools, and society

Adaptation: 1. A process by which living things develop structures and problem-solving mechanisms that enable them to thrive in a specific environment; 2. In cognitive developmental theory, a process of gradually modifying existing schemes and operations in order to take into account changes or discrepancies between what is known and what is being experienced

Adaptive problems: in evolutionary theory, problems that are likely to have occurred repeatedly in human evolutionary history, and the solutions to these problems influenced reproductive success

Adaptive self-organization: in dynamic systems theory, a process of emerging changes in response to new external conditions

Adaptive self-stabilization: the ability of a system to make internal modifications of the relationships among component parts in response to changes in the environment

Affects: emotions, feelings, or moods

Age constraints: restrictions about behavior based on age; being too young or too old

Age norms: in social role theory, age-based expectations about entry into or exit from certain roles

Age roles: participation in societal positions or functions based on chronological age, for example being eligible to vote at age 18

352

Agency: viewing oneself as the originator of action

Aggression: angry, competitive, and harmful behaviors directed toward the self and others

Aggressive drive: a force or psychological energy that promotes angry, competitive, or harmful behaviors

Anal stage: in psychoanalytic theory, a period of life during which the anus is the most sexualized body part; typically during the second and third years of life

Antisocial behavior: disruptive acts characterized by covert and overt hostility and intentional aggression toward others

Assimilation: in cognitive developmental theory, the process of incorporating objects or events into existing schemes

Assumptions: the guiding premises underlying the logic of a theory

Attachment behavior system: a complex set of infant reflexes and signaling behaviors that bring about caregiving responses from adults

Attention: the ability to focus on an object or task as well as to shift or redirect focus from one object to another

Attractors: in dynamic systems theory, recurrent patterns or stable states that emerge through the coordination of lower-level system elements into higher order organization

Autonomous morality: a relatively mature moral perspective in which rules are viewed as a product of cooperative agreements

Behavior: any observable action or activity

Behavioral complexity: the coordination and integration of skills to address the multiple and changing demands of the situation, including sequencing of responses, management of diverse demands, flexible modification, and self-regulation

Behavioral complexity scale: an approach to the measurement of behavioral complexity that permits one to distinguish small continuous changes as well as growth spurts; it suggests the direction of growth across three tiers, from action to representation to abstraction

Biological system: all those processes necessary for the person's physical functioning, including genetic factors, physical maturation, vulnerability to disease, nutrition, exercise, sleep and rest cycles, reproductive and sexual functions

Canalization: responsiveness, whether at a neural or behavioral level, is shaped and narrowed as a result of repeated experiences

Caregiving: responses of the caregiver to the infant's signals

Causal schemes: the ability to anticipate that specific actions will have specific consequences

Central conceptual structures: a theory of cognitive development which identifies networks of semantic modes and relations that have broad application within a domain, and which emerge in a progressive manner as a result of maturing central processing capacities and executive functions

Central process: in psychosocial theory, the dominant context or mechanism through which the psychosocial crisis is resolved

Change: modify or alter from one state, level of complexity or organization to another

Chaotic systems: in bioecological theory, environments that involve frenetic activity, lack of structure and routine, unpredictability, and high levels of background stimulation that interfere with or interrupt proximal processes

Classical conditioning: a form of learning in which a formerly neutral stimulus is repeatedly presented together with a stimulus that evokes a specific reflexive response; after repeated pairings, the neutral stimulus elicits a response similar to the reflexive response

Classification: the action of grouping objects according to some specific characteristics they all have in common, including all objects that show the characteristic and none that do not

Coercion theory: a model of how parents and children train each other through sequences of interactions so that the child's behavior is likely to become increasingly antisocial and aggressive, and the parents become increasingly unable to manage or regulate their child's aggressive behavior

Cognitive behavioral therapy: a form of psychotherapy that integrates many principles of classical conditioning, operant conditioning, and cognitive learning theory to help clients unlearn their problematic reactions and learn a new way of reacting

Cognitive behaviorism: the study of the many internal mental activities that influence behavior

Cognitive competences: knowledge, skills, and mental abilities

Cognitive map: in cognitive behaviorism, an internal mental representation of the learning environment

Cohort: in life course theory, a group of people who are roughly the same age and who go through the same historical period at about the same time

Collective agency: people's shared belief in their power to produce desired results as members of a group

Combinatorial skills: the ability to perform mathematical operations including addition, subtraction, multiplication, and division

Communion: commitment to and consideration for the well-being of others

Concrete experience: knowledge gained through direct experiences

Concrete operational thought: in cognitive developmental theory, a stage of cognitive development in which rules of logic can be applied to observable or manipulable physical relations

Conditioned reflexes: a type of learning in which a reaction is associated with a stimulus that one would not think would produce that reaction, such as salivating to the sound of a bell

Conditioned response (CR): in classical conditioning, a reflexive response that, through learning, is now controlled by a conditioned stimulus

Conditioned stimulus (CS): in classical conditioning, a previously neutral stimulus that, through learning, comes to control a response

Conflict-free sphere of the ego: basic adaptive functions such as perception, recognition of objects, logical problem solving, motor development, and language

Conscience: ideas about which behaviors and thoughts are improper, unacceptable, and wrong; carries out the punishing function of the superego

Conscious: mental capacities that contribute to awareness of one's immediate surroundings as well as one's thoughts, feelings, and actions

Conservation: the concept that physical changes do not alter the mass, weight, number, or volume of matter

Constancy: not modified; regular or continuous

Constructive web: a metaphor for thinking about development; the active, goal-oriented efforts of the actor in conjunction with the supportive structure of the physical and social contexts

Constructs: in theories, the unobservable processes or relationships

Context: the environment or setting, including physical settings, social groups, culture, and historical period

Continuous reinforcement: in operant conditioning, reinforcement is given on every trial

Control cycle: in life course theory, when a person loses control, or when personal freedoms are threatened, there is generally an attempt to preserve or regain control

Control parameter: in dynamic systems theory, the slowest or last component to reach a critical value before behaviors change or new behaviors emerge

Conventional morality: a stage of moral reasoning in which right and wrong are closely associated with rules created by legitimate authorities such as parents, teachers, or government officials

Core pathologies: in psychosocial theory, the destructive, defensive forces that result from the negative resolution of the psychosocial crises

Cultural tools: in cognitive social-historical theory, the artifacts and symbol systems that permit individuals to alter their environments and guide, regulate, and redefine themselves

Culture: the social, standardized ways of thinking, feeling, and acting that are shared by members of a society, and transmitted from one generation to the next, especially through childrearing practices, family arrangements, symbols, language, arts, stories, songs, and tools

Decentering: gaining objectivity over one's point of view

Defense mechanisms: techniques, usually unconscious, to alleviate anxiety caused by conflicting desires of the id and the superego in relation to drives and impulses

Demand features: in bioecological theory, characteristics of a person such as age, gender, or skin color that can invite or discourage interactions, depending on their social meaning

Development: change that occurs over time and has a direction

Developmental outcomes: in bioecological theory, positive or negative changes in competence as a result of the interaction of person, process, contexts, and time

Developmental stage: a period of life that is characterized by a qualitatively unique underlying organization and outlook

Developmental tasks: age-related skills and competencies that contribute to increased mastery over one's environment

Discrimination: in classical conditioning, the learner makes a response to a specific CS, but inhibits responding to stimuli that are similar to the CS

Disequilibrium: a condition in which changes in the organism or changes in the environment require a revision of schemes or mental structures

Dispositions: features of a person, such as temperament or motivation, that can alter the way a person engages a setting

Domains: fields or areas of focus, as in physical, cognitive, emotional, or social functioning

Drives: in psychoanalytic theory, sexual and aggressive forces that have a biological or somatic origin, and press for expression

Dynamic skill: the capacity to act in an organized way in a specific context; skills are adapted to the context in which the action takes place

Dynamic system: a system that continuously changes in order to carry out its functions and preserve its equilibrium or balance

Dynamic systems theory: a theory that attempts to explain how new, complex patterns or properties of behavior come into existence as a result of simpler components or processes that are already part of a system; it also seeks to address the reality of both variability and pattern in development

Dysfunction: difficulties on the part of the developing person in maintaining control and integration of behavior across situations; any condition that undermines adaptive competence

Ecological niche: habitat; the physical and organic features of the environment to which an organism is adapted

Ecology: scientific study of the interaction of organisms in their environments

Ego: in psychoanalytic theory, the mental structure that experiences and interprets reality

Ego development: the processes through which self-concept, self-esteem, and ego boundaries become integrated into a positive, adaptive, socially engaged person who is effective in assessing and responding to environmental demands

Ego ideal: a set of positive standards, qualities, and ambitions that represent the ways a person would like to be

Ego psychology: the study of the development and differentiation of the ego as integrative, adaptive, and goal-directed

Egocentrism: the perception of oneself and one's thoughts as central and compelling; the notion that others base their views and behaviors on one's perceptions

Electra complex: in psychoanalytic theory, a conflict that results from ambivalence surrounding heightened sexuality during the phallic stage, especially regarding a girl and her sexualized attraction to her father and a view of her mother as a rival for her father's affections

Emergence: in dynamic systems theory, a term that refers to the process of developmental change

Enactive attainment: personal experience of mastery

Encodings: in cognitive behaviorism, the construct that a person has about the self, the situation, and others in the situation

Environment: the surrounding physical, biological, chemical, social, and interpersonal features, especially those that affect the growth, health, mental activity, or behavior of an object or organism

Epigenetic principle: in psychosocial theory, a biological plan for growth such that each function emerges in a systematic sequence until the fully functioning organism has emerged

Equilibration: efforts to reconcile new perspectives and ideas with existing views

Equilibrium: a sense of balance in which one's schemes and structures provide effective ways of understanding and interacting with the environment

Ethology: the study of the functional significance of animal behavior in the natural environment from an evolutionary perspective

Evolutionary psychology: a field of psychology which draws upon principles of evolution to understand the human mind by considering the brain as a combination of mini-machines or subsystems that have evolved in response to the specific problems that humans faced in the thousands of years during which modern humans emerged from their hominid ancestors

Executive control: cognitive capacities associated with maturation of the prefrontal cortex; includes the ability to reject irrelevant information, formulate complex hypothetical arguments, organize an approach to a complex task, and follow a sequence of steps to task completion

Exosystem: in bioecological theory, one or more settings that do not involve the developing person as an active participant, but in which events occur that affect—or are affected by—what happens in the setting containing the developing person

Expectancies: in cognitive behaviorism, expectations about one's ability to perform, the consequences of one's behavior, and the meaning of events in one's environments

Experiential learning: a theory that emphasizes the essential role of experiences in the learning process

Extinction: 1. in evolutionary theory, a natural process through which a species fails to reproduce and eventually dies out; 2. in classical conditioning, when the CS is presented by itself for a number of trials without the UCS, the CR will be weakened and eventually eliminated; 3. in operant conditioning, the response strength declines after many trials when no reinforcement is provided

Feedback: in systems theory, information provided from the immediate environment and from past experiences that regulates behavior

Fitness: reproductive success

Fixation: in psychoanalytic theory, the continued use of pleasure-seeking or anxiety-reducing behaviors appropriate to an earlier period of development

Foreclosed: in psychosocial theory, a view of identity development in which the person has made commitments to a view of the self without experiencing any exploration or questioning

Forethought: the ability to represent the future situation in one's current thinking and anticipate some of the consequences of one's actions

Formal operational thought: in cognitive developmental theory, the stage of development characterized by advanced reasoning, hypothesis generating and testing, the ability to consider the interactions among multiple variables, and the ability to take a probabilistic view of the future

Free-rider: a person who does not contribute his or her fair share to the production of a resource, but shares equally in the benefits of the resource

Gender contentedness: a feeling of satisfaction with one's biological sex and related gender expectations

Gender preference: the development of a personal preference for the kinds of activities and attitudes associated with the masculine or feminine gender role

Gender role: expectations to perform distinct tasks, have access to certain resources, and display certain powers and attributes based on one's gender

Gender role convergence: a transformation in which men and women become more androgynous and more similar in gender orientation during later life

Gender role socialization: parental beliefs, attitudes, encouragement, rewards and punishments, and other discipline techniques which contribute to the child's understanding and enactment of gender roles

Gender role standards: attributes held by the culture for males and females; these attributes can include both precepts and sanctions

Gender scheme: a personal theory or mental construct about cultural expectations and stereotypes related to gender that guides one's preferences, self-concept, and interactions with others

Gender typicality: generally displaying the traits and preferences that are commonly associated with being a boy or a girl, a man or a woman in one's culture

Generalization: in classical conditioning, when a CS–CR bond is established, stimuli that are similar to but not exactly the same as the CS will also produce some measurable CR

Genital stage: in psychoanalytic theory, a period in which a person finds ways of satisfying sexual and aggressive impulses in mature, dyadic relationships, typically beginning with the onset of puberty

Genome: the full set of chromosomes that carries the inheritable traits of an organism

Goals: the results or achievements toward which effort is directed

Habit: in operant conditioning, the pattern of connections between the stimulus and responses, strengthened through repetition and the consequences that follow the response

Heteronomous morality: a view of morality in which rules are viewed as fixed and unchangeable insofar as they are established by a higher power or authority

Higher mental processes: in cognitive social-historical theory, the more advanced forms of thinking and problem solving, including language, symbolic representation, and logical reasoning

Higher order conditioning: in classical conditioning the transfer of the conditioned response to some symbolic representation of the conditioned stimulus

Historical time: in life course theory, the period of history during which a person lives; embedding developmental time in a historical context

Homeostasis: the system and the environment are in balance

Hope: in psychosocial theory, the prime adaptive ego quality of infancy; an enduring belief that one can attain one's essential wishes and goals

Human nature: characteristics that are shared by all humans as a species

Hypothesis: a tentative proposition that can provide a basis for further investigation

Hypotheticodeductive reasoning: a method of reasoning in which a hypothetical model based on observations is first proposed, and then tested by logically deducing the implications or consequences implied by the model

Id: in psychoanalytic theory, the mental structure that expresses impulses, wishes, and drives. Much of the content of the id is unconscious

Identification: the process through which one person incorporates the values and beliefs of a valued other, such as a parent

Identity: in cognitive developmental theory, the concept that an object is still the same object even though its shape or location has been changed; in psychosocial theory, a meaningful integration of one's roles and a view of oneself for the future that is acceptable and valued by society

Identity achieved: in psychosocial theory, a sense of commitment to family, work, political, and religious values and goals that follows a period of exploration and questioning

Identity diffused: in psychosocial theory, an inability to integrate various roles or to make commitments to specific goals

Imitation: repetition of another person or creature's words, gestures, and behaviors

Inclusive fitness: factors that promote the survival and reproductive success of others who share one's genetic ancestry

Induction: a form of discipline that points out the consequences of a child's actions for others

Information processing: how individuals make sense of the great amount of information that is present in their environment, how they analyze tasks in order to perform them effectively, how they translate their analyses into plans for action, and how they implement their plans

Innate behaviors: behaviors or action patterns that are present in some standard or shared form in all members of a species

Inner speech: the use of words and verbal thoughts to guide actions; inner speech is not meant to communicate with others, rather to support or direct one's own behavior

Insight: the ability to arrive at the solution to a problem through mental experimentation such as trial and error rather than having to try out each step in reality

Intentionality: as a component of agency, the ability to represent a future and to plan a course of action toward that future

Interdependent elements: in dynamic systems theory, the coordination and mutual influence of components within a larger system

Interdependent lives: events or changes that take place in one person have an impact on the lives of others, especially family members as well as close friends or co-workers

Intergenerational transmission: in life course theory, as children mature and form families of their own, they bring the experiences they have had as young children into their relationships as marital partners and parents; the beliefs, challenges, and resources of one generation are passed along to the next

Intermental: in cognitive social-historical theory, understandings and communications that occur between people through conversation and social interactions

Intermittent reinforcement: in operant conditioning, reinforcement is given on a schedule in which the number of responses or the time between responses is varied

Internalization: incorporating the values, beliefs, norms, or cognitive strategies of others into one's own ideas and strategies

Intervening variable: in learning theories, factors such as information and expectations that provide a bridge between stimuli and responses

Intervention: taking steps to alter the course of events; to make something happen

Intramental: in cognitive social-historical theory, similar to internalization; transforming knowledge that was observed in social exchanges outside the self and incorporating it into the way one thinks

Knowing: having awareness and knowledge; knowing is sometimes differentiated between knowing about and knowing how

Language: a system that allows for the communication of thoughts through sounds, words, and a grammar that combines words to convey meaning

Latency: in psychoanalytic theory, a period that begins following the resolution of the Oedipal or Electra conflict and lasts from about age 7 until puberty

Law of effect: a bond is established between the situation and the reaction depending on the feeling state accompanying the reaction

Law of exercise: the more frequently a stimulus–response connection is repeated, the stronger it becomes

Learned helplessness: after repeated exposure to uncontrollable negative events, an expectation forms that an outcome will not be influenced by any response that a learner makes

Learned resourcefulness: in the face of difficult situations, efforts to continue to address the task effectively, drawing on self-regulatory and self-control strategies, even when nothing seems to work

Life course: the integration and sequencing of phases of work, education, and family roles from childhood through later life

Life span: the typical length of life an organism can be expected to live; from birth to the end of life

Life stage: societally defined age-related status, as in childhood or adult; in developmental theories, a period characterized by a qualitatively unique organization and worldview

Linked lives: events or changes that take place in one person have an impact on the lives of others, especially family members as well as close friends or co-workers

Linked trajectories: in life course theory, the interconnections among long-term pathways in specific domains, such as the relationship of changes in one's role as a parent and one's role as a worker

Logico-mathematical knowledge: abstract concepts such as quantity, or similar or different, which are foundational to mathematical reasoning and problem solving

Longitudinal research: studies in which repeated observations of the same participants are made at different times in order to examine patterns of continuity and change

Long-term memory: a complex network of information, concepts, and schemes related by associations, knowledge, and use that can be drawn upon over time as needed

Lower mental processes: in cognitive social-historical theory, the cognitive abilities shared by infants and other animals, including learning through classical and operant conditioning

Macrosystem: in bioecological theory, the culture or society that frames the structures and relationships among the systems

Mediated learning: a community of learners where teachers model certain strategies for planning, summarizing, clarifying, and questioning the problem-solving process, and gradually turn these responsibilities over to the students

Mental activity: conscious as well as unconscious thoughts and feelings; knowledge acquisition and use; imagination, aspirations and plans, emotions, problem solving

Mesosystem: in bioecological theory, the interrelations among two or more settings in which the developing person actively participates

Metacognition: thinking about one's own thinking

Microsystem: in bioecological theory, a setting with particular physical characteristics and resources in which a person actively participates

Mirror neuron system: a coordinated network of neural areas that underlies a person's ability to observe and then re-create the actions of others as well as to understand the emotions and intentions of others

Modeling: in social learning, the process of learning by imitating a model

Models: in social learning, the people who are being observed

Moral reasoning: a cognitive aspect to morality based on assessments of intention, fairness, justice, and social obligations

Motive: a need or desire that causes or guides behavior

Multiply determined behavior: behaviors which are motivated by many desires or needs, some of which are conscious and recognized; others of which may be unconscious and outside of voluntary control

Mutations: changes in the DNA that result in the substitution, deletion, insertion, or reordering of some segment of DNA which then modifies subsequent developmental processes

Natural selection: in evolutionary theory, the basic mechanism that accounts for species change from the beginnings of life to the present; those individuals of a species best suited to the characteristics of the immediate environment are most likely to survive, reproduce, and rear their young to reach their reproductive potential

Negative feedback: in systems theory, information that reduces deviations from the norm and supports stability

Negative reinforcer: any stimulus that increases the rate of response when it is removed

Nested timescales: in dynamic systems theory, change takes place in different timescales, from milliseconds to months and years; these timescales are integrated in order to account for the emergence of complex behaviors

Neutral stimulus (NS): a stimulus that elicits a response of interest or attention, but does not elicit a reflexive response

Norms: collective expectations or rules for behavior held by members of a group or society

Object permanence: in cognitive developmental theory, a scheme achieved in infancy in which children are aware that objects continue to exist even when hidden or moved from place to place

Object relations theory: an extension of psychoanalytic theory that places more emphasis on human relationships, especially as they emerge in infancy, as a primary motivational force shaping personality and behavior

Observational learning: by observing others, one learns how a behavior is performed; when given the opportunity to perform the behavior, this information serves as a guide

Observations: descriptions of what happens

Oedipal complex: in psychoanalytic theory, a conflict that results from ambivalence surrounding heightened sexuality during the phallic stage; especially regarding a boy and his sexualized attraction to his mother, and a view of his father as a rival for his mother's affections

Open system: a structure that maintains its organization even though the parts constantly change

Operant conditioning: a type of learning in which a response is strengthened through repetition and through the consequences that follow the response; sometimes referred to as trial-and-error learning

Operation: an action or mental action that is performed on an object or set of objects

Optimal development: achieving one's highest potential

Oral stage: in psychoanalytic theory, a period of life in which the mouth is the site of sexual and aggressive gratification, typically during the first year of life

Organization: in cognitive developmental theory, the capacity to reduce information by creating structures or systems and then integrating or coordinating those systems

Organizational strategies: techniques that help preserve and retrieve information, manage more information by chunking or grouping bits of information together, and link new information with information that has already been stored

Parenting: the rearing of children

Person: in bioecological theory, one of the four elements that interact to produce developmental outcomes; significant aspects of the person include demand features, dispositions, and resources

Perspective taking: the ability to consider a situation from a point of view other than one's own

Phallic stage: in psychoanalytic theory, a period of heightened genital sensitivity in the absence of the hormonal changes that accompany puberty, typically starting during the third year of life and lasting until the child is 6

Physical state: in social learning theory, the state of arousal or excitement that provides information as one makes a judgment about whether one is likely to succeed or fail in a certain task

Plasticity: the capacity for adaptive reorganization at the neurological, psychological, and behavioral levels

Pleasure principle: in psychoanalytic theory, the instinctive drive to seek pleasure and avoid pain

Positive feedback: information that amplifies a variation and contributes to accelerated change in the same direction

Positive psychology: the study of the pleasant emotions of happiness and joy, the cognitive outlooks of optimism and hopefulness, and the adaptive, creative behaviors that result in mastery and efficacy

Positive reinforcer: any stimulus that increases the rate of response when it is present

Postconventional morality: the most advanced form of moral reasoning in which moral decisions are based on an appreciation of the social contract that binds members of a social system, and on higher values such as fairness and justice

Postformal thought: a qualitatively distinct kind of reasoning that integrates principles of logic and abstract hypothetical reasoning with contextual, relativistic, and subjective factors

Preconscious: a part of the mind just below conscious awareness from which memories and emotions can be recalled or retrieved

Preconventional morality: the most immature form of moral reasoning in which moral decisions are based on whether the act has positive or negative consequences, and whether it is rewarded or punished

Preoperational thought: in cognitive developmental theory, the stage in which representational skills are acquired; reasoning is based largely on perceptions rather than logic

Primary process thought: in psychoanalytic theory, the quality of unconscious thought derived from the pleasure principle that is characteristic of the id and is observed in dreams

Prime adaptive ego qualities: in psychosocial theory, basic adaptive capacities and strengths that emerge as a result of the positive resolution of each psychosocial crisis

Probabilistic epigenesis: in dynamic systems theory, the mutually influential relations among genes, behavior, and contexts which result in a highly variable, multiply determined path for development

Process: in bioecological theory, any activity or experience that takes place on a regular basis

Protective factors: conditions that help to minimize or buffer the harm associated with threats, or contribute to the person's ability to rebound following a crisis

Psychological system: all those mental processes needed to make meaning out of experiences, to learn, and to take action

Psychological tools: in cognitive social-historical theory, signs and symbolic systems, counting systems, and strategies for remembering

Psychosocial crisis: in psychosocial theory, a predictable life tension that arises as people experience some conflict between their own competences and the expectations of their society at each developmental stage

Psychosocial evolution: adaptive mechanisms that humans bring to bear in coping with modern day life as a result of information that is passed down from one generation to the next

Psychosocial moratorium: in psychosocial theory, a period of free experimentation and questioning before the final commitments associated with identity achievement are made

Punishment: in operant conditioning, a noxious consequence that follows an undesirable behavior

Qualitative change: modification in a basic attribute such as form, level of complexity, or organization

Quantitative change: modification in amount

Radius of significant relationships: in psychosocial theory, the nested circle of important individuals and groups in one's life; over time the breadth and depth of these relationships change

Range of applicability: in theory, the phenomena the theory is trying to explain

Reality principle: in psychoanalytic theory, a principle in which the ego protects the person by waiting to gratify impulses until a socially acceptable form of expression of gratification can be found

Reality testing: the ability to evaluate plans with an eye toward whether they can actually work given the characteristics of the situation

Reciprocal learning: similar to mediated learning; teachers model certain strategies for planning, summarizing, clarifying, and questioning the problem-solving process, and gradually turn these responsibilities over to the students

Reciprocal roles: social roles that are partially defined by the other roles that support them, such as student and teacher

Reciprocity: a scheme describing the interdependence of related dimensions such as height and width

Reflective observation: in experiential learning theory, thinking more about a topic, asking new questions, or generating hypotheses about this knowledge

Reflexes: a type of innate behavior; simple responses to simple stimuli

Reinforcement: in operant conditioning, any stimulus that makes a repetition of the response more likely

Repression: a defense mechanism where unacceptable impulses are pushed into the unconscious

Resilience: the ability to adapt successfully to events that threaten optimal functioning

Resources: in bioecological theory, features of the person including material assets, abilities, intelligence, and coping skills

Response: any behavior that occurs in reaction to the stimulus

Reversibility: a scheme describing the ability to undo an action and return to the original state

Risk factors: combination of conditions likely to impede optimal growth and disrupt development

Role: a set of behaviors with some socially agreed upon functions and for which there exists an accepted code of norms, such as the role of teacher, child, or minister

Role conflict: the state of tension that occurs when the demands and expectations of various roles conflict with each other

Role expectations: shared expectations for behavior that are linked to a social role

Role gain: addition of new roles

Role loss: subtraction of roles

Role models: people who can be observed to perform the behaviors associated with a role, and from whom one's own role enactment is learned

Role overload: the state of tension that occurs when there are too many demands or expectations associated with a role to handle in the time allowed

Role sequencing: the pattern of entry into and/or exit from roles; societies have expectations regarding the desirable or normative pattern, for example, getting married before having children

Role strain: the conflict and strain that arise when a person tries to meet the competing demands of multiple roles

Role taking: an essential socialization process through which the self-concept is formed as the person identifies with and internalizes the goals and values of society by enacting specific roles

Scaffolding: a more experienced person assists the learner in achieving new levels of competence by supporting what is already known and guiding the learner to incorporate new strategies that will advance mastery

Schedules of reinforcement: in operant conditioning, the frequency and regularity with which reinforcements are given

Scheme: in cognitive developmental theory, the organization of actions into a unified whole; a mental construct

Scientific concepts: in cognitive social-historical theory, the ideas, laws, and information that have been accumulated over generations as a result of systematic research, philosophy, and shared historical experience; as compared to spontaneous concepts

Scientific inquiry: a process for acquiring new knowledge through a combination of theory and systematic observation

Secondary process thought: reality-oriented, logical, sequential thinking

Self-efficacy: confidence that one can perform the behaviors that are required in a specific situation

Self-organization: in dynamic systems theory, spontaneous emergence of coherent, higher order forms through recursive interactions among simpler components

Self-reactiveness: the variety of processes through which a person evaluates and modifies actions

Self-regulation: a variety of strategies for the inhibition and control of thoughts and behaviors

Self-regulatory plans: strategies for achieving one's goals

Sensorimotor intelligence: in cognitive developmental theory, the first stage during which schemes are built on sensory and motor experiences

Setting: in bioecological theory, an environment characterized by patterns of activities, roles, and interpersonal relations experienced by the developing person

Sexual drive: impulses and motives directed toward the satisfaction of sexual desire

Sexuality: in psychoanalytic theory, the full range of physical pleasure, and impulses directed toward growth and renewal

Shaping: in operant conditioning, an approach to teaching complex behaviors by breaking the desired response into its major components. At first a response that is only an approximation of one element of the behavior is reinforced. Gradually new elements of the behavior are added, and a reinforcement is given only when two or three components of the response are linked together

Short-term memory: the capacity to encode and retrieve five to nine bits of information in the span of a minute or two

Signs: something that represents something else, usually in an abstract way, such as a word representing an object

Situational imperative: in life course theory, every situation has certain demand properties or requirements; when the situation changes, new behaviors are required

Social clock: norms regarding the timing of certain behaviors and pressures that create a sense of being on time, too soon, or too late

Social cognition: knowing about and understanding interpersonal behavior and the point of view of others

Social learning: learning that takes place as the learner observes and imitates others

Social role: a set of behaviors with some socially agreed upon functions and for which there exists an accepted code of norms, such as the role of teacher, child, or minister

Social time: the entry and exit from age-graded social roles, the sequencing of these roles, and the social and cultural meaning or expectations associated with these roles

Societal system: all those processes through which a person becomes integrated into society

Sociocultural: an approach to understanding behavior that views the individual, the interpersonal, and the cultural levels as operating together in an integrated fashion

Sociohistorical: an approach in which development is thought to occur in specific contexts at particular periods of time

Spillover: in social role theory, when the demands of one role intrude upon or interfere with the ability to perform another

Spontaneous concepts: in cognitive social-historical theory, generalizations drawn from daily, personal, direct experiences; as compared to scientific concepts

Spontaneous recovery: in classical conditioning, after extinction trials and some delay, the conditioned response reappears at a somewhat reduced level

Stages of cognitive development: in cognitive developmental theory, distinct periods of life during which a person's ability to understand and reason about the self, objects and their relationships, and others undergoes substantial, qualitative change

Stimulus: any event or energy source in the environment

Sublimation: a process that channels energy from impulses into activities that either symbolize the impulses or express them in a socially acceptable form

Subliminal perception: presenting words or images so rapidly that the person is not consciously aware of having perceived them, yet they influence attitudes and preferences

Superego: in psychoanalytic theory, the mental function that embodies moral precepts and moral sanctions; includes both the conscience and the ego ideal

Symbol: an object or image that represents something; often it incorporates a feature of the concept it represents

Symbol system: an interconnected set of symbols and signs that convey meaning in a particular culture; in cognitive social-historical theory, a psychological tool

System: a combination of interdependent elements that share some common goals, interrelated functions, boundaries, and an identity

System hierarchy: an adaptive feature of systems in which higher levels of the system have greater diversity of function, each one being comprised of subsystems that have more limited functions

Technical tools: in cognitive social-historical theory, physical artifacts

Theoretical learning: understanding of scientific knowledge by linking knowledge about concepts with knowledge about procedures

Theory: a set of interconnected statements, including assumptions, definitions, and hypotheses, which explain and interpret observations

Theory of mind: an integrated set of ideas about what a person understands about someone else's beliefs and desires

Time: in bioecological theory, one of the four basic elements that contribute to developmental outcomes; development occurs over time; both persons and contexts change over time; time has different metrics including micro time (e.g. how many minutes an infant and caregiver gaze at each other in an interaction); meso time (e.g. how many hours per week a child spends in childcare); and macro time (e.g. how many months or years a country is engaged in a war that disrupts families and communities)

Tools: in cognitive social-historical theory, both technical and symbolic devices that allow one to alter the environment; the tools of the culture shape the individual's actions and thought by linking goals and the means for achieving these goals

Trajectory: in life course theory, the path of one's life experiences in a particular domain, particularly education, work, and family

Transference: a person projects the characteristics of an internalized identification onto another person

Transition: in life course theory, the beginning or close of a role or event within a trajectory, such as graduating from high school or getting married

Trial-and-error learning: a type of learning in which improvement in problem solving is the result of the gradual association between a stimulus and a response

Turning points: critical events that bring about a significant change in one's commitments or a revision in one's trajectory

Unconditioned response (UCR): the natural reflexive response

Unconditioned stimulus (UCS): the stimulus that naturally produces a reflexive response

Unconscious: psychological processes that occur outside of awareness including wishes, fears, impulses, and repressed memories

Values: principles or qualities that are considered desirable

Verbal persuasion: encouragement from others

Vicarious information: in social learning, seeing a person similar to oneself perform a task successfully may raise one's sense of self-efficacy; seeing a person similar to oneself fail at a task may lower it

Vicarious learning: in social learning theory, learning by observing how others perform an action, and the consequences that follow the other person's actions; for example, whether the other person's action is followed by a positive reinforcement

Word meaning: in cognitive social-historical theory, the basic unit of analysis; the combination of speech and thought

Work–family conflict: in social role theory, when demands of work roles make it difficult to meet expectations for family role enactment

Work–family facilitation: in social role theory, when opportunities, resources, workplace policies, or competence associated with the worker role contribute to the ability to be effective in one's family roles

Work–family trade-offs: adjusting one's work life, for example by working fewer hours or changing to a different job, in order to meet family responsibilities

Worldview: a way of making meaning of the relationships, situations, and objects people encounter in daily life

Zone of proximal development: in cognitive social-historical theory, the theoretical space that captures the difference between what a person can do without assistance, and what the person can achieve with guidance and appropriate scaffolding; the emerging developmental capacity just ahead of the person's current level of functioning

Author Index

Note: Page numbers followed by 'f' refer to figures and followed by 't' refer to tables.

Subject Index

Note: Page numbers followed by 'f' refer to figures and followed by 't' refer to tables.